W9-DCI-083

REPORTS AND REPORTING

APPENDIXES

MONTGOMERY'S
AUDITING

PHILIP L. DEFLIESE, C.P.A.

MANAGING PARTNER, COOPERS & LYBRAND

PAST CHAIRMAN
AMERICAN INSTITUTE OF CERTIFIED PUBLIC ACCOUNTANTS

KENNETH P. JOHNSON, C.P.A.

PARTNER, COOPERS & LYBRAND

CHAIRMAN, AUDITING STANDARDS EXECUTIVE COMMITTEE
AMERICAN INSTITUTE OF CERTIFIED PUBLIC ACCOUNTANTS

RODERICK K. MACLEOD, C.P.A.

PARTNER, COOPERS & LYBRAND

A Ronald Press Publication
JOHN WILEY & SONS
New York / Chichester / Brisbane / Toronto

ISBN 0 471 06527-7

Library of Congress Catalog Card Number: 75–14944
PRINTED IN THE UNITED STATES OF AMERICA

10 9 8 7 6 5

To

ROBERT H. MONTGOMERY, C.P.A.
(1872–1953)

Author of the first six editions and
co-author of the Seventh Edition
of this book

ALVIN R. JENNINGS, C.P.A.

Co-author of the Seventh Edition

NORMAN J. LENHART, C.P.A.
(1894–1974)

Co-author of the Seventh and Eighth Editions

and

All the other partners and staff
of

COOPERS & LYBRAND

Who have contributed to the
furtherance of this work

Historical Perspective

Robert H. Montgomery (1872–1953) together with William M. Lybrand (1867–1960), Adam Ross (1869–1929), and T. Edward Ross (1867–1963) founded the firm of Lybrand, Ross Bros. & Montgomery in 1898, two years after the first CPA law was passed. The four had for some time previously practiced public accounting in Philadelphia.

Montgomery was a prolific writer and leader of his profession. He wrote many books, including a series on federal income taxes, and he was instrumental in the formation, and was president, of what is now the American Institute of Certified Public Accountants. Earlier, he also taught at Columbia University and the University of Pennsylvania.* He saw the need for a practical book on auditing and in 1905 and 1909 published American editions of *Dicksee's Auditing,* a British work. Noting the radical departure of American practice from Dicksee, he wrote the first American work on the subject, *Auditing: Theory and Practice,* in 1912. Seven subsequent editions followed from 1916 through 1957. For the Seventh Edition, co-authors Alvin R. Jennings and Norman J. Lenhart joined him and the book was renamed *Montgomery's Auditing.* The Eighth Edition, published after his death, was co-authored by Norman J. Lenhart and Philip L. Defliese. Comparisons of various editions reveal the development of public accounting in the United States.

During this period the firm flourished along with other major firms, paralleling the growth of business in the United States. In 1956, Cooper Bros. & Co. in the United Kingdom and abroad (founded in 1854) and MacDonald Currie & Co. in Canada (founded in 1910) joined Lybrand, Ross Bros. & Montgomery in forming the multinational firm of Coopers & Lybrand in recognition of the growing needs of international practice. Others have since joined and firms in 91 countries now serve clients of Coopers & Lybrand. Until 1973, the constituents retained their local names and used the Coopers & Lybrand name only internationally. In 1973, to eliminate the confusion of names, and in recognition of the integration of the firm's multinational practice, the constituents adopted the international name of Coopers & Lybrand and generally discontinued the use of local names.

Dropping the Montgomery name from a firm that had so long celebrated his contributions was not easy. However, his successors feel that the continued association of the Montgomery name with his major contribution to the literature of the profession is proper tribute to his memory.

---

*For a full account of Montgomery's contributions, see his autobiography *Fifty Years of Accountancy* (New York: The Ronald Press Co., 1939).

Preface

To those of us living and practicing in the profession in 1975, it often seems there can hardly be a worse time to publish a book on auditing with some expectation of durability. Problems beset the profession on all sides: the pace of change and the rising expectations of the public and government of the role the auditor plays; the threat of liability to both civil and criminal actions; the criticisms of the inadequacy of accounting and auditing—the state of flux posed by the Financial Accounting Standards Board, the committees of the American Institute of Certified Public Accountants, and the Securities and Exchange Commission—all point to a rather unstable period. The report expected in 1976 of the AICPA-sponsored Commission on Auditors' Responsibilities will, no doubt, contain far-reaching recommendations.

The present always seems a time of stress, and the future clouded, when so many things are happening all at once. Later they somehow always seem to fall into place. Thus has it ever been in our growing, but still very young, profession. In the prefaces of his various editions, Montgomery reported these convolutions over the years; he used his prefaces to expound his philosophies, hopes, and expectations. In the light of the present, a few excerpts are worthy of note.

On the pace of change and the problems, opportunities, and threats it poses:

From the Third Edition in 1921

Since the publication of the second edition of this book in 1916, the fluctuations in financial and business conditions have been more violent than any previous five years in the history of the world. We have had unparalleled inflation and partial deflation. . . .

From the Fourth Edition in 1927

. . . auditing principles under what we call normal conditions, even though when dealing with industry and finance as a whole, there does not seem to be any such thing as "normal conditions". . . .

From the Fifth Edition in 1934

... The economic adversities that befell the country laid bare or emphasized much in American business practice that is unsound and even reprehensible and there has been a general demand by investors, credit grantors, stock exchanges, and regulatory bodies for increased scrutiny of the accounts of businesses by competent independent auditors for the purpose of preventing a recurrence of such unsound practices.

And from the Seventh Edition in 1949

Recently, financial writers have written much about and freely criticized our presentation of financial reports. It's old stuff and not as important as it sounds. If it were really important, there would have been more changes than have taken place in the thirty-seven years since the first edition of this book. ...

The litigious times in which we find ourselves cause every professional to fear that any statement which he puts in print may be turned against him. Montgomery had a few things to say, over the years, about rising expectations, increasing professional responsibilities, and what should be done about them:

From the First Edition in 1912

... More is now expected of the auditor, and, happily, many of the profession have met this broader demand and have shown that the services of the practitioner must extend over the whole field of business activity. ...

From the Third Edition in 1921

... The future is bright because we have profited by our mistakes. ...

From the Fourth Edition in 1927

I have noticed a disposition on the part of some auditors to accept the advantages and evade the disadvantages which come with greater opportunities. Some auditors regard it as justifiable professional practice to examine accounts and avoid making any positive or affirmative statement that the accounts are correct or incorrect; they avoid the use of the word "audit" feeling it may involve them in a lawsuit; they cheerfully admit their inability to verify inventory quantities and values, as if it were a virtue to disregard the most important item in most balance sheets; they indulge in time-consuming corrections of trifling errors and other non-essential work and avoid the verification of details of importance.

In my opinion professional auditors should assume responsibilities comparable with their opportunities.

And from the Fifth Edition in 1934

With the growth of general public appreciation of the value and usefulness of the services of the professional auditor have come increased duties and responsibilities. More is expected of auditors than ever before. This responsibility the profession is ready to assume only to the extent that it represents reasonable demands. Auditors should not avoid reasonable responsibilities and liabilities, but, on the other hand, the profession must resist strenuously all efforts by national, state, or private action to broaden its responsibilities to a point where they become improper and unjustifiably burdensome.

And on another current issue—the adequacy of generally accepted accounting principles and whether they can be relied on to "present fairly"—we find:

From the Fifth Edition in 1934

I believe that good accounting practice must conform to good business practice. At the same time, I believe that most professional auditors have tried to follow good business practice in their professional work and that many business men, and particularly some regulatory bodies, have not as quickly recognized certain good and bad business practices. . . .

And from the Sixth Edition in 1940

Most of the complaints of recent writers relate to financial statements which would be considered either incorrect or inadequate in the light of the best practice. Accordingly, the correction of such statements calls for no new standards or restatements of principles. What has been forced upon us is a bewildering mess of state corporation laws, lawyers' opinions supporting the so-called incorrect statements, and various governmental regulations. In most cases, the only remedy needed has been a simple application of old and tried standards to statements reflecting violent departures therefrom.

One might very well say that there seems to be nothing new under the sun. It is a temptation to browse on through those old prefaces, and take heart from the thought that if Montgomery and his associates lived through their times, we may live through ours. But enough is enough: two enduring expressions are nearly the last of our quotes:

From the Third Edition in 1921

Good accounting practice is merely the practice of good accountants.

And from the Seventh Edition in 1949

. . . Good accounting practice and good business practice cannot remain long apart. . . .

In the eighteen years since the publication of the Eighth Edition much has happened that has advanced the art and technology of accounting and auditing, and we leave the differences between the two editions to speak for themselves. But most important is the change in public visibility of the auditor and his role in the functioning of our capital market, traumatic as that change has been. In 1957 auditors were most concerned about their responsibility to clients for failure to detect defalcations and other similar irregularities. Today clients readily understand and accept the limitations of the auditing process. Instead, the public—over 30 million stockholders—is more aware of the auditor and more concerned about his role in uncovering management's misrepresentations (a scarce occurrence in the 1950's) and other illegal or immoral acts. That issue needs sorting out, because only in an atmosphere of mutual trust can auditors relate to their clients in a meaningful and productive way. The question is whether the profession has oversold the implication of an auditor's opinion on financial statements; an insurance policy it is not! An activist SEC is pursuing matters of disclosure in many areas within and beyond financial representation, and is now even encouraging forecasting. And the FASB is searching for the light that will underlie basic concepts of accounting and the framework upon which all subsequent authoritative pronouncements should rest. Of the future we can be sure of only one thing—change!

Tempting as it is, we have deliberately restrained ourselves from opining on the many and sundry issues that face the profession today, such as price-level and current value accounting and new ways of auditing or reviewing interim financial statements. That is not the purpose of this book. Our job is to catalog the status quo for reference and study; future editions will note the changes as they come. We succumb to one more temptation to quote from the preface of Montgomery's Third Edition in 1921:

> It is a cause for congratulation that accounting is living up to the best traditions of a learned profession and is discarding obsolete theories and substituting new ones as rapidly as conditions warrant.... It is imperative that financial statements should reflect full and true financial conditions.

We can only concur.

PHILIP L. DEFLIESE
KENNETH P. JOHNSON
RODERICK K. MACLEOD

Acknowledgments

The long interval between the Eighth and Ninth Editions of this book requires explanation. At first the delay was occasioned by the many major accounting changes the AICPA's Accounting Principles Board was making and contemplating. More important, however, was the Firm's restudy of its auditing techniques occasioned by the emergence of recommendations in the late 1950's that statistical sampling techniques be considered as applicable to audit tests just when (in the Eighth Edition, page 49) we were convinced that our development of functional tests had matured. This led to a close re-examination of the nature and extent of audit tests and procedures, and the relevance of statistical sampling to the many facets of the auditing process, spearheaded by Thomas J. Cogan, C.P.A., an outstanding practitioner who served as my assistant until his death in 1968. The refinement, testing, field testing, and finally the articulation of the resultant integrated approach, described in Chapter 5, took time. It places statistical sampling in a minor role, because we are convinced that our experience has proved the merit of the systemized approach outlined, as opposed to a mathematical one.

We delayed publishing until we felt our approach was ready for exposure and until both our domestic and international practices were convinced of its efficacy. Much credit must go to our overseas partners in this connection, particularly the members of the Coopers & Lybrand International Committee on Accounting and Auditing and their associates.

It should be obvious therefore that this work has had the devoted attention, directly and indirectly, of many of my partners and staff, often at considerable personal sacrifice. It is impossible to honor each of them individually, much as I would like to, so I must do so with a collective expression of thanks and appreciation, particularly to my co-authors.

The book could never have met a reasonable standard of style, content, and consistency without the invaluable and arduous labors of Reed Storey, C.P.A., Ph.D., in content editing, Myra Cleary in style, grammar, and consistency editing, and Rosemary Trowsdale in endless typing. James Alfano, C.P.A., of our staff also provided valuable support.

P.L.D.

Introduction

This book is intended primarily for practicing certified public accountants. It should also be helpful to accounting and financial executives, bankers, underwriters, financial analysts, and lawyers. We trust it will merit the same attention from teachers and students of accounting and auditing as have earlier editions.

We have assumed a level of knowledge about business, finance, and accounting to be expected of a financial professional or of a student at an advanced stage of a course of study in business, economics, or accounting. As a result, we touch on fundamental subjects such as the organization of accounts and the double-entry system only to the extent necessary to discuss current professional problems.

Since the greater part of the work of professional independent auditors consists of examinations leading to opinions on financial statements intended for stockholders, creditors, and other nonmanagement users, substantially all of the book is devoted to that kind of examination. In the interest of size, we have not endeavored to bring together in this book a description of all of the matters that are, or might be, involved in the increasingly complex and sophisticated process of auditing as it is practiced by independent professional firms. Special investigations, acquisition audits, and the rest of the infinite variety of services an auditor is qualified and often called on to perform are not discussed, nor are the tax, consulting, actuarial, and other specialized services most firms provide. The valuable work of internal auditors and of auditors employed by agencies of government is beyond the scope of the book.

The book is intended to be an explanatory guide and a general reference work rather than a manual of specific procedures; therefore, we have concentrated on underlying logic and practical illustrations rather than specific rules of procedure of the kind that might be found in audit programs, internal practice manuals of CPA firms, or similar actual working directions. But we must add the caveat of previous editions: never will all the procedures outlined in this book be found necessary in any one audit.

As in previous editions, considerable emphasis is placed on the auditing aspect of the application of accounting principles. An auditor is more than a verifier of facts—his job is to scrutinize the translation of facts into accounting concepts and presentations, the highest form of the art. Thus, the accounting described in this book differs in its approach from that contained in many accounting and auditing texts.

Part I, consisting of the first eight chapters, sets forth our view of the theoretical and practical structure of an audit. Chapter 1 states the underlying theory, Chapter 2 describes the standards promulgated by the profession, Chapter 3 describes the central concept of internal control in terms that we believe facilitate its use in practice. Chapters 4 and 5 describe the auditing process and how and why auditors do what they do. Chapter 6 is a brief summary of the computer's impact on auditing: auditing computerized systems and using computers in auditing. Chapters 7 and 8 discuss organizing people to audit and to work harmoniously with clients' personnel.

In Part II, each of Chapters 9 through 16 is organized around one of the eight major activities or segments of the life cycle of a business through which economic activity is conducted and from which accounting aggregates are drawn for conventional financial statements. The rationale for that organization, which is different from that of earlier editions, requires explanation.

For many years auditing was organized almost precisely in parallel with the organization of financial statements. The audit program began with cash, proceeded through the accounts of the balance sheet and income statement, and ended with matters required for the statements and notes. The audit was planned and executed account by account, with some cross-referencing among related accounts.

As systems theory and related audit practice became more sophisticated, the interrelationship of accounts and the flow of data through them became more relevant. Auditors began to think of internal control as a system, and the concept of testing "from cradle to grave" came into being. From the resulting experience with viewing transaction processing systems from beginning to end grew an understanding of the significance to the accounts of the non-accounting aspect of many transaction flows. The next step was to organize the internal control testing phase of an audit in terms of transaction systems rather than accounts.

From that point it is only a short step to conceive of the entire accounting process—and, as a result, the entire audit—as falling into a number of related systems that produce the conventional financial statement accounts. Revenue and expense accounts measure the volume of transaction flow over a period of time, while the balance sheet accounts represent a cross section of the contents of the system at a given point in time. Thus, sales transactions flow through the revenue system, and the measurement of that flow is reported in the sales account; the accounts receivable balance at the end of a period is a measure of the total sales transactions still "in transit" at that time.

As elsewhere, the use of words having many meanings, such as "system" and "cycle," can be unnecessarily confusing. For purposes of differentiation and precision, we have in Part II introduced the term "segment" to describe the major transaction flows. The entire economic process in every organization consists of a cycle that begins and ends with cash. Cash is received, spent for the purposes of the enterprise, the product is delivered, and (if it is a successful product) more cash is received. Obviously, the major transaction flows are income and outgo of cash, but that simple division is too broad a generalization to be useful in describing auditing. It is convenient and useful to think of business operations, accounting, and auditing in terms of eight main types of transactions that make up segments of the cash-to-cash cycle.

Despite this difference in approach, the chapters in Part II retain the logical sequence of presentation of previous editions: a knowledge of the relevant accounting principles applied to a knowledge of typical transactions and related controls of the client provides a basis for the planning of the nature, timing, and extent of auditing procedures, culminating in fair presentation of the resultant financial statements.

Part III deals with reporting. The complex and still controversial subject of business combinations and consolidated financial statements is covered in Chapter 17; the presentation of financial statements, earnings per share, and notes in Chapter 18; and the auditor's report in Chapter 19. Chapter 20 describes the handling of, and reporting on, some commonly encountered assignments related to the ordinary examination which require special reports.

The aim in earlier editions of the book was to provide comprehensive coverage of generally accepted accounting principles. That is no longer necessary to the same extent because the authoritative literature is now much more comprehensive and is readily available in *AICPA Professional Standards,* which contains pronouncements of the FASB, APB, and their predecessors. Wherever pertinent, reference is made to sections or paragraphs in that publication. In most cases the original pronouncements (obtainable separately from the AICPA or FASB) are referenced as well. Reference is also frequently made to pronouncements of the SEC and other authorities. We believe the extracting and cross-referencing are most complete, but practitioners are cautioned to always consult the full texts. Nevertheless, the discussions of accounting principles and statement presentation in Chapters 9 through 16 and elsewhere will summarize the authoritative literature and elaborate on it as we think it will aid in understanding the underlying logic and its application in auditing practice.

References

References in this book to official pronouncements on accounting and auditing standards are as of September 1, 1975, and consist of the following:

> Statements and Interpretations of the Financial Accounting Standards Board (FASB), since 1974.
>
> Opinions, Statements, and Interpretations of the Accounting Principles Board (APB) of the American Institute of Certified Public Accountants (AICPA), predecessor to the FASB, 1959–1973.
>
> Accounting Research Bulletins (ARB) of the Committee on Accounting Procedure of the AICPA, predecessor to the APB, 1938–1959.

> Complete texts of all the foregoing may be obtained in original document form or found under topical headings in Volume 3 of the loose-leaf publication *AICPA Professional Standards* published for the AICPA by Commerce Clearing House, Inc., and cited herein as *AICPA Prof. Stds.*, vol. 3 (bound paperback versions are available periodically). Readers should note that the section and paragraph references are as of September 1, 1975, and that additional pronouncements will be inserted under appropriate topics as they are issued.

> Statements on Auditing Standards (SAS) of the Auditing Standards Executive Committee (AudSEC) of the AICPA, since 1974.
>
> Statements on Auditing Procedure (SAP) of the Committee on Auditing Procedure of the AICPA, predecessor to AudSEC, 1938–1973.

> Complete texts of the foregoing may be obtained in original document form or found in Volume 1 of *AICPA Professional Standards* published for the AICPA by Commerce Clearing House, Inc.

> Accounting and Auditing Guides for special industries, published by committees of the AICPA (available as separate AICPA publications).
>
> Accounting Series Releases (ASR) of the U. S. Securities and Exchange Commission (SEC) since 1934 (Nos. 1–176; available in SEC services).

―――

Although this book has been prepared primarily for use in the United States of America and outlines the standards and practices relevant to companies headquartered in the U. S. A. (regardless of location), its application is believed to be more universal. No references have been made to Standards published thus far by the new International Accounting Standards Committee (IASC) because such Standards are presently in harmony with U. S. A. pronouncements.

Contents

PART II   The Accounting Cycle

Typical Transaction Systems and Internal Control. Typical Transactions. *Auditing Procedures.* Objectives. The Audit Cycle.
Transaction Reviews. Functional Tests. Validation Procedures. Analytical Reviews. *Statement Presentation.* Basis of Carrying Investments. Balance Sheet Classification.

PART III Reports and Reporting

Part I

THEORY AND PRACTICE

1

Theory and General Principles

Purpose of Auditing

The Committee on Terminology of the American Institute of Certified Public Accountants (AICPA) stated in 1953 in Accounting Terminology Bulletin No. 1 that the most significant meaning of "audit" was:

> (4) An examination intended to serve as a basis for an expression of opinion regarding the fairness, consistency, and conformity with accepted accounting principles, of statements prepared by a corporation or other entity for submission to the public or to other interested parties.

That definition was updated and amplified but not basically changed in 1973 in paragraph 110.01 of Statement on Auditing Standards (SAS) No. 1, *Codification of Auditing Standards and Procedures:*

> The objective of the ordinary examination of financial statements by the independent auditor is the expression of an opinion on the fairness with which they present financial position, results of operations, and changes in financial position in conformity with generally accepted accounting principles. The auditor's report is the medium through which he expresses his opinion or, if circumstances require, disclaims an opinion.

3

That objective is frequently referred to as the "attest function" of certified public accountants. The standard form of report, also known as an "opinion" and less frequently as a "certificate," is as follows:

[Addressee]

We have examined the balance sheet of X Company as of December 31, 19—, and the related statements of income and retained earnings and changes in financial position for the year then ended. Our examination was made in accordance with generally accepted auditing standards, and accordingly included such tests of the accounting records and such other auditing procedures as we considered necessary in the circumstances.

In our opinion, the aforementioned financial statements present fairly the financial position of X Company at December 31, 19—, and the results of its operations and the changes in its financial position for the year then ended, in conformity with generally accepted accounting principles applied on a basis consistent with that of the preceding year.

[Name of Firm]

January xx, 19—

The auditor's report is discussed in Chapter 19. Although authoritative literature of the AICPA describes qualified opinions, adverse opinions, and disclaimers of opinion, as it must to be comprehensive, we emphasize that the objective of an *ordinary* audit examination is the positive, unqualified opinion illustrated above. Anything less is usually undesirable, and often unacceptable.

The public and any other "interested parties" are best served if the statements do "present fairly . . . in conformity with generally accepted accounting principles." Thus, an auditor has a responsibility to the public to take an active part in improving reporting practices in general and those of his client in particular. That responsibility cannot be overemphasized. It is indispensable to our approach to auditing, as will be apparent in the pages and chapters that follow.

Understanding—The Basis for Expressing an Opinion

We believe that the whole of auditing, with its complexities and growth into new areas, makes sense and can be comprehended in an orderly way by focusing on a simple concept: the purpose of any audit is to enable an auditor to understand the subject matter to the extent and in the particular terms needed to express an expert opinion. He must know enough about the subject matter on which the opinion is given to make it an informed opinion. An expert understanding of the subject matter is required for an expert opinion. Thus, an adequate professional understanding is the basis for an auditor's opinion on which he and others can rely with confidence.

However, an auditor's opinion must be defined within certain limits because auditors, like other experts, are qualified only within the limits of their expertise. Thus, more than a fine point of semantics is involved in limiting the understanding required to the frame of reference of the opinion to be expressed. One kind of understanding is required for an opinion on a company's financial statements, obviously another kind is needed for an opinion on the quality of the goods it produces, and still other kinds are necessary for opinions on personnel practices or management policies.

Standards that define what an auditor's opinion is supposed to mean are needed to avoid the confusion that would result if each user were left to supply his own. The AICPA's definitions of auditing limit the understanding to a particular technical context—*fairness of presentation of financial statements in conformity with generally accepted accounting principles consistently applied.*

The subject matter that an auditor must understand, and bring to bear in the process of his auditing, falls into two main areas: the body of theory and practice comprising generally accepted accounting principles, and the financial and accounting characteristics of the enterprise being reported on.

Understanding Generally Accepted Accounting Principles

A knowledge of generally accepted accounting principles is among the qualifications that an auditor must bring to the job. The accounting profession strives to assure that auditors possess those qualifications by regulating entry to the profession and by promulgating broad standards to which practitioners are expected to adhere. The most important of those standards are described in Chapter 2. The current state of generally accepted accounting principles is described as part of the discussion of each specific subject, starting with Chapter 9.

Understanding the Client Enterprise

Since the purpose of an auditor's examination is to understand the financial and accounting characteristics of the enterprise being reported on so as to reach an opinion, he should test every step of planning and carrying out his examination by asking: "Does this step add substantively to my understanding of the client's financial position or results of operations?" If it does, the auditor has a professional responsibility to take the step; if it does not, taking it would waste his and his client's time unless some other mutually agreed-upon objective is involved. This book describes many more auditing procedures than would be necessary in any single engagement; the above question is the simple and conclusive test to be applied to each procedure proposed for an engagement.

The integrity and reliability of presentations in financial statements depend primarily on two things: (1) the effectiveness of the company's accounting systems and the controls over them and (2) the fairness of its management's estimates, valuations, and judgments reflected in the statements. Thus, an auditor must understand not only a client's accounting systems, but also enough about the client's operations, management, and economic circumstances to be able to judge the fairness of estimates, valuations, and other judgments made. He must understand at least the following:

1. Accounting systems in use.
2. Systems of internal control.
3. Accounting principles used.
4. Characteristics of the operations of the client company that could have a financial or accounting impact.
5. Management policies and practices that could affect the reliability of financial and accounting controls and decisions.
6. Characteristics of the business environment that could affect financial statements.
7. Legal constraints, both present and potential, within which the enterprise must function.

Accounting Systems in Use. An auditor must understand the accounting systems that are *actually* in use. The reason that an auditor makes recurring tests of a client's systems of control, even though they may not change for many years, is the possibility that a system in use may have changed from the one that is supposed to be in use. That kind of discrepancy, although rare, is encountered in practice often enough to be recognized as a real possibility.

Systems of Internal Control. Accounting systems may produce erroneous information for any number of reasons. Business conditions can change without the changes being recognized by those responsible for accounting; those who operate accounting systems can become overworked, inattentive, or dishonest; accounting machines and computers can break down or malfunction. Much practical ingenuity has gone into devising control systems to prevent erroneous information

from being generated or to detect it at the earliest possible point. The more effective the control system, the more an auditor is entitled to rely on it and the less additional evidence he will have to gather. Understanding and evaluating the systems of internal control and the consequences of that evaluation for the auditor's work and his opinion are among the most important subjects of this book. Chapter 3 is devoted to defining and discussing internal control.

Accounting Principles Used. An auditor obviously must understand the accounting principles used by a client enterprise to make the specific statement about them that is required in the standard opinion. Chapter 4 describes the audit cycle and the way in which an understanding of accounting principles unfolds as an examination progresses. Understanding the accounting principles used is not a passive one-way comprehension of a static picture but is preferably a continuous dynamic process. An auditor is an expert in accounting principles and their general acceptance; therefore he should be, and often is, called on to recommend preferred accounting for transactions. He is thus often recommender, and then reviewer and evaluator, of the accounting principles employed by a client. Some commentators have seen that position as anomalous. In our opinion, however, it is both practically workable and socially desirable, as demonstrated throughout this book.

Characteristics of Client's Operations. An auditor's examination can meet professional standards even if he has limited knowledge of how a client does what it does. Thorough application of well-developed auditing procedures can nevertheless enable him to understand and test the accounting systems, internal controls, and accounting principles and to validate the resulting accounts. However, the better an auditor understands his client's operations, the more efficient his examination is likely to be, the more competent his opinion, and the greater his contribution to the client. Most experienced auditors agree that understanding a client's business is essential.

Evaluating management's estimates—such as estimates of cost to complete contracts, claim reserves required, or cost to be incurred in fulfilling product warranties—is a crucial part of most examinations. In those evaluations, an auditor has available a variety of time-tested procedures, practices, and practical rules of thumb that offer reasonable assurance of an acceptable conclusion. If he understands the operations of the enterprise under examination, he can select his procedures with more assurance or perhaps devise uniquely applicable procedures. He is often able to evaluate the estimates with less extensive or detailed procedures. He knows what he needs and how to ask for it, thereby minimizing the risk of poor communication and misunderstanding between auditor and client. And he can avoid naive or impracticable suggestions and focus his skills and experience on the accounting and control problems inherent in the operations of the enterprise. In short, understanding a client's operations always contributes to both efficiency and effectiveness of an examination.

Managers of businesses know that understanding operations is a full-time, never ending job. An auditor cannot understand a client's operations as well as the managers do, nor should he presume to do so. He should, however, strive to understand them as fully as possible within the limits of his function and his capabilities.

Increasingly, client management encourages auditors in their efforts to understand operations. It recognizes that a better informed auditor does a better job. He is more likely to be able to find ways to form his opinion in less time and with less effort, and more likely to notice opportunities for cost reduction or profit improvement.

Some accounting problems are caused by characteristics of the underlying operations or their controls (or lack of controls). For example, poor production controls might lead to excess inventory, excess cost, obsolescence, or decreased net realizable value. Or, poor controls over selling activities might cause difficulties in estimating liabilities for refunds on returned merchandise or costs of product warranties. Conventionally, an auditor deals with an accounting problem when it appears in the accounts. However, an auditor who understands the operations anticipates problems, understands their origin, and helps his client to forestall or correct them. Conversely, understanding operations also helps an auditor to be practical about apparent problems that may, in reality, not be problems.

There is no certainty in business life, and an auditor can never be absolutely sure that accounting or operational controls will operate as planned or that the accounts contain no errors or inaccuracies. The most he can hope for is "reasonable assurance" that he understands the accounts and controls and that his understanding is accurate. That is the reason for the questioning posture considered characteristic of the auditor—he must constantly say, "Give me evidence that I can rely on to be reasonably sure that what you say is true."

Management Policies and Practices. No experienced auditor fails to consider the policies and practices of management in deciding the extent of his auditing procedures. Some managements are highly disciplined and control-minded, and an auditor is justified in relying to a degree on those habits. Other managements, usually for economy reasons, de-emphasize systemization, discipline, and accounting accuracy. An auditor must also take that into account in deciding the extent of audit work required to afford him reasonable assurance.

Of course, reputable auditors prefer to associate only with managements that accept the basic tenets of accountability: honesty and integrity. Most auditors take precautions to try to discover and avoid discreditable associations. Though actual instances of them are rare, they are extremely difficult to handle when they occur.

Factors such as industry practice, habit, or simple ignorance are more likely than management dishonesty to create conditions that are not conducive to orderly accounting processes. An auditor who understands a management's policies and practices is able to deal effectively with difficult conditions by planning the timing, nature, and extent of audit tests needed to provide reasonable assurance, by anticipating problems that might arise and preparing for them, and by sympathetic persuading, when that is called for.

Business Environment. Financial position and results of operations are sometimes affected significantly by events that are completely outside of the areas controlled by management or the accounting systems of a client. Examples include devaluation of a foreign currency in which the accounts of a significant subsidiary are stated and the impact of financial difficulties of a major customer on realizability of inventories and collectibility of receivables.

An outside event that is more frequently encountered, and subtle and difficult to evaluate, is a gradual trend of business conditions in an industry, which will at some point affect the values of assets. When and how much to write down or write off unsuccessful ventures is one of the most difficult judgments reflected in financial statements. The better an auditor's understanding of the business environment, the better his ability to evaluate those judgments. Understanding the business environment, like understanding operating controls, enables an auditor to avoid excessive conservatism as well as naive optimism.

Legal Constraints. Every enterprise operates under the laws of the land and the terms of specific contracts and agreements. Failure to abide by legal constraints can create liabilities for damages or penalties or may even threaten the ability to continue operations or existence.

An auditor, although not an expert in legal matters, must read and understand loan agreements, labor contracts, leases, and other legal documents that affect finance and accounting. He must evaluate a client's compliance with tax statutes and regulations, which are often so complex and specialized that clients rely on their auditors and sometimes other experts for advice. He must understand reporting and other requirements of agencies that regulate certain industries, such as utilities, banks, insurance companies, and mutual funds. He must discern the accounting implications of purchase and sale agreements, merger plans, and complex security issues.

Specific legal constraints can be extraordinarily intricate, and understanding them is no easy task. That is especially so if they are designed in part to achieve a desired accounting result, as are the legal constraints in many agreements for mergers, leases, compensation plans, purchases, and complex security issues. Arduous as understanding some *specific* constraints may be, however, it is often not as burdensome as the effort to understand *potential* constraints and to decide when they may affect a client's financial position. In recent years, many clients and auditors have faced the difficulties of evaluating compliance with wage and price control regulations or the financial impact of environmental control regulations.

An auditor may rely on advice of a client's legal counsel with respect to compliance with legal constraints. If client's counsel is asked specific questions and answers them, an auditor is entitled to rely on those answers unless they are on their face clearly wrong or qualified or he has reason to believe that counsel may not have all relevant facts.

Since an auditor may rely on legal counsel, it is general practice for auditors to obtain letters of representation from counsel that enumerate actual and potential constraints and confirm compliance. A standard form of "liability certificate" and letters of representation (discussed in Chapter 10) aid both auditor and client in assuring that significant constraints are explicitly considered.

However, an auditor should not rely *implicitly* on client's legal counsel. The client may not have invited or permitted his counsel to address some of his legal restraints or problems. Pointed inquiry along those lines can ascertain whether such a situation exists.

Occasionally, an auditor encounters possible or actual acts that are purposefully illegal, a much more serious matter than a client's failure to comply through ignorance, error, or omission. Courses of action open to an auditor in that event are discussed in Chapters 2 and 5. Briefly, he should always seek the advice of his counsel. Even if the client is completely cooperative and eager to set the matter right, the potential complexities of the auditor's responsibility make it advisable to proceed cautiously and with professional advice.

Elements of Understanding: The Audit Equation

Understanding may be achieved in several ways. The fastest way is to inquire of others who are knowledgeable—either by reading what they have written or by interviewing them. Inquiry is essential in auditing, but it is not enough: understanding obtained through inquiry is secondhand, and the informant may be misinformed or deliberately deceptive. To provide a basis for a professional opinion, an auditor's understanding must be based on evidence: either the direct evidence of his own firsthand knowledge or evidence independent enough to serve as verification of the understanding.

There are different kinds of firsthand knowledge. In one kind, an auditor confirms the understanding gained through inquiry by firsthand contact with the underlying subject matter: he examines transactions and reperforms internal accounting control procedures. In that kind of firsthand evidence gathering, a tiny fraction of the available evidence is usually enough to afford reasonable assurance that the understanding is accurate.

In another kind of firsthand knowledge, an auditor makes his own observations to corroborate the understanding gained through inquiry and tests of the underlying matter. He may inspect the physical object or activity or he may make computations or reason logically to a corroborating conclusion. He may seek direct confirmation of a fact from a source outside the company. Even though the confirmation is not itself direct observation, the fact that it is received directly from an independent source gives it a high probability of veracity.

Both kinds of knowledge are necessary to an understanding adequate for an auditor's professional opinion. The understanding is based significantly on direct knowledge of the subject matter itself, but that is not enough because the subject matter can never be known to be entirely free of the possibility of intentional or unintentional error. Therefore, the understanding must also be based on some corroborating knowledge. That concept is fundamental to the logical structure of an opinion audit. We call it the "audit equation" because it can be stated algebraically as a reminder of the conceptual rigor of that logic:

$$\text{Knowledge of the subject matter} + \text{Corroborating knowledge} = \text{Understanding}$$

The equation is amplified in Chapter 2 and used as a basis for demonstrating the importance of internal control in Chapter 3 and for explaining auditing procedures in Chapters 4 and 5.

How Much Evidence Is Enough?

Ideally, an auditor wishes to have firsthand evidence to support every element of his understanding. Practically, he can never do so. To begin with, testing everything that could be tested is not economically feasible. Common sense tells him that some things can be accepted at face value and others cannot and that it may not be easy to tell which is which. And, probably most important of all, the critical points in an audit usually involve evaluating judgments of client management, which are themselves made in the face of uncertainty and in the absence of definitive information.

Thus, an auditor is constantly faced with the question of how far he needs to go: how many items to test to have an adequate sample, how often to test to have a basis for believing that the tested conditions hold true in the untested interval, and how much corroborating evidence he needs to validate a client's assertions.

The tension between the pressure of economics and the pressure of uncertainty results in a perennial quest for definitive rules that will tell an auditor, with reassuring certainty, exactly how much is enough. But there can be no certainty, and reliance on general quantitative rules would be an error of the most serious and fundamental kind. A rule tends to replace reasoned judgment exercised in the light of a unique set of facts and conditions. An auditor's opinion is the sum of his reasoned judgments. Therefore, he cannot evade responsibility for making them. Judgment about the extent of testing and other procedures is a critical ingredient in planning an audit; judgment about matters that cannot be fully corroborated is a critical ingredient in completing it.

While "rules" must be abhorred as both theoretically and practically dangerous, "guidelines" can significantly improve test selection judgments. Accumulated experience provides a "norm" of test size and type. The norm offers a shortcut to an advanced starting point for the reasoning process. Instead of starting with the question, "What do I need to do, and how much?" an auditor can start with, "Ordinarily, experience suggests I do thus and so; what reason do I now have to do the same, or more, or less?" That is why many auditors use standard auditing procedures and sample sizes, which have a valid place as long as they are used as aids to and not as substitutes for judgment.

Those judgments should not and need not be made on an intuitive or purely ad hoc basis. An explicit logic governs the nature and extent of audit tests, and it can be a rigorous guide to an auditor in planning his work. Explanation of that logic is the work of the next four chapters, and providing guides to its practical application is the purpose of most of the remaining chapters.

Relation of Auditor and Management

Auditors insist that the financial statements are representations of management. The most recent authoritative statement is in paragraph

110.02 of Statement on Auditing Standards No. 1. That position has been questioned from time to time, both by those who observe that auditors themselves often prepare the financial statements and by those who believe that financial statements should be reports *on* management rather than reports *by* management. The subject is discussed in more detail in Chapter 4, but two points are summarized here to keep the theory and practice of auditing in perspective: (1) the financial statements and the systems, procedures, policies, and decisions that support them are, and ought to be, primarily the responsibility of management because management alone can control the systems and the people, make decisions for the enterprise, and directly know the bases for and consequences of those decisions, and (2) an auditor should have a great deal to do with advising, helping, and sometimes urging or persuading clients to carry out the responsibility.

The function of an auditor's opinion on financial statements is to lend credibility to management's representations. It is sometimes assumed, however, that an auditor functions best if he detects misrepresentations and discloses them, or insists that they be corrected, or both. That assumption sets up auditors and management as adversaries. Auditors find themselves in the position of adversaries of management from time to time, often making headline news when they do. But those occasions are the exception rather than the rule.

The overwhelming majority of audit work is conducted on a different basis, which is far more serviceable and more in the interests of users of financial statements, the capital markets, and society in general. That basis can be kept uppermost in mind without losing sight of the possibility that conditions may arise unexpectedly that require the more sensational adversary relationship. It is best described as a harmoniously integrated operation designed to insure that both auditor and management contribute effectively to good reporting and investor protection (see "Related Party Transactions," Chapter 18).

Most managers are conscientiously interested in strong internal controls, sound accounting principles, and the best possible presentation of financial information to the public. Responsible managers recognize the social and legal necessity of an audit to lend credibility to their representations. They know that sound reporting enhances both the company's and its management's standing in financial circles. They expect, and often insist on receiving, advance counsel from auditors about prospective changes in accounting systems and controls, accounting principles to be used for prospective transactions, and all of the other decisions that ultimately affect financial statements. The integrity of the accounts and financial statements depends on and reflects the integrity of management. A willingness to consult auditors in advance about choosing the best practice manifests that integrity, and the availability of the independent auditor's objective point of view contributes to it.

Some observers think that cooperating with management can cause an auditor to get "too close" to a client to remain objective. That is a valid concern and auditors should actively guard against it. (Chapters 2 and 8 discuss bolstering and preserving objectivity.) However, a cooperative relationship between management and auditor is far too valuable to the social objectives that auditing serves to be inhibited unnecessarily. Prompt, reliable information is essential in today's fast moving, tightly organized financial markets. Decisions about accounting cannot wait for year end and an annual visit by an auditor. It is unacceptable to withhold until year end disclosure of the accounting effect of significant events and it is as bad or worse to change the effect by an "auditor's adjustment" after announcing quarterly or preliminary year-end results. If the interests of investors are to be served, auditors and clients have to work together throughout the year.

Thus, auditing practice in its optimal sense is preventive rather than corrective. It is a complex and sophisticated professional service which contributes to the economic viability of the enterprise under examination as much as it contributes to the enhancement of investor confidence in financial representations.

2

Standards and Professional Responsibilities

INTRODUCTION

Every profession must set high standards for the quality of its work because people unable to judge the work for themselves rely on it with irreversible consequences. Clearly, it is neither possible nor desirable

15

to relieve a practitioner of his professional responsibility by establishing detailed rules of conduct, because professional responsibility is the very quality that standards are designed to safeguard. Nevertheless, standards should be carefully defined and fully articulated to give a practitioner the clearest possible guides in his daily work.

The tug of war between individual exercise of professional responsibility and specific rules of conduct pervades every aspect of accounting and auditing. At the extremes, answers are clear: on the one hand, a professional practitioner cannot shed his responsibility; on the other hand, it is impossible to write rules to cover every possible combination of circumstances. It is between the extremes that tensions and frictions create controversy and anxiety: the question of how much uniformity should be required in accounting principles versus how much flexibility should be left to judgment; the question of to what extent standard sample sizes and auditing procedures should be spelled out versus to what extent the exercise of pragmatic judgments should be required, and so on. Although the specific subject matter of debate will change from time to time, it is unlikely that the debate itself will ever be concluded.

AUDITING STANDARDS

The membership of the AICPA has officially adopted ten broad statements collectively entitled "Generally Accepted Auditing Standards." The ten standards were amplified by the publication in early 1973 of Statement on Auditing Standards (SAS) No. 1, *Codification of Auditing Standards and Procedures*. The soundness and usefulness of the standards are demonstrated by their durability: nine of them were originally adopted in 1948 and have not changed basically since (although our understanding of several of them has come a long way). The tenth was adopted some years later, although the basic principle has been in existence as long or longer.

SAS No. 1 is at the present time the comprehensive authoritative statement on auditing standards. It encompasses and amplifies all previous pronouncements—the Statements on Auditing Procedure, numbered 1 through 54 and issued between 1938 and 1973. Four Statements on Auditing Standards have been issued since then, and others are in draft. All practitioners and those who need a thorough understanding of auditors' reports should study the Statements carefully. The ten generally accepted auditing standards are so significant that they are reproduced in this chapter with certain amplifying points from SAS No. 1, but this chapter is not a substitute for a complete reading of the Statement itself. The purpose of the chapter is to present the standards as an essential link between the theory of auditing and its actual practice, and to offer observations about the problems and opportunities encountered by practitioners in living up to them.

The ten standards are divided into three groups: general standards, standards of field work, and standards of reporting. Since the standards are interrelated and interdependent, they should be understood and acted on as a comprehensive whole rather than individually. All standards are quoted from SAS No. 1.

General Standards

Three general standards relate to the qualifications of an auditor and the quality of his work.

Training and Proficiency

The examination is to be performed by a person or persons having adequate technical training and proficiency as an auditor.

SAS No. 1 and No. 4 emphasize education, training, supervision and review, and continuing study to keep up to date with new developments. The accounting profession has stressed the need for continuing education in recent years, and Council (the governing body) of the AICPA has passed a resolution urging state regulatory bodies to adopt requirements for continuing professional education. Several states have done so, and the trend can be expected to continue and accelerate. Continuing education is a necessary part of the first standard, especially as new developments in accounting, auditing, finance, data processing, and business management continue to force change on practitioners. The emphasis on continuing education does not alter the primary role played by experience and on-the-job training in maintaining proficiency. Training on the job and within the professional auditor's office, planned development of well-rounded experience, and the importance of supervision and review are discussed in Chapter 7.

Independence

In all matters relating to the assignment, an independence in mental attitude is to be maintained by the auditor or auditors.

The significance of independence is indicated by the prevalence of the subject in the authoritative literature of the profession. It is found not only in SAS No. 1 and No. 4 but also in Rule 101 of the AICPA Code of Professional Ethics, the corresponding rules of professional conduct of the various State Societies and State Regulatory Agencies, and Rule 2-01 of Regulation S-X of the Securities and Exchange Commission (SEC). Rule 101 of the Code of Professional Ethics and Rule 2-01 of Regulation S-X deserve to be quoted in their entirety.

From the Code of Professional Ethics: Rule 101—Independence

A member or a firm of which he is a partner or shareholder shall not express an opinion on financial statements of an enterprise unless he and his firm are independent with respect to such enterprise. Independence will be considered to be impaired if, for example:

A. During the period of his professional engagement, or at the time of expressing his opinion, he or his firm
   1. Had or was committed to acquire any direct or material indirect financial interest in the enterprise; or
   2. Had any joint closely held business investment with the enterprise or any officer, director or principal stockholder thereof which was material in relation to his or his firm's net worth; or
   3. Had any loan to or from the enterprise or any officer, director or principal stockholder thereof. This latter proscription does not apply to the following loans from a financial institution when made under normal lending procedures, terms and requirements:
     (a) Loans obtained by a member or his firm which are not material in relation to the net worth of such borrower.
     (b) Home mortgages.
     (c) Other secured loans, except loans guaranteed by a member's firm which are otherwise unsecured.
B. During the period covered by the financial statements, during the period of the professional engagement or at the time of expressing an opinion, he or his firm
   1. Was connected with the enterprise as a promoter, underwriter or voting trustee, a director or officer or in any capacity equivalent to that of a member of management or of an employee; or
   2. Was a trustee of any trust or executor or administrator of any estate if such trust or estate had a direct or material indirect financial interest in the enterprise; or was a trustee for any pension or profit-sharing trust of the enterprise.

The above examples are not intended to be all-inclusive.

From Regulation S-X: Rule 2-01.   Qualifications of Accountants

(a) The Commission will not recognize any person as a certified public accountant who is not duly registered and in good standing as such under the laws of the place of his residence or principal office. The Commission will not recognize any person as a public accountant who is not in good standing and entitled to practice as such under the laws of the place of his residence or principal office.

(b) The Commission will not recognize any certified public accountant or public accountant as independent who is not in fact independent. For example, an accountant will be considered not independent with respect to any person or any of its parents, its subsidiaries, or other affiliates (1) in which, during the period of his professional engagement to examine the financial statements being reported on or at the date of his report, he or his firm or a member thereof had, or was committed to acquire, any direct financial interest or any material indirect financial interest; (2) with which, during the period of his professional engagement to examine the financial statements being reported on, at the date of his report or during the period covered by the financial statements, he or his firm or a member thereof was connected as a promoter, underwriter, voting trustee, director, officer, or employee, except that a firm will not be deemed not independent in regard to a particular person if a former officer or employee of such person is employed by the firm and such individual has completely disassociated himself from the person and its affiliates and does not participate in auditing financial statements of the person or its affiliates covering any period of his employment by the person. For the purposes of Rule 2-01 the term "member" means all partners in the firm and all professional employees participating in the audit or located in an office of the firm participating in a significant portion of the audit.

(c) In determining whether an accountant may in fact be not independent with respect to a particular person, the Commission will give appropriate consideration to all relevant circumstances, including evidence bearing on all relationships between the accountant and that person or any affiliate thereof, and will not confine itself to the relationships existing in connection with the filing of reports with the Commission.

An auditor, in common with practitioners in other professional fields, offers clients specialized technical skill and knowledge based on training and experience, but that is not all. Clients and others rely on him because they accept his professional integrity as an assurance that he will do what is expected of him, using his skill and knowledge to their fullest and placing his client's interest and the public interest ahead of his own. Professional integrity in any field depends ultimately on independence of mental attitude, i.e., objectivity. For example, a lawyer, traditionally his client's wholehearted advocate, does not serve his client well if he is not objective enough to say that a proposed course of action is wrong or reckless. A management consultant fails in his responsibility if he is not objective enough to make his professional judgment, however unpopular, understood by his client. Thus, up to a point, integrity, independence, and objectivity are qualities required of auditors in common with all professionals.

But an auditor's independence and objectivity must be visible and explicit rather than underlying and implicit. Clearly, the published opinion of an auditor has little value unless it rests unquestionably on those qualities. They are personal, inward qualities not susceptible of objective determination or definition, and are best maintained by the individual auditor's own conscience supported by his recognition that his principal asset is his reputation for independence and integrity. It is also important to the public's confidence in his opinion that his own respect for those qualities be made as apparent as possible.

SAS No. 1 and No. 4 emphasize *appearing* to be independent as well as *being* independent. The elusive and indefinable nature of the inward quality of independence has caused the accounting profession, led by the SEC, to attempt to spell out detailed prohibitions, not only against those activities or relationships that might actually erode the mental attitude of independence but also against those that might even suggest or imply a *possibility* of lack of independence. Many of those prohibitions reach extremes that might appear ridiculous to a layman, but they reflect the profession's concern about the appearance of independence. *For example:*

> No partner in an auditing firm, nor a member of his immediate family, is permitted to own even *one* share of stock of a client or affiliated company or even to participate in an investment club that does hold such shares, no matter what his personal fortune, the size of the company, or his distance from the actual work of the audit.

> An auditing firm may not have its employees' pension fund managed by an investment counselor that also manages a mutual fund client; there is no actual financial relationship, but there *might* be an *appearance* of lack of independence.

Rappaport describes the attitude of the SEC toward accountants' independence as evidenced by its cases and rulings.*

The greatest practical threat to an auditor's professional, independent mental attitude is that he is often selected, retained, or replaced at the sole discretion of the management on whose representations he is expected to report. An auditor is highly conscious that his independence is vital and that he must preserve the standards of the profession for the sake of his own reputation. Nevertheless, his relationship with financial management involves subtle pressures in matters requiring judgment, and he should avoid favoring an articulate, persuasive client who is at hand against a silent, impersonal public.

The profession, the SEC, and responsible leaders of the financial

---

* Louis H. Rappaport, *SEC Accounting Practice and Procedure,* 3d Ed. (New York: The Ronald Press Co., 1972), Chapter 26.

community have recognized this threat and have taken steps to deal with it. Some companies require that the selection and retention of auditors be ratified by the stockholders. The SEC requires public notice (Form 8-K) of termination of auditors, disclosure of any accounting disputes between client and former auditor within two years, and a letter from the auditor concurring in such disclosure. Those are worthwhile steps, but they mitigate rather than solve the problem.

An effective way to reduce the possibility of either the appearance or the reality of a potentially compromising relationship is for auditors to report to a committee consisting mainly of "outside directors" of a client company—directors who are neither officers nor employees and who are not closely related by family or financial ties to the company management. These "audit committees" have gained favor in recent years and were endorsed and encouraged by the Executive Committee of the AICPA in 1967 and by SEC Accounting Series Release No. 123 in 1972. Auditors and audit committees are equally concerned with independent judgments of financial decisions, and their mutual interests are strengthened by a formal working relationship. This subject is discussed in more detail in Chapter 8.

Due Care

Due professional care is to be exercised in the performance of the examination and the preparation of the report.

SAS No. 1 quotes a well-known legal definition of due care to the effect that a professional man is responsible for good faith, integrity, and diligence but not for infallibility.

The standard of due care is so basic to every responsible undertaking that it requires little discussion. We believe that the concept of understanding presented in Chapter 1 enlightens and safeguards the precept of due care. An auditor can test whether he is exercising due care in an examination by asking himself whether he understands what he is doing and why, and whether he understands the subject matter when he is finished.

The exercise of due care is also guided by the concept of materiality and relative risk which is discussed at length later in this chapter and in Chapter 5.

Standards of Field Work

Adequate Planning and Timing

The work is to be adequately planned and assistants, if any, are to be properly supervised.

SAS No. 1 gives examples of timeliness and discusses possible problems of timing and planning. Proper planning and supervision of field work are so fundamental to proper auditing that they require discussion at several points in Chapters 4, 5, 7, and 8.

Evaluating Internal Control

> There is to be a proper study and evaluation of the existing internal control as a basis for reliance thereon and for the determination of the resultant extent of the tests to which auditing procedures are to be restricted.

The importance of this standard, clearly recognized at least since 1947, has been increasing as internal control has become more sophisticated and as specialists have learned to construct systems that are demonstrably reliable. Chapter 3 is devoted to our analysis of the subject and its meaning to auditors.

Obtaining Competent Evidence

> Sufficient competent evidential matter is to be obtained through inspection, observation, inquiries, and confirmations to afford a reasonable basis for an opinion regarding the financial statements under examination.

The explanation of the standard in SAS No. 1 is important to understanding later chapters in this book. Therefore, major points of Section 330, "Evidential Matter," of SAS No. 1 are paraphrased or summarized here with references to the numbered paragraphs in the original source to enable a reader to follow them concurrently.

Paragraph .02 points out that "the measure of the validity of such evidence for audit purposes lies in the judgment of the auditor; in this respect audit evidence differs from legal evidence, which is circumscribed by rigid rules." Audit evidence is gathered in many different ways from many different sources, often more or less simultaneously. The specific pieces of evidence are interrelated in many supporting ways through the logical interrelationships inherent in accounting systems and clients' operations. Creating doubt or building confidence in an auditor's mind about the quality of his understanding is a cumulative matter, which grows both over time and across the spectrum of his examination. Therefore, a specific type of evidence may be more or less important at one time than another, or it may serve different purposes at different times or more than one purpose at the same time. The "admissibility" of evidence is determined by its contribution to the logic of developing an auditor's understanding and not by any inherent characteristic of the evidence itself.

The third standard of field work requires accumulation of evidential matter that is both sufficient and competent. Sufficiency relates to the quantity of evidence, competency to its quality and reliability. In simpler terms, the standard requires that an auditor believe both that the evidence he has examined is "good enough" and that he has examined "enough good" evidence.

Paragraphs .03 through .07 of Section 330 divide evidential matter into two main categories: underlying and corroborative evidence. Underlying evidence comprises the accounting data from which financial statements are prepared, including not only the formal journals and ledgers but also informal and memorandum records such as work sheets of computations, allocations, and reconciliations. Underlying accounting data are necessary but alone they are not sufficient to support an auditor's opinion.

Corroborating evidence is, as the name implies, matter available to an auditor that corroborates the representations in the accounts and financial statements. It includes documentary material showing the propriety of the accounting data, such as the approvals, endorsements, and cancellations on checks, vouchers, invoices, and the like; contracts and minutes of meetings; confirmations and other written representations of knowledgeable persons; results of direct observation, physical inspection, and computation; and conclusions reached through valid reasoning. A system of accounting records that is soundly conceived and carefully maintained produces an internal integrity and interrelationship of the accounting data, and evidence gathered in one area tends to corroborate that gathered in other areas.

The distinction between underlying evidence and corroborating evidence is fundamental. It is sometimes obscured because some kinds of underlying evidence are corroborative as well, and some documents serve both purposes: an invoice is part of the underlying evidence of the accounts, but the signatures, endorsements, references to contracts or purchase orders, and similar validating data on it are corroborative. "Underlying" is that which is part of the accounts, while "corroborative" always comes from outside the account or accounts being corroborated. That distinction, drawn under the third standard of field work, sets forth the same "audit equation" on the practical level of evidence as was stated in Chapter 1 on the theoretical level of "the understanding."

Chapter 1:

$$\frac{\text{Knowledge of the}}{\text{subject matter}} \ + \ \frac{\text{Corroborating}}{\text{knowledge}} \ = \ \text{Understanding}$$

Third standard of field work:

$$\text{Underlying evidence} \ + \ \frac{\text{Corroborating}}{\text{evidence}} \ = \ \frac{\text{Sufficient competent}}{\text{evidential matter}}$$

Paragraphs .08 to .15 of Section 330 strike again the persistent note that sufficiency of evidential matter is determined by an auditor exercising his professional judgment in particular circumstances. The amount and kind of evidential matter required depend on balancing many factors: materiality of the item under examination, materiality and relative risk of possible errors or irregularities, susceptibility of the item to unexpected change or misuse, the kind of evidential matter that is practically available, and the trade-off between the cost of obtaining evidence and its usefulness. An auditor must usually rely on evidence that is "persuasive rather than convincing," but he should search for all relevant evidential matter and evaluate it even if it appears to contradict other evidence and the representations in the financial statements. In other words, an auditor's attestation is a positive expression of an opinion and not a passive declaration of the absence of a negative opinion, and it is always based on "reasonable assurance" rather than certainty.

Our views on the amount and kind of evidence required in various circumstances are in Chapter 5, "Auditing Procedures—Their Nature and Extent," and elsewhere throughout the book, as pertinent. It should be noted that the foregoing discussion—which is concerned with evidence available to an auditor, from the client and elsewhere, to be gathered to arrive at his opinion—has no connection with the working paper evidence he retains to support his opinion. Evidence prepared by the auditor to demonstrate that his work was adequately done is discussed in Chapters 4 and 7.

Standards of Reporting

Adherence to Generally Accepted Accounting Principles

The report shall state whether the financial statements are presented in accordance with generally accepted accounting principles.

Obviously, an auditor must be thoroughly familiar with generally accepted accounting principles to comply responsibly with the standard.

The literature is vast on accounting principles and the meaning of "generally accepted." Nevertheless, the accounting profession has been severely and sometimes cynically criticized from both within and without for failure to be more precise and all-encompassing in promulgating generally accepted accounting principles.

Despite acknowledged deficiencies in generally accepted accounting principles, aggravated by some misunderstanding by non-accountants, the phrase is generally understood by practitioners. It stands for a large body of knowledge and practice which is useful and enduring and to a large extent consistent. A purpose of this book is to discuss in each of the appropriate chapters the current body of generally accepted accounting principles as we understand them. We recognize that some principles are changing so rapidly that statements of them may be outdated or incomplete by the time this book is published or soon thereafter. That is the nature of generally accepted accounting principles in a dynamic business environment. However, the main body of principles has demonstrated strength and durability under stress and can be expected to change only slowly, despite all the efforts that are being made currently to probe fundamentals and to reduce alternatives.

Accountants generally agree that the accounting principles referred to in the first standard of reporting and in the auditor's opinion are not fundamental truths or comprehensive laws, comparable to Newton's laws in physics, from which the details of practice are derived. Fundamental concepts of that nature may yet be discovered in accounting and the search for fundamentals continues. In the meantime, accountants have wrestled over the years with specific situations arising in practice and have developed and adopted numerous rules, conventions, and doctrines having "substantial authoritative support," which are now called principles. Some of those principles have been promulgated formally by an authoritative body of the profession or the SEC, but often they represent a consensus of professional bodies, prominent writers, and eminent practitioners. Those accepted conventions comprise the body of generally accepted accounting principles.

The Accounting Principles Board (APB) was the senior technical committee of the AICPA authorized to issue pronouncements on accounting principles from 1959 to 1973, during which period it issued thirty-one Opinions. Previously, the Committee on Accounting Procedure fulfilled that responsibility from 1938 to 1959 and issued fifty-one Bulletins. Until 1973, the AICPA issued interpretations of Accounting Principles Board Opinions, which are considered authoritative.

APB Opinions are generally accepted accounting principles for purposes of the first reporting standard, the auditor's opinion, and the Code of Professional Ethics. Since 1964, auditors' reports signed by Institute members have been required to disclose departures from APB Opinions (including Accounting Research Bulletins of the predecessor committee) unless a departure was disclosed in the financial statements themselves. Rule 203 of the revised Code of Professional Ethics adopted by the AICPA membership early in 1973 places the burden on the auditor to demonstrate that financial statements containing departures from APB Opinions can be in conformity with generally accepted accounting principles.

The Financial Accounting Standards Board (FASB), an independent private body with seven full-time members, replaced the Accounting Principles Board in mid-1973. Council of the AICPA has designated the Financial Accounting Standards Board as the authoritative source of accounting principles for Institute members and has given the Board's pronouncements on accounting standards the same status as Opinions of the Accounting Principles Board for purposes of the first reporting standard, the auditor's opinion, and the Code of Professional Ethics. The publications issued by the FASB include Statements (the equivalent of APB Opinions), interpretations, and exposure drafts.

There have been efforts to expand the first reporting standard to require auditors to report on "fairness" separately from generally accepted accounting principles. The reason for the movement is a belief in some quarters that it is possible to use generally accepted accounting principles in financial statements that do not present fairly and may in fact be misleading. Unfortunately, there has been some basis for that view in the past. Until the issue is clarified, auditors should adhere to the concept that fairness and generally accepted accounting principles are inseparable, even though that concept is not explicitly included in the formal standards. A principal reason is that "fairness" is too loose a term to be practical or useful unless it is defined in a specific frame of reference, i.e., generally accepted accounting principles.

Statement on Auditing Standards No. 5 deals with the issue. In reaching approximately the conclusion stated in the preceding paragraph, the Statement emphasizes repeatedly that the qualified phrase "presents fairly in conformity with generally accepted accounting principles" encompasses the judgment that events and transactions are adequately presented or described in terms of their substance. In our opinion, adequate recognition that substance must prevail over form, and that accounting principles employed must be appropriate in the circumstances, should settle the issue.

Consistent Application

The report shall state whether such principles have been consistently observed in the current period in relation to the preceding period.

The standard of consistency requires an auditor to say specifically in his report whether generally accepted accounting principles have been applied consistently from period to period; consistency within a period is presumed unless otherwise disclosed. The objective is to assure either that changes in accounting principles do not materially affect comparability of financial statements between periods or that the effect is disclosed. Chapter 19, "The Auditor's Report," contains a detailed discussion of the wording of an auditor's assertion about consistency and of the various possible exceptions.

Accounting Changes and Consistency. An accounting change resulting from a choice by management between two or more generally accepted accounting principles affects comparability of financial statements and requires specific comment by an auditor. Examples of that kind of change include a change from a declining-balance method of computing depreciation to a straight-line method, from the LIFO method to the FIFO method for inventory pricing or vice versa, and from the completed-contract method to the percentage-of-completion method of accounting for long-term contracts.

Of course, other factors also affect comparability, for example, changed conditions that necessitate changes in accounting and changed conditions that are unrelated to accounting. The effect of those other factors normally requires disclosure (covered by the third standard of reporting) but not specific comment by an auditor in his opinion. Since other effects on comparability are to be disclosed under the more general third standard, one might ask why the consistency of accounting principles is singled out for separate attention. The reason lies in the nature of alternative accounting principles—alternatives that are considered generally accepted may be substituted one for another, thus changing accounting results without any change in the underlying economic substance: a sound and sometimes necessary practice which is obviously susceptible to abuse.

Two recent pronouncements have significantly affected the application in practice of the consistency standard of reporting. Accounting

Principles Board Opinion No. 20, *Accounting Changes (AICPA Prof. Stds.,* vol. 3, Sections 1051 to 1051B) expanded and clarified the standards for disclosure of accounting changes in financial statements. Statement on Auditing Procedure No. 53, *Reporting on Consistency and Accounting Changes* (now incorporated in Section 420 of SAS No. 1), expanded the guidelines for applying the consistency standard to accounting changes.

Both the Opinion and the Statement distinguish changes in accounting principles from changes in accounting estimates or changes in a reporting entity. The three kinds of changes, called collectively "accounting changes," are further distinguished from other factors affecting comparability of financial statements between periods, including errors in previously issued statements, changes in statement classification, initial adoption of an accounting principle to recognize an event occurring for the first time, and adoption or modification of an accounting principle necessitated by transactions that are clearly different in substance from previous transactions. Of all classes mentioned, only changes in accounting principles and, sometimes, changes in a reporting entity require comment in an auditor's report under the consistency standard of reporting. Of course, the others may have to be either disclosed or commented on under the third standard of reporting.

Reason for Changing Accounting Principles. The most important advance in disclosure standards in APB Opinion No. 20, issued in 1971, is the requirement that a change in accounting principle be justified by a clear explanation of why the newly adopted principle is preferable. That requirement contrasts with the statement it replaces in Statement on Auditing Procedure No. 33, issued in 1963: "The reason for the change need not be stated" (Chapter 8, paragraph 7). It is an unusually explicit example of the extent to which the standards have evolved in the eight years between the two documents. We regard the requirement to justify changes in accounting principles as a profoundly important step toward expecting issuers of financial statements to explain the "why" of their accounting as well as the "what."

Change in Reporting Entity. The consistency standard applies to a change in a reporting entity only if the accounting change is not caused by an economic event. Thus, the standard does not apply if a change in the entity results from an acquisition or disposition of part of the business (including a business combination accounted for by the pooling-of-interests method in accordance with APB Opinion No. 16). It *does* apply if pre-existing subsidiaries or affiliates are added to or excluded from consolidated or combined statements.

Correction of Errors. Although correction of an error does not usually involve a change in accounting principle, some errors involve a wrong application of an accounting principle or selection of an unacceptable principle. Correcting those kinds of errors usually calls for comment in an auditor's report covering the corrected financial statements.

Change in Principle Versus Other Changes. Numerous practical problems arise in attempting to distinguish a change in accounting principle from the other factors affecting comparability of financial statements. The variety and complexity of business conditions encountered in practice are often difficult to interpret. Sometimes the interpretation has to be somewhat arbitrary. For example, APB Opinion No. 20 resolves the problem of distinguishing a change in accounting principle from a change in accounting estimate by requiring doubtful cases to be disclosed in financial statements as changes in estimates and to be considered by the auditor as changes in accounting principle coming under the consistency standard.

SEC Requirements. The SEC requires an auditor to disclose in his opinion matters that affect comparability as well as consistency, for example, a change in the remaining estimated useful life of assets. It is customary to make the disclosure in a middle paragraph of the report, but not in the last—or opinion—paragraph, to minimize possible confusion with the consistency standard. Those requirements are discussed by Rappaport.*

Adequate Disclosure

Informative disclosures in the financial statements are to be regarded as reasonably adequate unless otherwise stated in the report.

SAS No. 1 is general about what constitutes informative disclosures. The Opinions of the Accounting Principles Board, in contrast, contain detailed requirements for financial disclosures, which are authoritative but not comprehensive. They cover only the topics that the APB was able to address and not the vast area of financial information on which no authoritative pronouncements have ever been made, much of which is noncontroversial. More important, the intent of the third standard of reporting is that issuers of financial statements and auditors have a responsibility to assure that disclosures are adequate, regardless of whether a convention or precedent covers the matter. Identifying

* *Ibid.,* pp. 24·57–58.

matters of potential interest to financial statement users, deciding whether and how they should be disclosed, and then demonstrating the conclusion to the client are primary demands on an auditor's skill and judgment.

The leaders of the accounting profession and the SEC are understandably concerned about the attitude of "no rule, no disclosure" manifested by some issuers of financial statements. Court cases and items appearing in the press indicate that the concern is justified. However desirable that concern may be, it presents serious practical problems. For example, SAS No. 1, Section 430, notes the problem of disclosing confidential information or information that could harm a company or its stockholders. The matter is more difficult than the careful words of SAS No. 1 suggest. On the one hand, many managements sincerely believe that almost every additional disclosure requested or required is likely to result in a competitive disadvantage or other detriment to the company or its stockholders. On the other hand, directors, management, auditors, and their legal counsel have to worry about the possibility that a detrimental disclosure not made may be a basis for suit in the wake of subsequent difficulties, even if the cause of the difficulties is completely unrelated to the disclosure.

A prime example of that type of disclosure problem is the requirement to report sales and profits by line of business. In some companies, clear and significant competitive and other business disadvantages result from line-of-business reporting which reveals profits or losses of an important individual product. Resolution of that dilemma should be forthcoming in the next few years. In the meantime, auditors will face difficult judgments in their efforts to comply sensibly and realistically with the third standard of reporting. At least they are not alone; management and its legal counsel face the same problem.

One of the most significant trends of the mid-1970's is the increasing activity of the SEC in expanding its requirements for disclosures in financial statements under its jurisdiction. With a few exceptions, the SEC has been careful not to dictate accounting principles or practices, although it clearly has the authority to do so. Rather, through requiring detailed disclosure of accounting policies, the judgments surrounding them, and their effects on the financial statements, the SEC has been giving visibility to both good and questionable practices, thus obviously encouraging the former.

Expression of Opinion

The report shall either contain an expression of opinion regarding the financial statements, taken as a whole, or an assertion to the effect that an opinion cannot be expressed. When an overall opinion cannot be expressed, the reasons therefor should be stated. In all cases where an auditor's name is associated with financial statements, the report should contain a clear-cut indication of the character of the auditor's examination, if any, and the degree of responsibility he is taking.

An auditor's report must be painstakingly precise in spelling out the opinion expressed. Leaving the meaning of an auditor's opinion open to readers' inferences has long been inappropriate; it has now also become distinctly dangerous. In some instances, an auditor's failure to state his reasons for disclaiming an opinion has permitted inferences that were either more or less favorable to a client than was warranted. In other instances, users of financial statements cited ambiguity in an auditor's report as grounds for claims against him. Levy gives this example: *

> It was a major issue in the *Ultramares* case in relation to the alleged representation that the balance sheet was in accordance with the books, and it was one of the major issues resulting in the reversal which sent the case back for a new trial. Plaintiffs in the *O'Connor* case sought unsuccessfully to have the court submit to the jury the question of whether or not the characterization "Secured" in relation to assets in the balance sheet was a representation of fact as of knowledge.

The fourth standard of reporting was adopted specifically to prevent that kind of misunderstanding. From the time of its adoption, it has been accompanied by detailed recommendations for reporting in all conceivable circumstances and conditions (the fourth standard is discussed further in Chapter 19, "The Auditor's Report"). The standard is thus distinguished from the other nine generally accepted auditing standards, which are essentially broad, qualitative statements of ideals. The fourth standard of reporting is the basis for a detailed prescription because it is necessary for all auditors to use precisely the same words in the same circumstances to prevent misinterpretation of auditors' opinions and the responsibility they assume. The standard was amplified and updated by Statement on Auditing Standards No. 2, *Reports on Audited Financial Statements.*

MATERIALITY

Need for a Materiality Standard

A materiality standard is a practical necessity in both auditing and accounting. Allowing trivia to complicate and clutter up either the

---

* Saul Levy, *Accountants' Legal Responsibility* (New York: AICPA, 1954), p. 43.

auditing process or financial statements is wasteful and disorderly. Worse, it can cause inconsequential matters to obscure significant ones. Therefore, ignoring "items not material" is well-accepted practice: they are not disclosed in financial statements, they require no comment in an auditor's report, and they need not be corrected or adjusted in the accounts.

The concept is simple, but applying it in practice is not. These are some of the major questions: How is materiality of an item measured? Is materiality related to an effect on net income? An effect on the trend of net income? An effect on the balance of an item? Is materiality to be judged on the basis of individual items, categories of items, or the total of all possible items affecting the statements under review? If the total, is it the gross total or the net total?

Materiality is even more perplexing in the details of practice. Are some accounts subject to a lower or looser standard than others? Common sense calls for variations in "guesstimates" to be treated differently from factually based judgments and both to be treated differently from clear-cut errors, but how?

We have long believed, with others in the profession, that a standard —either a Statement of Financial Accounting Standards by the FASB or a Statement on Auditing Standards—is needed to guide practitioners on the subject of materiality. The concept of materiality is highly complex, is understood differently by different auditors, and is constantly alleged to be abused. The FASB is presently wrestling with the subject.

Pervasiveness of Materiality Questions

All kinds of questions about accounting for and disclosure of various items and events arise during the course of every audit, even one that is impeccably "clean" because of diligent auditing. Each question must be dealt with as two questions: First, how should the item or event be treated on its own merits? And second, is it material enough that the way it is treated affects the fair presentation of financial position or results of operations in the financial statements? The answer to the first question is of consequence only if the answer to the second—the materiality question—is affirmative. How materiality and relative risk affect the auditing process is also discussed in Chapter 5.

Obviously, an item that is clearly material is dealt with on its own merits and is not part of the subject under discussion. Also, material items are much less likely to be overlooked or accounted for incorrectly. Most of the questions of possible adjustments or disclosures raised by an audit involve both the question of correct treatment and the question of whether the item or event is material. Even if an item or event is clearly too small to be important, the question has to be dealt with because of the possibility that it may combine with others to accumulate to a material total.

The following are examples of items and events giving rise to possible adjustments or disclosures that may or may not be material:

Simple errors in the accounts—a mistake in a computation, an invoice payable that was overlooked.

Events requiring disclosure as unusual or nonrecurring, or segregation as extraordinary—occasional sales of productive assets used in the business, a casualty loss in a subsidiary warehouse.

Items possibly requiring prior-period adjustments—settlement of income taxes, a lawsuit, or wage contract negotiations.

Changes in the business entity—acquisition of a subsidiary company, consolidation of a subsidiary not previously consolidated.

Voluntary changes in accounting principles—adoption of a standard cost system that results in including certain production variances in the expenses of the year of occurrence rather than in inventory costs.

Changed conditions requiring new accounting—a new sales policy involving more liberal merchandise return privileges or product warranties, a change in a labor contract of a subsidiary that necessitates accrual of vacation pay.

Judgments or estimates—an allowance for estimated bad debts or for estimated obsolescence of inventory that could be larger or smaller.

In each of the above examples, the generally accepted accounting treatment is clear, but it is not clear whether failure to follow it would materially affect the financial statements.

A client's accounting staff decides how to account for and disclose most items and events before an audit begins. That is true even if the auditor is routinely consulted in advance about significant transactions; it is not practicable to consult the auditor on every unusual transaction, and those not clearly material may be either overlooked or routinely passed without review. The auditor must independently evaluate those judgments and reach his own conclusions about accounting, disclosure, and materiality.

The most sensitive category listed in the above examples is probably the last—judgments or estimates—because of the uncertainties involved, but differences of opinion between management and an auditor are also possible, and perhaps likely, in each of the other categories. Of course, the auditor should first discuss differences thoroughly with the client with the objective of reconciling them. However, even with the best of relations between client and auditor, several differences of opinion will usually remain as suggested "audit adjustments."

In companies that issue financial statement data periodically, financial management is understandably reluctant to change its initial judgments about accounting and materiality. By the time the audit is in progress, earnings for the year or three quarters of the year have been tentatively determined and reported to the president, the board of directors, and in many cases even the public. Even when management requests review of the accounts prior to any interim or year-end release, an auditor is unlikely to uncover all possible differences of opinion. Considerable embarrassment results if the preliminary figures are not borne out by the audited financial statements, even if the differences are small. Management, however responsible, is therefore interested in seeing that an auditor's suggested adjustments to the financial statements are "waived" as not material.

Score Sheets

Some auditors have adopted a general practice of keeping a record of potential audit adjustments, commonly called a "score sheet." As an audit progresses, each item, large or small, that an auditor thinks should or could be adjusted is first taken up with the client. Of course, if it is something the client has obviously overlooked or misjudged and there is agreement about its disposition, the accounts are adjusted and the item is of no further concern. If the client disagrees, or agrees but prefers not to adjust, the item is carried on the score sheet. The company under examination need not be especially complex to produce a score sheet covering several pages of working paper.

The auditor evaluates the score sheet as one of the concluding steps of the audit. More often than not, no single account is materially affected by the score sheet entries and the cumulative pluses and minuses net to an insignificant effect on individual classifications in the financial statements. The auditor then completes the audit and issues his opinion on the financial statements, and the score sheet becomes part of the evidential matter documenting his examination. It may also be useful in discussing with the client suggested improvements in his accounting procedures.

Sometimes, however, an auditor believes that the possible adjustments listed on the score sheet, although individually insignificant, accumulate to a total that is material to one or more of the items appearing in the financial statements—usually net income. The auditor then confers with the client to decide what to do.

The client may be able to produce further evidence to justify the initial treatment of some items or may agree to record some of them in the accounts or to disclose others. The discussions continue until enough score sheet items are resolved so that the auditor can conclude that the remaining items do not adversely affect the fairness of presentation of the financial statements.

Depending on the size and complexity of an organization, each score sheet item may have to be taken up with several levels of management. The first consultation, of course, is with the individual directly responsible, who must supply all the facts. Additional conferences may include his supervisor, and sometimes a plant controller and division controller, all of whom must concur in a decision. Often the deciding score sheet conference includes top management of the client company: the financial vice president and the chief executive. If discussions reach that level, two subjects should be probed: how to resolve the current score sheet problems and how to prevent similar problems from growing to such a magnitude in the future.

Rules of Thumb

The essence of materiality is that insignificant differences do not matter. The question of how large a difference may be before it matters has never been definitively answered in the literature of accounting and auditing. It was addressed in the famous *BarChris* case,* and the decision in that case included a number of issues of materiality. However, the reasoning in the *BarChris* decision was so intertwined with the specific facts of the case that it does not provide general guidance. The determination is still left to individual professional judgment, which can only be guided by some rules of thumb that are by no means uniformly accepted.

The figure most often given for the point at which a difference becomes material is 5%. That is, if the item under scrutiny is within 5% of what it might otherwise be, the difference is immaterial. Obviously, any rule of thumb, such as 5%, must be used with great caution and careful judgment. Sometimes 5% is clearly too broad a range. For example, small variations in trends are considered significant in companies with operational stability, such as public utilities, and the limit of materiality must be reduced to 3%, 2%, or less; otherwise, "immaterial" items would affect the trend. In recent years, the trend of annual earnings (up or down) has become of paramount interest to investors; consequently, whether an item is of sufficient mate-

---

* *Escott et al. v. BarChris Construction Corp. et al.,* 283 F. Supp. 643 (S.D.N.Y. 1968).

riality to influence the trend must receive careful consideration. (See a reference to this concept in APB Opinion No. 20, paragraph 38.)

Sometimes materiality of an item or event is clearly a function of the nature of the account. Little or no error is tolerable if precision is desirable and achievable, as in capital stock accounts where accounting does not require estimates or judgments. In contrast, inventory valuations can never be made with precision, and the threshold of materiality may be relatively high.

Some auditors believe that the standard of materiality should vary with the nature of the difference. If the difference arises from a clearcut error, the tolerance is smaller than for a judgment about classification or disclosure, and that in turn is smaller than for a difference in estimating collectibility, realizability, or some other uncertain future event.

Netting

The way items are added together or set off against each other can significantly affect evaluations of materiality. Some items or events are more significant than others, implying that some kinds should be evaluated individually while others may be evaluated in groups.

Netting separate items to determine the amount that is to be judged for materiality raises intricate questions that need careful attention. Is it acceptable, for example, to net the effect of an error against the effect of a change in accounting principle? Or to net an error in the beginning balance against an error in the ending balance? Clearly, both answers must be negative. Each change in accounting principle must be considered separately under the consistency standard, and APB Opinion No. 20 (*AICPA Prof. Stds.,* vol. 3, Sections 1051 to 1051B) calls for estimates and evaluations of materiality to be made afresh every year. Also, netting material items to obtain an immaterial total obviously violates the third standard of reporting. Otherwise, we see no harm in netting of, for example, insignificant differences in estimates against insignificant errors.

Summary

It should be clear from the foregoing discussion that a materiality standard is needed and also that it will not be easy to find one that can adequately encompass all the possible combinations of pertinent circumstances. In the meantime, each auditor has to try his best to judge what information might affect a reader's interpretation of the financial statements. If a decision might reasonably rest on a disclosure, it is material; if not, it is immaterial. For example, if one is buying an asset or a company at a price precisely measured by accounting results, small amounts become material; on the other hand, if one is buying or selling stock, prices may be affected by but are not derived directly from the financial statements, and a larger amount may have no effect on willingness to buy or sell. As rational as that criterion is, however, it is too subjective for easy or confident application.

RELIANCE ON OTHER AUDITORS

Frequently, an auditor, or members or employees of his firm, cannot examine the financial statements of one or more subsidiaries, divisions, or other components of a client company to be included in the financial statements on which he is reporting. Distance is usually the reason, but there are sometimes other causes, such as inadequate staff, a client's preference for another auditor, or a business combination during the period with a company that has another auditor. An auditor who cannot examine all the evidence that might be needed for his opinion must consider several questions before proceeding.

Accepting Principal Responsibility

The first question is whether his participation in the total engagement is sufficient to enable him to be responsible as principal auditor for an opinion on the financial statements as a whole. That decision does not depend only on the proportions of assets, revenue, and income that are subject to his own examination compared to the proportions examined by others, although those factors do significantly influence it. It also may be affected significantly by the relative consequences of issues and problems in the various components and by his knowledge of and contact with the entities involved.

The decision must rest on whether he can form an opinion based on an adequate understanding developed in accordance with the logic of the "audit equation." He cannot act as principal auditor if any essential part of that understanding is abdicated or defaulted to the other auditors. However, if he can complete the logic of the understanding through, for example, a review of the work of other auditors or by applying supplemental auditing procedures, there is no intrinsic limit to the extent of his reliance on the work of others. Within the rigor of that logic, there is an important qualitative difference in whether he wishes to accept full responsibility or to make it clear that he relies in part on others.

Accepting Full Responsibility

Once an auditor concludes that he can accept principal responsibility for an opinion, he must decide whether he will take full responsibility for the work of the other auditors. If he does, he omits reference to other auditors in his report, thus implicitly taking responsibility for the full examination. (See Chapter 19.)

An auditor should not rely blindly on the report of another auditor. Some rather dramatic examples of auditors who did and came to grief are available as object lessons. Rappaport * describes two of them.

An auditor who expects to rely on another with whom he is not acquainted should inquire about the other auditor's reputation and professional standing. Bankers and other credit grantors and other practitioners are among the sources having sufficient background, experience, and knowledge to give a reliable opinion. Inquiry is sometimes fairly difficult to complete satisfactorily, particularly if the other auditor is overseas. To locate someone who is clearly knowledgeable enough to give a valid opinion is not easy, and the inquiry is not always understood or the response not always sound in U. S. terms.

An auditor should also communicate directly with another auditor on whom he expects to rely. He should obtain a letter from the other auditor stating positively that he is independent as required by the rules of the AICPA and, if applicable, by the requirements of the SEC. SAS No. 1, paragraph 543.10(c), sets forth certain other minimum information to be ascertained by communication with the other auditor: that the other auditor is aware that the financial statements he examines will be included in financial statements on which the principal auditor will report; that the other auditor is familiar with generally accepted auditing standards and accounting principles in the United States and will conduct his examination and report according to those standards and principles; that the other auditor knows of relevant SEC requirements, if applicable; and that the other auditor will review matters affecting the consolidated statements, such as elimination of intercompany transactions and uniformity of accounting practices among the entities.

When an auditor takes full responsibility for the work of another auditor, he must be as satisfied with the quality of that work and with the results as if the work were done by his own assistants. Therefore, he will usually need to visit the other auditor, discuss the work done or to be done, review the audit program, and perhaps issue amplifying instructions and review the working papers. He may not need to do each of these every year, and some of them may be done by telephone

* *Op. cit.,* pp. 24·28–33.

or by mail, but an auditor's review of the work of another auditor for which he takes responsibility should be at least as thorough as his review of the work of his own staff. Some would say that an auditor who relies on the work of others should review it more carefully than he would the work done by his own firm.

Of course, an auditor may accept full responsibility for the work of another auditor without any of the foregoing procedures if the component reported on by the other auditor is not material in the financial statements as a whole. Then he may express an opinion with no inquiry about or contact with the other auditor, just as he may need no examination of an insignificant subsidiary to express an opinion on consolidated financial statements if no other auditors are involved.

Arrangements should be made in advance for the auditor to be free to communicate with the other auditor if the need arises; for example, to resolve questions concerning intercompany transactions or consistency in the application of accounting principles.

Identifying Other Auditor

A principal auditor who is unable to take the foregoing steps to assure himself of the quality of work and results of another auditor as if it were his own should not be willing to accept full responsibility for it. His report must then refer to the examination of the other auditor, indicating the division of responsibility for examining the financial statements. (Chapter 19, "The Auditor's Report," discusses recommended wording.) That reference is not a qualification of his opinion but an explanation of the scope of his examination. An auditor who refers to the examination of another auditor in his report need not assure himself about the work done by the other auditor to the same extent as if he accepted full responsibility for it. However, he must still inquire about the reputation and professional standing of the other auditor and communicate with him to assure that he is independent, that he knows how his report is to be used, and that the report will conform to generally accepted auditing standards and accounting principles in the United States. That is, even if an auditor does not take responsibility for the work of another auditor on whom he relies, he must inquire sufficiently to obtain positive assurance that his reliance is justified.

Other Precautions

The authoritative pronouncement, SAS No. 1, does not require it, but we believe that some or all of the review procedures described above are often highly desirable in certain circumstances, even if an auditor does not accept responsibility for the work of another. Examples of these circumstances are: if a component under examination is significant in the consolidated financial statements as a whole, if potentially important differences in auditing standards or accounting principles are known to exist in the other auditor's country of residence, or if particularly difficult auditing or accounting problems need to be resolved. Our experience is that auditors in other countries commonly believe sincerely that they understand U. S. accounting principles but in fact have not kept pace with the increasing number and complexity of APB Opinions, FASB Statements, and SEC Releases. We have seen problems go unrecognized concerning deferred tax accounting, accruals of deferred compensation and pension costs, and transactions in complex securities, to name only a few. We believe that an auditor serves his client best by including as an integral part of his examination periodic personal visits to auditors in foreign countries on whom he must rely.

CONFIDENTIALITY AND CONFLICT OF INTERESTS

Rule 301 of the Code of Professional Ethics of the AICPA states that a member ". . . shall not disclose any confidential information obtained in the course of a professional engagement except with the consent of the client." It almost goes without saying that Rule 301 is fundamental to auditors.

Requirement for Confidentiality

Common sense as well as the basic idea of auditing dictates that the auditor and not the client should decide what information the auditor needs and its relevance to his opinion. Efficient dispatch of audit tasks requires mutual trust and candor. Therefore, the client must be certain that, except for disclosures required by law and custom, the information he shares with the auditor will go no further without his permission. He must be assured of confidentiality and of the auditor's sense of responsibility for it.

Maintaining Confidentiality

At one time, auditors emphasized the need for confidentiality by imposing formal restrictions on their staffs. For example, a staff man was not even supposed to tell his wife, or anyone else, where or for which client he was working. The need to preserve confidentiality is now as great as ever, if not greater, but auditors handle the matter directly by constantly emphasizing to staff the need for and ethics of maintaining a client's confidence. Auditors have developed a reputation for being closemouthed, a good characteristic for an auditor to have and to pass on to his staff.

Despite auditors' emphasis on confidentiality, executives of some client companies worry about losing control of sensitive material through an auditor's staff. A client may believe that certain material is so sensitive that he cannot be comfortable with an auditor's general assurances about the character and training of his audit staff. If access to the material is necessary to the auditor's opinion, the client has no alternative but to grant access; if he wishes to limit that access to the auditor in charge, the auditor should respect the client's scruples.

Most attitudes are less extreme and the manager or senior field auditor can gain access to restricted data by promising to keep his working papers in a separate, confidential file. Although awareness of clients' sensibilities in that respect is important, we have observed that clients' fears generally tend to subside as the working relationship is strengthened and mutual confidence grows.

Insider Information

An auditor and his assistants have the same responsibilities as management for handling insider information: not to turn it to personal profit nor to disclose it to others who may do so. Those responsibilities are clearly encompassed in the general injunctions of the Code of Professional Ethics quoted earlier: independence forbids personal profit and confidentiality forbids aiding others. The point deserves emphasis because the ways in which insider information may be used, even inadvertently, are many and subtle, and because society's heightened standards of accountability have focused attention on the responsibility of all insiders to use their information impartially.

Conflict of Interests

Some clients' fears that secrets will be passed on to competitors are so great that they refuse to engage an auditor whose clients include a competitor; others are satisfied with assurances that the staff on their engagement has no contact with the personnel of a competitor. The price paid by a client for so high a degree of confidentiality is the loss of industry expertise that can be provided by auditors who are familiar with more than one company in an industry. Our experience is that the risk of leakage of information having real competitive value is slight.

A more difficult and quite common conflict of interests results if two clients of an auditor do business with each other. For example, an auditor of a commercial bank client is also likely to have clients among the bank's depositors and borrowers. Suppose the auditor observes the September 30th physical inventory of a client who is also a borrower at the client bank, and finds a substantial shortage. Under the terms of the loan agreement with the bank, audited financial statements are not due at the bank until the next March 31st. The client understandably wants time to determine the cause of the shortage and whether it is real or not. What does the auditor do? He is faced with a practical conflict of interests that is quite apart from problems of potential formal legal liability or expression of an opinion on either set of financial statements. The requirements of principle and of practice are irreconcilable. On the one hand, he must not use his insider information from one client to profit by improving his relationship with the other client. On the other hand, it is absurd for him to pretend that he does not know what he does know. One party will be unhappy if he does nothing; the other party will be upset if he does anything.

The way out of the dilemma is clear in principle, although following it in practice may be difficult. Court cases seem to have clarified a client's responsibility. As soon as a significant event—good or bad—happens, it should be disclosed to all concerned. Neither the client bank nor the client borrower has priority, and the incidental fact of their parallel relationship with the auditor should not affect the handling of the matter. The auditor's duty is to persuade his client to make the necessary disclosures—to the other party if it affects only the two, and publicly if it affects the public.

If the client management refuses, the auditor must treat the incident as he would a significant problem in the financial statements; he must decide whether he can continue to serve the client. Usually he will consider going to the board of directors, and in some cases to the SEC and the stock exchanges, and to anyone else he knows is affected. Those are very serious steps, and whether to take them is as weighty a decision as an auditor can ever be called on to make. But he would risk even more serious problems by favoring his own clients over other concerned parties.

Another problem of confidentiality and conflict of interests may result if a client company that is considering the possibility of acquiring another company engages its auditor to examine that company. What happens to the auditor's findings and to whom does he owe his duty of confidentiality? Our practice in those circumstances is to obtain written confirmation from the chief executives of both companies regarding the extent and limitations of the auditor's responsibilities to each. Usually that confirmation approves delivering the findings to the acquiring company, but only after discussing them with the company to be acquired.

THE AUDITOR AND FRAUD OR ILLEGAL ACTS

The objective of an "opinion audit" is an opinion on financial statements regarding fairness of presentation of financial position and results of operations of a client company. It is not specifically designed to prevent or detect theft, embezzlement, and the like. An audit can never be designed to *prevent* fraud, although certain kinds of auditing have some deterrent effect. Special audits can be designed for the purpose of *detecting* certain types of fraud, but other ways of discouraging and discovering dishonesty of employees are more effective and less costly (see "Preventing or Detecting Fraud," below).

The unique function of an opinion audit has been clearly defined for decades, and auditors generally understand the limits of an audit in detecting fraud or illegal acts. Nevertheless, many laymen persistently believe that searching for dishonesty and illegality is a major purpose of an audit. The accounting profession, collectively and individually, often sounds self-serving and defensive in emphasizing limits on responsibility assumed by auditors, especially when stockholders are deceived by massive fraud that includes false and misleading financial statements, as evidently occurred in the *McKesson & Robbins* and *Equity Funding* cases. The following paragraphs describe our opinion of a reasonable standard of responsibility, a standard which we believe the pronouncements of the AICPA have expressed or implied.

Fraud As It Relates to an Auditor's Responsibility

While there are many kinds of fraud and dishonesty, for the purposes of this discussion all fraudulent acts fall into one of two categories: those of nonmanagement and those of management (i.e., the top executive group). That is to say, there is dishonesty that can occur in spite of management's efforts to prevent it, and there is dishonesty that occurs only because management wills it.

The extent of collusion—the number of people who conspire to commit the fraud—has an important bearing on whether it can or should be detected by an audit. On the one hand, it is axiomatic that the greater the number of people who know about an illegal act, the more difficult it is to continue to conceal it. On the other hand, if collusion—either management or nonmanagement—is systematic and well disciplined, all evidence of the fraud can be suppressed or altered so as to make it virtually impossible to detect by presently recognized auditing procedures.

The significance of the fraud to the financial statements obviously affects its significance to the audit. An auditor should not seek to detect insignificant and immaterial items—whether the result of fraud or not—and should not be held responsible for failing to do so.

Thus, three characteristics of fraud affect an auditor's responsibility for detecting it: whether it is significant to the financial statements, whether collusion effectively conceals it, and whether it is management or nonmanagement fraud.

Preventing or Detecting Fraud

Any discussion of an auditor's responsibility for discovery of defalcations and similar irregularities must be conducted with the perspective that a responsible management relies on many provisions for protection against that type of loss, and the last—and least—of all of these is the audit.

The most important provision for protection is the system of internal control, the subject of Chapter 3. As described at length in that chapter, internal control serves several purposes; safeguarding assets and discouraging both purposeful and accidental unauthorized activity are two of them. Systemization and disciplined adherence to the system are basic. Physical security, such as safes, storerooms, guards, gates, and locks, together with systems and disciplines that restrict access to those secure places, are required to protect assets from damage or pilferage by outsiders as well as insiders. Segregation of duties—having the work of one employee check that of another—serves to promote efficiency and accuracy and also makes it necessary to organize collusion to conceal fraud or errors. Finally, good supervisory controls, including internal audit, should serve to warn management of conditions that could make fraud possible.

Other provisions for protection are careful investigation of the background of an individual given a position of trust, responsibility, or temptation, and adequate fidelity bond insurance. Insurance indemnifies a company for losses that are discovered and also provides a deterrent to dishonesty on the part of a bonded employee. The bonding company also helps in investigating the character of those bonded.

Thus, a management interested in preventing or detecting employee fraud has the means for doing so without relying on an auditor. An appropriate function of an auditor in the system of protection is evaluating it and pointing out weaknesses or opportunities for improvement, not supplementing it or duplicating it by making tests for the purpose of detecting fraud. Although some auditors explicitly assume that function in special examinations, it is not yet required by the standards applicable to the ordinary examination.

Management policies can be circumvented by collusion on the part of employees, either among themselves or with outsiders. Active supervisory control is the only means of preventing or detecting employee collusion. For example, collusion between purchasing agents and vendors can be discouraged by sound systems and procedures, but it can be prevented or detected only by close, continuous supervision of the activities and relationships of those exposed to the temptation. An audit can test those activities, but auditing can never substitute for adequate supervision.

If management carries out its responsibility for internal control, including provisions to protect against loss from fraud, an auditor is entitled to rely on those controls to insure the accuracy of the accounts underlying the financial statements, including their freedom from error resulting from undetected employee fraud.

Fraud on the part of management is an entirely different matter. By definition, it is willful circumvention of the principles of good management, especially accountability. Its usual objective is to publish false and misleading financial statements that deceive stockholders and creditors, rather than to steal assets, although occasionally both are involved. Both law and business custom have attempted to protect the public against it, by statute, by civil and criminal penalties, and by such customs as having boards of directors that include nonmanagement people. Another important custom, increasingly supported by securities laws and regulations, is the independent audit.

Responsibility for Fraud and Illegal Acts

The following is an excerpt from SAS No. 1, the authoritative statement of the accounting profession:

> In making the ordinary examination, the independent auditor is aware of the possibility that fraud may exist. Financial statements may be misstated as the result of defalcations and similar irregularities, or deliberate misrepresentation by management, or both. The auditor recognizes that fraud, if sufficiently material, may affect his opinion on the financial statements, and his examination, made in accordance with generally accepted auditing standards, gives consideration to this possibility. However, the ordinary examination directed to the expression of an opinion on financial statements is not primarily or specifically designed, and cannot be relied upon, to disclose defalcations and other similar irregularities . . . . [or] deliberate misrepresentation by management. . . . [Paragraph 110.05]

That is to say, an auditor has essentially the same responsibility for fraud and illegal acts as for other factors that may affect his opinion. His examination must be thorough enough to provide him with reasonable assurance that fraud, misrepresentation, and similar irregularities do not materially affect the financial statements.

An auditor's examination may, of course, reveal fraud, but two kinds of fraud are likely to escape detection, even in an audit that is carefully planned and well executed: immaterial fraud and material fraud that is skillfully concealed, especially through collusion of several parties to the fraud. Some types of defalcations or thefts are too small to distort financial statements, no matter how significant they may be in moral principle or to the perpetrator's own fortunes. Likewise, financial statements are unaffected by significant fraud that, by accident or design, is hidden in the same expense category in which the loss would be recognized if it were discovered. A company may suffer losses in many ways: management may be incompetent, sales policies may be ill-advised, costs may be higher than necessary, operating losses of various kinds may be suffered, and defalcations may be concealed through improper or unauthorized charges to cost or expense accounts. All such elements are reflected in the statement of income, and it is not necessary for the various types of losses to be segregated for an auditor to give his opinion on the presentation of the results of operations for the year.

The possibility always exists that management can perpetrate and conceal a fraud so skillfully that no clue shows, even to an auditor who diligently and intelligently complies with generally accepted auditing standards. An auditor could expand his examination significantly without finding a clever fraud; he can never expand it far enough to be certain of detecting all fraud. In general, an examination extended beyond the evidence needed for reasonable assurance of absence of irregularities that might affect the financial statements meets steeply diminishing returns—the added ability to detect fraud is rarely worth the added effort and cost.

Extending procedures in an effort to disclose defalcations does not serve the best interests of either the auditor or his client. Some years ago, a committee of the AICPA explored the matter with representatives of a large number of surety companies. As a result, a number of surety companies representing a substantial percentage of the fidelity bonds written in the United States signed a letter, addressed to the Institute, stating that they would not assert claims, under their rights of subrogation, against auditors if affirmatively dishonest or criminal acts or gross negligence on the part of the auditors were not involved. The letter further stated that claims would not be asserted unless an impartial committee of three non-accountants concluded, after a hearing, that the circumstances warranted that action.

As indicated in Chapter 1, although an auditor is not a lawyer, he is expected to be generally familiar with laws governing business and rules of regulatory commissions affecting the accounting of his clients. An auditor cannot, however, be responsible for a policing program to see that all government regulations are followed. If, as a result of his tests, indications of what may be illegal transactions appear, and the client's legal counsel agrees that illegal acts are involved, the auditor should so report to the board of directors or, in extreme cases, to the stockholders. He should also receive the client's legal counsel's written opinion as to the client's liabilities resulting from such transactions. If a substantial contingent liability is believed to exist because of illegal acts, the auditor should insist that necessary reference to the liability be made in the financial statements or qualify his opinion.

If an auditor finds that improper payments have been made, it once was considered sufficient to report them to the board of directors, and if the board of directors approved them to receive a certified copy of minutes covering the approval. That still may be adequate for closely held companies, but it may not go unchallenged for public companies. The morality of many long accepted business practices is being increasingly questioned. In our opinion, the issue is not a passing one, but may signal a trend toward expecting disclosure of—and auditors' attention to—questionable acts that could be criminal, regardless of their materiality to the financial statements. If so, both management and auditors are facing a real challenge in discovering how to respond to the demand—the direction or form of that response is not at all clear.

In summary, an auditor must have evidence affording a basis for concluding with reasonable assurance that the financial statements are free of material error, including deliberate misrepresentation. His auditing procedures must be designed to that end. He is responsible for diligently seeking that evidence and intelligently evaluating it, and *most of the time* doing so prevents or detects management fraud. However, it cannot always detect a cleverly concealed, collusive fraud, and an opinion cannot and should not be taken as a guarantee (see "Related Party Transactions," Chapter 18).

On occasion, a client may engage an independent auditor to make a special fraud-oriented examination, either as an adjunct to the opinion audit or as a separate engagement. A special examination may be necessary or desirable, for example, if suspicions of fraud are aroused or other problems come to light. Regularly recurring examinations for that purpose are seldom desirable, however, for reasons given in a preceding section. The same time and money could be spent more effectively to improve systems design or to employ and train a special internal audit staff to watch over parts of the company that may be especially susceptible to fraud.

Avoiding Misunderstanding

Auditors must, of course, avoid misunderstanding with clients about the responsibility for discovering fraud, defalcations, and similar irregularities. Most auditors recognize the necessity of a written communication spelling out mutual understanding of functions, objectives, and responsibilities regarding an audit examination. In fact, written agreements about audit examinations are so important that they should not be limited to the subject of responsibility for detecting fraud but should cover all important aspects of an engagement. This can be covered in the engagement memorandum (Chapter 7) or management letter (Chapter 4).

Discovery or Suspicion of Fraud

Chapter 5 discusses the alternative courses of action an auditor may follow if his review of the systems in use indicates weaknesses that could permit fraud. However, when fraud is discovered or suspected during an ordinary audit examination, an auditor's reaction may range from merely pointing out to the client an apparently insignificant incident, through requiring a special investigation to determine the magnitude of a potential problem, to the extreme of withdrawing from the engagement because of inability to form an opinion. The auditor should satisfy himself as to whether a potential loss is of such magnitude that it will affect his opinion on the financial statements. He may well take into consideration the circumstances in which his suspicions were aroused. For example, peculations from an imprest fund would normally be expected to be of less consequence than those arising from "lapping" accounts receivable collections. In any event, the appropriate level of client management should be fully advised of the situation. If the auditor has established to his own satisfaction that a probable loss is not so material as to affect his opinion, the client should decide whether to pursue the matter further. If the auditor has reason to believe that a material loss from defalcations or similar irregularities exists, he has no alternative but to request that the amount be reasonably determined. The decision, whether the initial determination is to be made by the client or by the auditor as an additional assignment, would, of course, be made by the client. If the determination of the probable loss is made by the client, the auditor should satisfy himself of its reasonableness by appropriate tests.

ACCOUNTANTS' LEGAL LIABILITIES

The subject of accountants' legal liabilities is complicated and whole volumes are devoted to it. It cannot be covered comprehensively in a book such as this, but mention of this growing area must be made in any discussion of professional responsibility. At the risk of oversimplification, there follows an outline of the current status of this subject.

Liability to Clients

Liability to clients is relatively easy to describe. An accountant is "in privity" with his client. In other words, his services are performed pursuant to a direct contractual relationship with his client. In these circumstances, it has been clear under common law that a professional is liable to his client for simple negligence. Needless to say, if an auditor is liable to his client for his simple negligence, he is also liable to his client for gross negligence or fraud. For many years, auditors have been careful to make it clear to clients that an ordinary audit is not intended to disclose defalcations and similar irregularities, and so failure to discover one should not be a basis for suit. (See "Responsibility for Fraud and Illegal Acts" earlier in this chapter.) Responsibilities regarding unaudited statements are covered in Chapter 19.

Liability to Third Parties

Determining the proper scope of an accountant's liability to third parties is a more complicated matter. Conceptually, the problem is to balance the accountant's reasonable right to protect himself from the claims of unknown (and sometimes innumerable) persons who he had no reason to suspect would rely on his work, against what is viewed as the important public policy of protecting ever increasing numbers of third parties who rely upon financial statements from the adverse effects of incompetent performance by professionals.

The *Ultramares* Rule

The first authoritative, and probably most influential, effort to deal with this balance was that of Judge Cardozo of New York in the 1931 case of *Ultramares Corp. v. Touche*. That decision firmly established the rule that an accountant is liable for his simple negligence only to someone with whom he is in privity. However, the opinion indicated that an accountant could be liable to third parties if his conduct involved fraud, or gross negligence tantamount to fraud.

The *Ultramares* Rule has been significantly eroded in the years since 1931. The erosion began with judicial decisions that held that accountants should be liable for simple negligence to persons who they specifically knew would rely upon their opinions with respect to particular financial statements even though they were not in privity. That principle was in due course further eroded to the effect that an accountant was liable for simple negligence not only to known third parties, but also to any reasonably limited and reasonably definable class of persons whom the accountant might reasonably expect to rely upon his opinion with respect to financial statements.

The Federal Securities Laws

This process of erosion was probably given direction and emphasis by certain provisions of the Securities Act of 1933 and the Securities Exchange Act of 1934, statutes which, like the erosions of the *Ultramares* Rule, contemplate the possibility of large numbers of persons relying upon financial statements and accountants' opinions thereon.

To the end of protecting such persons in certain circumstances, Section 11(a) of the Securities Act of 1933 provides as follows:

> In case any part of the registration statement . . . contained an untrue statement of a material fact or omitted to state a material fact required to be stated therein or necessary to make the statements therein not misleading, any person acquiring such security . . . may . . . sue . . . every accountant . . . who has with his consent been named as having . . . certified any part of the registration statement . . . with respect to the statement in such registration statement . . . which purports to have been . . . certified by him.

Section 11(a) thus establishes what on its face appears to be a standard of absolute liability. There is, however, an escape clause in the form of Section 11(b), which provides that if, with regard to a portion of a registration statement made upon his authority as an expert, an accountant had, after reasonable investigation, reasonable ground to believe and did believe the statements made therein were true and there were no omissions to state material facts, he is relieved of the liability imposed by Section 11(a). Section 11(b) establishes the so-called "due diligence" defense.

Section 11 thus provides a rule that is comparable to the increasingly prevalent common-law rule of liability for simple negligence to known and reasonably limited classes of third parties. While Section 11 involves a different burden of proof than the common-law rule (under Section 11, the plaintiff, having established that the registration statement contains an untrue statement of material fact, does not have to prove the accountant's negligence; rather the accountant must prove his own freedom from negligence), it does provide for liability to a class of known and reasonably limited third parties (the purchasers of securities in a public offering) on the grounds of the accountant's simple negligence. Section 11 has not received much attention recently, principally because it applies only to registered public offerings of securities, subject to the safeguards of the Securities Act of 1933, and not to routine purchase and sale transactions in securities. Moreover, the statute of limitations (one year) is relatively short.

For many years, then, accountants were sued principally either at common law, with plaintiffs continually attempting to erode the *Ultramares* Rule, or, where the type of transaction permitted it, pursuant to Section 11 of the Securities Act of 1933. Of late, however, another section of the federal securities laws has received increasing attention in connection with claims against professionals. Section 10(b) of the Securities Exchange Act of 1934, and Rule 10b-5 thereunder, have developed remarkably over the past 15 years, so that now hardly any securities litigation fails to allege a violation of these provisions. Rule 10b-5 contains broad (and some say vague) proscriptions providing that:

> It shall be unlawful for any person . . . by the use of . . . interstate commerce . . . to make any untrue statement of a material fact or to omit to state a material fact necessary in order to make the statements made, in the light of the circumstances under which they were made, not misleading. . . .

The courts have spent an immense amount of time defining standards for liability under Rule 10b-5. Although it appears to establish a rule of absolute liability regardless of motive or intention, the courts have held that in fact an element of guilty knowledge or intention is required. Consequently, at least to date, simple negligence has not been considered sufficient to establish primary Rule 10b-5 liability. However, there is a developing tendency for plaintiffs to charge that an accountant's negligence has "aided and abetted" the fraudulent acts of management, and that the accountant should, therefore, not totally escape monetary liability to the plaintiff.

In any event, there is, and has always been, sufficient room for doubt as to what is simple and innocent negligence and what is conduct from which an inference of guilty knowledge can be drawn that, particularly of late, professionals (both accountants and attorneys) have increasingly found themselves named as defendants in Rule 10b-5 litigation. It is important to note that since Rule 10b-5 applies to any purchase or sale of any security, it can be used by a plaintiff with respect to both registered public offerings and any other transactions in securities. Moreover, the applicable statute of limitations varies from state to state and it is not uncommon to have a lawsuit four to five years after the event alleged to give rise to liability.

The concept of "class actions" has developed along with Rule 10b-5. Simply stated, class actions are litigations in which one or a relatively small number of plaintiffs can sue on behalf of a very large number of allegedly injured persons. Indeed, one of the prerequisites of a class action is that the number of potential claimants be so large that it would be impracticable for each of them to sue individually. When class actions come into play, the dollar amount of potential liability can expand almost astronomically, thereby making the class action technique, in the hands of less than ethical plaintiffs, a formidably coercive weapon. In fact, the class action technique has been sufficiently abused to prompt a counter trend; as the result of a recent Supreme Court decision, a class action plaintiff must bear the cost (often quite substantial) of notifying all other potential parties to the suit.

Criminal Charges

Another trend, deeply disturbing to all members of the profession, is to charge auditors with criminal liability when they are associated with financial statements subsequently discovered to have been misleading. Although to date there have been only four prosecutions (Continental Vending, Four Seasons, National Student Marketing, and Equity Funding) producing the conviction of eight individuals, it is clear that the defense of compliance with generally accepted accounting principles prevailing when the statements were issued will not deter a jury from finding criminal liability when, in their judgment, fair disclosure has not been made. Thus, errors of judgment in not requiring adequate disclosure of certain matters known to the auditor, even though no personal gain can be shown to inure to him, may result in criminal liability in certain circumstances. Although the cases are few, they serve as the sternest possible warning to all auditors to be careful when acting in areas of ambiguity or uncertainty.

Civil Regulatory Remedies

Accountants are also subject to sanctions that do not involve criminal penalties or the payment of damages. The SEC, as the principal government regulatory agency charged with enforcement of financial reporting standards, has two civil remedies available to it: a civil injunctive action, or a disciplinary proceeding under Rule 2(e) of its Rules of Practice. Either remedy may be sought against an individual accountant or a whole firm. The sanction most frequently exercised by the SEC is the civil injunctive action through which, as in any equity proceeding, the SEC seeks to enjoin the defendant from further violations of the federal securities laws. Under currently prevailing standards, such injunctions are available only against those who the SEC can persuade a court are likely to violate the federal securities laws again if not enjoined. Prior to the end of the last decade, such actions were almost always brought only against the "business interests" involved in the issuance and trading of securities. Since then, a significant trend toward bringing such proceedings (civil and criminal) against professionals, both accountants and lawyers, has developed.

Under Rule 2(e), the SEC:

> May deny, temporarily or permanently, the privilege of appearing or practicing before it in any way to any person who is found . . . (ii) to be lacking in character or integrity or to have engaged in unethical or improper professional conduct, or (iii) to have willfully violated or willfully aided and abetted the violation of any provision of the federal securities laws . . . or the rules and regulations thereunder.

As SEC enforcement activities go, such proceedings are relatively infrequent and, since they are generally conducted privately and confidentially, usually do not receive the kind of public notice given other SEC enforcement activities. Suspensions and disbarments are rare. However, SEC actions that are publicly disclosed can obviously have a significant impact on a professional's practice and that of his firm, and have recently resulted in censures and sweeping sanctions requiring outside review of the internal procedures of the accounting firms involved and limitations on the acceptance of new clients (e.g., SEC ASRs No. 144, 153, 157, and 173).

Serious departures from standards and codes of professional conduct can also result in the suspension or revocation of an auditor's Certified

Public Accountant's certificate by State Boards of Accountancy. The AICPA Code of Professional Ethics and the equivalent Codes of State Societies and State Boards also contain prohibitions against unethical and unprofessional conduct, such as advertising and solicitation; their complete texts should be consulted.

CONCLUSION

Formal pronouncements by the profession concerning auditing standards and responsibilities of professional auditors must of necessity be carefully worded in the broadest possible terms. As a result, a layman or newcomer to the profession may mistake them for bland abstractions without real-life substance. On the contrary, they are practical working precepts. Living up to them is fraught with real and difficult problems, and the consequences of misjudgment are severe. There is therefore a constant tendency among practitioners to seek detailed rules of conduct and procedure. The profession has successfully resisted that temptation for the most part. Exceptions, such as the fourth standard of reporting, are based on important reasons for assuring that, to the extent possible, the same circumstances have exactly the same consequences.

Public expectations are clearly changing in the direction of demanding more from an auditor; for example, he is expected to examine and report on more aspects of an enterprise, assume more responsibility, and lead the way toward more and better disclosures. Those rising expectations are not yet reflected in the formal standards or other authoritative literature of the profession; many are not yet articulated well enough to begin serious discussion of them. A period of rapid change has grave consequences for an auditor—actions he takes today will be scrutinized and judged, perhaps unfairly, in the future in the light of standards yet to be recognized and accepted. In the present circumstances, each practitioner must keep a watchful and objective eye on his own performance and, if in doubt, be guided by the maximum rather than the minimum standard of acceptable professional conduct. In the meantime, the AICPA has formed a special commission on auditors' responsibilities to ascertain the public's expectations of the auditor and the ability of the profession to fulfill those expectations. From the report of that study, expected in 1976, further guidance along these lines may be obtained.

3

Internal Control

INTRODUCTION

Internal control has long been recognized as fundamental and indispensable to modern auditing. The recognition emerged gradually in the early days of the profession as auditors sought to explain the practical discovery that, for most purposes, an examination of every transaction was seldom necessary. In recent years, understanding of internal control and its relationship to auditing has deepened, in part as a result of the advances in cybernetics and in the technology of control made by management scientists and computer specialists.

The changing concepts of internal control and the struggle to articulate them in the form of a concise and practical guide to practice can be traced through earlier editions of this book and recurrent articles in the *Journal of Accountancy* and elsewhere. As the theory and practice of management continue to evolve, it is to be expected that concepts of control and the practice of them will likewise change. Practicing auditors should therefore approach this discussion and the official pronouncements of the profession as perhaps the latest, but certainly not the last, word on the subject. The latest official publication appeared as Statement on Auditing Procedure (SAP) No. 54 in 1972 and is now incorporated as Section 320 of Statement on Auditing Standards (SAS) No. 1. The Section is a complicated and thoughtful forty-page document that is worthy of careful study by every practitioner. It discusses the subject in somewhat different terms than we use here, but our approach is entirely consistent with it.

DEFINITIONS AND OBJECTIVES OF INTERNAL CONTROL

The profession's formal definition of internal control, originally published in 1949 and repeated in subsequent publications, including SAS No. 1 (paragraph 320.09), is a succinct and serviceable starting point for explaining the place of internal control in the theory and practice of auditing:

> Internal control comprises the plan of organization and all of the coordinate methods and measures adopted within a business to safeguard its assets, check the accuracy and reliability of its accounting data, promote operational efficiency, and encourage adherence to prescribed managerial policies. . . . a "system" of internal control extends beyond those matters which relate directly to the functions of the accounting and financial departments.

The quotation defines three kinds of internal control, based on the three objectives it outlines: internal administrative or operational control (to "promote operational efficiency, and encourage adherence to prescribed managerial policies"), internal accounting control (to "check the accuracy and reliability of . . . accounting data"), and internal check (to "safeguard . . . assets").

Internal Administrative or Operational Control

Broadly, the prime responsibility of business management is to operate an enterprise at a profit, or within the available resources if it is a not-for-profit organization. In both types of business, management must produce its products or services at acceptable cost; it must develop markets in which they can be sold at proper prices; and, because pressure of competition, changes in customer demand, and other factors cause obsolescence, it must develop new or improved products or services.

To accomplish those objectives, management must develop policies to promote efficiency in every area of activity, such as purchasing, production, distribution, and research; implement those policies through proper personnel selection, training, and compensation; communicate the means of effecting them; and police performance through operating supervision and controls. For example, competitive bidding requirements may reduce material purchase costs; standards based on time and motion studies may promote efficient use of labor; quality control may sustain a policy of selling only first-grade merchandise; comparison shopping may aid in maintaining competitive selling prices—broadly speaking, all are "controls." In this book the "plan of organization and all of the coordinate methods and measures adopted within a business to . . . promote operational efficiency, and encourage adherence to prescribed managerial policies" are referred to as "internal administrative" or "operational" controls (the terms are interchangeable).

Operational controls are distinguishable from the other two areas of internal control by their primary operating purpose, and in many instances they may be exercised by operating rather than financial or accounting departments. In other instances, they may be based on or integrated with accounting data, or more than one purpose may be served by the same controls. For example, certain administrative controls may be based on data or information furnished by accounting or financial departments, such as operating budgets·and reports of expenditures. On the other hand, some internal administrative controls, especially those of a physical nature, may also serve the purpose of internal accounting control or internal check procedures. The problem of defining where accounting control ends and operational control begins is one of conceptual and semantic significance only; in both theory and practice it is better to accept a broad, imprecise distinction as reflecting the fact that the two overlap in many ways.

Internal Accounting Control

Controls that "check the accuracy and reliability of . . . accounting data" or, to put it more precisely, controls that are designed to bring about accurate and suitable recording and summarization of authorized financial transactions are termed "internal accounting controls." The responsibility for the installation and maintenance of internal accounting controls is clearly that of the accounting (or financial) department.

Equally clearly, those controls are of prime interest to the independent auditor who is to report on the financial statements drawn from the records the controls are designed to protect. An auditor should, of course, consider whether seeming weaknesses in controls exercised through accounting means are compensated for by operational controls, physical measures, or close supervision by management.

Internal Check

Internal check comprises those accounting procedures or physical, statistical, or other controls designed to safeguard assets against defalcations or other similar irregularities or against avoidable loss from other causes. Some forms of internal check of a physical nature, such as fences, gates, watchmen, and inspection of outgoing material or personnel, are ordinarily the responsibility of operating departments. The accounting department is usually responsible for the installation and maintenance of those internal check controls that may be achieved through accounting procedures or by proper segregation of accounting duties. Coordination among departments is, of course, necessary for an efficient system.

SAP No. 54 Definition

SAP No. 54 (SAS No. 1, paragraphs 320.27 and 320.28) revised and expanded the definitions of administrative control and accounting control, as follows:

.27 *Administrative control* includes, but is not limited to, the plan of organization and the procedures and records that are concerned with the decision processes leading to management's authorization of transactions.[1] Such authorization is a management function directly associated with the responsibility for achieving the objectives of the organization and is the starting point for establishing accounting control of transactions.

.28 *Accounting control* comprises the plan of organization and the procedures and records that are concerned with the safeguarding of assets and the reliability of financial records and consequently are designed to provide reasonable assurance that:

   a. Transactions are executed in accordance with management's general or specific authorization.

   b. Transactions are recorded as necessary (1) to permit preparation of financial statements in conformity with generally accepted accounting principles or any other criteria applicable to such statements and (2) to maintain accountability for assets.

1 This definition is intended only to provide a point of departure for distinguishing accounting control and, consequently, is not necessarily definitive for other purposes.

c. Access to assets is permitted only in accordance with management's authorization.

d. The recorded accountability for assets is compared with the existing assets at reasonable intervals and appropriate action is taken with respect to any differences.

The first paragraph distinguishes administrative controls that do not enhance accounting control from those that do. The second paragraph highlights internal check in subparagraphs (a) and (c) but incorporates internal check as part of accounting control. The definition calls explicit attention in subparagraph (d) to a fact that is too often taken for granted: accountability is a management responsibility, and exercising it calls for validating recorded accounts.

Achieving Internal Control Objectives

Controls are fundamental to all organizations and managements; they are not merely inventions of accountants and auditors to make their lives easier. Even in rudimentary or haphazard activities, someone has to keep track of tools and materials, of who has done what, and who owes what to whom. As organizations become larger, it becomes more necessary to use formal control procedures to assure that employees' actions are consistent. As stated earlier, administrative or operational control is the most pervasive of the kinds of control.

In practice the three objectives of administrative control, accounting control, and internal check can be achieved in many ways. In some instances all three may be embodied in the same procedure; in other cases each may require a separate procedure. For example: a formal, specialized receiving department can "promote operational efficiency" by providing for efficient receipt, inspection, and forwarding of all items received; it can "check the . . . reliability of . . . accounting data" by checking and documenting quantity and condition of goods received; it can "safeguard . . . assets" (discourage defalcations) because it has a place in the organization separate from ordering goods, disbursing funds, and keeping records. As the definition implies, internal control usually involves "coordinate methods."

Safeguarded assets and reliable records are necessary to the effective functioning of any enterprise, large or small. Every responsible accountant, or an owner doing his own bookkeeping, wishes to record transactions accurately, avoid errors in the accounts, and minimize the task of locating errors that do occur. Even the smallest business can control access to its cash and merchandise by keeping them locked up when not in use, record its activities in a checkbook, and reconcile the checkbook with its bank statements regularly.

As soon as the size of a business and the volume of transactions permit, the usefulness of such control procedures as double-entry bookkeeping, controlling accounts for receivables and payables, and periodic trial balances is universally recognized. Wherever opportunity offers, routines are divided so that one task double-checks another, documents are numbered and accounted for to safeguard against omissions, and predetermined standards are established to draw attention to transactions that are unusual and possibly erroneous.

Today bookkeeping machines, tabulating equipment, and computers have mechanized much of the bookkeeping process and permitted controls to be systematized. In the course of designing more complex equipment and systems, much has been learned about the theory and practice of building in self-checking and error-detecting routines and of disciplined adherence to systematized requirements for documentation, authorization, and the like. The lessons learned are equally applicable to simple or manual systems.

As a result, we have been able to generalize and simplify our concepts of internal accounting control and internal check. We can identify the few fundamental elements that must be present in one form or another in every transaction and then describe the limited number of actions that can be taken to achieve control objectives, no matter what the pattern of transaction flow or the sophistication of data processing technology.

Every transaction has to go through certain steps: it has to be authorized, initiated, executed, and recorded. For purposes of internal accounting control and internal check, the system should make reasonably sure:

1. That *only* legitimate and appropriate transactions are authorized, initiated, executed, and recorded,
2. That *all* authorized transactions are initiated, executed, and recorded as intended,
3. That errors in execution or recording are detected as soon as possible.

It can be argued that the whole of control is summed up in the third general objective above, since the processing of an unauthorized transaction or failure to process an authorized one can be considered an error; however, the evaluation of internal accounting control and internal check is facilitated by singling out the two types of errors for separate attention. It should also be noted that, while internal control aims at preventing or discouraging unauthorized transactions and errors, it must be organized to recognize the fact that absolute prevention is impossible. Therefore, it is necessary to attempt to provide reasonable assurance that both types of errors will be detected if and when they occur, usually by building a series of control points into a system. Since controls have a cost in time and money, there is always an economic judgment for management to make: whether a further degree of control or assurance is worth the cost of providing it. Like all judgments, it contains a large element of subjectivity and mistakes are not uncommon—over-control seldom makes headlines, but the result of under-control frequently does.

INTERNAL CONTROL AND AUDITING THEORY

Since an auditor is concerned primarily with the reliability of accounting data, his interest in controls has traditionally been much narrower than management's. An opinion on financial statements can be formed without considering a whole range of matters of daily concern to management that do not affect the reliability of accounting data: number of calls made by salesmen, the diligence of purchasing agents' bid solicitation, adherence to the preventive maintenance schedule, and so on. We question, however, whether an auditor should limit his interest to the narrower area of accounting controls. There are many instances in which operational controls affect the reliability of accounting data in direct and indirect ways; they are discussed in subsequent chapters. Furthermore, auditors today are better qualified by education and experience to understand the broader concerns of managerial and administrative control and to put that understanding to work in auditing operational controls to aid client management.

While the authors believe that the broader view is far better for both auditor and client and may come to be accepted, the discussion in this chapter is restricted to the conventional, narrower definition of internal accounting control and internal check cited previously.

The discussion of the third standard of field work in SAS No. 1 and in Chapter 2 points out that audit evidence consists of underlying evidence and corroborative evidence. Reasonable assurance cannot be achieved by relying exclusively on either type of evidence, but, short of those extremes, there is a distinct and direct trade-off: the better the underlying evidence, the less corroborating evidence is needed and vice versa. If the underlying evidence of the accounts is very reliable, an auditor needs minimal corroborating evidence; for varying degrees of less-than-total reliability, an auditor requires more corroborating evidence.

Internal control determines the degree of reliability of underlying evidence. However, optimum internal control cannot provide perfect assurance. Reasonable assurance of the reliability of the accounts is the best that can possibly be achieved.

Weaknesses in internal control—the absence of certain expected control features—do not necessarily result in erroneous underlying evidence, but merely permit the *possibility* of evidence being erroneous. The accounts may be properly maintained and the data valid, but the possibility of error reduces the degree of reliance that can be placed on the controls. That is why auditors refer to "weaknesses" in internal control—the absence of a control feature does not make the system poor, or wrong, but simply weak. In that case, better corroborating evidence can often make up for the weakness, for audit purposes, by establishing the validity of the underlying evidence of the accounts.

Thus, an auditor's evaluation of internal control establishes the first term of the audit equation: how much he can rely on the underlying evidence of the accounts. The value of that term then determines the value that the other term must take, that is, how much corroborating evidence he needs. That is what is meant by the second standard of field work: "a proper study and evaluation of the existing internal control" is the basis "for the determination of the resultant extent of the tests to which auditing procedures are to be restricted."

An auditor's response to a weakness in control is more subtle and complicated than simply "more" auditing procedures. If his evaluation of internal control causes him to decide to shift reliance from underlying to corroborative evidence, that shift may, depending on circumstances, call for adopting auditing procedures that might not ordinarily be necessary, or for changing the timing of certain procedures, or for increasing the size of test sample comprehended in a standard auditing procedure, or a combination of all three. Often, however, the shift may require a qualitative change in the nature of certain auditing procedures that increases their importance, instead of a quantitative increase in audit work.

INTERNAL CONTROL AND AUDITING PRACTICE

Because many companies today have effective internal controls, auditors expect to find them operative as a matter of course. However, the auditor must always be alert to the possibility of a breakdown. One of the easiest ways for an audit to "overrun" its budget and deadline is for an auditor to overlook control weaknesses until it is too late. He then finds himself involved in extensive unplanned account validation or reconstruction, which can be an expensive and demanding undertaking. *For example:*

A company acquired its first computer and undertook accounts receivable processing as the first system to be converted. The auditor's suggestions for control features to be incorporated in the system design were ignored (as were other elements of good management, such as adequate instruction and training of originators and users of data). By the time the auditors arrived to make a "proper study and evaluation of the existing internal control" it was too late. The accounts receivable were out of control, and the issuance of financial statements was delayed several months while the balances were validated or written off as uncollectible.

A company had a large inventory of spare parts. Controls over receipts and issues and the posting of perpetual inventory records were very loose, as indicated by the prevalence of adjustments resulting from cycle counts. The company did not feel that the potential benefits justified the substantial cost of designing a well-controlled system. The auditor accepted the perpetual inventory records as the basis for preparation of financial statements as long as an appropriate sample of test counts corroborated management's view that the probable error in the perpetual records was not material and had not changed significantly from the prior year. One year the auditor's sample failed to corroborate that view. The auditor first suggested an additional, more extensive sample of test counts and then, when that did not provide the necessary assurance, said he could not arrive at an opinion unless the company took a complete and very expensive physical inventory.

Thus, the practical application of the second standard of field work can be a matter of the most serious concern, both to auditor and client. Obviously, an evaluation of internal control is not "proper" under the standard if either the study itself or the auditor's resultant plans and actions are perfunctory.

The following sections describe the fundamentals of internal accounting control and internal check and relate them to the broader subject of administrative or operational control. Chapters 4 and 5 describe the auditor's evaluation process, the tests he should make to confirm it, and the actions he should take as a result. The chapters in Part II describe typical examples of internal control as it is found in practice.

CHARACTERISTICS OF INTERNAL ACCOUNTING CONTROL
AND INTERNAL CHECK

Only a limited number of basic steps are involved in internal control and check. To prevent unauthorized transactions, all transactions must be properly authorized and documented. To assure the processing of authorized transactions as intended, it is essential that an organization have an adequate system and competent, honest people to operate it. Secondly, it must have adequate documentation. Numerical control over documents can be established and systems of open holding files and reminder lists can be set up to keep track of transactions and guard against their going astray. To prevent or detect errors, adequate documentation, authorization, and subsequent examination are necessary; other controls include double-checking computations, validity checks, control totals, and reconciliations. Thus, much the same kinds of control operations are called for no matter what the objectives or transactions.

We have identified only three conditions required for control and only thirteen kinds of control activity that can possibly be applied to accounting transactions, or any other kind of data processing for that matter. The exact number depends on how one defines his terms and distinguishes among similar kinds of activity, and it is not important. What is important is that the activities can be remembered easily. They may take many different forms, some of them extraordinarily complex, and their adaptation to different circumstances—and an auditor's evaluation of them—is a large part of the practice of accounting and auditing and of the subject matter of this book. The effort to follow those ramifications and adaptations can be confusing, frustrating, and exhausting. It is less so if one keeps in mind that the functions and general objectives of control are quite simple and that choices among means of achieving them are limited.

Control can be classified on three levels: first, the conditions under which control can take place; second, the basic control operations performed directly on transactions, either individually or in groups; and, third, control activities that serve to enforce, supervise, and maintain discipline over the operations and their results. Under different conditions one control activity may be more important than another; as a general rule, the conditions permitting control and the discipline over it are always more important than the specific control operations themselves, since the latter are unlikely to function well without the former.

CONDITIONS OF CONTROL

Certain basic conditions must exist before control is possible: there must be some degree of systemization, competent people to operate the system, and documents that record transactions and what is done with them.

Systemization

A systematic plan is fundamental to the control of any operation. Most accountants accept the idea that a double-entry accounting system is a basic necessity for all but the simplest enterprises. The more explicitly any operation is defined, the easier it is to carry it out reliably and to keep it under control. Ideally, everyone involved in an operation should know exactly what should and should not be done under every possible condition, including how to handle unauthorized, incomplete, or erroneous transactions. Without a system, control is impossible, or at best infinitely more difficult and time-consuming, and the risk of out-of-control events is infinitely greater. Thus, the system itself is perhaps the most fundamental control, and the more effective it is, the more effective the other controls are likely to be.

The degree of systemization directly affects an auditor's plans from the very start, as demonstrated in detail in Chapters 4 and 5. He is entitled to assume, as a minimum, the existence of an organized set of records because without it there is unlikely to be underlying evidence reliable enough to permit an opinion on the financial statements as a whole. If there is a formal chart of accounts, the probability that the accounts themselves are reliable is increased. If there is a division of tasks, if control duties are separated from operations, and if the tasks and assignments are set forth in a formal procedures manual, the prospects of reliability are better.

Competence and Integrity

Systems and all other control procedures are useless unless the people assigned to carry them out do so conscientiously and consistently. Each person must have a level of competence adequate to the task and enough personal integrity to feel a sense of responsibility for it. Usually, competence and systemization go together, but one is found without the other often enough to justify examining them separately. The competence and integrity of individuals in an organization are influenced by many factors: the organization's reputation and physical location; its personnel selection, retention, and training policies; the difficulty of the work; the amount and quality of supervision; and the degree of systemization. Sometimes the people must be selected in the light of the work to be done; sometimes the system, the supervision, and the work itself have to be modified to be appropriate to the level of competence available.

Competence has long been recognized as having an important bearing on control. Some auditors take it into account implicitly, almost intuitively, and seek more evidential assurance that controls are functioning properly when they believe the level of competence is low. Others believe that auditing is more effective if competence is explicitly evaluated, in the light of systemization and the kinds of discipline exercised, as a condition having a direct impact on the amount and kind of testing an auditor should do. Also, explicit attention to that condition reminds an auditor to keep alert for changes in personnel or subtle changes in their attitudes that could call for re-evaluation.

Documentation

Data must be recorded for many organizational purposes: communication between people, analysis, accountability, and control. Many financial data serve several organizational purposes simultaneously: adequate description permits correct accounting and helps prevent errors in processing and recording, and is also basic to communication. Some documentation is required solely for control purposes: performance of activities is documented, usually by initialing or other means of identifying the performer, to fix responsibility and permit supervision of it. Some documentation required primarily for control purposes contributes secondarily to other purposes: numbering of documents is primarily a means of providing accountability to insure that all authorized transactions are fully processed, but it also serves to identify documents when they are needed for other purposes.

Documentation is inherent and implicit in systemization. It is enumerated as a separate condition of control because it is an essential prerequisite to adequate control. Obviously, without complete and accurate description of a transaction, its authorization, and each operation through which it passes, exercise of control over it is not possible.

BASIC CONTROL OPERATIONS

If control over accounting data is analyzed into its most basic elements, it becomes apparent that there are only three kinds of control operations:

Making sure that data are valid by checking them to something else (validation),

Making sure that all data that should be present are present (completeness checks),

Making sure that computations or clerical operations are correctly performed (reperformance).

These three basic operations appear in many forms; a few common ones comprise very nearly all the control activity an auditor is likely to encounter. We have identified three forms of validation, four of completeness checks, and two of reperformance. Again, the exact number and names are not important; it is their common characteristics that are worth noting.

Before describing the basic control activities, it is well to pause to define three terms that must be used repeatedly in discussing auditing: "validate," "verify," and "confirm." Though used as synonyms in daily conversation, these terms are differentiated in auditing, sometimes somewhat differently in different contexts. As used throughout this book, "validate" is the general term meaning to establish the truth, accuracy, or relevance of a fact or figure by corroborating it in some way. "Confirm" is used in a specialized sense in auditing: to validate through requesting corroboration by another source (usually outside the organization) having direct knowledge of the fact or figure being validated. "Verify" means to validate through an auditor's own investigation of the facts, examination of supporting data, or reperformance of computations.

Forms of Validation

The following paragraphs discuss three common forms of validation.

Authorization

The primary control over individual transactions is the act of authorizing them. Authorization consists of someone comparing a proposed transaction with plans, conditions, constraints, or general knowledge of what constitutes propriety, and deciding that it is or is not valid. The act of authorization is the principal means for making sure that only legitimate and appropriate transactions are processed and that all other transactions are rejected. It can be delegated to particular individuals who document their performance by initialing the transaction document. It is increasingly being automated by specifying in advance the conditions under which a type of transaction will be automatically authorized. For example, a production order can be automatically authorized when the on-hand amount of an inventory item falls to a predetermined point requiring replenishment. It should be noted that, for control to exist, some form of authorization *must* be carried out before, after, or during transaction initiation and execution.

There is potential confusion in two common uses of the term "authorization." The control operation of *authorizing individual transactions* must be distinguished from that aspect of systemization that *spells out which members of an organization are authorized* to do what. For a transaction to be properly authorized, the authorizer must be delegated the authority to do so: that is, the *act* must be carried out by a person or under the conditions recognized by the system as having the *right* and *competence* to do so.

Comparison

Several control operations consist of comparing a figure with another figure arrived at independently. Often a reconciliation is called for in making a comparison. The reconciliation procedure, common throughout auditing, consists of identifying *legitimate* differences between items being compared and tracking down and correcting *unacceptable* differences. Common examples of validation by comparison are bank reconciliations; reconciliations of detail balances to control accounts; physical counts of cash, securities, inventories, or other assets; and confirmation of balances with debtors or creditors. Since those control procedures are also auditing procedures, they are described in detail in the appropriate chapters that follow.

Validity Checking

Transactions can be checked in various ways for compliance with the rules of the system, thus validating their propriety. In its most elementary form, validity checking consists of examination of a transaction by someone who understands the accounting system, to see that it has been accomplished in accordance with prescribed procedures. In a more sophisticated system, validity checks are built into the system itself to test each transaction against predetermined expectations. It is common to provide for validity checks at as many points as possible in a transaction processing system in order to detect errors as soon as possible after they occur.

Following are some typical validity checks:

> A transaction document can be matched to an independently originated document as evidence of its validity. For example, vendors' invoices can be matched with receiving reports and purchase orders.

Data can be checked against predetermined standards or lists of acceptable norms. For example, the unit price of an item can be checked to a standard price list.

A transaction can be checked for compatibility with its source or destination. For example, entries to the cash account must come from regular receipt or disbursement sources, or payroll charges must be entered only in labor accounts.

The internal consistency of recording a transaction can be validated by arithmetic relationships such as check digits.

Each of the above examples can be carried out by a supervisor who is knowledgeable about the whole processing system, it can be systematized and carried out by a properly instructed clerk, or it can be built into a computer program and carried out automatically during computer processing.

Other validity checks can be incorporated in a comparison type of control. For example, during a count of cash or securities or a confirmation of receivables, both the asset and the record of it can be checked for validity; as part of a bank reconciliation, signatures and endorsements on cancelled checks can be scrutinized.

Forms of Completeness Checks

Four forms of completeness checks are described below.

Numerical Sequencing

The best means of making sure that transactions are not lost in processing is to number them as soon as (or preferably before) they originate and then account for all the numbers after they have been processed. Numbering documents is part of the documentation condition; the control operation is the act of checking to see that all numbered documents complete the expected processing. The possibility of purposeful or accidental errors in the numbering process is reduced if the numerical sequence is printed in advance on the forms to be used for documenting transactions. If the chance of error or misuse is not considered a significant hazard, the numbering is often originated simultaneously with the document. For example, a computer preparing checks in the course of an accounts payable processing run can be programmed to number the checks sequentially.

Control Totals

A classic way to make sure that all transactions are processed through a particular step or series of steps is to total the critical numbers before and after processing: the assumption is that the processing is correct if the two totals agree. There is, of course, a possibility of one error exactly offsetting another error or omission, but the possibility is slight. Control totals do not provide control in themselves; they provide information by means of which control is exercised. The actual control operation is the comparison of two totals and the searching out and correction of errors giving rise to differences. A reconciliation may be called for, as described under "Comparison" above.

Control totals appear in many forms. The whole double-entry system is a structure of control totals because the totals of the debits always have to equal the totals of the credits, whether in individual entries or the accounts as a whole. Batches of transactions may be totalled before transcription or other processing. A control total over some kinds of computations can be established by making the same computations in the aggregate. Comparison can be conceived of as a completeness check as well as a form of validation: a bank reconciliation and proof of cash validate the cash balance and also check the completeness of processing of cash transactions.

Holding Files

Another common check on completeness is to make a list of transactions or keep a file of copies of originating documents and delete items from the list or file as processing is completed. The open items on the list or in the file provide information that permits the control operation of checking the list or file and taking action on transactions that should have been completed and were not.

The most common examples of holding files are the file of purchase orders waiting to be matched with receiving reports and invoices, and the file of sales orders waiting to be matched with shipping orders and billings. Any document that originates a transaction can go into a holding file until matched with similar evidence of completion. Many balance sheet accounts can be viewed as essentially open holding files: accounts receivable and accounts payable are open files of incomplete cash receipts and cash disbursements transactions; inventory accounts are open files of incomplete production transactions. Provision should always be made, and usually is, for periodically reviewing and taking action on items that remain in an account for an unusually long time.

Reminder Lists

Some kinds of authorized transactions can be overlooked if their timely processing is not controlled by suitable reminder lists. Common examples are filing invoices payable by due dates and keeping calendars of tax payment due dates. Controls over compliance with legal and contractual constraints are usually in the form of reminder lists: checklists or questionnaires enumerating the conditions to be complied with.

Forms of Reperformance

Two forms of reperformance are discussed in the paragraphs that follow.

Double-Checking

The most obvious and elementary way to catch errors is to double-check anything that might be in error. Someone simply repeats—reperforms—the activity being controlled. The initial performer can check himself, but the control procedure is strengthened and internal check is added if another person does it.

Every clerical and physical activity in a business can be double-checked—originating data, transcribing data from one document to another, physical counts, computations, and so on. Double-checking can be detailed and specific, consisting of complete reperformance of the initial activity. Or, if absolute accuracy is not considered worth the cost of detailed double-checking, forms of "partial double-checking" consist of scanning the results of a completed operation to discover gross errors or double-checking a number of items selected at random.

Obviously, double-checking is relatively expensive. If there is no substitute for it, it is often possible to design a sampling procedure based on statistical principles that affords reasonable assurance of detecting an intolerable incidence of error. Good systems design calls for providing, wherever possible, some other form of control over errors that is more economical than double-checking.

Pre-Audit

The most comprehensive way to review transactions for authorization, completeness of processing, and errors in processing is for someone knowledgeable to examine transactions in detail just before they are completed—a form of reperformance known as pre-audit. Pre-audit is distinguished from double-checking by the level of sophistication of the operation and the performer: double-checking implies simple, detailed, often mechanical reperformance, while pre-audit implies subsequent evaluation and judgment, with or without detailed reperformance. It is distinguished from internal audit (discussed later in this chapter) by its place in the system. Pre-audit is a late stage in the transaction processing system and therefore not independent of its supervisors, while internal audit is separate and apart from the transaction processing system and usually reports to a higher level of management.

Pre-audit was a common operation in earlier days when the theory and practice of control were less developed than they are now. It is gradually disappearing in favor of the types of disciplinary controls described below.

DISCIPLINARY CONTROLS

We have categorized four kinds of control operations as "disciplines" because in different ways they share the characteristic of monitoring, enforcing, or "disciplining" accounting activity, including the basic controls, and its results. Disciplines are important because their presence affords reasonable assurance that the basic accounting and control operations are functioning as designed at times other than those selected for formal auditing. Their value has been implicitly recognized for many years, but we believe they deserve much more explicit consideration than they have received in the past. Three disciplines are necessary features of an adequate system of control, and one is an optional feature whose value is becoming increasingly recognized.

The necessary features are segregation of duties, restricted access, and supervisory controls. Segregation of duties causes the work of one person to act as a discipline over the work of another. Restricted access is a necessary discipline to prevent unauthorized activity of all sorts, from loss or misuse of assets to loss or misuse of the general ledger. These two disciplines have long been recognized and associated with the objective of internal check. The function of the third feature, supervising the system and those who operate it, has an obvious effect on accuracy and reliability.

The optional feature is internal audit. An internal audit function reviews and "disciplines" the adequacy of accounting and control activities.

Segregation of Duties

The separation of one activity from another serves several purposes. Quite aside from the objectives of control, it is usually more efficient to specialize tasks and people. For example, it is usually better to select and train one person to handle cash or the spare parts inventory exclusively and another person to keep the records than to try to find, train, and supervise someone versatile enough to handle the assets and also keep the records. The relative costs must be evaluated in each instance. Most often, efficiency is attained only when the volume of activity justifies specialization.

However, the control features of segregation of duties are important enough to be adopted whether efficiency results or not, and often even if inefficiency is the consequence. If two parts of a transaction are handled by different people, each serves as a check on the other. For example, one bookkeeper can process a day's cash receipts and another post the receipts to the accounts receivable records. Checking the total of the postings to the total receipts provides some assurance that each operation was accurately performed. Segregation of duties also serves as a deterrent to fraud or concealment of error because of the need to recruit another individual's cooperation (collusion) to conceal it.

Restricted Access

If unauthorized transactions are to be prevented, whether they constitute theft or simply well-intentioned activity not consistent with the system, it is necessary to restrict access to all items that could be used to initiate or process a transaction. Restricted access is most commonly thought of in connection with negotiable assets—cash, securities, and sometimes inventory and other items that are easily convertible to cash or personal use. It applies equally to access to the books and records and the means of altering them—unused forms, unissued checks, check signature plate, files, computer room, computer tape storage, ledgers, and everything important to the accounting process. Systemization and discipline should aim at restricting access to those individuals who are competent and can be held responsible.

In its simplest form, restricted access is evidenced by physical security—a safe, a vault, a locked door, a storeroom having a custodian, a guarded fence. Physical safeguards are useless, however, without a discipline that prevents unauthorized persons from entering. The discipline can be automated to some degree. Issuing a key to only one person is an elementary form of automated authorization to enter a locked area; or, computers can be programmed to reject commands or transaction data unless specific tests for authorization and propriety are met. Physical security measures should also protect assets and records from physical threat such as accidental destruction, deterioration, or simply being mislaid.

Many of the defalcations that have come to the authors' attention resulted from failure to maintain the disciplines of segregation of duties and restricted access to assets and records.

Supervisory Controls

Supervisory controls are of two types:

1. *Built-in controls, or supervisory internal check.* Accuracy and reliability are added to the features of segregation of duties and restricted access if the tasks performed by some persons provide a check on the work of others. Many built-in supervisory controls can be designed so that transaction processing cannot be completed unless control conditions are met, a control-enhancing feature in itself. For example, an approver of vouchers for payment sees that the proper persons (e.g., those in the purchasing, receiving, and voucher preparation departments) have signed off for their roles in the processing of the payment before giving approval, and payment cannot be made (except through oversight) without that approval.

2. *Superimposed controls, or supervisory administrative check.* Supervisors or administrators should regularly ascertain that each participant in a system is attending to his or her assigned functions. They must see that reconciliations are made regularly, control account balances agree with details, numerical sequences are accounted for, and the like. Supervision of this kind is basic and necessary; however, since it is "superimposed," transactions can be processed even if the controls are inoperative.

Together with systemization, supervision is essential to control operations. If supervision exists, it provides the means for correcting other weaknesses. Without adequate supervision, the best of accounting systems and control procedures run the risk of becoming erratic or undependable on short notice. Under pressure, systems and disciplines may be shortcut or bypassed, reconciliations omitted, errors and exceptions left unattended, and documents lost, mislaid, or simply not posted to journals and ledgers. Supervisory and administrative personnel may be drawn into the day-to-day work of processing data and correcting errors, and so find themselves less able to perform their supervisory control duties.

Effective administration is in part a pervasive, intangible quality of management. Subjective as it may be, an auditor can recognize the absence of good administration and take steps to modify his audit program as a result. (The effect on an audit program of a weakness in or absence of any of the necessary disciplines is discussed briefly later in this chapter and in detail in Chapter 5.)

Even in a well-designed system, lack of supervisory controls may be signalled by problems in the accounts: an inordinate number of errors and exceptions, backlogs and bottlenecks, and instances of prescribed procedures that are not followed. If problems proliferate and it appears that supervisors are bogged down with detail or have inadequate knowledge of the matters for which they are responsible, an auditor is on notice that he had better not rely on the continuity of other control procedures, no matter how well designed.

Superimposed controls consist of specific, observable routines for regularly assuring supervisors that the specified conditions of control and the required basic control operations are maintained. Adequate administrative routines require documentation of their performance: checklists; exception reports; initials evidencing review of batch controls, bank reconciliations, vouchers, and the like; log books for review routines; and written reports. When control routines are documented, an auditor can test them to obtain evidence of the quality of supervisory controls.

Internal Audit

An additional level of discipline is provided by an internal audit function. Just as the basic double-checking operation verifies the propriety of a basic processing activity, the internal audit function double-checks the functioning of other control processes, including the disciplines. The work of internal auditors provides evidence when data processing functions are being effectively performed, a warning system when they are not, and a deterrent to substandard performance of routines subject to audit. The internal audit function is discussed at length in Chapter 8.

OPERATIONAL CONTROLS

The relationship between administrative or operational controls and accounting controls was described at the beginning of this chapter. Although operational controls aim primarily at efficiency of operations and adherence to policy, they have a feedback type of disciplinary effect on the efficiency of the accounting control system. Modern systems use a great deal of financial data to help management control operations. It is gradually being recognized that in these systems the operations serve to control the financial data almost as much as the data control operations. *For example:*

Sales, production, and on-hand inventory data are used in a modern inventory system to forecast production needs and trigger production orders. That information, which is also essential to the financial accounting system, controls production planning to such a degree that the production planning department serves as an effective control over the accuracy of the financial data. The operational users of the system are constantly checking the accuracy of inventory balances, thus substituting in part for formal inventory cycle count procedures.

The comparison of actual income statements and balance sheets with budgeted figures is widely used as a tool of managerial control over departmental operations. If the budgets are actively used by management, the operations serve to a degree as a control over the accuracy of the financial statements, because an error in the data processed would cause a variance that would have to be explained by an operating manager. However, one should guard against the tendency of managers to accept without question favorable variances, which may shelter errors and make discovery more difficult.

Standard costs are a managerial accounting tool used to identify variations from plan. Comparing actual to standard also helps to identify accounting errors, thus serving as an internal accounting control.

Other operational controls, some of them apparently remote from the accounting system, can have an important bearing on the accounts and financial statements. Thus:

Effective sales forecasts and inventory and production management help to prevent inventory overstocking and obsolescence.

Effective credit management helps to minimize bad debt losses.

Effective maintenance programs help to minimize maintenance costs and, by prolonging the life of equipment, depreciation charges.

Since operational controls can have a profound effect on financial position and results of operations and can, on occasion, substitute for accounting controls, they are an appropriate subject of interest to an auditor. If he does not understand them or ignores them, he can no doubt still do an audit according to professional standards. He may test where he need not or he may worry about accounting problems that are adequately taken care of through operational controls. Or he may be forced into unplanned extension of audit work if operational weaknesses unexpectedly result in financial statement problems such as inventory obsolescence or bad debt losses. But he can finish his audit effectively, though perhaps not efficiently, and express an opinion on the financial statements.

If he *does* understand operational controls, however, he will be able to plan a more efficient and effective engagement by relying on the controls, where appropriate, and by recognizing the potential for problems if the controls are weak. And he will have infinitely more opportunity to be of help to his client through an objective review of and comments on operational as well as accounting controls.

In our opinion, an independent auditor will be expected someday to evaluate operational controls as part of his examination. In the meantime, there will be a rather difficult transitional period as the expectations of clients and an auditor's ability to meet them rise at an uneven rate. An auditor must take special care to make sure that management and others, such as audit committee members, understand the extent to which he is in a position to comment on operational controls.

INTERNAL CONTROL AND AN AUDITOR'S EVALUATION

Effect on the Audit

Audit tests of controls and the effects of control evaluation on other auditing procedures are part of the subject of Chapter 5, "Auditing Procedures—Their Nature and Extent." A summary preview of that material is necessary for the purpose of completing this discussion of the effect of control on an audit.

Conditions of Control

The conditions of control have to exist to some degree before an audit is possible. Without basic systemization, competence, and documentation, there is very little to audit. There may be systems work, and accounting work, and an auditor may be willing to do both, but there must be books and records to audit. Beyond the basic groundwork, the better the conditions of control, the better and more reliably the basic controls and disciplines can function. An auditor can focus his attention on the controls themselves, while retaining the perspective of the underlying influence of the conditions of control.

Basic Controls

In any system for processing transactions, an auditor can look for the basic control or controls that assure validity, completeness, and accuracy of the amounts recorded in the accounts. Since clients are interested in detecting errors as early as possible, many systems have several control points. An auditor is interested only in the accuracy and reliability of accounts supporting the financial statements. He may therefore be able to focus on one control that affords reasonable assurance of reliability, and consider the others redundant. If there is a gap in the system of basic controls, an auditor can first try to persuade his client to close it, and, if unsuccessful, he can usually design auditing procedures to apply to the underlying data to determine whether they can be relied on for his purposes.

Thus, a weakness in basic controls is likely to cause an auditor primarily to expand his testing, but may also change the timing and nature of some of his tests.

Disciplinary Controls

The disciplines provide the auditor (and client) with assurance of the continuity of basic controls. Thus, a weakness in discipline results primarily in a shift in the timing of auditing procedures from interim to year end and, sometimes, in more or different kinds of testing.

Two of the disciplines—segregation of duties and restricted access— are closely identified with the internal check objective of control. It has been an accepted rule for many years that a weakness in internal check usually requires a change in the timing of auditing procedures, while a weakness in basic controls usually requires a change in the extent of auditing procedures. As our understanding of control develops, it becomes clear that the other disciplines also contribute to continuity of control and therefore affect the timing and sometimes the nature of auditing procedures. It is thus the functioning of the disciplines, rather than the coincidental serving of the internal check objective, that determines the effect on audit tests.

Furthermore, our understanding of control makes it clear that the disciplinary controls reinforce and raise the first term of the audit equation: the reliability of the underlying evidence is enhanced by effective monitoring of the basic internal controls. With effective disciplinary controls, and better understanding of them, many of the account validation procedures previously considered basic may become unnecessary. Other traditional auditing procedures may take on the nature of *tests of controls* rather than validations of the underlying data. Thus, the evolution of our concepts of internal control permits an expansion of the limits within which the audit equation holds true: effective disciplinary controls tend to limit the need for gathering of corroborative evidence.

The Auditor's Interest and Management's Interest

Since control is essential to effective organization, management needs assurance that controls are functioning as intended. An auditor's interest in internal control is similar to that of management, but it is not quite identical. Some of the similarities and differences are worthy of comment.

Management needs meticulous, detailed accuracy. An error in an individual customer's account or an individual budgetary line item causes inconvenience (and possibly poor public relations) at best, and wrong decisions or losses at worst. An auditor, on the other hand, is interested primarily in the overall fairness of presentation of financial statements. Since he can tolerate a range of error that is not material for his purposes, he can be satisfied with fewer controls than management can. That is not to say that auditors should tolerate looseness or inaccuracy; on the contrary, a "loose" system can result in errors or uncertainties in the aggregate as well as in details. Rather, since management's interest in details is or should be far greater than an auditor's, the auditor should be doubly warned if he encounters inattention to controls.

Management is interested in detecting and correcting errors as soon as possible in the transaction processing system. As a result, controls are usually built in at several points in the system, perhaps at every step. An auditor is interested mainly in whether the resulting account balances are reliable. If one control assures reliability of the resulting account balance, an auditor need not test all of the others, which he can consider redundant for his purposes. The auditor does not have to be concerned over every weakness in control.

Management is interested in designing control systems that function reliably and routinely with as little management attention as possible. An auditor's interest must be in the existing system of internal control as a basis for determining the first term of the audit equation. Auditors are often called on to review systems in the design stage and advise on the controls that should be included in the design—a highly desirable practice, since complex systems are difficult to change once implemented. However, it cannot substitute for evaluating and testing the system of internal control once it is in existence, which is called for by both the theoretical logic of the audit equation and the practical observation that a system can be altered intentionally or unintentionally between the design stage and the operating stage.

There is a high degree of mutual responsibility and dependence between auditor and management. Management is responsible for the functions of accountability and control, and obtaining an independent audit is part of those functions. An auditor is responsible for his opinion and for arriving at it with professional diligence and efficiency. He is explicitly responsible for evaluating the system of controls toward that purpose and only by implication for advising on weaknesses that are thereby disclosed. Management is dependent on the auditor for his share of the accountability function;

the auditor is dependent on management for establishing and maintaining the accountability and control systems. Their symbiotic interdependence is an indispensable fact. Even if it were not indispensable, it would still be a highly desirable condition of effective investor protection.

The Internal Control Questionnaire

An auditor evaluates internal control by first gaining an understanding of the whole system of transaction processing, then identifying the controls, and finally determining which ones afford reasonable assurance of the reliability of the resulting accounting data. He tests those controls to obtain firsthand evidence that they are functioning. Since control objectives and the means of achieving them are limited in number and much the same from one system to another, most auditors find that both efficiency and effectiveness are greatly enhanced by identifying and listing expected controls and then using the list on all or most engagements. The result is the familiar internal control questionnaire.

The questionnaire can be organized so that questions are classified according to control objectives and each question refers to the presence of a possible desirable control operation that fulfills the related objective. A negative answer indicates the possibility of a control weakness and requires the auditor to consider its effect on the reliability of the underlying evidence. The absent control may have no significant effect on the reliability of the information produced by the system, or other control operations may compensate for the omission. In those cases, a negative answer simply directs the auditor toward thinking through that conclusion. On the other hand, the omission may have actual or potential significance, necessitating a specific shift in the audit logic toward reliance on corroborating evidence. In any event, a negative reply in the questionnaire requires an explicit, rational response, and, usually, documentation of the conclusion. Without that explicit connection between controls and the audit effort, an auditor risks lapses in the logic of his audit plans.

An alternative is to organize the internal control questionnaire in terms of expected results, rather than expected control operations. Thus, instead of the following questions:

> Are purchase orders that are approved by a responsible official required for all expenditures?

Are vendors' invoices matched with purchase orders and receiving reports?

Are invoices, purchase orders, and other data in support of cash disbursements furnished to the signer of checks?

there might be the following:

How are cash disbursements authorized?

The latter method requires a narrative response embodying explicit consideration of the same factors of significance, compensatory controls, and audit response as described above. Its advantage is that it focuses on the control objectives and requires considerably fewer questions; its disadvantages are the difficulty of analyzing the narrative responses in terms of identification of control weaknesses and the possibility that an important control may be inadvertently omitted from consideration.

4

Auditing Procedures—
The Audit Cycle

INTRODUCTION

The standard short-form auditor's report states that "our examination was made in accordance with generally accepted auditing standards, and accordingly included such tests of the accounting records and such other auditing procedures as we considered necessary in the circumstances." The first assertion is that a reporting auditor understands and has measured up to the standards of the profession described in Chapter 2. The second assertion is that he has exercised his professional judgment to select the particular combination of auditing procedures that meet the profession's standards in the unique set of circumstances encountered in the examination.

His explicit assumption of responsibility for making a professional judgment should not be taken for granted. It means that the auditor has looked at a particular set of facts and circumstances, thought about the standards of the profession, and decided what to do, and is willing to be held responsible for his decision. It implies that he did not rely on preconceived rules and also that his decision was based on more than a whim. It implies an orderly process of reasoning from particular facts to a specific conclusion about a course of action, a process that has to be both practical and logical.

The logical basis for selecting auditing procedures is described in the next chapter. The practical process an auditor goes through in approaching an examination is the subject of this chapter: deciding what needs to be done, planning it, doing it, and preparing to repeat the process in a recurring engagement. Auditing is continuous—the end of one examination blends into the beginning of the next, and each succeeding examination is built on the experience of prior ones.

A first examination of a new client requires the most comprehensive and explicit development of the audit process and, more often than not, more extensive auditing procedures. For that reason, the audit cycle is presented in this chapter in terms of a new engagement. In subsequent engagements the full cycle is repeated, but many of the steps can be eliminated, shortened, or de-emphasized.

INITIAL ASSUMPTIONS

An auditor approaching a recurring engagement is guided by his prior experience with the client and the reasonable assumption that circumstances have not changed significantly since the previous examination. An auditor approaching a new engagement has to make some initial assumptions about the client, to decide where and how to begin his examination. He bases those assumptions on his own and other auditors' experience with other clients and he adopts them tentatively, recognizing that subsequent steps in his examination will prove or disprove them. The assumptions adopted are implicit in the starting point he chooses, but the audit will be better planned and executed if he explicitly identifies and evaluates them.

Existence of Conditions of Control

An auditor should be able to assume that a new client has, at least to some degree, the conditions of control identified in Chapter 3: systemization, competence and integrity, and documentation. Some elements of each of those conditions are necessary for an organization to function, and an unqualified auditor's opinion may be difficult or impossible to arrive at without them. Common sense and experience indicate that, in the absence of advance information to the contrary, it is unrealistic to expect either the best or the worst possible conditions. An auditor should therefore start his examination on the assumption that a reasonable degree of internal control exists. As he proceeds through the steps of the audit cycle, he will have ample opportunity to expand or contract his work as increasing knowledge alters the initial assumption.

Competence and Integrity of Management

One of the conditions of control is competence and integrity of those involved in the accounting and control process. An auditor is also entitled to make the same initial assumption about the management of his client. The assumption is valid because it is true in most cases and is fundamental to the concept and purpose of an opinion audit. If the assumption of management competence and integrity, including honesty, is not justified, another type of examination may be possible, but not one that permits an expression of an opinion on financial statements.

An auditor's position vis-à-vis client dishonesty was discussed in Chapter 2. As that discussion makes clear, an auditor is not entitled to hold to an unverified assumption of competence and integrity throughout his examination. The examination must produce evidence on which to base a positive belief that the assumption holds true. Thus, auditing procedures at various stages of the audit cycle provide cumulative reasonable assurance that gross instances of incompetence or attempted dishonesty will come to light, although instances not having a material effect on the financial statements may not be detected. The alternative courses of action open to an auditor who discovers that he can no longer rely on the assumption of competence and integrity are discussed in Chapter 5.

Scope of Examination Defined by Audit Equation

Another initial assumption is that the audit equation defines the scope of the examination. That is, the examination can concentrate on underlying evidence plus corroborating evidence because they constitute sufficient competent evidential matter to provide reasonable assurance that the account balances are reliable. Although the audit equation defines the entire examination in almost every audit, there are enough exceptions to the rule for the assumption to be recognized as only an assumption and challenged from time to time throughout an audit cycle. Sometimes external events or management actions unrelated to the accounting process or the financial statements have a significant impact on them. Since events of that kind are rare, they may well escape management attention. Therefore, an auditor should constantly challenge his initial assumption about the focus of his attention by being alert to all events affecting his client, even those apparently unrelated to the subject of the audit, and to their potential effect on financial statements and disclosures.

THE AUDIT CYCLE

For purposes of description, every audit cycle can be conceived of as comprising eight major steps:

1. Understanding the client's systems,
2. Recording the understanding,
3. Preliminary evaluation of internal control,
4. Confirming the operation of controls,
5. Definitive evaluation of internal control,
6. Completing the audit,
7. Reviewing the financial statements, and
8. Issuing the opinion.

Clients' affairs are dynamic, changing, and of infinite variety, and so are audits. The eight steps may vary in relative importance from one audit to another and they seldom will appear as separate, isolated steps. However, whether carried out in sequence or in combination, all eight are found in one form or another in every engagement.

1. Understanding the Client's Systems

Chapter 1 sets forth the purpose of an audit examination: to understand the subject matter. An auditor's first task in an audit of a new client is to obtain, as quickly as possible, sufficient understanding to enable him to plan his audit program. Understanding a new client in the breadth and depth required for the ideal relationship described in Chapter 1 takes time, but the essentials can be assimilated rapidly. In recurring engagements, the accumulated experience of prior audits provides most of the necessary background, but even then an auditor often has reason to undertake some or all of the following procedures to update and clarify his earlier understanding.

Preliminary Homework

At the earliest stages of his contact with a new client, an auditor can learn much about the industry and its particular problems—and perhaps about the company itself—through research in business publications and in publications of the client company, such as annual reports and news releases. He can also get valuable information about some industries from audit guides published by the AICPA or from authoritative books written by accounting practitioners in specialized fields.

Trade associations in some industries publish a large volume of material, and a scan of some recent issues may suggest matters of current concern in the industry. Trade association material is usually too detailed and technical to contribute much to a speedy grasp of a new client's principal financial and accounting problems, but many auditors like to keep abreast of it as part of maintaining an understanding of their client's business environment. In short, an auditor should have an understanding of the client's industry; in some firms, the trend toward industry specialization is increasing.

Previous Auditor's Working Papers

If a client changes auditors, professional custom calls for the predecessor to make some information in his working papers available to the new auditor. The prior working papers can be a convenient source of information about the accounting system, internal control system, and accounting principles used by the client, as well as the composition of beginning balances of individual accounts. However, most of this information can also be obtained from the client.

The usual procedure is for the client to notify the previous auditor of the decision to change auditors and to request his cooperation with his successor. The two auditors then arrange a mutually convenient time and place to review the working papers. The client should be happy to pay both auditors for time and expense involved because the cost will be amply repaid in more efficient and effective service from the new auditor. However, the working papers are the property of the auditor who prepared them, and he is under no compulsion to accede to the request that he share them with a successor. Most auditors see no reason not to oblige if the request is within reason and relationships among the parties are not ruffled by unusual conditions.

Interviews

If properly conducted, initial interviews with a new client's management and supervisory personnel can be the most effective part of an examination. Interviewing is a special skill, and an auditor should cultivate it by every means available (Chapter 8 discusses the subject in more detail). Through interviews, even brief ones, he can quickly gain a comprehensive initial understanding of the client. The more thorough his initial understanding, the more systematic will be his planning and execution of audit tests and other phases of the examination.

Interviews should be designed to elicit information contributing to each of the levels of understanding described in Chapter 1: the client's accounting systems, internal controls, accounting principles, operations, management policies and practices, business environment, and legal constraints.

The most basic interviews, of course, are those with a sufficient number of client personnel who are knowledgeable about accounting systems and controls and can provide the auditor with a relatively thorough understanding of the company's accounting, internal control, and related activities and how they are carried out. In these interviews, questions and answers can be highly detailed and specific because an experienced auditor and knowledgeable accounting executives of a client company know clearly what is wanted. Deciding how many interviews are required is a matter of judgment, and avoiding omissions or duplications may be difficult in a large or complex operation. Some auditors like to interview those who perform accounting functions, as well as their supervisors, at the beginning; others defer interviews with nonsupervisory personnel until later, usually during the testing process.

Members of top management should be interviewed to learn about plans and policies that may affect the financial statements and also to establish a solid common understanding about the scope of the auditor's work and his responsibilities. No one likes unpleasant surprises: the auditor wishes to guard against the discovery at the last minute of a management action or decision having important financial statement implications, and management wishes to make sure that its decisions have no unanticipated financial statement implications. Good communication between top management and an auditor is a continuing necessity.

An auditor should also interview a sufficient number of personnel who are immediately responsible for operations, to gain an understanding of the main features of the operations and of potential problem areas having implications for internal control or financial statements. Auditors or clients are sometimes reluctant to "take up the time" of operating managers, but a skilled interviewer can learn all he needs to know from a supervisor or middle manager in a short period of time. As a rule, potential interviewees are happy to oblige after proper introduction, and the time is a good investment in more intelligent planning of the audit and evaluation of the results.

In the course of his interviews with top management and operating management, an auditor should inquire about business conditions and important legal covenants or regulatory conditions. He can thus gain the beginning of a significant background understanding of operational problems, management policies, the business environment, and legal constraints affecting the financial statements.

A growing number of companies, both public and private, are establishing audit committees of the board of directors (auditors' relationships with audit committees are more fully discussed in Chapter 8). If a committee exists, an auditor should arrange to meet with and interview the committee chairman in the early stages of the examination. He should understand the committee's expectations, and the committee should understand the auditor's intended scope of work.

During his interviews, an auditor will be referred to many different kinds of records and documents; he should collect copies of those documents that he believes will be necessary or helpful, both for the basic understanding of client affairs and for later reference during an audit. Examples are:

Legal documents, such as by-laws, articles of incorporation, minutes of directors' meetings, loan agreements, contracts, and leases,

Procedures manuals,

Organization charts, job descriptions, and other descriptions of the client company,

Policy statements and written planning summaries for the company or principal departments,

Memoranda explaining important or unusual transactions and their accounting treatment, and

Copies of internal management accounting reports, such as budgets, financial statements, cost reports, and variance reports.

Plant and Office Tours

A tour of offices and principal plants contributes significantly to an auditor's initial understanding of a new client. A walk through a client's office can tell an experienced auditor a great deal about the company's accounting system and controls. The quality of systemization and discipline is visible in physical arrangements and work habits as well as in the accuracy of the accounts. Similarly, a plant tour provides a preliminary "feel" for control problems and additional understanding about the company and its operations.

If a company has widely dispersed operations, especially overseas, a principal auditor must consider whether he should spend the time and money to visit significant outlying plants and offices. Technically, the standards of the profession do not require these visits. Nevertheless, we believe it is always worthwhile for a principal auditor to visit significant operations, no matter how distant. The initial cost is virtually certain to be recovered through more effectively planned and coordinated auditing procedures and through an increased ability to counsel management on accounting problems relating to the outlying operations. There is no substitute for contact with management on the scene and with the local auditors, whether of the auditor's own or another firm.

Procedures Manuals

Many companies, particularly large, complex ones, maintain extensive manuals of practice and procedures. An auditor should always obtain a complete set of procedures manuals covering accounting and asset control activities. The extent to which it is useful to obtain manuals of activities peripherally related to accounting, such as purchasing and personnel practices, depends on the circumstances of the client's systems. Although procedures manuals can often help to clarify an auditor's understanding of a particular phase of a client's system, they are for the most part too detailed and extensive to contribute effectively to his initial effort to gain an understanding of the client. Instead, manuals serve as major reference sources as the audit progresses.

2. Recording the Understanding

During interviews and plant tours, an auditor receives a great many impressions in a short period, sometimes about operations or systems that are highly technical or complex. Explanations he hears may be poorly worded or oversimplified, and he may forget or misunderstand them. Accordingly, it is essential that he make a rough record of his understanding as he goes along, to be filled in and confirmed later.

A record of understanding usually consists of two parts:

A broad summary of the auditor's overall understanding of the business, organization, management plans and policies, etc., supplemented by relevant documents collected in the review phase, and

A detailed summary of accounting procedures and controls.

The latter must be more detailed because it is the basis for a preliminary evaluation of internal controls and the planning of audit tests. The summary may be either narrative or graphic, so long as it provides an intelligible description of the accounting systems, procedures, and controls as the auditor understands them initially.

Flow Charts

While narrative descriptions of accounting systems, procedures, and controls can be perfectly satisfactory, we prefer flow charts. The process of preparing a flow chart provides a format and a discipline that assist the preparer in thinking through his understanding. The schematic form of a flow chart highlights both gaps in the auditor's understanding and discontinuities or weaknesses in the flow of data or control over it. A flow chart can also be read more rapidly by a reviewer or subsequent auditor.

Transaction Review

The completeness and accuracy of the recorded understanding should be checked by the first series of audit tests: the transaction reviews. The auditor should trace a transaction of each type through the entire system, comparing the processing and control steps to those recorded in the flow chart or narrative. The nature of transaction reviews and how to do them is discussed at length in Chapter 5.

3. Preliminary Evaluation of Internal Control

Purposes of Preliminary Evaluation

The first term of the audit equation requires an auditor to obtain evidence of the extent to which he can rely on the underlying accounts of the client. That evidence is gathered through audit tests; to decide what to test and how much, the auditor must make a preliminary evaluation of the system of internal control. The primary purpose is to identify which controls afford reasonable assurance that the affected accounts are accurate and reliable. Those are the controls that should be tested.

A corollary purpose is to identify controls that do *not* need to be tested. Malfunction of insignificant or redundant controls would not affect reliance on the final validity of the accounts, and controls that are known to be unreliable need not be tested because they must be disregarded in any event (disregarded for audit purposes; an auditor would not ignore problems that should be attended to by his client).

The preliminary evaluation also consists of identifying apparent control weaknesses: that is, the absence of expected or desirable control operations. Apparent weaknesses should be discussed at once with responsible client personnel. The auditor's preliminary understanding may be in error or incomplete, and the client may be able to improve upon it. There may be compensating controls elsewhere in the system. Or, if the auditor has identified a weakness that could materially affect the examination, early discussion with the client may allow time to plan and implement corrective action. That course is always preferable to one involving extended audit scope. (The next chapter contains a more extensive discussion of the alternative courses of action open to an auditor who discovers weaknesses in internal control.)

Internal Control Questionnaire

For the reasons given in Chapter 3, most auditors find an internal control questionnaire helpful in evaluating control systems. A comprehensive questionnaire reminds an auditor of possible control features and identifies and highlights those missing from the system under review. Although a questionnaire is a useful and generally applicable tool, it is not essential to an adequate evaluation of controls, particularly if the auditor has carefully prepared flow charts to aid in spotting control deficiencies.

A comprehensive, general-purpose internal control questionnaire may be completely inapplicable in small companies, in simple systems within larger companies, or in companies with special characteristics. Some auditing firms have developed a separate, simplified "small business" questionnaire, and there are a number of specialized questionnaires tailored to particular industries: insurance companies, banks, hospitals, and hotels, to name a few.

Audit Program

The preliminary evaluation of controls provides a basis for drafting the audit program. An audit program is a list, generally in detail, of steps to be performed in the course of an examination. It controls the nature and extent of the examination; aids in arranging, timing, and distributing the work; guards against possible omissions and duplications; and provides part of the evidence of work done. We believe that an audit program is necessary for adequate planning and supervision of an engagement under the first standard of field work. As a practical matter, the pressures of a new engagement often preclude actual writing of an audit program before work begins. If necessary, an experienced auditor can plan and supervise the work of assistants and require adequate documentation of that work without a written program. He should document his plans by committing the program to writing as soon as possible.

Recurring Engagements

Drafting an audit program completes the first phase of an audit cycle. That first phase is extensive in an initial engagement, sometimes involving more work than the remainder of the examination. In contrast, it may be only a small part of the work in a recurring engagement, consisting of brief meetings with key client personnel to consider changes in the client's circumstances since the previous year, conducting transaction reviews, and reviewing the audit program for possible revision. Even so, it is no less essential.

Both client and auditor need to beware of a dangerous tendency to treat changes perfunctorily. A client can easily forget changes that have taken place during the year because he has become accustomed to them by the time an auditor inquires. An auditor can easily treat matters reported to him as trivial and fail to think through their implications. In each recurring engagement, he must remember that gradually changing conditions can easily outdistance an audit program, making it a misleading guide to the nature and extent of examination required.

Accordingly, an auditor should exercise special care in planning a recurring engagement. If he finds he has started audit tests based on last year's program before reviewing his understanding with the client, conducting his transaction reviews, and checking his audit program, he should re-examine his approach to maintaining and updating his understanding of the client.

4. Confirming the Operation of Controls

Clearly, an auditor should confirm as much of his understanding as possible. As a practical matter, he could have been misinformed by his interviews and other inquiries. As a matter of principle, he has to obtain competent evidence to satisfy the first term of the audit equation and the third standard of field work.

Functional Tests

Although every audit step throughout the cycle (including simply spending time on a client's premises and with client personnel) tends to confirm an auditor's understanding, this is one principal purpose of testing the compliance of a system with prescribed control procedures. The other objective is to provide evidence permitting reasonable assurance that control systems are in effect, are operating as prescribed, and can be expected to continue to do so throughout the period under examination.

Transaction reviews confirm the completeness of an auditor's understanding. Functional tests provide the evidence on which he can base conclusions about the apparent effectiveness of controls. Both kinds of tests are discussed in detail in the next chapter; as noted earlier, the only controls that need be functionally tested are those on which the auditor explicitly intends to rely for reasonable assurance of the accuracy of the accounts.

5. Definitive Evaluation of Internal Control

Functional tests will either confirm or alter an auditor's understanding of the client's accounting systems and controls. Either way, he has definitive firsthand knowledge with which to plan the balance of the audit, revise the audit program if necessary, and possibly make constructive suggestions to the client.

If his understanding, as confirmed by functional tests, reveals either weaknesses in accounting controls or opportunities for improvements, he should, of course, take up his observations with responsible members of management. Management is always interested in an auditor's observations if they are informed, competent, and significant. Significance usually relates to the level of management—lack of control over travel advances should probably be taken up with an accounting supervisor rather than with the president, while a failure to monitor compliance with environmental protection regulations would be of interest to the president but perhaps not to an accounting supervisor. Significance is also determined by the preferences of management—some presidents, and even some directors, are interested and involved in matters like travel advances.

Management Letter

Discussion of apparent weaknesses and problems that is cooperative and constructive and aims at exploring possible courses of action is by far the best way to communicate findings to clients. The real work, and the positive contribution made by an auditor's observations, takes place in discussions with client management.

Usually these discussions are confirmed in a formal letter to a representative of the client—the so-called "management letter" or "suggestion letter." Some companies request such a letter, or the audit committee of the board of directors may require it. Even though no letter is required by professional standards or specifically requested by the client, it is in the interest of both auditor and management to have a written record of their discussions for future reference.

Auditors take pride in their management letters because the letters are a constructive contribution to the financial strength and viability of their clients. The breadth, depth, and variety of suggestions in the letter depend on the vigor, skill, and imagination of the auditor. Whatever his basic abilities, he should strive to bring them all fully to bear in assistance to his client.

The best time to discuss with a client weaknesses in controls and related problems and to write a management letter is at the conclusion of the functional tests and the definitive re-evaluation of controls. That point marks the end of the second phase of an audit cycle and ideally occurs at a time when both auditor and management have time to consider the auditor's findings. It should preferably take place sufficiently before the year end to permit corrective action that can affect the scope of the auditor's remaining work. Sometimes, however, the pressure of other demands on both the client and the auditor causes formal delivery of the management letter to be deferred until after year end.

6. Completing the Audit

An auditor's judgment of the extent and timing of account validation and other substantive tests needed to complete an audit is based on the understanding of internal control gained and confirmed in the first two phases of the cycle. If the client has effective basic controls and disciplines, the auditor may be able to satisfy himself about the integrity of the accounts with limited substantive tests. In terms of the audit equation, internal control determines the degree of reliability of the underlying evidence, which in turn determines the amount of corroborative evidence to be obtained through substantive tests.

Substantive tests, which consist of validation tests, analytical reviews, and other auditing procedures, are defined and described at length in Chapter 5 and in specific detail in the auditing procedures sections of Chapters 9 through 16. For the purpose of describing the audit cycle in this chapter, substantive tests refer to all audit procedures other than transaction reviews and functional tests, and the term "validation" has the general meaning used in Chapter 3: to establish the truth, accuracy, or relevance of a fact or figure.

Validation of Principles and Judgments

Validation is more than checking that assets and liabilities exist and are carried in the accounts at the proper amounts, and that transactions are properly authorized and recorded in the correct accounts. Validation also includes identifying and evaluating the accounting principles used and, perhaps even more important, evaluating a client's judgments that affect valuation estimates. As noted in earlier chapters, evaluating value judgments is probably the most sensitive and difficult of an auditor's duties, but it is inescapable. In subsequent chapters, we examine and comment on specific valuation and estimating problems and alternative solutions available to an auditor.

Validation of Accounts

Auditors have traditionally and customarily paid most attention to balance sheet accounts, validating by one means or another that each account is fairly stated, neither larger nor smaller than it should be. Practically, that is the easiest thing to do. We believe that emphasizing balance sheet accounts is also theoretically sound, even though the income statement has received greater attention from investors in recent years.

Sufficient assurance that the income statement is fairly stated is provided by the process of validating the accuracy and consistency of balance sheet accounts at the beginning and end of a period, and by an internal control system that is tested and found to be sound and functioning. Income statement accounts are logically and inextricably related to one or more balance sheet accounts: the income statement accounts measure the "stream" of transactions flowing through the business, and the balance sheet accounts represent the results of transactions that are "in transit," so to speak, at a balance sheet date. Therefore, measuring the in-transit amounts at beginning and end by validating the balance sheet accounts also validates the stream between, provided the accounting system is under reasonable control.

Years ago, validation focused almost entirely on the year-end balance sheet. Exceptions were rare and were approached with great caution. Now it is more common to focus most validation procedures on dates other than the year end, except in companies that are very small or have particularly volatile operations, or whose controls and disciplines are absent or temporarily inoperative. Public companies wish to close their accounts and release net income figures as soon as possible after the year end, and that does not allow enough time for all validation procedures to be performed between the year end and the release date. Moreover, since accounting controls and disciplines are becoming more sophisticated, both because of the improved state of the art and because the demand for dependable interim figures is increasing, their presence reduces the risk of undetected error between validation dates and year end.

Thus it is necessary, as well as possible and practicable, to perform most validation procedures before the year end. It is also theoretically sound: with adequate controls, it should be acceptable for validation to take place earlier than the end of the accounting period.

Justification of Interim Validation of Year-End Balances

How can an account balance on a given date (the fiscal year end) be validated by examining the balance on another, earlier date? There are two principal reasons: (1) reasonable assurance that the accounting and control systems are operating satisfactorily and (2) the logical, interrelated structure of an enterprise's accounts and operations.

Continuity is an important feature of a strong control system. The necessary disciplines described in Chapter 3—segregation of duties, restricted access, and supervisory controls—are so categorized because they are necessary to assure continuity. The optional discipline of internal audit is not necessary, but it strengthens the assurance of continuity when it is present. If an auditor's evaluation of the accounting and control systems discloses no material weaknesses in the basic controls and the necessary disciplines, this provides "reasonable assurance that errors or irregularities . . . that would be material in the financial statements being audited would be prevented or detected within a timely period by employees in the normal course of performing their assigned functions" (SAS No. 1, paragraph 320.68). Therefore, validation of a balance during the year, plus appropriate reliance on the operation of internal control for the balance of the year, gives an auditor reasonable assurance that the balance at year end is also valid.

The reasonable assurance provided by adequate internal control is reinforced by the fact that the kinds of items susceptible of early validation are integral parts of an enterprise under examination. They are interdependent, and an auditor may rely on that interdependence in validating account balances. For example, a certain amount of cash is needed to operate; a certain level and "mix" of accounts receivable are an integral part of the flow of sales; raw materials, work in process, and finished goods flow through the inventory "pipelines" to cost of goods sold, which is in turn related to sales. The same is true of plant and equipment, accounts payable, most accruals, and major revenue and expense accounts. The interrelationships are like those among the heart, lungs, blood, and brain of a living thing: if one stops, they all stop; if one malfunctions seriously, it affects the others. An auditor's focus is not on the individual items composing an account balance, but rather on the balance itself, not in isolation but as it relates to all other balances in the financial statements.

Thus, analytical reviews, including reviews of account activity and comparisons of account balances, provide evidence that all interrelationships and the control systems are maintained throughout the remainder of the period after validation. That evidence is additional assurance that a year-end balance is probably as valid as a comparable balance validated earlier.

There are, of course, circumstances in which accounts should not be validated at other than year end. If the item to be validated is very large, out of the ordinary, or subject to significant change during the relevant time period, it is not necessarily subject to the logic of integral relationships. If internal controls, particularly the disciplines, cannot be relied on, reasonable assurance of continuity is lacking. Sometimes year-end validation is simply more economical to perform and more certain in its results. Even in those situations, however, it may be possible to carry validation work to a point that will permit completing it at the critical time with relatively little additional work.

Validation in Last Quarter

As a practical matter, validation procedures are not often undertaken earlier than the last quarter of a fiscal year, even though it is theoretically acceptable to do so. The main reason is that current events affect valuations and judgments, and current conditions can change within a few months in a fast moving economy. Thus, calendar-year companies seldom take physical inventories earlier than the end of September, October, or November; usually, the auditor confirms receivables in the same period.

Procedures at and After Year End

If most of the substantive procedures are applied at the end of a month in the last quarter of the year, the typical fast year-end closing calls for tight planning and precision performance. Validation procedures for most accounts can be limited to some or all of the following: analytical reviews and comparisons of year-end balances, account activity, fluctuations, and the like; confirmation of large or sensitive items; tests of cutoffs; and reviews of problems that have been previously identified. Large or unusual transactions can be sought out for scrutiny. Reviews and inquiries must be made about substantive changes in the business or in the system of internal control, and in a search for subsequent events or commitments affecting the financial statements.

Audit activities at year end are likely to follow a pattern similar to the following:

Working papers evidencing earlier validation procedures are reviewed, account by account, and inquiries made about changes in systems and controls.

Activity since validation in each account is scanned to detect obviously unusual items or fluctuations. Inquiries, and possibly tests, are made to re-evaluate at year end the problems revealed by earlier examination.

Account balances and other matters that can be confirmed are confirmed.

Journal entries, trial balances, consolidating work sheets, and drafts of financial statements are meticulously scrutinized and double-checked.

Logical relationships among accounts are reviewed, and the information is brought up to date.

The "score sheet" and memoranda of problems identified earlier are brought up to date, reviewed, and discussed for a last time with management of the client. Sometimes, further tests are required to obtain reasonable assurance on the status of a problem.

Last-minute inquiries are made throughout the client organization. Written representations of management are customarily obtained on some matters, such as inventories and liabilities.

7. Reviewing the Financial Statements

Although the financial statements are technically the responsibility of a client's management, they are in practice always the result of the continuing process of consultation between auditor and client. The auditor provides his expert advice on many matters, such as accountability procedures, accounting entries, disclosures of events and accounting policies, and wording of notes to financial statements.

The extent of the auditor's participation varies widely. At one end of the spectrum is a well-staffed company which prepares the format of the financial statements and a draft of the text of the annual report in nearly final form before the end of the fiscal year. The auditor reviews these statements and offers his suggestions for improving their form or content or both. At the other extreme is the client who, usually because of inadequate staff, permits his auditor to carry out the task of preparing the financial statements and reviews them when the auditor delivers a completed draft.

A time-honored mental picture, still current in the profession, portrays an auditor sitting down with his client to explain what the financial statements mean. No doubt that picture is still accurate in many instances, but an auditor has compelling business and professional reasons to avoid a relationship in which a client relies to that extent on his auditor. The decisions reflected in the financial statements are the client's responsibility, and common sense as well as good professional conduct dictates that an auditor should not take on that responsibility. Further, the financial statements contain information useful to management, even in small businesses, and, we believe, an auditor has a professional responsibility to help a client learn to use that information in day-to-day operations.

In concept, the review of financial statements follows validation procedures in an audit cycle because validation procedures are supposed to assure an auditor that all problems affecting the financial statements have been brought to light. If validation procedures reveal previously unrecognized problems of valuation or financial statement presentation, the audit cycle should be considered imperfect because the event is evidence that the auditor's understanding of the client was previously imperfect. Moreover, the client's system of internal control should be considered faulty because it should have detected the problem. Although unforeseen problems will continue to be a regular fact of life— neither client nor auditor can completely control the course of events— every possible effort to prevent them is worthwhile.

8. Issuing the Opinion

Most engagements have a deadline for release of audited financial statements or data taken therefrom. An auditor should not sign an opinion until he is satisfied that all procedures specified in the audit program have been completed as planned and that all possible questions have been brought to his attention, answered properly, and recorded in the working papers. A well-planned audit aims to have field work procedures completed sufficiently in advance of the deadline to permit a thorough review of the working papers by the manager or partner.

Working Paper Review

The review of working papers is important enough to deserve being called the capstone of the audit. It should be so closely related to the final review of financial statements that one can hardly be distinguished from the other. It requires an experienced and fully knowledgeable professional to bring together all of the planning, effort, and documentation to make sure that procedures are adequate and appropriate, that they have been performed properly, that conclusions reached are objective and logical, and that there is a properly documented basis for an informed opinion. The reviewer must evaluate the completeness of the audit program in the light of the results of the tests, the quality of work done by the performing auditors, the quality of the client's judgments and decisions and the auditor's review of them, the adequacy of the working paper record, and the quality of the resulting understanding. Furthermore, the exacting and inconclusive nature of most audit tasks makes it imperative that every piece of work be reviewed for completeness and logic by another qualified professional.

The review is a complex and demanding task of such critical importance that accounting firms are constantly seeking ways to help the reviewer by providing aids such as checklists, standardized procedures, and policy bulletins, while simultaneously trying to guard against routinized performance of a highly judgmental task. The quality of the review, and therefore of the audit, rests on the professional diligence and sense of responsibility of the reviewer. There is no way to substitute for those qualities or compensate for their absence. Although he can be guided and supported by aids such as those listed above, and by a clear understanding of the logic of the audit, the reviewer cannot and should not be relieved of the burden of responsibility for understanding all that he needs to understand to be able to give his opinion on the financial statements.

In practice, the review rarely works as smoothly as it does in theory. There are delays by client personnel, unexpected auditing or valuation problems, an assistant who falls ill or cannot complete his assignment on time, and innumerable other possible hindrances. Increasing public pressure for the fastest possible release of significant information causes deadlines to be drawn constantly tighter. Under the pressure of a deadline the risk of oversight or misjudgment is greatest. Experienced auditors resist that pressure and make sure that they review an integrated set of financial statements supported by a coherent working-paper summary of questions and judgments before committing themselves, explicitly or implicitly, to an opinion on the financial statements or to approving release of any part of them.

It is a good practice to go further than that. The number of judgments entering into financial statements, many of them made at the last minute and under pressure, represent more responsibility than one auditor should be asked to bear alone. Many firms require that the financial statements be reviewed by a second qualified professional before release of any figures. Simply calling for review is of dubious value unless the reviewer is provided with positive means of going directly to the matters of judgment. One means of insuring effective review is to prepare a formal memorandum of matters for the attention of the reviewer, which can be kept up to date and reviewed as the audit progresses. The memorandum briefs the reviewer on significant matters arising during the audit and serves as a point of departure from which he can make inquiries aimed at evaluating the quality of the primary auditor's understanding.

An auditor should carefully integrate the working papers and systematically file and index them. It is particularly important to include all memoranda prepared covering points considered in the review process or discussed in closing conferences with the client. Since court cases have turned on the presence or absence of a record in working papers, auditors must be exceptionally careful to keep an accurate record of exactly what they did, said, and thought.

The exact nature of the "working paper review" by the manager or partner has been variously interpreted. Many years ago it consisted of a schoolmasterly critique of the preparer's personal attributes, such as penmanship and neatness, as much as the content of the papers. In recent years, some auditors seem to have emphasized protection against legal action, others the fixing of responsibility, and others the independent "second guessing" of judgments. If working papers are voluminous, the task of review is a large one and differences in approach can be significant.

Whatever other purposes the review may have, its primary purpose must be to make sure that the logic of the audit is complete and properly documented. The logic, based on the audit equation, calls for evidence in the working papers that: the underlying systems were understood, tested, and evaluated; the evaluation was translated explicitly into a program of corroborative auditing procedures; the results of those procedures either confirmed the evidence of the accounts or led to a rational exploration of differences; and the results support each detail disclosed in the financial statements.

That logic has to be reviewed by one person—the auditor in charge of the engagement. He has to obtain assurance, directly or indirectly, that the working papers do support the logic of the audit and he has to investigate and explain—not suppress—any that do not. He may delegate to another reviewer a portion of the review that focuses on a well-defined segment of the audit logic. For example, evidence that the physical inventory was properly taken is part of the audit logic, and the principal reviewer must know that the working papers contain that evidence; however, he may ask another competent person to scrutinize all of the working papers of test counts and tests of pricing and summarization to make sure that they confirm the propriety of the inventory. The principal reviewer alone must be responsible for bringing together all of the logic; therefore, the delegation of review responsibility should be based on a rational plan relating to the audit logic and not on assumptions as to the nature of the papers or the competence of the other reviewer. If part of the review is delegated, the subordinate reviewer's conclusions should be documented so that they can become part of the written record of the audit logic.

Reviewing: Form Versus Substance

The working papers preserve the work of the audit and its results for the future, and therefore auditors give the working paper review much attention. The risk of that attention is that so much emphasis on the after-the-fact reflection of the audit can cause the real substance of the audit to be viewed in less than its proper perspective. Working papers are a means to an end, not an end in themselves.

The real substance of the audit is doing it: planning it intelligently and logically, executing it diligently and perceptively, and especially supervising it so that the real review is continuous and active. By the time working papers are reviewed, they should contain a complete record of each step and each mental process involved in reaching the final judgments and conclusions. If an audit is properly planned, executed, and supervised, the working paper review should be nothing more than the final control over a result already accomplished and a means of determining that all items of significance have been considered in reaching an audit conclusion. Confusion of the working paper review with the substance of the audit is likely to create problems.

If the evaluation of audit findings is left for the working paper review, it is obviously too late. The reviewing auditor does not have time for adequate exploration and analysis of problems and it is too late for corrective action. As a matter of course, problems identified by the audit are usually dealt with as soon as they come to light and not left for the working paper review. Instances of problems that were not identified until the review are frequent enough to afford recurrent proof that to leave them for the review is completely unworkable as a general practice.

Therefore, auditors are constantly seeking improved means of continuous review and communication while an audit is in progress. Various systems of formal and informal reporting have been developed. In recent years, a much larger fraction of total audit time has been devoted to "supervision." In our opinion, the concept of "understanding," kept explicitly in mind throughout an audit, aids in that process. An assistant auditor should be required to understand the purpose and result of his work and to understand why a particular finding is significant or insignificant. The supervising and reviewing auditors should be required to understand the work of their assistants while it is in progress and its implications for the client's financial statements and control systems.

Another problem that may be created by delay of the supervisory review is the question of how to complete the review before the opinion date for large, diversified companies that are accustomed to issuing, within three weeks of the year end, summary figures from financial statements approved by the auditors. Obviously, an audit cannot be completed and all the working papers reviewed within that period of time, yet an auditor cannot risk shortcutting his professional responsibilities simply to meet a deadline.

The answer is that the review—and the supervision of the audit—is done before the year end and as the work progresses. An auditor who understands the logic of the audit and also understands his client knows what needs to be reviewed to complete the documentation of that logic. He can therefore plan the steps necessary to complete the logic of the audit, assign the delegated portions of the review, and go directly to the critical working papers in time to see that the logic is complete and properly documented before the deadline.

RENEWING THE CYCLE

The end of one audit usually blends into the beginning of another. The final stages of an audit may stretch out over a period of weeks or months. After the statements are issued, tax returns may need to be prepared, statements filed with the SEC, or special-purpose statements given to lenders or government agencies. There may be a meeting with the audit committee of outside directors to prepare for or a stockholders' meeting to attend. There is also administrative cleanup: records of time spent must be collected, analyzed, and compared with budgets, and fee billings must be processed. That is the natural time to begin planning next year's audit cycle—to agree on locations to be visited, timing of physical inventories, assignment of tasks to the client's staff, and actions to eliminate problems encountered in the examination just concluded.

Once an auditor–client relationship is working well, the audit cycle is continuous throughout the year. An auditor maintains his understanding of a client by frequent contacts at all levels of the client organization. Problems and unusual transactions are raised and resolved early. The audit tests themselves become a periodic means of confirming that neither management nor auditor has overlooked anything important in their continuing effort.

5

Auditing Procedures—
Their Nature and Extent

INTRODUCTION

An auditor has to understand his client's systems and be acquainted with the mode of operations before he starts his audit. That statement seems elementary and even redundant after the extensive discussion in Chapters 1, 3, and 4. But it deserves emphasis because in the past it was common to begin various audit tests before or while internal control was evaluated. As a matter of policy, large amounts of routine checking and reperformance of clerical functions were expected. Those and similar practices somehow implied that certain kinds and amounts of testing were required no matter what a client's characteristics or conditions.

Clearly, there should be no testing for testing's sake in a well-conceived audit. Every audit procedure test has (or should have) one or more specific practical purposes determined by its place in the audit logic. That place, in turn, is determined by the characteristics of the client: its business, the nature of the transactions, the kind of accounting system and data processing equipment, the type of controls, the materiality and relative risk of error in the data being tested, and so on.

TESTS VERSUS PROCEDURES

Auditors use the term "test" in a variety of contexts, as this chapter will illustrate. It is frequently used interchangeably with audit "procedure." Obviously, testing is an audit procedure, and conversely all audit procedures are for the purpose of testing the validity and reliability of financial statement data. Audit procedures are often performed on a "test basis," meaning that a given procedure is applied to some, but not all, of the subject matter under examination. For example, the auditor's confirmation of account balances with customers is a well-recognized audit procedure. Its objective is to test the validity of the receivable balance in the balance sheet. In many instances, this procedure is performed on a test basis, with the number of accounts selected for confirmation depending on the particular circumstances of the audit. This interchangeable usage of "test" and "procedure" seldom causes any confusion in practice.

LOGIC AND TERMINOLOGY

All audit procedures and tests are aimed at one or more of the following purposes:

Confirming the auditor's understanding of the client's systems and procedures,

Obtaining evidence that controls are functioning so as to permit reliance on the underlying accounts,

Validating a fact or representation, such as an account balance, or

Corroborating a relationship among accounts.

Even a beginning auditor must understand the purpose of a test and know enough about the client to recognize the place of the test in the logic of the audit. Otherwise he should not be doing the test.

Many different words have been used to describe and classify audit tests. One system of terminology is not necessarily better than another unless it makes precise communication easier among auditors and outside the profession or helps in understanding the purpose of each test, when and how to do it, and when and how to alter it in response to changed conditions. One problem of terminology is that all of the words used in auditing are common ones which have meanings and usages beyond their application in auditing. They can therefore too easily be construed differently. The word "test," for example, has common meanings in schoolrooms and chemistry laboratories which are different from its meaning in auditing. Even in auditing, each auditor's understanding of the kind and amount of activity involved in a "test" may be different from that of other auditors.

A logical interrelationship among terms and consistency in their usage is therefore essential; so is precise definition if that is possible. With those objectives in mind, we use the terminology of Statement on Auditing Procedure (SAP) No. 54—now Section 320 of Statement on Auditing Standards (SAS) No. 1—supplemented by some terms that we have found consistently useful because they can be defined meaningfully and related to one another through the audit logic outlined in earlier chapters.

SAP No. 54 introduced the terms "tests of compliance" and "substantive tests" into the authoritative literature of the profession in 1972:

The purpose of tests of compliance is to provide reasonable assurance that the accounting control procedures are being applied as prescribed. [Paragraph 320.55]

. . . The purpose of . . . [substantive tests] is to obtain evidence as to the validity and the propriety of accounting treatment of transactions and balances or, conversely, of errors or irregularities therein. [Paragraph 320.70]

Since the purpose of audit procedures or tests is to develop "sufficient competent evidential matter" to justify the auditor's opinion, the kinds of audit tests needed are related to the kinds of evidence required. The discussion of the third standard of field work in Chapter 2 concludes with this formulation:

$$\frac{\text{Underlying}}{\text{evidence}} + \frac{\text{Corroborating}}{\text{evidence}} = \frac{\text{Sufficient competent}}{\text{evidential matter}}$$

The validity of underlying evidence is established by the results of tests of compliance or functional tests. Underlying evidence comprises the accounts themselves, including the books of original entry, ledgers, and work sheets that produce the aggregate numbers in financial statements. Functional tests provide the means by which an auditor may be reasonably assured that he can rely on the internal control system to assure the validity of the underlying evidence.

Corroborating evidence is established by means of substantive tests. Corroborating evidence comes from outside the accounting system and substantiates the results of the system. It comprises items such as confirmations by outsiders; the validating signatures, endorsements, and initials on documents; and information acquired by observation, physical examination, computation, or reasoning. Substantive tests provide means external to the accounting system by which an auditor may be reasonably assured that account balances and other information emanating from the system are valid. Substantive tests involve two classes of auditing procedures: "tests of details of transactions and balances, and analytical review of significant ratios and trends and resulting investigation of unusual fluctuations and questionable items" (SAS No. 1, paragraph 320.70). We use the terms "validation procedures" and "analytical reviews" to identify the two classes.

The relationships described may be shown schematically:

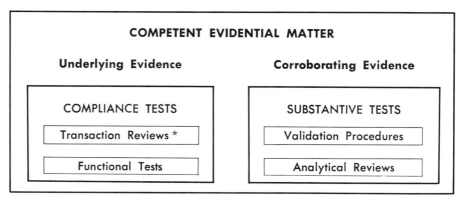

* Transaction reviews are part of the process of understanding the system and are therefore not technically compliance tests; however, they are so classified in paragraph 320.52 of SAS No. 1 because their purpose is to aid in designing functional tests.

We categorize auditing procedures in this fashion for purposes of discussion or conceptualization; the distinctions are never mutually exclusive. Every transaction review contributes something to functional testing and often to validation and analysis as well. Every validation procedure and analytical review contributes something to the understanding of and confidence in the system of internal control. And any specific procedure may at one time be a compliance test and at another time a substantive test. Also, the boundaries of the boxes should be seen as fluid: at one time or another each audit test may constitute a greater or smaller part of the whole body of evidence.

Each of the categories of tests in the schematic diagram fits one of the purposes set forth at the beginning of the chapter:

> Transaction reviews *confirm an auditor's understanding* of a client's systems and controls.
> Functional tests *provide evidence that controls are functioning* properly.
> Validation procedures *substantiate* account balances.
> Analytical reviews *corroborate relationships among accounts.*

The logic of the audit equation is that if transaction reviews and functional tests reveal no reason to doubt the reliability of the underlying evidence, an auditor is justified in minimizing (but not eliminating) validation procedures and analytical reviews. If a transaction review or functional test reveals the possibility of doubt about the reliability of the underlying evidence, that doubt can often be removed or reduced sufficiently by validation testing and analytical reviews. The relationship is as direct and specific as the audit equation implies —it is complicated only by the possibility of alternative reactions because there may be several ways to remove a doubt.

Each of the categories of tests is discussed in turn in this chapter. In the concluding section, the rationale for the size and method of selection of audit test samples is discussed.

MATERIALITY AND RELATIVE RISK

Materiality was discussed at length in Chapter 2. Obviously, both quantity and quality of audit effort should be in proportion to the significance of the subject matter—its materiality in relation to the financial statements as a whole. *For example:*

Inventories of an industrial company are a major element of the balance sheet and a major determinant of net income. They are therefore a major focus of audit procedures. Inventories of a public utility or an educational institution, on the other hand, vary less from year to year and are not usually material; hence, audit attention is correspondingly minimal.

Relative risk is another dimension, so to speak, of the materiality principle. Auditors have always recognized implicitly that the allocation of their efforts, and the direction of their vigilance, should be affected by the relative risk of error or misstatement in a particular environment. Usually, but not always, materiality and relative risk go together. *For example:*

Relative risk accompanies materiality in the inventory comparison described above. Inventories of an industrial company, as well as being material, are likely to present complex problems of control, valuation, and accounting principle. On the other hand, the property, plant, and equipment accounts may be even more material (in value) than inventories in the balance sheet of an industrial company, but they usually offer much less relative risk from an audit verification standpoint, and audit effort is allocated accordingly. Conversely, plant accounts of a public utility company are important because of their relationship to the rate base.

This example suggests the importance of being explicit about response to relative risk. An auditor must understand clearly why he must usually invest less effort on some accounts and more on others, so that he can react promptly and decisively when significant risk of error or misstatement arises. The principle of materiality and relative risk is pervasive, affecting every statement about audit procedures.

Finally, the financial soundness of a business has a bearing on the degree of risk an auditor may safely assume. There is less pressure on the successful concern to window-dress, to understate expenses or inflate sales, or to conceal liabilities. An auditor must consider that the newly organized business struggling for a foothold, or the established business fallen on hard times, may endeavor to postpone write-offs and conceal pledging of assets and creation of liabilities.

TRANSACTION REVIEWS

The first steps in the audit cycle consist of obtaining and recording an understanding of the client. The several levels and kinds of understanding are described in Chapter 1; the most fundamental to auditing are the accounting systems and the systems of control. Having inquired about the systems and made records or flow charts of the resulting descriptions, an auditor should confirm his understanding by examining the systems himself.

He does that by tracing each significant type of transaction from its inception to conclusion—"from cradle to grave"—to make sure that he has identified all significant processes and has noted and evaluated each phase of the transaction flow. In our opinion, the cradle-to-grave concept is most important. In the past, auditors often tested cash transactions under the cash section of an audit program, revenue and accounts receivable transactions under another section, and so on. Under such a segmented approach, a significant part of many transactions that originate and are acted on outside the accounting department can be neglected. *For example:*

> The integrity of inventory accounts is significantly affected by activity in storekeeping and purchasing departments.
> The integrity of revenue accounts is significantly affected by the strength of the sales department's control over customer orders and credit requests.
> The entries for estimates of uncollectible accounts and losses on contracts in process are based on data that originate and may be almost entirely processed and evaluated in operating departments; the accounting department may have little more to do with the transaction than to process the resulting entry.

It is thus imperative, we believe, that an auditor examine transactions from cradle to grave if he is to be sure he understands the system adequately. Apparently, however, some auditors do not believe that transaction reviews are necessary—at least in the meticulous detail that we recommend—since SAP No. 54 does not require them. We believe there is a serious gap in the logic of an audit unless an auditor confirms his understanding of the system with an adequately documented transaction review before proceeding to test the identified controls.

Types of Transactions

Usually it is not hard to identify and define the major systems for processing transactions. Every enterprise, no matter what it does, carries out certain basic business activities which must be controlled and accounted for. Those activities are so common that Chapters 9–16 are organized around them: the selling activity, the buying activity, the production activity, the property activity, and the income tax, investment, cash management, and financing activities.

Identifying subsystems or types of transactions within the major activities is much harder. A company may have several separate modes of buying, selling, or producing activities. The different activities may have the same or different accounting systems, or the systems may be different up to a point at which they combine; for example, invoices from several different purchasing activities may be brought into a single accounts payable department. Conversely, the systems may be the same up to a point and then become different; for example, products may take different routes in the later stages of production or distribution. Sometimes identical transactions may be handled as separate types because of special arrangements with customers or buyers. An auditor must do his best to identify those distinctions in the course of a transaction review as part of his attempt to understand the system.

In addition to a variety of types of transactions within each of the major systems, a client may have unique subsystems or parts of systems, usually to facilitate monthly or quarterly closings or to provide for regular or periodic estimates or judgments basic to financial statement preparation. *For example:*

> A system may be needed to compensate for a gap in a conventional transaction system: a procedure for pricing and recording unmatched receiving reports or for identifying and recording invoices received after the end of a period.
>
> Special systems may be required to accumulate data needed to determine revenue or expense: gathering of data to permit the computation of federal income tax, estimates of cost to complete contracts for percentage-of-completion accounting, or estimates of pension liabilities or insurance claim reserves.
>
> Extensive systems or subsystems may be required to make the evaluations called for in the exercise of management's accountability function: loan quality reviews by lending agencies, evaluation of unearned revenue balances by transportation companies, or a system for taking, pricing, and evaluating physical inventory by merchandising companies.

Some of the preceding examples illustrate subsystems that are likely to be activated only once a year or once a quarter. In those cases, an auditor is likely to make the review together with preparing for validation tests during the current year. The transaction review, however, is necessary under the logic of the audit equation to make sure that the system is well enough understood and is operative.

Although not imperative, it is worth considerable effort to identify types of transactions and subsystems before starting transaction reviews. An auditor will obviously undertake to review only those types that he has identified. Therefore, poor identification may lead to too little testing and the necessity to replan or even repeat the testing program. However, the audit cycle contains safeguards against errors of omission. The transaction review itself may reveal overlooked types of transactions. If not, the validation tests and analytical reviews are almost certain to do so, perhaps inconveniently late but not too late for effective completion of the audit. It is likely to be particularly difficult in new engagements to be sure that all significant types have been identified in the initial phase.

Definition of Types of Transactions

The term "type of transaction" is differently understood by different auditors. Some believe it to be very broad—"sales" is one type of transaction and "purchases" another. Some believe it to be very narrow—transactions with each customer or supplier or transactions entering into each account are considered separate types.

We define the term in the light of the logic of the audit equation. The purpose of making compliance tests is to obtain evidence of the reliability of controls that assure the validity of the underlying evidence. Therefore, the term "type of transaction" must be defined in the light of the conrols an auditor is aiming to evaluate. Thus, transactions are of the same type if they are of the same nature and are subject to the same controls.

This clear conceptual definition often becomes considerably less clear when applied in practice. The following paragraphs describe the most common situations.

Transactions Processed in Different Locations
By Different People

If a transaction system is adequately systematized and disciplined, that is sufficient reason to believe that the same controls prevail in all locations covered by the system. In the absence of evidence to the contrary, all similar transactions through the system can be considered to be of one type.

If the systemization or discipline does not assure uniform processing, the same transaction in different locations may have to be considered a different type of transaction for purposes of transaction review. In that event, a separate review of each type of transaction at each location may be necessary. If noted weaknesses are not considered serious or the relative risk of resulting misstatement is not high, it may be acceptable for an auditor to rotate his visits among the various locations and accept as relatively small the risk of undetected variation from the system in locations not visited.

If there is a weakness in any of the conditions of control so that there can be no reasonable assurance that different people in the same location exercise control in the same way, an auditor's response should not be to do more transaction reviews but rather to choose among the alternative responses to an identified weakness in internal control. Those responses are described in a later section of this chapter.

Transactions Originating in Different Ways

Transactions originate in a variety of ways that is potentially infinite. That does not mean that every different point of origin gives rise to a different type of transaction. As a practical matter, efficient processing and control of transaction data requires systemization beginning at the point of origin, or as near it as possible. With adequate systemization, different points of origin can be subject to the same controls, and therefore considered of one type.

Nevertheless, it is inevitable that different kinds of activity will require different systems for originating transactions. At a minimum, for example, an accounts payable system must provide for "non-purchase order" items as well as those processed through the purchasing department with a purchase order. It may also have to provide for "rush items," or distinguish between items that can be documented on receiving reports and those that cannot, or accommodate any of a variety of other conditions.

In some organizations, it is not possible to systematize the origination of transactions. In that event, an auditor may review a transaction from every point of origin. Or, if the number of points is large, it may be a better application of audit logic to recognize the control problem, look for the compensating controls, and make functional tests of them.

When transactions differ because of different points of origin and there are no compensating controls, the control that causes the differences is usually the approval or authorization control. Thus, an office manager approves payment of a rent bill, the building superintendent approves a fuel bill, etc. Although the same disbursing procedure is used, they are different types of transactions for an auditor's purpose. A scan of account classifications and a review of types of entries in each usually supplies clues to types of transactions for review purposes.

Types of Transactions That Combine or Divide

Most systems are designed to combine different types of transactions into a single type at one or more points. *For example:*

Sales orders and service orders may be different types of transactions as they are processed through the sales and order entry departments, but become a single type when transmitted in the same type of document to the billing department.

Export orders and domestic orders may be distinct types of transactions, processed separately through the credit and billing departments, but may be combined into a single type for accounts receivable recording and cash collection procedures.

Conversely, export and domestic orders may be exactly the same for order entry, packing, and shipping purposes but separate for accounts receivable recording and cash collection procedures.

As systems become more sophisticated and particularly as they are computerized, transactions may be batched or combined with other transactions into one total, thus completely losing their diversity at some point in the system.

The definition of "type of transaction" applies without qualification in those cases: the types of transactions are different when they follow different routes or are subject to different controls; they are the same type from the point at which they merge into a common system.

Apparently Identical Transactions Controlled Differently

Auditors must be alert to conditions that cause apparently identical transactions to be, in substance, different types. *For example:*

A consumer goods company manufactures products which fall into four distinct seasonal sales patterns: Easter, Summer, Fall, and Christmas. Superficially, the products and their marketing differ little from season to season, and the accounting system is the same all year round. In fact, however, the "Christmas rush" causes so many handling, processing, and recording problems that a transaction review of any other seasonal shipment is meaningless or even misleading for an evaluation of controls at the Christmas season.

In the example given, there are at least two different types of transactions. Identifying that type of situation is especially difficult in an initial audit. The broader levels of understanding described in Chapter 1—knowledge of the operations, the management policies, and the business conditions—help make the identification but even at best an auditor must be prepared for surprises.

Transaction Type Identified Late in the Audit

What happens if an auditor discovers late in the audit cycle that he has overlooked a significant type of transaction? The answer depends entirely on the circumstances. There is no point in going back through the whole audit process as it applies to that type of transaction solely to observe the theoretical structure of the audit logic. In many cases, it may be necessary to do so for the practical purpose of deciding what to do: an understanding of the system has to be recorded and confirmed so as to plan required functional and validation tests. If the condition is discovered in the validation procedures phase, timing may require that the auditor go directly to the kind of validation procedures he would employ if he were not to rely on controls over the unevaluated type of transaction. Even if time permits, he may decide that the client's failure to identify the type of transaction and advise him of it in advance may be sufficient evidence of possible weakness in supervisory control to require particular attention during validation procedures.

How To Make a Transaction Review

An auditor can select for review the first transaction of a given type that comes to hand. He can start anywhere in the system and proceed in either direction. It is customary to start at the point of inception because at that point there is likely to be the greatest number of types of transactions and the clearest distinction among types. But, in our opinion, starting at inception is not essential; frequently, starting at the end is more convenient. Generally, a completed transaction is reviewed, but sometimes characteristics of the system (as in some computerized "real-time" systems) may necessitate tracing a "live" transaction from inception to conclusion.

A reviewing auditor should scrutinize each step in the processing of the selected transaction, starting with why and how it originated. He should check the computations, reviews, and approvals performed and note how they are documented. He should check the transcriptions from one document to another and note how those linkages are controlled. He should ascertain the purpose and trace the disposition of copies of documents evidencing the transaction and of other documents prepared from them.

Throughout the test an auditor should keep in mind the basic control operations described in Chapter 3, observing the methods of validation, completeness, and reperformance. He should watch for evidence that those operations are present and are completed, and he should look for evidence of the presence of the necessary disciplines. Those operations and each step in performing them should be documented in a flow chart or other record of the auditor's understanding.

The mechanical process of tracing the steps in the transaction is not important, but the resulting comprehensive understanding of the system and how it works is critical. Therefore, an auditor should make sure he understands each step, how it is done, the reason for it, and how it relates to other steps. Equally important, he should explicitly consider the reasons for differentiating types of transactions and the potential impact of that differentiation on the financial statements. *For example:*

> A new type of customer may present a new collection problem; different treatment of different customers may create problems of price control or price discrimination, express or implied warranties, or commitments for future cost or possible contingent liabilities; different types of transactions often have different income, sales, or excise tax consequences.

How Many Transactions To Review

Since the objective of a transaction review is to confirm an auditor's understanding of the flow of data through the system, there is no theoretical or practical reason for him to examine more than one of each type of transaction. Many auditors are troubled by that assertion, perhaps partly because it departs so much from the large-volume testing of transactions prevalent in earlier days. They test more than one of each type of transaction—how many more is a subject of inevitably inconclusive debate—and justify doing so by citing the possibility that a single transaction selected for testing may not be representative of the whole.

There is no significant risk that a review of one transaction will lead to a misleading conclusion, however, if the client's system is understood adequately. If the transaction selected is not representative, it is a separate type of transaction, and that fact should be identifiable. The key to adequate transaction review is thus the identification of the different types of significant transactions. The audit process rests on the skill, experience, and judgment applied in identifying types of transactions. If the auditor has done this adequately, there is no reason for him to review more than one transaction of each type to confirm his understanding of the flow of data through the system.

Another reason many auditors examine more than one transaction is an uneasy feeling that something could be wrong and that the examination of one transaction can hardly be expected to reveal it. But finding what is wrong with the system is not the purpose of the transaction review; the purpose is to confirm the auditor's understanding of the system. From that understanding he identifies the key controls on which he plans to rely and then tests them by means of *functional* tests. A satisfactory functional test, not a transaction review, provides a basis for a conclusion that all transactions of a given type are likely to be processed uniformly.

Therefore, pursuant to the logical development of an audit, a review of one transaction of each significant type is enough to confirm an auditor's understanding of the system, but only if the types of transactions are adequately identified. That means that most of the time and emphasis in a transaction review should be devoted to evaluating the system and identifying the controls rather than to the review process itself. That thought is worth repeating because auditors should not treat transaction reviews perfunctorily.

As noted earlier, there are points in most transaction systems at which different types of transactions are brought together and are then processed in the same way. If one transaction of each different type is selected for review, a question arises of what to do when the types are combined, that is, whether all of the selected transactions must be followed through the entire system. In our opinion, following through the entire system after transactions merge is unnecessary. If several types of transactions merge into one, only one need be reviewed through the latter processing stages. The merging point can be considered the "grave" of the other types.

How Often To Review

Each significant transaction system should normally be reviewed each year on a recurring engagement. As a practical matter, that principle is tempered by an auditor's knowledge of his client's management policies and practices. In a stable, highly organized company (the two seem to go together), an auditor who is satisfied that radical changes have not taken place may be content to test some of the types of transactions on a rotating basis and confirm his understanding of others by means of inquiry. The frequency of a transaction review for that kind of company depends on the auditor's judgment of materiality and relative risk (discussed previously): the more significant a type of transaction and the greater the risk of error or changes in the system, the more frequent and intensive should be the review.

Strict adherence to an auditor's main objective does not call for review of insignificant types of transactions. An auditor should make sure that his client understands that and should obtain from the client explicit agreement about evaluation of insignificant types of transactions. Analytical reviews (discussed below) will catch the rare occurrence of one that might suddenly blossom into significance.

FUNCTIONAL TESTS

Purpose

The purpose of functional tests is to gather evidence that controls on which an auditor intends to rely are functioning and may be expected to continue to do so. Functional tests follow transaction reviews in the logic of an audit because transaction reviews identify the controls to be tested. Functional tests precede substantive tests because the evidence of functional testing provides the basis for determining the nature, extent, and timing of substantive tests to be made. Substantive tests also serve as further confirmation of the existence and functioning of controls.

What To Test

The purpose of functional testing dictates that all controls that are necessary to provide reasonable assurance of the reliability of financial statement aggregates should be tested. Conversely, *only* those controls should be tested. Good systems design calls for many controls that an auditor can ignore because they are redundant or because they are control operations that do not directly affect financial statements; he can ignore others because available validation procedures make relying on them unnecessary or uneconomical and still others because the resulting data are not material in the financial statements.

Distinguishing between controls on which he should rely and those on which he need not or should not is a good test of an auditor's understanding of the subject of internal control and of his client. The distinction should be made explicit so that the logic of the audit is complete.

Since clients are interested in the reliability of all their control operations and not solely those that contribute to an auditor's objective, many expect auditors to test the entire control system. That is a worthwhile service which can often be provided with little increase in time and cost, but it is not essential to an auditor's objective.

Key Controls and Redundant Controls

Some auditors believe that there is always a key control in a transaction system, which renders the others redundant. If so, only that control need be tested. *For example:*

> The control operation of taking a physical inventory periodically and reconciling it to the inventory balances in the accounts usually renders redundant an auditor's concern about the controls over the perpetual inventory records.

To determine redundancy, an auditor looks at the transaction system and asks himself which controls offer assurance of the reliability of the resulting account balance. A properly drawn flow chart identifies the control point or points. A well-designed internal control questionnaire can help direct attention to expected controls and also to the logic of redundancy.

Since the key control may not always exist or be readily identifiable, however, the reasoning process must allow as well for evaluating and testing the cumulative effect of controls. Often, deciding which controls or how many are really key controls is essentially a matter of subjective judgment. *For example:*

> All of the basic control operations described in Chapter 3 may be present in a typical accounts payable system:
> *Authorization* by means of purchase orders;
> *Comparison* of invoices with purchase orders, receiving reports, vendor lists, etc.;
> *Validity checking* of account coding, payment terms, vendor eligibility, etc.;
> *Numerical sequencing* of purchase orders, vouchers, and checks;
> *Control totals* over preparing vouchers, disbursing cash, and posting accounts;
> *Holding files* of unmatched purchase orders, receiving reports, and invoices, and of approved invoices awaiting payment;
> *Reminder lists* of due dates of invoices awaiting payment;
> *Double-checking* of clerical entries on purchase orders or invoices; and
> *Pre-audit* of the documents by the check signer.

Which of those is the key control? To decide which controls to test, an auditor must refer to the purpose of the control:

> *Only legitimate and appropriate transactions processed.* Initial authorization, pre-audit, and perhaps validity checking, if designed to that

end, should detect inappropriate transactions. If an auditor decides that one control can be relied on for that purpose, the others become redundant.

All authorized transactions processed. Numerical sequencing, holding files, control totals, and reminder lists serve as completeness controls. An auditor may select one for testing and consider the others redundant. His selection may be based on some characteristic of the system that renders one control more reliable than the others, or on ease and economy of testing, or on simple preference.

Errors prevented or detected. Comparison, double-checking, control totals, validity checks, and pre-audit all serve to prevent or detect errors. Since errors can occur anywhere in a system, an auditor probably chooses the final error-detection routine as the control to rely on. If pre-audit exists, it is ordinarily the final error-detecting control. If pre-audit does not exist or is not considered to be conclusively reliable, the auditor may have to test the final control operation on the individual transaction—double-checking or comparison—and subsequent controls over groups of transactions such as control totals.

As the last item illustrates, two or more controls are sometimes required for cumulative assurance, but testing of all controls is seldom necessary. Usually, reference to the three purposes of control will help to clarify the alternatives in an auditor's decision about which controls he should test.

How To Test

There are only two ways to test control functions. The operation can be done over again to see that it was done right the first time, an act that we call "reperformance," or the execution of the operation can be observed. In general, basic control operations can be reperformed, whereas disciplines must be observed. There are exceptions and considerable overlapping in applying that general rule—for example, evidence of supervisory controls and segregation of duties can be observed in the course of reperforming basic controls, and internal audits can be reperformed as well as observed.

In the past, auditors have tended to prefer reperformance as an audit test because its basis is documentary evidence of the initial performance and it can be done at the auditor's convenience. In view of the importance of the disciplinary controls, we believe that observation of the disciplines should receive at least as much attention as reperformance. Often some documentary evidence of the performance of supervisory controls exists; inspection of that evidence is equivalent to observation.

The following categories of control described in Chapter 3 as the basic control operations can each be tested by reperformance:

Authorization. Examining some transactions to see that each conforms to company policy and that there is evidence of appropriate authorization.

Comparison. Examining a file of completed transactions to see that the documents supporting each transaction agree with each other as expected or that necessary reconciliations have been completed and that there is evidence of the comparison having been made as part of routine control operations.

Validity checking. Reperforming the control operation, for example, by examining signatures and endorsements, matching purchase invoices against supporting documents, checking the account coding, or recomputing check digits.

Numerical sequencing. Examining files of completed documents to see that all numbers are accounted for and that there is evidence that the function of sequence checking has been regularly performed.

Control totals. Reperforming the operation of adding a file and checking one total to another or noting evidence that the operation has already been performed.

Holding files. Examining a sample of completed transactions and reperforming the matching operation that is the basis for relieving a holding file. Testing a holding file usually involves observation of the open holding file as well as reperformance of completed transactions.

Reminder lists. Checking a reminder list to see that it is complete and comprehensive and reperforming the activities that the reminder list controls, noting evidence of the timeliness of original performance.

Double-checking. Checking a sample of transcriptions, extensions, footings, and the like to confirm that previous double-checking was effective.

Pre-audit. Reperforming the pre-audit of transactions and noting evidence of initial performance.

An auditor may reperform two or more control operations in a single test if the necessary evidence of the operations is contained in the same document.

All other controls must be tested by observation. Systemization, competence and integrity, and documentation are pervasive underlying conditions which are under constant observation, implicitly or explicitly, throughout an audit. Segregation of duties, restricted access, and supervisory controls are explicit disciplines, which can be sought out for observation. Internal audit can be tested by observation as well as by reperformance, by arranging for joint examinations with a client's internal auditors. Operational controls can be observed in use.

How To Select and Document Functional Tests

The auditor in charge of an engagement decides which functions to test, how to test them, how many to test, and how to select the items for testing. Although he can do so on the basis of experience and judgment alone, he usually relies on the accumulated experience of others—represented by an internal control questionnaire—to identify usual control practices, a specimen form of audit program to suggest appropriate tests, and sometimes procedures manuals to specify the extent of testing under various conditions. Those generalized aids must always be adapted or expanded to fit particular circumstances. His decisions on functional tests are then set forth in the audit program.

To preserve the integrity of the tests, the auditor performing them must select the items to be tested rather than have the client make the selection. Having done so, he can use the assistance of the client's clerks to search the files and to assemble the material for his examination.

Auditors differ about the degree of documentation required for functional tests. Some believe that initialing the audit program is enough. However, we believe it is necessary to identify to some degree the documents examined (so that they can be re-examined if necessary) and the tests applied to them.

How Many To Test

The purpose of a functional test is to gather evidence supporting a conclusion that controls exist and are functioning and may reasonably be expected to continue in an untested interval. Once the controls are identified, how many instances of their functioning must be reperformed or observed to permit a conclusion?

The size of functional test samples has been the subject of extensive debate in the auditing profession. Some auditors believe that enough testing should be done to permit valid inferences according to the rules of statistical theory. Some believe that it is seldom, if ever, valid to extrapolate the results of a test to a significant period before or after the test date. Much of the debate stems from the subjective and judgmental nature of audit evidence and the fact that audit evidence is generally "persuasive rather than convincing" (Chapter 2, the third standard of field work). And, under conditions of uncertainty, the answer to "How much is enough?" is inevitably governed to some extent by personal predilection.

In our opinion, the principal reason for the lack of agreement is a futile effort to establish a single rule that will apply to all functional tests. That effort is unlikely to be productive because several factors affect the degree of confidence an auditor may need to have in a specific system of controls, and he must take all of them into account in deciding how much evidence he should gather through functional testing of the control processes. The most significant are:

The effectiveness of disciplinary controls.
The difficulty of maintaining control.
The importance to the auditor of the data being controlled.
The kind of control.
The auditor's confidence in the system.

Effectiveness of Disciplinary Controls

As previously discussed, management has a more immediate interest than an auditor in having a systematic means of preventing lapses in control or detecting them as they occur—that is, of assuring the continuity of control. If management is successful in establishing such a system of disciplinary control, an auditor can evaluate it, test it, and rely on it. Thus, while one purpose of a functional test of the basic control operations of a client is to confirm their existence and functioning, it should also confirm—sometimes by concurrent observation—the existence and functioning of the disciplines, if they exist. If control operations are systematized and well disciplined, the test should provide an auditor with sufficient basis for an opinion that the systems and disciplines will continue to function in preventing or detecting lapses in basic controls. That opinion is ordinarily reinforced and confirmed as later steps in the audit cycle furnish additional evidence of the continued operation of the disciplinary controls.

If the functions of an internal audit department include reviewing and testing basic controls, a single test of the underlying data to confirm the quality of the internal audit function usually provides a basis for using internal audit reports as evidence of continuing reliability of basic controls.

In some companies, the influence of disciplinary controls is apparently neutral, giving no basis for either believing or doubting that they provide reasonable assurance of continuity of basic controls. An auditor then has to obtain direct evidence of continuity, which he can usually do in the following ways:

> Test data can be selected to span the period under examination up to the date of the functional test. Since functional testing is ordinarily done before validation testing—perhaps about half to three-quarters of the way through the fiscal year—this first step does not provide evidence of continuity throughout the balance of the year, although absence of lapses in the test data provides the beginning of reasonable assurance.
>
> Validation tests later in the year and analytical reviews at year end ordinarily provide evidence sufficient to permit a conclusion that controls are continuing to function during the balance of the year.
>
> If validation tests are completed considerably before the end of the fiscal year, some auditors advocate additional functional testing at or near the end of the year. In our opinion, if none of the earlier audit evidence from either functional or validation tests gives reason to doubt the continued functioning of the controls, the analytical reviews customarily employed in the later stages of the audit cycle should be an adequate test of continuity without more functional tests.

Sometimes disciplinary controls are nonexistent or ineffective even though the basic controls apparently exist. The company may be too small, systems may not be working properly, morale may be poor or employee turnover high, or supervision may be in the hands of people whose competence and diligence are open to question. In these cases, an auditor must seek more and better evidence to assure himself of continuity of control. He can consider three possible reactions:

> Shifting his validation procedures to the end of the fiscal year and perhaps increasing their extent,
>
> Increasing the extent and intensity of his analytical reviews, and
>
> Validating account balances by extensive vouching of transactions (see "Kinds of Validation Procedures," later in this chapter, for a description of "vouching").

These procedures may ultimately satisfy an auditor that he can rely on the system for his purposes for the current year. But he should remember that management's control requirements are more stringent than his, and controls that are currently lax are in danger of becoming totally unreliable in later years. An auditor pursuing the ideal standard of auditing would feel that he had a duty to present to management the facts and his evaluation of them. That is his positive, constructive reason for going on record with his control evaluation; an equally compelling reason is to protect himself against subsequent client criticism. If disciplinary control is nonexistent or ineffective, an auditor would be well advised to say so in a management letter.

Difficulty of Control

The simpler, more tangible and straightforward the accounting process, the more likely it is to continue to function properly; the more complex or intangible the process, the greater the risk of error or omission and the more difficult it is to control. *For example:*

> A simple payroll calculation of rate times hours, although subject to human or machine error, is less so than a calculation of payroll under a complex group-incentive piecework system. Moreover, the simple calculation can be controlled by examining the relationship of total hours to total dollars, an act which is easily documented. In contrast, the only ways to control the complex calculation may be either reperformance, which is prohibitively expensive, or a judgmental review, the quality of which cannot be documented.
>
> The evaluation and approval for payment of claims in an insurance company is often a high-volume, yet complex and judgmental, task. The quality of processing can vary and is much more difficult to control than, say, the relatively straightforward and controllable processing of premium notices and receipts.

In both examples, an auditor should seek more extensive evidence of the adequate functioning of the control over the complex operations than of that over the simple and straightforward operations.

Importance to the Auditor of Data Being Controlled

Obviously, a control having a direct bearing on a significant item in the financial statements needs to be relied on more heavily than one having an indirect or less significant impact. *For example:*

> If the physical inventory and its reconciliation to the accounts is the only significant control over the annual cost of goods sold and year-end inventory, that control deserves as much or more attention from an auditor as all of the combined control processes over accounts payable described in an earlier example.
>
> Control over the data entering directly into the sales account, the inventory account, or any other financial statement aggregate is more important than control over the data used for such estimates as pension expense or warranty reserves, because the latter are based on so many judgments and assumptions, which will be subject to analytical reviews.

Controls over the computation of federal income tax liability are usually more important than controls over payroll tax computations because the former is a larger and more significant item.

Significance affects an auditor's need for assurance in two ways. Directly, he obviously needs a firmer basis for reasonable assurance as the type of transaction becomes more significant; he does not need to test insignificant types at all. Indirectly, the more significant the type, the more important it is to the client and the greater the relative risk of management's bypassing or intervening in the routine of processing and control to record an out-of-the-ordinary adjustment or change of estimate.

The Kind of Control

Controls over individual transactions obviously differ significantly from controls over groups of transactions or areas of activity. Controls over individual transactions operate much more frequently than controls over groups of transactions, and each operation is less significant to the aggregate. However, since controls over groups of transactions are often validation procedures, adequate performance at the end of an accounting period can compensate for inadequate performance earlier in the period. An auditor therefore ordinarily makes a closer scrutiny of controls over groups of transactions than of controls over individual transactions, but he is content to examine a smaller number of group controls.

Confidence in the System

The evaluation of controls is a cumulative process which improves with each step in an audit cycle. Judgments of earlier years carry over in recurring engagements (assuming no significant changes in procedure or personnel) and reinforce judgments in the current examination. Accumulating evidence and experience increases an auditor's confidence in a client's system of controls and in his own evaluation of them, and that increasing confidence influences the degree of testing.

The Need for Judgment

The size of the sample required to afford reasonable assurance of the existence and continuity of internal control varies according to the interaction of at least the five factors discussed. The sample may be relatively small and selected at a specific time or it may be extensive and selected to cover the entire time span under examination. Since the several factors can interact in complex ways, it would be a serious mistake to relieve an auditor of the responsibility for thinking through his judgments by establishing arbitrary rules for sample size or selection methods.

However, some auditing firms, apparently for the purpose of promoting uniformity of practice, have established guidelines for sample size and sample selection methods. We believe that guidelines of any type should be accompanied by an admonition that they cannot be accepted as substitutes for judgment and that users should understand the procedure for well-reasoned departures from them. The same applies to arbitrary rules for application of statistical sampling techniques.

RESPONSE TO CONTROL DEFICIENCIES

Either transaction reviews or functional tests may reveal gaps in the control system. If a control is nonexistent, the transaction review should disclose the fact; if a significant control exists but is not functioning, the functional test should discover it.

Simple Weaknesses

To repeat an observation from Chapter 3: the absence of an explicit control feature does not necessarily make the system or the underlying data poor or wrong, but simply weak. The weakness removes an auditor's objective basis for maximum reliance on the underlying data. It therefore calls for an explicit response in accordance with the logic of the audit equation.

The audit equation implies that the inevitable result of observed weaknesses in control is additional substantive testing. All of the literature on auditing, beginning with the second standard of field work (". . . evaluation of the existing internal control as a basis for . . . determination of the resultant extent of the tests . . ."), carries the same implication. In practice, however, an auditor who has discovered a significant control weakness has a number of alternative courses of action open to him, and planning additional auditing procedures should ordinarily be almost the last resort.

The first step, as always, should be to discuss the problem with the client so that auditor and client may agree on the facts and jointly examine the alternatives. The most desirable solution from everyone's point of view is for the client to correct the problem by making necessary changes in the system. That is often a simple enough matter: a control procedure such as a reconciliation can be instituted with retroactive effect, duties can be reassigned so as to establish a necessary discipline, or those responsible for a malfunctioning control can be reinstructed or retrained.

If changing the system is not possible, the next best solution is for the client to undertake supplementary procedures that will assure everyone concerned—client primarily and then auditor—of the integrity of the data involved. Sometimes that can go so far as to require a complete reprocessing of affected data.

In either solution, the client's activity results in a new set of control conditions which the auditor should test and evaluate.

A third possible solution is to change the timing or the nature of certain normal minimum substantive tests. *For example:*

> A transaction review of a production cost system may show an absence of control over material lost, stolen, destroyed, or damaged in the course of production ("shrinkage"). Unless the auditor can be reasonably assured that shrinkage is not potentially significant, a solution might be to take the physical inventory at the year end instead of at an interim date.

A change in the client's system, either to control inventory shrinkage or to identify it on a timely basis, would clearly be preferable. But shifting the date of the physical inventory is a better solution than planning additional audit testing.

A fourth alternative, to be employed only if the other three are not possible, is for the auditor to compensate for a deficiency in control by as much additional effort as is required in the circumstances. The kinds of additional effort and the circumstances calling for them are described under "Effect on Auditing Procedures" hereafter.

The extension of auditing procedures is an undesirable solution for at least two and possibly three reasons. First, it is more costly and less productive for the client than any of the first three solutions. Second, and perhaps more important, it corrects nothing and leaves the control problem to plague both client and auditor in the future. Third, procedures can be extended only so far, and in extreme cases may not be sufficient in scope to give the auditor the degree of assurance that he is seeking.

A fifth alternative, which is extreme indeed, is for auditor and client to accept the problem as insoluble. The auditor then must decide whether he can issue a qualified opinion or must issue a disclaimer or adverse opinion.

That hierarchy of responses to control deficiencies is another illustration of the pervasive principle that the best auditing is preventive. Identifying and correcting a control problem is much better for the company, its investors, and the auditor than for the auditor to make up for the weakness by extensive auditing procedures, and both are better than reporting to the public that an unresolved problem exists.

Purposeful Deficiencies

Most control weaknesses are accidental lapses. An auditor must nevertheless be prepared for those rare situations in which the lapses are intentional. Control weaknesses that are purposefully fostered to facilitate or conceal fraud are unlikely to be readily apparent. A principal ingredient of business deceit and theft is a careful and often ingenious effort to keep the evidence of its existence to an insubstantial and highly equivocal minimum.

An auditor whose suspicions are aroused is in an extremely delicate position and must proceed with caution. His responsibility for fraud was discussed in Chapter 2: he is responsible for expressing an opinion on the fairness of presentation of financial statements, not for certifying to the absence of fraud, but he must have reasonable assurance that fraud which undermines financial position is not present. He cannot ignore warning signs, but neither can he make accusations based only on suspicions nor should he design procedures intended primarily to detect fraud.

The particular circumstances of individual situations will, of course, largely determine the proper course of conduct of an auditor who suspects that control weaknesses may permit or conceal fraud. As a general rule, it is best simply to use exceptional care in adhering closely to the logic of the audit. Weaknesses in internal control require an auditor to seek additional corroborative evidence: it is the fact of the weakness, not the possibility of fraud, that determines his response. If weakness in control is coupled with poor discipline of the sort that might arouse suspicion, an auditor is required to place less reliance on underlying evidence and more reliance on corroborative evidence. His reason for extending substantive tests if accounting controls are weak, or altering their timing if internal check is weak, is the logic of the audit, and it does not require him to raise the question of fraud or imply taking responsibility for it. If weaknesses in control are so serious that the underlying evidence is rendered totally unreliable—which could happen if systemization and disciplinary control are extremely poor—an auditor can have no basis for an opinion and his only alternative is to so inform the client.

Effect on Auditing Procedures

If the best among the alternative responses to a control weakness is for an auditor to shift his reliance to corroborative evidence, the action he takes varies with the kind of control that is deficient. To maintain the integrity of the audit logic, the action taken should be explicitly related to the weakness and its possible consequences for the financial statements.

If any one of the necessary disciplinary controls is weak, the basis for believing in continuity of control is weakened or nonexistent. That is true of segregation of duties, restricted access, and supervisory controls. The most common response is likely to be a shift of validation tests from an interim date to the year end. Without the basis for believing in continuity of control, an auditor does not have one of the two logical reasons for believing that interim tests validate a year-end balance.

Depending on the nature of the deficiency, an auditor might also increase the amount of validation testing. He might, for example, check in detail rather than test-check period-end cutoffs and plan a larger number of inventory test counts and receivable confirmations, either in anticipation of errors or as a basis for statistical inference. He might decide that he should examine all negotiable assets at the same time, either at year end or by a surprise count.

If systemization and/or disciplinary controls are weak enough to raise doubts about the accuracy of the account classifications appearing in the income statement, substantive tests of those accounts may afford the necessary assurance. Those tests might be more detailed analytical reviews, possibly supplemented by vouching a large and representative enough sample of transactions to permit inferring a conclusion about the total account.

If one or more of the basic controls over transactions or groups of transactions—the completeness, validation, and reperformance checks described in Chapter 3—are missing or unreliable, the response is likely to be much more limited and specific. If a required reconciliation is not reliably made, an auditor can do it himself. If he is in doubt about authorizations, completeness checks, or validity checks, he can vouch a large enough sample of transactions to reach a conclusion about the reliability of the underlying data.

It was recognized many years ago that weakness in internal check called primarily for shifting the timing of substantive tests and sometimes also for additional testing, while weakness in the basic internal accounting controls called primarily for additional testing. That still holds true; it is now increasingly recognized that weakness in disciplinary controls also can affect the timing and nature of validation procedures.

SMALL COMPANIES AND RUDIMENTARY CONTROL

Small companies and some that have not been previously audited often have rudimentary controls. Auditors of those companies must consider whether there is need for functional tests if they already know that controls are weak or nonexistent.

The logic of the audit equation states that underlying evidence and reliance on it are basic to an auditor's opinion. At a minimum there must be accounts to audit. The underlying system has to be understood and the understanding confirmed. Thus, a transaction review, at least, is called for in every company being audited. The transaction review may be simple if the systems are simple. The conclusion reached after the transaction review may be to rely on controls, which must then be functionally tested; it may be to proceed directly to substantive tests because there is not sufficient reason to rely on controls; or it may be to institute remedial action before attempting an opinion audit, if the accounts are so unreliable that this alternative is warranted. As indicated previously, it may be unnecessary to complete an internal control questionnaire, or a special "small business" questionnaire may be useful.

Functional tests may or may not be needed, depending on the results of the transaction review. Even in a one-bookkeeper operation, the accounting system can be well organized, the attitudes toward order, discipline, and accuracy exemplary, and the competence of the bookkeeper outstanding. If so, functional tests may provide evidence that those conditions are present, and the auditor may be able to complete his examination with little extension of tests. Because internal check is lacking, particularly the discipline of segregation of duties, he is likely to decide to perform validation tests at year end instead of at an interim date. But he may not need more extensive validation procedures if the functional tests reveal no significant exceptions or problems. He may decide to rely more than otherwise on comparison and analyses of the interrelationship among accounts to identify misclassifications or unusual conditions—again because inability to segregate duties makes control over that type of error difficult. But, under the favorable conditions cited, extensive verification of transactions or similar vouching is not required.

Even in smaller organizations it is possible for the control conditions of systemization, competence, and documentation to exist. It is also possible for all of the basic control operations to be executed to the extent applicable and to maintain the discipline of restricted access. But it is usually not possible to have segregation of duties or supervisory control. As a result, an auditor is unlikely to be able to obtain reasonable assurance of the continuity of controls from functional tests alone. His possible responses in that event are discussed earlier in the chapter; in brief, the simplest thing to do may be to perform validation tests at year end, thus gaining sufficient assurance that controls continued to function throughout the period.

If any of the favorable conditions cited above is significantly lacking, an auditor may be able to compensate for it and still render an opinion on the financial statements. Clearly, if he already knows he cannot rely on some or all controls, functional tests of those controls serve no purpose. His time and attention are better devoted to sufficiently extensive account validation and other substantive tests.

If an accounting system and the competence of a bookkeeper are so unreliable that an auditor must virtually reconstruct the accounts, he must consider whether he can give an opinion on the financial statements, because the data may be too unreliable to provide a basis for an opinion.

Maintaining independence is a constant problem with smaller company clients. It is a short step from an auditor's drafting journal entries based on errors and omissions he has discovered to actually preparing journal entries, closing the accounts, and even keeping them. It is also a short step from giving advice on judgments a client must make for financial statement preparation (inventory valuation, for example) to making them for a client. Managements of smaller clients are often willing to leave those judgments to auditors. Therefore, an auditor must review his relationship frequently, preferably with the client, both to make sure that the client understands and exercises the judgments for which he is responsible and to make sure that the auditor adheres to the standards of the profession.

VALIDATION PROCEDURES

The principal objective of validation procedures is to substantiate an account balance—usually a balance sheet account, but sometimes an income or expense account. In addition, validation contributes to the same objectives as compliance tests: the examination of the results of individual transactions as reflected in balance sheet aggregates tends to confirm an auditor's understanding of the system and to provide additional assurance that controls are functioning. The absence of errors or exceptions in validation tests is strong evidence that the underlying accounts are reliable; conversely, a significant incidence of unexpected error is a clear indication that either an auditor's understanding of the underlying system is not complete or controls have not functioned to prevent or detect errors.

Statement on Auditing Procedure No. 54 (SAS No. 1, paragraph 320.28) includes validation as a part of the accountability function of internal control, thereby emphasizing that account validation is a management responsibility as much as an auditor's procedure. It is primarily good management, and only incidentally a contribution to good auditing, for the company to check the accuracy of the accounts by validation procedures, such as reconciling bank accounts, counting inventory, sending statements to customers, and the like. Once that fact is recognized, it follows that auditors' validation procedures can become essentially functional tests of a client's validation procedures.

Validation Procedures Versus Functional Tests

The dual purpose of many validation procedures has been recognized for several years. Describing it is rendered easier by reference to the schematic logic of the audit equation. A validation procedure—such as a reconciliation—that reperforms a client's procedure obviously provides evidence of the functioning of control, which contributes to confidence in the underlying data. At the same time it provides the auditor performing it with his own corroborating evidence.

When confidence in the first term of the equation is maximal, a given procedure is more of a functional test than a substantive test. That can permit greater flexibility in deciding both timing of the procedure and the amount of data to be examined. When the primary objective of the procedure is a substantive test because of doubt about the reliability of underlying evidence, the nature of that doubt may affect the design of the procedure, as described above in the section, "Effect on Auditing Procedures." In any event, both objectives must be kept in mind in planning validation procedures and in evaluating the results.

Kinds of Validation Procedures

There are a few common kinds of validation procedures and techniques, which can be described here in general terms. The specific applications of each of the techniques to particular accounts and types of transactions are described in detail in the chapters in Part II. Virtually all validation procedures consist of confirmation, physical inspection, reperformance, or vouching. The techniques of reconciliation and account analysis also play an important part in many validation procedures.

Confirmation

Confirmation is a favorite among validation procedures because it is usually relatively fast and efficient. It consists of asking a third party to confirm a fact. Almost any fact may be confirmed, but confirmation in auditing applies most often to account balances, and sometimes to transactions or non-accounting facts. Confirmation is most effective if the third party is independent (i.e., an outsider) and presumably has no interest in the outcome of the audit. It is still a good procedure even if the confirmer belongs to the organization being audited or was otherwise involved in the transaction being confirmed.

Since confirmation procedures have been subverted on occasion, an auditor should take reasonable precautions to preserve their integrity, but he should not conduct himself as though he expected fraud. For example, confirmation requests, correctly addressed, should be controlled by an auditor's representative until mailed in an envelope with his own return address; confirming replies should be mailed directly to the auditor by the confirmer; and the auditor should examine the replies for obvious questions of authenticity, but he is not expected to detect forgeries of documents or signatures.

Often, but not always, confirmation is called for in the exercise of management's accountability function. The practice of sending statements of account to customers, depositors, and the like is a form of confirmation in the exercise of that function.

Physical Inspection

Inspection of the physical matter represented by accounts is a validation procedure with obvious merit. Although it is often time-consuming and accurate identification of the items under inspection is sometimes difficult, there is no better way to corroborate an account balance. (The link between asset and account balance—that is, the pricing—must of course be validated as well.) Physical inspection is essentially an accountability procedure and so should be employed by management with the auditor participating or observing.

The practice of taking inventory of most kinds of physical assets at least once a year has been accepted as elementary good management for a long time. Most companies arrange for physical counts of cash, securities, inventories, and the like at convenient times during a year. Some companies take inventory of property, plant, and equipment from time to time. If an account represents legal contracts such as insurance policies, mortgages, or leases, it is good practice to inspect and account for those documents periodically. The participation of the auditor in such physical inspection is not essential (except as otherwise indicated in this book) although it is frequently desirable.

When an auditor inspects assets or documents, he does so as an auditor and not as an appraiser, handwriting analyst, lawyer, or other kind of expert. He is entitled to ask for reasonable assurance that the material being inspected is what it is represented to be, and he can exercise common sense in evaluating that assurance. It is unreasonable and uneconomical to expect him to do more. In unusual circumstances, the advice or opinion of an appraiser or other appropriate expert may have to be sought to provide the reasonable assurance.

In the past, unannounced "surprise counts" were a favorite auditing procedure. The objectives were several: to validate the existence of the asset, to test compliance with prescribed procedures, and to check on employee discipline. In the light of the logic of the audit, surprise counts have limited usefulness. The element of surprise has no purpose other than to serve as a deterrent to undesired conduct by custodians of assets; as such it serves a disciplinary function. An audit purpose is served by a complete count of negotiable assets—preferably of all negotiable assets simultaneously—if disciplinary controls are weak, but the element of surprise is seldom necessary.

Reperformance

Many account balances are based on computations, and the only way to validate them is to reperform the computation. Some computations are quite simple and straightforward, for example, most of the accrued and prepaid accounts. Some computations can be so extensive that they are computerized: inventory pricing, and depreciation and amortization computations are examples. Others can be extraordinarily complex and involve highly specialized technical knowledge: the accruals of federal income tax and pension expense, for example. Many computations are based on or include the results of judgment.

An auditor's validation procedure consists simply of reperforming the computation. If a judgment is involved, he reperforms the reasoning process leading to the judgment. Reperformance may be either complete and detailed, or an overall computation of the aggregates, or a rough computation to check on the reasonableness of the results.

Vouching

Vouching consists of scrutinizing the evidence supporting a transaction and judging whether it is in order, appears bona fide, serves a proper business purpose, and is properly accounted for. Vouching was traditionally the bulk of an auditor's work. It is still a necessary and sometimes an indispensable procedure. But since evaluation of systems has replaced extensive transaction verification, vouching has become a much smaller fraction of an auditor's effort.

The procedures of confirmation, inspection, reperformance, and vouching can be employed singly or in combination and the effort can be simple or extensive and complex. Two common techniques that are employed in implementing validation procedures are described in the paragraphs that follow.

Reconciliation

Reconciliation consists of bringing two figures into agreement by identifying differences. Two independently accumulated totals of the same amounts are likely to be different because of items in transit, items treated differently, or errors. Reconciliation consists of identifying the specific differences and classifying them as pure reconciling items, which in time will clear themselves or otherwise require no adjustment, or as items that should be recorded to change one total or the other. Reconciliation may be detailed, as are most bank account reconciliations, or partial, as is common for physical counts of inventories. For example, if a physical count of an inventory differs from the account balance, transactions before and after the count are usually examined for in-transit items, and the account balance is then adjusted for any unreconciled difference, even though it is recognized that a more extensive search might explain the difference. However, significant unreconciled differences should be investigated by either the client or the auditor.

Reconciliation is a basic audit technique but it is even more a basic technique of management accountability. Reconciliations should be a routine part of management's system of control and accountability for the purpose of preventing or detecting errors. Therefore, although auditors commonly prepared many reconciliations in the past, it should now be the rule rather than the exception that reconciliations are prepared by clients and reviewed or tested by auditors.

Inexperienced preparers often incorrectly assume that a reconciliation is complete once all differences between the two figures being reconciled are identified and explained. For accountability purposes, however, the validation process is not complete until all corrections of errors and other entries affecting the accounts are recorded. For audit purposes, the process is not complete until all reconciling items are traced to their proper disposition: completion of in-transit transactions and recording of adjustments.

Account Analysis

To an auditor, "to analyze an account" means to break down and summarize the details of an account in a way that is meaningful for the intended purpose. An understanding of an account is greatly facilitated by meaningful analysis; conversely, analyses prepared in terms of irrelevant summary categories are completely useless. Auditors should be specific about the purpose of an analysis and the form it should take.

There are two main kinds of account analysis. One is an analysis of activity in which the kinds of additions and deductions are summarized. The other is an analysis of the composition of a balance in which the major items or categories of items are identified. Account analysis may sometimes be employed in internal control and accountability procedures, but it is primarily an audit tool. The auditor uses account analyses as a basis for validation tests and for analytical reviews, which are described in subsequent sections of this chapter.

Extent of Validation Procedures

Validation tests performed should be sufficient to afford reasonable assurance that the balance in an account is fairly stated. That implies that the major portion of the balance in the account should be validated by one of the procedures described above. However, there are several reasons for an auditor to tolerate less than 100% validation. One reason for departing from 100% validation is the significance of an account. Spending much time to validate an insignificant balance is obviously unnecessary. In practice, every account in a client's financial statements receives some kind of validation procedure. Insignificant accounts may receive no more than a "review," but that review substantiates the balance within the range of materiality appropriate to the financial statements as a whole.

Another reason for departing from the assumption of 100% validation is the nature of the account. Some accounts can be validated substantially by examining a few of the items composing the balance. A characteristic of many accounting aggregates is that a relatively small number of fairly large items accounts for a large portion of the total.

An auditor may validate all or most of the large items and a few of the remaining smaller ones. If there are no important errors in the items tested, the auditor can accept the remaining untested balance as not material or as not offering a significant risk of undetected error.

If the number of items composing an account balance is large and no single item is significant in relation to the total, an auditor may reach valid conclusions about the total by validating a fairly small sample of the items. The choice between judgmental and statistical approaches to the selection of samples is discussed in the concluding section of this chapter.

A third reason for less than 100% validation is confidence in the internal control and accountability systems. Validation tests may be minimal if an auditor has substantial confidence in the reliability and integrity of the accounts. Conversely, if that confidence is lacking, validation tests may be extended up to 100% verification of an account balance. Innumerable examples appear in the auditing procedures sections of Chapters 9–16. The following illustrate the point:

> Cash balances are best validated by reconciliation of the account balance to the balance confirmed by the bank. An auditor with confidence in a client's controls may simply review and test some of the client's reconciliations.
>
> The extent of an auditor's confirmation of accounts receivable or physical inspection of inventory items is in inverse proportion to his confidence in controls; with maximum confidence, he may need to validate only a small number of accounts receivable or inventory items.
>
> The validation of accounts payable may range from a small vouching test of a well-controlled system to an extensive test, possibly including confirmation if controls are not present.

In summary, the validation procedures and techniques available to an auditor are few enough in number and simple enough in concept to be readily understood and applied. The extent of their application depends on the significance of the account, the nature of the account, and the auditor's evaluation of the pertinent controls. His skill is tested more in determining their extent and in perceptively evaluating the errors and exceptions revealed.

Errors and Exceptions in Validation Procedures

It is in the nature of the accounting process that validation tests produce apparent discrepancies in the best of circumstances. Most discrepancies have routine explanations pertaining to items in transit or errors or adjustments properly detected by the system and in process of correction. Some discrepancies can be quite difficult to understand and evaluate. Clearly, all have to be adequately explained for a test to be meaningful. Auditors have traditionally called an unexplained discrepancy an "exception."

A way of handling exceptions is for an auditor to arrange with his client beforehand for an appropriate knowledgeable person on the client's staff to investigate them. An auditor need not investigate the exceptions independently, as that may be inefficient. (If he has evidence of fraud or is engaged to seek it, of course, he has to conduct his own investigation.) His purpose in an opinion audit is to validate an account balance, and reviewing the client's explanation of an apparent exception is part of that validation process.

An auditor's attention is therefore more appropriately directed toward a critical evaluation of the client's explanation of an exception. He must understand the nature of the exception and the explanation of it in terms of its implications both for the client's system and for the account balance under examination. He must consider the possibility that even a single, fairly small error that appears to be innocent may warn of a potentially significant loss of control. *For example:*

> Among the exceptions appearing in the confirmation of a sample of accounts receivable of a consumer goods distributor were a few replies noting that credits for returned merchandise were not reflected in the balances. Inquiry indicated that the credits were in process in the client's system, a routine occurrence. However, further investigation revealed that, for various reasons, the client was experiencing a serious back-up in processing and recording the credits and the returned merchandise was being included in inventory well before the credits reducing accounts receivable were recorded. As a result, amounts for the same merchandise were, for a period, shown in both inventory accounts and accounts receivable. Thus, a careful scrutiny of apparently innocent exceptions to accounts receivable confirmations uncovered a potentially significant misstatement of sales and receivables which might have been overlooked by both client and auditor.

The evaluation of exceptions revealed by validation tests is a critical point in an audit. It calls for skill, perception, penetrating realism, judgment, and sometimes persistence. Its importance cannot be overemphasized because it is at this point that an auditor can most readily fail in his mission.

The reason is that the only evidence of previously unrecognized problems is likely to be a very slight, fleeting glimpse of something that "doesn't quite fit." If the client has innocently overlooked the problem, it is usually because he has accepted a plausible explanation for it, which he passes on to the auditor together with other routine explanations. If the client's motives are not innocent, the explanation offered to the auditor is very likely to be designed to be even more plausible. An auditor's unique contribution, his opinion based on objectivity, requires him to evaluate independently both the incident and its explanation.

That principle is easily stated and is consistent with the popular notion of an auditor as a sharp-eyed skeptic. It is not easy to practice. Substantially all of the information received by an auditor in the course of his work is factual, accurate, truthful, and routine. His challenge is to pick out for investigation the one false note in several thousand. Since he is not infallible, it is an extremely demanding assignment.

One unnecessary obstacle to penetrating evaluation can be removed if an auditor is careful to understand and distinguish between the dual implications of an exception to a validation test. The exception must be evaluated for its implications for both the accuracy of the account and the continuity of controls. If the test is viewed solely as a verification of an account balance, the control implications may be missed; if the test is viewed as a test of control compliance, the extrapolation of an exception to its implied impact on the account balance may not be made.

If exceptions reveal significant problems, an auditor has the same possible responses from which to choose that were described earlier in this chapter in connection with functional tests.

Timing of Validation Procedures

In the majority of audits, validation procedures are carried out before year end, usually sometime in the last quarter of the fiscal year, for reasons described in Chapter 4. Briefly, validation of balance sheet accounts before year end is acceptable if there is no reason to suspect weaknesses in internal control and the accounts represent assets or liabilities that are an integral part of the enterprise. Earlier validation must be linked to the year end by analytical review.

If an auditor determines that the controls are particularly unreliable, he is not, of course, entitled to rely on validation tests other than at or close to year end. Year-end tests are also sometimes necessary for other reasons. *For example:*

The volatility of a company's operations or of certain accounts may be so great that tests at other than year end are worthless.

Few auditors would fail to check year-end market values of marketable securities and commodities.

An interim review of the salability and net realizable value of high-style or highly seasonal consumer goods would not provide a basis for conclusions on year-end balances.

Most companies that are too small to be able to maintain control systems strong enough to permit interim validation testing do not have a compelling need for early release of audited financial statements. Since their lenders and stockholders are willing to wait a reasonable period after the end of the fiscal year for financial statements, an auditor can plan all of his validation procedures on the year-end balances and wait for an orderly closing of the accounts to complete his work. Sometimes it is more efficient and economical to do so, even if not required by the condition of the company's accounting and control systems. The fact that the bulk of an audit is carried out at or after the end of the fiscal year is no excuse, however, for neglecting early planning and the continuing contact that enables an auditor to maintain his understanding of a client.

ANALYTICAL REVIEWS

The fourth category of auditing procedures is described in paragraph 70 of SAP No. 54 (paragraph 320.70 of SAS No. 1) as "analytical review of significant ratios and trends and resulting investigation of unusual fluctuations and questionable items." Its purpose is to corroborate the logical interrelationship among accounts and to identify and explain all significant changes or abnormalities.

Auditors use the word "review" incessantly, and so it is worthy of careful definition. If analyzed, it refers to one or a combination of four activities: reading, scanning, comparing, and validating by logical relationships.

Reading

An audit program that says "review the loan agreement" or "review the minutes" means to read them, looking for matters of financial and accounting significance. It should go without saying that an auditor must then think through what he reads to a conclusion about the impact on the financial statements—an effort that may involve sophisticated, complex analysis and discrimination between form and substance. Every significant document—from obvious financial ones to distantly related ones such as union contracts—must be read and analyzed.

Scanning

To "review the activity in the account between interim and year end" means to look at the summary entries and investigate those that are larger or smaller than are to be expected in that account, those that originate from an unexpected quarter, or those that in any other way strike the auditor as out of the ordinary. The words usually instruct one *not* to dig into details—words such as "analyze" or "vouch" are used for that—but only to scan.

Comparing

To "review the account balances" means to compare balances with the corresponding balances in one or more other accounting periods or in the budget. It is customary to review monthly income and expense account totals and investigate and obtain explanations for fluctuations. If an account has been validated before year end, the year-end balance is "reviewed," that is, the balance is compared with the validated balance and all unexpected deviations are investigated.

Validating by Logical Relationships

An auditor with experience and a little ingenuity can find ways to validate the reasonableness of account balances by examining logical relationships among them. He can relate inventory balances to cost of goods sold, accounts receivable to sales, payables to expenses, and so on. He can correlate units shipped, received, or on hand with dollar balances of sales, purchases, or inventories. He can correlate independently generated but related data, such as sales and cost of goods sold, and he can reconcile movements into and out of accounts with related beginning and ending balances.

Validation by means of the logical relationships among independently generated account balances is attractive—when it works well, it gives a great deal of confidence for relatively little work. It is so attractive, in fact, that inexperienced auditors can waste a great deal of valuable time trying to make comparisons and reconciliations that are not practicable in the circumstances. Worse than the waste of time is an auditor's dilemma once the validation procedure has been attempted and has failed: did it fail because it was not practicable or because there was something wrong with the account being validated? He is usually forced into further investigation to seek assurance that it is not the latter.

Thus, validation by logical relationships should be approached with great caution. The procedure should be based on a thorough understanding of the client's systems and operations and should be designed in cooperation with client personnel knowledgeable about the characteristics of the subject under examination. It can then be a powerful, sophisticated audit tool.

Combinations

The phrase "review the financial statements" implies a combination of all four activities. The reviewer is expected to read the statements, scan the figures, compare them with prior figures, examine the logical relationship among accounts, and analyze all the thoughts and impressions created in the process.

Items To Be Reviewed

Several examples of analytical review have been given in the foregoing discussion, as well as the proposition that unique reviews may be constructed for specific client situations. The following are typical audit program instructions for common analytical reviews:

Compare monthly income and expense account balances and investigate fluctuations.

Compare balance sheet accounts month-to-month and with the prior year and investigate fluctuations.

Review budget variances and evaluate explanations of the reasons for variances.

Review unit product costs and compare with those of prior periods.

Compute significant ratios (ratios would be specified) and compare with those of the prior period (or with those of the industry or competitors if available) and explain changes.

Read minutes of meetings of the board of directors and all significant contracts and documents; trace financial items into the financial statements.

Review the activity in the accounts between interim and year end and investigate unusual items.

Review journal entries.

Extent of Analytical Reviews

The extent of analytical reviews, like that of validation procedures, depends on the significance of the account, the kinds of data available, and the auditor's evaluation of the controls. Insignificant accounts either are not reviewed or receive a broad cursory review unless the auditor is making an intensive detailed review for additional assurance that controls are functioning. The more extensive the statistical, managerial, and budgetary data, the greater the possibility of analytical review. In some audits, more extensive analytical reviewing can replace some validation procedures, while in others, it contributes to a greater degree of understanding and assurance of the accuracy and reliability of the accounts. Weaknesses in internal check—a one-bookkeeper accounting system is a good example—lead to more intensive and detailed analytical review in preference to extensive transaction vouching.

Thus the procedures in the analytical review category produce a sort of subjective, deductive type of audit evidence. Instead of the objective type of evidence showing "it is there or not there," which results from the other auditing procedures, analytical reviews produce a cumulative diminution of uncertainty as each expected relationship is found to be in place.

SAMPLING

The concept of audit samples is based on the generally valid and mathematically verifiable assumption that analysis of a representative sample taken from a group of items accurately reveals the characteristics of the group as a whole. The concept and practical applications of sampling have been a part of auditing for generations. For years, the literature of the profession has been filled with discussions of methods and techniques of sampling, and the subject is still one of some controversy.

As with every other term used in auditing, part of the discussion stems from different usage, resulting in attaching different meanings to the term. Some treat "sampling" as synonymous with "testing," so that any piece of evidence examined is a sample or part of a sample. Within that broad usage, the idea of inferring a conclusion about the whole from a sample of the parts can be encompassed without being precise about how it is done. Some would correct that imprecision by restricting the term to samples from which conclusions can be drawn according to strict, mathematically verifiable rules.

In this discussion, the unqualified word "sample" or "sampling" refers to any examination of items of data for a purpose that goes beyond the specific item. The term "inference sampling" is used when the purpose is to infer the characteristics of the whole from the characteristics of the sample. Inference sampling can be either "statistical"—based on the rules of mathematical statistics—or "judgmental"—based purely on the judgment of the sample designer.

Limited Role of Statistical Inference Sampling in Auditing

We subscribe to the concept of sampling and to the validity of the various methods and techniques in the circumstances to which they apply. Our definition of the nature and extent of audit tests places inference sampling in an important but relatively small role in an ideal audit. Furthermore, if inference sampling is called for, sample selection is usually best based on an auditor's judgment in the light of his understanding of the audit objective and characteristics of the subject matter. The subject of the place of inference sampling in auditing is not settled, and some auditors take issue with the foregoing statements. Therefore a brief explanation is in order.

The kinds of audit tests and their purposes can be repeated and summarized as follows:

> *Transaction review:* to confirm an auditor's understanding of the flow of data.
>
> *Functional tests:* to gather evidence that controls are functioning, thus permitting reliance on the underlying accounts.
>
> *Validation procedures:* to substantiate an account balance by confirmation, physical inspection, reperformance, or vouching.
>
> *Analytical review:* to corroborate a logical relationship among items or accounts.

Inference sampling is of limited application for those purposes. For transaction reviews, one transaction of each type is enough. That transaction is a sample of the structure of a system, but tracing it does not permit inferences about the validity of other transactions. For analytical reviews, sampling is inapplicable. Inference sampling is useful only in special cases of functional tests and validation procedures.

For functional tests, examination of one item demonstrates the existence of the control, and, in most cases, examination of a few items demonstrates that the control is functioning and that there are disciplinary controls that reasonably assure its continued functioning. The expectation of continuity of control is the conclusion for which the test is designed. It is the observation of the disciplinary controls that permits the conclusion rather than inference based on relating items examined to all items.

When discipline is neutral or absent and continuity of control is not reasonably assured, inference sampling is required to obtain a basis for reasoning from specific examples to a conclusion about the whole. In our opinion, when inference sampling about the continuity of control is the purpose of functional tests, the variety of influences (described earlier in this chapter) on the amount of evidence needed calls for selecting the sample size on the basis of judgment. When controls are so weak they cannot be relied on to assure the accuracy of the accounts, validation procedures are called for, and statistical inference sampling of the underlying data may provide that assurance. An adequate sample of transactions found to be error-free or nearly so permits an inference that the same holds true for all transactions.

Validation procedures other than the above example usually do not involve inference sampling. An auditor validates an account by validating a single figure in its entirety, by validating the major part through examining a small number of large items, or by observing and testing the client's validation procedure. The latter two may involve sampling, but not inference sampling. In a limited number of instances, all items in an account may be considered homogeneous, no one of them may be significant in relation to the total, and the total number may be large. In those circumstances, inference sampling may be the most effective method of choosing items to test in validating the account balance.

There are two reasons why inference sampling, once of major significance to every audit, is now reduced to an important but relatively small place in most audits at a time when mathematically based methods of sample selection and evaluation are improving.

The first is a radically improved understanding, by all concerned, of systems of all kinds and how they should be controlled. That understanding probably developed concurrently with applications of the computer to business systems. Auditors now know that the structure of a system can be designed to minimize the risk of random error and to maximize the probability of its detection should it occur. A given business system thus need not—and should not—be considered as an unknown universe of data subject to random errors of unknown incidence that must be sampled to infer its characteristics before the data can be relied on.

The second development is the increasing reliance of auditing theory on understanding through logic and evaluation rather than through the mechanical accumulation of evidence. That theory and its implications for the design of an audit have been set forth in the preceding chapters.

Appropriate Uses of Statistical Inference Sampling

However, even though its use may be limited, statistical inference sampling is essential for the purposes to which it is applicable. An auditor needs to be able to recognize the conditions in which those procedures may be appropriate or preferable. The following are the most common:

1. The reliability of control is uncertain, and the consequences of deficiencies may or may not be significant. For example, if the accuracy of perpetual inventory records of raw materials is doubtful but not sufficiently questionable to require a year-end physical inventory, the auditor or client may count a sample of the raw material items and, on the basis of the results of that sample, draw inferences about the accuracy of the inventory records.

2. The auditor or client wishes to test the accuracy of an extensive nonrecurring procedure that cannot be controlled by systemization. For example, retail companies commonly accrue accounts payable only at the end of a fiscal year through an extensive routine of examining subsequent payments and recording those applicable to the fiscal year. An examination of a sample of payments not so recorded permits inferences about the accuracy of the cutoff procedure.

3. The data processing system is not under control and no valid conclusions can be drawn from the system itself. If the volume of data is too large to permit verification, it may be possible to validate an account balance through statistical inference. For example, an inventory of a very large number of homogeneous items on perpetual inventory records may not have been physically counted and may not be subject to adequate accounting controls over receipts and issues; or posting to a very large number of small accounts receivable may be inadequately controlled. In either example, a properly designed statistical sample could permit an acceptable inference about the probable total dollar value of inventory or accounts receivable. Given the stated assumption that control over postings is not reliable, an auditor would have a serious question about the possibility of giving an unqualified opinion. But he might be able to do so if he were sufficiently versed in statistical sampling and the results of his sample were satisfactory.

4. Auditors are often engaged to evaluate certain facts about a universe of data in special assignments in which the examination of relatively small samples under statistical sampling principles permits valid conclusions. Examples are: audits of freight bills, audits of travel expense for compliance with company policy, and audits of insurance claims for propriety of processing.

It should be noted that the above sampling procedures are not necessarily audit tests. Rather, whether performed by auditor or client, they are part of the client's accountability function—the responsibility to establish the integrity and reliability of accounting aggregates. A constant awareness of an auditor's primary objective—an understanding as a basis for an opinion—is vital to an effective and efficient audit, and other objectives, such as supplementing the client's procedures or controls, should be separately identified. We believe that, in all but a few audits, techniques involving inference sampling are appropriate to the second category of objectives rather than to the first.

Sampling procedures in an audit provide part of the body of audit evidence that is cumulative and corroborative through the interrelationships described in earlier chapters. Therefore, sampling results seldom stand as the sole basis for a conclusion. For that reason, judgmental sampling, instead of the more rigorous technique of statistical sampling, is usually acceptable in audit practice.

Statistical sampling is a powerful and sophisticated tool in the unusual circumstance where there is relatively little knowledge of the nature of possible weaknesses or errors in a relatively large "universe" of fairly homogeneous items, but a definitive conclusion is required within a known degree of error. Although that circumstance may rarely arise, there is no substitute for statistical sampling if it is needed. Most auditors do not need to apply it frequently. All auditors should be knowledgeable about the basic concepts of statistical sampling and the circumstances in which it may be applicable and practicable. However, the specialized skill required for effective use of statistical sampling is not, in our opinion, an essential part of an auditor's qualifications. Appendix A describes how statistical sampling techniques are applied.

6

Electronic Data Processing and Auditing

INTRODUCTION

The computer has become so much an integral and accepted part of business and accounting that it is universally acknowledged as one of the most significant technological developments of the twentieth century. Its effect on modern business methods has been dramatically rapid and far reaching, its uses are increasing both in number and sophistication, and the ultimate characteristics of "the computer era" are still the subject of imaginative conjecture. Its effect on auditing has been recognized in Statement on Auditing Standards (SAS) No. 3, *The Effects of EDP on the Auditor's Study and Evaluation of Internal Control.* That Statement introduces the subject as follows:

> Section 320.33 of SAS No. 1 discusses methods of data processing as follows:
>
> Since the definition and related basic concepts of accounting control are expressed in terms of objectives, they are independent of the method of data processing used; consequently, they apply equally to manual, mechanical, and electronic data processing systems. However, the organization and procedures required to accomplish those objectives may be influenced by the method of data processing used.
>
> Because the method of data processing used may influence the organization and procedures employed by an entity to accomplish the objectives of accounting control, it may also influence the procedures employed by an auditor in his study and evaluation of accounting control to determine the nature, timing, and extent of audit procedures to be applied in his examination of financial statements. [Paragraph 2]

The computer affects auditors in two direct ways and a third, indirect way. First, an auditor must understand the nature of data processing, as well as the character of the controls incorporated in data processing systems, to be able to perform meaningful tests and to evaluate control conditions pursuant to the first term of the audit equation. Second, an auditor should take advantage of the power and flexibility of the computer to improve the efficiency of his audit. A third, broader, and possibly ultimately more important impact of computers on auditing is the effect of computer systems theory and practice on our understanding of control and, as a result, our conclusions about the nature and extent of audit tests.

The Conceptual Impact

Before computers could be used effectively in accounting, it was necessary to develop an extensive and rigorous theory of control. That exercise illuminated and expanded auditors' understanding of internal control, and forced them to think more precisely about it, although it did not fundamentally change it.

The audit logic described in the preceding chapters is universal: it does not vary on the basis of whether the auditor or the client uses a computer or any other data processing method. A client has the same responsibility to control data and to produce reliable financial statements. An auditor has the same need to understand his client and the same responsibility to gain evidence that the underlying data may be relied on. The evidence is gathered in the same way: through "cradle to grave" understanding of the system, through identifying significant controls, and through testing those controls for evidence of functioning.

Clients' Use of Computers

Even though basic principles and objectives remain the same, electronic methods of handling and storing data have created entirely new forms of accounting systems and records. "Machine-readable" records are invisible or unreadable to the human eye. Auditors have therefore had to develop new techniques and relate them to new systems.

"Bookless" accounting systems and the complete disappearance of "the audit trail" have been widely predicted. When they materialize, if they do, auditors will have to adapt conventional procedures further, and there is no doubt that they will discover how to do so. As yet, however, interests more compelling than those of the independent auditor require that audit trails and eye-readable accounts and records be preserved. The needs of customers, suppliers, company management, and regulatory agencies for tracing transactions, verifying results, and retrieving data preclude full realization of the computer's abilities to condense information and handle complex accounting functions with a minimum of human interaction. Thus, auditors' responses to clients' use of computers remain an evolutionary adaptation of traditional procedures rather than a revolutionary development of new procedures.

Auditors' Use of Computers

From the beginning of the computer era, it was clear that if clients could use computers so could auditors. Efforts to do so have had three kinds of practical results. First, a number of computer programs, some of them "general-purpose," have been developed to carry out a variety of common audit tasks related to validation procedures. Second, auditors have learned to use clients' computers through using both clients' programs and specially written programs to perform functional and validation tests. Third, "timesharing" computer facilities are proving increasingly useful to make a variety of computations and analyses that previously were not economically feasible. Those developments are described briefly in the concluding portion of this chapter.

HOW COMPUTER SYSTEMS OPERATE

The specifics of how computer systems of various sizes, types, and models are assembled and operated is a subject in itself. It is not necessary to go into it here because a practicing auditor must understand his client's computerized accounting system in depth, and any other reader can follow the logic of auditing as it applies to electronic data processing (EDP) from the limited background given here.

EDP accounting installations range in size from a typewriter-size terminal connecting an office with a powerful and versatile computer on a "timesharing" basis, or a small self-contained unit operated by a single specialist, to multimillion-dollar complexes staffed by hundreds of persons. Obviously, control conditions vary accordingly.

Processing Data

Whatever the size, the function of EDP is basically the same. Data are fed to the installation in conventional "eye-readable" form and converted to "machine-readable" form (some data, such as telephone toll-call data, can be originated in machine-readable form). The computer processes the data as instructed by its "program" and either stores them or sends the results back to the user, or both. The ways in which data are fed to the computer, and in which the computer accepts and processes them, are described in specialized terms: for example, sequential batch processing and random access processing; integrated systems, on-line data capture, real-time systems, and data-base systems.

Functions Within an EDP Installation

Each of the following functions has to be carried out in every EDP installation. In very small ones, the functions may occur virtually simultaneously, or all may be handled by one person; in larger ones, they are carefully defined, controlled, and documented.

Request for Service

A user has to let it be known that EDP service is required: a new "application," a modification or enhancement of an existing application, a change in number or format of reports, etc. The requests must be reviewed and approved (see below), logged, and controlled—usually by a numerical control which is subsequently used for identification in the systems and programming documentation.

Systems Design

An adequately experienced specialist must design the system (or review available "software packages" to satisfy the system needs). In all but the most elementary systems, there are several levels of systems design varying from general—block diagrams of the system concept—to specific—detailed flow charts and specifications.

Programming

The specifications for the system must be translated into detailed instructions to the computer for each step required of it.

Systems Technical Software Support

Medium-sized to large EDP organizations have a separate group of technical software support personnel, usually identified as "systems programmers," responsible for installing and maintaining the "operating system," as distinguished from the "applications systems." The operating system manages, directs, and controls the activities of the computer and related equipment through detailed instructions for processing applications, handling errors and other problems, keeping records, and maintaining security controls.

Testing

The programmed system has to be tested to make sure it produces the desired results and does not produce undesired ones. Since programming is always a demanding task and often a complex one, testing and "debugging" can be a lengthy process. The "systems acceptance function" (see below) plays an important role in the testing process.

File Conversion and Parallel Run

Files must be converted from the old system to the new. It is customary to run the new system "in parallel" with the old for a period of time to minimize the risk of interruption or loss of data due to unforeseen "bugs."

Operations and Filing

Once converted, the system must be operated, files maintained and safeguarded in "libraries," and reports produced on a reliably regular, orderly, and timely basis.

User Review and Approval

Since EDP is a service function, it must satisfy the needs of its users at a reasonable cost. Since it is an esoteric and specialized function, users cannot evaluate its cost-effectiveness on a casual or implicit basis. Therefore, user review and approval—even of simple systems—must be formalized and explicit, or it risks being neglected or becoming a source of friction within the organization. A good way to organize the function is for an "EDP Steering Committee" of user executives to have decision-making responsibility, supported by a staff of specialists who can make detailed reviews and recommendations at several stages in the design of a new application.

The Systems Acceptance Function

The primary objective of the systems acceptance function is to ascertain that data processing control requirements, as set forth in the design specifications, are operating as approved and achieving the desired results. While control is the primary objective, adherence to other standards and procedures—such as documentation and programming guidelines—can be monitored at the same time. The function thus assures that EDP systems being developed conform to management's specifications for the EDP function as it fits into the overall company organization.

The systems acceptance function should review each new system at several points in its development, such as:

Finalization of systems design,
Completion of detail specifications,
Completion of programming,
Development of test plan,
Production of meaningful test results,
Accomplishment of file conversion,
Establishment of system parallel methodology,
Completion of parallel run period, and
User review and approval.

While designers of the system should be expected to be mindful of established control and other standards, the systems acceptance team provides a valuable perspective, both as a result of its independence and as a result of being able to review and evaluate a visible body of results.

The results of the systems acceptance function should be documented either by sign-off procedures as the systems documentation develops or by issuing reports to management.

INTERNAL CONTROL IN COMPUTER SYSTEMS

Internal control in an EDP system comprises exactly the same control operations as were described in Chapter 3, although their form and relative importance may be different. The conditions of control and the necessary disciplinary controls—systemization, competence and integrity, documentation, segregation of duties, restricted access, and supervisory control—are far more important than in manual systems. There are two principal, interrelated reasons for this.

First, computer systems process large masses of data without necessarily leaving visible links. Data can be irretrievably lost or misdirected and the amounts of data involved in a single malfunction could be significant. If the computer is deliberately abused, all eye-readable evidence can be obliterated, and the results of manipulation magnified to extraordinary proportions by the power of the computer.

Second, the control procedures in some EDP systems are performed by relatively few employees, and any one of them may be in a position to cause significant malfunctioning of the system either accidentally or purposefully. Without well-maintained conditions of control, and especially disciplinary controls, the possibilities for abuse of the system by users, programmers, or machine operators are great: an operator can erase a master file or use the wrong transaction file for updating a master file, a programmer can modify a program so as to process data incorrectly, or a user can introduce data that destroy the integrity of the system.

The possibilities for abuse of the computer have been clearly recognized and described in the literature on the subject, and so have the control measures needed to minimize them. The control measures are often viewed (incorrectly) as costly to implement, or (also incorrectly) as inhibiting or even preventing realization of the computer's full potential for speed and efficiency. It took a number of failures—some of them spectacular—to prove that control is even more necessary in computer systems, no matter how costly or inconvenient. In fact, the study of how to control computer systems can be credited with bringing into focus the importance of the conditions of control and disciplinary controls, and their relationships to basic controls, all of which were described in Chapter 3.

SAS No. 3 sets forth the same understanding of the importance of the conditions of control and disciplinary controls, and of their relationships to basic controls, although the terminology is slightly different. The SAS uses "general controls" rather than "conditions of control" and uses "application controls" in a sense that roughly parallels our categories of "basic controls."

Conditions of Control

The complexity of EDP systems, together with their characteristic large volumes of data and high speeds, means that they cannot function efficiently unless the operations are planned with meticulous accuracy. Thus, the conditions of control—systemization, competence and integrity, and documentation—are required for operational effectiveness as well as for their contribution to control.

Systemization is established by means of a written plan of organization, clear assignments of authority and responsibility, and written procedures and standards of performance. The latter should spell out in detail management's standards for documentation, program cataloging, and activity record keeping; security measures over data files, program libraries, and the computer room; authorizing requests for data processing; designing, programming, testing, and approving changes or new applications; and operating the computer and maintaining files.

Competence and integrity must be maintained by supervisory control over hiring, promotion, and assignment of personnel.

Documentation in EDP systems takes on a slightly different and much more important meaning than in manual systems. EDP documentation is the definition of a computer system and all of the procedures, both human and machine, required to carry it out. Without it, no one other than the designer can understand the system fully, and he may forget or may leave the company's employ.

There are three kinds of documentation: systems documentation, program documentation, and operations documentation. Systems documentation should include: systems narratives, systems flow charts, forms for input source documents, data file layouts (cards, tapes, disc, etc.), data element definitions, data file retention instructions, report layouts, data capture procedures, and description of controls. The elements of program documentation are: processing flow charts, a narrative description of each program in the system, data file layouts, decision tables, source program listings, job control language listings, sort parameters, and sample reports. Each computer program in the system should be supported by the following documentation: processing flow chart showing the required input files, output files, and reports; computer set-up instructions showing device assignments, output forms, card stock, etc.; program halt messages and remedial action; restart and recovery procedures; estimated run time and maximum run time; emergency procedures; and output file destinations and retention instructions.

Documentation is essential to effective control. Also, it is required as a means of operational efficiency so that system analysts and programmers can understand the system when working on it to maintain and enhance it, so that supervisors can review and evaluate the work being done, and so that work can be passed along in an orderly manner to another department, to the next shift, or to a successor on the job. To accomplish those purposes, documentation must be meticulously accurate and complete, and kept up to date for every change in the system. Ideally, systems and programming documentation is developed initially during the design phase and refined and completed during the programming and implementation phases—and reviewed at each stage by the systems acceptance function.

Documentation standards will vary from one organization to another due to type of equipment, hardware configuration, programming languages, and the numbers and experience levels of personnel. The organization's written procedures and performance standards should spell out the documentation standards expected and the control procedures to be exercised over development and maintenance activities. Supervisors should review the documentation manuals periodically to make sure prescribed standards are being adhered to. No system should be considered in "production status" unless documentation has been completed, reviewed, and approved in conformity with established standards.

Basic Controls or "Application Controls"

The basic control of authorization is fundamental in EDP: authorization of requests for data processing and authorization of every transaction submitted to EDP for processing. Basic controls are also built into the system in the design stage or into the computer "hardware" itself. Control features inherent in the computer's hardware and built into the operating system are used both to provide control over operations and to detect hardware malfunctions. As in manual systems, control features are useless unless they are properly monitored,

and errors and corrections are followed up by responsible and knowledgeable personnel.

Data Processing Request Authorization

Requests for data processing systems, modifications, and enhance-
ments (e.g., new systems program modifications, addition or deletion
of programs, change in report distribution, etc.) usually originate in
the user department or from within the data processing department in
conjunction with the user department. Regardless of origin, all requests should be reviewed and approved by (1) an executive independent of EDP activities, (2) the internal auditor, (3) user department
management, (4) EDP operations management, and (5) systems and
programming management.

Transaction Authorization

Just as in manual systems, some responsible individual must authorize the initiation of every transaction. No one in EDP should be
authorized to initiate transactions. When originating data are "hard
copy"—invoices, issue slips, and the like—authorization can be the
conventional approval initialing. When transactions are originated
manually in machine-readable form—from point-of-sale recorders or
remote terminals, for example—authorization must be in the form of
the disciplinary control of restricting access to the equipment to those
responsible for authorizing as well as initiating transactions. When
the data are originated automatically, as are telephone toll-call charges,
the activator of the system is the authorizer of the transaction, and any
checking or approving routines are built into the mechanics of the
system.

Operating Systems Controls

An operating system consists of a series of programs that perform
various functions such as scheduling and supervising the application
programs, allocating storage and peripheral devices, and handling
errors and restarts. Operating systems also include control routines
to prevent and detect errors, for example, validity checks of internal
leader and trailer records, which may include file name, record counts,
block counts, volume identification, date, and retention period. In
advanced systems, more complex control functions may be performed,
such as preventing two or more terminals from attempting to simul-

taneously update one record, or restoring data in process when the system goes "down."

Hardware Controls

Error detection and correction controls are similarly built into most computers. These controls, such as redundancy checks, duplicate process checks, and equipment checks, can be depended on to detect and, in some cases, correct errors due to machine malfunctions. Hardware controls may also be incorporated into data entry and data transmission devices as required.

EDP controls have the same objective as any others: to provide reasonable assurance that no unauthorized transactions are processed, that all authorized transactions are processed, and that errors are prevented or detected as promptly as possible. Every transaction has to be authorized, and either the computer itself or someone in the EDP control function must check incoming data for authorization. There must be means for recording for control purposes all data originated, all data received by EDP for processing, and all data processed.

There are many kinds of EDP systems, and they can employ some or all of the basic controls described in Chapter 3. For example, some use numerical sequencing and some rely on batch control totals; double-checking through "key verification" is used for critical data; and the frequent use of validity checks has been noted above.

Systems that include remote terminals and operate on a random access, on-line basis have to rely on more sophisticated controls, in combination with disciplines and care on the part of users. Validity checks can be built into the computer to check on the validity of the user code, location, data entered, and files accessed. Access logs can be maintained by the computer and reviewed for propriety of the activity. Users can double-check their input, maintain control totals of data transmitted, and restrict access to the terminal.

Disciplinary Controls

Together with systemization, disciplinary controls are the most important elements of EDP control, because basic controls can easily be neglected or bypassed without meticulous discipline. It is disciplinary controls that provide reasonable assurance of the consistency and continuity of basic controls. Furthermore, there must be control procedures to insure that disciplinary controls are maintained. The written procedures required for proper systemization should provide in detail for segregation of duties, restricted access, and supervisory control—and, where available, internal audit.

Segregation of Duties

Between Users and Data Processing.   The system should not permit data processing personnel to initiate transaction data, authorize transactions, initiate master file changes, establish or maintain input controls, correct rejected items, or reconcile output controls.

Within Data Processing.   Systems design, programming, operations, and library functions should all be segregated—if possible, in separate departments. The duties of software support programmers should be segregated from those of applications programmers. A member of one function should not be authorized or permitted to act in another function. Policies and procedures should explicitly preclude:

Programmers and systems analysts operating the computer.

Programmers and systems analysts having access to production machine-sensible programs and data files.

Unsupervised access to the computer room by programmers and systems analysts.

Computer operator access to program source listings and systems and programming documentation.

Computer operators performing program changes, and programmers and systems analysts placing program changes in production status.

Unauthorized access to programs and data files by operations' and programming personnel.

Operations personnel having any control function responsibilities (other than the limited duties of reconciling processing results to predetermined batch or file controls so as to allow further processing), such as reconciling reports, tracing and correcting rejected items, selecting and filing data files, distributing output reports, and the like.

If the systems design and programming functions are not segregated from the computer operations function, protection against unauthorized program and data file modifications is compromised. Knowledge of data file structure, program logic, algorithms, and limit tests, coupled with an opportunity to operate the computer, provides an environment in which it is possible to circumvent the authorized controls of the systems. If there is also access to corporate assets, the opportunity to misappropriate them is obvious.

An important dimension of control over programs is independent review and approval before executing program changes. After a program or system becomes operational, its integrity must be preserved. All new programs and changes to operational programs should be approved by an individual charged with quality assurance responsibilities. This control should be exercised before the programs are implemented to determine whether they have been authorized, tested, and documented. The operations group should never authorize new programs or changes, but they should ascertain that the changes have been approved before placing the programs in production status. The operations group may request changes that they believe will improve operational efficiency, but they should not have the final authority to approve those changes. As part of the supervision of operations, a responsible individual should review all activity involving the program libraries.

Restricted Access

Restricted access to data files, program libraries, equipment, and documentation is even more important than the same discipline in manual systems. Proper access controls assist in the prevention or detection of deliberate or accidental errors caused by the unauthorized or incorrect use or manipulation of a computer program, data files, or the computer. Access should be limited to those individuals authorized to process or maintain particular systems.

Data Files. Data files—either master files or transaction files—should be subject to "library" procedures. That is, the files should be controlled by a "librarian" who has no computer operations or programming responsibilities. The librarian should account for the movement of data files in logs which indicate recipient, application, volume number, retention period, creation data, and other pertinent information. The movement of data files should be restricted to the operations area (especially, data files should not be stored in or released to the systems/programming area). An effective system should further ensure that retention periods on files are adhered to and that the erasing of files is properly authorized. In more sophisticated installations, automated library procedures may be in effect to ensure that the correct version of the data file has been utilized.

Program Libraries. In most data processing installations, computer-executable programs are maintained on disc or magnetic tape files controlled by the operating system. Those files are called "program libraries," a term not to be confused with the physical storage "libraries" for data files, referred to above. Additionally, to facilitate maintenance of source programs, source statements may also be stored on these media. The same degree of control exercised over data files should be in effect for program libraries.

There are several librarian software systems that support many of the techniques needed for controlling programs and, in some cases, data files. A librarian software package can provide effective control if care is exercised over the procedures used to authorize modifications of programs within the library. If these procedures are not rigidly controlled, the integrity of the system can be seriously compromised.

Other File Security Procedures. Program libraries, important master files, transaction files, and documentation should be periodically "backed-up" by duplicating them and storing the duplicates at a safeguarded offsite location to assure that records can be reconstructed in the event of destruction of the current files. The specific backup requirements should be established by the management/user/systems team.

The above procedures may necessitate a full-time librarian working on all operating shifts. Sometimes, however, a librarian works only on the prime shift and supervisory personnel are assigned to the function for other hours of operation. Small installations may require only a part-time librarian. If the librarian works on the prime shift only, the files scheduled to be run during other periods can be made available while the remainder of the library remains inaccessible.

Equipment. Access to computer hardware, including terminals and remote job entry devices, should be limited to those individuals authorized to operate the equipment. A properly designed EDP installation should include physical safeguards over the equipment and restricted access to the computer room. These safeguards may range from internal policies and procedures to locked doors that can be opened only by authorized operations personnel.

Documentation. Program documentation, including source statement listings, source programs, and other documentation of program logic, is a valuable asset which should be subject to restricted access to preclude its unauthorized use. Access to documentation should be limited to those persons who require it for the performance of their duties (i.e., systems analysts and programmers). Program logic should not be accessible to computer operators. Operators should be supplied with run manuals, which include instructions detailing how to operate a specific program or set of programs.

Supervisory Controls

Myriad activities are performed simultaneously within the operations area by the computer and an assortment of peripheral equipment. Careful supervision is required to ensure that those activities are conducted in accordance with established operating procedures.

Activity is usually documented by logs produced by the computer itself simultaneous with processing, either typed out by the console typewriter or, in more sophisticated installations, recorded on discs and printed on the high-speed printer. In some smaller installations, where a computer-produced log is not a standard option, a detailed operations log, recording how all computer time is spent, should be prepared by the operator. If a computer-generated log is available, all operator activity during file set-up and processing should be automatically recorded.

The volume of the console log print-out makes review a difficult but not impossible task. Increasingly, automated "job accounting information" (JAI) systems have been incorporated within the computer's operating system. Examples of this technique can be found in installations utilizing such systems as Hasp, Grasp, or systems management facility (SMF) files. These software aids can produce statistics [e.g., central processing unit (CPU) time, device and storage usage requirements, data set activity, CPU downtime, operator interventions, idle time, etc.], which can provide useful information in monitoring the operations from both an efficiency and disciplinary control standpoint. Regardless of which technique is used, details should be maintained of all re-runs, unusual processing halts, operator interventions, and operating system overrides for careful follow-up.

These logs should be reviewed by an individual with sufficient knowledge to evaluate the activity and its results, determine whether it is appropriate, and recognize departures from established operating disciplines. The individual performing this review may, for example, cross-reference the console log (or the manually prepared operations log) to the SMF file or to the predetermined, independently controlled processing schedule. This would help to ensure that all computer processing is carried out in accordance with authorized operating instructions and that, when combined with appropriate computer library procedures, only authorized programs are executed.

To be effective, the logs must be subject to procedures that prevent their loss or destruction; e.g., the computer-produced log should be printed on prenumbered paper and controlled and reviewed by supervisory personnel.

Internal audit or the "systems acceptance" function can be given copies of authorized programs and all authorized changes. Periodically those independently maintained programs can be run through the computer for comparison with the production programs, so as to detect any differences, which should then be scrutinized and traced to an approved program change request.

REVIEW AND EVALUATION OF INTERNAL CONTROL

Objectives

The objectives of reviewing and evaluating internal control of an EDP system are the same as for other systems: determining the extent to which the auditor may rely on underlying data because they are subject to controls that are functioning as planned and may reasonably be expected to continue to function. The means for achieving the objectives are also the same: understanding the system, confirming operation of controls, identifying the significant controls, and testing those controls. The specific tasks involved differ considerably from those in manual systems, but only because computer systems are organized and operate differently from manual systems. The following paragraphs illustrate how the general principles set forth in Chapters 3, 4, and 5 may be adapted to computerized accounting systems.

An auditor can gain sufficient competence to evaluate the EDP parts of a system as competently as he evaluates the rest of a client's systems through outside training and working with others experienced in EDP. However, in all but the simpler EDP installations, it may be more effective to delegate the evaluation and testing of internal controls related to EDP to a specialist who works as part of the audit team. That is because EDP is a highly technical field, and a client large enough to use it is likely to require a team of auditors contributing in various ways to the in-charge auditor's overall understanding of the client and its systems. An EDP audit specialist can understand the EDP system more quickly and more thoroughly than a non-specialist, and furthermore, he may be helpful in devising ways to use the computer in the audit.

Understanding the System

In evaluating internal control, an auditor must gain an understanding of: first, controls that operate on and through the overall data processing organization, and second, the controls related to each transaction processing system or, as it is commonly called in computer terminology, each "application." The understanding of each system should start at its beginning—the "cradle," which is usually well before data enter the computer—and should go beyond the computer to the "grave."

Linking EDP Reviews With Other Reviews

Obviously, it would be a serious gap in the logic of the audit to treat the EDP part of a transaction processing system as a separate "black box"; an auditor must understand the whole flow of transaction processing up to, through, and beyond the computer. As described in Chapter 5, different types of transactions can merge into one as they travel through a processing system. Guided by the rigor of the audit logic, an auditor must either assure himself that types of transactions merge for control purposes prior to or upon entering an EDP installation, or treat each one as a separate application. The fact that EDP is highly technical, and is discussed separately here, does not imply that the review of EDP controls is anything other than an integral part of a properly coordinated audit.

Overall Organization Controls

As noted in the previous section, systemization, documentation, and discipline are especially important to EDP, for operational efficiency as well as internal accounting control. An auditor should therefore expect to find written organization charts, assignments of responsibility and authority, procedures manuals, and standards of performance. Someone knowledgeable about the client's overall EDP organization can help the auditor to understand that documentation and the control features built into it.

Application Controls

The route that an application takes through the computer can best be understood from the client's systems flow charts and block diagrams, guided and supplemented by discussion with systems designers. A client may prepare an overview flow chart which will contribute to an auditor's understanding by highlighting the control operations.

A questionnaire is especially useful in evaluating internal control for EDP installations. Since the conditions of control and disciplinary controls are so important, a questionnaire can help an auditor to make sure that he has considered all important matters. Most auditors who use internal control questionnaires have a separate, specifically designed questionnaire for EDP installations.

Confirming the Operation of Controls and Functional Testing

In EDP systems, examining the documentation of the system and tracing out the flow charts and narrative descriptions of the systems, programs, and operations requirements should result in identifying the key controls to be tested. Also, tracing transactions through the system is included in some of the procedures used in functional tests of application controls (see "Tests of Application Controls" below). Therefore, transaction reviews are not discussed separately from functional tests.

Tests of Disciplinary Controls

The following are examples of functional tests of disciplines.

Where the client has an automated data file library management facility, review the reports created by the facility for evidence of adherence to established standards and procedures.

On a test basis, obtain copies of key programs from the source statement library and compare them to the independently controlled latest authorized source listing maintained by system development.

Where the client utilizes a program management library facility, review the activity reports on a test basis and trace a sample of activity back to approved data processing request forms, noting requisite approvals, adherence to standards, and proper modification of existing documentation.

On a test basis, cross-reference the computer log to the job accounting report and from there to the job processing schedule.

If the log is manually prepared, ascertain on a test basis that all time (CPU and Wall Clock) is accounted for and reconcile the log to job scheduling.

On a test basis, evaluate the reasons for re-runs, processing halts, and unusual operator interventions; determine that they have been resolved in accordance with established operating procedures.

On a test basis, investigate any departures from the established job processing flow.

Request a directory search and determine, on a test basis, that the program names in the library are authorized program names.

Review the procedure for electing control options in the operating system and observe it in action to ascertain whether the client has implemented the manufacturer's security and job accounting routines, where applicable; determine that these routines are utilized in accordance with established policy.

Review the console logs and determine that all "initial program loads" (IPL) have been performed in accordance with operating requirements and that any departures have been adequately documented.

Review the client's policy regarding the bypassing of data file label halts and scan the console log for adherence to this policy.

Tests of Application Controls

Tests of controls over specific applications also serve to confirm that disciplines are functioning. If disciplines appear sound—that is, consistency of control functioning is reasonably assured—an auditor may be able to limit his functional testing of application controls. If an auditor has found disciplines to be weak or absent, he usually has to give up reliance on controls and plan for validation tests, although he may possibly find compensating controls in the applications area.

There are four ways in which application controls can be tested:

1. Manual controls (i.e., those performed by people rather than the computer) can be reperformed and evidence of their execution examined. For example, manually prepared batch controls can be reperformed and the record of regular batch control preparation and follow-up examined.

2. In applications that are simple enough so that output reports can be compared directly to input data, the auditor selects data, manually reperforms the functions the computer program is supposed to be performing, and traces the results to the output reports. If the results are equivalent, the auditor can conclude that the program has been implemented—at the time of his test—in conformity with the documentation.

3. In more complex systems, where output reports may not be available to allow tracing of the computer processing by manual reperformance, the auditor may use the computer by processing test data. He must first calculate by reference to the systems and program documentation what results should be generated by the computer program. He must then develop a "test deck"—a body of test data—process it through the program, and compare the results with those expected. If they are equivalent, the auditor can conclude that the program has been implemented in conformity with the documentation.

It should be noted that in the "test-deck" procedure, the auditor is relying on the documentation as a basis for designing his tests. He is also relying on the systems design, acceptance, and operating disciplines to insure that the programs contain no unusual procedures that may not be disclosed by use of a test deck. The test-deck procedure has many variations, including trace routines and integrated test facilities.

[A trace routine is a program that runs in parallel with a production program to print out a sequential record of the steps in the production program that have been executed. An integrated test facility (ITF) is a set of accounts representing a unique, artificial accounting grouping (e.g., company, division, department) that serves to accumulate data as part of the normal processing cycle solely for testing purposes. This grouping is ideally controlled by the internal audit staff. After the grouping is established, artificial master records are created, similar to those in actual accounts. The tester then evaluates which controls are to be tested and prepares the test-deck data accordingly. The test information goes into the system along with the regular production data and passes through the application and all of the controls. Those test transactions that pass all controls and generate an acceptable result are segregated in the ITF. An ITF is a method used to avoid the problems connected with the possibility of test-deck data "adulterating" the regular records of bona fide transactions.]

Often the auditor may make use of test procedures that the systems acceptance or internal audit function has designed. These procedures involve test decks, integrated test facilities (also used by operations), and ongoing quality assurance procedures. The auditor, once he has become familiar with them, may readily adapt them to his work. Where they are carried out on an ongoing basis by a quality assurance or internal audit function, the auditor should review that function to be assured of the quality of its work; he can then adjust the scope of his work accordingly.

4. The auditor may review the computer program instructions and compare the results to the documentation for conformity. He can then cause the programs that he reviewed to be "compiled" (i.e., converted into the specific language routine used by the computer), and compare them to those actually in use by the computer. The number of program reviews necessary to validate the reliability of the documentation is dependent on systems design, acceptance, and operating disciplines. If these disciplines are of high quality and consistently functioning, the auditor may have confidence that the documentation is faithfully represented in the computer programs. The number of times he would apply this procedure during the period under review is determined by the reliability of the disciplines.

The analysis of programs is generally performed by a programming specialist, who reports the results of his review to the auditor for evaluation. The analysis is usually manually performed; however, there are automated procedures that can aid in this analysis. The comparison of programs to those cataloged on the computer can be performed automatically through the use of specialized computer software.

Where more advanced systems, such as data base, are in use, the auditor may make extensive use of systems software to confirm the operation of controls. An example is the "Internal Query Facility" used under the IBM/IMS systems. It is encouraging to note that many computer vendors are actively working with auditors to provide such software as part of these systems. Further, many installations have designed specific software for their own purposes, which may be used by auditors in functional tests of controls.

Error Control (Edit and Validation)

One area that should usually be tested and evaluated with special care is error control. Controls are useless unless errors detected are themselves controlled, examined, and properly disposed of.

Computer systems typically "reject" transactions not passing control point tests, whereas manual systems typically correct the error at the control point at the time it is discovered. A computer's speed and efficiency would be seriously diminished if it were required to stop and correct every error encountered, so it is customary for computers to reject abnormal items and continue processing normal ones. The rejects must then follow a special segment of the transaction processing system.

There should be a system for recording and establishing control of rejects, examining the reason for a reject, correcting it, and re-entering the transaction. An auditor should review and understand that system in the same way that other transaction systems are reviewed. The important controls—those over documentation of rejects, completeness and timeliness of corrections, and authorization for re-entry —should be identified and tested.

In addition, an auditor should give explicit attention to the reasons for items appearing in the reject cycles. As noted elsewhere, any kind of audit "exception" may be the slight visible evidence of an unrecognized weakness that could be potentially serious.

Review of Systems During Design

Ideally, the auditor should participate in the systems acceptance function and should review new systems for adequacy of controls as they are being designed. It is much easier to correct control deficiencies in the design stage, and sometimes audit routines can be built into a system. Evaluating a system in the design stage does not make it unnecessary to re-evaluate it when it is completed and in the production stage, because many changes might be made in the interval.

WEAKNESSES IN EDP INTERNAL CONTROL

In 1975, it appears to be fairly generally accepted that the conditions of control and basic controls over the flow of data are important. It is not so generally accepted that the disciplinary controls—restricted access, segregation of duties, and supervisory controls—are even more important. It is not at all unusual to find program documentation lacking, unrestricted access to tape libraries, programmers operating computers, and so on.

If an auditor encounters those conditions he should react as he would to any serious weakness in internal control, even though basic controls appear to be functioning adequately. His alternative reactions are described in Chapter 5. He should do his best to convince his client to correct the weakness. Failing that, he should try to persuade his client to adopt accountability procedures that would compensate for the weakness in the computer department: verifying payrolls, confirming accounts receivable, taking physical inventories, and the like. As a last resort he must rely on his substantive tests, expanding them or changing their nature or timing as appropriate. If that fails, he must consider a disclaimer of opinion. The fact that weaknesses in disciplinary controls have apparently not resulted in errors does not relieve an auditor of his responsibility to follow the rigorous logic of the audit equation. Ultimately, it does not relieve the client of his basic management responsibility for accountability and control, and an auditor should remind his client of that fact as often and persuasively as possible.

USING A CLIENT'S COMPUTER IN VALIDATION TESTS

An auditor can usually execute his validation tests in the same way whether his client has a computer or not. Often the testing can be more efficiently carried out if the power of the computer is recognized and used. More important, a more rigorously penetrating test can often be designed using the computer. The use can be simple, such as programming the computer to print (under the auditor's control) confirmation requests. Or it can be more sophisticated, such as in the selection and evaluation of statistical samples or in making analytical reviews. The range of possibilities in between is infinite, depending only on an auditor's ingenuity in identifying or devising ways to use the computer's basic ability to scan, select, compare, and compute. The computer may be used in validation tests in several ways, such as through general-purpose audit programs, specially written audit programs, and review and use of a client's programs.

General-Purpose Audit Programs

Almost every large accounting firm and several other organizations have prepared a generalized set of audit programs in a computer language suited as nearly as possible for general use. Each set of programs bears an efficient sounding name—ours is Auditpak II. While there are some variations in capacity and capability, they all include programs for making comparisons, selections according to a formula or specified criteria, mathematical computations, sorts and summaries, and lists and print-outs in a variety of forms.

Most general-purpose audit programs represent a pragmatic trade-off between irreconcilable practical constraints; the ways in which that trade-off has been made are the principal differences among the various programs. The greater the emphasis on ease of use and accessibility by untrained or unspecialized personnel, the less the flexibility, capacity, and efficiency of the program, and vice versa.

Examples of tasks for which general-purpose audit programs can be used are:

> Price out and foot a physical inventory file, compare quantities to perpetual records and to records of test counts, and compare prices to a standard cost file.

> Age an accounts receivable file into specified aging categories, foot the file, subtotal records by account number, select accounts for confirmation, print confirmation requests, and compare receivable balances to cash receipts received subsequently.

> Foot a payroll file, scan the file for hours or dollar amounts in excess of prescribed limits, and select records for further detail testing.

> Extend and foot a security portfolio file and compare market prices or quantities to an independent source.

> Compare account balances, actual against budget, and print out details of the accounts that show fluctuations beyond a specified tolerance.

Special-Purpose Audit Programs

General-purpose programs can handle many common audit situations. However, there are instances—such as where an auditor is dealing with a highly sophisticated system or where complex audit tasks must be performed—in which it is more efficient to write a new program than to make extensive modifications to a general-purpose program. In such situations, the auditor (aided by a computer audit specialist) writes one or more programs to perform tasks designed to accomplish his specified audit objectives.

Review and Use of Client's Programs

It is not unusual for an auditor to find that a client has programs that will satisfy his audit needs or for the client to be able to write such programs relatively easily. In those instances, the auditor may use the client's program, but only after he (usually with the aid of an EDP audit specialist) has thoroughly reviewed the program logic so that he has the requisite assurance that the program is designed to perform the procedures he has specified.

In addition, an auditor must take the steps necessary to preserve the integrity of the audit logic and the evidence supporting it. That holds true whether he is using a general-purpose, special-purpose, or client program. An auditor should, for example, be present at the running of his program and satisfy himself that he understands the equipment on which it is located, where it is compiled and executed, where the data files are located, and where his output is being produced.

Using the Computer

An auditor should periodically review his audit program for the specific purpose of identifying tests involving a large volume of repetitive tasks, such as scanning, selecting, comparing, checking mathematics, footing, and the like. He should then estimate the time to be saved by using the computer to perform those tasks and compare it with the time required to set up the computer application. Both estimates are so much affected by the characteristics of the client's system that it is impossible to generalize about the size of a task that should be considered for computer application.

Increasingly, systems are being developed that, due to their complexity and the disappearance of conventional eye-readable hard copy, require the use of computer-assisted techniques in completing an audit. Therefore, auditors must learn to use the computer and to become familiar with the various software techniques that are available and can be adapted to the objectives of functional tests as well as those of validation tests.

USING OTHER COMPUTERS

The growth of timesharing computer facilities has made it possible for every auditor to have access to a large-scale computer from his own or a client's office. Timesharing computer services are used today mainly for professional accounting services other than auditing: for example, tax computations, financial analysis and planning, and helping clients with extensive accounting computations such as depreciation.

However, timesharing computers can be used effectively in audits if extensive computational processes must be performed on relatively small amounts of data. Timesharing programs can be used in statistical sampling to generate random numbers for use in selecting accounts from a given file and to make the computations necessary to evaluate the results of the sample. They can be used to perform standard computations such as depreciation and to make or test complicated computations such as amortization, present value, imputed interest, and actuarial estimates.

The timesharing computer is a fairly new audit tool. It is to be expected that its applications to auditing will multiply as auditors experiment with it and gain experience in its use.

COMPUTER SERVICE CENTERS

Many organizations use outside contractors to process some or all of their accounting data. Computer service centers have proliferated and grown into a well-established industry. The service centers are usually subsidiaries of banks or computer manufacturers, or independent companies devoted to that activity.

For many years there were uncertainties and differences of opinion about the division of responsibility between a service center and its customer companies for control of the data being processed. That condition was reflected in differences of opinion about an auditor's responsibility for reviewing internal controls over records produced by a service center. The AICPA Audit Guide, *Audits of Service Center Produced Records,* issued by the Auditing Standards Division in 1974, points out that both customer ("user") companies and their auditors must take the same responsibility for control of data processed by service centers as for data processed internally. The methods of accountability exercised by a user company and of review and evaluation by an auditor are exactly the same as those described in this and earlier chapters. Use of a service center should have no effect on the audit cycle or the nature and extent of auditing procedures, other than the relatively minor administrative complications of arranging for access to the service center.

When a service center processes data in exactly the same way for each of a large number of users, it is clearly inconvenient and uneconomical for the auditor of each of the users to make an independent review of the system. The practice has therefore grown of producing one audit report on which all of the user auditors rely in the exercise of their responsibilities. The Audit Guide spells out the detailed requirements for that "third party review": the scope of the review, the time period it should cover, the content of the report, and its use by others. An example of a third party reviewer's report is included in the Guide.

Some auditing firms have established computer service centers for servicing their clients. According to Interpretation 101-3 of the Rules of Conduct of the Code of Professional Ethics, auditors may provide computer services (for non-SEC-regulated companies) without impairing their independence, so long as the client institutes all transactions, and is able to assess the validity of the financial statements produced from the computer records.

7

Administration of the Audit

INTRODUCTION

Effective audits don't just happen. Every audit is a complex mixture of activities requiring meticulous coordination and scheduling. Unless the auditor's staff is well organized and the audit efficiently administered, even the most skilled auditor cannot produce his best results. Organization of an office and administrative management of audits are prerequisites to efficient and effective implementation of technical standards and procedures.

Large audits can be complex, fast moving operations involving up to several hundred people; it is hardly an exaggeration to call running such audits a form of generalship. But any audit, even a small one requiring only a few days of a senior auditor's time, can go out of control or become perfunctory as a result of organizational or administrative deficiencies. The subject thus requires more than passing attention. We give it attention that is descriptive rather than definitive because good administration is a matter of day-to-day discipline, diligence, and attention to detail more than of formulating plans and principles. When things are going smoothly, auditors may tend to forget that good administration is a demanding and important job.

Statement on Auditing Standards (SAS) No. 4, *Quality Control Considerations for a Firm of Independent Auditors,* for the first time brings many of the elements of good administration formally within the profession's generally accepted auditing standards. The SAS recommends establishing policies and procedures to maintain independence; assign adequate personnel to engagements; insure adequate consultation and supervision; control practices in hiring, professional development, and advancement; monitor acceptance and continuance of clients; and inspect for effectiveness of all those procedures.

Administration of an audit involves everyone connected with the engagement to a greater or lesser degree. Even the newest assistant does his part in the proper preparation of working papers and time reports. The subject is discussed under five main headings:

Planning.
Supervision.
Recording the audit: working papers.
Reviewing, classifying, and filing working papers.
Administrative wrap-up.

PLANNING

Planning the technical performance of an audit engagement was described in Chapter 4; this chapter concentrates on administrative planning. Administrative and technical planning are inseparable, and one is of little use without the other. There are several steps in the planning process; they do not necessarily follow in the order described.

Planning With Client

Audits may once have been sufficiently routine and self-contained to be planned without reference to a client, but that time is past. The first step in planning an engagement is to discuss with the client new developments that may require attention and any requests he may have for changes in staffing, timing, or scope of work. Working with a client is so important to effective management of an engagement that the entire next chapter is devoted to it.

Engagement Memorandum

It is always a good discipline to put a summary of the plans in writing in an engagement memorandum. It helps to ensure that they are complete, specific, and logically organized, and it serves as a guide for an auditor and his assistants in executing the plans.

An engagement memorandum is important even when it is not shared with the client, but many auditors prefer to submit the memorandum formally to the client, accompanied by a fee estimate and understanding of limitations on fraud detection (Chapter 2). That memorandum, or letter, serves as a basis for discussion and agreement on such matters as locations to be examined, scope of each segment of the examination, timing of each step, and division of work between client's staff and auditor's staff. If conditions subsequently change, it can provide a reference point for orderly reconsideration of audit plans and fees.

Audit Program

An auditor should review the audit program on the basis of an updated understanding of the client, his circumstances, and his needs, and revise the program as necessary. An audit program is essentially an administrative device for instructing staff in the work to be done; it also serves as a control over the performance of the engagement. It should spell out the steps to be performed and their objectives in sufficient detail to guide assistants and to serve as an understandable record for reviewers and subsequent planners.

Although "standard audit programs" were once the subject of considerable debate, there is no theoretical justification for their use today. An auditor needs to understand each client and to design auditing procedures in the light of that understanding according to the logic of the audit equation; each audit must be tailored to the particular needs of a particular client.

The review and revision of the audit program is usually the responsibility of the manager, and the partner generally reviews the manager's judgments. To do so, the partner has to have at hand at least the results of the internal control evaluation and possibly other working papers that document the logic of the audit as it is expressed in the audit program. Both manager and partner should document the exercise of their responsibility by signing the audit program when it meets with their approval.

Time Budget

The time required to complete each step in an engagement should be estimated based on the audit program and the experience of prior years. A time budget is necessary not only to estimate fees but to control the work and guide assistants in the type and quantity of effort expected of them. A time budget is usually drawn up by broad divisions of the audit, but better control is possible if it is detailed by individual program steps.

The importance of close control over time cannot be overemphasized; extra time spent at each of several steps in an examination can result in an unfinished audit as the deadline approaches, and possibly in fee problems with clients. Clients seldom object to additional fees for handling a problem that is properly identified and discussed with them in advance of undertaking additional work to deal with it.

Timing

Although a time budget identifies the amount of time to be spent on each program item, it does not specify when or in what order the work is to be done. Thus, an additional part of planning an engagement with a client is to decide on dates and times for various phases of the audit. The budgeted time can then be scheduled in light of the plan.

Assignment Forecasts

Once an auditor knows what kind of staff he needs, for how long, and when, he can prepare an assignment forecast for his own planning purposes and notify his firm's assignment department. An assignment forecast may simply specify a staff category: "senior," "staff accountant," etc., or it may specify the staff by name.

Both auditor and client benefit from year-to-year continuity of staff on an engagement; it saves time at almost every step and results in a more effective audit because more thorough knowledge of a client is gained by repetition. However, a periodic "fresh approach" through rotation of staff is ordinarily desirable. The most practical approach is to plan an orderly rotation. One of the assistants assigned to an engagement may be designated as understudy for the senior. After he is qualified by sufficient experience, he is assigned as a senior, and the previous senior is assigned to another engagement or perhaps to the supervisor's role. That process of planned movement of staff through the various positions on an engagement or from one engagement to another is a useful, desirable, and sensible system. Although it seldom works perfectly because of staff changes or changes in clients' plans, it is well worth the effort to minimize the alternative dangers of the inefficiency of completely new staffing on the one hand and the diminished effectiveness that results from growing stale on the other.

For some engagements, continuity of staff and early identification of replacements is important for another reason. If a client is engaged in certain kinds of "classified" work for the government, audit staff may have to obtain clearance for access to it. Security clearance may be routine or it may take some time, and that time must be allowed for by early identification of those who need the clearance.

Instructing Staff

A most important and often overlooked final step in the planning process is carefully instructing staff members about what is expected of them. The objectives of the audit should be explained, the timing of the various phases discussed, and the responsibilities of each individual understood and accepted. An audit task undertaken without a clear understanding of its objective, the time it is expected to take, and how it fits into the whole audit entails a serious risk of inefficient or ineffective performance.

SUPERVISION

Good administrative supervision is vital to effective auditing, not only to maintain staff efficiency but also for the healthy development of the professional skills of audit staff. Supervision is hard to develop because professional men proverbially prefer *doing* the work of their profession to *managing* it.

Supervision is today recognized as so important that on many engagements as much as one-fifth to one-fourth of total audit time is devoted to it. While that situation in itself presents potential problems of control and maintaining efficiency, the time is usually well spent. The total audit time is likely to be much larger without effective supervision.

Supervision starts with assigning tasks and taking time to make sure that each task and its objectives are understood. It continues with frequent discussions between supervisor and assistants for the purpose of keeping both informed and providing continuous advice and direction to assistants. That means discussions among partner, manager, and staff accountants; on large audits personal visits to many different groups and locations may be required. While the audit objective concludes with review of the finished work of assistants, the broader objectives of supervision are not completed until the conclusions of the review are discussed with assistants and their performance evaluated.

Many firms require those supervising audit engagements to prepare written personnel reports on each assistant. The personnel reports are accumulated to provide a basis for performance evaluation, salary review, and promotion. Some firms require those preparing personnel reports to discuss them with the individuals being reviewed. Whether required or not, a good supervisor interested in training and developing his assistants ensures that all aspects of the job, including training and individual performance, are frankly discussed before the audit team breaks up.

One of the essential qualities of good supervision is adequately instructing and motivating assistants so that the process of evaluation and conclusion is continuous, problems are discovered and aired early, and communication is on-the-spot and not after-the-fact. The working paper review is an essential feature of an audit, but it should ideally be a final type of control to make sure that nothing has been missed by the supervision process. Auditors are constantly trying to devise aids to facilitate early identification and evaluation of problems. Checklists, questionnaires, and standard formats for meetings and memoranda are useful, and the effort to improve them should continue. However, there are no substitutes for strong, active, and intelligent supervision by supervisors, managers, and partners at the scene of the engagement.

RECORDING THE AUDIT: WORKING PAPERS

Working papers are both the tools of the auditing profession and the documentary evidence of an auditor's work. Those two functions may conflict—the papers on which an auditor sketches out his questions, uncertainties, alternatives, and indecisions are necessary for that purpose, but that documentation of his work may be harmful in the hands of a hostile litigant. The problem of using working papers as *working* papers and at the same time rendering them unassailable to an attack in the courts is one with which the accounting profession has wrestled for years. The only practical solution is to do the audit properly and then take the time to put the file in order—a sometimes uninteresting but always necessary practice. How to do it is discussed under "Evaluating Working Papers," later in the chapter.

SAS No. 1

Guidelines for the content of working papers are set forth in paragraph 338.05 of Statement on Auditing Standards (SAS) No. 1.

Although the quantity, type, and content of working papers will vary with the circumstances, they generally would include or show:

a. Data sufficient to demonstrate that the financial statements or other information upon which the auditor is reporting were in agreement with (or reconciled with) the client's records.

b. That the engagement had been planned, such as by use of work programs, and that the work of any assistants had been supervised and reviewed, indicating observance of the first standard of field work.

c. That the client's system of internal control had been reviewed and evaluated in determining the extent of the tests to which auditing procedures were restricted, indicating observance of the second standard of field work.

d. The auditing procedures followed and testing performed in obtaining evidential matter, indicating observance of the third standard of field work. The record in these respects may take various forms, including memoranda, checklists, work programs, and schedules, and would generally permit reasonable identification of the work done by the auditor.

e. How exceptions and unusual matters, if any, disclosed by the independent auditor's procedures were resolved or treated.

f. Appropriate commentaries prepared by the auditor indicating his conclusions concerning significant aspects of the engagement.

An auditor prepares working papers covering all of those matters in the normal course of his work. To serve as the formal documentation envisioned by SAS No. 1, it is necessary only that the working papers be prepared with the care needed to make them legible, coherent, and consistent.

We would add to the above list of the technical functions of working papers the following practical functions. The working papers should include or show:

Information needed to prepare tax returns, reports to the Securities and Exchange Commission, and other similar reports.

Historical data bearing on questions that may later be the subject of research by the auditor or discussions with the client.

Content and Format

The content of working papers cannot be standardized. Working papers should be designed to fit the circumstances and needs of a particular auditor, a particular engagement, and a particular subject being examined. Most working papers are relatively straightforward, but a great deal of ingenuity and skill is needed to design a working paper that can reduce a complex subject to a readily comprehensible schedule or analysis. Every experienced auditor can recall instances in which the most sophisticated talent available misunderstood or entirely missed the real significance of a difficult transaction until the proper working paper analysis unlocked the puzzle.

Although the content of working papers must be individual, the format should not be. Every group of auditors should adopt a standardized format so that working papers can be organized systematically for use during an engagement, for ready access for reference or review, and for orderly filing for future reference. Every working paper should be headed, dated, and initialed at the time the work is performed, using a standardized format:

> *A heading* identifies the client and the subject of the working paper;
> *Dating* not only provides evidence of the time of preparation but also facilitates tracing the sequence in which steps were performed and helps to plan the timing of similar work in the next examination; and
> *Initialing* completes the documentation and also helps reviewers or subsequent users to know from whom to seek additional information.

Every working paper should contain an explanation of the procedures followed (unless the information is included elsewhere in the working papers, e.g., in an audit program) and the result of the procedures. Sometimes those are obvious from the computations or other data recorded; sometimes a narrative explanation is required. Some firms use a standardized group of symbols as a shorthand documentation of procedures: the time-honored "tick marks."

Notwithstanding the diversity required by the variety of conditions encountered in practice, some categories of working papers have common characteristics, which are worthy of comment.

Trial Balance

The trial balance in most audits no longer serves its original purpose—the work sheet on which an auditor brought a client's accounts into balance and entered his numerous adjustments to them. Now accounts are for the most part kept in balance at all times, or the client balances and adjusts them before the auditor even looks at the trial balance. Nonetheless, the trial balance remains the key working paper in many audits because it is the one on which all underlying working papers are integrated, referenced, and summarized into the aggregates in the financial statements.

Transaction Reviews

Working papers recording transaction reviews should identify the specific transactions selected for review and each step in the transaction flow that was reviewed. Sometimes the identification of the transaction is on a separate working paper from the identification of the steps in a flow because the latter is most conveniently recorded in the form of a flow chart or narrative, which can be carried forward from year to year as long as the system remains unchanged. Listing the transaction steps on a columnar sheet is a convenient time-saver in audits of stable systems. Then a separate column can be used to record the review each year, and the sheet will serve for more than one year.

Functional Tests

Functional tests are most often recorded by a description of the tests performed and the data tested. Sometimes a functional test requires preparing a schedule, such as a bank reconciliation or a proof of cash, or a list of items to be extracted from files or to be checked to data in another location. If so, the schedule or listing prepared can serve as the working paper.

Some auditors believe that signing off an audit program instruction is sufficient evidence in working papers of the performance of functional tests. We prefer the additional evidence given by working papers showing reasonable identification of items examined in functional tests, identification of exceptions, if any, and the auditor's resulting conclusions.

Validation Procedures and Analytical Reviews

Validation procedures are most often evidenced by some kind of account analysis presenting both the account information and an indication of the evidence examined and auditing procedures followed. Neither a transcription of entries in an account nor a copy of a client's records is an account analysis. Rather, an account analysis is a summary of the meaningful aggregates or entries contained in the account. Analyses of accounts were more fully described in Chapter 5.

Analytical reviews are often evidenced by computations made by an auditor in the course of the review. If so, the items of the computation must be adequately identified for later understanding. Analytical reviews are sometimes carried out by examining client data. If so, working paper evidence consists of a narrative description of the review and its results.

Memoranda of Exceptions and Unusual Matters

Questions, exceptions, or unusual matters that arise must be recorded in the working papers pending explanation or resolution. That explanation or resolution may result from further auditing procedures, consultation with the client, or the auditor's own research and reasoning. Recording all questions in the working papers is imperative. The steps taken to resolve them should be detailed, persons involved in the resolution identified, and the resulting conclusions completely explained. It is not acceptable simply to check off a question or record a cryptic answer such as "cleared." Explanations of material matters should be complete and conclusive, and should be summarized in a separate listing of "Matters for the Attention of Partners," which should be reviewed by the partner in charge of the engagement.

REVIEWING, CLASSIFYING, AND FILING WORKING PAPERS

Audit documentation is critical, both for purposes of legal issues that may be raised and for planning later audits. Thus, five routine matters require careful attention:

Reviewing working papers,
Evaluating and classifying them for retention,
Indexing them for convenient reference,
Developing and maintaining permanent files on each client, and
Complying with varying legal requirements for records retention.

Reviewing Working Papers

The important task of reviewing working papers was discussed at length in Chapter 4. The point was made there that one reviewer must be responsible for following through the logic of the audit and making sure that it is documented in the working papers. He may delegate portions of the review on a controlled basis. Many firms require a review by another person of the documentation of all procedures, judgments, and conclusions.

Working papers are voluminous, occupying several filing cabinets on large engagements. Administrative control of the working paper review and its documentation is therefore a task in itself. One way to do it is to require a reviewer to initial each working paper and the cover of each file. Better documentation results if each reviewer prepares a memorandum of his work and his conclusions.

The primary responsibility for the working paper review is usually assigned to the manager, including responsibility for controlled delegation of portions of the review. The partner is responsible for an independent review. If he participated in the work, believes the issues are sensitive or specialized, or otherwise feels the need for another point of view, he has available a second partner or specialist partner for consultation.

As emphasized in Chapter 4 and above, the substantive review of the actual work done and conclusions reached should take place long before the final review and integration of the working papers. That final review is necessary to insure that nothing has been overlooked.

Evaluating Working Papers

Every audit produces some working papers that need not be retained. Thus, as an audit concludes, working papers that have no bearing on the understanding that forms the basis for the auditor's opinion should be discarded to permit the working paper file to constitute, as nearly as possible, a concise, logical, tightly knit body of support documenting the auditor's examination, his understanding, and the basis for his opinion.

Choosing between relevant and irrelevant data is easier said than done, however. Young staff members, eager to do a noteworthy job, persistently write accounts of mountainous "problems," which perspective reduces to molehill proportions. And sometimes working paper analyses of complex transactions go through several formats before the subject matter is properly understood. Material such as registration statements also commonly goes through several printer's proofs.

Opinions differ as to whether relevant but redundant papers should be retained and the extent to which altering or rewriting papers to clarify the record is appropriate. The only generalization that can be stated unequivocally is that the working papers must be carefully reviewed to make sure that no questions are unanswered and that no gaps or loose ends remain in the recorded trail of logic.

Since working papers often include copies of client documents and records, auditors must decide which ones to retain in the working paper files. Usually material available in client files need not be retained, but some exceptions should be noted, such as:

Copies of important contracts or agreements that are in themselves evidence of the authenticity of transactions or that may need to be referred to subsequently, and

Work sheets of auditors' inventory test counts and accounts receivable confirmation replies and their results, which provide evidence of procedures followed.

Filing Working Papers

As portions of an audit are completed, auditors are greatly tempted simply to bundle the papers together rather than take the time to sort, index, and file them. That is always false economy—even if nineteen out of twenty working papers are never needed again, the twentieth will often be needed badly and its immediate availability will more than pay for the cost of good housekeeping.

Working papers should be retained according to a uniform system that is intelligible to everyone involved and provides for ready retrieval of needed papers. Following is an outline of one system that works well in practice:

> Separate sections are set up for major categories of working papers: report draft, financial statements, trial balance, audit program, time analyses, notes and memoranda, and cash, receivables, and so on, account by account.
>
> The financial statement items are keyed by reference letters to the trial balance, which in turn is keyed to a summary working paper in the front of each account section.
>
> The working papers in each working paper section or file binder are numbered (A–1, A–2, etc.) and an index of working paper numbers and subjects is prepared and filed in the front of the section or binder.
>
> Notes, memoranda, program items, and related working papers that are filed in different sections are cross-referenced by means of the index letter and numbers.

Permanent Files

Some audit papers apply to each recurring engagement and should be retained in a separate permanent working paper file. Copies of some material—the certificate of incorporation, by-laws, bond and note indentures, union agreements, important contracts, organization charts, accounting policies and procedures, and perhaps flow charts of the accounting and internal control systems—apply year after year and thus can be more easily located in a permanent file than in the file of a single year's working papers.

Other papers more useful in the permanent file include:

> Working papers with historical significance, such as analyses of capital accounts,
>
> Schedules of key ratios and comparisons that facilitate comparison of long-term trends, and
>
> Other key material that either remains stable or serves as a useful point of departure for several audits.

Audit programs and internal control questionnaires are usually kept in separate files similar to the permanent file.

Permanent files should be reviewed annually and updated and weeded out if appropriate. Permanent files tend to become unwieldy with outdated or irrelevant data. Superseded documents of historical, but no longer current, significance can be filed in a "superseded permanent file," identified, and retained as long as the auditor in charge deems necessary.

Storage and Retention of Working Papers

Legal requirements for records retention vary from state to state, and an auditor should make sure that he understands and complies with those to which he is subject. Generally speaking, auditors keep the latest two or three years' working papers available for ready access. Older files are transferred to safe storage and retained for a longer time, and ultimately they are destroyed under reasonable safeguards. In the meantime, the working papers are legally the property of the auditor.

ADMINISTRATIVE WRAP-UP

After the audit is completed and the working papers reviewed and filed, there are both technical and administrative loose ends to wrap up. The special reports, tax returns, and similar matters are likely to have due dates which act as a professional discipline, but it is easy to let administrative matters slide. Everyone knows that to be a costly luxury, but without tight administrative control it can happen.

Time analyses must be completed and budget variances analyzed. Billings must be prepared and processed. The audit program should be revised preliminarily in preparation for the next engagement. Ideally, the next engagement should be planned with the client, as part of the wrapping-up process. In many well-organized engagements, the end of one audit constitutes the beginning of the next.

MAINTAINING THE QUALITY OF PROFESSIONAL PRACTICE

How to maintain, and enhance, the quality of practice is a major concern of all reputable accounting firms. Preventing lapses as far as possible and detecting them promptly if they occur are important functions of office organization. The best prevention, of course, is careful screening and training so that only professionals of strong character, high standards, and penetrating intelligence are admitted to positions of responsibility. Some firms go to great lengths to screen prospective partners and managers.

Besides screening, quality control is best maintained by the old rule, "Two heads are better than one." Some firms make two partners responsible for each audit examination. Most firms have specific formal procedures for consultation among partners to make sure that difficult or sensitive decisions are made jointly by those directly responsible and those most experienced and knowledgeable in the particular subject matter. However, those procedures should not grow to the point where they obscure or dilute the individual's professional responsibility for making a decision and accepting the consequences of it or where they impede prompt response to client needs. Maintaining a dynamic and productive balance between prompt professional service and maximizing the contribution of senior management and specialists to the quality of service is a responsibility of office organization.

A third quality control technique is a form of internal audit. In some multi-office firms, teams of auditors are organized to examine practices in offices other than their own. They do so by "reperforming" one or more audits; examining the transaction flow charts, audit programs, and working papers; and following through the logic of the audit. Through discussion with audit personnel responsible for the engagement, they determine and evaluate the level and quality of the audit staff's understanding of the client. The examinations must of necessity be of a limited sample of engagements, but within a period of a few years the work of each partner and manager comes under scrutiny. The same kind of internal audit can be organized within an office. The control operations discussed in earlier chapters can be observed in the practices described above.

8

Working With a Client

INTRODUCTION

It is an evident, though seldom mentioned, fact that an audit is an examination not only of books, accounts, and financial data but also of what people are doing: accounts they are keeping, controls they are maintaining, financial representations they are making, ways in which they are dealing with the business events coming before them, and financial decisions they are making. An audit has to be carried out on the client's premises with the client's personnel. Auditing is thus inescapably a process of dealing with people.

Without the ability to communicate well with clients' personnel, all of an auditor's skills are useless to his client and to himself. Auditing involves getting people to do things, most often things they would not otherwise do or choose to do, and often to change things they are doing. An auditor has to relate more than acceptably to clients' personnel because a successful audit depends on enlisting the active and positive cooperation of the client's accounting staff, because the resolution of differences of opinion calls for reservoirs of goodwill and mutual trust and sometimes extraordinary powers of persuasiveness, and because auditing requires auditor and client to work together with a high degree of confidence in one another.

The subject of working with a client deserves emphasis for another reason. Young or inexperienced auditors, fresh from recent advanced learning, may find it difficult to deal with the mature personnel in a client's organization, who may be steeped in their own way of doing things. Auditors spend their time reviewing the work of others and may be tempted to interpret their hindsight as superior judgment. An auditor may be better educated and have a broader point of view than some of the accountants, clerks, and storekeepers with whom he comes in contact. He must exercise tact, and suppress the sense of accomplishment that naturally follows a discovery that something can be corrected or improved.

In today's environment, auditor, management, and client's staff understand the auditor's function and work together to accomplish it. An auditor can expect the respect and courtesy due a professional because his role is better understood, and a client can expect the same. The partner and other senior personnel on an auditing engagement are kept humble by the difficulty of the problems they face and the decisions they must make; it is worth their while to take the time to make sure that assistants and associates share that attitude.

INVESTIGATING POTENTIAL CLIENTS

Most auditors seek to know of the reputation and business standing of potential clients. That procedure is simply good practice, and potential clients should not take it as casting a doubt or slur on the contemplated relationship. On the contrary, they should take comfort in an auditor's efforts to maintain the quality of "the company he keeps."

Sometimes the inquiry is easy and brief. The potential client may be well known in the community, or there may be mutual business associates. In some instances, more formal inquiry is called for.

The initial investigation should give the auditor an adequate understanding of his client. However, he should be alert to circumstances that might call for further inquiry. For example, if a client company is purchased or client management is replaced by persons unknown to the auditor, another investigation would be in order.

INTERVIEWING

The first phase of an initial engagement consists of interviewing members of the client's staff and executives for the purpose of understanding the client. The most demanding or difficult parts of later stages of an examination usually involve interviews or conferences to solve problems, decide among alternatives, or iron out differences of opinion. Thus, gathering information, often sensitive information, quickly and efficiently and without giving offense, is a fundamental skill. To some extent, effective interviewing is a function of the personality of the auditor but, to a considerable extent, it can be learned through instruction and improved with practice.

If an auditor initiates an interview, he should carefully plan and prepare for it. He should identify the objective of the interview and do all the advance homework he can. An executive is quick to spot "fishing expeditions" and time-wasting fumbling and becomes impatient with them. Since the ultimate purpose of an interview is always to gather enough information to enable an auditor to understand a given subject, he has no business asking for an interview until he has defined the subject he wishes to understand. At the same time, he must keep in mind that an interview may well produce unexpected information important to his purpose.

The ability to establish a relationship conducive to the effective exchange of information is a subtle personal skill. An auditor has to be alert and flexible enough to detect and respond to his subject's expectations. Some people feel it is bad manners to plunge immediately into business before getting acquainted; others are impatient to get on with it. If introductions are properly made, most executives are willing to give an auditor all the time he needs and to share their thoughts candidly with him. An auditor can usually build on that initial goodwill simply by being personable and observant.

Attentive listening is one of an interviewer's most valuable skills. Students of the subject have long recognized a tremendous difference between listening and actually hearing what is said. Many people in conferences and interviews listen primarily for the purpose of detecting opportunities to interrupt with their own thoughts. Others listen for such extraneous objectives as picking up material to support their own beliefs or even simply to get a required task over with. Once an interviewer recognizes the nature of those distracting motives, he can block them out and concentrate on hearing what the interviewee is saying. Anyone, no matter how sophisticated, is gratified by undivided attention, and an interviewer inevitably benefits from giving it.

Keeping control of an interview is vital, but it is also important to avoid structuring it to such a degree that the interviewee is precluded from volunteering pertinent information. Encouraging an interviewee to expand on his thoughts without losing track of the objective of the interview is a skill that improves with practice.

Ordinarily, an initial interview is not expected to be the last, and an auditor intends to establish a continuing working relationship with his client's people. Accordingly, it is important to foster and retain the goodwill of an interviewee. One effective way to do that is to make sure that he learns the results of the interview: for example, how it enabled the auditor to carry out his function more effectively, how the auditor reacted to questions raised or problems discussed, and how others responded on the same subjects. The pressure of time and other demands often makes that kind of feedback difficult, but seeing that it gets done is always worth the effort.

In summary, interviewing is both an art and a rational technique that is fundamental to effective auditing. (In fact, the word "auditor" means hearer, both in its archaic meaning describing the work of a professional auditor and in the more general current usage of the word.) Every practicing auditor would do well to study the subject of interviewing and not leave it to chance and innate personality.

PLANNING

It is always in the interest of both client and auditor to discuss the engagement plan together and to take the time to do it right: to learn the objectives and to establish timetables and assignments. An auditor can thus be assured of the availability of data and client personnel, and the client can use his advance knowledge of the auditor's requirements to schedule them into his staff's routine without disruption. Occasionally the client can suggest a more effective means of achieving a given objective, or auditor and client together can identify and resolve problems before they affect the examination.

Careful, cooperative planning can be carried out without relieving an auditor of his responsibility for determining the scope of his examination. The auditor always retains that responsibility but he fulfills it better by seeking the assistance of his client.

WORKING WITH CLIENT'S STAFF

Even in the best planned, smoothest running engagement, an auditor and his assistants need to ask a great many questions and make a great many requests of a client's staff. At times, the client's staff assists the audit staff directly or indirectly in preparing schedules and analyses, searching files or accumulating test data, and processing such tasks as accounts receivable confirmations. Clearly, courtesy and consideration are called for, both in minimizing the number and duration of interruptions and in making sure that auditor and client know that the purpose is understanding the subject matter and not policing it.

An auditor must accommodate himself to his client's working habits. Different clients prefer different degrees of formality. Some are informal and do not appear to care whether formal channels of communication are observed. For those clients, an auditor should adopt a similarly relaxed attitude. Some are formal and disciplined, and an auditor must behave accordingly. In some client offices, outsiders, including auditors, are expected not to address employees directly but to go first to supervisors. Others clients prefer to designate one or several persons to act as liaison with auditors.

Most companies have written and unwritten customs covering dress, conduct, working hours, and the like. An auditor should take pains to respect his client's wishes and to fit unobtrusively into the office routines. An otherwise excellent working relationship can be spoiled by such apparently trivial matters as members of the audit staff arriving late, working in shirt sleeves, or otherwise disregarding a client's sensibilities.

WORKING WITH INTERNAL AUDITORS

More and more companies are establishing internal audit departments. The function has grown in size and stature, and professional societies of internal auditors have been established which offer specialized courses, conferences, and publications devoted to the subject. The term covers a wide variety of activities. An internal audit department may:

Function as a part of the internal control and internal check system, focusing heavily on matters such as surprise cash counts and inventory checks.

Function essentially in parallel with the independent audit function as described in this book, focusing on the evaluation of systems and validation of account balances.

Be broadly responsible for evaluating compliance with company policies and practices.

Be interested primarily in operational audits and in developing sophisticated functions that are not only valuable in themselves but also serve as management training grounds for rising executives.

Devote its time entirely to special projects or to responsibility for parts of the system, such as bank reconciliations or voucher approval, to the point where no time is left for internal auditing as such.

Since the term "internal auditing" encompasses so wide a variety of activities, an outside auditor approaching a new client should make sure that his understanding of the internal audit function is as comprehensive as his understanding of the client's other systems. He should also start early to become acquainted with the internal auditors because they are likely to be the group in a client's office with whom he will be working most closely and most often.

The activities of an internal audit department usually overlap those of an independent auditor to a significant degree—sometimes they are completely parallel—but their purposes and functions are different. An independent auditor's function is to understand the client's systems as a basis for relying on the end results of those systems so as to give an opinion on the financial statements. An internal auditor's function is to understand the company's systems in order to see that company policy is followed and that the systems function with maximum efficiency at minimum cost. An independent auditor can perform an internal auditor's functions, but it is usually preferable to have this done by those more intimately knowledgeable about company policies and practices. Internal auditors could often perform an independent auditor's function, although the results would lack the essential quality of independence. Sometimes internal auditors do make formal opinion audits for their employer managements of, for example, a potential acquisition or performance under a royalty or franchise contract.

Since the independent auditor and the internal auditor have so much in common, they must work together to minimize duplication. Of course, minimizing duplication is always desirable to reduce both the cost of the work and the interruption and inconvenience to the operations under examination. At the same time, however closely he works with internal auditors, an independent auditor must also objectively evaluate their work because they are an important disciplinary control in the client's overall system of internal control.

To make a "proper study and evaluation" of an internal audit department, an independent auditor should read applicable job descriptions, study audit programs, review time budgets and work schedules, examine samples of working papers, and read all of the internal auditors' reports for the period before the time of the examination. The understanding thus gained can be confirmed by examining, either separately or jointly, some of the same systems examined by the internal auditors. If the independent auditor's findings coincide with those of the internal auditors, he can properly conclude that their work is satisfactory according to his standards.

Once he has a clear understanding of the internal audit operation and has confidence in it, an independent auditor can plan audit steps in cooperation with the internal audit staff.

Cooperation

The work programs of internal and outside auditors can be integrated, with no loss of control, so that they are consistent with and complement one another rather than duplicate or overlap. In a decentralized or diversified company, the internal auditors may examine some divisions and departments and the independent auditors others, rotating their assignments from examination to examination and exchanging and making use of one another's working papers and findings. Or, the two groups may undertake concurrent examinations of the same subject matter, dividing the tasks between them.

In other circumstances, the independent auditor may plan a type of controlled reliance on the internal auditors. For example, the internal auditors may prepare listings, account analyses, or tests for the independent auditor to test-check, or they may process and mail accounts receivable confirmations with requests that replies be sent directly to the outside auditor's office.

In terms of audit theory, a degree of reliance on internal auditors is justified on the principle that a capable, well-functioning internal audit department provides disciplinary control so reliable that an independent auditor can limit his testing of other parts of the system.

Planning

Effective cooperation between independent and internal auditors requires extensive and sometimes imaginative planning. Duties and tasks of each group must be carefully defined and assigned. The participants must agree on the caliber of personnel to be assigned to each task, the extent of testing to be performed, and the form and content of working paper documentation to be provided. The internal auditors should be able to make worthwhile suggestions concerning the outside auditor's plans, and vice versa. The groups should agree on working relations between them, particularly on the manner in which audit findings are conveyed to management—preferably jointly.

WORKING WITH MANAGEMENT

An auditor who has a satisfactory relationship with a client will have occasion to work with the chief executive officer, the chief financial officer, and various members of the corporate staff, such as legal counsel, tax specialists, the financial public relations department, corporate development officers, and planners. Those contacts present opportunities for interesting and challenging assignments. For his basic purpose of understanding his client well enough to have a basis for an opinion, contacts with management are important to an auditor because they are likely to provide him with an opportunity for insight into his client's operations and problems which enhances that gained through the audit.

Chief Executive

Most chief executives got where they are by making efficient use of their time, and they want their business contacts to be brief and to the point. As a result, chief executives and auditors sometimes meet only when a problem too large or difficult for anyone else to resolve requires them to come together. In those circumstances, the likelihood of a productive meeting satisfactory to both parties is reduced. We believe that meaningful contact between the auditor and the chief executive officer is highly desirable. The auditor should know what the president or chairman expects of him. The chief executive should know the auditor well enough to be able to call him directly when he needs him: for example, to advise on a confidential acquisition or other transaction in the planning stage, to help with a confidential financial or accounting problem, or to resolve a problem between auditor's and client's staff.

Above all, both executive and auditor should make every effort to communicate thoroughly and precisely enough to prevent surprising one another. The auditor–client relationship is not functioning the way it should if the chief executive initiates transactions having unexpected accounting implications or the auditor suddenly presents new disclosure requirements affecting the president's plans. The extent of the contact between them depends on the president's needs and the auditor's ability to be useful. The contact may sometimes become extensive. At a minimum, the auditor should meet with the chief executive annually to report on his activities and prospective developments in financial reporting.

Chief Financial Officer

An auditor who is broadly experienced and has a proper understanding of his client is inevitably a valuable adjunct to the chief financial officer and his assistants. He can contribute his expertise in accounting and financial reporting drawn from his experience with other clients, and can provide a relatively objective point of view. He is a source of informed, knowledgeable comment on events and decisions facing the financial officers. A financial officer cannot be expected to share his plans and problems with an outsider unless he trusts and respects him completely. That confidence cannot be given; it must be earned by a demonstrated competence and desire to be helpful.

An accumulation of earned goodwill is even more important if the time comes for an auditor to disagree with his client about an important matter and to press his point of view with insistence. It is much easier to arrive at the best course of action under the pressure of difficult circumstances if the parties have previously worked together successfully; it may be impossible to find a constructive solution if they have not.

Financial executives have a wide range of views about the value of the contribution of their auditors, as evidenced by various published and unpublished studies. Those views no doubt reflect a corresponding range of experience. To some extent, an auditor's innate ability, including the depth and breadth of his character and experience, determines the contribution he can make. A more significant determinant is his willingness and ability to accommodate his skill and talent to a client's particular needs and style, so that he does, in fact, contribute rather than disturb, distract, or impede.

Corporate Staff

In all but the smallest companies an auditor today must expect to be involved with a variety of members of the client's corporate staff who are working on problems directly or indirectly related to accounting and auditing. The range of possible problems covers the whole spectrum of business activity: there may be merger negotiations, labor contracts, lease or purchase decisions, fair trade, or, in the recent past, price controls, to name a few. An auditor may be initially invited into a group to review and approve the accounting treatment of proposed transactions before the fact rather than afterward. An auditor who is adequate to the challenge will be able to offer more than that: he will have expertise and, quite likely, ideas to contribute to improve the solution.

That kind of activity can become extremely time-consuming. An auditor may be pleased that his contribution is recognized and sought, but he may also be concerned about neglecting other responsibilities and even about getting so involved as to jeopardize his independence. In our opinion, the time simply must be made available. A professional person has a duty to bring all his skill and competence to bear where his client needs it. Moreover, an auditor does his basic job much better if he evaluates plans rather than records of events that have already taken place. His understanding of a client is enhanced by every meeting he attends. Every involvement in client financial affairs contributes to his opinion on the resulting financial statements. He must, of course, take care to preserve his objectivity while discharging his professional responsibility.

The distinction between traditional, essential audit tasks and constructive, informative peripheral services is rapidly vanishing. Some see in its disappearance a salutary trend. In earlier days, the audit was the focus of the auditor–client relationship and encompassed the bulk of activity, with other services being incidental, sporadic, and often gratuitous. The direction in which we are heading with some clients is toward a broad, multifaceted contribution of accounting and auditing skills of which the audit is only one recurring activity. The trend is salutary because an audit that is an integral part of a whole range of services is more effective and probably less expensive for the client. However, that trend can easily be misunderstood by general management, directors, or outsiders. It is therefore important that all practitioners who are engaged in that kind of sophisticated service make sure that interested nonfinancial parties understand how and why an auditor's special assignments contribute to a more effective audit without endangering his essential independence.

THE AUDIT COMMITTEE

In our opinion, the move toward audit committees of outside directors has been beneficial to management, directors, stockholders, and the auditing profession. Auditors and outside directors have some common interests which are vastly strengthened by interaction between them. A properly active and involved audit committee serves to protect the corporate interest by overseeing the auditor and, at least to some extent, company management.

The protection takes both a theoretical and a practical form. Theoretically, the existence of an audit committee of outside directors is a demonstration that all parties are attending with due diligence to their duties to the stockholders concerning financial reporting and disclosure. An audit committee reinforces an auditor's independence, while an auditor provides an independent source of information to the directors; management's support of the relationship demonstrates a sense of accountability. Practically, an audit committee brings a number of specific benefits to the auditor–client relationship.

An audit committee permits the directors—particularly those who serve on the committee for a number of years—to assess the alertness and energy of the auditor, the scope and limitations of his work, the quality of client–auditor relations, and the quality and variety of contributions that the auditor makes to the viability of the company and to investor protection. Members of audit committees can also accumulate an understanding of the sensitive areas and potential trouble spots in the company's financial affairs, which may prepare them to cope with a troublesome problem should it develop.

An audit committee also gives a sharper focus to the auditor's activities. Anticipating and preparing for directors' questions forces an auditor to look at his work and at the company's affairs from the broadest possible perspective. The auditor and the company's financial management soon learn that the audit committee is distinctly not pleased to learn of existing and unresolved problems, but that they have a keen and appreciative interest in hearing about problems that have been recognized, attacked, and disposed of. That is the real and practical value of an audit committee: it forces both auditor and management to take a more aggressive approach toward solving problems that they might otherwise be inclined to learn to live with.

Except for the first year that an audit committee is established or during the development of some special problem, a few meetings a year should probably suffice. The auditor may submit, in advance, a written report on the scope of his activities both in the prior year and as planned for the coming year. Sometimes he may also be asked for a letter of comment and recommendations. The directors should discuss with the auditor the areas for which he is held responsible and, more importantly, those for which he is not responsible. The directors should be acquainted with the degree of the auditor's involvement in special work and should understand how that special work might affect the basic audit function. They should inquire about sensitive areas—the potential trouble spots and areas on which an auditor concentrates.

The literature on this subject reports that some audit committees perform recurring tasks, such as reviews of audit programs. In our opinion, that is not always desirable because an audit committee works best on an "exception" basis. The time spent reviewing audit programs could better be spent discussing and understanding significant judgments reflected in the financial statements or the design of the company's control systems.

Much of the literature on the subject, including the pamphlet published by the AICPA,* recommends that an audit committee meet separately with an auditor and with members of management. Separate discussions in private meetings can result in questions and misunderstandings arising from different interpretations of the subjects discussed, and a subsequent joint meeting with management is then required to resolve them. Of course, either party should be able to call a private meeting when a matter is so serious that confidential discussion seems advisable. However, in most cases, an audit committee should insist that problems be faced jointly by the auditor and financial management and, if necessary, reported to the committee jointly. Usually, brief private meetings are held as a matter of form, and if substantive matters come up, all parties are requested to join in the discussion of them. The working relationship established in the routine annual meetings should provide a basis for an orderly approach to most problems.

In our opinion, an auditor should take the lead in recommending the formation of an audit committee and in advising on its functioning. Auditors are the experts in their field and the focus of the committee's purpose; hence, they should have the most to contribute to it. An auditor's initiative in that respect is propelled to some extent by self-interest: most directors are men of broad experience and substantial standing in the financial community. Accordingly, an auditor needs their views in resolving the difficult judgments he is sometimes called on to make; he also welcomes their recognition and good opinion of his work.

FEES AND BILLING

Audits are expensive, and while clients are usually willing to pay a fair fee, they understandably wish to minimize the expense. Auditors enjoy their professional work but sometimes view the billing and collecting of fees as an administrative chore. Nevertheless, the handling of fee arrangements is a necessary element of working with a client. Properly planned and controlled, the task can be handled smoothly and quickly.

The key element is an auditor's sympathy for his client's needs and the pressures upon him. While those vary, the most common one is budgetary. No matter how delighted a financial executive may

* *A Statement on Audit Committees of Boards of Directors* (New York: AICPA, 1967).

be with an auditor's contribution, someone in the company is likely to regard the audit as a necessary evil and to consider one audit as good as another. To deal with that attitude, a client needs to know what the audit will cost, why it has to cost that amount, and what he might do to minimize the cost. He needs to know about and have some degree of control over changes before they happen.

The experience of contractors over the years has developed the methodology for estimating project costs, controlling them, and foreseeing changes. The methodology is easily applied to recurring audit engagements, making it possible to treat them in much the same way. Set up in that fashion and accompanied by the kind of detailed cooperative engagement planning recommended elsewhere in this chapter, fee problems usually disappear.

Fee negotiations may be the responsibility of the chief internal auditor, controller, financial vice president, or audit committee. Some audit committees take on that responsibility to make sure that corporate management does not unduly restrict the scope of audit activity through fee pressures.

As in any other economic enterprise, the most definitive test of success is the customer's willingness to pay for the product: the tenor of the fee discussions is an accurate barometer of an auditor's success in working with his client.

Part II

THE ACCOUNTING CYCLE

9

The Revenue Segment

REVENUE, ACCOUNTS RECEIVABLE, AND RELATED ACCOUNTS

205

INTRODUCTION

Accounting for revenue, accounts receivable, and related accounts is discussed in this chapter in two parts: short-term transactions characteristic of the bulk of modern business activity and long-term transactions characteristic of certain industries. Typical of the first type of transaction is an ordinary sale for cash or on account: a customer elects to buy, the enterprise delivers and renders an invoice, and the customer accepts and pays, all within a short time. Typical of transactions in the second category are installment sales, long-term contracts, and some leases: production or delivery by the enterprise, payment by the customer, or both may occur over a long period.

Although some short-term revenue transactions can present accounting and auditing problems, it is the transactions that extend over several accounting periods that most often involve serious questions about when to recognize revenue and related profit, and difficult estimates and judgments may be needed to answer them.

DEFINITIONS

The key terms of the chapter are defined in the following paragraphs.

Revenue is defined in APB Statement No. 4, *Basic Concepts and Accounting Principles Underlying Financial Statements of Business Enterprises (AICPA Prof. Stds.,* vol. 3, Section 1026), as:

> . . . a gross increase in assets or a gross decrease in liabilities recognized and measured in conformity with generally accepted accounting principles that results from those types of profit-directed activities of an enterprise that can change owners' equity . . . . Revenue under present generally accepted accounting principles is derived from three general activities: (a) selling products, (b) rendering services and permitting others to use enterprise resources, which result in interest, rent, royalties, fees, and the like, and (c) disposing of resources other than products—for example, plant and equipment or investments in other entities. Revenue does not include receipt of assets purchased, proceeds of borrowing, investments by owners, or adjustments of revenue of prior periods. [Paragraph 1026.12]

Revenue is thus the general term applied to all receipts from operations, as distinguished from receipts from so-called capital transactions. Revenue is more general and all-inclusive than other frequently used terms such as gross sales, gross income, or operating revenue.

Accounts receivable has not been formally defined in the same way, but its meaning is generally understood. Accounts receivable are claims against customers and others arising from the business activities of an enterprise; that is, they are revenue not yet received in cash. Since extending credit is virtually universal in modern business activity, accounts receivable are found in almost every enterprise. Trade accounts receivable are generally short-term, often outstanding for little more than the "in-transit" time needed for sellers and buyers to process transactions—shipping, billing, receiving the goods, inspecting them, processing the invoice for payment, and processing the cash receipt.

Accounts receivable sometimes result from transactions other than those with customers in the ordinary course of business; for example, from sales of plant and equipment or investments or from loans to employees or other non-customers.

Notes and acceptances receivable are formal evidences of amounts due. They are usually more readily negotiable, though not necessarily more collectible, than accounts receivable.

Unbilled and accrued receivables result from accounting recognition of revenue without concurrent notification to the customer. *Unbilled* indicates that an invoice is expected to be sent later, as in the case of amounts accrued under cost reimbursable contracts or contracts accounted for by the percentage-of-completion method. *Accrued* refers to amounts for which collection is expected when due without formal invoicing, such as interest, rents, or royalties. For convenience, all of those receivables are included in accounts receivable in this chapter unless the context necessitates discussing them separately.

Sums receivable from stock subscriptions and similar capital transactions are rarely considered accounts receivable. They are excluded from this chapter because they involve no revenue and are discussed in Chapter 16, "The Financing Segment." Also excluded are transactions entered into for investment purposes, which are part of Chapter 14, "The Investment Segment," and receivables involving the refund of expenses, such as refunds of amounts paid for goods returned to vendors, covered in Chapter 10, and income tax refunds, which are covered in Chapter 13.

Unearned revenue and deferred income are the general terms used for accounts that reflect various kinds of advance payments made for goods and services not yet delivered. Some common kinds are advance payments on contracts, unexpended balances of grants, magazine subscription sales, transportation and entertainment ticket sales, and unearned discount on loans.

Most companies have one or more major sources of revenue, usually called "sales" or "gross income," and several relatively less significant types of miscellaneous revenue, often called "other income." The category of a given type of revenue depends on the principal business activities of an enterprise: sales may be "other income" to a utility or an educational institution; interest and dividends from investments may be the "gross income" of an investment company.

• ACCOUNTING PRINCIPLES

Two basic questions must be answered to account for revenue and accounts receivable:

When should revenue and a related receivable be recognized?
How much revenue should be recognized?

All accounting principles affecting revenue and accounts receivable deal with one or both of those questions. The longer the transaction takes to consummate, the more complex the questions can become: a simple sale over the counter for cash, which is completed in a moment or two, causes few, if any, accounting problems; a long-term contract or long-term lease may raise difficult problems of timing and amount of revenue recognition.

TYPICAL SHORT-TERM TRANSACTIONS

When To Recognize Revenue

The usual time for recognizing revenue in a commercial or industrial enterprise is when assets are sold or services rendered. The underlying reason is the "realization principle" explained in paragraphs 149 to 153 of APB Statement No. 4 (paragraphs 1026.13 to .17 of *AICPA Prof. Stds.*, vol. 3). The principle is often called the "sale basis" of revenue recognition:

> P–2. *Realization*. Revenue is generally recognized when both of the following conditions are met: (1) the earning process is complete or virtually complete, and (2) an exchange has taken place. [Paragraph 1026.14]

The earning process is defined as "all of the profit-directed activities of an enterprise that comprise the process by which revenue is earned . . ." [Paragraph 1026.13].

Applying the Sale Basis

A legal claim against a customer arises when a service is performed for him or when title to goods passes to him. Technically, accounting under the sale basis should follow and reflect the legal reality, and a receivable and the related revenue should be recognized when a customer receives services or title to goods.

In many transactions, however, the time and place at which legal title passes are obscure or inconvenient to identify for accounting purposes. For example, title does not pass in shipments FOB destination, or in shipments on drafts accompanied by bills of lading, until the buyer receives the merchandise or the drafts are paid; installment sales contracts may include complicated provisions to enable a seller to retain legal title during the collection period. In those examples, the earning process is "virtually complete" well before title passes.

Usually, the most convenient point for recording a sale is when goods leave a seller's premises, either in the hands of a customer or in the hands of a common carrier for shipment to a customer. The counter clerk's sales slip or the shipping document authorizes preparation of a billing, which is the basis for an entry recognizing revenue and an account receivable.

Variations of the Sale Basis

Revenue transactions that are not in the form of a sale of goods often require variations in the procedure, but they usually follow the essence of the realization principle or sale basis. Nine common examples follow.

1. Utilities Services. Electric, gas, water, and telephone services are delivered continuously but are ordinarily billed once a month or less frequently, at various dates ("cycle billing"). As a result, some services delivered have not been billed at any period end. The majority of regulated electric and gas companies do not record unbilled revenue at the end of a period. However, some companies measure or estimate the amount of unbilled services and recognize it by recording an unbilled receivable.

2. Performance Under Contracts. Many cost reimbursement type contracts give the seller the legal and practical right to bill as soon as materials are purchased or service is performed. Preparing formal invoices is a clerical function similar to billing utility charges. Recording revenue and an unbilled receivable based on performance is preferred practice.

3. Rents, Interest, Royalties, Etc. Some kinds of revenue, such as interest and some rents and royalties, accrue as time passes because they are payments for the right to use assets for specified periods. Some rents, most royalties, and similar kinds of revenue accrue on the basis of performance of some kind by the licensee, such as dollars of sales volume or barrels of crude oil lifted. The contractual basis of accrual—time or performance—determines the way revenue and receivables are recognized.

4. Sales on Consignment. Merchandise is frequently shipped to a distributor on consignment, which means that legal title, risk, and responsibility for the goods remain with the seller, who has no claim against the consignee (other than for return of the consigned goods) until the merchandise is sold. The handling of the goods and the paperwork for the transaction may be in every respect the same as a regular sale. However, no revenue or account receivable should be recorded until the consignee sells the goods.

5. Sales With Right To Return. In some industries the customer has, by contract or custom, the right to return and receive credit for goods, regardless of reason. Frequently the customer is allowed to delay payment until he resells the goods. In these transactions, the customer's ultimate acceptance (or resale) is critical in determining whether an exchange has taken place. This is particularly crucial when the industry is seasonal, as in toys, seeds, fertilizer, farm equipment, etc., and the normal resale period just precedes or follows the manufacturer's fiscal year end. When these rights or customs exist, recording of sales should be delayed (or reversed) pending customer advice, or consignment accounting may be more appropriate. Sales involving "puts" or special guarantees should not be recorded until all rights expire.

6. *Unearned Revenue.* Some services are billed and paid before being delivered; for example, transportation, subscriptions to periodicals, some rents, and contracts for television programs. Since the seller earns revenue only by performing the contracted service, recording cash received or a receivable for the sale results in recognizing "unearned revenue," which should be recorded in a balance sheet account bearing that title. Unearned revenue is then reduced and revenue recognized as the service is delivered, usually based on some statistical measure such as tickets collected, passengers counted, copies mailed, or number of showings.

7. *Advance Receipts.* Unearned revenue should also be recorded for sales contracts that require a customer to pay part or all of the purchase price before goods or services are delivered. "Down payments," "progress payments," "security deposits," and a variety of other arrangements are common. If the full price is received in advance, accounting for the unearned revenue is the same as that described in the preceding paragraph.

Partial advance receipts give rise to the additional problem of relating the receipt to the uncollected balance of the sale price on the one hand and to the recognition of earned or unearned revenue on the other. In some cases, such as utility security deposits and deposits of the "last month's rent in advance" required in many leases, the recording of receivables and revenue is independent of accounting for the deposit, and it is necessary only to keep the deposit separately identified to permit "closing out" one against the other when the time comes. In a few instances at the other extreme, a legal right to an entire uncollected balance arises upon receipt of an advance, and it is appropriate to record the uncollected balance as a receivable and credit unearned revenue for the selling price. In most transactions involving advances, however, the revenue and receivable are not recorded until goods are delivered or services performed.

8. *Grants and Appropriations.* A grant or appropriation for work to be performed is a type of advance receipt. Governmental agencies

are the principal grantors and nonprofit organizations the common recipients, but grants and appropriations appear in all types of organizations. Receipts are accounted for in the same way as unearned revenue, usually in an account entitled "unexpended balances," and recognized as revenue as costs are incurred for performance of the work.

9. *Tuition and Dues.* A large part of the revenue of educational institutions and clubs is for the privilege of attending or using the facilities for a given period. Charges for tuition and dues are usually billed in advance for a period of attendance or membership of a year or less, and the revenue is recognized (usually ratably) over the period in which the services are rendered. Problems result, however, if a lump-sum collection covers a long-term membership or a series of lessons. Some proprietary educational enterprises, for example, offer "lifetime" contracts or discounts for prepayment of long-term tuition contracts. Prorating those amounts to periods of performance of services and estimating how much of the prepayment relates to services that will be demanded and how much may be forfeited by the customer can be difficult.

Revenue Cutoff

Most questions of when to record revenue and receivables for typical short-term transactions involve the transition from one accounting period to the next. The time that goods are shipped or services rendered is usually known. The necessary information is provided by adequate documentation of the date of shipment or delivery to a common carrier, and a reliable system for summarizing and recording the facts of large numbers of transactions. Nevertheless, questions inevitably occur in the attempt to divide a continuous revenue stream at the end of one period and beginning of another. Following are two examples of types of problems that may be encountered.

1. *Intentional Acceleration or Delay of Sales.* Management of a company that recognizes sales and receivables at the time of shipping goods may mount an all-out effort in the last few weeks of the year to accelerate filling and shipping of customer orders, thus increasing shipments and revenue over the level that would otherwise prevail. Conversely, management may order shipments to be halted or delayed to hold down sales and income. Those actions are a prerogative of management, and the accounts must reflect the results of the decisions. However, if sales returns or allowances early in the next year are higher than ordinary, indicating that the necessary "exchanges" have not taken place, those consequences should affect the measurement of revenue recognized, as discussed later in the chapter.

2. Extraordinary Complexity. Accurate accounting for revenue earned by transportation companies can be extremely difficult. Rate and fare schedules are sometimes complex, and rates or fares for a unit of freight or a passenger may be different, depending on routing, carriers involved, and other factors. Usual practice where precise pricing is difficult or untimely is to estimate revenue arising from delivery of service using the best available statistical average—revenue per passenger, per passenger mile, per passenger carried on a given route, and the like. The balance of unearned revenue is verified at least once a year by accounting for or estimating the details composing it. (The section on typical transaction systems and internal control later in the chapter describes the most common procedure.)

Revenue Recognized Before or After Sale

Certain exceptions to the realization principle or sale basis are generally accepted. Revenue is sometimes recognized at completion of production, not at sale, on certain precious metals and farm products. The characteristics that permit that exception are immediate marketability at an assured sale price, unit interchangeability, and sometimes the difficulty of determining unit costs [Accounting Research Bulletin No. 43, Statement 9 of Chapter 4 (*AICPA Prof. Stds.,* vol. 3, paragraph 5121.15), and Chapter 1A, paragraph 1 (Section 4010)]. Some of those products are accounted for as by-products (next section). Revenue is often recognized as construction progresses for certain long-term construction contracts and as cash is collected for certain installment sale contracts. Both are discussed in the section on long-term transactions in this chapter.

Sales That Reduce Cost

Proceeds from some kinds of sales are usually accounted for as reductions of cost rather than as revenue. Examples are sales of scrap, sales of by-products, and sales from a company store or cafeteria.

Intracompany and Intercompany Sales

Transfers of semifinished and finished products from one department or plant to another are sometimes recorded as sales at current market prices for management accounting purposes. Several distinct stages in the manufacturing process between raw materials and finished stock characterize some businesses. Manufacturing operations may be organized so that the finished product of one division or affiliated company may be a raw material of another. A primary purpose of accounting for transfers of products within a company as sales is to show departmental or plant results as if they were separate entities. However, intracompany sales are not revenue to a company as a whole and should be segregated in the accounts to facilitate eliminating them from the company's income statement and eliminating the related "unrealized" profit from inventories.

Sales between affiliated companies are usually recorded at current market prices to enable each company to produce separate financial statements. However, intercompany sales are not revenue in a consolidated income statement; they should be segregated in the accounts to facilitate their elimination and the elimination of the related unrealized profit from inventories. Consolidated financial statements are discussed in Chapter 17.

Sale and Leaseback Transactions

A company may construct a building or equipment, sell it to an unaffiliated entity, and then lease the same building or equipment under the terms of a long-term lease. Earlier practice, at least of some companies, was to record the sale price as revenue (usually resulting in a gain on the sale) even though the seller would clearly return it to the purchaser as rent over the term of the lease. In 1964, APB Opinion No. 5, *Reporting of Leases in Financial Statements of Lessee (AICPA Prof. Stds.,* vol. 3, Section 5351), concluded that a sale and subsequent leaseback of property should not usually be considered independent transactions. No gain or loss should be recognized on the sale except in rare circumstances, such as if a loss would have been properly recognized without the sale and leaseback transaction. The gain or loss should be recorded as a deferred credit or deferred charge and amortized over the period of the related lease.

How Much Revenue To Recognize

The general rule for measuring revenue is given in paragraph 151 of APB Statement No. 4 (paragraph 1026.15 of *AICPA Prof. Stds.,* vol. 3):

> The exchange required by the realization principle determines both the time at which to recognize revenue and the amount at which to record it. . . . Revenue recognized under the realization principle is recorded at the amount received or expected to be received.

The amount received or expected to be received in most individual transactions is the exchange (sale) price, often less a cash discount or other discount or allowance that is expected to be taken. Since the exchange or sale price is often, though not always, the invoice price, measuring revenue begins with the invoice price.

Invoice Price

An invoice price may include sales tax, excise tax, freight out, and similar items that may or may not properly be included in revenue. The treatment of excise taxes varies from industry to industry and even within the same industry. For example, some distillers include the substantial excise taxes on liquor sales in revenue and in expenses, while others separate the taxes by recording a liability rather than revenue at the time of sale. Accounting for sales taxes also varies. A suggested rule is: a charge that is legally imposed on a buyer (for example, most sales taxes) should not be accounted for as revenue; in contrast, a charge that is legally imposed on the seller and passed on to the buyer like other costs (for example, an excise tax) should be included as part of the seller's revenue. However, the rule is not universally followed.

Industry practice also varies on whether revenue is the total price paid or only that portion of the price related to the value added by the seller. For example, a stockbroker or real estate broker recognizes as revenue only the commission for his services as broker and not the full value of the property involved in the transaction. The transaction is seen as a rendering of service for a fee rather than as a purchase and sale of property. On the other hand, most construction contracts are accounted for "gross" or "broad"—all material and labor costs are included in the expenses of the contractor-seller and are included as revenue with the contractor's fee, even though the costs are rebilled to the customer as incurred.

Reductions of Invoice Price

The amount "expected to be received" from sales is often less than the invoice price. Sellers customarily allow buyers a discount for prompt payment and permit them to pay less or return goods that are damaged or substandard. Even cash sales are subject to price rebates to dissatisfied customers. Some sales will be returned for credit or refund, the price on others will be adjusted, and some sales on account will prove uncollectible. Which specific transactions will be in those categories cannot be known at the time they are recorded.

Thus, revenue for a period is measured by deducting from the invoice price of sales an estimate of the total of doubtful accounts, discounts, returns, and allowances or adjustments that are expected to reduce the amounts to be received from the sales. Alternatively, revenue is recorded in the amount of invoice prices and an expense is recorded in the same period for estimated adjustments or uncollectible accounts. Accounts receivable are carried in a balance sheet at estimated net realizable value by deducting those same items from the face amount of receivables.

For many companies, the adjustments and uncollectible accounts are insignificant in relation to revenue and receivables, and so they are not recorded. That fact does not eliminate management's responsibility for periodically making the necessary estimates, so as to confirm that conditions have not changed.

The various deductions from sales and accounts receivable are normally accounted for separately, not only because the bookkeeping is more convenient but also because the separate amounts often provide useful information. In financial statements, revenue may be reported net of the deductions or the deductions may be shown separately, reducing "gross sales" to "net sales." Some companies report the deductions among the expenses in an income statement on the theory that discounts and uncollectible accounts are a financial expense and allowances for unsatisfactory goods are a product expense. In principle, however, revenue deductions are different from expenses that involve past, present, or future expenditures of funds. In auditing, as well as in accounting, they ideally belong in the revenue–receivables segment rather than in the expense–payables segment.

1. *Doubtful Accounts.*   Uncollectible accounts should be written off as soon as they are recognized as such, but usually they cannot be identified until long after the related sales. Therefore, an estimate of the uncollectible accounts included in accounts receivable at a balance sheet date is needed to measure revenue of a period (or the expense related to revenue) and net realizable value of accounts receivable. The estimate is customarily recorded as an allowance for doubtful accounts, which is deducted from accounts receivable in a balance sheet.

An allowance for doubtful accounts may be estimated by a formula, such as a percentage of sales for the period or of accounts receivable at the end of the period. A formula is convenient and practical for calculating periodic additions to the allowance, but it is a tool, not a principle. The appropriateness of a formula must be checked from time to time by a judgmental evaluation of the collectibility of the receivables themselves.

The basic tool for evaluating collectibility of accounts receivable is an "aging" analysis that lists each individual account item according to the period of time it has been outstanding. The usefulness of the aging process is based on the presumption that the longer an account remains outstanding, the less likely it is to be collected. Although not always true, that presumption is broadly valid.

Aging is only a starting point for evaluating collectibility of accounts receivable. The age of an account is not in itself a conclusive basis for evaluation. "Aged" accounts receivable should be examined by people who are knowledgeable about the company, its customers, and the economic and business factors affecting both, and those knowledgeable people should estimate the probable total of accounts receivable that may ultimately prove uncollectible. That estimate cannot be precise, but experienced credit executives whose past judgments have been confirmed or corrected by experience can be relied on to produce practically useful results.

There are two methods of handling the accounting entries for doubtful and uncollectible accounts. Under one, uncollectible accounts are written off against revenue, and the balance of the allowance account is adjusted from time to time as new estimates are made. Under the other, accounts written off as uncollectible reduce both accounts receivable and the allowance, and the allowance is replenished by a periodic journal entry charging revenue. Collections on accounts previously written off are usually added to the allowance for doubtful accounts.

2. *Sales Returns and Price Adjustments.* Sales returns are cancellations of earlier sales and involve return of merchandise. Price adjustments or allowances are credits to customers for errors in pricing, shipments of the wrong merchandise, defects in quality, shortages in shipments, and the like. Most companies that produce standard items permit customers to return unwanted goods. Even those whose product is specially designed or custom built, and therefore not usually returnable, must sometimes allow a price adjustment to a dissatisfied customer. Product warranties or other guarantees may involve a price concession instead of repairing or replacing the product. Whether the policy of a company is limited or generous, both revenue and accounts receivable are overstated to the extent that they include sales of items that will be returned or prices that will be adjusted, and both should be reduced by an allowance for returns and price adjustments.

Evaluating the adequacy of an allowance for returns and adjustments can be based in part on recent experience. However, that previous experience should be tempered by knowledge of recent economic conditions and sales policies that may significantly affect returns. Sometimes returned goods may unexpectedly become a significant problem. *For example:*

A supplier to automobile manufacturers produced and shipped a product according to schedules of estimated requirements set forth in a "blanket purchase order" from a customer's purchasing agent. Then automobile sales slumped, production schedules were cut back, and the customer returned unneeded inventory equal to more than a month's sales. That return alone wiped out more than 10% of the supplier's gross profit and most of the net income for the year.

Late in a fiscal year, a distributor of a number of lines of consumer goods adopted a "substitution" policy: instead of notifying a customer that an item ordered was out of stock, the company simply substituted and shipped another similar item. A few months later, volume of returned goods began to grow sharply as customers returned the unwanted substitutes.

As those examples illustrate, only people thoroughly acquainted with a company's marketing and sales policies and economic circumstances can estimate reliably the amount needed as an allowance for returned goods and price adjustments.

Estimated returns of goods should be accounted for by reversing the sales entries: sales and accounts receivable should be reduced by the amount of the sale price, and cost of goods sold should be reduced by the cost of merchandise expected to be returned to inventory. Where the effect on receivables and inventories is not significant, the accounting entries are often shortcut by merely reducing sales and receivables by the amount of the gross profit on estimated returns.

3. *Sales Discounts.* Discounts are adjustments of sale prices and should be deducted from both sales and accounts receivable. Three classes of discounts are commonly encountered: trade discounts, quantity discounts, and cash discounts. Trade discounts are ways of setting prices for different classes of buyers. Quantity discounts, as the name implies, are price reductions that vary with the quantity ordered. Both kinds are usually deducted in invoicing and therefore are excluded from amounts initially recorded as sales and accounts receivable. Neither trade discounts nor quantity discounts treated in that way cause accounting problems, and an allowance for trade or quantity discounts is normally not needed.

Cash discounts are offered to buyers to induce prompt payment. Most buyers try to take cash discounts because the effective rate of discount is high in relation to the cost of money, but not all discounts are taken. Technically, sales for a period should be reduced by cash discounts taken plus estimated discounts yet to be taken, and accounts receivable at the end of the period should be reduced by the estimated related cash discounts to be taken in the future. However, cash discounts are seldom material in relation to either revenue or accounts receivable. Therefore, cash discounts taken are sometimes classified as "other expense" rather than as a reduction of revenue, and discounts not yet taken are ignored if not material in amount.

4. *Other Revenue Reductions.* Less common deductions from revenue, accounts receivable, or both include disallowed costs plus related contractors' fees on government contracts and "unrealized" losses on translation of foreign currency receivables into terms of domestic currency. A company's marketing and sales policies may also result in other allowances or adjustments of selling price and receivables. Whatever the specific nature of the allowance, the accounting principles are the same as those already described, and someone knowledgeable about the circumstances of the adjustment or allowance should estimate the amount by which receivables and revenue should be reduced.

Adjustment of Estimates

Measuring revenue and receivables involves numerous estimates, which often prove inaccurate and require correction in later periods. APB Opinions No. 9 and 20 (*AICPA Prof. Stds.,* vol. 3, Sections 2010 and 1051 to 1051B) require accounting for changes in estimates as elements of current or future revenue rather than as corrections of revenue of the period in which the original estimate was made. The only exception to that rule is that revenue of prior periods should be restated for significant errors stemming from mathematical mistakes, mistakes in applying accounting principles, or oversight or misuse of facts that existed in the earlier periods. Changes based on new information, later developments, or better judgment are not corrections of errors but changes in estimates to be accounted for currently or prospectively.

LONG-TERM TRANSACTIONS

Elements of transactions that extend over more than a year often complicate the basic process of determining the timing and amount of revenue recognition. The sale itself is often relatively less important in some of those transactions than in a typical short-term revenue transaction, and the sale basis of revenue recognition is not useful in some kinds of long-term transactions. This chapter is devoted to problems of revenue recognition; problems of cost recognition are discussed in other chapters, but some aspects of costs are summarized here because they are inseparable from the accounting principles applicable to revenue.

The accounting profession has issued a number of pronouncements affecting recognition of revenue in long-term transactions:

"Government Contracts," Chapter 11 of Accounting Research Bulletin (ARB) No. 43 (1953; *AICPA Prof. Stds.*, vol. 3, Sections 4041, 4042, and 4043).

ARB No. 45, *Long-Term Construction-Type Contracts* (1955; *AICPA Prof. Stds.*, vol. 3, Section 4031).

APB Opinion No. 7, *Accounting for Leases in Financial Statements of Lessors* (1966; *AICPA Prof. Stds.*, vol. 3, Section 4051).

"Installment Method of Accounting," paragraph 12 of APB Opinion No. 10, *Omnibus Opinion—1966 (AICPA Prof. Stds.*, vol. 3, Section 4020).

"Amortization of Debt Discount and Expense or Premium," paragraphs 16 and 17 of APB Opinion No. 12, *Omnibus Opinion—1967 (AICPA Prof. Stds.*, vol. 3, Section 5361).

APB Opinion No. 21, *Interest on Receivables and Payables* (1971; *AICPA Prof. Stds.*, vol. 3, Sections 4111 and 4111A).

APB Opinion No. 27, *Accounting for Lease Transactions by Manufacturer or Dealer Lessors* (1972; *AICPA Prof. Stds.*, vol. 3, Section 4052).

Accounting for Retail Land Sales (1973), an AICPA Industry Accounting Guide.

Accounting for Profit Recognition on Sales of Real Estate (1973), an AICPA Industry Accounting Guide.

Accounting for Franchise Fee Revenue (1973), an AICPA Industry Accounting Guide.

Those pronouncements are extensive, detailed, and often complicated. It helps in understanding them to keep in mind that, although they have generally emerged from the handling of specific problems, they show a remarkable degree of adherence to the basic principles of revenue recognition already described.

Those basic principles generally require, subject always to the collectibility of the revenue, both an exchange transaction and performance of the activities that earn the revenue. Performance commonly precedes sale in short-term transactions, and sale is normally the key event in recognizing revenue. However, performance following sale or a sales contract is the basis for recognizing unearned and accrued revenue, as described earlier in the chapter.

In long-term transactions, the emphasis often shifts from sale to performance because significant elements of a transaction frequently remain to be performed after sale. Implementing the principles can become extraordinarily complex and often involves difficult judgments about what constitutes performance, when it occurs, and how much revenue pertains to different elements of performance.

The fact that the collection of cash is spread over a long period does not in itself require deferring recognition of revenue. The Opinions and other pronouncements consistently limit application of the installment method, under which revenue is recognized as cash is received, to transactions in which collectibility of the revenue is not reasonably assured (APB Opinion No. 10, paragraph 12). That is because a schedule of cash collections is seldom related to either sale or performance, the bases in principle for recognizing revenue. If the collectibility of the sale price can be reasonably anticipated, revenue should be recognized as soon as an exchange occurs and performance is complete or virtually complete, even though the sale price is collectible over several years and income tax is payable as installments are collected.

Long-Term Contracts

Long-term contracts have become an increasingly important feature of business activity in recent decades. Construction of a ship, a large building, or a nuclear power plant may extend over several years; development of an airport control system or an urban transit system may take a decade; contracts for sophisticated research may also cover long periods.

Customarily, a pattern of payments is negotiated as part of a long-term contract. The payment pattern may range all the way from full payment in advance to no payment until satisfactory completion of the contract, but it usually involves a series of "progress payments."

Recognizing revenue from many kinds of long-term contracts at the time of sale or delivery—the point considered most significant in short-term transactions—is unsatisfactory because it produces fluctuating revenue and net income that do not fairly represent the actual course of economic activity. Nor is the pattern of payments a good basis for revenue recognition because it is negotiated on the basis of the financial needs of buyer and seller, which do not necessarily reflect performance under a contract.

If possible, recognizing revenue based on the pattern of actual performance under a contract is preferable. The profession formally recommended in ARB No. 45 (*AICPA Prof. Stds.*, vol. 3, paragraph 4031.15) that revenue on long-term contracts be recognized as work progresses by the percentage-of-completion method if "estimates of costs to complete and extent of progress toward completion of long-term contracts are reasonably dependable." The completed-contract method is preferable if "lack of dependable estimates or inherent hazards cause forecasts to be doubtful."

Since ARB No. 45 was published in 1955, companies have increasingly been expected to use the percentage-of-completion method because growing sophistication of management and better information systems have increased management's ability to plan and manage long-term projects. Inability to prepare dependable estimates of cost to complete contracts is therefore increasingly considered substandard practice. Even if "inherent hazards" of contracts or other factors beyond management control make recognizing income imprudent until contracts are completed, management is expected to prepare and use estimates of cost to complete to evaluate, among other items, *the possibility of a loss on a contract*. Under either method, *an indicated loss* must be recorded.

Unit Price Method

Many long-term contracts cover production of a number of units—for instance, fifty airplanes—at a specified price per unit. In those cases, revenue is recognized as in any other sale: in the amount of the specified price as each unit is delivered. Costs must be allocated to units completed, in process, and yet to be started; those allocation problems are discussed in Chapter 11. Unit price accounting is often thought to be apart from the subject of long-term contract accounting, but it is not: unit price contracts are equally subject to the uncertainties of estimates of cost to complete and the requirement that any losses be anticipated and recorded.

Percentage-of-Completion Method

Under the percentage-of-completion method of accounting, revenue and accounts receivable are recognized in proportion to the degree of completion of a contract. A common procedure is to recognize as revenue the same fraction of the total contract price as the costs incurred to date bear to the estimated total cost to complete the contract: the "cost-to-cost" method. Occasionally, some other basis for recording percentage of completion is more accurate, reliable, or convenient: for example, architects' or engineers' estimates of stage of completion or a physical measure of stage of completion such as the number of production operations completed. Different estimates of stage of completion can be used to corroborate each other.

Ordinarily, if at any time the estimated total cost to complete exceeds the total contract price, thus indicating a loss on the contract, the entire loss should be recognized. However, anticipating the entire loss may not be required if the loss contract is one of several related contracts that together are expected to produce a profit, or if the contract was intentionally taken at a predicted loss without irrevocable delivery commitments. (In the latter case, the contract may be likened to a research and development "cost-sharing" contract.) In either instance, the rationale for taking the loss contract, and for recognizing the loss on a percentage-of-completion basis, should be explicit and documented.

The key to percentage-of-completion accounting is the estimate of cost to complete. It is often a difficult and perplexing key. Technical engineering and production problems abound in attempting to foresee with reasonable accuracy the length of time and magnitude of effort that will be needed to complete a contract to the satisfaction of the customer. Even with those aspects resolved as well as possible, numerous accounting questions and problems can arise. The following paragraphs give a few examples.

Should material costs be included in costs incurred? On some kinds of contracts, all or most of the material is purchased at one time, sometimes before work is started. If material costs were 70% of the total contract cost, for example, and all materials were purchased in advance, including material costs incurred in the cost-to-cost percentage-of-completion formula could result in recognizing 70% of the revenue and related gross profit before work even began. Conversely, in engineering/construction contracts, the major elements of material and subcontract costs are likely to occur late in the period of performance. To avoid either kind of bias, revenue can be recognized as consisting of two elements. The first is simply reimbursement for costs incurred, and the second is the profit on the contract. The second element can be recorded on the basis of a rational measure of performance, most often the ratio of labor cost or labor man-hours incurred to total estimated labor cost or man-hours. Some contractors analyze total contract profit into elements related to material cost, engineering cost, construction cost, and the like and recognize revenue on separate percentages of completion of the various elements.

Should a learning curve be anticipated? In unit price contracts, the first unit produced costs significantly more to construct than the thirtieth, and the thirtieth costs more than the seventieth, because efficiency improves with repetition and experience. Some contractors anticipate a "learning curve," both in bidding for contracts and in estimating cost to complete. Others estimate cost to complete by simply extrapolating the cost of the first few units over all units under contract. Disregarding the learning curve results in conservative (high) estimates of cost to complete, thus deferring some or all of the profit on the contract until later stages of completion. When the learning curve can be shown to exist on the basis of the client's past performance on similar contracts, it is a factor that can be taken into account. If potential production problems involving threatened or implied additional costs call for esti-mating higher later costs, those facts should also be recognized and taken into account explicitly.

How many separate but related contracts may be treated as one for accounting purposes? Often a contract is deliberately accepted at a loss because of related profitable contracts. Those related contracts may ac-tually be approved by the customer before the contractor accepts the first, they may be informally promised by the customer, or they may merely be hoped for. Recognizing revenue on the basis of the estimated cost to complete all related contracts is often appropriate if one or more of the group of contracts is deliberately undertaken at a loss that may be considered an investment in the other contracts. It is, however, often extremely difficult to assess the probability that the related contracts will be obtained. Only reasonable certainty of performing profitably in the near future on related contracts actually received can justify ignor-ing a probable loss on a contract.

How should incentive provisions be accounted for? Many contracts contain schedules of rewards and penalties for exceeding or falling short of various performance standards. Determining when they should be reflected in revenue is often difficult. Usually they are ignored until the later stages of contract completion when the likelihood that they will take effect becomes reasonably assured.

How can the effects of price redetermination and renegotiation be anticipated? Many government contracts and some non-government ones contain provisions for audit of contract costs and redetermination of the contract price based on allowed and disallowed costs. For many years, government contracting agencies, the accounting profession, and interested contractors have been trying to reduce areas of uncertainty in contract costing, but contract costs still remain largely a subject for negotiation. Allocating overhead is a particularly difficult matter: for example, allocating between contract and non-contract activities and between present and future periods. Contract price adjustments result-ing from redetermination should be anticipated and reflected in reve-nue, but in practice that is often difficult to do.

Percentage-of-completion accounting for revenue usually requires several separate balance sheet accounts. An "unbilled receivable" is normally used to record revenue recognized. As bills are prepared, appropriate amounts are transferred from the unbilled receivable to an account receivable. Progress payments received are kept separately in an appropriate account. Accounts receivable, unbilled receivables, and progress payments received are usually disclosed separately in a balance sheet.

Completed-Contract Method

Under the completed-contract method of accounting, no revenue or receivable is recognized until a contract is completed or virtually completed. Until then, only expected losses are recognized. Costs incurred and progress payments received are accumulated and may be offset against each other in a balance sheet to show the net investment or net excess receipts on individual contracts. Consistent with contract cost accounting under the methods described above, and contrary to cost accounting principles for inventories in general (Chapter 11), general and administrative expenses are usually accumulated and deferred as assets until the contract is completed and revenue is recognized. (The reason is that general and administrative expenses are reimbursable under terms of most contracts.) Unless a contractor has numerous contracts that are continually being completed, the completed-contract method results in fluctuating revenue and net income.

Cost Accounting Standards Board

In 1970, the U. S. Government created the Cost Accounting Standards Board (CASB) and gave it the power to set uniform accounting rules for government contract costing. By mid-1975, the CASB had issued a number of standards. Most of them articulated long-held generally accepted accounting principles, but some mandated one among several formerly acceptable alternatives. The CASB standards have the force of law, and—while they technically apply only to government contracts—they may be expected to exercise an authoritative influence over all contract accounting.

Revenue and Long-Term Receivables

Long-term receivables from customers often complicate revenue recognition by raising problems of both collectibility and timing of revenue. A long collection period usually makes estimating collectibility more difficult than for short-term receivables, and the continuing relationship between buyer and seller often obscures whether or not the revenue is fully earned at the time of sale. Often the question is how much revenue to recognize at time of sale and how much to recognize later.

Factors that may affect revenue recognition in long-term transactions include (1) difficulty of estimating uncollectible accounts for some kinds of installment receivables, including those for retail land sales and franchise fees, (2) contractual requirements for significant performance by a seller after sale, especially if significant costs may be incurred long after a sale but before the related receivable is fully collected, and (3) effective interest rates that differ significantly from those specified in notes or contracts receivable.

Difficulty of Estimating Collectibility

The principle for recognizing revenue from sales involving long-term receivables is the same as for sales involving short-term receivables. The amount of revenue and related cost is determined by estimating amounts of uncollectible accounts, discounts, returns, and other allowances. The installment method of recognizing revenue, though widely used in computing taxable income for federal income tax purposes, rarely applies. The installment method, which recognizes gross profit on the basis of collections of cash, applies only if ". . . receivables are collectible over an extended period of time and, because of the terms of the transactions or other conditions, there is no reasonable basis for estimating the degree of collectibility" [APB Opinion No. 10, paragraph 12, footnote no. 8 (*AICPA Prof. Stds.*, vol. 3, paragraph 4020.01, footnote no. 1)]. Even then, the cost recovery method, which recognizes equal amounts of revenue and expense as cash is collected but no profit until all costs are recovered, may be preferable to the installment method.

The AICPA has published three Industry Accounting Guides dealing with industries where both collectibility and timing of revenue recognition are frequent problems. They are *Accounting for Retail Land Sales, Accounting for Profit Recognition on Sales of Real Estate,* and *Accounting for Franchise Fee Revenue.* The Guides are lengthy and detailed and should be studied carefully by anyone concerned with those specific subjects.

The Guides affirm, in different words, the principle that sales should be recognized when an exchange takes place and performance is substantially complete, and that an estimate of uncollectible amounts should be made. The installment basis is rejected by two of the Guides unless "collection is not reasonably assured" (*Land Sales,* paragraph 17, and *Franchise Fee Revenue,* pages 9 and 10). Detailed conditions for "reasonable assurance" are spelled out in the *Land Sales* Guide.

The installment and cost recovery methods are used if revenue cannot be recognized at the time of sale because collectibility of receivables cannot be reasonably estimated. Those methods cannot adequately account for revenue deferred to await significant performance by a seller after sale—they are unrelated to questions of performance except as delayed or unsatisfactory performance may adversely affect collectibility of receivables. Methods that recognize revenue on the basis of performance are discussed in the next section.

Performance by Seller After Sale

Revenue should not be recognized before it is earned. Therefore, revenue earned by activities occurring after the time of sale should be recognized on the basis of performance of those activities, regardless of whether a related receivable is long- or short-term. Transportation services, rent, and subscriptions to periodicals are examples, described earlier in the chapter, of revenue recognition based on performance rather than sale. The Accounting Guides referred to above contain examples of long-term receivables which have been discussed recently in the AICPA literature.

Unearned revenue should be recorded if amounts related to a long-term receivable are not fully earned at the time of sale. For example, the Guide on *Retail Land Sales* specifies that part of the sale price for a lot be allocated to the sale of the unimproved land and part to the constructed improvements required by the contract. For want of a better method, the Guide requires that allocation of revenue be based on total expected cost—cost incurred and estimated to be incurred. The Guide on *Profit Recognition on Sales of Real Estate* calls for deferring all or part of the profit on a sale if the seller "continues to be involved" with the property by managing it, developing it, arranging financing, guaranteeing a return, and the like.

The same principle, but with a slightly different explanation, is described in the Guide on *Franchise Fee Revenue,* pages 4 to 9. The Guide rejects spreading the fee pro rata over the life of the franchise agreement on the grounds that a franchisor performs his obligations early in the franchise relationship, long before the end of the agreement. Separate fees and royalties normally compensate the franchisor for continuing services rendered after the franchise is established. Recognizing the franchise fee as revenue at the inception of a franchise relationship was similarly rejected because the sale of a franchise normally requires certain services that remain largely unperformed at inception.

The Franchise Committee in effect broadened the definition of "sale" to include substantial performance of a franchisor:

> Substantial performance as to the franchisor means that (1) he has no remaining obligation or intent—by agreement, trade practice or operation of law—to refund any cash already received or to excuse nonpayment of any unpaid notes; (2) substantially all of the initial services of the franchisor required by the contract have been performed; and (3) any other conditions which affect consummation of the sale transaction have been met. [Page 8]

Since performance is incorporated into the definition of a sale, the total initial franchise fee is recognized as revenue at one time, rather than being spread over time as is revenue allocated to improvements of land in land sales contracts.

The Committee's solution to its particular problem is probably satisfactory, but it should not become a precedent because of its extremely limited application. That is, accepted principles of revenue recognition contain two prerequisites for recognition: an exchange and performance of the earning activities. The Committee in effect has rolled the two into a single standard, a procedure that will cause significant problems if a sale occurs in one accounting period and the related performance occurs in another. To describe a franchisor's performance as "consummation of the sale transaction" does no particular harm because of the nature of a franchise transaction: it usually is completed at a fairly specific point. In principle, however, distinguishing a sale from later performance by a seller is preferable. A principle that recognizes some revenue at sale and some at performance not only applies generally but also avoids the confusion that could result from attempting to stretch a "sale" over several periods.

Revenue Recognition and Effective Interest Rates

The accounting profession was concerned a few years ago about transactions in which the parties negotiate a price that appears to include two elements: an exchange price of the product bought and sold, and interest on the use of money that is inherent in the right to defer all or part of the payment for a prolonged period. Recording the entire sale price as revenue at the time of sale results in recognizing unearned interest as revenue. The same concern applies to other transactions involving long-term receivables in which the parties either specify no interest rate or specify a rate that differs significantly from the going rate of interest for receivables of the same general terms and risk.

If no interest factor is specified by the parties to a transaction that clearly involves the long-term use of money, interest must be approximated or imputed, a matter involving difficult judgments. APB Opinion No. 21, *Interest on Receivables and Payables (AICPA Prof. Stds., vol. 3, Sections 4111 and 4111A)*, describes the possible consequences of a significant difference between the rate of interest specified in a receivable and the prevailing interest rate: "Unless the note is recorded at its present value . . . the sales price and profit to a seller in the year of the transaction and the purchase price and cost to the buyer are misstated, and interest income and interest expense in subsequent periods are also misstated" (paragraph 4111.01). The Opinion gives an example of imputation in paragraph 4111A.01.

The difference between the present value and the face amount of a receivable is a discount or premium. It should be amortized so that interest from the receivable is recognized at a constant rate on the outstanding balance of the receivable until fully collected. That rate is the discount rate used to compute present value of the receivable, and the accounting is the so-called interest method [APB Opinion No. 12 (*AICPA Prof. Stds.*, vol. 3, paragraphs 5361.01 and .02)]. Other methods that result in essentially the same interest income may be used. For example, the method known as "sum of the months' digits" or "Rule of 78" (the sum of the digits 1 through 12 equals 78) usually produces results comparable to those of the interest method. Straight-line amortization of a discount or premium should not be used if the result is materially different from that of the interest method.

Opinion No. 21 recognizes that determining present value of a long-term receivable is often difficult. It permits measuring revenue from a sale in exchange for a long-term receivable by approximating either the sale price of the asset sold or the market value of the receivable, whichever is the more clearly determinable. If neither can be estimated with reasonable accuracy, the present value of the receivable may be determined by discounting the interest and principal at an imputed rate of interest. The Opinion describes the factors to be considered in choosing an imputed rate, specifying that it should normally not be less than "the rate at which the debtor can obtain financing of a similar nature from other sources at the date of the transaction" (paragraph 4111.12).

Revenue from Leases

Rent revenue is normally recognized as it is earned, that is, as time passes, and unearned rent or accrued rent receivable is recorded when the rent collected does not correspond to rent revenue earned. That method of accounting for lease revenue is often called the "operating method."

However, some lease transactions are accounted for as having the substance of financing the sale of the leased property. A simple example shows the major characteristics of the two different methods. The assumed facts illustrated are:

> Company A manufactures a piece of equipment at a cost of $35,000 and has it available for sale or lease at January 1, 19x1.
>
> The equipment has an estimated useful life of five years and has no scrap value.

Operating Method

On January 1, 19x1, Company A leases the equipment to Company B for five years, beginning January 1, 19x1, and ending December 31, 19x5, for $10,000 annually payable each year in advance. Company A uses the operating method; it recognizes revenue as the rent is earned and depreciates the asset by a straight-line method based on the five-year estimated life, resulting in a profit in each of the five years:

Rent revenue	$10,000
Depreciation of equipment	7,000
Income from leased property	$ 3,000

Company A's profit for the five years totals $15,000.

Financing Method

Company A uses the financing method, which accounts for the lease as equivalent to the sale of the property, resulting in a long-term receivable from Company B. Company A recognizes an immediate gross profit of $6,700, representing the difference between cost ($35,000) and the present value of the five payments using a rate of 10% as the rate of discount ($41,700). This is equivalent to the normal selling price. Interest on the receivable is then recorded as follows:

Year	Uncollected Receivable at December 31	Interest Earned
19x1	$34,870	$3,170
19x2	27,356	2,486
19x3	19,019	1,735
19x4	10,000	909
19x5	-0-	-0-
Total interest		$8,300

The total income is the same under the financing (sales) method ($6,700 plus $8,300 interest = $15,000) as under the operating method, but it is recognized in a different pattern—more in the earlier and less in the later years of the lease period.

Lease Transaction Variations

The example illustrates the two basic methods. However, they may appear in combination depending upon possible variations in the transactions. *For example:*

1. Company A might have leased the equipment to Company B and then assigned the lease (not the property) to Company C for $41,700. Company A could recognize the gross profit immediately by treating the transactions as a sale and an assignment of a receivable. Company C would recognize the interest earned from the long-term receivable as it is earned.

2. Company A might have sold the equipment for $41,700 to Company C (a finance or leasing company) which in turn would lease the equipment to Company B under the same terms, producing the same aggregate accounting result.

3. If Company C borrowed the purchase price (or a portion of it) at an effective rate of less than 10%, a transaction known as a "leveraged lease" would result (see below).

Leveraged Leases

In a "leveraged lease" transaction a lessor finances a large part of his cost with a nonrecourse third-party loan with terms that effectively relieve him from actual or potential liability because the lender is willing to rely entirely on the security of the property and the lease. The lessor-borrower's investment, which may be as little as 20% of cost, is recovered in the early years of the lease through a combination of rent receipts and income tax savings resulting from deductions for interest and accelerated depreciation. It is argued that the lessor should recognize revenue from the transaction in proportion to his unrecovered net investment, since that investment is his only economic contribution to the transaction and he has no direct liability. In many cases, however, that theory must be substantially qualified or is even negated by the test of collectibility, because full utilization of the tax benefits and the projected cash flow sufficient to completely recover the investment cannot be considered reasonably assured in the early years of a lease. The issue remains unresolved. The SEC's ASR No. 132 requires that the transaction have sufficient substance to support lease accounting.

Choice of Method

The methods of accounting for lease revenue and their combinations cannot be applied indiscriminately. APB Opinion No. 7, *Accounting for Leases in Financial Statements of Lessors (AICPA Prof. Stds.,* vol. 3, Section 4051), and APB Opinion No. 27, *Accounting for Lease Transactions by Manufacturer or Dealer Lessors* (Section 4052), describe the circumstances in which each type of accounting is appropriate. Presently there is no pronouncement that covers leveraged leases.

In general, revenue should be recognized by the operating method if a lessor retains significant risks or rewards of ownership or is unable to estimate reasonably the collectibility of amounts due or amounts of future costs under the terms of the lease; many leases obligate the lessor to service the equipment. Accounting for leases as equivalent to sales, that is, by the financing method, is an example of accounting for the substance of a transaction rather than its form when it appears that a sale by a manufacturer or dealer has really taken place. That often requires dividing a transaction into its elements—an element of sale and an element of long-term financing—and accounting for the elements separately. Banks and financing and leasing companies that purchase property for the purpose of financing a long-term lessee normally use the financing method for accounting purposes, but might use the operating method for income taxes (including accelerated depreciation); that combination would give rise to deferred income taxes (see Chapter 13).

The APB Opinions referred to above are complicated, and a reader should consult them, particularly to understand fully the accounting for leases as financing or sale transactions. For example, a manufacturer- or dealer-lessor must account for a lease transaction with an independent lessee as a sale if at the time of entering into the transaction (1) collectibility of the payments required from the lessee is reasonably assured, (2) no important uncertainties exist concerning the amount of costs yet to be incurred under the lease, and (3) any *one* of the following conditions is present:

(i) The lease transfers title to the property to the lessee by the end of its fixed, noncancelable term; or

(ii) The lease gives the lessee the option to obtain title to the property without cost or at a nominal cost by the end of the fixed, noncancelable term of the lease; or

(iii) The leased property, or like property, is available for sale, and the sum of (1) the present value of the required rental payments by the lessee under the lease during the fixed, noncancelable term of the lease (excluding any renewal or other option) and (2) any related investment tax credit retained by the lessor (if realization of such credit is assured beyond any reasonable doubt) is equal to or greater than the normal selling price or, in the absence thereof, the fair value (either of which may be less than cost) of the leased property or like property; or

(iv) The fixed, noncancelable term of the lease (excluding any renewal option) is substantially equal to the remaining economic life of the property. (This test cannot be complied with (1) by estimating an economic life substantially equal to the noncancelable term if this is unrealistic or (2) if a material contingent residual interest is retained in the property.) [Paragraph 4052.04]

Accounting for a lease as equivalent to a sale and accounting for leveraged leases have the effect of accelerating the recognition of income in periods earlier than under the operating method, a result sometimes called "front-ending." As long as they truly reflect the substance of the transactions, they are superior to the operating method. Whatever the pattern of revenue recognition, its propriety must always be subjected to the collectibility test. Revenue should not be recognized unless there are no significant contingencies for repayment or inability to collect.

• TYPICAL TRANSACTION SYSTEMS AND INTERNAL CONTROL

TYPICAL TRANSACTION

There are seven steps in the initiation and execution of every kind of sale. Sometimes the steps may be simple, close together, and even combined with one another; sometimes one or more of them may be protracted and complex. The following is a generalized description of the steps and related controls an auditor might expect to find. Records and controls for activities such as the planning of a product, seeking customers, and convincing them to buy are operational activities not closely linked to accounting; their cost is accounted for in the selling expense segment rather than the revenue segment.

Receipt and Acceptance of Customer's Order

A customer's order acts as a three- or four-part authorization for making a sale: receipt of an order is a customer's authorization; acceptance of the order after review of its terms is the sales department's authorization; review for credit results in authorization by financial management to extend credit to a customer; sometimes review by production is necessary for authorization to make quality and delivery commitments. Those authorizations are a "basic control," in the terminology used in Chapter 3; they should be documented by some kind of initialing or distinctive stamping of the order form.

Preparation of Order Form

A standard form fills an operational need to facilitate the uniformity of order processing, but the form also serves to establish initial control over an order and its further processing. That documentation is best done as early in the system as possible, preferably as soon as the order is received and before the first step is completed. Order forms should be under effective control. One control is numerical sequence, established by using prenumbered forms. Another is a holding file, such as a backlog listing of open customers' orders, or an open file of control copies of order forms from which fully processed orders are deleted from time to time.

Confirmation of Order

Good control over error or misunderstanding requires confirming an order with the customer when that is feasible. That is a "validity check" in the classification of controls in Chapter 3. In many businesses, the substantial cost of changing or cancelling an order after it has been processed more than justifies the cost of the confirmation procedure; in others, a formal contract is required. In some companies, however, order processing time is so short that confirmation is not practicable; in others, the cost of confirming exceeds all possible value.

Preparation of Execution Instructions

In many systems, the instructions for all the steps necessary to execute a sale completely can be prepared on one form in one step. If considerable work is involved in execution, such as fabrication to a customer's specifications, it may be necessary to prepare execution instructions in several steps. Generally speaking, the steps in executing an order are requisitioning, packing, shipping, and invoicing. A customer's order may be requisitioned from stored finished goods inventory, from the factory by means of a production order, or from suppliers by means of a purchase order. A packing slip is needed to instruct the proper department to gather and prepare the order for shipment. A shipping order is needed for the shipping department to prepare routing, schedule necessary transportation, and authorize release of the goods. Each department needs sufficient copies of the instructions to enable it to advise related departments of its action and also to retain in its own files evidence of performance.

Control over execution should be through numerical sequence, a holding file, or both. If execution involves a number of steps, a holding file is preferable because it affords ready access to information on uncompleted transactions. In many systems it is useful to prepare and partially complete the invoice form as part of this step; the invoice form can then serve as a holding file for control over the other execution steps. Sometimes invoices are not prepared until requisitioning, packing, and shipping are completed; then a copy of the order form serves as a holding file. Either way, the control operation consists of matching the control file with notices of performance by each of the executing departments and examining the file periodically to discover and investigate transactions overdue for completion.

Physical Execution: Withdrawal from Stock, Packing, and Shipping

Control within the executing departments is most often operational or supervisory, but there can be accounting control similar to that described in the previous step: a holding file of execution instructions, which are cancelled by notice of performance.

Control outside the executing departments is likewise maintained through comparing documents evidencing performance with the holding file of original execution instructions, by accounting for the numerical sequence of documents, or both.

Completion of Invoice and Billing of Customer

Control over originating an invoice is established by authorization of billing, which is in turn based on proper supporting documents: customer's order, shipping order, and so on. Authorization is often "automated" by originating an invoice automatically when the supporting documents are accumulated. Control over the accuracy and propriety of invoice data should be provided: terms, prices, extensions, footings, and the like should be double-checked. Double-checking can be done by qualified persons, or some or all of it may be mechanized or computerized. Comparisons and validity checks may also be made to price lists, customer lists, and the original customer order.

Recording for accounting purposes usually begins with this step (except for transactions in which invoicing is a later step, such as unbilled revenue or accrued income). In many modern systems, invoices are recorded as part of the operation that originates them; in others, they must be "posted" to the records. Numerical sequencing and control totals are the most common controls.

Collection of Invoice

Generally, collection of a billing in accordance with its terms may be expected in the ordinary course of business, but controls are needed to identify those that are late, in error, or delinquent. A useful step in the collection process is the preparation of periodic customers' statements of account—a form of validity checking. A further control is provided by aging of accounts receivable and credit department follow-up of overdue accounts. There should be properly qualified approval of write-offs, adjustments, credits, and all other non-cash credits to accounts receivable—an authorization control.

Accounts receivable balances that have been written off should be kept under memorandum control and reviewed by responsible officials from time to time.

Cash receipts typically come in the mail or over the counter, usually accompanied by an identifying sales slip, bill stub, listing, or invoice number. Whatever the form or manner of receipt, documentation should be established at once by listing the pertinent data and establishing control totals: collections by mail should be listed by names and amounts, receipts over the counter should be listed on cash register tapes or counter sales slips recorded in the presence of customers, and receipts from collectors or outside salesmen should be accompanied by listings when received. Restricted access should be established as soon as possible, preferably by depositing all receipts in a bank. Items not suitable for immediate deposit, such as postdated checks or checks made out for improper amounts, should be documented separately and appropriately safeguarded.

Whatever the medium of documentation, it should be controlled by numerical sequence. There may be several different media: counter sales slips from different departments, cashiers' receipts, collectors' or route salesmen's receipts, remittance advices, lists of checks, register tapes, and the like. The documentation from each source of receipt should be controlled by its own numerical sequence. Often, receipts are listed once a day and the date of the list serves as the numerical sequence.

Cash receipts preferably should be processed throughout in identical batches so that the completeness of the processing can be controlled by comparison of the totals of the batches. For example, the total of the initial documentation batch should be compared to the total of the bank deposit batch and to the total of the batch of postings to customers' and other accounts.

Illustrations of Typical Transactions

The seven steps described above are always present, whether in condensed or expanded form. The following are some common examples:

> Over-the-counter retail sales may condense the seven steps into a short personal encounter. The customer orders orally, and the clerk accepts, checking authorized sales terms and perhaps checking the customer's credit standing with the appropriate central department; the sales slip combines all the paperwork, sometimes including the stock withdrawal notice (or the tag removed from the goods to be sold may constitute the requisition); the clerk physically executes the sale; the customer pays, or the sales slip is forwarded to the billing department

for invoicing; control is provided by the prenumbered sales slip or the cash register tape.

In sales under contract, the first three steps may be complex and protracted. There may be requests for proposals, bid preparation, bidding, and extended contract negotiations.

In large sales, such as construction projects, long research projects, or large numbers of items to be constructed and delivered over a period of time, the physical execution step may be extensive.

In providing continuing services, such as electricity or telephone services, the first four steps are performed once for each customer and execution is continuous thereafter. Revenue from rents, royalties, and interest is similar. A system for periodic reporting of the amount of service delivered is needed to initiate the billing.

In transportation services, the billing and collection may come before physical execution and at a different time from the receipt, acceptance, and confirmation of the order. A customer buys a ticket or a token and uses it when he chooses.

Returns

The system must provide for authorization and execution of returns, allowances, and discounts. In the nature of things, these transactions are likely to be less well controlled than the sales transactions: the volume of sales transactions is large enough to permit systemization and discipline, while returns and allowances are likely to be sporadic, problematic, and lacking in common characteristics. Accordingly, it is important to establish accountability over returns and allowances as early as possible.

A routine for preparing receiving reports for *all* goods received (next chapter), including returned goods, is essential. Returned goods may go through the same receiving routine as other receipts or may be processed through a separate receiving area, inspection system, and paperwork system. The returns must then be authorized, that is, reviewed and approved by a responsible official.

Returns should be recorded in the accounts as promptly as possible so as to correct the balances of revenue and accounts receivable. In practice there are often delays in recording returned goods: they must be inspected for condition and alleged defects investigated; correspondence with the customer may be required about the reasons for return, possible substitution, and the like. There is a natural inclination to delay the processing of returns; periodic review of the open file of receiving reports is ordinarily the best means for controlling those tendencies.

Sales allowances are even more difficult to control than returns because they often constitute reductions of invoiced amounts and accounts receivable based on judgment of the validity of customer complaints. They should be controlled by operational policies specifying who may authorize allowances and under what conditions. Forms and reporting procedures should be adopted to establish prompt documentation, authorization, and accountability. Investigation of uncollected receivables should reveal unrecorded allowances.

Accountability

The management function of accountability is aided by adequate documentation of the execution of the basic controls. Exercising the accountability function involves periodic checking on the functioning of the controls.

The numerical sequence of originating documents—customers' orders, sales invoices, counter slips, and so on—should be accounted for to identify missing or misdirected items. The various holding files throughout the system—unfilled customers' orders; unmatched stores' issues, shipping orders, or invoices; and unrecorded returned merchandise reports—should be reviewed regularly and appropriate action taken on items remaining open beyond the usual processing time. The review should be made by someone sufficiently independent and responsible to understand the action that is required and to take it. Evidence of performance should be recorded in logs or other records.

Accounts receivable are the most important of the holding files. At frequent intervals, detailed accounts receivable should be reconciled to the control account; the reconciliation serves as evidence of performance. Statements of account should be sent to customers. Aging analyses should be prepared and reviewed critically by persons responsible and knowledgeable enough to take appropriate action on overdue accounts; they should sign the analyses to record satisfactory completion of the review.

One of the most difficult functions in exercising accountability is comparing unearned revenue accounts with their supporting detail. Occasionally, that can be accomplished by a simple footing of individual customers' account balances—the credit equivalent of accounts receivable (for example, students' advance deposits on tuition and advance payments on contracts or grants). For most unearned revenue accounts, however, the supporting detail is not under accounting control, and the reconciliation task is sometimes so arduous that it is done infrequently.

The usual method of exercising a comparison control for unearned revenue is to establish a "cutoff" date. Thereafter, all tickets received for services delivered (or evidence of subscriptions delivered) are sorted into those purchased before and those purchased after the cutoff date. Those purchased before the cutoff date are priced, and the total is accumulated. After a period of time (often several months) sufficient to allow for the use of substantially all the services purchased before the cutoff date, the balance of the unearned revenue account as of the cutoff date is adjusted to equal the total of the identified services purchased before and unused at the cutoff date.

If development of actual data for comparison with the control of unearned revenue balances is considered impracticable or prohibitively expensive, adequate accountability often can be exercised by computing the statistical relationship of the balance to the volume of services purchased and delivered. Statistical procedures of that nature must be used with caution because unrecognized changes in circumstances may render them invalid.

Disciplinary Controls

The disciplinary controls, particularly restricted access and segregation of duties (internal check), have special significance in the handling of cash, for obvious reasons. Cash and cash records should be safeguarded at every point. Cash should be deposited in a bank account without delay and kept in as secure a place as possible until it is deposited. Cash records should likewise be protected against tampering, physical loss, and destruction.

If the size of a business or organization permits, each of the tasks connected with handling and recording cash should be performed by persons acting independently of one another. Those who list the cash should be independent of those who safeguard it or prepare it for deposit, and both should be independent of those who record amounts in customers' and other accounts; each of those groups should have no other duties related to cash. Someone independent of all of those functions should compare the resulting control totals, should receive and investigate items charged back by the depositary bank, and should handle other correspondence in connection with receipts.

See Chapter 15, "The Cash Segment," for a more detailed discussion of disciplinary controls over cash.

Miscellaneous Income and Receivables

Almost every company has sources of revenue that are incidental to its principal operations. A company selling goods and services may have incidental rents, royalties, sales to employees, and so on; a college, hospital, or investment company may have incidental revenue from sales to outsiders. Records and controls of incidental revenue often tend to be casual. While the cost of control should never exceed its potential benefits, it is good business to guard against the possibility of substantial losses of incidental revenue by establishing controls similar to those outlined for the typical transaction.

LONG-TERM TRANSACTIONS

Long-Term Contracts

The same seven steps of initiation and execution are present in long-term contract transactions as in a typical short-term revenue transaction, but they may be widely separated and almost unrelated. Negotiation of a contract, which is the customer's order, and authorization for its performance may be widely separated in space, time, and personnel from execution of the contract. Billing is likely to follow a schedule specified in the terms of the contract and may have no direct relation to execution of the contract. Execution may be spread over a long period of time, and the point at which it is completed may be difficult to identify. Therefore, recording revenue must be related to recording the performance of the contract, and the controls over recording performance become the controls over recording revenue. Those controls are described in Chapter 11, "The Production Segment."

The basic control over the amount of revenue recorded on the basis of contract performance (percentage-of-completion method) is the estimate of cost to complete. When contracts are initially bid, costs are estimated, contract prices are negotiated, and the ratio between the two is easily established. As costs are incurred under the contract, revenue is usually recorded proportionately. Periodically, cost to complete must be re-estimated: since revenue is fixed (unless contract provisions permit specified changes), a change in estimated cost requires recognizing a change in the ratio of revenue to cost for accounting purposes. Since costs do commonly change, regular, conscientiously prepared estimates are essential.

The more detailed and specific an estimate, the better the control it provides. Years ago, estimates of cost to complete frequently were based on little more than a project engineer's guess about the percentage of completion. An engineer's guess is no longer sufficient, but it frequently serves as a check on the detailed judgments made.

Preferably the estimates should be prepared in detail and subject to accounting and disciplinary controls. The estimates should include detailed analyses of original bills of material, with items still to be obtained priced at currently estimated prices. Initial estimates of various kinds of labor should be analyzed in detail and compared with experience to date. Judgments must be applied in extrapolating current experience into the future. The smaller and more specific the items extrapolated, the smaller the risk of error. The more times a contract is examined and the judgments made and remade, the better the estimates are likely to be.

The preparation of estimates of cost to complete should be systematized, with detailed written systems and procedures and requirements for responsible review and approval of judgments. Each step should be carefully documented to facilitate review and approval. No matter how well organized, or how carefully performed and documented, however, estimates of cost to complete can never be more than estimates. Errors in judgment are inevitable, but the likelihood of error is minimized if judgments are exercised according to a well-established, well-controlled routine.

Other Long-Term Transactions

All the transaction processing steps are also present in installment sales, long-term receivables, franchise transactions, retail land sales, leases, and other long-term transactions. Although the accounting principles may be complicated and difficult to understand, the basic steps in recording and controlling them should not be. The only difference from the typical transaction is that performance of some of the steps is long delayed or spread over several periods. Delayed performance may be evidenced by a buyer's deferred payments, a seller's agreement to provide certain services in the future, or simply the fact that the transactions cover a period of time, as do leases.

The only effect of long-term performance on transaction systems and controls is the obvious one of dealing in longer time periods. There must be reminder lists or holding files of payments due and other contractual steps to be performed to serve as control against omission or delay. Reminder lists and subsystems for periodic computing and recording of the portions of transactions currently eligible for recognition are necessary. And the periodic review of judgments about collectibility, interest factors, future costs, and the like becomes more difficult, more judgmental, and more critical to the accurate measurement of periodic revenue.

• AUDITING PROCEDURES

OBJECTIVES

The objectives of auditing procedures for revenue and receivables are to provide evidential matter (both underlying and corroborative) that is sufficient and competent to give an auditor reasonable assurance that:

Revenue accounts and related income and expense accounts include the transactions that they purport to represent.

Accounts receivable are authentic and probably collectible.

Judgments on which valuations, allowances, and deferred income are based are arrived at rationally and responsibly.

Descriptions, classifications, and related disclosures are adequate and not misleading.

All loss contingencies are identified and recorded or disclosed.

THE AUDIT CYCLE

The revenue–accounts receivable segment, like all the others, must be examined in terms of the full audit cycle described in Chapters 4 and 5. The accounting and control systems must be understood and evaluated in the context of the financial statements taken as a whole. Functional tests must be made, and account balances must be validated by substantive tests as corroborative evidence to provide a basis for an auditor to understand, evaluate, and form an opinion on the accounting principles employed, the reasonableness of revenue, accounts receivable, and related accounts as presented in the financial statements, and the adequacy of the financial disclosures. The full cycle of auditing must be viewed as a whole, integrated process and not as separate steps.

Transaction Reviews

Chapter 5 presents a detailed discussion of how to make a transaction review, how many to make, and how often. A critical factor in efficient and effective transaction reviewing is adequate identification of significant types of transactions. Identifying significant types of transactions in the revenue segment probably calls for more attention than in other segments because the dynamics of marketing and customer service continually create pressures for new types of sales activity or for special treatment of certain transactions. A transaction is a different type for an auditor's purposes if the control processes that affect the accuracy of amounts recorded in the financial statements or the authenticity or collectibility of an account differ from the control processes over other transactions.

If the control processes differ in areas that do not affect the financial statements, the differences can be ignored for audit purposes. Accordingly, the extent of an auditor's interest varies from situation to situation. *For example:*

> Controls over the authorization, execution, and recording of the invoice preparation and billing function are invariably important, and any variation in the handling of those functions and the related control procedures gives rise to a different type of transaction for an auditor's purposes.
>
> Controls over the initial recording of sales orders interest an auditor because they may contribute to the strength of controls over the accounting function, but they are less important than the first example because they are not directly related to entries in the accounts supporting the financial statements.
>
> Sales department controls over the review of sales orders or over the confirmation of orders with customers usually (but not always) have a lower order of importance to an auditor because their effect on the financial statements is still more remote and indirect. They still interest him, nonetheless, because a misunderstanding of a customer's request or a sale on unintended terms could raise questions about the collectibility or authenticity of the resulting receivable.
>
> Controls over statistical analyses of the order backlog might not concern an auditor at all if they have no bearing on his objectives.

Possible different types of transactions cannot be definitely enumerated because of the infinite variety of economic activity that an auditor encounters and the almost equally great variety of possible ways of processing and controlling transactions. A new customer or market might create a different type of transaction in one company but receive identical handling in the mainstream of transactions in a competitor company. One company may have a prescribed uniform system for handling all but exceptional sales, while another company may elect different types of processing and related controls for sales from different departments or sales to different customers. The following list is intended only to suggest the variety of differences that an auditor must be alert to and must evaluate:

> Export sales and domestic sales.
> Partial shipments and complete shipments.

Shipments from stock and shipments on special orders, drop orders, or custom fabrication.

Company-made products and purchased products.

Consignment sales and direct sales.

Packaged goods and bulk goods.

Sales to jobbers and distributors and sales to users.

"Dated" invoices and current invoicing.

"Shipped to one, billed to another" and shipped and billed to same addressee.

Government sales and non-government sales.

Chain store customers and individual customers.

Large, regular customers and small, occasional customers.

Sales to outsiders and sales to affiliates or employees.

Charge sales and cash sales.

Industrial sales and customer sales.

Parts sales to "OEM" customers and sales to distributors or end users.

As more fully described in Chapter 5, a substantial effort to identify significant types of transactions before testing commences is conducive to an efficient and effective audit, but it is not essential. The transaction review itself and other steps in the audit cycle provide means for identifying types of transactions missed in the initial understanding.

Functional Tests

An auditor must identify the control operations and how they work and adapt his program of functional tests accordingly. Also, although each processing step needs controls, their importance to an auditor varies with their relative influence on financial statements, and functional tests must be designed with that relative importance in mind. The following is a generalized example of a representative program of functional tests of a revenue–accounts receivable segment.

Order Control

The procedure for establishing control over customers' orders is usually not of primary importance to an auditor because a lost or overlooked order generally has no accounting significance, and accordingly the procedure need not be tested. In special situations, however, the procedure may be a key link in the series of controls that provide reasonable assurance that all shipments are billed and all bills are for bona fide shipments. In that event, the audit program might call for a functional test such as the following:

Documentation and customer authorization: From the customer order backlog report (or the file of order forms), select x customer orders; trace recorded data to the original customer order and related documents.

Authorization: Examine evidence of sales department and credit department approval.

Instruction Control

The preparation of execution instructions is usually significant because it is the first step in originating an invoice. The functional test of control over that step consists of examining invoices and is usually combined with tests of those same invoices for other purposes. For purposes of illustration, representative program instructions are set forth separately for each step:

Select x invoices at random; trace them to the customer's order; note evidence of double-checking, validity checking, and approval. Trace data on invoice to execution instructions if not prepared simultaneously.

Invoice Control

Contrasted with earlier processing steps, control over the completion of invoices and billing of customers is always essential because it controls the basis for an accounting entry and documentation of accounts receivable. As such, it is the focus for a greater intensity of functional testing. The following functional tests might be called for in an audit program:

Authorization and completeness: Select x invoices; examine supporting customer order and shipping order and trace invoice data thereto. Inspect open file of unmatched orders and shipping reports. Obtain and evaluate explanation for all delayed items. Examine evidence that the file is reviewed regularly for delayed items.

Double-checking and validity checking: Select x invoices; check prices against price lists; check payment terms, discount, and allowances against authorized lists; examine evidence of double-checking and supervisory approval; check account coding.

Control totals: Select x invoices; trace to sales journal and to receivable posting medium. Compare sales journal total to total of accounts receivable posting journal (or to batch controls or other cross-check of accuracy of entry to sales journal). Examine evidence that those comparisons are made on a regular basis, and reviewed and approved by supervisors.

In practice, all of the above tests and those in the earlier examples could be combined in one program instruction and applied to the same sample of invoices. In doing so an auditor must be careful that he does not permit the separate objectives of each to become confused.

Collection Control

Since the financial consequences of controlling customers' payments are obviously important, there should be a functional test of the cash receipts controls. For example:

> Select *x* paid invoices (or cash receipts postings if system does not identify paid invoices); trace to initial documentation listing, to bank deposit duplicate listing, and to detail accounts receivable ledgers; compare totals of initial list, bank deposit, and accounts receivable posting and trace to cash book and general ledger. Note evidence that control totals and comparisons are made regularly, and reviewed and approved by supervisors.

Unit Control

In some accounting systems, numbers of units are an integral part of the system and control is as important as control over dollar amounts. For example, the number of units shipped or billed might be accumulated for extension at an average or standard cost for the cost of goods sold entry. A thorough cradle-to-grave transaction review should identify systems in which control over units is significant. If it is, the functional test of controls over documentation, summarization, and recording of dollar amounts usually can simply be expanded to include unit amounts as well.

Validation Procedures

When auditors think of auditing accounts receivable, they usually think of confirmation by direct communication with debtors. That is because confirmation by direct communication has been one of the very few specifically required generally accepted auditing procedures for more than thirty years, during which it has been the subject of extensive official and unofficial literature of the profession. This emphasis was unfortunate, however, to the extent that disproportionate attention to the confirmation procedure may distort the cumulative, corroborative, interrelated context within which all auditing procedures must be viewed.

Confirmation is one validation procedure among several, just as validation tests are one kind of audit evidence among several. Tests of the sales and accounts receivable cutoff (described later) are also important to validation, and in many instances so is examination of cash receipts after the examination or confirmation date. Confirmation establishes only authenticity of accounts (and not conclusively at that); other procedures are needed to establish collectibility of accounts, however authentic they may be. For that purpose, analytical reviews of the judgments and valuations entering into estimates of collectibility are the critical elements. As with other tests, confirmation procedures contribute to the evaluation of internal control and to analytical reviews, just as other procedures contribute to establishing the authenticity of receivable balances.

Unless internal control weaknesses are found or unless such discontinuities as seasonality or other kinds of fluctuation remove the basis for "reasonable assurance" of continuity, validation tests of receivables are usually made before the year end. The practical necessity and theoretical justification for doing so were discussed in Chapter 4.

Reconciliation of Detail to Control

General ledger control account balances should be compared with totals of individual accounts receivable, discrepancies between the two investigated, and appropriate adjustment made by the client. That is a routine accountability procedure, which should be carried out regularly by the client. An auditor should check trial balances of accounts receivable prepared by the client to the individual ledger accounts in detail or, if internal control is satisfactory, on a test basis. Footings of the trial balance should be checked to the extent deemed appropriate. Reasons for recurring discrepancies between control and detail should be determined and investigated.

Confirmation of Receivable Balances

Confirmation of receivables (including notes, acceptances, and other receivables) by direct communication with debtors is a universally accepted auditing procedure. The applicable professional standard was restated in paragraphs 331.01 and 331.03 of SAS No. 1, issued in 1973, as follows:

> Confirmation of receivables and observation of inventories are generally accepted auditing procedures. The independent auditor who issues an opinion when he has not employed them must bear in mind that he has the burden of justifying the opinion expressed. [Paragraph 331.01]
>
> Confirmation of receivables requires direct communication with debtors either during or after the period under audit; the confirmation date, the

method of requesting confirmations, and the number to be requested are determined by the independent auditor. Such matters as the effectiveness of internal control, the apparent possibility of disputes, inaccuracies or irregularities in the accounts, the probability that requests will receive consideration or that the debtor will be able to confirm the information requested, and the materiality of the amounts involved are factors to be considered by the auditor in selecting the information to be requested and the form of confirmation, as well as the extent and timing of his confirmation procedures. [Paragraph 331.03]

1. Selection of Accounts for Confirmation. On the basis of his review of internal control and of the audit logic described in Chapter 5, an auditor should decide whether all or only part of the accounts should be confirmed and, if the latter, the basis for selecting the accounts to be confirmed. Accounts receivable selected for confirmation should usually include a representative portion of both the dollar amount and the number of accounts; they may include all accounts with balances over a selected amount and a number of smaller accounts taken in numerical or alphabetical sequence, accounts with old unpaid items, and accounts written off during the period under review. In certain circumstances, selection of the accounts to be confirmed may be made by use of statistical sampling methods (Chapter 5). The selection should exclude accounts for which replies to requests for confirmation cannot reasonably be expected, such as those with certain government agencies, foreign concerns, and some large industrial and commercial enterprises that use a voucher or computerized system that makes confirmation impracticable.

An experienced auditor usually confirms accounts that appear unusual. The confirmation of accounts with zero or credit balances should be considered. A credit balance suggests the possibility of an incorrect entry, especially if internal control is weak. Confirmation of an account receivable should not be omitted merely because payments or other credits have been recorded since the confirmation date. Occasionally a client requests that accounts in addition to those selected by the auditor be included among the accounts to be confirmed, usually in the hope that the confirmation request may speed up collection; an auditor may properly accede to those requests.

Accounts and notes receivable that have been discounted or pledged should be confirmed with lenders, so that any liability or contingency is brought to the auditor's attention. Confirming receivables with those with whom they have been discounted or pledged does not preclude an auditor from requesting confirmation from the debtors as well, particularly if the client is responsible for collections.

As a rule, so as to preserve the integrity of the confirmation process, the auditor takes care that his plan for selecting accounts and the accounts actually selected for requesting confirmation of balances are not revealed beforehand to his client. However, if the client does not wish statements or confirmation requests sent to certain debtors, the auditor should be satisfied that there is an adequate reason before acceding to the request. He may wish to employ alternative procedures to satisfy himself, insofar as possible, that those accounts are authentic and accurate in amount. As indicated in Chapter 19, an auditor may not wish to assume the risk of expressing an unqualified opinion in that situation.

Since confirmation is usually a validation test, the basis for extrapolating confirmation results into a conclusion about the total accounts receivable balance must be valid. The logic is either (a) a large enough fraction of the total dollars is confirmed that the materiality of the remainder, or the relative risk of error in it, is negligible or (b) the sample confirmed is representative so that valid inferences about the total can be drawn from it. That conclusion can properly be drawn whether the sample is selected judgmentally or on the basis of statistical sampling. Chapter 5 discusses that point.

The mechanical process of selecting accounts to be confirmed should be controlled by the auditor to maintain the integrity of the validation procedure. If the accounts are maintained in handwritten or machine-written form, he can either scan the accounts and make his selection on the basis of the judgments outlined above or he can use a random selection routine. If the accounts are maintained by computer, he can scan a printout and mark selected accounts for calling out of the computer; alternatively, he can use a computer program to call out some or all of the accounts having the characteristics he has decided to emphasize. That use of the computer is described in Chapter 6.

2. Confirmation Procedures. After selecting the accounts for confirmation, an auditor should observe the following procedures in processing the requests. They are applicable to both negative and positive methods of confirmation (which terms are described and compared in the following sections of this chapter):

> Names, addresses, and amounts shown on statements selected for confirmation should be compared with the debtors' accounts. Thereafter, the auditor should maintain control over statements selected for confirmation until he has mailed them; this does not preclude use of appropriate client personnel to assist the auditor, under his supervision.
>
> Proof that the total of the debtors' accounts from which selection has

been made agrees with the control account should be obtained through adding machine tapes or a computer or accounting machine trial balance printout of individual receivable balances, prepared by the client and tested by the auditor.

Requests for confirmation, together with postage-paid return envelopes addressed to the auditor, should be mailed in envelopes showing the auditor's address as the return address. If the client objects to using the auditor's address, returns may be addressed to the client at a post office box controlled by the auditor, and the post office should be directed to forward mail to the auditor after the box is surrendered.

All requests should be mailed by the auditor; he may use the client's mail room for mechanical processing under his control, but he should himself deposit the completed requests with the Postal Service.

Undelivered requests returned by the post office should be investigated, corrected addresses obtained, and the requests remailed by the auditor.

The purpose of those procedures is not so much to protect against possible fraud on the part of the client (although that possibility is clearly implied) as to preserve the integrity of the confirmation procedure as a valid proof of authenticity. The proof is less conclusive if there is the possibility of accidental or purposeful interference with direct communication with debtors, and an auditor should take all reasonable steps to minimize that possibility.

3. Negative Confirmation. The negative method of confirmation is a request that a debtor communicate directly with an auditor only if the statement balance is considered in any way incorrect. It is the most frequently used method. Since the auditor expects debtors to reply only if they wish to report differences, he may assume that no reply signifies the debtor's acceptance of the balance in the absence of any reason to believe the contrary.

It is important to impress on debtors the necessity for communicating directly with the auditor when discrepancies exist. If an auditor has reason to believe that the negative form of confirmation request will not receive consideration, he should not be satisfied that he has complied with generally accepted auditing procedures in sending out that form of confirmation request. In that respect, paragraph 331.05 of SAS No. 1 states in part:

> ... The negative form is useful particularly when internal control surrounding accounts receivable is considered to be effective, when a large number of small balances are involved, and when the auditor has no reason to believe the persons receiving the requests are unlikely to give them consideration. If the negative rather than the positive form of confirmation is used, the number of requests sent or the extent of the other auditing procedures applied to the receivable balance should normally be greater in order

for the independent auditor to obtain the same degree of satisfaction with respect to the accounts receivable balance.

If statements of account are not mailed at the time confirmations are requested, or if statements are not to be sent to debtors, a letter form of request may be sent. With appropriate changes of language to express the negative form, the form of positive confirmation letter shown in the following section may be employed.

If statements are sent to debtors, they may be inscribed by means of a rubber stamp or have a sticker affixed reading somewhat as follows:

PLEASE EXAMINE THIS STATEMENT CAREFULLY.

If it is not correct, please write promptly, using the enclosed envelope *and giving details of all differences,* to our auditors,

[Name and Address of Auditors]

who are now making their periodic examination of our accounts.

Unless you promptly report a difference to our auditors, they will assume that you consider the statement to be correct.

Remittances should not be sent to the auditors.

It should be noted that the request is worded as coming from the client. Even though the auditor drafts the request, prepares it, and selects the accounts, all confirmation requests should be made in the client's name because the relationship exists between client and customer (or client and creditor, when liabilities are being confirmed) and information about it should not be given out to a third party without authorization.

The value of negative confirmation requests has been the subject of much discussion. Although the incidence of debtors who simply ignore and discard requests is unknown and unmeasurable, the results can nonetheless be relied on to an appropriate degree for two reasons:

Since the objective of confirmation is reasonable assurance of the authenticity of the aggregate accounts receivable, not of any single account, a discrepancy is significant only if it is evidence of a condition that affects a great many accounts (unless that is true, use of negative confirmations is not appropriate). There is a very high probability, amounting to "reasonable assurance," that some debtors receiving negative confirmation requests will be either responsible enough or incensed enough to report differences. Measuring the impact of the discrepancy then becomes another procedure for the client and the auditor.

Confirmation of accounts receivable is only one in a series of procedures constituting the body of evidential matter. Audit evidence is cumulative, and one procedure tends to corroborate another. Therefore, the possibility of a margin of error can be tolerated in a single procedure because its purpose is to corroborate other evidence rather than to serve by itself as the sole basis for a conclusion.

Depending on the circumstances of an engagement, negative confirmation requests may be supplemented by requests for positive confirmations, particularly of larger balances.

4. Positive Confirmation.   The positive method of confirmation is a request that a debtor reply directly to an auditor stating whether the amounts and other details shown on a statement or letter submitted for confirmation are correct.   It may be used for all accounts or for selected accounts, such as those with larger balances, those representing unusual or isolated transactions, or others for which an auditor needs greater specific assurance of authenticity and accuracy.   The request may be conveyed by a letter or directly on the statement by means of a rubber stamp impression or an affixed sticker.   To facilitate replies the auditor should enclose a postage-paid envelope addressed to himself.

Because the form of the request specifically asks for a reply, an auditor may not assume that failure to reply indicates that the debtor agrees with the reported balance.   Second requests should be sent, and sometimes third requests by registered mail.   Replies to "positive" requests may be facilitated if an auditor furnishes the details of the individual items included in the balances.   Those procedures may be particularly helpful if the debtor's system of accounting does not readily permit identification of account balances.   If an auditor fails to receive positive confirmation of a substantial number of accounts or of a material dollar amount of receivables, he should employ alternative auditing procedures, as described later.

The positive method of confirmation is called for if there are indications that a substantial number of accounts may be in dispute or inaccurate or if the individual receivable balances are unusually large or arise from sales to a few large customers.   Rule 17a–5 of the Securities and Exchange Commission and identical Rule 532 of the Board of Governors of the New York Stock Exchange require positive confirmation of *all* accounts receivable and accounts payable of stockbrokers.

It is impracticable for an auditor to determine the genuineness or authenticity of signatures on replies to confirmation requests.   Replies are received from debtor corporations signed by officers unknown to the auditor and also from individuals signed by others as agents, trustees, or guardians whose authority is unknown to the auditor.   If the signature on a reply does not agree with the name of the account in the records, an auditor should determine whether the client has written evidence of the authority of the person signing the reply. If not, the auditor should consider the account unconfirmed and mail a second request appropriately worded to obtain a properly signed reply. It may be desirable on bank and brokerage engagements to request the client to supplement the confirmation procedure by reviewing signatures for genuineness and authenticity; auditors are not expected to be able to detect forgeries.

Experience has shown that a form of positive request that requires a minimum of effort on the part of the recipient produces greater response. The request may be made by letter or by a request affixed to the statement. The letter form is designed for use if statements of account are not to be mailed to debtors or if the confirmation requests are sent separately from the statements. It is designed so that, when the amount shown is in agreement with the debtor's records, he need only sign his name in the space provided and return the letter in the envelope enclosed with the request. Following is an illustration of the letter form:

[Date]

[Name and address of debtor]

Dear Sirs:

In accordance with the request of our auditors [name and address of auditors], we ask that you kindly confirm to them your indebtedness to us at [date] which, according to our records, amounted to [amount].

If the amount shown is in agreement with your records, please so indicate by signing in the space provided below and return this letter directly to our auditors in the enclosed envelope. Your prompt compliance will facilitate the examination of our accounts.

If the amount is not in agreement with your records, please inform our auditors directly the amount shown by your records with full details of differences.

Remittances should not be sent to the auditors.

Very truly yours,

[Name of client]

The above stated amount is correct as at [date].

_____

[Debtor of client]

_____

[Title or position]

If statements of account prepared by a client are to be used for positive confirmation requests, they may be sent in duplicate with an appropriately worded request (often imprinted on the statement) that the debtor acknowledge the correctness of the statement by returning the duplicate, duly signed, directly to the auditor. A variation is the form of monthly statement in which the balance owing and the name of the debtor appear in two places, one of which is separated from the main body of the statement by perforations. The coupon may be torn off, signed by the debtor, and returned directly to the auditor.

5. *Confirmation Procedures as Affected by Mechanization.* Auditors have found that replies to confirmation requests are sometimes difficult to obtain if a debtor's accounts payable processing centers are dispersed in various localities or if mechanized or automated systems are in use. That is true of a number of government departments and agencies as well as of many large industrial and commercial enterprises. In many instances, however, those difficulties have been overcome with care and ingenuity; for example, an auditor may determine in advance the location of the records he desires to confirm and may (1) alert the customer in advance that a confirmation request is to be made, (2) mail the request to arrive before the confirmation date, (3) supply details of the balance to be confirmed, such as invoice dates, numbers, and amounts, or (4) confirm specific transactions rather than an account balance.

An auditor can often make effective use of mechanization or computerization of a client's accounts receivable systems. Selection rules can be programmed and the files of detail accounts searched automatically, lists and analyses can be prepared, and sometimes the confirmation request can be printed as part of the machine "run." Several general-purpose computer programs are available that are designed to aid in the confirmation process. Chapter 6 discusses their purpose.

6. *Exceptions to Confirmation Requests.* Replies from debtors to requests for confirmation should reveal whether the receivable balances confirmed are substantially correct. They frequently disclose a variety of differences and exceptions that require consideration. An auditor should examine all replies and evaluate them carefully, but he need not ordinarily investigate exceptions reported in replies.

Investigation by the auditor may consume more time than the significance of the exceptions warrants; most often the exceptions are neither material in amount nor indicative of serious weaknesses in the accounting or control systems. Many exceptions reported ordinarily prove to be payments in transit or shipments not received at the confirmation date rather than discrepancies. Other reported exceptions, usually involving small amounts, result from disputes over allowances, discounts, shipping charges, or returned merchandise.

After the auditor has made a copy or other record for control purposes, investigation of replies may properly be turned over to a responsible client employee whose regular work does not involve responsibility for cash, receivables, or credit functions. The auditor should review the employee's findings and if he feels it necessary, employ additional procedures to be satisfied that the account is valid.

If the discrepancies reported suggest a possible pattern of control weakness, or are significant in amount, the auditor has to decide what further auditing procedures are necessary to satisfy himself as to the receivable balances as of the balance sheet date. Chapter 5 discusses the alternatives open to him.

Procedures in Lieu of Confirmation

If replies to confirmation requests cannot reasonably be expected or if the number and character of replies to positive confirmation requests are not satisfactory, an auditor should attempt to satisfy himself as to the validity and accuracy of receivable balances by alternative procedures.

Receivables from governments are frequently not capable of being confirmed; in such cases, the auditor satisfies himself by examining the relevant contracts, shipping documents, public vouchers, and evidence that the agency has acknowledged receipt of shipment. In other cases, in addition to the procedures suggested in the succeeding paragraphs under the heading "Other Validation Procedures," an auditor may wish to vouch transactions for a period around the balance sheet date. Some procedures that might be employed include tracing individual sales invoices and collections to their source; footing underlying records and checking daily postings to control accounts; checking arithmetical accuracy; checking the accuracy of cash discounts and other discounts allowed; reviewing returns and trade discounts; and accounting for numerical sequence of sales invoices and cash receipts reports. The auditor may substantiate sales and the resulting accounts receivable by examination of orders, sales contracts, and shipping documents; collection of receivables may be checked by examination of subsequent cash receipts, cash remittance advices, and other records. In this respect, an effective procedure is to assume current physical control of cash receipts and to subsequently compare the record of receipts with daily accounts receivable postings.

Other Validation Procedures

In some circumstances, even though receivable balances have been confirmed, an auditor may consider it advisable to compare, on a test basis, billings, shipping memoranda, and other data with recorded transactions in accounts receivable for some period. Those tests should be made for a period immediately preceding and immediately following the fiscal year end and may be made as a part of the functional testing of internal accounting control. They should also help to determine that a proper sales cutoff was made. Improper cutoffs may result from errors or intentional recording of sales in an improper period because of bonus arrangements, sales quotas, royalty agreements, income tax considerations, or for other reasons.

If merchandise is billed to customers and held for them, care must be exercised to exclude that merchandise from inventory and to determine that the customers have authorized billing before delivery.

An auditor should usually examine credit memoranda issued during a period after the close of the fiscal year to determine that reported annual sales were not inflated and that proper provision has been made for discounts, returns, and allowances.

If an auditor finds that consigned goods are treated as sales and included in receivable balances, with a resulting anticipation of profits, the unsold goods in the hands of consignees (which should be confirmed) should be adjusted to the basis of like items in the merchandise inventory and reclassified as inventory. If the goods appear to be salable at an adequate margin of profit, related charges, such as freight paid by the consignor, may be added to the inventory costs.

If an auditor test-checks extensions of invoices as part of a functional test of billings, he should note whether discounts that have been allowed conform to the client's policies as indicated by price lists or sales contracts.

An auditor should read sales contracts with selling agents and other agreements affecting receivables to insure that matters such as title to accounts receivable, time of billings, method or time of payments, commissions, and special discounts do not escape his attention.

An auditor should examine receivables other than trade accounts— such as debit balances in accounts payable, claims, and advances—by reviewing the transactions as recorded in the accounts and noting supporting evidence. The precise nature of those accounts should be determined for purposes of the scope of audit testing, evaluation of their collectibility, and their classification in the balance sheet. Confirmations should be obtained by direct communication with debtors to the extent considered reasonable and practicable. Although those receivables may not be significant in amount, if they are not subject to satisfactory internal accounting control and internal check, the logic of the audit equation may require greater relative emphasis on substantive tests than for trade receivables.

An auditor should determine that drafts sent for collection are recorded in the accounts, either separately as drafts receivable or included in accounts receivable. He should inquire of the banks with which drafts have been deposited for collection or from which loans or advances on account of foreign shipments have been obtained to ascertain whether drafts have been pledged against loans or advances. Drafts in the hands of collection agents should be confirmed and their status determined as of the balance sheet date. Since an auditor cannot always use the usual confirmation procedures to substantiate receivable balances from foreign debtors, the existence of drafts may help to substantiate those balances.

Analytical Reviews

Collectibility

The collectibility of receivable balances should be reviewed to determine the amount of allowances necessary to state the receivables at their net realizable value as of the balance sheet date. The starting point for a review of collectibility is an aging analysis—sometimes called an aged trial balance. A client should prepare periodic aging analyses as part of his accountability function; if that is not done, an auditor should request that one be prepared for his use in the examination. In either case, the auditor should establish the accuracy of the analysis by testing the aging of some of the accounts; he should also test the footing of the analysis and compare the total to the ledger total of receivables.

Often computers are, or can be, programmed to produce an aging analysis as a by-product of the reconciliation of detail accounts to control accounts. Alternatively, an auditor may be able to provide his client with a general-purpose computer program that can age accounts. In some cases, it may be desirable to employ statistical sampling and extrapolate the results of aging a representative selection of accounts to conclusions about the total.

In reviewing an aging analysis, the most obvious characteristic to evaluate is the number and dollar amount of overdue accounts. However, an auditor should probe more deeply than that and scrutinize a number of accounts closely for evidence of special situations (such as "dated" invoices) that might indicate collectibility problems. An auditor's purpose in inquiring into those matters is not to judge the collectibility of each individual account examined, but to gather evidence supporting judgments, first on the adequacy of the client's investigation and evaluation of individual accounts (a management function usually performed by the credit manager), and second on the overall reasonableness of the allowance for doubtful accounts.

Past-due receivable balances and other unusual balances should be reviewed with the credit manager to obtain information on which to base an opinion as to their collectibility. Files of correspondence with collection agents and debtors should be examined. Past experience in collecting overdue accounts should be related to current balances as a guide to probable current collectibility. Changes in the number and size of overdue accounts and possible changes in business conditions affecting collectibility should be discussed with the credit manager.

As a result of those reviews and discussions, an auditor should understand the basis for the client's estimate of an adequate allowance for doubtful accounts. His own evaluation of the evidence, together with his common sense and experience, provides a basis for judging whether the allowance is reasonable.

An auditor should scan revenue and receivable transactions after the balance sheet date, including sales, cash receipts, discounts allowed, rebates, returns, and write-offs; those transactions—or their absence or an unusual increase or decrease—may reveal abnormal conditions affecting collectibility at the balance sheet date. Events after the close of the fiscal period are often the best proof of whether the receivable balances at the balance sheet date are actually what they purport to be.

An auditor should determine whether receivables have been sold with full or partial recourse. If so, he should investigate them and evaluate the possibility of losses through default of the debtors.

Approvals for notes and accounts receivable written off during the year should be examined.

Notes and acceptances receivable, past due or current, may themselves be indicative of doubtful collectibility, unless trade custom is to take notes, because accepting notes for overdue accounts receivable is a common practice. The origin of notes should be determined because current notes may sometimes represent renewals of matured notes or acceptances. If usual trade practice is to obtain notes or acceptances from debtors of high credit standing, the collectibility of the notes should be considered in the same way as that of other receivables.

The collectibility of notes against which collateral has been pledged may depend on the value of the collateral. If collectibility of significant collateralized notes in the ordinary manner is in question, an auditor may find it desirable to have an independent appraiser value the collateral.

Receivables from affiliates, directors, officers, and employees should be reviewed to determine that they have been properly authorized and are actually what they purport to be. If loans have been made over a long period of time, past experience often throws light on the intentions of the debtors. It is good practice to review those receivable accounts even though they appear to have been settled before the balance sheet date, especially to see whether the advance or loan was renewed after the balance sheet date. Those that in fact represent advances or loans should be segregated and so described. Disclosure on the balance sheet of receivables from affiliates, directors, officers, and employees does not reflect on the integrity of those debtors.

Other Analytical Reviews

Relationships of revenue accounts among one another and to related accounts should be reviewed analytically and compared with those of prior periods, those anticipated in budgets, and the like. Usually various sales analyses are prepared for management purposes, and an auditor can obtain copies for his review. If management data are not available, the auditor can design work sheets on which he or the client's accounting staff can enter the data to be reviewed.

The most common relationships between accounts are the ratios of accounts receivable to sales, various allowance accounts to sales, and cost of goods sold to sales. It may also be useful to relate sales of certain product lines to one another. The ratios and the balances in the accounts themselves should be compared from month to month and with the corresponding period of the prior year. Trends and fluctuations should be noted and explanations sought for unusual patterns. Sometimes sales can be related to units sold or produced and the trend of an "average unit price" examined.

AUDITING PROCEDURES: SPECIAL CONSIDERATIONS FOR PARTICULAR TYPES OF REVENUE

For the most part, the auditing procedures described above are adaptable to the great variety of circumstances encountered in practice. One auditing procedure may take on greater significance than another, or certain procedures may be used more extensively, but on the whole the elements of the audit are similar. Some of the more common variations that require emphasis on particular procedures are the following:

Cash sales;

Consignment sales;

Interest, some rents, and similar fixed payments for the use of property;

Royalties, production payments, and similar variable revenue;

Income from investments;

Gifts and donations;

Dues, tuition, and similar payments for enrollment;

Revenue from services, such as hotels and hospitals;

Deferred income or unearned revenue; advance receipts for future services;

Revenue from long-term receivables, and

Revenue from long-term contracts.

Cash Sales

If the sales for cash are significant, internal control and internal check are especially important. Cash sales are characteristic of relatively small unit value goods, which often are easily converted to cash and at the same time are difficult to keep under strict physical and accounting control. And, of course, cash itself is easy to lose or misappropriate. Therefore, management is likely to be deeply concerned with maintaining the conditions of control and the disciplinary controls, especially regular and systematic accountability routines, segregation of duties between handlers of merchandise and handlers of cash, limited access to cash and merchandise, and close supervision. An auditor's examination of revenue from cash sales should focus more heavily on those controls than on cash counts and inventory checks because, however important the existence of the cash at a single date, the ongoing control over cash and the recording of sales is more significant to a client and to an auditor.

Consignment Sales

Receiving confirmation from a consignee of sales for the account of a client and of inventory on hand is sufficient in most cases. There are important exceptions, however, for which more rigorous and specific procedures are required. Chapter 11 discusses when and how to validate consignment inventories.

Rents, Interest, and Similar Fixed Payments For the Use of Property

Revenue from fixed payments can usually be validated fairly easily by overall computation of amounts due and comparison with amounts actually recorded. Usually, a client prepares a list of the properties, loans, and so on, and the related income. An auditor should test the list by examining leases, loan agreements, and similar contractual bases for the revenue, noting and evaluating all special terms having financial statement implications. He should evaluate operational and accounting controls over receipt and recording of revenue, including measures for controlling and accounting for the vacancy rate in rental properties. He should note and evaluate delinquencies and arrearages, including implications for the realizability of the related assets. He should always confirm some or all significant loans receivable, and he may wish to confirm leases and similar contractual obligations.

As described in the section on accounting principles, there are various methods of recognizing revenue from use of property, particularly leased property. An auditor must evaluate not only the method employed but also the alternative methods so as to have a positive basis for concluding which of them most clearly reflects the economic facts of his client's business.

Royalties, Production Payments, and Similar Variable Revenue

Many kinds of revenue are based on a stipulated variable, such as production or sales. Usually, the buyer of a right subject to variable payments for its use is required to report from time to time the amount of the variable and the computation of the resulting payment to the seller. If the amount of revenue is not significant, most companies simply accept the payor's statement after a superficial scrutiny for reasonableness. In that event, an auditor can do much the same. He can examine the agreement on which the payment is based, compare receipts with those of the prior year, and possibly request confirmation that all amounts due have been reported and paid. If amounts are significant, contracts usually provide for independent audit of the accounting for the variable, either by the seller's auditor or by an independent auditor acceptable to him. Satisfactory audit reports on the payments ordinarily provide an auditor with reasonable assurance that the related revenue is fairly stated.

Income from Investments

Chapter 14 discusses auditing procedures for income from marketable securities and investments.

Gifts and Donations

Accountability for donations can be a problem because they are rarely covered by contract and they lack a delivery of goods or services to provide concurrent evidence that the revenue is due. If gifts are received centrally—as in development offices of colleges, hospitals, museums, and similar institutions—reasonably good control procedures can be established: properly supervised opening of mail and recording of receipts, segregation of duties between handling and recording, early accountability through means such as prenumbered receipt forms, and so forth. An auditor can test and evaluate those procedures in the same manner as described for testing control over conventional sales.

If donations are received by numerous volunteers—as in many agencies financed by "annual drives"—control is likely to be poor because management may feel that it is impolitic or impossible to ask volunteers to submit to control procedures. In those cases, an auditor may have to make it clear in his report that he cannot take responsibility for an opinion that all donations were recorded and that he reports only on "recorded receipts."

However, it is possible to establish adequate control over volunteer solicitations in the right circumstances, as the systems in use in many United Way drives have proven. Solicitation forms are prepared in advance, and their issuance to volunteers, processing, and return are controlled. The possibility of abuse is thus minimized though not eliminated. In those cases, an auditor can test and evaluate the systems and controls and usually obtain reasonable assurance that gift revenue is fairly stated.

Dues, Tuition, and Similar Payments for Enrollment

An auditor can usually validate tuition and similar revenue rather easily by checking receipts to membership or registration records. Sometimes the validation can be done on an overall basis: numbers of members or students times annual dues or tuition. Sometimes it is necessary to check or test-check individual items from accounting records to the membership or registration rolls.

Revenue from Services, Such as Hotels and Hospitals

Control and accountability for service revenue should be the same as for sales of products: documentation of transactions and of receipt of cash or billing for services. Auditing revenue from services is generally the same as auditing sales of products. Often there are independently generated statistical data, which can be used to corroborate revenue through analytical review: numbers of rooms cleaned, beds made, meals served, and the like.

Deferred Income or Unearned Revenue; Advance Receipts For Future Services

Sometimes accounting systems provide trial balances of detailed items supporting deferred income or unearned revenue balances: for example, students' advance payments of tuition. In those cases, an auditor can obtain the necessary assurances by reviewing and checking the trial balance to the control account and examining and testing individual items.

More often transactions flowing through unearned revenue accounts are not controlled in detail. The input to the account may be on one basis—for example, ticket sales or subscription receipts—and the relief of the account may be on a different basis—a statistical measure of service delivered such as revenue per passenger mile or per issue delivered. In those cases, the accountability function requires the client to make a periodic analysis or "inventory" of the account balance. That inventory consists of a detailed scrutiny of underlying data, for example, of subscription records or of transportation tickets subsequently "lifted." It can often be an extremely arduous and time-consuming effort, comparable in many ways to physically counting inventories. For that reason, the date selected is usually based on practicality and convenience, and it seldom coincides with the fiscal year end.

An auditor should observe and participate in the analysis in the same way that he observes and tests physical inventory procedures. He should observe and test the client's procedures and evaluate the results. If the results are satisfactory, that is, if controls appear adequate and the resulting adjustment of the account balance is small enough to indicate that the method of relieving the account is reasonably accurate, then the auditor can be satisfied with analytical reviews of activity and balances between the audit date and year end.

Often, a client believes that an unearned revenue "inventory" is impossible or prohibitively expensive. For a transit company, for example, the unearned revenue balance represents tokens in the hands of the public, and there is no way—short of changing the token—to identify those purchased before a given date.

If the client cannot or will not validate the balance, neither can the auditor. He can nevertheless usually obtain reasonable assurance that the balance is fairly stated in relation to the financial statements as a whole. He can pay particular attention to functional tests for assurance that all revenue commitments sold—tickets, tokens, subscriptions, and the like—are controlled and promptly recorded and that amounts transferred from unearned to earned revenue are accurately and consistently computed and well controlled. He can relate the balance to the pattern of sales and service activity and investigate changes in the ratio relationship. As long as transfers to revenue for estimates of lost and unused items are made only on a conservative basis, he can conclude that the amount has a bias toward overstating the liability for service to be rendered.

Revenue from Long-Term Receivables

Receivables collectible over a long period are subject to the same auditing procedures as other receivables, but the evaluation of collectibility takes on added importance. In addition, a client's policy and procedure for computing imputed interest, where that factor is present, must be reviewed and checked.

Revenue from Long-Term Contracts

Audit evidence for revenue from long-term contracts is obtained from the various means management uses to monitor and control fulfillment of contract terms and the allocation of revenue to fiscal periods. A client should provide an auditor with an analysis of each contract and the change orders that act as amendments. In many instances, an analysis prepared for management purposes will suffice, but in others an analysis will have to be prepared especially for audit purposes. Depending on the size and significance of the contracts, the auditor can check or test-check the analysis to underlying data, including the contract itself, the accounting for costs incurred to date, the estimates of cost to complete each contract, and the amounts of revenue recorded in the period under audit.

The Contract

Contracts selected for testing should be examined for authorization, payment terms, and special features such as penalties, incentives, escalation clauses, price redetermination, limitation of payments, termination provisions, and change orders. Since contracts are often highly complex technical and legal documents, the examination can be a difficult and time-consuming task. Also, since many contracts with the government or with suppliers to the government involve restricted access under federal security regulations, it may be necessary for an auditor who is to examine the contracts to obtain in advance the appropriate security clearance.

Costs Incurred

Costs incurred are part of the production segment, and therefore auditing procedures employed in evaluating controls over costs and substantive testing of costs incurred, where that is necessary, are described in Chapter 11.

Estimate of Cost To Complete

The estimate of cost to complete is the most critical element in accounting for revenue and unbilled receivables under long-term contracts, and also in evaluating the need to provide for estimated losses. An auditor should review his client's procedures for preparing estimates of cost to complete, preferably far enough in advance of his examination to suggest changes that might facilitate it. He should test the compilation of the estimates by reviewing underlying data, such as manning tables, labor rate schedules, bills of material, and schedules of material received and still to be received. He should make analytical reviews and comparisons, such as comparing the details of the estimate of cost to complete to the details of the original cost estimate supporting the contract bid, or comparing evidence of physical completion, such as numbers of units completed, with the percentage of completion indicated by cost estimates. He should talk with the engineering and production supervisors who make the critical judgments entering into the estimates so as to understand the bases for their judgments and the degree of confidence with which they are made.

Preparing estimates of cost to complete is one of management's most difficult tasks, and evaluating them is correspondingly difficult for an auditor. The better an auditor understands his client's operations and business conditions, the better he will be able to understand the estimate of cost to complete. The better he understands the estimating process, the more efficiently he can complete the evaluation, thus minimizing his own time and inconvenience to the client. If the estimates are diligently and responsibly prepared and communication between auditor and client is open and candid, an auditor can obtain reasonable assurance that the estimates are accurate enough.

Price Redetermination

The possibility of contract price redetermination or of renegotiation liabilities can have material financial statement effects, and an auditor must evaluate the need for or the adequacy of the client's allowances. Since estimating the results of redetermination or renegotiation is highly subjective, an auditor's evaluation is correspondingly difficult. A client's previous experience in price redetermination or renegotiation audits is helpful evidence. If potentially serious questions about possible price redetermination or renegotiation arise, an auditor without substantial knowledge of the pertinent regulations is well advised to seek the advice of specialists.

Billings and Collections

An auditor should also check or test-check billings on contracts to ascertain that they are in accordance with contract terms. Confirmation of billed accounts receivable may need the special efforts described earlier for receivables from government agencies. An auditor should pay particular attention to old outstanding items because contracting agencies ordinarily pay promptly unless the balance is disputed.

• STATEMENT PRESENTATION

REVENUE

Sales and Operating Revenue

APB Opinion No. 9 (*AICPA Prof. Stds.*, vol. 3, paragraph 2010.28) states that "the income statement should disclose revenues (sales) . . . ." The terms generally used are "net sales" or "sales," although occasionally the phrase "after deducting returns and allowances" may also appear.

Material amounts of sales to parent companies, subsidiaries, or other affiliates that are not eliminated in consolidation should be disclosed and the transfer pricing policies explained. If excise or sales taxes included in billings to customers are significant, the amounts and the manner of accounting for them should be disclosed.

Similarly, important factors influencing the interpretation of sales or comparability with other companies are usually disclosed. Thus, in reporting sales under long-term contracts, financial statements should indicate, generally in a note, the method used to record revenue: for example, the percentage-of-completion or completed-contract method. When revenue includes significant amounts of contract costs incurred directly by the customer, that fact and the total amount should be stated. Also, significant amounts of sales or revenue (and related net income) by foreign subsidiaries should be disclosed, usually in a note.

Rule 5–03 of Regulation S-X requires reporting companies to disclose "gross sales less discounts, returns and allowances," showing separately, if practicable, sales to parents and subsidiaries and sales to others. A similar requirement covers the disclosure of operating revenue. The term "gross sales" distinguishes amounts received from sales of products from "operating revenue," amounts received for services. The two captions may be combined if the smaller of the two is not more than 10% of the total.

Other Income

Ordinarily, items making up other income may be combined and shown as a single amount in the income statement—frequently net, without a separate statement of other expense. If the nature or size of a particular item might be significant in appraising the results of operations, however, separate disclosure is usually desirable. The equity in undistributed earnings of unconsolidated subsidiaries and joint ventures (Chapter 14) is often stated separately, with the amount of dividends received from those companies shown parenthetically or in a note.

SEC requirements for disclosures of items of other income are somewhat detailed and are stated in Rule 5–03 of Regulation S-X, as follows:

Dividends. State separately, if practicable, the amount of dividends from: (a) Securities of affiliates, (b) marketable securities, and (c) other securities.

Interest on securities. State separately, if practicable, the amount of interest from: (a) Securities of affiliates, (b) marketable securities, and (c) other securities.

Profits on securities. Profits shall be stated net of losses. No profits on the person's own equity securities, or profits of its affiliates on their own equity securities, shall be included under this caption. State, here or in a note referred to herein, the method followed in determining the cost of securities sold, e.g., "average cost," "first-in, first-out," or "identified certificate."

Miscellaneous other income. State separately any material amounts, indicating clearly the nature of the transactions out of which the items arose.

Revenue Deducted from Costs

Receipts or other credit items that are recoveries or reductions of costs and expenses are deducted in the financial statements from the related costs, usually without separate disclosure. Cash discounts on purchases, sales of scrap, sales of by-products, and income from production-supporting activities such as a cafeteria are examples.

RECEIVABLES

Statement presentation of receivables involves consideration of description, classification, and segregation. The minimum requirement is adequate and informative disclosure of the nature of receivables and the bases of related allowances.

Description

If only the term "accounts receivable" or "receivables" appears on a balance sheet among current assets, a reader is justified in assuming that the amount so described is deemed to be collectible from trade debtors (customers) of the company within the period customary for the trade or industry.

Receivables from customers may be described in terminology customary in a particular trade or business; thus, the term "premiums receivable" may be used by insurance companies, and "rentals receivable" by real estate owners.

If receivables include distinct categories that are individually material, reporting them separately is usually appropriate: for example, notes and acceptances, installment accounts, accounts pledged as collateral, accounts past due, and notes discounted.

It is desirable to segregate unsecured notes and accounts from those against which collateral is held. Careless use of the word "secured" should be avoided; its use may be construed to mean that the collateral can be promptly converted into cash sufficient to satisfy the note. That may or may not be true. A so-called "secured" note may be worth no more than the ultimately realizable value of its collateral. Suggested presentation in those circumstances might be along the following lines:

Note receivable (with collateral—which should be described generally, both as to nature and present value).

If the amounts of nontrade and certain types of trade receivables are significant, they should be separately identified and described (see "Related Party Transactions," Chapter 18). Those that may require separate disclosure include:

Receivables from affiliated companies,

Receivables arising from sales to employees (other than ordinary-course-of-business sales of the company's products or services),

Receivables from officers, directors, and stockholders,

Receivables from transactions outside the ordinary course of business,

Receivables from the U. S. Government,

Unbilled amounts under long-term, cost-plus-fixed-fee, and cost-plus-incentive-fee contracts,

Receivables on terminated contracts, and

Claims for refund of federal income taxes.

If receivables from other than trade debtors are not significant, they may be grouped in one figure and described as, for example, "Other receivables."

Classification and Segregation

Financial statements ordinarily should distinguish between current and noncurrent assets and current and noncurrent liabilities. Receivables arising from ordinary transactions of the business that reasonably may be expected to be collected during the normal operating cycle are classified on the balance sheet as current assets, usually immediately after cash and marketable securities. Chapter 3A of Accounting Research Bulletin No. 43 (*AICPA Prof. Stds.*, vol. 3, Section 2031) sets forth certain principles governing the classification of assets and liabilities as current or noncurrent. It states in part:

> . . . A one-year time period is to be used as a basis for the segregation of current assets in cases where there are several operating cycles occurring within a year. However, where the period of the operating cycle is more than twelve months, as in, for instance, the tobacco, distillery, and lumber businesses, the longer period should be used. Where a particular business has no clearly defined operating cycle, the one-year rule should govern. [Paragraph 2031.05]

The Bulletin also states that installment or deferred accounts and notes receivable that generally conform to normal trade practices and terms within the business may be included in the term *current assets*.

The Securities and Exchange Commission, in Rule 3–11 of Regulation S-X, has also established criteria for classification. The text of that rule is:

> Assets and other resources classed with cash and its equivalent as current assets shall be reasonably expected to be realized in cash or sold or consumed within one year. However, if the normal operating cycle of the company is longer than one year, generally recognized trade practices may be followed with respect to the inclusion of items such as installment receivables or inventories long in process: *Provided,* An appropriate explanation of the circumstances is made and, if practicable, an estimate is given of the amount not realizable within one year.

In statements prepared in accordance with Regulation S-X, notes receivable and accounts receivable must be shown separately, and accounts receivable are segregated as trade accounts receivable and other accounts receivable. In other published financial statements, those distinctions are not always made.

Notes and acceptances receivable arising in the ordinary course of business may be combined in one amount. They are frequently shown in combination with accounts receivable under a common designation, such as "Notes and accounts receivable" or merely "Receivables." Material amounts of trade installment notes or receivables should be stated separately.

The statement presentation of notes receivable varies according to industry custom. In some industries notes are given by concerns of the highest standing, whereas in others notes may be considered an' indication of weakness. Demand notes are not necessarily current, and care should be taken in classifying them as such, especially if interest is not being collected currently.

Interest accrued on notes may be included with the face amount of the notes provided the caption indicates that it is.

Auditors should be alert to long-term contracts that provide for progress payments and have clauses permitting the debtor to withhold certain amounts until completion and final acceptance of the work. An auditor should determine whether the receivable represented by the retained amount is properly includable among current assets at the balance sheet date.

Significant amounts of receivables from subsidiaries and affiliates should be stated separately. Collection of those accounts before the balance sheet is released does not justify deviation from that practice. Whether receivables from subsidiaries and affiliates are current or noncurrent depends largely on the expectation of realizing them in cash. Even if those accounts arise from current transactions, they may in effect represent long-term advances in the form of a revolving fund and should accordingly be classified as noncurrent assets.

Receivables from employees arising in the ordinary course of business are sometimes stated separately on the balance sheet, although opinions differ as to the necessity for that segregation. Some people contend that employees are customers even though they may be granted special discounts and that their accounts can often be collected more readily than those of other customers. Unless receivables from employees represent a substantial portion of the total receivables from trade debtors or special circumstances require disclosure, there seems to be little reason to segregate them.

Significant receivables from directors, officers, principal stockholders, and other related parties—other than those arising in the ordinary course of business—should be stated separately on the balance sheet. The distinction between those receivables and trade receivables rests on the possibility that the relations between debtor and creditor are such that affiliation or self-interest may influence prompt and full collection.

Material credit balances in accounts receivable should be classified as liabilities unless they can properly be offset against debit balances. Often they represent advances to be applied against unbilled orders and are similar to unearned revenue. If significant in amount, they should generally appear among the liabilities, grouped separately as customers' advance payments. Similarly, material debit balances in accounts payable that are not direct offsets to related credit balances should be included in the balance sheet with accounts receivable.

Receivables arising from transactions other than sales in the ordinary course of business may include advances to salesmen and others, loans to officers, and claims against creditors or refundable income taxes. Not infrequently they include amounts that are rarely settled in cash: for example, charges to vendors for goods returned to them are often settled by other shipments. Those items, as well as deferred charges to operations, such as rents paid in advance and similar items, should not be included under the caption "Accounts receivable." Claims for tax refunds resulting from carryback provisions of the Internal Revenue Code should be shown as current assets if collection is reasonably assured within the normal operating cycle of the business.

Receivables arising from subscriptions to capital stock should not be included in receivables for the reason stated in Chapter 16. Formerly, it was customary to classify them as receivables, but now that treatment is not acceptable; they should be shown as a deduction from capital stock subscribed in the capital section of the balance sheet.

Receivables under contracts usually consist of items billed and costs accumulated but not yet billed. Since billed items and unbilled costs differ in character, they should be distinguished on the balance sheet if the amounts involved are material. Advances or progress payments received under contracts may be offset against receivables if there is good reason to believe that the advances will be applied in payment of those receivables. The amount of the offset should be clearly disclosed. If an advance is considered to be equivalent to a revolving fund to be liquidated near the completion of the contract, it should be shown as a liability.

Under provisions of long-term contracts, progress payments may be more or less than costs incurred. Progress payments and costs incurred should be presented net for each contract; a debit balance in one contract should not be offset against a credit balance in another. As a result, there may be two captions in a balance sheet: an asset, "Unbilled costs and fees under long-term contracts, less $XX progress payments" and a liability, "Progress payments under long-term contracts, less $XX unbilled costs and fees."

Claims under terminated contracts are usually classified with current assets unless disagreements or other conditions indicate the possibility of an extended delay in collection. Material termination claims should be separately captioned. Partial payments received against a claim should be deducted from the related receivable. Termination claims payable to suppliers and subcontractors represent liabilities to third parties and should be classified as liabilities, with appropriate cross-references, rather than offset against the claims receivable.

Receivables Pledged, Sold, or Discounted

If receivables are pledged against loans, the amount pledged should be indicated in the description of the receivables and also in the description of the loan liability or in a note.

If receivables are sold under a repurchase guarantee, the portion of the net proceeds withheld by the buyer should be shown as a receivable by the seller. The balance associated with the repurchase guarantee that could become a liability should be disclosed in the balance sheet or in a note.

The total amount of receivables discounted is usually disclosed in a note, although it may be shown among the assets on the balance sheet with a contra liability or by deducting the discounted items from the aggregate receivables, leaving a net amount representing receivables not discounted.

Allowances Deducted from Receivables

APB Opinion No. 12 (*AICPA Prof. Stds.*, vol. 3, Section 2044) includes a statement about "valuation allowances for losses such as those on receivables . . . ," as follows:

> It is the Board's opinion that such allowances should be deducted from the assets or groups of assets to which the allowances relate, with appropriate disclosure. [Paragraph 2044.02]

Thus, receivables may be shown on the balance sheet either gross, less the allowance, or net, with the amount of the allowance indicated in the caption.

Disclosing the amounts of individual allowances is not considered necessary if a combined allowance for doubtful notes and accounts receivable is deducted from the sum of the related asset amounts. Other allowances, such as those for cash discounts, collection costs, or decrease of profit because of expected returns of merchandise, should be shown the same way, or, alternatively, they may be combined in one amount with the allowance for doubtful receivables, provided that treatment is indicated in the caption.

Deferred finance or interest charges on installment accounts receivable at the balance sheet date should be classified in the balance sheet as a deduction from the receivables, either directly from the installment accounts or from the sum of the receivables as part of the total allowance. (Commercial banks are one exception: unearned interest on discounted loans is usually shown as a liability, although the question of reclassifying that item as a deduction from loans is under periodic discussion.) Unearned rentals recorded by leasing companies should be deducted from the aggregate amount of the related rentals receivable on the balance sheet in the manner set forth in paragraph 14 of APB Opinion No. 7 (paragraph 4051.14 of *AICPA Prof. Stds.*, vol. 3).

Unamortized discount or imputed interest that causes a receivable to be recorded at an amount different from its face amount is not a liability or deferred credit separable from the obligation that gives rise to it and therefore should be presented in the balance sheet as a deduction from the face amount of the note or account receivable.

Unearned Income

The theoretical division of unearned income into the portion that is a liability for the cost of service contracted for and the remainder, which is deferred profit on the sale, is usually ignored. Unearned income is presented as a liability, usually current.

10

The Buying Segment

PURCHASES, COSTS, EXPENSES, ACCOUNTS PAYABLE, AND RELATED ACCOUNTS

BUYING SEGMENT AND COST OR EXPENSE SEGMENT

This chapter covers the "buying segment" common to every business: the acquisition of goods and services for use in the business to produce revenue in exchange for payment or promises to pay. It is part of the larger "cost segment," in which the costs of some goods and services acquired are accounted for as assets until they are used, while the costs of others are accounted for as expenses of the period of acquisition. It comprises almost all expenses, all assets whose costs become expenses when they "expire," and all liabilities incurred to acquire the assets and expenses of the segment.

Accounts Included in Chapters 11, 12, and 13

Since the typical cost segment is too large to be covered in a single chapter of this book, its discussion is divided among this and the following three chapters.

The production segment is discussed in Chapter 11. It can also be called *the inventory segment* or *the cost of goods sold and operating expense segment*. In general, *cost of goods sold* includes all costs incurred in purchasing or producing goods for sale, excluding costs remaining in inventory at the end of a period. It may also include additional items such as losses from reducing cost of inventories to market, royalties paid for the right to manufacture a product or use a patented process or equipment, and amortization of preproduction and tooling costs. It is often reduced by sales of by-products and disposable value of scrap. Estimated costs of warranties, guarantees, and other commitments to future expenditures are also sometimes included in cost of goods sold although more often they are included in other expense categories. *Operating expense* is the term that designates costs and expenses incurred to produce revenue from services. Unfortunately the term is not descriptive and is easily confused with selling, general, and administrative expenses—cost of services rendered would be a more descriptive term which would be comparable to cost of goods sold.

The long-term asset segment is discussed in Chapter 12. It can also be called *the depreciation, depletion, and amortization* segment. It accounts for costs that are spread over the useful lives of assets lasting many years, including plant and equipment, leasehold improvements, and other depreciable assets; mineral deposits, standing timber, and other depletable natural resources; and intangible assets, including goodwill and deferred charges.

The income taxes segment is covered in Chapter 13, because the complexities of that unique type of expense call for separate treatment.

Accounts Included in the Buying Segment

Selling Expenses

Selling expenses include salesmen's salaries, commissions, and expenses and other costs of selling products or merchandise such as advertising and overhead of the sales department. Items such as costs of warehousing or other storage of completed products pending sale, estimated losses from uncollectible accounts, and credit and collection expenses are frequently included in selling expenses, although it is equally acceptable to treat the former as product cost and the latter two as administrative expense or "other expense." Costs of products sold below cost to induce buyers to purchase other products, less proceeds of their sale, are occasionally classified with selling expenses as promotional expenses.

In the insurance industry, commissions paid to agents are the most significant selling expense. Generally, most of such commissions are paid by the insurance company out of payment of the first few premiums. Since, in most instances, the related policies are in effect and create revenue for years beyond the year of issue, the first-year commission expense and related "acquisition expenses" must be deferred and amortized over the policy lives to achieve a proper matching of revenue and expenses during all the periods the insurance is in force.

General and Administrative Expenses

General and administrative expenses include salaries and expenses of corporate executives and of the general offices and departments such as accounting and credit, corporate expenses such as transfer agents' fees, costs of reports to stockholders, certain taxes, and legal and auditing fees. Other expenses unrelated to manufacturing or selling but within the usual activities of an enterprise are also commonly included in this category.

Combining selling expenses and general and administrative expenses in published financial statements is increasingly common practice. Some of the more significant of the individual expenses are described briefly in the following paragraphs.

Research and Development Expenses

Expenditures for experimental, research, and development activities are characteristic of most industries in which it is necessary to find new processes and products and to improve existing ones. Although those expenditures generally relate to future rather than current production, they are usually recognized as expenses as incurred. As more fully described in Chapter 12, until the issuance of FASB Statement No. 2 (*AICPA Prof. Stds.*, vol. 3, Section 4211), deferring those expenditures as assets was permissible if future periods, rather than the period of incurrence, clearly benefited from them and continuing value at least equal to the amount deferred was reasonably assured. The reasons for not deferring experimental, research, and development costs are usually more persuasive—future benefits may be intangible and impossible to measure, the length of the future period to be benefited may be impossible to determine, and continuing value of the expenditures may be uncertain. Accordingly, FASB Statement No. 2 requires research and development expenses to be expensed as incurred. At the time of its effective date (January 1, 1975), all unamortized research and development costs were required to be written off retroactively.

Research and development expenses are usually disclosed as a separate item in income statements when significant; disclosure in a note or otherwise is required in statements filed with the SEC.

Pension Expense

Expenses of pension plans are significant in most companies and, if so, should be disclosed in a note with a brief description of the significant features of the plan.

Rent Expense

Rentals under long-term leases require disclosure; they are treated in Chapter 12 because the expense is related to long-term asset use.

Maintenance and Repairs

Costs of maintenance and repairs are stated separately by companies for which the item is significant, such as utilities and transportation companies. Other companies may disclose the amount.

Other Expense or Other Deductions

A miscellaneous category is needed, and certain items have been designated other expenses or other deductions as a matter of long-standing custom. The most common items included are cash discounts on sales (preferably deducted from sales instead), interest (if not significant), and losses on disposition of assets.

Interest Expense

Interest, including amortization of debt premium and discount, is separately stated if significant.

Income Taxes

Income taxes are a significant expense item for most companies; the measurement, classification, and allocation of income taxes between periods is often complex and difficult. Accordingly, this subject is more fully covered in Chapter 13.

Prepaid Expenses

Prepaid expenses are costs, most often for services but sometimes for assets such as stationery and supplies, that have been paid for in the routine of the buying segment but apply to future periods or to the production of future revenue—for example, insurance, rent, and taxes. Prepaid expenses often relate to time and are amortized to expense as time passes.

Accounts Payable

Accounts payable is the collective term used to describe specific amounts owed, usually for goods and services. In a narrow sense, it means amounts due on open account to suppliers of merchandise, materials, or supplies, evidenced by sellers' invoices. But the term is also used broadly to encompass not only suppliers' balances but also the amounts often known as accrued expenses or accrued liabilities. Most items in an accounts payable balance are the results of transactions "in transit" in the ordinary course of business—transactions that were recorded on receipt of sellers' invoices and are in the process of being approved and processed for payment. However, the "in-transit" stage may sometimes be quite long. It is a time-honored custom for companies that are short of funds to finance themselves partly through the good nature and patience of their suppliers; conversely, tough competition may make suppliers relatively eager to offer extended payment terms to obtain sales.

Accrued Liabilities

Accrued liabilities or accrued expenses are items for which liability is acknowledged and reasonably determinable but that are not yet payable. Most accrued liabilities accumulate (accrue) with the passage of time—for example, interest, rent, property taxes—or with some service or activity—for example, payrolls, royalties, sales commissions, income taxes. Accrued liabilities are often included in accounts payable.

Agency Obligations

Most companies collect funds that belong to someone else. That is, funds collected are held in trust, either for the contributor or for a third party, and the collecting company has a liability for the funds held in trust. The most common types of trust or agency obligations arise from payroll withholdings for various purposes: income taxes, social security taxes, insurance premiums, union dues, charitable contributions, installment payments to purchase stocks or bonds, and others. Sales taxes collected and deposits received by utilities from customers are other common examples.

Loss Contingencies

For many years prior to the publication of FASB Statement No. 5, *Accounting for Contingencies (AICPA Prof. Stds.,* vol. 3, Section 4311), the term "estimated liabilities" was used for expenses and losses recognized in the accounts, and "contingent liabilities" was used for expenses and losses disclosed in financial statements or notes but not formally recognized in the accounts. Statement No. 5 defines both as "loss contingencies" and requires accrual of those loss contingencies meeting the criteria quoted below. Since the terminology in that Statement is different from, but not inconsistent with, prior practice, the terms "contingent liability" and "loss contingency" are used interchangeably in this book.

Estimated Liabilities

Estimated liabilities are those loss contingencies that should be accrued under FASB Statement No. 5. The Statement requires *both* of the following conditions for accrual:

> a. Information available prior to issuance of the financial statements indicates that it is probable that an asset had been impaired or a liability had been incurred at the date of the financial statements. It is implicit in this condition that it must be probable that one or more future events will occur confirming the fact of the loss.

b. The amount of the loss can be reasonably estimated. [Paragraph 4311.08]

A variety of transactions involve commitments to expend funds in the future. Often the amount of future expenditure cannot be known precisely, and estimates are necessary. Product warranties and guarantees are common, and there can be no certain knowledge of how many claims may be paid. In the insurance industry, the major item of "estimated liabilities" is, for property–casualty companies, the estimate of reserves for known losses payable and for losses estimated to have been incurred but not reported to the insurance company as of the balance sheet date and, for life insurance companies, the actuarially determined policy liabilities for future policy benefits under life, annuity, accident and health, and other contracts. Some future expenditures may be more objectively determinable; for example, the cost of definite service schedules, the cost of deferred maintenance or deferred compensation, and the cost of completing promised development under land sales contracts may be fairly well known.

Contingent Liabilities or "Loss Contingencies" That Are Not Accrued

Contingent liabilities are unrecorded obligations relating to past events that may arise on occurrence of a future event deemed to be possible but not probable. If the event were probable, the liability would be real, even though estimated, and not contingent.

FASB Statement No. 5, referred to above, defines a contingency as ". . . an existing condition . . . involving uncertainty as to possible gain . . . or loss . . . that will ultimately be resolved when one or more future events occur or fail to occur." It thus refines the definition of contingent liability in the previous paragraph and changes the terminology to "loss contingency."

• ACCOUNTING PRINCIPLES

GENERAL PRINCIPLES *

The same accounting principles apply throughout the cost or expense segment, although different problems may require different

---

* Sources for this discussion include APB Statement No. 4, *Basic Concepts and Accounting Principles Underlying Financial Statements of Business Enterprises* (1970), paragraphs 65 and 145–164 (*AICPA Prof. Stds.*, vol. 3, paragraphs 1023.26 and 1026.09–.28); APB Opinion No. 16, *Business Combinations* (1970), paragraph 67 (*AICPA Prof. Stds.*, vol. 3, paragraph 1091.67); FASB Statement No. 5, *Accounting for Contingencies* (*AICPA Prof. Stds.*, vol. 3, Section 4311); and Accounting Terminology Bulletin No. 4, *Cost, Expense and Loss* (1957). The first two have at least partially superseded the terminology bulletin.

emphasis. This discussion is thus prefatory to all four chapters on costs and expenses, but additional principles are discussed in each. Two major accounting conventions that are significant in all four chapters are the convention of "matching costs with revenue" and that of "anticipating losses."

Matching Revenue and Cost

Income determination in present-day accounting is essentially a process of relating revenue and costs to accounting periods. Revenue is normally assigned to periods first, using the principles described in Chapter 9. Costs are then related either to the revenue or to the period. For example, cost of goods sold is directly related to the product or merchandise included in sales revenue of the period; in contrast, administrative expense is usually assigned to a period and is deducted from whatever revenue is assigned to that period.

Cost

Cost is a price or a sacrifice of value—something of value given up— usually to obtain something else of value. Several kinds of costs are discussed in accounting literature, the most important of which are a price actually paid for an asset (acquisition cost or historical cost), a price that would currently be paid to acquire an asset already held (replacement cost or reproduction cost), and a foregone return from alternative uses of an asset (opportunity cost or economic cost).

The costs used presently in accounting are predominantly historical or acquisition costs. An asset is initially recorded at the price paid to acquire it, and revenue is normally recognized only when an asset is sold. Consequently, changes in the value of an asset between purchase and sale are rarely recognized except to reduce or remove costs of assets assumed to be used up or lost. Replacement cost is used occasionally: for example, to apply the rule of cost or market, whichever is lower. Opportunity cost is an economic concept and is not used in present-day accounting practice.

The most authoritative definition of acquisition cost is now found in APB Opinion No. 16, paragraph 67 (*AICPA Prof. Stds.,* vol. 3, paragraph 1091.67): ". . . the amount of cash disbursed or the fair value of other assets distributed . . . [or] the present value of the amounts to be paid." That definition conforms to common definitions of cost. Accountants also often use "cost" to mean the basis on which assets are carried in balance sheets, thus stretching its meaning to cover fair values of assets or services received by donation.

Costs, Expenses, and Assets

Expenses are "expired" costs. That is, expenses are costs that relate to present (and sometimes past) revenue and are deducted from current revenue to measure net income for the current period. In contrast, many—but not all—assets are "unexpired" costs, costs that relate to future revenue and are carried forward as assets, or "deferred," until the period in which the related revenue is recognized. The unexpired costs then expire and become expenses of that period. Those assets are costs that are presumed to benefit future periods; expenses are costs of assets or services consumed or expired without producing some tangible or specifically determinable future benefit with continuing value.

Although there is a technical distinction between "cost" and "expense," the two terms are often used loosely and even interchangeably: for example, some may refer to "maintenance cost" and others to "maintenance expense." That use seldom causes confusion, but it is desirable to maintain consistent usage in a given context.

The following illustrates the relation between some important kinds of unexpired and expired costs:

Cost of	Unexpired Cost (Asset)	Expired Cost (Expense)
Merchandise purchases	Merchandise inventory	Cost of goods sold
Materials used Direct labor Factory overhead	Inventories of: Work in process Finished goods	Cost of products sold (or cost of goods sold)
Buildings, automobiles, store fixtures, lathes, and the like	Plant and equipment, furniture and fixtures	Depreciation
Crude oil deposit	Oil and gas property	Depletion
Three-year insurance policy	Prepaid insurance	Insurance expense
Parking lot on leased property	Leasehold improvement	Amortization of leasehold improvement
Patented process	Patent	Amortization of patent

Cost (meaning acquisition or historical cost) is the most common basis of accounting for significant assets or services acquired and for almost all assets and services consumed, that is, expenses. Net income for a period is "realized" revenue less "expired" costs of the period.

Expenses, Assets, and Liabilities

In principle, most expenses arise in the way just described—unexpired costs (assets) expire and become expenses of the period of expiration. Companies buy assets, not expenses, so that the theoretical sequence of stages of a typical cost in an enterprise is (a) the enterprise acquires an asset (unexpired cost) by paying cash or by incurring a liability which is later settled by paying cash, (b) the cost of that asset is carried in the balance sheet until related revenue is recognized, and (c) the cost becomes an expense of the period for which the revenue is recognized or expires for other reasons.

Practically, however, attempting to account for all expenses as assets first is not worth the trouble. The length of the time from acquisition to expense varies from a moment for some costs to several years for others. Normally, costs incurred and expiring within the same accounting period are recognized as expenses as incurred, unless recognizing an asset is for some reason more convenient or more meaningful. Only costs likely to remain unexpired beyond the period of incurrence have to be recorded as assets to "match" them correctly with revenue.

Examples of items that, although sometimes recorded first as assets, are usually recorded directly as expenses either when cash is paid or by accruing a liability are:

> Employment costs, which include not only salaries and wages but also numerous related costs—employment taxes, pensions, insurance, vacation and sick pay, bonuses, and sometimes education and training and medical facilities.
>
> Repairs and maintenance of plant and equipment, which must be maintained at an efficient operating level and repaired when they break down.
>
> Taxes, including both income taxes and other taxes imposed by various federal, state, local, and foreign governments.

Anticipating Losses

A longstanding tenet of accounting is that the major principle of "matching costs and revenue" is superseded whenever necessary by the other major principle of "anticipating losses." In the terms used above, that means that an "expiration" of value is recognized when it occurs even though it may be due to accident or events beyond the control of the enterprise.

From time to time in the past, problems and confusion have arisen about the measurement and timing of anticipated losses. Critics have accused some companies of anticipating excessive losses in a poor year to relieve later years of expenses for asset expirations. As a result of APB Opinion No. 30 (*AICPA Prof. Stds.*, vol. 3, Section 2012) and FASB Statement No. 5 (Section 4311), the principle now appears clearly established that it is proper to recognize liabilities and losses in value of assets resulting from events up to the balance sheet date, provided the amount can be reasonably estimated, but it is not proper to anticipate losses to be incurred from future events, even though they are related. That principle is discussed in more detail in connection with specific kinds of anticipated losses, below and in Chapters 11 and 12.

One limited exception to this pervasive rule of recognizing losses immediately is the practice in utility accounting—where the rate-making process is recognized as a controlling factor (see "Public Utilities" in Chapter 13 and "Regulated Companies" in Chapter 19)—of deferring and amortizing some kinds of losses (and gains) with regulatory commission approval.

RECORDING COSTS

Accounting principles for costs incurred and expired and related assets and liabilities revolve around two basic questions. They are essentially the same two questions as those discussed in Chapter 9 for revenue and related receivables. Each may apply separately to the two major sides of a typical cost or expense segment:

When should a cost incurred—usually an obligation to pay—be recorded, and when should a cost expired be recorded?

How much liability, cost, or expense should be recorded?

When To Recognize a Liability, an Asset, or an Expense

A cost is incurred at the moment cash is paid or a legal obligation to pay originates. A cost expires and an expense arises at the moment assets are sold, consumed, or lost without producing another identifiable asset. A cost usually is incurred and expires at different moments, but both events are accounted for as a single occurrence as long as both fall in the same accounting period. Cost incurrences are generally recorded by consistent application of practical procedures rather than by strict adherence to legal rules. The timing of cost expirations is dictated by (1) the need to "match" costs with revenue and (2) the overriding requirement that losses be anticipated.

When To Record Costs Incurred

Cost incurrence and the related liability are seldom recorded until after the legal obligation occurs, simply because it takes time to process the record of a transaction. Usually the most convenient point to initiate recording a cost is when the goods or services are received, whether that point is technically before or after title passes. Actual recording usually follows receipt by a few days—goods received must be inspected, receipt must be documented and matched with the seller's invoice, the documents must be approved and processed, etc. As long as the same rules are consistently followed, that lag causes no problems except around the ending of accounting periods, when precise timing can be critical. Accurate and consistent cutoff of transactions is important, and a periodic routine must be established to search for and record unrecorded costs and liabilities existing at the end of a period.

When To Record Costs Expired

The timing of a cost expiration is determined either by its presumed relation to revenue recognized or, in the absence of that relation, by its relation to the period of consumption [APB Statement No. 4 (*AICPA Prof. Stds.*, vol. 3, paragraphs 1026.19 to .25)]:

> Some costs—for example, cost of goods sold and sales commissions—are associated directly with sales revenue and are recognized as expenses of the period in which related goods are sold.
>
> Some costs—for example, depreciation and insurance—are presumed to relate indirectly to revenue or periods and are assigned to periods by a formula or other "rational and systematic" means (costs associated with a period by those means may be recognized either as expenses of the period or as costs of goods produced during the period).
>
> All other costs are presumed to be costs of the period of their incurrence, either because they relate to that period or because they cannot reasonably be presumed to relate to any future period.

Costs in the first two groups are often recorded as assets because they are associated with tangible property and are presumed at incurrence to relate to specific future revenue or determinable future periods. They may be charged to expenses before their expected expiration dates at any time they no longer provide discernible future benefit.

Accruals and Prepayments

An asset or liability must be recorded whenever an expense is recognized in a period other than the one in which it is incurred. A prepayment results if cash is paid (or if a liability is recognized) before the cost expires. Conversely, recognizing an expense that has not already been recorded as a liability results in accruing a liability. For example, if property tax is payable in September (as it is in many jurisdictions), monthly statements for January through August would include a property tax expense and an increasing liability for accrued property tax payable. Statements for September through December, after the tax is paid, would also include a property tax expense, but the liability would be replaced by a decreasing asset for prepaid property tax.

The need to record an expense to determine net income often results in recognizing an expense and a liability before a legal obligation to pay exists. For example, the cost of repairing automobiles or electrical appliances sold under warranty clearly relates to the revenue from sale of the product, but may not be incurred until one or more accounting periods later. An estimated expense and liability are therefore accrued to determine income correctly for the period of sale, even though no legal obligation will exist until some units of the product break down. The accounting concept of a liability is thus broader than many legal definitions of a liability.

Distinction Between Prepayments and Other Assets

Fundamentally, there is little difference between prepayments and assets such as inventories, plant and equipment, and intangibles: all are unexpired costs expected to be of benefit in the future. Prepayments are often assumed to be less readily realizable than inventory or equipment, but that does not necessarily follow: it may be easier to realize cash on the contractual right to cancel an insurance policy than on custom-built, single-purpose tangible property.

The distinction between prepayments and deferred charges is based on the difference between current and noncurrent, as modified by custom and materiality (prepaid insurance, for example, and many types of deposits do not expire for more than a year). The prepaid expense category is seldom material in financial statements, and noncurrent items that are not material are included in prepaid expenses for convenience. If deferred costs (debt expense and deferred pre-operating expenses are the most common) are material and will expire over several years, they are classified as noncurrent deferred charges.

How Much Cost or Expense at Incurrence

Acquisition cost is ". . . the amount of cash disbursed or the fair value of other assets distributed . . . [or] the present value of the amounts to be paid" to acquire an asset or service (see "Cost" above). That amount is known at the time the transaction is executed in the majority of instances. Purchases of goods and services are invoiced in specific prices and terms. Invoices can be checked against purchase orders and other supporting documents. Wages and salaries, taxes, rent, royalties, interest, and similar costs accumulate according to contracts, statutes, or other specifications and can be accrued by following those terms. When an insurance or warranty claim is honored, the amount is specified and agreed on.

Problems of how much to record can arise if an invoice price does not equal the cost incurred because of discounts or additions, such as freight or insurance on goods purchased, or if for some reason the price is unknown and must be estimated (as is the case in losses payable by property–casualty insurance companies). Both kinds of problems are discussed at appropriate places later in the chapter. The most serious questions about how much to record arise if several assets are acquired at a "basket" price or the "fair value of other assets distributed" is not readily determinable. Both questions are most often encountered when businesses are acquired; they are discussed in detail in Chapter 17 on business combinations.

How Much Expense at Expiration

Accounting for short-term expiration of costs is relatively straightforward because expense is recorded either as a liability is incurred or over a short and specific period of time. Accounting for cost expiration that is widely separated in time from incurrence presents some of the most complicated and difficult problems in accounting. Cost expirations related to estimates of future costs are covered in this chapter; those related to inventories, fixed assets, and income taxes are covered in succeeding chapters.

PRINCIPLES APPLYING TO SPECIFIC ITEMS

The accounting principles described so far apply to the broad cost segment generally. The remainder of this section on accounting principles describes the principles affecting the major items of the typical buying segment.

Purchases and Accounts Payable

Purchases of assets and services that are paid for in cash as the cost is incurred cause few, if any, accounting problems. The amount of cash paid fixes the cost, and the nature of the expenditure usually determines its asset or expense classification.

Purchases on open account from trade creditors likewise cause few problems. Cost should always be recorded net of trade discounts, which are essentially pricing devices and should not be recorded in the accounts (cf. Chapter 9). In principle, cost should also be recorded net of cash discounts, and discounts to be taken should be estimated and deducted. However, cash discounts are usually immaterial, and accounting for estimated discounts is troublesome. Two common practices are used, and either is usually acceptable if used consistently: (1) recording costs and accounts payable at amounts before deducting cash discounts and recording discounts taken as miscellaneous income, or (2) recording costs and accounts payable net of all discounts and recording discounts lost as miscellaneous expense. The latter is preferable.

Invoices commonly show itemized costs, with separate charges for taxes, freight, insurance, and other items included in the total invoice price. In principle, those charges are part of the acquisition cost of goods or services received and should be allocated to the individual items in the invoice. That allocation is usually too burdensome in practice, and the additional costs are often recorded separately. They may be recorded as expenses of the period of acquisition; a preferable procedure for purchases of materials is to increase the cost of all items by a fixed percentage for "purchasing overhead" costs and to reconcile periodically the estimated and actual "overhead" charges.

Notes Payable and Other Formal Evidences of Indebtedness

A variety of formal evidences of debt are commonly used in or related to purchases of goods and services:

Short-term notes payable are sometimes issued to suppliers or others to finance inventories or receivables.

Trade acceptances are frequently used to finance domestic purchases for short periods and may be issued on individual invoices or monthly statements. Trade acceptances have stated maturities, may be discounted by the seller who draws them, and are presented for payment through the holder's bank. Ordinarily they do not represent a lien on goods purchased.

Commercial letters of credit are extensively used to finance imports. A letter of credit is a guarantee by a bank extending credit to a buyer so that drafts drawn by a seller against the buyer in compliance with stipulated terms will be honored when presented for payment. Drafts drawn by a seller against a letter of credit may be sight drafts or time drafts. Sight drafts require payment on presentation; time drafts have stated maturities. Time drafts are customarily discounted by a seller of merchandise at his own bank, which forwards the drafts for acceptance and payment at maturity to the bank that issued the letter of credit. The buyer's bank pays sight drafts and accepts time drafts on the basis of shipping documents which evidence receipt of the merchandise.

Purchases of goods and services involving formal evidences of debt follow the same general principles as purchases on open account. They are recorded at cost—the invoice price or amount due. Cost excludes interest on interest-bearing or discounted instruments.

A significant number of transactions involving drafts and acceptances payable may require departure from the usual practice of recording purchases and payables when goods or services are received. Recording "goods in transit" and "drafts and acceptances payable" may be necessary to maintain control of those transactions as well as to assure timely recording of costs and liabilities incurred.

Agency Obligations

Accounting principles for agency obligations are usually quite simple: funds collected for others must be recorded and accountability maintained until the funds are turned over at the required time to the principal for whom they are held in trust. That often means maintaining separate accounts for each item or for each group of related items. Payment to the principal must usually be accompanied by a detailed accountability report to enable him (or it) to account properly for the funds.

Sales Taxes, Payroll Withholding, Etc.

Many agency obligations are specified in statutes or agreements, and the accounting should conform to the specified details. For example, sales and excise taxes are usually fixed as a percentage of taxable sales or sales value; amounts withheld from employees' wages and salaries for income taxes and social security taxes are established by statute or government regulation; amounts withheld from employees for pension contributions, insurance premiums, bond or stock purchases, dues, charitable contributions, and the like are specified in agreements with employees or labor unions.

A liability is recorded as amounts are collected from customers or employees, sometimes by identifying specific amounts and sometimes by applying appropriate percentages to base amounts. The liability remains until discharged by remitting funds to the appropriate government agency, insurance company, pension fund trustee, labor union, or other recipient.

Deposits

A company may receive deposits from employees, customers, or others, either for safekeeping or as part of an agreement for sales or services. For example, a school may hold funds of the athletic association, the drama club, the student loan fund, or the vending machine concession; a utility company holds customers' deposits for service; several kinds of companies hold customers' deposits for the use of returnable containers; landlords hold tenants' deposits on leases. A deposit normally will be refunded or otherwise reclaimed by the depositor, sometimes with interest. Some deposits will be held for a long time, however, and some will never be reclaimed because customers lose receipts or forget or die or move away without reclaiming the deposit, returnable containers are broken or lost, or other factors intervene.

A liability is recorded when a deposit is received and is removed or reduced when a deposit is refunded. Tenants' deposits often become the rent for the last period under a lease. Balances should be scrutinized periodically; unclaimed deposits or estimates of unclaimed deposits may be recorded as income unless other disposal is required by law. Under the laws of some states, for example, certain unclaimed deposits revert to the state after lapse of a statutory period (the law of escheat). Interest payable on the deposits, if any, should be accrued as earned, but as a practical matter it is often recorded at the time of refund rather than accrued, when the amount is not material in the aggregate.

Wages or Other Payments Unclaimed

Unclaimed wages and old outstanding checks are a form of agency obligation that differs from others in not having the feature of periodic detailed accountability to outsiders. Separate liabilities should be recorded and detailed accountability maintained, especially of unclaimed wages, because the escheat laws of some states require them to be turned over to a state agency after a specified time.

Accrued and Prepaid Expenses

Recording accrued and prepaid expenses is normally a straightforward procedure. The cost of each service and the time over which it expires are usually known more or less precisely and can be computed readily with only minor technical problems. The exceptions are estimated expenses, which are discussed separately later in the chapter.

The mechanics of accounting for prepaid and accrued expenses may be handled in two ways. In principle, a prepaid expense or accrued liability is recorded when payment is made or a liability is incurred, and the expense is amortized or accrued as the cost expires. An acceptable alternative procedure, which is often convenient, is to recognize expenses when liabilities are incurred and to compute and record prepaid or accrued amounts at the end of each accounting period.

Rent

Rent expense for a period can normally be calculated readily. Even if rent depends on a variable, such as sales, it is usually known by the end of a period. Amounts prepaid or unpaid at the end of a period are likewise usually readily calculated.

Interest

Interest expense is also, under normal conditions, easily calculated and accrued—it is a matter of applying an appropriate interest rate to a balance during a period. Interest rates are generally specified; however, sometimes the rate must be estimated or interest must be imputed at a rate different from a specified rate [see Chapter 9 and APB Opinion No. 21 (*AICPA Prof. Stds.*, vol. 3, Sections 4111 and 4111A)]. The problem in those instances is in determining an appropriate rate, not in accruing the expense. Once a rate is determined, accruing interest is a matter of computation.

Commissions

Commissions payable, usually to inside or outside salesmen, are ordinarily a routine accrual of the period of the related sale. Sometimes, however, a commission system includes a number of complications designed to assure salesmen of a minimum income or "draw," to provide incentives to achieve certain objectives, or to prevent payment of commissions for sales subsequently rescinded.

Commissions should be accrued in relation to sales made or services rendered even though the sale price remains uncollected. If necessary, both expense and liability can be reduced by commissions on estimated sales that may ultimately prove not collectible. Debit balances in commissions payable that represent drawings in excess of commissions earned should not be carried forward as assets if they are really minimum compensation of salesmen for the period. If a commission plan requires offsetting future commissions against excess "draw," experience with the pattern of commissions usually provides a basis for judging whether excess "draw" can be earned out in a reasonable period.

Commissions paid by insurance companies to their agents must be deferred and amortized over the estimated lives of the policies sold so as to match that expense with the premium revenue to be received.

Salaries, Wages, and Payroll Taxes

Gross pay is recorded as an expense or cost of assets, net pay is recorded as an account payable or disbursement, and deductions or withheld amounts are recorded as agency obligations. At period end, salaries and wages not yet payable are accrued.

Payroll taxes are readily computed as soon as the amount of the payroll is known. Ceilings on pay subject to certain taxes result in accruing the larger part of tax liability in the early months of a year; some companies therefore record the total amount as prepaid taxes as it is paid early in a year and amortize it to spread the expense over the entire year.

Vacation Pay, Sick Pay, and Similar Employee Benefits (Other Than Pension Plans)

Vacations with pay are almost universal practice in the United States, and the amount of vacation granted to each employee often depends on length of service. A variety of other benefits have similar characteristics: allowable paid time off due to illness may accumulate annually or up to a maximum cumulative total, entitlement to severance pay may increase with length of service (severance pay is common and may be substantial in European and South American countries), allowances for extended vacation may depend on length of service (such as thirteen weeks of vacation after each five years of service).

Vacation and similar plans may be formal and specific. Those spelled out in formal contracts, such as union contracts, usually provide for some form of vesting; that is, they specify conditions under which an employee's right to a benefit becomes assured no matter what happens. Some benefit plans, though not provided by formal contracts, are explicitly promised to employees in published memoranda or booklets. Estimated costs in a formal and specific plan should be accrued over the period of service in which the benefits accumulate.

Some informal plans are as firmly established as formal ones. Vacation and sick pay may be expected because of long-established custom. Severance pay or "ex gratia" pensions are acknowledged customs in some foreign countries. A liability for benefits should be accrued in those circumstances even though no vesting occurs and estimating the amounts to be paid may be difficult. The liability should be accrued by recording expenses over the period of service during which employees are presumed to earn the expected benefits.

As a practical matter, the doctrine of materiality may cause a problem in applying the principle that the cost of benefit plans should be accrued during the period of service. Benefits may start out as an insignificant matter, and both the benefits and their costs may grow gradually over many years. As a result, annual charges to expense are based on actual costs incurred, and recording a liability for accrued costs as well would result in a "doubling up" of expense in the year of change. Since the omitted liability is not material in the balance sheet, many such benefit plans (other than pension plans) continue to be accounted for on a cash basis rather than the preferred accrual basis.

Deferred Compensation

Companies often agree to defer part of an employee's compensation until later years, usually after the employee retires. Deferred compensation in the United States is normally based on a contract or formal plan, but informal arrangements are possible. APB Opinion No. 12, *Omnibus Opinion—1967 (AICPA Prof. Stds.,* vol. 3, paragraphs 4064.01 to .03), provides that deferred compensation should be "accrued in a systematic and rational manner." The amount to be accrued may be explicit. Usually, however, deferred compensation is a specified payment each year after an executive or employee retires for a specific number of years or until death. The accrued expense and liability for each year of service may have to be estimated actuarially based on mortality tables. "Systematic and rational" accrual may be accomplished by a variety of methods. Some companies accrue the estimated liability on a straight-line basis, which results in an equal expense for each period benefited; others accrue on a present-value basis, which results in an increasing expense because of interest on the accrued liability. Either way, the liability at the end of the term of active employment should at least equal the present value of the deferred payments not yet due.

Stock Compensation

Distributions to employees by a corporation of its stock or of options to buy its stock may require accruing compensation expense. However, not all plans for distributing a corporation's stock to its employees are compensation plans and not all distributions under compensation-type plans result in recording compensation expense under present generally accepted accounting principles.

Some stock distributions to employees have primary purposes other than compensating employees. For example, employee stock purchase plans are often part of a corporation's efforts to secure equity capital or to encourage widespread ownership of stock by employees. Those plans are "noncompensatory" as long as the purchase price is not lower than is reasonably required to interest employees generally or to secure the desired funds. The Accounting Principles Board has concluded that at least four characteristics are essential in a noncompensatory plan:

> . . . (a) substantially all full-time employees meeting limited employment qualifications may participate (employees owning a specified percent of the outstanding stock and executives may be excluded), (b) stock is offered to eligible employees equally or based on a uniform percentage of salary or wages (the plan may limit the number of shares of stock that an employee may purchase through the plan), (c) the time permitted for exercise of an option or purchase right is limited to a reasonable period, and (d) the discount from the market price of the stock is no greater than would be reasonable in an offer of stock to stockholders or others. [APB Opinion No. 25, *Accounting for Stock Issued to Employees (AICPA Prof. Stds.,* vol. 3, paragraph 4062.07)]

Compensation is almost invariably involved in awards, grants, or bonuses of stock to employees and may be involved in grants of options to buy stock over extended periods. Generally awards of stock or options to buy stock are granted to a limited number of officers and key employees for current or future services or to induce continued employment or greater effort in managing the company so that its success will be reflected in the market value of the stock. An option agreement usually provides that, during a specified period and on performance by the grantee of stipulated conditions, the grantee may at his own election exercise the option in accord with its terms. In recent years, traditional option and award plans have been supplemented or replaced by more complex plans and arrangements, often involving an award of a variable number of shares of stock or a variable option price. "Variable" plans almost always involve compensation under present generally accepted accounting principles.

Compensation expense from awarding stock or granting rights or options to buy stock to employees should be accrued over the period of related employees' services, which may be spelled out in the plan or agreement or may need to be inferred from the circumstances. The offsetting obligation to distribute stock is not technically a liability, although it may sometimes be settled in cash, but is similar to a stock subscription (described in Chapter 16).

Determining the amount of compensation is the major accounting problem in recording compensation from awarding stock or granting stock rights or options. The traditional principle, expressed in ARB No. 43, Chapter 13B, "Compensation Involved in Stock Option and Stock Purchase Plans" (*AICPA Prof. Stds.*, vol. 3, Section 4061), is that the compensation equals the amount by which the fair value at the date of grant of the stock to be received exceeds the amount an employee must pay to receive the stock. Applying that principle results in recognizing:

> Compensation expense equal to the fair value of the stock at date of grant if stock is awarded to an employee at no cost to him, but
>
> No compensation expense if the option or purchase price at least equals the fair value of the stock at date of grant of the option or right.

Some compensation expense is recognized in situations falling between those limiting cases.

The result described above followed from two conclusions of the Committee on Accounting Procedure in the ARB: (1) the value of an option should be measured at the date of grant, and a grantee's later gains and losses should not affect the measure of compensation, and (2) measuring the value inherent in a restricted future right to buy shares of stock at a price at, or even above, the fair value of the stock at the date of grant was impracticable. Thus, the fair value of the stock at the date of grant became the only objective measure of the value of an option and the basis of recording the stock option transaction.

The latest pronouncement on stock compensation plans and agreements is APB Opinion No. 25 (*AICPA Prof. Stds.*, vol. 3, Sections 4062 and 4062A), issued in October, 1972. The Opinion was prompted by the increasing use of "variable" plans, but the Board reviewed the status of Chapter 13B of ARB No. 43. The major issues on which views differed are summarized in paragraph 5 of the Opinion:

> Some accountants believe that compensation cost for all compensatory plans should be recorded at the date of grant or not later than the date of exercise. They believe that past experience and outside evidence of values can overcome difficulties in measuring compensation. Other accountants be-

lieve that compensation need not be recorded if an employee pays an amount that is at least equal to the market price of the stock at the date of grant and that problems in accounting for compensation plans pertain to plans in which the number of shares of stock or the option or purchase price cannot be determined until after the date of grant or award. Still other accountants, although they agree in principle with the first group, believe that progress will result from specifying the accounting for plans with variable factors but leaving Chapter 13B of ARB No. 43 in effect with modifications while the entire topic of accounting for compensation involving stock is studied. [Paragraph 4062.05]

The Board chose the third course: Opinion No. 25 modified Chapter 13B of ARB No. 43 but did not change the basic accounting for stock options if the total option price is known and at least equals the total market value of the stock at date of grant. The Opinion contains, in paragraph 10, two significant modifications of prior principles:

Quoted market price of stock awarded or optioned is specified as the measure of value to be compared with the amount an employee pays, if any, to determine the amount of compensation expense from awarding of stock or granting of a stock option. That change affects all grants if the fair value of the stock differs from its quoted market price.

The measurement date for determining compensation is specified as the "first date on which are known both (1) the number of shares that an individual employee is entitled to receive and (2) the option or purchase price, if any." That change affects only the "variable" plans and agreements because the measurement date for the more traditional-type plans remains the date of award or grant.

When the measurement date is later than the date of grant, compensation expense should be accrued in each intervening period on the basis of the fair (market) value of the stock at the end of the period. Accounting for "variable" awards or options may thus involve accruals of compensation, and perhaps reversals of accruals, at the end of each period between grant date and measurement date, depending on the quoted market price of the stock involved.

Opinion No. 25 is complex and cannot be adequately summarized in a few paragraphs. It also discusses other matters, such as accounting for income tax benefits of stock compensation arrangements. Readers should therefore refer to the Opinion for a more complete description of accounting principles for accruing compensation expense from issuing stock to employees.

Taxes Other Than Income Taxes

The principal types of taxes paid directly by business enterprises, other than income taxes and those explicitly or implicitly included in the prices paid for goods and services purchased, are those based on sales, on payrolls, on property valuation, real or personal, and sometimes on the balance sheet or some other measure of the whole business entity. The statutes and regulations are necessarily complex and varied, and there are difficult accounting and legal questions about what items should be taxed and what their value is.

These taxes are usually routinely assessed and paid, and measuring how much to record presents little difficulty: for example, it may be necessary to estimate a current year property tax rate before it is publicly announced. However, if there are unsettled disputes at the end of an accounting period, judgments about the outcome must be made in much the same way as for income taxes (see Chapter 13).

It has long been accepted that a tax is an expense of the period covered by the services for which it is assessed, or is directly related to the transaction giving rise to it, such as sales or payroll (see Section 4081 of *AICPA Prof. Stds.,* vol. 3). Almost always the period covered by property and franchise taxes is a year. There are differences of opinion about what year is covered by a given assessment: the calendar year, the taxpayer's fiscal year, or the taxing authority's fiscal year, and so on. The differences of opinion can be tolerated because taxation is proverbially recurrent and so no material distortion of income will result as long as a method is consistently followed.

For some state or local corporate excise or franchise taxes, it can be unclear whether the tax applies to the current year, even though payable in a subsequent year, or whether the tax is for the privilege of doing business in the subsequent year even though measured by the financial statements of the current year. Usually, the local Society of Certified Public Accountants provides guidance on a common approach to such questions. The principles applicable to state franchise taxes based on net income are usually the same as for federal income taxes (see Chapter 13).

It is generally, though not universally, accepted that a tax levied on a buyer and collected by a seller is accounted for as an agency collection —neither revenue nor expense of the seller—while a tax levied on a seller is both revenue and expense even though it is explicitly billed to the buyer. There are exceptions to that general rule which have become sanctioned by long-standing practice.

ACCRUING ESTIMATED EXPENSES

Estimated Expenses

Several kinds of accrued expenses already discussed involve more or less routine estimates of expenses and liabilities. For example, the property tax rate, and therefore the total tax bill, is often not known until well into the year to which the tax applies. An estimate of taxes for the year, based on prior years' experience and prediction of probable changes, is required to accrue property taxes during the year. Estimates may also be needed at year end if the tax year does not correspond to a company's fiscal year.

Some accruals are mostly routine but may involve complications. For example, estimating the number of units to accrue royalty expense and royalties payable may be complicated if the unit cost of royalties involves step rates based on volume.

Some accruals present major accounting problems because they involve long estimating periods or become intertwined with questions of accounting principle. Some of those—warranties and guarantees, deferred maintenance, pension costs, losses on operations of discontinued businesses, insurance company reserves for claims and other future policyholder benefits, and self-insurance—are discussed specifically later in the chapter, following a brief discussion of other points that pertain to estimated expenses generally.

Most estimates of expenses involve accruals, but occasionally estimates must be made of the amount of prepaid expense items. For example, certain insurance premiums, which are usually prepaid, may be significantly reduced later by dividends. Since insurance expense should be based on cost, which is the amount paid less dividends, dividends should be estimated, based on prior years' experience.

Correcting Estimates

Accruing expenses and liabilities based on estimates inevitably results in later adjustments when the cost becomes known. How best to correct errors of estimate has long been a subject of disagreement in accounting, and the theory is not entirely clear. However, the principles that guide practice are unequivocal:

Treatment as prior period adjustments should not be applied to the normal, recurring corrections and adjustments which are the natural result of the use of estimates inherent in the accounting process. [APB Opinion No. 9 (*AICPA Prof. Stds.*, vol. 3, paragraph 2010.23)]

> . . . a change in accounting estimate should be accounted for in (a) the period of change if the change affects that period only or (b) the period of change and future periods if the change affects both. A change in an estimate should not be accounted for by restating amounts reported in financial statements of prior periods or by reporting pro forma amounts for prior periods. [APB Opinion No. 20 (*AICPA Prof. Stds.*, vol. 3, paragraph 1051.31)]

Estimating and correcting estimates are continuous processes, and changes in amounts of accrued liabilities almost always affect the related expense of the period of change.

Loss Contingencies That Should Be Accrued

Estimated expenses and liabilities that should be accrued must be distinguished from loss contingencies that should not be accrued. Estimated expenses have been incurred and will be paid, but the amount of the expense and related liability is not known and must be estimated. Many other loss contingencies have not been incurred and will not be paid unless some specific event occurs in the future, or the potential amount of a loss contingency may not be subject to reasonable estimation. Sometimes this distinction is hard to make; for example, the costs of making good on product warranties are an expense of the period in which the products are sold (because experience shows that such costs are incurred at time of sale) and should be estimated and accrued even though the specific amount to be paid is not known. But amounts that might be assessed in a pending lawsuit for damages will become an expense and liability only if the case is lost. They should not be accrued but they should be disclosed.

Major contingent liabilities (loss contingencies that should not be accrued) and their characteristics are discussed later in the chapter.

Product Warranties and Guarantees

The sale of products often carries a commitment to perform some kind of activity in the future. The commitment may be explicit and measurable: for example, to install equipment sold, to prepare a site for it, to perform a specified schedule of service or maintenance routines on it, or a similar specific contractual obligation. The cost of fulfilling such a commitment can usually be estimated accurately and competently, and few major accounting problems result.

The commitment may, however, be implicit or explicit but not readily measurable: for example, warranties to replace defective parts, warranties against defective workmanship, or a general business policy to "guarantee satisfaction." Estimating the ultimate cost of general or implicit warranties is difficult at best but is especially problematic if the warranty is new and untried. Nevertheless, the best estimates possible have to be made to match the cost of product warranties and guarantees with revenue resulting from related sales. Estimates can be improved with experience. But past experience, however helpful as a guide to expectations of the future, must be tempered by judgments of current economic conditions and marketing policies.

The usual procedure in accounting for estimates of product warranties and guarantees is to recognize the cost of rendering the repair or replacement services as an expense as incurred and to estimate future cost and adjust the accounts at least annually. Equally appropriate, though unusual, is a practice of accruing an amount of expected future cost as each sale is recorded and recording actual costs incurred as reductions of the accrued liability. In the latter case, an annual estimate of future costs is still necessary to evaluate the balance of the liability. We noted in Chapter 9 that customers' claims under warranties and guarantees are sometimes satisfied by adjusting the sale price rather than by repairing or replacing the product. If so, the accounting involves reducing revenue rather than accruing expenses, but the same considerations apply.

FASB Statement No. 5 notes, in paragraph 4311.25, that inability to make a reasonable estimate of product warranty liability precludes accrual under that Statement, but it also raises a question about whether a sale should be recorded until the liability can be estimated.

Deferred Maintenance

Repairs and maintenance for most operations consist of constant small recurring expenditures with an aggregate cost about the same from year to year. In some plants, major repairs and renewals are required less frequently and their cost represents a significant outlay whose timing is to some degree under the control of management. For example, refractory and steel companies may reline their furnaces every four or five years; gas utilities may paint their storage tanks at similar intervals; roofing and siding, elevator systems, and heating and air conditioning plants of major buildings need overhauling only after long but reasonably predictable periods.

It is accepted practice in some industries to accrue the cost of major maintenance over several years by recording an annual expense based on the estimated cost of the anticipated maintenance and either the elapsed time or amount of usage until it is required. Actual expenditures then reduce the liability. Sometimes only specific estimated costs of major repairs and renewals are accrued; sometimes an entire average annual repair and renewal cost is estimated and accrued.

We believe that accounting for deferred maintenance costs is not as widely practiced as it should be. Putting off repairs and renewals to reduce expenses is a tempting way to improve current income at the expense of the future. Failure to estimate and accrue maintenance, repair, and renewal costs is often defended on the grounds that professional literature contains no explicit statement requiring their accrual, or that they are not material or too difficult to estimate.

Paragraph 4 of Chapter 6 of ARB No. 43, which was in effect from 1953 until superseded by FASB Statement No. 5 (*AICPA Prof. Stds.*, vol. 3, Section 4311), stated in part: ". . . it is deemed desirable to provide, by charges in the current income statement, properly classified, for all foreseeable costs and losses applicable against current revenues, to the extent that they can be measured and allocated to fiscal periods with reasonable approximation." FASB Statement No. 5 superseded that quotation and did not specifically address deferred maintenance so it is not clear whether it is no longer desirable to provide for that "foreseeable cost." However, some kinds of deferred maintenance appear to fit the Statement's criteria for "loss contingencies that should be accrued" quoted on page 280 above, because the value of the asset is thereby impaired. Therefore, the issue must be considered unclear, and failure to account for deferred maintenance cannot be considered unacceptable.

It is considered good maintenance practice for engineers to inspect plant and equipment regularly to estimate future repair and maintenance needs. Some companies now translate those estimates or "inventories" into estimated costs by time periods and accrue them.

Pension Costs

Widespread adoption of pension plans for employees, frequent broadening of pension benefits, and variations in plans have created a number of accounting problems in estimating liabilities for pension costs and allocating those estimated costs among periods of employees' service. Recent federal legislation mandating vesting and other guarantees with respect to private pension plans complicates this process further. The concept underlying accruing pension costs is relatively simple, but complications can make the computations and estimates extremely complex, normally requiring the use of actuarial assumptions and estimates.

Accrual Versus Funding

Accountants generally agree that the costs of providing pensions to employees after retirement are expenses of the periods of employment. For "defined contribution" plans, the accounting is relatively simple, because the annual pension expense is defined, not estimated. For "defined benefit" plans, actuarial estimates of the amount and timing of contributions and benefit payments can be complicated. The following simplified example illustrates some of the basic elements of defined benefit pension plans.

Employee X is hired by Company A on January 1 of year 1. He will retire in 10 years and will be paid a pension of $1,000 on January 1 of each year 11 through 15. (Note, however, that pensions normally are for life.)

Company A may either pay the pension benefits directly to X or may "fund" them: pay an outside agency—perhaps an insurance company or a pension fund—to be responsible for pension benefits when they become due. Several ways of providing for payments to retired employees or "contributions" to funding agencies are possible.

1. The company pays the pension benefits as they fall due each year 11 through 15—a method aptly called "pay-as-you-go."

2. The company buys a five-year, 5%, single-premium annuity for X at the end of the tenth year. The cost is $4,546, the present value at 5% of the five pension benefits. The method is called "terminal funding."

3. The company deposits $2,791 at 5% interest when X is hired. That amount accumulates to $4,546 at the end of ten years and will be used to pay the pension benefits to X as they become due. The method is a prepayment and thus is at the opposite extreme from pay-as-you-go and terminal funding. It is seldom used, principally because it tends to tie up funds for long periods, often at a relatively low return.

4. The company deposits $361 at 5% interest on December 31 of each year 1 through 10 to accumulate the $4,546 needed at the end of year 10. This method is a common form of actuarial funding and may have numerous variations—for example, the contributions to the funding agency may increase over time.

The way pension benefits are paid or funded does not necessarily determine the accounting for pension costs. Pay-as-you-go and terminal funding methods, for example, do not allocate pension costs to periods of employment and therefore cannot be accepted as methods of recognizing pension expenses. Funding is essentially a financial rather than an accounting matter. Nevertheless, accruing costs and paying them are clearly related and may involve some of the same concepts.

Accrual and prepayment accounting techniques can be applied to any pattern of payment of pension costs to allocate costs among accounting periods. To illustrate, costs can be allocated to the ten years that X is employed on a straight-line basis (equal amount to each period) for each of the payment patterns in the example:

Payment Pattern	Amount of Payments	Number of Payments	Total Payments	Allocated Cost of Each Year
1	$1,000	5	$5,000	$500
2	4,546	1	4,546	455
3	2,791	1	2,791	279
4	361	10	3,610	361

Complicating Factors

The varying amounts in the table are due to interest (5% in the example) and stem from differences in the payment patterns. Differences in payment patterns and the impact of interest over long periods are factors that complicate accounting for pension costs.

Numerous other factors also complicate pensions, introducing problems not present in the simplified example. Among them are length of life of employees (since most pensions are for life), employee turnover, future compensation levels, vesting rights, and possible retirement ages. Three crucial factors in the example besides the rate of interest—years to retirement, amount of pension benefit, and number of benefit payments to be received—must usually be estimated, often years in advance and for large numbers of employees with varied employment records, types of pension rights, and life expectancies. Estimating the impact of factors such as employee turnover and mortality of retired employees is sometimes further complicated by recent federal legislation mandating vesting rights in certain circumstances, which give at least partial benefits to some employees despite employment changes or inadequate service records, and supplementary benefit provisions, which continue benefits to wives, husbands, and children after deaths of eligible employees.

Other complicating factors include costs of "past service" and "prior service," two technical actuarial notions that have long been sources of disagreement among accountants concerned with accruing pension costs. In nontechnical terms, past service costs and prior service costs are pension costs attributed to employee services before a pension plan was adopted or before changes in a plan increased benefits, and are thus distinguished from "normal cost"—pension costs attributed to current and future employee services.

Although accountants generally agree that past and prior service costs should not be accounted for as corrections of income of prior periods or otherwise charged directly to retained earnings, they disagree on how to accrue those costs or even whether they need to be accrued at all. One area of disagreement involves whether past and prior service costs pertain to the employee group at the time a plan is started or changed or to the plan itself, which covers a continuing employee group as a whole. That difference affects the period over which past and prior service costs are accrued—one group would accrue them over the remaining service lives of the particular employee group, while the other would accrue them over a somewhat longer period. A third group disagrees with both and holds that accruing normal cost and an amount equivalent to interest on unfunded past and prior service costs accrues all of the pension costs that a company will ever pay.

We have found it necessary to refer to actuarial computations and concepts several times in the foregoing brief discussion. Most companies find that they must use actuarial methods to estimate the values required to manage their pension programs. Actuaries have developed several actuarial cost methods to estimate amounts and incidences of future pension benefits. Although actuaries' efforts have been largely devoted to questions of funding and other management concerns rather than to accruing pension expenses for accounting purposes, most actuarial cost methods can be used in accounting.*

APB Opinion No. 8

Accounting for pension costs is now guided primarily by APB Opinion No. 8 (*AICPA Prof. Stds.*, vol. 3, Sections 4063 to 4063B). The Opinion was a response not only to the increasing importance and complexity of pension plans but also to specific criticisms of then existing pension accounting. Some companies used legal interpreta-

---

* Descriptions, which were written primarily for accountants, of actuarial assumptions, concepts, and methods can be found in two appendixes to APB Opinion No. 8, *Accounting for the Cost of Pension Plans (AICPA Prof. Stds.*, vol. 3, Sections 4063 to 4063B); Ernest L. Hicks, *Accounting for the Cost of Pension Plans* (Accounting Research Study No. 8); and two *Accounting Interpretations of APB Opinion No. 8*, published by the AICPA—Julius W. Phoenix, Jr., and William D. Bosse, *A Discussion of the Background and Requirements of APB Opinion No. 8*, and Frederick P. Sloat, *Actuarial Considerations Involved in Pension Costs Under APB Opinion No. 8*.

tions showing limitations on liabilities for unvested pension benefits to defend minimum accruals, or even no accruals, of pension costs. Many companies showed wide year-to-year fluctuations in pension expenses, including no pension cost for some years. The Accounting Principles Board attributed those fluctuations to several factors, prominent among which was a tendency to base pension expense for accounting purposes on pension cost funded. The amount funded was often in turn affected by several factors not relevant to accruing pension costs, such as recognition of actuarial gains and losses in a period, fluctuations in company earnings, availability of funds, and income tax rates. The Board also noted the effect of varied accounting for past and prior costs.

The Opinion showed a rare unanimity—the Board agreed on most major points. The Opinion contained one major compromise, however, in establishing minimum and maximum limits on pension cost accrued in a period rather than specifying a single method of accruing costs. That range stemmed primarily from disagreement about accounting for past and prior service costs. The majority of the Board preferred full accrual of those costs but concluded that the maximum and minimum procedure was a distinct improvement over existing practice during a time when accounting for pension cost was in a transitional stage.

The following is a highly condensed summary of the major conclusions of Opinion No. 8:

> Pension costs should usually be accrued on the assumption that the plan will continue indefinitely, even though its continuation technically may be at the company's discretion and its legal obligations are interpreted as limited. Experience shows that plans do continue, and accounting for pension cost should not be discretionary.
>
> Annual accrual of pension expense and liability should be based on consistent application of an accounting method that uses an acceptable actuarial method. It should not be *less* than normal cost increased by an interest equivalent on unfunded prior service cost (including past service cost) and an amount for vested benefits, if needed. It should not be *more* than normal cost increased by 10% of past and prior service costs (considered separately until each is amortized) and an interest equivalent on differences between amounts accrued and amounts funded, if any. Accounting for past and prior service costs is a major difference between the minimum and maximum accruals—only interest on unfunded amounts is included in the minimum while 10% of the costs are included in the maximum. The inclusion of an amount for vested benefits in the minimum accrual is extremely complicated in the Opinion. Essentially, it is intended to insure that total pension cost accrued (whether funded or not) at

least equals vested benefits as defined in the Opinion. Since applying that test every year might result in fluctuating accruals because of the vesting accrual, however, the Opinion in effect allows twenty years to bring the total accrual into line with vested benefits.

All of the actuarial cost methods discussed in Appendix A of the Opinion (and in Section 4063A) except terminal funding are acceptable for accruing expenses and liabilities for pensions if the actuarial assumptions are reasonable and the method is applied consistently in conformity with other provisions of the Opinion. The same test applies to other possible methods. The terminal funding method and the pay-as-you-go method (which is not an actuarial method) are unacceptable because they do not accrue pension costs before retirement.

Actuarial gains and losses, both realized and "unrealized," should be averaged or spread over 10 to 20 years to be consistent with the long-range nature of pension costs. Short-term fluctuations in market prices of fund investments, sporadic gains and losses from sales of investments, and changes in assumptions about future benefits or earnings should not result in fluctuating pension cost accruals.

Since accrual of pension cost does not depend on the amount funded, and some pensions may not be funded at all, differences are to be expected between total accrued pension cost and pension benefits funded. Those differences are accrued or prepaid expenses. An amount equivalent to interest on the accrued liability or prepayment should be added to or deducted from the current accrual of expense.

Those conclusions are, of course, elaborated on in the Opinion, which also contains other conclusions.

Opinion No. 8 represents a significant step forward from earlier practice in accounting for pension costs. In concept, we favor full accrual of pension costs, including prior and past service costs, although we would not necessarily accrue them over the remaining service life of the employee group existing at the time of adoption or change of a plan.

The enactment of the Employee Retirement Income Security Act of 1974 again focused attention on pension cost accounting. The FASB thereupon placed the subject on its technical agenda to determine whether changes are needed. In the meantime, it has reaffirmed the applicability of Opinion No. 8 in its Interpretation No. 3 (*AICPA Prof. Stds.*, vol. 3, Section 4063-1).

Losses from Discontinued Operations

A major convention of accounting requires that all losses be anticipated and recorded when a decision is made to discontinue a segment of a business. Considerable time and cost are usually required to dispose of the operations after the decision has been made, and continuing operations at a loss is often necessary to complete commitments or minimize the total loss on discontinuance and disposal.

Before APB Opinion No. 30, *Reporting the Results of Operations— Reporting the Effects of Disposal of a Segment of a Business, and Extraordinary, Unusual and Infrequently Occurring Transactions* (1973; *AICPA Prof. Stds.,* vol. 3, Section 2012), customary practice was to estimate and record as an extraordinary item all anticipated losses, including losses on continuing the operations to be disposed of. Thus the financial effects of a decision to discontinue a segment of a business were shown as a single extraordinary amount in the period of the decision. The Opinion does not change the convention or principle that all probable losses from disposal should be estimated and recorded in the period of the decision to discontinue operations. However, the Opinion does (1) change the disclosure, (2) define "disposal of a segment of a business," "measurement date," and "disposal date," and (3) describe how losses are to be measured.

At the measurement date (date the decision is made to discontinue), probable gain or loss from disposing of the discontinued segment should be estimated. That estimate must take into consideration the effects of continued operations between the measurement and disposal dates. Estimated losses on disposal should be recognized at the measurement date, but gains should be recognized only at the disposal date.

Gains or losses from operating the discontinued segment should be recognized in the usual way by matching costs of the operations with revenue from sales, but they should be disclosed separately from results of continuing operations. Results of operations of a discontinued segment and gain or loss from disposal of that segment should be shown together on an income statement, apart from both results of continuing operations and extraordinary items. The Opinion specifically states that neither is an extraordinary item.

Recording an estimated loss on disposal of discontinued operations is similar to accruing other estimated expenses, with one significant exception: no liability accrues. Rather, the offsetting item is a valuation account that in effect reduces the carrying value of the segment being disposed of to its estimated net realizable value, even though the valuation account may be included among the liabilities in a balance sheet.

"Self-Insurance"

Most companies insure against losses from fire or other casualties; that is, they buy insurance that will reimburse them, in whole or in part, for financial loss resulting from fire, workmen's compensation claims, liability to customers, and the like.

Some companies assume the burden of risk of loss over their own large number of relatively small exposures to certain types of losses. They pay no premiums for the risks they assume themselves and are said to be "self-insured." Until 1975, when FASB Statement No. 5 (*AICPA Prof. Stds.,* vol. 3, Section 4311) prohibited the practice, many self-insured companies estimated possible future losses and accrued an expense annually in a "reserve for self-insurance."

Self-insurance accounting was controversial. The decision of the FASB was based on the argument that casualty losses in companies other than insurance companies do not accrue like wages or rent but arise only if a casualty occurs. An insured company pays for protection, and those payments are an expense of the periods to which the insurance applies. In contrast, an uninsured company must bear the loss itself. Since an uninsured company is different from an insured company, the argument goes, accounting that makes them appear alike is misleading.

In years past, a "surplus reserve" for self-insurance (created by reserving a portion of retained earnings) was used as a means of advising readers of company practice; however, losses were required to be charged to income as they occurred. Although the practice is rare, FASB Statement No. 5 specifically permits it.

Loss Reserves and Reserves for Future Policy Benefits In the Insurance Industry

Probably the most challenging accounting (and auditing) task in the property–casualty insurance industry is estimating adequate reserves for losses. Great care and sound judgment must be exercised in making loss estimates because losses paid to policyholders, with few exceptions, represent the largest single cost of doing business in this industry. Particularly in the so-called "casualty" lines (workmen's compensation and personal injury), it may be, and frequently is, years before the aggregate amount of a reported loss is finally known. Since deficiencies (or, less frequently, redundancies) in aggregate loss reserves must be made up by charges or credits to the category of income and expense known as "underwriting results" in the period in which they emerge, it can be seen that even a small percentage variation in the amount of the aggregate loss reserves can have a substantial effect on underwriting results and accordingly on net income for an accounting period. That problem and others peculiar to the property–casualty insurance industry are dealt with at length in the **AICPA** Industry Audit Guide, *Audits of Fire and Casualty Insurance Companies* (1966).

The life insurance industry has its own unique problems in establishing proper reserves for future benefits to policyholders and other policy liabilities. All insurance companies are subject to regulation in those states in which they are licensed to transact business, one feature of which is filing periodic financial statements (at least annually) with the state regulatory authorities. While some latitude in methods of reserving is permitted in these "statutory" financial statements, life insurance companies must compute their reserves using actuarial standards acceptable to the regulatory authorities. The standards include mortality assumptions and maximum interest rate assumptions which are incorporated into published reserve factors.

Since the primary role of the insurance regulatory authorities is protection of the interests of the policyholders, the reserve factors described above and other statutory reporting requirements tend to produce statutory financial statements that are very conservative compared with financial position and results of operations presented in accordance with generally accepted accounting principles. To deal with this problem, the AICPA published, in 1972, an Industry Audit Guide, *Audits of Stock Life Insurance Companies*. This Guide gives thorough coverage to the accounting and actuarial techniques that must be applied to convert the statutory reserves to the basis of generally accepted accounting principles. In broad terms, the techniques involve the substitution of realistic factors based on the company's own experience (with provisions for adverse deviations) for mortality, rate of interest earned on funds invested, withdrawals (termination of their policies by insureds), and expenses. It is beyond the scope of this book to describe the methodology of those conversions, which, as noted above, is discussed in the Guide extensively.

CONTINGENT LIABILITIES OR LOSS CONTINGENCIES THAT SHOULD NOT BE ACCRUED

The term "contingent liability" should be used in accounting to designate a possible liability that (1) arises from past circumstances or actions, (2) may become a legal obligation in the future, and (3) if paid, will result in a loss or expense or perhaps an asset of doubtful value. Losses that may arise from possible future events that are general risks are sometimes wrongly referred to as contingent liabilities. For example, the possibility that property may be damaged by tornadoes in certain sections of the country does not create a contingent liability and requires no recognition in financial statements.

Disclosure of Existence

The existence of contingent liabilities should be recognized and appropriately disclosed. The fact that a precise amount cannot be established does not justify failure to disclose the existence of a material contingent liability. The question of whether a contingent liability should be disclosed is one of the most subjective of the many judgments affecting financial statements, and contingencies can never be evaluated with complete confidence. However, an accountant's natural inclination to anticipate losses is a healthy balance for the natural optimism that management may have toward contingent liabilities.

Even though contingent liabilities are not recorded formally in accounts, a record should be kept of estimates of possible liabilities and their amounts. Some companies keep memorandum accounts that not only provide information needed to disclose contingent liabilities but also provide control over possible liabilities.

Contingent Liabilities of Indeterminable Amount

Contingent liabilities are, by definition, possible but not probable or admitted. The following may describe either actual or contingent liabilities, depending on the degree of certainty or probability of liability:

Matters in litigation, such as alleged patent, copyright, or trademark infringements or breach of contract;

Possible claims by employees for back compensation under laws whose interpretation is uncertain;

Proposed additional taxes for prior periods that a company believes are unwarranted;

Possible liability for refunds arising from renegotiation that a company believes are unjustified;

Claims that counsel believes may be adequately defended—the amount of liability, if any, will be fixed by judge or jury after the balance sheet date;

Guarantees of a new product.

Liability under product guarantees may be uncertain when a new product is introduced and experience gives no indication of the likelihood of claims. Estimated liabilities arise once experience shows that claims are probable. A company should determine whether amounts claimed under various types of litigation or government regulation represent actual or contingent liabilities. Advice of legal counsel may be helpful, or even required, to make that kind of determination.

Potential assessments of policyholders for abnormal losses of mutual insurance companies are not usually considered contingent liabilities because assessments are so infrequent.

Contingent Liabilities of Determinable Amount

The amounts of many contingent liabilities are usually determinable; it is their becoming actual liabilities that is in doubt. Common examples include the contingent liability of a secondary obligor if a primary obligor defaults in payment, such as liabilities that may arise from the following transactions:

> Sale, pledge, or assignment of accounts receivable or installment obligations in which the transfer involves a liability to the seller, pledgor, or assignor in the event of non-collection.
>
> Discount, sale, or transfer of notes receivable, trade acceptances, bank acceptances arising under commercial letters of credit, or domestic and foreign drafts;
>
> Endorsement of notes;
>
> Accommodation endorsement of commercial paper;
>
> Guarantee of indebtedness (interest or principal) of others;
>
> Sale of real estate subject to a mortgage with a vendor's liability continued under a bond;
>
> The portion of insurance coverage that an insurance company cedes to (reinsures with) another company (the reinsurer).

In most of those examples, the amount of the contingent liability is the maximum possible loss, not necessarily the actual loss, that may be suffered. If accounts receivable are sold with recourse, for example, it is highly unlikely that all will prove uncollectible by the assignee. By custom, contingent liabilities of this type must be disclosed even though the probability that a liability may arise is remote.

Most of the contingent liabilities mentioned above may result in contingent assets; that is, a right of action by endorsers or guarantors against the primary obligor ensues if they become liable on his default. In exceptional circumstances, contingent liabilities may be fully offset by contingent assets that would be acquired if the liabilities became actual. The fact that contingent assets may arise on default does not relieve a company of the responsibility for disclosing those contingent liabilities; the necessity of payment by the secondary obligor is generally prima facie indication of doubtful value of a claim against the primary obligor.

Accounts Receivable Sold

Ordinarily an account receivable may be assigned legally without notifying the debtor of the assignment. However, an assignment of an account receivable is valid in some states only if some act, such as the filing of public notice, is performed.

Accounts receivable sold are usually guaranteed, and the vendor is obligated to make good the default by assigning other accounts receivable or returning cash if the debtor fails to pay. Less frequently, accounts receivable are sold outright without guarantee, and the vendor has no continuing or contingent liability.

Accounts receivable may be guaranteed for a consideration, a condition found in the relationship between textile mills and their factors. Estimated probable losses should be accrued and reflected in financial statements of the factor or guarantor. The amount of loss that is possible, not probable, should be disclosed in the balance sheet as a loss contingency or contingent liability.

Drafts Sold

Drafts against foreign shipments are often sold to banks at the time goods are shipped, and the cash received is credited to a customer's account. The accounts will not disclose the amount of contingent liability on those drafts, but that information may be available in a subsidiary record.

The terms on which business is conducted with customers in foreign countries may range from 30 to 120 days or longer. Therefore, a large portion of drafts drawn against foreign shipments and sold to banks in the last few months prior to the end of a period may be outstanding at the balance sheet date; contingent liability for those unpaid drafts should be disclosed.

Guarantees, Endorsements, and Acceptances

Guarantees of debt, endorsements of promissory notes, and accepted drafts or bills of exchange all give rise to contingent liabilities. Although the governing law is technically different for each, the business purpose is the same: the guarantor, endorser, and acceptor acknowledge a contingent liability to pay the debt evidenced by the basic document if the primary obligor defaults.

Guarantees of Subsidiaries' Obligations

Good accounting practice requires full disclosure in a parent company's financial statements of contingent liabilities arising from endorsements and guarantees of subsidiaries' obligations and commitments—such as those for merchandise to be delivered at future dates—that mature beyond the date of a balance sheet. That kind of guarantee is not, of course, disclosed as a contingent liability in a consolidated balance sheet of the company and subsidiaries because the primary obligation is shown as a liability of the consolidated group.

Parent companies sometimes guarantee specified dividends or interest on securities of subsidiaries in the hands of the public. If the guaranteed amounts in arrears have not been paid by a parent company, the liability and the fact of guarantee should be recorded in the accounts of the parent company and the subsidiaries.

COMMITMENTS

A contingent liability does not arise merely because a company decides, either through its internal authorization procedures or by formal contract, to purchase inventory, securities, or other assets. Contracts or orders to buy are referred to as "commitments" and ordinarily require no recognition in the accounts until the asset is received. However, the existence of material commitments is usually disclosed in notes to financial statements. If contracts to purchase contain clauses providing penalties for cancellation, a penalty cost should be accrued if cancellation is considered probable. Chapter 11 discusses losses on commitments to purchase inventories.

● TYPICAL TRANSACTION SYSTEMS AND INTERNAL CONTROL

TYPICAL TRANSACTION

Every purchase goes through about the same steps: determining needs; shopping for the best means of satisfying them and the best price; ordering the item; receiving, inspecting, and accepting it; storing or using it; recording the transaction; and paying the invoice. Large or infrequent purchases may be subject to special scrutiny, but the process is still basically the same. Conceptually, payrolls are part of the buying segment, but practical differences in the handling of payrolls make the conceptual parallel not particularly useful.

In this chapter we deal with normal repetitive buying of goods and services—the "typical transaction," including payrolls as a separate type of transaction—and then with variations on it.

Determining Needs

The buying segment starts when someone identifies a need, which may occur in several different ways. *For example*:

Raw material inventory replenishment needs may be determined manually or automatically when stock on hand reaches a reorder point or when a bill of materials for a job order is prepared. Sometimes sophisticated computerized systems identify needs and simultaneously execute much of the buying system. See Chapter 11, "The Production Segment," for an outline of ordering techniques and controls.

Needs for occasional goods and services are identified and described by the user, usually on a requisition form which has to be approved (authorized) by the person (who may be the same as the user) responsible for the budget expenditure category.

Recurring services such as utilities, telephone, periodicals, or janitorial services are identified only initially and are thereafter provided continuously without further request.

Specialized services, such as insurance, legal, advertising—and auditing —are usually identified by a specialist.

Needs for fixed assets are usually identified by engineers, planners, capital budgeters, or executives.

Controls over requisitioning are often informal because a requisition, as such, does not appear to have accounting or asset safeguarding significance. The purpose of control over requisitions is often thought to be solely so that the initiator may follow up on the processing of his request. Requisitions may be in numerical sequence, but most often the only control is simply a holding file of copies of unprocessed requisitions in the user department.

Authorization control is usually exercised at two points. First is approval of the requisition by the supervisor having budgetary responsibility for that category of expenditure. The second level of authorization control is review of the requisition in the purchasing department prior to processing. Sometimes another type of control may be provided by comparison of items requisitioned with predetermined standards or approved lists.

Strong controls over requisitioning are important to minimize the danger of overstocking—either tying up cash in assets that may be lost or become obsolete, or wasting cash through over-use of services. Control can be exercised only through operational measures for independently determining the optimum level of expenditure and establishing it as the operational goal: examples are determination of economic order quantities and stock reorder points, analytical review and determination of expenditure budgets, and cost justification procedures for unusual expenditure requests.

Recurring services present a particular control problem. Users can be depended on to originate requests when they need a subscription to a periodical, for example, but are not so dependable in "derequisitioning" the subscription when it is no longer needed. The only control over continuing payments for redundant services is periodic operational review by persons knowledgeable enough about the activity to be able to determine the optimum level of expenditure.

Ordering

Preferred practice is to have a purchasing agent shop for sources, negotiate terms, and place orders. The purchasing function has become so well established in modern business that a specialist purchasing agent is considered essential for every enterprise of any size.

The purchasing department receives requisitions and establishes control over them. The handling of requisitions prior to actually placing purchase orders is a subject in itself—specialized skill or experience is needed for the most efficient grouping of items, concentration of orders to obtain volume discounts while also maintaining multiple sources of supply, effective bid solicitation, placing of blanket orders, negotiating schedules for vendor production and storage prior to delivery, and all the other ramifications of getting the best possible prices and services. It is a skill easily neglected or abused, as the cost of doing it poorly is an opportunity cost which cannot be measured by conventional accounting means. The subject of purchasing, and operational controls over the activity, is beyond the scope of this chapter.

Controls within the purchasing department comprise principally systemization through explicit, detailed policy and procedure statements, discipline of purchasing agents, and supervisory review, often supplemented by exception reporting and operational audit.

The purchase order is the execution instruction that authorizes a vendor to deliver and bill on certain terms (the terms should be complete and specific as to delivery time, routing, and quality of materials as well as number and price; otherwise those terms are dictated by the supplier). The purchase order in well-organized systems also authorizes the receiving department to accept the goods described and the accounting department to pay on acceptance by the receiving department. Since the purchase order authorizes execution and recording of transactions, control over it is of great importance.

The basic controls over purchase orders consist of some or all of the following:

Prenumbering of purchase orders and subsequent accounting for all numbers to guard against loss or misdirection.

Holding files of open purchase orders in the purchasing and accounting departments and periodic review of the files to monitor timely execution of orders.

Double-checking purchase order preparation: data transcribed from requisitions and master files of data on vendors, prices, etc.; extensions and footings; account distribution, etc.

Segregation of the functions of accounting and receiving so that they are independent of the functions of the purchasing agent and of one another and can therefore serve as a control mechanism.

Disciplinary control over accounting for purchase orders consists initially of review and approval of purchase orders prior to issuance. That review can be mechanized in part: prices can be compared with standards or averages of past experience, or purchase orders with small dollar amounts or routine characteristics can be mechanically passed for less detailed review. Disciplinary control is also afforded by budgetary systems that require explanations of differences between actual expenditures and budgeted amounts. Additionally, in some systems the requisitioner receives a copy of the purchase order; his review of it for conformity with his expectations constitutes a disciplinary control.

Some specialized goods and services cannot be ordered by a purchasing agent because the technical and performance requirements are too esoteric, or in some cases are even unknown, and must be negotiated directly between the ultimate user and the vendor. That situation is likely to be a persistent and sometimes highly sensitive problem for most companies because of the conflict between overall organizational, operational, and fiscal control, which calls for centralized specialized purchasing, and the desires of individual users, almost all of whom are likely to believe that they can get better quality and service by dealing directly with vendors. Deciding where to draw the line between operational autonomy and organizational efficiency varies from company to company, but even in extreme situations some specialized services are allowed to bypass the purchasing function. In those cases, adequate accounting control is provided by a requirement that the specialist-user approve the invoices—a procedure enhanced by the discipline inherent in budgetary control.

Sometimes purchase terms call for payment by sight drafts, acceptances, or other negotiable commercial paper. If that occurs frequently, a system should be established for segregating those purchase orders and notifying the accounting and treasury departments of the existence of the liability.

Sometimes purchases must be made on the spot or in foreign countries having primitive exchange systems. Buyers should have a systematic means of reporting commitments made and terms negotiated.

Receiving, Inspecting, and Accepting

Most enterprises receive a volume and variety of goods and are required to give receipts for them on delivery; thus companies must have an organized means for doing so—even if it consists only of informal instructions to the office receptionist. The receiving function should be organized to serve control purposes and in most modern businesses it is. In companies engaged in production and distribution, the volume of receiving is so large that the receiving function is lodged in a separate, formally organized department.

The receiving function should inspect goods for conformity with specifications on purchase orders. Quantities should be verified by counting, weighing, or measuring. Some systems provide for omitting quantities from the copy of the purchase order sent to the receiving department to improve the likelihood of independent verification of quantities; other companies believe that procedure is inefficient or easily bypassed. In the process of verifying quantities, the receivers should also verify quality insofar as possible, including freedom from shipping damage. If laboratory tests are necessary to verify quality, a sample sent to the laboratory and subsequent distribution of reports of the results of testing are an extension or subroutine of the receiving function.

Acceptance of a shipment must be reported to the purchasing and accounting departments, most often by forwarding to them copies of the original purchase order or receiving report.

Receiving is primarily a physical rather than a data processing function, and thus controls within the function are largely supervisory. Restricted access to the department and segregation of its function from those of ordering and recording enhance the discipline of the system. Failure to record part of a receipt should be controlled by subsequent follow-up of differences between the receiving report and the vendor's invoice.

Services and some goods are received directly by users. Procedures for originating receiving reports from user departments may be prescribed, but they are difficult to maintain and control. The usual procedure is to forward the vendor's invoice to the user for approval and acknowledgment of receipt.

Storing or Using

Once received, goods must be forwarded to the requisitioner. In most companies the volume of receipts requires locating the facilities for storage of purchased goods close to the receiving department. Controls over receipt, storage, and issuance of purchased goods are covered in the chapter on inventories. The procurement control loop is closed when the requisitioning department compares the goods physically received with its file copy of the original requisition. Some systems call for forwarding evidence of that comparison to the accounting department before the invoice is approved for payment.

Recording

An asset or expense and the related liability are often recorded on receipt of a vendor's invoice for goods or services. Authorization for recording can be routinized: a clerk can be authorized to record invoices that are properly approved by an authorized representative of the requisitioning department or invoices that match related purchase orders and receiving reports as to quantities, prices, and other terms.

Failure to establish control over vendors' invoices early in the process is a common control weakness, which can have especially negative consequences if many invoices must be routed for approval to operating officials whose main interests are directed elsewhere. Unless the flow of invoices can be closely controlled, it is advisable to establish documentation and numerical control by some means such as immediate entry in an invoice or a "pre-voucher" register.

Once invoices have been authorized, the recording process consists of, first, recording the correct amount in the proper account and period, and second, correctly summarizing and posting the records. A clerk should check the arithmetic on the invoices, either by recomputing it or comparing it with purchase orders to verify the amount. The accounting distribution must be double-checked and entered (sometimes an initial entry is made on the purchase order). As cutoff for the end of an accounting period approaches, a clerk must check that invoices are recorded in the proper period.

Supervision over the clerical processes of authorization and recording is exercised by review and approval of transactions by a responsible, knowledgeable individual. Sometimes invoices are approved by supervisors prior to processing for cash disbursements; sometimes supervisory review takes place when the check is signed.

Summarization and posting can consist of manual entry in a voucher register from which totals are posted to ledgers, or of conversion of invoice data to machine or computer input. In either event, control is provided by double-checking the entry or conversion, batch or control totals, or both. Assigning voucher numbers to the invoices early in the recording process and subsequently accounting for the sequence of numbers, and periodic review of open files of items awaiting processing also serve as controls over the omission of items from the recording process.

Discipline over the summarizing and posting process is provided primarily by supervisory review of reconciliations, trial balances, and open file follow-up. Segregating the duties of those who prepare invoices, approve them, post the detailed records, maintain control accounts, and make the reconciliations and follow-up also enhances discipline. Secondary levels of discipline are provided by budgetary controls and variance analyses.

Payment

Controls over the cash disbursements process are organized to provide all practicable and reasonable assurance that no unauthorized payments are made, all liabilities are paid on time, an accurate record is made of each payment, and unclaimed items are adequately identified, controlled, and ultimately cancelled.

Basic controls to prevent unauthorized payments consist of various measures, such as cancellation, to prevent reprocessing of documents a second time or processing of unauthorized documents. Cash disbursements personnel should be independent of those who originate authorized documents. Signed checks should be processed in such a way as to keep them out of the hands of unauthorized persons (segregation of duties); unissued checks should be safeguarded (restricted access); authorizing documents should be cancelled upon processing (documentation); the final approving authority, usually the signer of the check, should have evidence of the authorization, propriety, and control processing of supporting documents (pre-audit).

All acknowledged liabilities should be paid on time to take advantage of cash discounts, minimize controversy with suppliers, and maintain the enterprise's credit rating. Vouchers approved for payment are usually filed by due date, and control over timely processing is provided by periodic reviews of open holding files—unmatched receiving reports and invoices and overdue open items appearing on the accounts payable reconciliation of detail to control.

Accurate recording of payments is controlled by establishing numerical sequence of checks prior to preparation, maintaining a detailed check register, accounting for the numerical sequence of checks entered in the register, and comparing paid checks returned by the bank with the check register.

Old outstanding checks appearing on the bank reconciliation should be removed from the cash disbursements records and accounted for separately. After appropriate inquiry into the reasons for long outstanding checks, they should be cancelled, payment stopped at the bank, and the accounts adjusted either to reverse the original entries or to record the items in a liability account.

Discipline over the cash disbursements process is provided by the check signer's review of supporting documentation, and by supervisory review of evidence of reconciliation and follow-up of the series of holding files of unmatched documents, of the accounts payable trial balance, and of the bank statement (see Chapter 15).

Payrolls

Payroll processing is the one function that is most likely to be similar from one organization to another. Over the years, payroll systems have become highly organized and generally well controlled. The sequence for payroll transaction processing, theoretically the same as the sequence for purchase transactions, differs importantly in practice. The functions of requisitioning, shopping for, and purchasing labor have less accounting significance than they do in a purchasing system, while control over receipt of services, recording, and payment has relatively more accounting significance.

Leaving the subject of control over the efficiency of labor for the chapter on the production segment (Chapter 11), the following paragraphs describe the controls to be expected in a typical payroll transaction processing system.

Authorization to employ and pay should be prepared independently of the immediate user (employer or supervisor) and of those responsible for preparing the payroll. Preferred modern practice is to lodge that responsibility in the personnel department, which signs on an employee and in the process creates records authorizing employment at a particular job or in a particular department, the rate of pay, and payroll deductions. The personnel department should also be responsible for originating termination notices. Control may be exercised by prenumbered employment and termination notices, the sequence of which is subsequently accounted for, or by personnel department review of payroll data.

Evidence of performance of services should be produced in the form of time reports or clock cards, which should be controlled first by supervisory review and approval. Control is also provided by comparison of payroll costs to standards or budgets or by reconciliation to production cost or job order records. If pay is based on production rather than time, as in piece work or commissions, the quantity basis should be similarly approved and reconciled to available data.

The computation of pay can be simple or exceedingly complex, manual or fully mechanized. In any event, the controls consist basically of double-checking the computation or of control totals derived from a separate calculation of the aggregate amount. The self-interest of employees and their ready access to the personnel and accounting departments also act as a control, at least over underpayment.

Accounting distribution may be similarly complex and may be manual or automatic. Accounting distribution for purely financial purposes is not ordinarily difficult to control because the wages of most employees are charged to the same account from one period to another. Accounting distribution for detailed cost accounting systems may call for extensive computation and allocation of pay among cost centers; in those cases control is usually exercised by batch proof, supplemented by the discipline of variance analysis.

The computation of payroll deductions is governed either by statute (in the case of payroll taxes, etc.) or contract (union agreement, group insurance contract, or agency agreements with charitable organizations, credit unions, etc.). The authorization to make deductions from an individual's pay ordinarily comes from the personnel department which, in turn, obtains written authorization from the employee. Cumulative records of deductions are required for each employee, and the posting to the cumulative records acts as a control total for comparison to the amounts withheld from each payroll.

Payment of a payroll is usually by check, most often prepared as an integral part of the computation procedure. Control over payroll disbursements made by check is much the same as control over cash disbursements of accounts payable.

Cash payrolls, once common, are becoming a rarity, primarily because of the additional care required in maintaining control over currency and the increasing availability of personal banking. The handling of cash payrolls can be turned over to specialized contracting agencies, in which case the control problems become those of the agent. If a cash payroll is handled by the company, each payroll should be accounted for on an imprest basis. The required denominations of currency and coin should be pre-tallied, preparation of pay packets should consume all the currency drawn for that purpose, and the pay packets should be totalled after preparation for balancing to the imprest total.

Pay packets should be controlled until turned over to employees in exchange for signed receipts. Some companies turn the pay packets over to employees' supervisors for distribution, a less desirable practice than having someone independent of the supervisors make the distribution. Unclaimed amounts should be listed at once, kept under control, and returned to cash if unclaimed after a short period of time.

In all but the smallest organizations, the recognized advantages of segregation of duties are not difficult to achieve. In the accounts payable system, the duties of requisitioning, purchasing, receiving, recording, and handling disbursements are segregated as a matter of operational logic and efficiency as well as good accounting control. Similarly, the personnel department is independent of the accounting department and the foreman who approves clock cards is independent of both departments. The handling of payroll checks or cash should be separate from all three.

EDP Controls

Payroll is usually one of the first applications to be computerized as a company moves into electronic data processing, with purchases and accounts payable not far behind. The kinds of controls that can be expected are described in Chapter 6, "Electronic Data Processing and Auditing."

Returns and Credits

Every credit due an enterprise, either because goods were returned or because something about the purchase was unsatisfactory and an allowance was negotiated, is an asset equivalent to a receivable. It is important therefore that credits be controlled as carefully and completely as possible. That is easier said than done, however, because credits are apt to be non-routine, infrequent, random events which are difficult to systematize.

Returns have to be prepared for shipping back to the vendor, and thus the shipping department should have a routine for originating controlled notification to the accounts payable and purchasing departments at the time purchased items are returned. Control can be exercised through a subsystem similar to that used in controlling sales (described in Chapter 9, "The Revenue Segment").

Allowances, adjustments, and occasional returns originating in departments other than shipping should be subject to a procedure, preferably formalized in writing, for notifying the accounting and purchasing departments of a dispute or claim found to be due. Since no positive means exists of controlling compliance with that type of routine, periodic inquiry of all knowledgeable people throughout the company should be made as to the existence of unrecorded claims or allowances.

Prepaid Expenses, Accrued Liabilities, Agency Accounts, And Other Liabilities

Control over prepaid expenses, accrued liabilities, agency accounts, and other liabilities is provided initially by administrative procedures to insure timely attention to the required entries. Reminder lists—calendars or tickler files to alert those responsible to payment due dates—should be maintained. Orderly recording of accruals and amortization is best assured by a system of routine recording of standard monthly journal entries. Because periodic adjustment is usually required, periodic supervisory review of the balances of the accounts and the amortization computations is essential.

Some liability and agency accounts require full-fledged transaction systems which should be subject to the controls described in Chapter 3. Some examples are: payroll withholdings (usually part of the payroll system), customers' deposits, and commissions payable (which may be comparable to either the payroll or accounts payable system).

• AUDITING PROCEDURES

OBJECTIVES

The objectives of auditing procedures for purchasing and accounts payable are to provide evidential matter that is sufficient and competent to give an auditor reasonable assurance that:

> Expense accounts include all costs and expenses applicable to the period and also all losses and estimated future expenses that should be reflected in the period, and classification is consistent with the accounting system and generally accepted accounting principles.
>
> Accounts payable are properly authorized, represent the correct amounts of currently payable items, and reflect all outstanding obligations.
>
> Prepaid and accrued accounts are comprehensive and properly stated.
>
> Account descriptions, classifications, and related disclosures are adequate and not misleading.
>
> All loss contingencies are identified and recorded or disclosed.

It is simply in the nature of things—the structure of businesses and accounting transactions—that liabilities are more likely to be understated or omitted from the accounts than overstated, and any inclination to improve financial statements only adds to that likelihood. Therefore, auditing procedures in the purchasing–accounts payable segment concentrate heavily on seeking evidence of omitted or understated liabilities, but without ignoring the possibility of overstatement.

THE AUDIT CYCLE

As described in Chapter 5, functional tests must be made to obtain evidential matter giving reasonable assurance that the systems work as planned and can be depended on to continue doing so and therefore that the underlying evidence of the accounts may be relied on.　Account balances must be validated by substantive tests to provide such additional (corroborative) evidence as an auditor needs to supplement his reliance on the system of internal control.　Those tests provide an auditor a basis for evaluating and forming an opinion on the accounting principles employed, the presentation of accounts payable, expenses, and related accounts in the financial statements, and the adequacy of the financial disclosures.

Transaction Reviews

Some of the initial steps in the buying segment have no effect or only an indirect effect on amounts entering into the accounts.　In a buying system, the beginning of the transaction is the purchase requisition.　A company may have several different kinds of purchase requisitioning systems, and each system may—or may not—give rise to a different type of transaction.　For example, the raw material requisitioning system may be quite different from the system used for requisitioning goods and services by operating departments, and the system for requisitioning items of property, plant, and equipment may be different from both.　Since those systems by nature are not of the same type, they are unlikely to be subject to the same control operations. And similar transactions may represent different types of transactions when control operations differ or because systemization and disciplinary control are so loose as to permit each department to create or alter its own systems.

Most of the different requisitioning systems in effect combine into one or a few types of transactions in the purchasing department (purchases that do not go through the purchasing department are obviously a different type of transaction). The purchasing department may put all purchase requisitions through the same control processes (in which case they represent only one type of transaction from that point on), even though separate purchasing agents or sub-departments may handle different categories, such as raw material purchases, purchases of services, and purchases of capital items. More often, purchasing departments use different systems based on the size or nature of an item. Also, if receiving procedures differ, distinctions must be maintained.

It is increasingly common in making a transaction review of the buying segment to review the operational control processes within the purchasing department: the controls over competitive bidding, conflicts of interest, contract and blanket purchasing, vendor volume and performance statistics, and so forth. Reviewing those operational controls does not add greatly to total audit time and it can produce observations that are useful to the client. However, while it contributes somewhat to an auditor's understanding of his client's affairs, it cannot be regarded as a necessary step in the audit. Some auditors carry out that review routinely and gratuitously; since it is an additional service, it is technically preferable to agree on it in advance with the client.

Purchases that do not go through the purchasing department are obviously a different type of transaction from those that do, but they are often handled so informally that it is hard to tell whether they constitute one different type or several different types. Most often the requisitioning and ordering routines are not standardized among departments, but the purchases come together at a common control point, usually the voucher clerk, before being recorded in the accounts. In that instance, the review of the different types of transactions in a departmental requisitioning process can usually be combined with the functional test of the control point.

Purchases made through bills of exchange (such as drafts and acceptances) should be subject to controls that identify them and establish early accountability, and they should be considered a separate type of transaction. Purchases made by travelling buyers obviously constitute a distinct type of transaction.

The receiving department plays an important part in the purchasing transaction system. The receiving report, which records the activities of the receiving department, is generally attached to the invoice at the time it is processed for payment. Some auditors believe that the receiving department should be visited and its activities observed in the course of the transaction review. Others are content to scrutinize receiving reports for evidence of proper performance, including provisions for control and supervisory approval of reports. Much depends on whether receiving activities for all procurement are centralized and procedures are uniform or whether they are scattered and diverse.

Usually, all types of transactions except payroll come together in the system for vouchering accounts payable and cash disbursements. Often a separate system exists for large, urgent, or otherwise unusual payments, which is subject to different control procedures and constitutes a separate type of transaction. However, once different types of transactions have converged, there is no need to distinguish among transactions passing through the accounts payable system for purposes of transaction review or functional tests just because they represent purchases of different kinds of items or are charged to different accounts. The only basis for differentiation is differing control procedures.

Viewing his objective strictly, an auditor has no need to review insignificant types of transactions, such as the petty cash system or the reimbursement of personal expenses, if he is satisfied that no aggregate effect on the financial statements could occur. However, the scrutiny of those minor but easily abused types of transactions—principally to advise the client of weaknesses—is so much a part of the auditor's traditional procedures that many auditors continue the practice. Whether it is continued or omitted, it is well for the client to be fully informed about the matter.

Payrolls are ordinarily processed in different batches: those for different departments and weekly, biweekly, monthly, and executive payrolls. They are different types only if they are subject to different control systems; for example, payrolls based on piece work must have different controls from those based on time. The payrolls of different departments may enter into the cost accounting system (Chapter 11) differently and thus be subject to transaction review in connection with the cost accounting system. Executive and administrative payrolls are also dissimilar.

In an initial examination an auditor may wish to review several or all of the different kinds of payrolls to confirm his understanding that they are subject to the same control procedures and therefore are the same type of transaction. Once he has done so, he should have no need to review more than one of each type in subsequent audits, if he is satisfied that there have been no changes in controls.

Functional Tests

Following is a generalized example of a representative program of functional tests of a purchasing–accounts payable segment, which illustrates how control functions are identified and functional tests designed.

Control Over Requisitions

The first step in the segment, the requisitioning system, does not have a direct effect on the accounts since a requisition does not give rise to an accounting entry, and the loss of control over requisitions, whatever operational problems it might create, does not necessarily create accounting problems. (One significant exception to that generalization is the encumbrance system of accounting used by units of government and related agencies, in which the requisition does give rise to an encumbrance entry.)

Therefore, an auditor may conclude that he has nothing to gain by functionally testing the requisitioning system. On the other hand, he may conclude that the requisitioning system establishes important initial conditions of documentation and accountability, which contribute to control over purchase orders and invoices, and accordingly that functional tests do contribute to the building of cumulative confidence in the system.

In that event, he would be interested in testing two control functions: control over documentation and authorization of requisitions, and control over execution of authorized requisitions. Test data for the second function are generally found in the requisitioning department; test data for the first function can be found in the files of the purchasing department or the requisitioning department, whichever is more convenient. The functional test audit program might read:

Select x requisitions: examine for completeness of descriptions, quantities, instructions as to delivery dates, etc.; trace to underlying computations or control data; note evidence of approval and authorization.

Examine holding file of unfilled requisitions; note evidence of periodic review; inquire into old or otherwise unusual items.

Examine file of completed requisitions; note evidence of accounting for numerical sequence; inquire into gaps in numerical sequence (many requisitioning systems employ a permanent, repetitively used "travelling requisition," in which event the controls consist of holding files rather than prenumbering; there might be a holding file for requisitions ordered but not received).

Control Over Purchase Orders

Since the purchase order formally authorizes the execution of a purchase transaction, and often its recording and payment, controls over preparation and processing of purchase orders are ordinarily of more interest to an auditor than controls over the requisitioning system. His interest is in the completeness and accuracy of purchase orders as authorization for transactions and in the evidence of supervisory review and approval. Since his interest in vendors' invoices is approximately the same—completeness, accuracy, propriety, and approval—functional tests of purchase orders are most often combined with functional tests of control over vendors' invoices.

Control over the proper and timely execution of all purchase orders is maintained either by an open holding file of uncompleted purchase orders, a numerical file of completed purchase orders, or both. The control file should be examined as part of the functional testing. The functional test program might read as follows:

Select x paid invoices: trace invoice data to comparable data on accompanying purchase order and receiving report.

Examine purchase order for completeness: numbering, dating, description, quantity, price, delivery date, quality specifications, routing; examine evidence of double-checking of purchase order; examine evidence of approval.

Examine vendors' invoices for evidence of double-checking and validity checking.

Examine evidence of approval for payment and of cancellation after payment; examine evidence of payment according to invoice terms.

Examine open file of uncompleted purchase orders and inquire into reasons for old or unusual items; examine evidence of exception reports and other follow-up of old unfilled purchase orders.

Operational Controls

The objective of an operational control functional test can be incorporated in an examination of purchase orders or accounting control functional tests with little additional effort if an auditor understands the principles of operational controls over purchasing. The purchase order files (perhaps those in the purchasing department rather than the paid invoice files) can be examined for evidence of competitive bidding, accumulation of vendor performance information and alternative source information, and evidence of follow-up and "expediting." During the testing, observations can be made of the quality of systemization and discipline.

Control Over Raw Material

In most companies the bulk of purchases are for raw materials and thus there is a tie-in between the functional testing of controls over the purchasing segment and that over the raw material inventory segment. The functional test of the linkage can be originated either from the raw material inventory data or from the purchasing data. In the latter case, the functional test program might read:

> For raw material purchase invoices included in the above test trace to posting to perpetual inventory cards; test the tie-in of posting control totals to purchase voucher register totals.

Control Over Receiving

Some auditors consider performing functional tests of controls in the receiving department necessary. While it may be worthwhile to observe the functioning of the receiving department in connection with the transaction review to make sure that it is properly understood, we see no purpose to be served by a separate functional test of the operations of that department. If it is observed that the receiving department functions independently and that it produces the paperwork required to inform the accounting department and other interested persons adequately, then failures in control can be expected to be insignificant or to be brought to light elsewhere in the system.

Control Over Invoices

Some purchases are authorized independently of the purchasing department; usually the number of those purchases is significant and the processing constitutes at least one separate type of transaction. Functional test program instructions might be as follows:

> Select x non-purchase order invoices: scrutinize for propriety; examine evidence of double-checking and validity checking, approval by requisitioner and approval for payment, cancellation on payment, and payment in accordance with terms.

The functional test over recording and summarization of properly authorized, executed, and approved invoices might be as follows:

For invoices examined in above tests:
1. Trace to voucher register, thence to cash disbursements book or register, thence to cancelled check or, if not available, copy of check or check register.
2. Examine evidence of batch controls, double-checking, or other controls over the posting or conversion process.
3. Test-check footings of voucher register and cash disbursements book.
4. Trace postings of voucher register and cash disbursements book to control accounts.

Reconciliation

All but the most rudimentary accounting systems can be expected to include the control features of reconciling the detail of accounts payable to the control account and reconciling cash disbursements to the bank statement. Those operations should be functionally tested, but doing so also constitutes a validation test; they are therefore discussed in the next section.

Control Over Returns

Unless returns are clearly insignificant, controls over them should be functionally tested, perhaps as follows:

Select *x* credits for returned goods: examine underlying evidence of reason for return, correspondence with vendor, and acceptance by vendor; examine evidence of review and approval; trace to accounts payable; trace to posting to raw material perpetual inventory records.

Control Over Payrolls

In testing controls over payrolls, an auditor wishes reasonable assurance that the system accurately records all costs and expenses and related liabilities for salaries, wages, and related benefits. He should also keep in mind the factors influencing the amount of his functional testing, which were described in Chapter 5: the effectiveness of disciplinary controls, the difficulty of maintaining control, the importance of the resulting data, the kind of control, and the degree of his confidence in the system. Since payrolls are a large element of cost in almost every enterprise, are made up of a large number of transactions, and are usually well organized and easy to test in quantity, there is a tendency for payroll functional tests to exceed those required by rigorous application of the rationale recommended in this book.

However minimal the functional test of payrolls may turn out to be, it cannot be eliminated. The following might be an audit program instruction:

Select *x* payroll transactions (the selection might be from different payrolls if the auditor is so inclined).

Trace authorizations for name, rate of pay, and deductions to personnel department records; note authorization by employee and approval by personnel department.

Examine personnel department controls over authorizations for employment, termination, and changes in rates of pay.

Trace above transactions to clock cards or time reports; note evidence of double-checking and approval.

Test control over computations of gross and net pay (double-checking, control totals, etc.).

Check accounting distribution of gross pay and payroll deductions.

Trace net pay to check (or employee receipt in the case of cash payroll); note numerical sequencing and control totals.

Control Over Prepaid and Accrued Accounts

Technically speaking, functional tests of controls over prepaid and accrued accounts must be considered. However, validation is usually simple enough and so it may be unnecessary to rely on controls—in which case functional tests are unnecessary. Also, as noted in the preceding section, control over those accounts consists of supervisory review and scrutiny of the accuracy of account balances. Since that is exactly what an auditor does in validating the account, a single test may serve for both purposes.

Validation Procedures

In most audits it is not necessary to apply validation procedures to cost and expense accounts, except to the extent that validation tests of balance sheet accounts at the beginning and end of a period tend also to validate the related cost and expense accounts. As noted in Chapter 4, it is both theoretically sound and practically convenient to focus validation testing on balance sheet accounts. Reasonable assurance that the system produces accurate and reliable expense accounts is ordinarily obtained through functional tests corroborated by analytical reviews such as comparisons of income and expense accounts.

Validation tests of accounts payable, and liability accounts in general, are heavily weighted toward providing assurance that there are no material unrecognized or unrecorded liabilities. Questions rarely arise about possible overstatements of accounts payable because the balance consists of items that have been scrutinized and acknowledged before being recorded. Accrued liabilities can be overstated or understated if final determination of the actual liability differs from the estimates on which the accrual was based. For the most part, however, the greatest risk in accounting for the buying segment, whether the system of internal control is strong or weak, is that liabilities will go unrecognized or unrecorded. Another important objective of accounts payable validation tests is obtaining evidence of the adequacy of the client's accountability procedures for recorded liabilities.

Tests for Unrecorded Liabilities

Unrecorded liabilities may stem from several sources.

Late Invoices. In even the most well-controlled systems some purchases or other commitments are not recorded until the related invoice is received, and some invoices are not received until after the accounts for a period have been closed. The sooner after the end of a period that the accounts are closed, the more unrecorded late invoices are likely. Thus, it is a virtually universal auditing procedure to examine the voucher register, cash disbursements book, file of vendors' invoices, or whatever other convenient record exists for a short period after the end of the fiscal year to discover items that should have been recorded as liabilities of the year.

Companies aim for an audit opinion date as soon after the end of the fiscal year as possible, in some instances after approximately three weeks. That does not provide much time for testing for late invoices. Adequate control over the timely recording of liabilities and commitments is prerequisite to an early closing and early opinion date; if the results of interim tests of the system are not satisfactory, an auditor should not agree to an early opinion date.

Some kinds of late invoices can be ignored even if they are relatively large in amount. If working capital, current ratios, and so on are not at the critical point, recording raw material purchases may not be significant since doing so increases both current assets and current liabilities (assuming a physical inventory taken at year end is not used to adjust the inventory and expense accounts). Similarly, recording the liability for recurring charges such as utility bills may not be important if a comparable lag in the preceding year results in twelve months' charges to expense.

An examination of subsequent files for late invoices cannot, of course, bring to light those that have been deliberately withheld. That should not happen and is one reason for the liability certificate (discussed below). No responsible executive will sign a liability certificate with the knowledge that an unrecorded liability has been withheld.

In some companies the examination of vendors' invoices received subsequent to year end is an extensive accountability procedure required to compensate for weak or absent controls over accounting cutoff. In those instances, an auditor can observe and test the client's procedures in much the same way as he observes and tests physical inventory procedures. One of the auditor's tests is a test examination of subsequent invoices to ascertain whether the client's procedures have gone far enough.

Test of Cutoff. This test is intended to prove that all transactions applicable to a period are recorded, no transactions applicable to the succeeding period are recorded, and all transactions are recorded in full. If the basic transaction documents are in numerical sequence, an auditor can note the number of the last receiving report used on the cutoff date, the last voucher recorded, and the last check issued (or other basic transaction documents). He can trace the receiving report to the perpetual inventory records and to accounts payable or the listing of open unmatched receiving reports and note that no higher numbers are listed. He can do the same for the last voucher number, tracing it to the voucher register and cash disbursements book. He can trace the last check issued to the cash disbursements book and voucher register and the list of outstanding checks in the bank reconciliation.

If the basic transaction documents are not prenumbered, it may be necessary to trace out a sample of documents both before and after the cutoff point to obtain sufficient evidence that the cutoff was properly made.

Unmatched Receiving Reports. Another test for unrecorded liabilities is to examine files of receiving reports unmatched with recorded invoices. Companies that have a significant volume of those items usually have a routine for accumulating them at the end of the fiscal year and recording them through a journal entry. Whether or not that routine is in effect, the receiving department cutoff and the existence of in-transit items can be tested.

Purchase Commitments. Purchase commitments should be tested to determine whether they constitute liabilities or require recognition of loss. In companies with operations that make the likelihood of purchase commitments remote, an auditor may be content with a simple inquiry of purchasing agents. If conditions indicate otherwise, he may wish to examine files of open purchase orders.

Year-End Inquiry. All organizations have liabilities incurred and commitments made at a year end that are unrecorded. Most companies are sufficiently well organized that the total of those items is unlikely to be significant. In some far-flung, decentralized organizations the possibility may be significant enough to merit a procedure for formal inquiry of department heads, supervisors, and other responsible officials as to knowledge of unprocessed invoices, unrecorded commitments, or contingent liabilities.

Letter of Representation (Liability Certificate)

It is general practice for an auditor to request from his client written representation that, to the best of the client's knowledge and belief, all liabilities have been entered in the accounts or disclosed to the auditor. That procedure is desirable since it (1) provides written evidence that the auditor made proper inquiry of company officials about liabilities not otherwise determinable from the records, and (2) documents explicitly the representations made to him. The information should be obtained and the letter dated as near as possible to the date of completion of field work; some auditors take pains to have the letter signed and dated on the same day as the opinion.

The representation letter should be signed by a chief executive and usually also by the officer responsible for accounting. In rare instances, an officer or chief executive may refuse to sign the letter. If an auditor desires to express an opinion in the face of that refusal, he should satisfy himself that the refusal is not based on serious reservations or intentional misrepresentation.

In our opinion, however, it is difficult to conceive of circumstances in which, after the issue has been tactfully explained, it would be possible to express an opinion in the face of a refusal to sign a representation letter. The refusal inevitably creates doubt about the accuracy and completeness of other evidence. An executive is expected to understand his legal and moral responsibility for financial statement representations; if he does, he can see that the representation letter only spells out some of those responsibilities but does not increase them. Thus, refusal to sign the letter must be taken as a signal either of withheld evidence or of inadequately understood responsibilities; either destroys the basis for an audit opinion.

The specimen letter on pages 336 and 337 may be modified to meet special requirements. If a business has a type of liability not common to business in general, it is advisable to refer specifically to that liability in the letter.

It should be understood that a representation letter complements an auditor's examination and is not a substitute for auditing procedures. It is a valid piece of corroborative evidence because, as noted at the beginning of Chapter 4, an auditor is entitled to rely on an assumption of competence and integrity of his client's executives. It is thus competent evidence but not sufficient in itself.

Letter From Counsel

It is similarly general practice to obtain written representation from a client's attorneys about the status of suits, threatened litigation, or other actual or contingent liabilities. If more than one firm of attorneys is employed or if there is an "in-house" legal department as

MANAGEMENT REPRESENTATION—LIABILITIES
[Client's letterhead]

[Name and address of auditors]

Gentlemen:

In connection with your examination of the financial statements of [name of company] as of [balance sheet date], and for the [current period] then ended, I hereby state that, as of [balance sheet date], to the best of my knowledge and belief:

1. All liabilities have been recorded on the books of account, including the liability for all purchases to which title had passed prior to the balance sheet date.

2. No asset of the company was pledged, or is now pledged, as collateral for any liability, except as follows:

3. There were no unused balances of letters of credit outstanding, except as follows:

4. There were no "loss contingencies" that were *not* disclosed in the notes to the financial statements and:

   • for which there was at least a reasonable possibility that a loss or an additional loss may have been incurred, or
   • that represent guarantees of a third party transaction even though the possibility of loss may be remote, or
   • that occurred after the balance sheet date and indicate that an asset may have been impaired or a liability may have been incurred after that date,

   except as follows:

   (I understand the term *loss contingency* to mean those matters described in Financial Accounting Standards Board Statement No. 5, *Accounting for Contingencies*, which you furnished to me.)

5. No losses will be sustained as a result of purchase commitments in excess of normal requirements or at prices in excess of the prevailing market prices, nor are there any agreements to repurchase items previously sold that have not been recorded in the financial statements.

6. There were:

   (a) No commitments for purchase or sale of securities or to repurchase the company's stock or any other securities; no options given by the company, including options on company's capital stock; and no bonus or profit-sharing arrangements, except as follows:

   (b) No other commitments, contracts (including foreign currency forward exchange contracts), or leases that, in my judgment, might adversely affect the company, except as follows:

7. All material transactions between related parties have been appropriately disclosed in the financial statements, or notes thereto, except as follows:

   (I understand the term *related parties* to include, among other things:

   The company; its "affiliates"; "principal owners," "management," and members of their immediate families; entities for which investments are accounted for by the equity method; any other party with which the company may deal when one party has the ability to significantly influence the management or operating policies of the other to the extent that one of the transacting parties might be prevented from fully pursuing its own separate interests; and any other situation in which another entity has the ability to significantly influence the management or operating policies of the transacting parties, or in which another entity has an ownership interest in one of the transacting parties and the ability to significantly influence the other, to the extent that one or more of the transacting parties might be prevented from fully pursuing its own separate interests.

   The term *affiliate* means a party that directly or indirectly, through one or more intermediaries, controls, or is controlled by, or is under common control with, a specified party. *Control* means the possession, direct or indirect, of the power to direct or cause the direction of the management and policies of a specified party whether through ownership, by contract, or otherwise.

The term *principal owner(s)* means the owner(s) of record or known beneficial owner(s) of more than 10% of the voting interests of the reporting entity. The term *management* means any person(s) having responsibility for achieving the objectives of the organization and the concomitant authority to establish the policies and make the decisions by which such objectives are to be pursued. It would normally include members of the board of directors, the president, secretary, treasurer, any vice president in charge of a principal business function (such as sales, administration or finance), and any other individual who performs similar policy making functions.)

8. There were no defaults in principal, interest, sinking fund, or redemption provisions with respect to any issue of securities or credit agreements, and no breach of covenant of a related indenture or agreement, except as follows:

9. Contractual obligations for plant construction and purchase of real property, equipment, and patent or other rights amounted to approximately $_____ at the balance sheet date.

10. There were no agreements under which any of the liabilities of the company had been subordinated to any other of its liabilities nor were any receivables owned by the company subordinated to any other liabilities of the debtor companies, except as follows:

11. There were no lines of credit, commitments for borrowings, or compensating balance arrangements, including those by or for the benefit of others, in existence during or at the end of the year, except as follows:

(I understand that a "compensating balance" is defined for this purpose as that portion of a demand deposit (or a time deposit or certificate of deposit) maintained by a corporation (or by any other person on behalf of the corporation) which constitutes support for existing borrowing arrangements of the corporation (or any other person) with a lending institution. Such arrangements would include both outstanding borrowings and the assurance of future credit availability.)

12. Federal income tax returns have been examined and reported upon by the Internal Revenue Service through _____; returns of the years since _____ are still open; the provision for unpaid federal income taxes reflected in the balance sheet is adequate to cover any additional assessments resulting from examinations already made or from those to be made by the Service. [Where appropriate include foreign and state taxes on income.]

13. The latest stockholder, director, and executive committee meetings were held on the following dates, respectively:

Stockholders _____

Directors _____

Executive Committee _____

14. No events have occurred subsequent to [balance sheet date] that would require adjustment to or disclosure in the financial statements.

Very truly yours,

_____

[Name of company]

_____   _____

[Date signed]   [Name of chief financial officer signing and title]

_____   _____

[Date signed]   [Name of chief executive officer signing and title] well as outside counsel, separate requests should be made of each. Usually identifying the attorneys to whom letters should be addressed is no problem, but sometimes, especially in complex companies, one or more attorneys may be overlooked or omitted. In the course of his other procedures an auditor should be alert for evidence of the work of attorneys, who should be identified for purposes of requesting a representation letter.

A suggested form of request follows:

[Name and address of legal counsel]
Dear Sirs:

In connection with their [usual] examination of our financial statements as at [balance sheet date], our auditors, [name and address], have requested information regarding pending or contemplated litigation in which we are involved or represented in any way. They particularly desire information as to estimated minimum and maximum amounts of our contingent assets or our contingent liabilities, direct or indirect, from issues unresolved, from contracts and agreements involving disputes, or from outstanding judgments as of the date of your reply.

We shall appreciate your courtesy in promptly supplying the requested information directly to our auditors. Brief summaries of the current status of cases in litigation, amounts at issue, and causes of action will be appropriate, supplemented by such additional information as you feel will assist them in arriving at an opinion concerning our financial position. Please inform them also as to amounts due you or accrued and unbilled for services and costs advanced as at [balance sheet date].

A return envelope is enclosed for your reply.

Very truly yours,

_____

[Name of Client]

As noted in the discussion of "legal constraints" in Chapter 1, an auditor is not qualified to judge a client's compliance with many kinds of legal and regulatory constraints, nor can he rely on client's counsel for an overall certification of compliance because counsel may not have been alerted to a possible compliance problem. He is, however, competent to judge whether a systematic means exists for detecting and evaluating possible constraints and to understand the resulting conclusion. In the event of doubt about compliance with a specific legal constraint, an auditor may ask the client to specifically direct counsel's attention to the question in his request for information. That should be done only after discussion with the client, however, because the request may involve counsel in additional research for which the client will incur a fee.

In 1975, letters of representation from counsel to auditors are a subject of controversy. Lawyers are concerned on the one hand about revealing highly sensitive information and on the other about their liability if they do not. Accountants cannot accept a refusal to make information available from an audit client, but audit evidence is cumulative in an auditor's judgment. If other evidence is satisfactory for that judgment, an auditor may decide that he need not insist on a letter from counsel. The issue is under study by representatives of both professions and by the SEC, and an orderly resolution is to be expected.

Confirmation of Balances With Vendors

For years auditors have had differences of opinion about whether it is necessary or even desirable to request vendors' confirmation of accounts payable balances. In the authors' view, confirmation is a valid procedure but necessary only in special circumstances. The reason lies in the fundamental difference between a payable balance and a receivable balance.

A receivable billing originates in the client's organization and has to be accepted by the customer to be authentic; thus, without confirmation its authenticity may be considered in doubt. On the other hand, a payable invoice originates in a vendor's organization and is scrutinized and accepted in the client's organization before being recorded. It is thus validated both by vendor and client.

A reason often given for confirming accounts payable is not so much to confirm the validity of recorded balances as to confirm the absence of unrecorded items. However, if the buying segment is adequately systematized, it should not be necessary to do so because the functioning of systematic requisitioning, ordering, and receiving activities provides reasonable assurance that liabilities are properly authorized and recorded.

Confirmation may be called for in the absence of continuity and integrity of the buying segment and if the auditor is seriously concerned about unrecorded invoices. If, for example, the voucher register or invoice files are destroyed by catastrophe or incompetence, confirmation may be necessary to provide evidence as to whether accounts payable balances are properly stated. It may likewise be necessary if dishonesty is suspected, but in that case an auditor is engaged in a kind of examination different from an ordinary audit.

Thus, confirmation of the ordinary trade accounts payable detail has more the character of an internal accounting or accountability procedure, undertaken to compensate for accounting or control deficiencies, than of an audit test. If it is undertaken, the confirmation procedure is parallel to that described in Chapter 9 for the confirmation of accounts receivable, except that an additional step of circularizing known vendors with zero balances is included. Particular concern should be given to past-due items, and an aging may be desirable if payments are not customarily current.

In contrast to routine accounts payable, unusual payable balances should be confirmed with creditors. Unusual balances may not be subject to the systemization and other controls of the ordinary buying system; they may result from complex or unusual negotiations for which it is desirable to have evidence of acceptance by the creditor, or the balance may be significant enough so that the simple procedure of requesting confirmation cannot be omitted.

Confirmation of accounts that result from internally generated activity and therefore are not validated in the same way as trade accounts payable is also good practice. Depositors' accounts in banks are an example.

Other Tests for Unrecorded Liabilities

The analytical reviews described later in this chapter serve a number of audit purposes; in making them, an auditor should be alert for evidence of unrecorded or contingent liabilities. The examination of minutes, contracts, leases, etc., may give evidence of commitments that might or might not result in liability. Examinations of fluctuations in account balances and comparisons of relationships among account balances could point the way toward unusual transactions or omitted liabilities.

Tests of Recorded Liabilities

Accounts Payable Trial Balance. The detail of accounts payable should be balanced to the control account as a routine part of the client's accountability procedures. An auditor should obtain the trial balance—usually an interim one—and test it for purposes of validating the accounts payable balance and functionally testing the client's accountability procedures. He should agree the total of the trial balance with the general ledger, foot or test-check footings, and trace a sample of entries on the trial balance to the underlying documents, usually vendors' invoices. He should scan the trial balance or the underlying detail for old or otherwise unusual items and obtain and evaluate explanations for those noted.

If that and all other tests are completed satisfactorily, an auditor does not, technically, need to test the year-end trial balance; however, it is so easy to do that most auditors do at least examine the year-end trial balance for evidence that it has been conscientiously completed.

Inventory Reconciliations. In connection with the reconciliation of raw material physical inventories to perpetual records and control accounts (Chapter 11), investigation of the causes of errors in recorded balances also serves to corroborate accounts payable balances and accountability procedures.

Debit Balances. The underlying causes of debit balances in accounts payable should be investigated. They may represent overpayments: if so, an auditor should consider whether they are collectible either through application against future purchases or in cash; confirmation may be desirable. He should also consider how an overpayment may have arisen and whether it is the result of deficiencies in accounting or operational controls. A debit balance may be related to an unrecorded offsetting liability, which should be discoverable from examination of the underlying data.

Accountability for Imprest Funds. A variety of activities are accounted for through imprest fund systems: petty cash expenditures, travel and personal expenses, some kinds of salesmen's commissions, and sales of inventory on consignment. Usually, no one of the imprest funds is significant and often they are not significant in the aggregate. If they are not significant, an auditor may conclude that he need only observe that there is a procedure in effect to record and account for imprest fund activity. If they are significant or if his client expects him to do so, he may examine or count some or all of the funds and verify the cutoff. Usually he will determine that the imprest funds have been reimbursed at year end so that the related expenses are recorded in the proper period.

Agency Accounts. The balances of agency accounts should be supported by a trial balance of the detail accounts. For many agency accounts the balance at the end of a period is remitted to the principal shortly thereafter, so that an examination of the remittance voucher and the supporting detail serves to validate the period-end balance. Some accounts, such as unclaimed wages and customers' deposits, are not currently remitted; in those cases an auditor should examine and test a trial balance reconciling detail to control and scrutinize the underlying details for unusual items.

Prepaid and Accrued Accounts. Many prepaid and accrued accounts are insignificant and an auditor may consider it sufficient simply to compare the balance with the corresponding balance of the prior period and scan the activity during the period. On the other hand, since prepaid and accrued accounts often afford insight into unusual elements of regular transaction systems and may therefore contribute to an auditor's understanding of the systems, many auditors scrutinize individual accrued and prepaid accounts even though balances are insignificant. The usual procedure is to examine the contractual, statutory, or other basis for the liability, to recompute the computation of the periodic accrual and of the balance as of the dates selected (which may be either interim or year end), and to test the logic and arithmetic. For many accrued liabilities and some prepaid expenses, the accrual or prepayment is based on an estimate of a liability which cannot be determined precisely; in that case, the basis and rationale for the estimate should be reviewed, compared with prior experience, and evaluated in the light of related circumstances.

Analytical Reviews

Because of the variety of expense accounts in most accounting systems, analytical reviews may be more extensive for the buying segment than for other segments.

Variance Reports

If they exist, variance reports and analyses of actual costs and expenses against budgeted amounts should be examined. Explanations of variances should be critically evaluated both for their adequacy and for the light they may shed on the accuracy and authenticity of the accounts.

Comparative Review of Balances

Balances of expense and related balance sheet accounts can be compared from month to month and with those of the prior year to identify trends and fluctuations. The underlying causes of trends and fluctuations should be thoroughly understood and evaluated for their implications for other accounts. Unusual transactions should be vouched by examining underlying evidence.

Ratio Analysis

In a stable business, accounts tend to establish stable relationships one to another, and changes in relationships may signal conditions requiring accounting recognition. Pertinent ratios should be computed and compared with corresponding ones for prior periods; for example, cost of goods sold to sales; selling expense to sales; general and administrative expenses to sales; inventories to cost of goods sold; accounts payable to disbursements; unit costs or departmental costs to related volume of activity.

Journal Entries

Journal entries should be reviewed for unusual items. In most companies with a large volume of journal entries, routine recurring ones are "standardized," and ordinarily an auditor's review can be limited to nonrecurring or nonstandard journal entries.

Account Analyses

Most auditors wish to analyze the details of certain accounts that they regard as sensitive; for example, legal expense. An auditor can request the client to prepare the account analysis and assemble the underlying documentation for his scrutiny.

Examination of Legal Documents

An auditor's examination of important legal documents contributes to many phases of an audit, not least of which is his evaluation of the liability accounts. He should read minutes of directors' meetings, all important contracts, agreements, and leases, and correspondence supporting significant negotiations; in the course of doing so he should be alert for commitments, contingent liabilities, and covenants having financial implications.

Effect of Weaknesses in Internal Control On Substantive Tests

If an auditor is not willing to place maximum reliance on internal control but does not consider it so deficient as to conclude that there is no adequately organized system, he has to lean more heavily on substantive tests to provide the corroborative evidence he needs. Of the substantive tests described above, he would lean most heavily on the following:

> More extensive post-balance sheet testing of vendors' invoices and cash disbursements for possible unrecorded liabilities.
>
> A physical inventory coordinated with accounts payable cutoff at the end of the year instead of or in addition to an interim inventory.
>
> More intensive scrutiny of agency accounts and accrued and prepaid accounts.
>
> More intensive and detailed analytical reviews.
>
> In some cases, confirmation of balances with vendors.

In those few instances in which an auditor regards the internal control system as marginal and questions whether it can be relied on at all, he can take a sufficiently large sample of accounts payable transactions (possibly determined according to the principles of statistical sampling) as a basis for a conclusion as to whether the underlying accounts are reasonably stated.

Substantive Tests: Specific Accounts

The foregoing sections focused on the generic nature of audit tests, which should be understood because it remains the same whatever the circumstances. Most of the accounts discussed in this chapter function routinely as a part of the buying segment, and the auditing procedures previously described can be applied to them with little adaptation. Trade accounts payable, accrued salaries and wages, and most of the agency accounts and accrued and prepaid expense accounts are in that category and require no further comment. The following paragraphs focus on some accounts that commonly have particular characteristics worthy of note. The variety of conditions found in practice makes it impossible to be comprehensive: the comments can only illustrate the kinds of adaptations of basic tests that may be called for.

Loss Contingencies

Auditing loss contingencies is one of the most difficult aspects of many examinations, and the variety of conditions encountered makes it impossible to describe an auditor's task definitively. Even in the best and most responsibly managed companies a condition requiring evaluation as a contingency can be overlooked. Thus, both auditor and client should take special pains to search for those conditions. Following are the kinds of steps usually taken.

1. Inspection of Minute Books. An auditor should insist on inspection of the minutes of meetings of stockholders, the board of directors, and executive and other committees of the board for the period under examination and up to the date of his report. Those minutes may reveal contracts, possible or pending litigation, and other matters indicating contingencies to be investigated.

2. Inspection of Contracts. An auditor should examine contracts and agreements to which his client is a party and, among other matters, be alert for provisions that may create material contingencies.

3. Inquiry and Discussion With Officers and Employees. The possibility of loss contingencies should be reviewed with management. Frequently the review brings to light the existence of liabilities not determinable from the accounts. Management's statement as to loss contingencies is included in the representation letter illustrated earlier.

4. Information from Bankers and Attorneys. Contingent liabilities may be revealed by banks' replies to confirmation requests suggested in Chapter 15; those may include a request for a statement of the client's liabilities as acceptor, endorser, or guarantor of notes, drafts, and acceptances.

An auditor should obtain information from the client's attorneys about the status of suits and pending litigation; that information may reveal possible liabilities of substantial amount. The client's records should be scanned for the names of attorneys who have been engaged or to whom retainers or fees have been paid, and usually information should be requested from all of them.

5. *Accounts Receivable Discounted.* Accounts receivable may have been discounted with banks or discount companies and the recourse aspect not recorded in the accounts. An auditor may find a clue to the existence of those receivables if the accounts indicate discount transactions such as payments of interest. Indications of such dealings should be investigated.

6. *Commitments of Subsidiaries.* An auditor should inquire about commitments of subsidiaries guaranteed by the parent company. Those may not appear in the parent company's records but may represent a contingent liability.

7. *Guarantees of Indebtedness of Others.* A corporation may guarantee payment of the principal amount of bonds of another corporation and perhaps also interest and sinking fund payments. If the guarantor is a parent company and the indebtedness guaranteed is that of an affiliate or subsidiary, the existence of the guarantee should not be difficult to discern. If there is no apparent relationship between the guarantor and the obligor corporation, and the guarantor has not been called on to make payments under the guarantee, an auditor must rely for his information on review of corporate minutes and inquiries of officials of the guarantor corporation. Past transactions may indicate the existence of a guarantee, for example, properties subject to a bond issue that have been transferred to another corporation with the transferor guaranteeing new substitute bonds issued by the transferee.

8. *Other Unliquidated Claims.* Although it is customary to insure against liability for damages claimed by employees and the public, insurance policies usually do not cover unlimited liabilities and not all companies carry adequate insurance. Furthermore, unusual claims for damages may arise from alleged breach of contract, failure to deliver goods, antitrust violations, existence of foreign substances in a company's product, and other causes. An auditor should inquire about possible liabilities of that general character.

Some claims may not be referred to counsel. For example, salesmen may claim commissions in excess of those paid or accrued, or employees who have been dismissed may claim salaries or other compensation for uncompleted terms of service. Those claims are often handled as purely administrative matters and may not be referred to counsel unless they are substantial in amount. If an auditor learns of a possible material loss contingency for those claims, such as from an entire union, he should request the opinion of client's counsel with respect to the probable liability.

9. *Judgments.* Occasionally a company disputes a claim, resorts to litigation, and has a judgment entered against it. If the case is appealed and a bond is given pending final decision, execution of the judgment may be stayed. Such a judgment is seldom entered in the accounts because many businessmen consider recording judgments an admission of liability and do not permit a claim that they propose to fight to be shown as a liability.

The existence of judgments may be detected in several ways. An inspection of lawyers' bills may furnish a clue. If a company is able to pay but does not do so on principle, an auditor may not find it difficult to learn the facts. If a company obviously is in serious financial difficulties, an auditor may suspect that judgments have been obtained. In any event, he should request a written statement from a responsible executive as to judgments of which he has knowledge; in unusual circumstances he may even request an independent report based on a search of public records.

10. *Undisclosed Liabilities.* One of an auditor's most difficult tasks is determination of liabilities to which no direct reference appears in the accounts. Clues to those obligations may be discovered in unexpected places, and an auditor should be constantly alert for indications of their existence.

Responses to requests for confirmation of bank loans may list as collateral securities or other assets that do not appear on the records. Those may be borrowed from affiliated companies or others.

The assignment of fire insurance policies on merchandise or materials is likely to indicate the hypothecation of inventories, with a corresponding liability that may be unrecorded.

Distributors of nationally advertised branded merchandise sometimes enter into agreements with agents and franchised dealers to supply advertising and demonstration materials or reimburse them for a part of advertising costs they have incurred. An auditor should examine those contracts for undisclosed liabilities.

Manufacturers of machinery and equipment often sell their products at a price that includes cost of installation. An auditor should determine that estimated cost of completing the installation of equipment sold has been recorded in the same period as the profit from sale of the equipment.

The cancellation of purchase commitments frequently involves a penalty. Particularly in a period of declining prices, an auditor should consider the possibility of liabilities arising from those cancellations; correspondence with the creditors may be necessary.

In an audit of a contractor's accounts, interrogation of executives and employees may disclose important portions of jobs supposedly finished that require additional work at the contractor's expense or certain contracts in process that are expected to result in losses. Matters of that kind are not always ascertainable from the accounts, but the information must be sought nevertheless. The letter of representation as to liabilities generally includes reference to contracts that might adversely affect a company.

If a client does not carry insurance, an auditor should satisfy himself as to the provision for unsettled claims as well as those incurred but not reported at statement date.

Accrued Pension Costs

An auditor must understand the contractual and other arrangements giving rise to pension costs and be aware of the requirements of the Employee Retirement Income Security Act of 1974 so as to ascertain that the expense and liability have been determined in accordance with generally accepted accounting principles. The significance of pension costs to most companies and the effect of a possible misstatement of those costs on the fairness of presentation of the financial statements usually calls for specific substantive testing by an auditor. He should first obtain a copy of the company's pension plan and the actuary's most recent report, read them, and abstract the points that affect the financial statements, such as the following information:

1. A description of the essential provisions of all plans in effect, including eligibility requirements, bases for determining benefit payments, and available vesting rights.
2. Actuarial cost methods used, actuarial assumptions, bases for providing for past service costs, and method of dealing with actuarial gains and losses, including unrealized appreciation and depreciation.
3. Dates and frequency of valuations, bases of stating plan assets, and sources of data from which actuarial determinations are computed.
4. Details of charges to expense and funding contributions for the year.
5. Changes during the year in actuarial cost methods or assumptions for accounting and funding purposes.

6. Value of prior service costs and vested benefits not provided for at beginning and end of year.
7. Value of vested benefits arising during the year.
8. Amount of actuarial gains and losses arising during the year.

The following auditing procedures are illustrative of those that might be applicable to the audit of pension costs other than under insured pension plans:

1. Review and test employee data (given to the actuary) on which the actuarial calculations are based (that may generally be accomplished through analytical review of the data and comparison with related internal reports, statistics, or other information, sometimes supplemented by compliance tests).
2. Compare data relating to pension costs to prior year's data for changes affecting comparability.
3. Determine whether any employees possibly entitled to participate in a plan have been excluded from the actuarial calculations and, if so, obtain an estimate of the maximum effect of the omission on pension expense.
4. Review the reasonableness of the actuarial assumptions to ascertain that all pertinent factors are included. While auditors are not actuaries, it is part of an auditor's professional qualifications to understand in general terms what methods and assumptions are reasonable and necessary.
5. Obtain reasonable assurance that pension fund assets are properly valued.
6. Determine whether termination of the plan is pending by inquiry, reading minutes, etc.
7. Determine that pension expense is within the limits established by APB Opinion No. 8. (*Note:* The FASB has possible amendment of that Opinion on its agenda.)

Other Employee Benefits

Liability at year end for vacation pay, contributions to employees' welfare funds, or other fringe benefits should be reviewed. If vacation periods are based on length of service, a detailed computation of the accrued liability is normally prepared by the client. An auditor should review the method used and make sufficient test-checks of the computation to determine that the amount accrued is substantially correct. He should estimate the amount of the accrual on an overall basis, regardless of whether a detailed computation is available for testing.

A published statement of company policy may create liabilities for rights that accrue to employees even without formal labor contracts. Opinion of counsel may sometimes be necessary to determine whether there is a legal liability at the balance sheet date. Contracts and policies of that nature do not always clearly indicate whether employees' rights accrue ratably over a period or come into existence in their entirety at a specific date.

An auditor must be alert for possible liabilities arising from employee benefits so customary as to constitute an implied promise. Sick pay, severance pay, and some kinds of bonuses and pensions are examples.

Travel Expense and Commissions

An auditor may obtain a list of employees with expense accounts and make appropriate tests to determine whether all expenses have been reported and recorded in the accounts of the proper period. He may test related post-balance sheet entries to determine whether any should have been recorded in the period under examination.

Bonuses and Profit-Sharing Plans for Officers and Employees

An auditor should determine that the liability is computed in accordance with the authorization and plans in effect.

Amounts due officers and employees under profit-sharing plans become a liability in the period during which the profits are earned. If the exact amount of the liability cannot be definitely fixed until a later date, it must be estimated at the balance sheet date.

Royalties

In determining the amount of royalties payable at a given date, an auditor should examine royalty and licensing contracts and extract important provisions for his permanent files. Many contracts provide for a minimum royalty regardless of whether a liability for royalties accrues on a unit basis. Oil and gas producing companies frequently enter into leases that require periodic payments even when no oil or gas has been produced. Those payments are usually termed "lease rentals."

Coal leases often call for minimum annual payments regardless of whether the leasing company extracted coal. Publishing companies enter into agreements with authors that provide for a sliding scale of royalties dependent on the number of copies sold.

An auditor should attempt to determine from a royalty contract whether the payments are actually royalties or whether, in fact, they represent payments for the purchase of a patent or other property covered by the agreement. If the contract is in reality a purchase agreement, the asset and liability should be set up at the date of the contract and depreciation or amortization of the asset charged to expense. So-called royalty payments should not be charged to expense if they represent a reduction of the purchase liability. If provisions of a royalty contract are not clear, an auditor should request a legal interpretation of ambiguous provisions.

Royalties Based on Sales. If royalty payments are based on sales, computations may be checked against recorded sales. Selective tests of statements of royalties due may be made to substantiate recorded amounts.

Royalties Based on Production. In some instances royalty payments are based not on sales but on the quantity or value of goods produced. In that instance an auditor should review documents on file supporting amounts accrued and make suitable tests of underlying data. If accounting records are not kept in sufficient detail to furnish the essential data, it may be necessary to analyze production records to obtain the required information.

Confirmations. If data on which a royalty is based are solely in the possession of lessors or vendors, it is desirable to secure from them statements of liability under royalty agreements. A request for confirmation may bring to light important differences in interpretation of contract provisions.

Interest Payable

Many liabilities bear interest. Occasionally accounts payable bear interest and an auditor should explore that possibility. Loan accounts of partners and corporate officers usually bear interest; judgments, overdue taxes, and other liens often bear interest at high rates. If bond interest is in default and the indenture provides for interest to accrue thereon, the amount should be estimated and recorded.

The computation of accrued interest at the balance sheet date normally can be checked with little or no difficulty.

Advance Payments and Deposits

An auditor should make appropriate tests of advance payments and deposits to determine that the total of the detail records agrees with the control accounts. Material amounts should be confirmed by correspondence with depositaries or other recipients.

Dividends Declared But Unpaid

An auditor should check the computation of the liability for cash dividends declared but unpaid at the balance sheet date by multiplying the number of shares outstanding at the date of record by the rate of dividend declaration of the board of directors.

Unclaimed Dividends

Frequently stockholders cannot be reached and dividend checks may be returned by the post office. The liability for unclaimed dividends may remain undischarged for some time, and an auditor may examine evidence on a test basis to support charges and credits to the account.

Many large corporations, particularly those that have numerous stockholders or bondholders, turn over to fiscal agents the details of dividend or bond interest payments. Under those arrangements, the corporations usually consider their dividend or interest obligations discharged when they deposit the amount of the aggregate required payments with the fiscal agent. In those circumstances, an auditor is not concerned with unpaid dividend checks or uncashed bond coupons, which become obligations of the agent. He should, however, investigate the handling of unclaimed dividends no longer an obligation either of the agent or of the corporation because of the statute of limitations.

Provisions for Uninsured Claims and Losses

An auditor should form an opinion as to whether balances in claim liability accounts seem adequate for possible claims or losses resulting from known events up to the balance sheet date. In doing that he is guided by the client's experience, the experience of other companies in similar activities, and inquiry of company personnel and legal counsel. If the company maintains a claims department, an auditor may wish to review available reports of claims pending, claims settled, and company estimates of costs of final settlement.

Prepaid Insurance

An insurance register or schedule of prepaid insurance should show for each item:

Policy number
Insuring company
Coverage (type and amount)
Co-insurance
Date of policy
Expiration date
Prepaid amount at beginning of period
Premium paid during period under review
Charge to expense in the period
Prepaid amount at end of period

If an insurance register is not maintained, a schedule of prepaid insurance should be prepared, preferably by the client's staff. An auditor should check or test-check the data shown in the register or schedule. Insurance policies and vouchers supporting premiums should be examined on a test basis; in addition to the items tabulated above, an auditor should note beneficiaries, special assessment clauses, and evidence of liens on the insured property. If original insurance policies are not available for inspection, an auditor should determine the reason. Since lenders often hold insurance policies as collateral for loans, the absence of policies may indicate the existence of liens on the property. An auditor should request the client to obtain the policies (or copies) for his examination. He should request confirmations from the insurance companies or brokers particularly with respect to possible retrospective premiums. If there is evidence that insurance is in effect for which the client has not been billed, appropriate liability, expense, and prepaid amounts should be recorded.

Computations of amounts prepaid at the end of a period may be checked approximately. If the company is a going concern, the basis of computation is customarily pro rata, not the short cancellation rate. Prepaid liability and compensation insurance, if premiums are based on payrolls, may be checked by a review of payrolls since the effective date of the policies to determine that charges to expense appear proper. Premiums due may exceed advance payments so that at the end of a period there may be a liability rather than a prepayment. Total prepaid insurance per the register or schedule should be compared with the general ledger.

An auditor is usually not an expert in determining insurable values, and he has no responsibility for management's decisions concerning insuring risks, but he may render helpful service to his clients by calling attention to differences among the amount of coverage, the insurable value (if available), and the recorded amount of insured property.

Fidelity bond coverage should be reviewed to determine that requirements of by-laws or company policy have been met and that the amount of coverage seems adequate. If the amount of fidelity bond coverage appears to be inadequate, an auditor should urge a reappraisal of the requirements.

Prepaid Taxes

An auditor should determine that the amount of prepaid taxes is actually an expense applicable to future periods. Reference should be made to local tax bills and laws because taxes are imposed by state and local authorities under statutes that vary widely in their provisions.

Significant variances in prepaid taxes at the beginning and end of a period should be investigated.

Prepaid Commissions

The propriety of amounts of prepaid commissions should be investigated. If commission expense is a material item, an auditor may wish to examine contracts with salesmen or obtain from management an authoritative statement of the terms of employment; he should see that the salesmen are still employed by the company. Commission records or other evidence of commissions earned may be reviewed; entries in the salesmen's accounts may be traced from commission records and cash records. If there are many salesmen, the examination may be limited to the accounts of only a few of them or to the entries for only a limited period. Transactions of the last month of the period may be reviewed to determine that commissions have been allocated to the proper period. An auditor should be satisfied that balances are in fact prepaid expenses which will be matched with revenue of future periods, and not current period compensation. Confirmation of prepaid commission accounts may be requested from salesmen. If there is a subsidiary ledger for prepaid commission accounts, the balance of the general ledger account should be compared with the trial balance of the subsidiary ledger and differences investigated.

As noted earlier in this chapter, commissions to insurance agents and other policy acquisition costs are significant factors in the insurance industry, both property–casualty and life. For "statutory" financial reporting, acquisition costs must be charged to expense as incurred; under generally accepted accounting principles, they must be deferred and amortized over the lives of the related policies or over the estimated future premium paying periods. Detailed procedures for examination of these "deferred acquisition costs," including tests of future recoverability of these assets, are described in the AICPA Industry Audit Guides, *Audits of Fire and Casualty Insurance Companies* and *Audits of Stock Life Insurance Companies*.

Advances to Employees for Expenses

Advances to salesmen and other employees for expenses may be tested by an examination of cash disbursements, expense reports, and cash receipts. If employees are advanced amounts as working funds on an imprest basis, an auditor may examine reimbursements in the month following the end of the period to determine whether expenditures of material amount prior to the end of the period have been reimbursed. Advances may be confirmed by correspondence with employees. The general ledger account should be compared with the subsidiary ledger and differences investigated; the individual balances may be aged and old balances scrutinized. Unusual advances to officers should be identified.

Prepaid Pension Costs

Sometimes a company's method of accounting for pension costs calls for making contributions to its pension fund in excess of the amount chargeable to expense for the year. The resulting "prepaid pension cost" balance should be substantiated in the same way as the more usual accrued liability for pension costs described earlier.

Inventory of Supplies

Inventories of supplies, if substantial in amount, should be subjected to the same auditing procedures as those described in Chapter 11 for inventories.

Unamortized Debt Discount and Expense

An auditor should determine that accounting for unamortized discount, redemption premium, and expense on retired or refunded bonds is in accordance with the accounting principles set forth in Chapter 16 under "Long-Term Debt Financing." He should check the computation of amounts charged to expense or capitalized by charges to construction during a period.

Suspense Debits and Credits

Every chart of accounts contains a resting place for debit and credit items for which the final accounting has not yet been determined: the officer responsible may not have decided which expense account should be charged; the job order or cost center or subaccount may not have been opened up yet; there may be some unresolved question about the handling or propriety of the item. In the great majority of cases the suspense debit and credit accounts may be quite active in the course of a year, but all the issues should be resolved and the accounts closed out by the end of the fiscal year. An auditor may wish to test balances at an interim date and inquire into the disposition of items because doing so may contribute considerably to his understanding of the kinds of accounting problems that can occur and the implications for the system of internal control. In the rare case of balances remaining at the end of the fiscal year, an auditor should inquire searchingly into the reasons why proper distribution is not determinable. Particularly in the case of suspense debits, a client commonly and understandably often wishes to carry in the balance sheet items in dispute which someone in management "just doesn't want to give up on." If those debits are significant, an auditor needs evidence that they are likely to have a realizable value or to benefit future operations, and are therefore properly classified as assets.

STATEMENT PRESENTATION

LIABILITIES

Introduction

In presenting liabilities and deferred credits on a balance sheet, current liabilities are usually listed first and totalled. Noncurrent liabilities follow—long-term borrowings, deferred compensation, estimated losses, deferred taxes—and finally minority interest in consolidated subsidiaries. This distinction between "current" and "noncurrent" is of importance in the determination of working capital, discussed in Chapter 18. FASB Statement No. 6 (*AICPA Prof. Stds.*, vol. 3, Section 2033) requires a total of current liabilities; in certain industries, such as insurance, real estate development, and leasing, that total has generally not been considered significant information and accordingly has not been shown.

Accounting Research Bulletin No. 43, Chapter 3A (*AICPA Prof. Stds.*, vol. 3, paragraph 2031.07), states:

> The term *current liabilities* is used principally to designate obligations whose liquidation is reasonably expected to require the use of existing resources properly classifiable as current assets, or the creation of other current liabilities. As a balance-sheet category, the classification is intended to include obligations for items which have entered into the operating cycle, such as payables incurred in the acquisition of materials and supplies to be used in the production of goods or in providing services to be offered for sale; collections received in advance of the delivery of goods or performance of services; and debts which arise from operations directly related to the operating cycle, such as accruals for wages, salaries, commissions, rentals, royalties, and income and other taxes. Other liabilities whose regular and ordinary liquidation is expected to occur within a relatively short period of time, usually twelve months, are also intended for inclusion, such as short-term debts arising from the acquisition of capital assets, serial maturities of long-term obligations, amounts required to be expended within one year under sinking fund provisions, and agency obligations arising from the collection or acceptance of cash or other assets for the account of third persons.

A one-year period is generally considered the basis for segregation of current liabilities from long-term or noncurrent liabilities. A period longer than one year is used when the operating cycle is longer than a year; its use should be disclosed in a note to the financial statements.

Regulation S-X of the Securities and Exchange Commission defines current liabilities in Rule 3-12, as follows:

> Obligations which are payable within one year or whose liquidation is reasonably expected to require the use of existing current assets or the creation of other current liabilities shall be classed as current liabilities. However, if the normal operating cycle of the company is longer than one year, generally recognized trade practices may be followed with respect to the exclusion of items such as customers' deposits and deferred income, provided an appropriate explanation of the circumstances is made.

Subgroupings of current liabilities are frequently listed in the order in which they will become due. An exception is notes payable, which is often stated as the first item of current liabilities even though other current liabilities may be paid before the notes are due. Subgroupings generally shown separately, if material, are notes payable, accounts payable, accrued expenses, cash dividends payable, income taxes payable, and current installments of long-term debt.

Accounts Payable

If the term "accounts payable" is not qualified, a reader is justified in assuming that it represents amounts due trade creditors as a result of ordinary business transactions. Amounts payable to trade creditors are normally due currently, except if extended time payments have been arranged. Current debit balances that are not direct offsets to accounts payable, if material, should be segregated and reflected in the balance sheet as current assets.

Accounts payable other than to trade creditors may be grouped in a separate total including items such as customers' credit balances, advance payments and deposits, royalties payable, taxes collected on behalf of taxing authorities, payroll withholdings of other items such as union dues and hospitalization and group insurance premiums, and claims or awards. If an individual item is significant it should be stated separately. If cash collected or received for the account of third parties is segregated as restricted deposits and classified as a noncurrent asset, the related liability should be shown as noncurrent. If the cash is included in current assets, the liability is also current.

Advances from directors, officers, and employees and cash dividends payable are frequently stated separately. Rule 5-02 of Regulation S-X requires for financial statements filed with the Securities and Exchange Commission that "dividends declared" and amounts payable, other than items arising in the ordinary course of business, to "underwriters, promoters, directors, officers, employees and principal holders (other than affiliates) of equity securities" be stated separately. If the amount of cash dividends declared but unpaid has been deposited with a disbursing agent, the deposit and related liability may be shown on the balance sheet or they may be omitted and the dividend treated as paid. Disclosure of the omission in a note to the financial statements is desirable.

Accounts payable to affiliated companies and other related parties should be stated separately.

Receivable and payable balances with the same person should not generally be offset against each other if no right of offset exists or if separate settlement of those balances is expected. An account due to a vendor may be discounted and thus could represent a liability to a third party.

Security Deposits

Under uniform systems of accounts prescribed by public utility regulatory bodies, security deposits are reflected as current liabilities.

Lessors often require a deposit from a tenant to be applied as payment of rent for a final period of a lease. Since the lessor's obligation involves a long-term deferment of delivery of the service, the deposit need not be classified by the lessor as a current liability until a year before expiration of the lease.

Returnable Containers

Containers are usually returned within a fairly short period of time, and the related liability is generally classified as current. However, if experience indicates that containers are not returned promptly, it is proper to estimate the portion of the total liability that will not be refunded within one year for classification as a noncurrent liability. The liability for deposits on containers is frequently reflected as noncurrent by certain industries, for example, beverage companies. Although classification as noncurrent is considered less appropriate than current classification, it may be regarded as permissible provided the containers are not included in current assets.

Accrued Expenses

Obligations of a continuing character, not due at the balance sheet date and often likely to be larger in amount at maturity, are sometimes grouped with accounts payable and sometimes presented separately from those based on completed transactions. In a detailed statement the various types of accrued expenses may be shown separately because they reflect different phases of a business, but it is not improper to combine them in one amount if they are not abnormal in character or amount. The kinds of accruals represented may be indicated in the caption.

Liability for Taxes

The estimated liability for income taxes remaining after the payment of required installments is usually stated separately, entitled "Accrued income taxes," "Estimated federal, state, and foreign income taxes," "Provision for taxes," or a similar caption. Under APB Opinion No. 10 (*AICPA Prof. Stds.*, vol. 3, Section 2032) the offset of securities against taxes payable, formerly considered acceptable practice in a number of instances, is no longer acceptable except "when it is clear that a purchase of securities (acceptable for the payment of taxes) is in substance an advance payment of taxes that will be payable in the relatively near future, so that in the special circumstances the purchase is tantamount to the prepayment of taxes" (paragraph 2032.03).

Provisions for deferred income taxes should be included among current liabilities to the extent that they relate to receivables or other items (such as inventories stated on the percentage-of-completion basis) that are classified as current.

Extended Vacation Allowances

If recording a liability for vested rights in extended vacation allowances is deemed necessary, the amount of the liability should be allocated between current and noncurrent on the basis of the amounts expected to be payable within and beyond one year, respectively. If the adoption or revision of extended vacation plans has, or may have in the future, a material bearing on comparability of financial statements, disclosure of the effect is desirable.

Advances and Liabilities Under Government Contracts

The balance sheet treatment of liabilities to the government, resulting from renegotiation, was discussed in Chapter 9. Reference should also be made to ARB No. 43, Chapter 11A (*AICPA Prof. Stds.*, vol. 3, Section 4041) dealing with cost-plus-fixed-fee contracts, which recommends that advances made by the government to finance those contracts may be offset, with appropriate disclosure, against work-in-process inventories (if they represent payment for the work) or accounts receivable arising from billings to the government (if the advances represent payment of billings); in other circumstances, they should be shown as a current liability.

Advance payments on government contracts are frequently made on the basis of a percentage of inventory accumulated for performance of the contract. Title to the inventory may vest in the government, with the company having a claim against the government for its equity in the inventory. Percentage advances or progress payments may be treated as deductions from inventory. Disclosure should be made that title to the applicable inventory is held by the government.

Contracts terminated by the government often stipulate that a contractor may recover allowable costs incurred to date of termination and, possibly, a related portion of estimated profit. Advances and partial payments made by the government on terminated contracts are usually deducted separately from amounts of termination claims. Loans under which those claims have been pledged as collateral should be shown as current liabilities, whether or not guaranteed by the government.

A contractor may arrange one or more subcontracts with other companies for portions of the work. The termination claim liability of the contractor to subcontractors is finally determined by their approved claims and is then included as a part of the contractor's termination claim. Subcontractors' claims are treated as current liabilities (at actual or estimated amounts), and the same amounts are included in the receivable for the contractor's termination claim.

Loss Contingencies

Product Guarantees

The estimated liability under product guarantees may be included under current liabilities or noncurrent liabilities, or apportioned between them on a reasonable basis, as circumstances indicate.

Trading Stamps and Profit-Sharing Coupons

The liability for trading stamps and profit-sharing coupons may be approximately allocated, as appropriate, between current and noncurrent liabilities, based on the estimated period of redemption.

Provisions for Repairs and Renewals

Provisions for recurring maintenance jobs such as relining furnaces, repainting stores, renewal of tanks, and the like are shown among noncurrent liabilities. It is not customary to assign an amount of those liabilities to current liabilities.

Other Estimated Liabilities

Estimated liabilities for items such as deferred compensation, pension liability (other than amounts to be paid to a funding agency, which are current liabilities), workmen's compensation, severance pay, contract losses, and the like are usually classified as noncurrent liabilities. If the portion due within the next operating cycle can be reasonably estimated, it is properly includable as a current liability. If the existence of a liability is admitted or probable, but circumstances do not permit a reasonable estimate of its amount, disclosure of the facts should be made in a note to the balance sheet. If the amount may be material, an auditor should consider whether qualification of his opinion is necessary.

Disclosure of Contingent Liabilities

If the amount of contingent liabilities involved is or may become material, its existence should be recognized and appropriately disclosed in the balance sheet or notes thereto. The fact that a precise amount cannot be established is no justification for failure to indicate the existence of a material contingent liability.

FASB Statement No. 5, referring to loss contingencies of the type formerly termed contingent liabilities, requires that:

> . . . disclosure of the contingency shall be made when there is at least a reasonable possibility that a loss or an additional loss may have been incurred.[6] The disclosure shall indicate the nature of the contingency and shall give an estimate of the possible loss or range of loss or state that such an estimate cannot be made. Disclosure is not required of a loss contingency involving an unasserted claim or assessment when there has been no manifestation by a potential claimant of an awareness of a possible claim or assessment unless it is considered probable that a claim will be asserted and there is a reasonable possibility that the outcome will be unfavorable. [Paragraph 4311.10]

> [6] For example, disclosure shall be made of any loss contingency that meets the condition in paragraph .08(a) but that is not accrued because the amount of loss cannot be reasonably estimated (paragraph .08(b)). [Quoted under "Estimated Liabilities" at the beginning of this chapter.] Disclosure is also required of some loss contingencies that do not meet the condition in paragraph .08(a)—namely, those contingencies for which there is a *reasonable possibility* that a loss may have been incurred even though information may not indicate that it is *probable* that an asset had been impaired or a liability had been incurred at the date of the financial statements.

Contingent liabilities are not stated in dollar amounts in the same manner as direct liabilities on a balance sheet because the fact rather than the amount of liability is in doubt. For example, while the amount of notes receivable can be stated in dollars, the contingent liability for notes sold is not actual at the date of the balance sheet; the liability for damages, if any, for breach of contract may not be determinable until awarded by a jury and approved by a court. Therefore, the existence of contingent liabilities is most frequently disclosed in a note. Sometimes a caption "Contingencies (Note ——)" appears on the liability side of a balance sheet immediately preceding the capital section; that procedure is generally followed in financial statements filed with the Securities and Exchange Commission. The position of the notation on a balance sheet is not important, but a clear statement of significant information is.

Whether a contingent liability is material is sometimes a troublesome question. The potential amount involved may be large, but the possibility of the contingent liability's becoming actual may seem remote. FASB Statement No. 5 requires that the contingent liability for receivables discounted be disclosed even if not material in amount, because readers of a balance sheet may be interested in how the company obtains working capital.

Clients often resist disclosure of contingent liabilities, believing that the information might be detrimental to the company or its stockholders. It is sometimes argued that a balance sheet stating the existence and amount of lawsuits or other claims for which a company denies liability might be construed as admission of liability. An auditor should, of course, give full consideration to the position of his client, but usually it is possible to explain a contingent liability and at the same time avoid harmful admissions. A statement may suffice that the amount of a contingent liability is indeterminable at the balance sheet date but may be substantial and that counsel considers the possibility of its becoming a determined liability of material amount to be remote.

Notes and Acceptances Discounted

After the date of discounting notes or acceptances but before maturity, the amount of the contingent liability of the endorser, usually expressed as the principal amount of the notes or acceptances discounted or sold with recourse, should be disclosed. It is not sufficient to state that notes or acceptances have been discounted without stating the amount. An example of a note disclosing that type of information is as follows:

As of December 31, 19__, the Company was contingently liable in the amount of $_____ on notes receivable sold to banks with provisions for repurchase.

Letters of Credit

Some creditors and creditors' organizations have urged that unused amounts of commercial letters of credit should be disclosed on balance sheets of companies to which banks have issued letters of credit. The authors believe that disclosure is rarely essential to a proper understanding of financial position, but there is no objection to disclosing the information in a note, such as "Unused balances of commercial letters of credit at December 31, 19__ were $_____."

Other Disclosures of Contingent Liabilities

Contingent liabilities arising from sales of accounts receivable and drafts, endorsements and guarantees, and the like should be disclosed. It is worth repeating that in many instances the amount of the contingent liability represents the maximum possible loss. The actual loss eventually suffered, if any, may be substantially less, because seldom does a primary obligor default on all sold or discounted paper and in many instances a claim arises that may eventually offset the immediate loss. On the other hand, care should be exercised to avoid a misleading implication as to the likelihood of realization of a claim.

COSTS AND EXPENSES

Cost of Goods Sold

In a multiple-step income statement, cost of goods sold is shown as a single item subtracted from net sales to show gross profit. In a single-step income statement, cost of goods sold is listed together with other expenses and the total is deducted from total revenue to produce income before income taxes. Occasionally, cost of goods sold is not shown as a separate item, but total costs and expenses are broken down according to their nature, such as cost of materials, salaries and wages, employee benefit expense, depreciation expense, and the like.

For financial statements filed with the Securities and Exchange Commission, Rule 5-03 of Regulation S-X requires the disclosure of "the amount of cost of tangible goods sold as regularly computed under the system of accounting followed" and also "the amount of beginning and ending inventories . . . and . . . the basis of determining such amounts" (described further in Chapter 11). If sales and operating revenue are combined, as discussed in Chapter 9, cost of goods sold and operating expenses may also be combined. Otherwise, the amount of operating expenses (representing the cost of services sold) should be stated. There should be separate disclosure of purchases from and services rendered by a parent, subsidiaries, and other affiliates.

Depreciation and Amortization Expense

Chapter 12 discusses disclosure requirements in the statement of income for depreciation and amortization expense.

Lease Expense

Rental expense is generally classified according to the nature of the premises leased; for example, rental of production facilities is part of manufacturing cost while rental of a warehouse for storage of finished goods is usually classified as selling expense. Disclosures required in connection with leases are dealt with in Chapter 12.

Experimental, Research, and Development Expense

The nature of experimental, research, and development activities generally determines their classification in an income statement. If the activities have little or no current relationship to the manufacturing function, the expenses may be presented in a separate category or combined with an appropriate grouping of other nonmanufacturing expenses. In other instances, their principal relationship may be to current manufacturing activities, thus justifying inclusion of all or a part of those expenses in cost of goods sold. However classified, FASB Statement No. 2 (*AICPA Prof. Stds.*, vol. 3, Section 4211) requires the total to be disclosed.

Pension Costs

Paragraph 46 of APB Opinion No. 8 (paragraph 4063.46 of *AICPA Prof. Stds.*, vol. 3) sets forth certain requirements for disclosure of pension costs in financial statements or a related note, as follows:

1. A statement that such plans exist, identifying or describing the employee groups covered.
2. A statement of the company's accounting and funding policies.
3. The provision for pension cost for the period.
4. The excess, if any, of the actuarially computed value of vested benefits over the total of the pension fund and any balance-sheet pension accruals, less any pension prepayments or deferred charges.
5. Nature and effect of significant matters affecting comparability for all periods presented, such as changes in accounting methods (actuarial cost method, amortization of past and prior service cost, treatment of actuarial gains and losses, etc.), changes in circumstances (actuarial assumptions, etc.), or adoption or amendment of a plan.

The changes in accounting methods mentioned in item 5 above are discussed in Chapter 2. Changes in actuarial assumptions that stem from altered conditions, although not an accounting inconsistency, do affect comparability and accordingly should be disclosed if material in the current year or expected to be material in the future. Those changes may be based on experience or on current or prospective changes in employment conditions.

The disclosure requirements of Opinion No. 8 are generally in accord with those of the Securities and Exchange Commission for financial statements filed with the SEC, except for two items. Rule 3-16 (g) of Regulation S-X calls for "a brief description of the essential provisions" of plans in effect and, for a plan that has not been funded or otherwise provided for, "the estimated amount that would be necessary to fund or otherwise provide for the past service cost of the plan."

Other Expense

The extent to which details of other expenses are disclosed in financial statements depends on their significance. Frequently, they are combined and presented only in total or combined with items of other income to show one figure for miscellaneous income, **net, or miscellaneous expense, net.**

The Securities and Exchange Commission requirements are somewhat detailed and are stated in Rule 5-03 of Regulation S-X, as follows:

Interest and amortization of debt discount and expense. State separately: (a) Interest on bonds, mortgages, and similar debt; (b) amortization of debt discount and expense (or premium); and (c) other interest.

Losses on securities. Losses shall be stated net of profits. No losses on the person's own equity securities, or losses of its affiliates on their own equity securities, shall be included under this caption. State, here or in a note referred to herein, the method followed in determining the cost of securities sold, e.g., "average cost," "first-in, first-out," or "identified certificate."

Miscellaneous income deductions. State separately any material amounts, indicating clearly the nature of the transactions out of which the items arose.

Extraordinary Items

Until the publication of APB Opinion No. 30 (*AICPA Prof. Stds.,* vol. 3, Section 2012) in 1973, many large items of expense were classified as extraordinary items. The Opinion narrowed the definition of an extraordinary item, causing most items to be classified as "Other expenses." That Opinion and the extraordinary item category are described in Chapter 18.

11

The Production Segment

INVENTORIES, COST OF GOODS SOLD, AND RELATED ACCOUNTS

INTRODUCTION

Inventories and the production segment constitute perhaps the most pervasive, significant, and difficult subject in accounting and auditing and indeed in business management generally. The subject is pervasive because most enterprises have to carry amounts of goods in transit, awaiting or in process of production, or available for servicing customers. The subject is difficult because problems inevitably arise in keeping track of items, evaluating their condition and salability, and determining costs, in addition to other management problems of attaining maximum production and distribution while minimizing cost, investment, and risk.

From a strict accounting point of view, inventories are unexpired costs at a balance sheet date, awaiting matching with future revenue. (That concept is discussed at length in Chapter 10.) Thus, Statement 2 of the profession's official pronouncement on inventory pricing [ARB No. 43, Chapter 4 (*AICPA Prof. Stds.*, vol. 3, Section 5121)] declares:

A major objective of accounting for inventories is the proper determination of income through the process of matching appropriate costs against revenues. [Paragraph 5121.03]

Inventories and the production segment are vital to an enterprise because success is measured in large part and often primarily by the ability to manage production efficiently and economically. But an auditor's interest, and the subject of this chapter in its most basic sense, is restricted to the accounting point of view: the physical existence of inventories, measurement of cost, and estimates of realizable value. However, since management's control over production is a principal determinant of the amount of inventory on hand, its costs, and its realizable value, an auditor is compelled to give greater heed to operational controls in this segment than in any of the other segments.

Fundamentally, only three questions about inventories are of interest to an accountant or an auditor:

Do they exist?
What is their cost?
What is their realizable value?

For convenience, the discussion of accounting principles is organized under the headings of those three subjects.

• ACCOUNTING PRINCIPLES

THE GENERAL RULE: LOWER OF COST OR MARKET

The two fundamental principles governing accounting for the buying segment, discussed at length in Chapter 10, are the principle of matching costs with revenue and the principle of anticipating losses. Both are brought together in the general rule for carrying inventories: cost or market, whichever is lower. "Cost" incorporates the first principle: inventories are unexpired costs carried forward in a balance sheet to await matching with future sales revenue. "Market" recognizes the second principle: if realizable value falls below cost, the loss is anticipated by writing inventory carrying values down to realizable value.

PHYSICAL EXISTENCE

What Constitutes Inventory?

Chapter 4 of ARB No. 43, "Inventory Pricing" (1953; *AICPA Prof. Stds.,* vol. 3, Section 5121), is still the profession's authoritative pronouncement on the subject. It is referred to hereafter simply as Section 5121. Statement 1 defines inventory as follows:

> The term *inventory* is used herein to designate the aggregate of those items of tangible personal property which (1) are held for sale in the ordinary course of business, (2) are in process of production for such sale, or (3) are to be currently consumed in the production of goods or services to be available for sale. [Paragraph 5121.02]

That definition distinguishes items to be included in inventory from other costs that are either intangible or held for purposes other than production or ordinary sale. The costs of inventories become cost of goods sold when they are sold "in the ordinary course of business." Property acquired for purposes other than sale in the ordinary course of business does not become inventory upon a decision to sell it.

Supplies are sometimes classified as inventory and sometimes as prepaid expenses. Technically, only supplies entering into manufacturing should be included in inventory under the definition given, and selling and administrative supplies on hand should be classified as prepaid expenses. Usually, however, supplies are not of great significance, and the distinction between manufacturing supplies and other supplies is often disregarded.

It is sometimes unclear whether tools and spare parts should be classified as inventory or as equipment. If an item is expected to last more than a year, it should be classified as equipment; if it is ordinarily consumed "currently" (in the words of the Statement), it should be included in inventory of supplies. Tools and parts, like supplies, are usually not a major item in the balance sheet, and so their classification need not be an issue. However, see Chapter 12 for handling of instances where the question is significant.

Inventories usually consist of tangible personal property—as the definition states—with very few exceptions. Large amounts of the intangible results of labor—such as design and production engineering or similar technological effort—are often expended in creating inventory items. Costs related to those intangibles may be accumulated in inventory in considerable amounts and for a considerable time before a tangible product with which they can be associated begins to take form. Contract research and similar accumulations of intangible products or services, although technically unbilled receivables, are sometimes classified as inventories until billed and are included in this chapter. Intangible costs held for use in the business, rather than for sale, and other costs that may be deferred, are covered in Chapter 12.

When Are Items Includable in Inventory?

The legal test of title is often disregarded for accounting purposes as a matter of convenience or business practice. For example, sometimes purchases in transit that are legally owned because title has passed may not be recorded as inventory until after receipt and inspection of the goods and validation of the vendor's invoice. Similarly, shipments under arrangements such as installment sales, C.O.D. sales, and certain export sales are normally recorded as sales and the items removed from inventory even though the seller commonly retains title to protect himself.

Nevertheless, the rule of legal title must often be respected and reflected in the accounts if significant amounts are involved. For example:

If goods received but not recorded at a balance sheet date may be significant in amount, a company should have a means for "picking up" and recording the inventory and related liability.

Significant amounts of goods in transit, title to which is legally vested in the buyer, should be included in the buyer's inventory; goods in transit shipped FOB buyer's plant should, of course, be excluded from his inventory.

Consigned goods are inventory of the consignor until the consignee reports their sale.

Goods on approval or trial should be in the inventory of the legal owner; demonstration models may be unsalable and more properly classified as equipment.

Under many government contracts, title to inventory passes to the government when partial payments are made on the contract. When the percentage-of-completion method is used in accounting for long-term contracts (Chapter 9), revenue is recognized and related costs are deducted from revenue as production or construction progresses; the assets involved are thus primarily receivables rather than inventories. Therefore, inventory technically owned by the government or other buyer is often not shown as inventory by the contractor.

There are two major alternatives to percentage-of-completion accounting for long-term contracts. If the completed-contract method is used, costs incurred on a contract are usually shown as costs of inventory, reduced by partial payments received. Contractors that use the unit-of-delivery method, which recognizes revenue and cost of goods sold in proportion to the fraction of total contract units delivered to the customer, reflect unbilled costs as inventory. When title to such inventories is held by the customer, that fact should be disclosed.

What Constitutes "Held for Sale in the Ordinary Course of Business"?

Changes in business conditions can create doubt about whether items on hand are salable "in the ordinary course of business." Past experience is often a helpful guide but it is seldom conclusive, especially in volatile markets or for new and untried products.

As a rule of thumb, a supply of inventory items that does not exceed the amount anticipated to be sold in a reasonable period, say one year, does not raise a question of salability. But doubts about salability arise when the number of units on hand exceeds a year's expected sales. If economies of production or purchase dictate that items be manufactured or purchased in large lots to be sold over several years, those items are properly included in inventory—subject, of course, to tests for realizable value (discussed below).

Difficult judgments are required if a new and untried product is manufactured or purchased and no historical basis for estimating its acceptability exists. A reasonable number of items produced according to a well-organized marketing study of customer needs may appropriately be classified as inventory.

MEASUREMENT OF COST

Statement 3 of Section 5121 defines cost of inventory:

> The primary basis of accounting for inventories is cost, which has been defined generally as the price paid or consideration given to acquire an asset. As applied to inventories, cost means in principle the sum of the applicable expenditures and charges directly or indirectly incurred in bringing an article to its existing condition and location. [Paragraph 5121.04]

The definition is relatively simple and straightforward. Inventory cost includes costs of acquiring and producing goods for sale. It excludes all selling costs and all general and administrative costs except those clearly related to production.

Putting the definition into practice is not simple, however, for several reasons:

> The cost of goods acquired for resale or for use in production is rarely as simple as the invoice price of items purchased.

Complications proliferate in determining the cost of manufactured products and products in the process of manufacture; cost accounting is a complex and highly developed branch of professional accounting, which affects the cost of inventory in several ways, including allocating costs to products and periods and to production and nonproduction departments and thence to units of product processed.

Cost of inventory may be measured by several different methods; inventory costs are usually aggregates—units of inventory are rarely purchased or produced individually—and many costs are allocated two or more times before being related to specific units of inventory.

Interchangeable units of merchandise or products usually have different costs, creating difficulties in determining which costs should be used to value the inventory of items on hand and which costs should be assigned to items transferred or sold.

Cost of Purchases

Cost of purchased goods or materials is the invoice price, less discounts, plus other costs of acquiring the goods or materials. Trade and quantity discounts should always be deducted from the invoice price. Cash discounts (usually two per cent or less), which are properly reductions of inventory costs, are sometimes reflected as a reduction of cost of goods sold.

Transportation charges (including those incurred after acquisition for shipping goods or materials to a branch plant or warehouse), import duties, insurance, warehousing, and handling costs are all part of acquiring merchandise or materials and bringing them to their "existing condition and location." They are therefore appropriately added to invoice price to obtain inventory cost. However, for practical reasons they are often accounted for as items of manufacturing overhead rather than as cost of items purchased. Some cost accounting systems add a "material overhead" factor to the cost of purchased materials to cover costs associated with acquiring, handling, and storing of materials.

Cost of Production

The same general cost principles that apply to purchases apply also to determining the cost of finished and semifinished products, including costs of material used, labor, and a reasonable allocation of manufacturing overhead.

Useful financial statements can be consistently prepared using fairly simple inventory costing practices. However, the complexities of modern manufacturing processes, which often convert raw materials into products of a radically different nature or appearance, necessitate adequate, and sometimes elaborate, cost accounting systems. Financial reporting and internal accounting control are much better served by cost systems that account for costs of production and the resulting inventories. A cost system is even more important in providing information for orderly management of production and marketing of the resulting product.

The principles of cost systems and cost accounting are too extensive to be set forth here in detail. The following paragraphs summarize those applicable to inventories presented in financial statements that are in accordance with generally accepted accounting principles.

Material Cost

Material cost is the cost of material that becomes physically part of products. Other materials, such as oils for lubricating machinery or washroom supplies, are normally included in overhead.

Materials may be purchased and stored for use when required or they may be ordered as needed and put into production as received. Materials are usually categorized as raw materials inventory even though they may consist of manufactured parts and subassemblies. The raw materials inventory is reduced and production or work-in-process inventory is increased as materials are placed in production.

Cost of production should include raw material put into process, which is generally more than the material in the end product because of waste and shrinkage. Cost systems attempt to distinguish between normal and abnormal shrinkage. Normal waste and shrinkage is included in inventory as part of the cost of producing the units of product that emerge. The cost of abnormal shrinkage during a period should be accounted for as a separate expense or loss and should not be included in inventory at the end of the period.

Cost of production should be reduced by cost recoveries, such as sales of scrap and by-products. A by-product is distinguished from a "common" or "joint" product (discussed hereafter)—the value of a by-product is not significant in relation to total production cost. Customarily the selling price or recovery value of scrap and by-products is simply credited as a reduction of overall production cost.

Material cost of one division, subsidiary, or affiliate may often be the sales of another. Therefore, if the selling division or subsidiary records a profit, intracompany or intercompany profit in inventory must be eliminated in consolidation, to reduce the inventory to cost.

Labor Cost

Labor cost consists of wages and related employment costs of employees directly engaged in production. Wages of supervisory and support personnel, such as storekeepers and repairmen, are usually called indirect labor and included in overhead. Payroll taxes, pension costs, and similar employment costs of production employees are also sometimes included in overhead for convenience.

The distinction between labor and overhead is clear in concept, but complexities of technology and the proliferation of labor categories have clouded it in practice: in what category are the specialists who set up the production machines, production schedulers, engineers, and methods men? Except in unusual cases, it does not matter for accounting purposes whether particular labor cost is classified as labor or overhead, as long as the classification is consistently maintained from period to period.

Before the development of managerial cost accounting systems, labor cost was an inventoriable cost regardless of whether it was efficient and productive. Now, many systems identify the cost of "idle time," "rework time," and similar nonproductive categories. Some accountants believe that nonproductive labor cost should not be included in the cost of products carried forward in inventory. Others believe that some inefficiency is inevitable and is as much a cost of producing a product as other labor cost. Within the range of normal operating activity, either view is acceptable, but labor costs resulting from unused or excess capacity should not be included in inventory.

Manufacturing Overhead

Manufacturing overhead represents those manufacturing costs that cannot be associated directly with units of product. That is, overhead is all production cost except direct material and direct labor costs. It usually includes indirect labor (such as wages of supervisory production and factory administrative personnel), indirect materials (supplies and other small items not usually accounted for individually), depreciation, maintenance, light and power, heat, certain taxes, and all the other indirect costs of running a factory. Production engineering is commonly included in overhead but engineering of an experimental nature may or may not be included. Production overhead should not include selling expenses, and generally should not include general and administrative expenses.

Items of overhead that vary with production—such as some indirect labor and materials, social security taxes, vacation pay and pension costs, and power—are often classified as variable overhead, and others that depend primarily on time—such as rent, depreciation, insurance, and real estate taxes—are classified as fixed overhead. Many costs are semifixed or semivariable. For example, cost of supervision tends to remain stable over relatively small variations in production but changes if variations in production are relatively large.

Variable and fixed overhead costs are sometimes called direct overhead and indirect overhead, respectively, to indicate how they vary with production. That usage is often confusing because of the other uses of those terms in accounting, but it is nevertheless common, as in "direct costing."

Direct costing is a method of inventory overhead pricing that includes as costs of inventory only costs that vary with production. Fixed overhead costs are considered to be expenses of providing productive capacity rather than costs of producing products and are included in expenses of the period of incurrence.

Controversy has surrounded the method since it was widely advocated a quarter of a century ago, concerning its acceptability for pricing inventories in financial statements purporting to be in accordance with generally accepted accounting principles. Almost no one challenges its usefulness in many internal accounting reports for management. The literature generated by the controversy is vast, but arguments for and against direct costing have not changed much recently. Interest in and applications of direct costing also seem to have leveled off after spreading rapidly during the 1950's.

Proponents of direct costing argue that the method both is theoretically sound and provides information that is more useful than that provided by conventional "absorption costing." The method formally recognizes the ideas underlying flexible budgets, break-even analysis, and profit–cost–volume relationships and results in an income statement that shows the *contribution margin* (sales less variable costs) of each product or segment—the amount it contributes toward fixed costs and profits. Proponents further argue that: the effect on net income of variable and fixed costs is vital information not provided by conventional accounting; direct costing results in a better matching of costs with revenue because reported net income always varies directly with sales and cannot, as it can with conventional methods, increase with increases in production even though sales decrease; and costs related to products should be included in inventory and deducted from revenue when the products are sold while those related to time should be recognized as expenses of the period to which they relate.

Opponents of direct costing do not deny the usefulness of information about variable and fixed costs but point out that it can be disclosed without dislocating the determination of net income to the extent inherent in direct costing. They hold that fixed costs are not costs of facilities that should be charged against income as incurred, but rather part of the costs of production. Further, they believe that over-head application is a means of properly dividing the cost of production between that which is sold and that which has been retained in inventory.

Although committees of the AICPA have not spoken specifically and directly on the acceptability of direct costing, the preponderance of opinion among spokesmen for the Institute is that the method is not encompassed within generally accepted accounting principles. The Securities and Exchange Commission refuses to accept financial statements based on the method, and the Internal Revenue Service explicitly prohibits it for federal income tax purposes.

Methods of Determining Inventory Cost

Costs may be gathered by items or groups of items—the "job cost" system. Or they may be first charged to production departments or processes and aggregated, and the resulting departmental or process cost assigned to the related production—the "process cost" system. Material and direct labor can usually be directly associated with a process or job. Overhead for the most part cannot, and is usually allocated to processes or jobs on some systematic basis. The most common basis is in proportion to direct labor—either dollars or hours—though many systems have developed other bases. As long as it is rational and systematic and consistently applied, any reasonable method of overhead allocation is presently acceptable for financial statement purposes.

Assigning costs to products is so complex in many production operations that no one determines precisely the actual cost of a unit or item. Rather, the unit costs that are used to state inventories at cost are useful approximations or averages resulting from the application of several cost accounting methods. Among the most significant methods involved in determining the unit costs of manufactured products are actual cost, standard cost, and joint cost. The retail method is commonly used to estimate inventory cost in certain kinds of mercantile operations. The methods discussed are sometimes alternatives to each other but may be used together in a single entity.

Actual Cost

An actual cost system records and assigns to processes and jobs the actual costs incurred. Total production costs of a period are assigned to (absorbed by) units produced during the period. Product costs are not determinable until production is completed for a period, and the method does not distinguish between fixed costs and those that vary with the level of production. Consequently, if cost levels remain constant and production is down, unit costs will be higher.

Actual cost thus has at least two major shortcomings: costs of production and inventory cannot be known until after the end of a period, and unit costs are excessively sensitive to changes in the volume of production, especially if there are significant fixed costs. It is therefore seldom used in its pure form. At a minimum, overhead is usually applied to production by use of normalized overhead rates even though materials used and labor may be recorded at actual cost.

A normalized overhead rate avoids fluctuations in unit costs caused by variations in production levels. As a result of the inevitable differences between actual and estimated levels of production, the actual overhead expense usually is different from that applied to production. This underabsorbed or overabsorbed overhead can be accounted for in two ways. If it is believed that unabsorbed overhead costs cannot be associated with product and therefore with potential revenue, the variance is excluded from cost of inventory and charged off in the period it arises. The more common practice is to treat the variance as a proportionate adjustment of the aggregate cost of goods sold and ending inventory.

Standard Cost

In a standard cost system, predetermined or standard costs are assigned to material and production operations and product standard costs are derived. The actual costs incurred are measured against the appropriate standards, and variances (differences between standard and actual costs) are determined for each significant function. Standard material quantities may be computed from actual consumption data of earlier periods or bills of material established by engineering studies, standard labor hours from actual production records or from time studies, and standard overhead rates from estimated overhead expenses applied to production at normal or expected capacity—all usually extended at prices and wage rates current at the time the standards are set.

Realistic standard costs for inventory valuation should reflect normal operations that may reasonably and practically be attained under the operating conditions expected during the period, not theoretical goals that cannot possibly be realized.

A simple standard cost system usually produces six or seven variances:

Material price
Material quantity or usage

Labor rate

Labor hours or time

Overhead volume or capacity

Overhead budget or spending

Overhead efficiency (separate variance only with certain standards)

Most of the common standards can be refined, and most of the common variances can be analyzed further if necessary. Standard costs may readily be adjusted to approximate actual costs for purposes of inventory valuation when that step is considered necessary. All that is needed is to allocate accumulated variances between inventories and cost of products sold.

However, standard costs that are realistically determined are frequently an appropriate basis for inventory valuation. Unfavorable variances that reflect inefficiencies or abnormalities of various kinds should be recognized as current losses or expenses rather than added to inventory cost. Variances caused by differences between actual and standard wage rates or material prices, and other variances that represent changed conditions rather than inefficiencies or abnormalities, should be allocated to inventories and cost of goods sold rather than being recognized as current gains or losses.

Many companies that use standard costs recompute the standards annually to reflect current conditions and price year-end inventory at the new standards for the following year. That practice can result in pricing some inventory in excess of cost if prices have increased significantly near the end of a year. Care must therefore be taken to avoid recognizing profits from inventory price changes before sale; usually a reasonable estimate can be made of the excess of new standard cost over actual cost included in ending inventory, and the aggregate ending balance adjusted accordingly.

Joint or Common Costs

Many manufacturing processes generate more than one product from the same material, particularly in industries such as chemicals, petroleum, lumber, meat packing, leather, and canning. Products that are inevitably produced together—that is, production of one necessarily results in production of the other(s)—are known as joint products or common products. Costs of the products after the point at which the individual products become identifiable are usually called separable or added costs; they can be identified with individual products in the same way as costs of products produced separately. Costs before that point are known as joint or common costs; they must be allocated to individual products by a reasonable method.

Assigning joint costs to individual products is necessary to measure the profitability of each product and also to determine inventory cost, but there is no way to ascertain the actual costs of individual joint products. Joint costs are allocated to individual products by two accepted methods, both of which have numerous variations:

> On the basis of some physical measure, such as number of units, weight, or volume.
>
> On the basis of relative sales value of the products at the "split-off" point, which often must be computed by deducting from ultimate sales value identifiable costs incurred after split-off.

The essence of the relative sales value method is that all joint products from the same operation appear to be about equally profitable. The assumption of equal profitability of joint products is at least as justifiable as any of the infinite number of possible assumptions involving varying relative profitabilities, particularly when the output of product cannot be varied by changes in the process.

Therefore, a method of allocation of joint costs should not be used if it tends to show one joint product as significantly more profitable than others unless there is objective justification for doing so.

By-products are joint products of relatively insignificant value. Accounting for them as joint products is not worth the trouble, and the so-called by-product method is practicable and reasonable. By-products are in effect assigned costs equal to their net sales value by deducting their net sales value from total production costs. The net production cost is allocated to the remaining product or products.

Retail Method

The retail method, as its name implies, is used by merchandisers selling on the basis of established selling prices. They find it useful to maintain inventory records and price physical inventories at selling prices for control purposes. It is essentially a method of establishing selling (retail) prices of goods acquired based on predetermined markon percentages applied to the cost of the items and subsequently accounting for the merchandise stocks at their retail price amounts. Physical inventories are also priced at retail and compared with inventory records to discover physical shortages or shrinkage. The essential steps of the method are:

> Purchases at cost for each line or department, including transportation and similar charges, are added to opening inventory valued at cost.

Purchases at retail prices are added to opening inventory valued at retail, and that total is further increased by markups and related retail adjustments.

The total retail amount is compared with the total cost amount to determine the percentage of cumulative markon: i.e., the relation between retail and cost for the period.

The aggregate of opening inventory and purchases at retail is reduced by sales, markdowns, discounts and allowances, and shrinkage to determine ending inventory at retail.

Ending inventory valued at retail is reduced by the percentage of cumulative markon to obtain an estimate of the ending inventory valued at cost or less.

The retail method results in an estimate of inventories approximating the lower of cost or market because any change downward in established selling price automatically results in an adjustment of cost to market. The percentage of cumulative markon that is used to reduce retail to cost is determined from the original retail price plus markups but is applied to retail after markdowns. The reduction from retail to cost is thus larger than if the percentage were computed including both markups and markdowns.

Since shrinkage inevitably exists in retail merchandise operations, estimates of shortages or provision for shrinkage are customarily recorded periodically, usually based on a percentage of sales. When shortages are revealed by physical inventory, provision for shrinkage is adjusted.*

Methods of Determining Inventory Movements

Individual units in inventory lose their identity, especially if they are numerous and interchangeable. Costs of acquisition or production change from period to period, however, and it makes a difference in measuring net income whether goods sold or transferred were acquired or produced during the current period or in earlier periods. Sometimes, depending on the cost system in use, it makes a difference whether they were acquired or produced early or late in the same period. Unless units of products or goods can be identified as they move through production and inventories, assumptions about their movements are required to separate costs that should remain in inventory from those that should be transferred to other inventories or to cost of goods or products sold. Even if identification is possible, accountants often prefer to rely on those assumptions.

* More exhaustive discussions of the retail method are found in H. F. Bell and L. C. Moscarello, *Retail Merchandise Accounting,* 3rd Edition (New York: The Ronald Press Co., 1961), especially Chapters 6 and 7.

Specific Identification

In custom or contract work, units or lots of inventory are often identifiable and unique. Costs are traceable to specific jobs or lots, and the most accurate matching of costs and revenue results from identifying costs specifically associated with each job or lot both in inventory and as it is sold. (Despite this desirable feature, use of the specific identification method is not required when the advantages of another method are deemed to be overriding: for example, the LIFO method might be preferable in some instances.)

The identity of specific units or lots, however, may not be useful for accounting purposes when items in inventory are homogeneous. Under those conditions, specific identification is costly to maintain and tends to create opportunities to select the lots to be sold in ways that may distort periodic income. Most accountants agree that homogeneous units should be accounted for using a consistent assumption about inventory cost flows.

Assumptions of Cost Flow

According to Statement 4 of Section 5121:

> Cost for inventory purposes may be determined under any one of several assumptions as to the flow of cost factors (such as first-in first-out, average, and last-in first-out); the major objective in selecting a method should be to choose the one which, under the circumstances, most clearly reflects periodic income. [Paragraph 5121.05]

Whereas it was once thought that the assumptions should approximate the physical flow of goods, the most important criterion now is that the assumption chosen should most clearly reflect income. The Statement refers to "flow of cost factors," not to "flow of inventories." The choice among the different assumptions now rests primarily on different views about how income should be measured. The Statement mentions three assumptions; we will discuss four: first-in first-out, average, last-in first-out, and normal or base stock.

1. First-In First-Out. Accounting for cost of goods sold under the first-in first-out (FIFO) method is based on the assumption that the goods first received or produced are the goods first used or sold. Consequently, inventory remaining on hand at the end of a period is priced at the latest cost. The original justification for FIFO was that it probably approximates the physical flow of inventories most of the time in many businesses. Using or selling the oldest units on hand is generally good merchandising policy, and most companies try to follow it.

Under the "flow of cost factors" criterion the justification for FIFO is that the inventory amount carried in a balance sheet should reflect current unexpired costs, and income should be measured by the difference between revenue and the sum of unexpired costs at the beginning of a period plus current costs expiring during the period.

2. *Average.* Accounting for cost of goods sold under the average method (often called the weighted or moving average method) is based on the assumption that units in inventory become mixed or commingled in such a way that units used or sold are drawn from both opening inventory and subsequent purchases or production. An average unit cost of inventory is determined by adding the quantities and costs of items purchased or produced during a period to quantities and costs of items in the opening inventory and dividing the total costs by the total quantities. That average is applied to determine cost of inventories on hand and cost of goods or products sold. The average method may involve more effort to maintain than FIFO in cost systems relying on manual clerical computation, but it probably requires less computational effort in mechanized or computerized systems.

The justification for the average method is that the cost and profitability of a particular sale should not be affected by the purely theoretical accident of which cost an accountant chooses to assign to it.

3. *Last-In First-Out.* Accounting under the last-in first-out (LIFO) method is based on the belief that operations require a certain minimum quantity of inventory at all times and that increases in the value of that basic inventory should not be reflected in income. Costs of goods or products consumed or sold are determined at the latest costs, and inventory is priced at the earliest costs, to avoid including in reported income the effect of a changing acquisition price on a more or less fixed quantity of inventory.

The justification for LIFO is that the most useful concept of income results from matching current costs with revenue stated in terms of current sales prices. Physical flow of inventories need not be in accord with the LIFO assumption, and LIFO is now rarely defended with arguments that some kinds of inventories actually are managed by removing first the items most recently acquired or produced.

Adoption of LIFO has stemmed largely from its advantage of deferring payment of income taxes on increases in inventory values almost indefinitely if prices rise continually over long periods, coupled with a provision in the Internal Revenue Code that LIFO cannot be used for tax purposes unless it is also used in financial statements. Thus, in times of rising prices, LIFO results in lower reported earnings than other methods, and vice versa. In 1975, LIFO is receiving renewed attention in the light of concerns about continuing inflation, and a number of major companies have adopted the method. See Appendix B for a description of the major methods of accounting for LIFO inventories.

4. Normal or Base Stock. Accounting under the base stock method is founded on the same assumption as accounting under LIFO, and both methods have as their primary objective elimination from reported income of so-called "inventory profits and losses." The base stock method is an accepted accounting practice and has long been used by some companies engaged in processing basic raw materials, although its use for federal income taxes is no longer permitted by the Internal Revenue Service. The LIFO provisions of the tax law represent to a considerable extent a substitute for the normal or base stock procedure.

However, the normal or base stock method differs from LIFO in several respects. The basic inventory that is assumed to be required at all times for normal operations is fixed under the base stock method as to both quantity and price. Increases above or decreases below the fixed quantity, unless they result from changes in plant capacity or in manufacturing processes, are considered to be temporary. They reflect management's short-term appraisal of future markets, availability of materials, or other conditions and are priced in inventory at current cost determined by one of the more conventional cost bases or at market price, if lower than cost. Thus, current costs that have not been incurred by a company may be included in determining costs of goods consumed or sold. LIFO, in contrast, is a cost method in the sense that it uses no costs not already actually incurred. Increases in a LIFO inventory above the base quantity are priced in layers at the cost existing when each increase occurs, and decreases come from the most recent increase, which may have been several periods earlier. When low cost layers are thus liquidated, reported earnings are increased.

Comparison of Methods

FIFO maximizes the effect on reported income of price changes during a period of rising prices; ending inventory values are the highest of the various assumptions and cost of goods or products sold is the lowest; therefore, reported income is the highest.

LIFO is the opposite of FIFO. It minimizes the effect on reported income of price changes during a period and, in times of rising prices, results in the lowest inventory value and lowest reported income of all methods except base stock. The base stock method produces results much like those of LIFO, sometimes valuing inventory a little higher and sometimes a little lower, with a corresponding effect on reported income. Under both of the latter methods, inventory is stated at costs that may be substantially different from current costs.

Using the average method tends to dampen the effect of price changes, and the results of the method usually fall between those of FIFO and LIFO.

FIFO and average methods are well established though often criticized for creating fluctuations in reported net income. LIFO and base stock methods are also accepted but have been criticized in recent years as artificial. Some accountants prefer the base stock method over LIFO, claiming that base stock has more advantages and fewer disadvantages. However, its unacceptability for income taxes has clearly inhibited its use, and LIFO is far more prevalent than base stock.

ESTIMATES OF MARKET OR REALIZABLE VALUE

Acquisition cost is the principal basis of stating inventories, but current selling prices and current costs are used in two ways in accounting for inventories:

Some inventories are stated at selling price or at amounts derived from selling price, such as net realizable value.

Applying cost or market, whichever is lower, requires determination of both replacement or reproduction cost and net realizable value.

Inventories at Selling Prices

Stating inventories in excess of cost results in recognizing profits before sale. Nevertheless, revenue is occasionally recognized before sale, as described in Chapter 9, and inventories are therefore occasionally stated at selling prices or net realizable value—estimated selling price less estimated costs to complete and sell.

Statement 9 of Section 5121 describes specific limited circumstances in which selling prices or net realizable value are an acceptable basis for valuing inventories:

Only in exceptional cases may inventories properly be stated above cost. For example, precious metals having a fixed monetary value with no substantial cost of marketing may be stated at such monetary value; any other exceptions must be justifiable by inability to determine appropriate approximate costs, immediate marketability at quoted market price, and the characteristic of unit interchangeability. Where goods are stated above cost this fact should be fully disclosed. [Paragraph 5121.15]

Products valued under those conditions should be stated at net realizable value; sales price is acceptable only if no further costs are involved to complete and dispose of the inventory.

Although using net realizable value is acceptable if the conditions described are met, the trend in recent years appears to be toward more conventional methods of valuing inventories for the types of products mentioned. In any event, we emphasize that mere difficulty of determining cost is the least persuasive justification for using net realizable value. The primary justification for the method is that an inventory is immediately salable at quoted market prices.

Cost or Market, Whichever Is Lower

One of the fundamental conventions of accounting is that losses should be recognized immediately on discovery. Since that principle takes precedence over that of matching of costs with revenue, inventory losses are recognized currently to the extent they can be determined, and cost of inventory in excess of its utility is not carried forward in balance sheets.

The Principle

Statement 5 of Section 5121 advises:

> A departure from the cost basis of pricing the inventory is required when the utility of the goods is no longer as great as its cost. Where there is evidence that the utility of goods, in their disposal in the ordinary course of business, will be less than cost, whether due to physical deterioration, obsolescence, changes in price levels, or other causes, the difference should be recognized as a loss of the current period. This is generally accomplished by stating such goods at a lower level commonly designated as *market*. [Paragraph 5121.07]

Loss of utility is considered an event of the period in which the loss is discovered and therefore its cost is an expense of that period. When an inventory item or group of items is written down to market at the end of a fiscal year, that written-down value becomes its "cost," and it should not subsequently be "written up" if market value increases (*AICPA Prof. Stds.*, vol. 3, paragraph 5121.05, footnote 2). Recoveries in a later interim period of write-downs recorded in an earlier period of the same fiscal year *should* be recorded as gains (*AICPA Prof. Stds.*, vol. 3, paragraph 2071.14).

"Market"

The purpose of valuing inventories at the lower of cost or market is to record all known losses, not to permit shifting of profits from one period to another. Section 5121 is based primarily on the assumption that cost and selling price move together so that a decrease in replacement cost of inventory signals a decrease of utility requiring recognition of a loss. If sales price does not decrease with replacement cost, however, inventory will not be sold at a loss but at a normal profit. Conversely, if sales price decreases but replacement cost does not, a loss (or at least a lower profit) will occur even though replacement cost does not signal the decrease in utility. Statement 6 of Section 5121 describes how market—the indication of utility of inventory—is determined:

> As used in the phrase *lower of cost or market* the term *market* means current replacement cost (by purchase or by reproduction, as the case may be) except that:
>
> (1) Market should not exceed the net realizable value (i.e., estimated selling price in the ordinary course of business less reasonably predictable costs of completion and disposal); and
> (2) Market should not be less than net realizable value reduced by an allowance for an approximately normal profit margin. [Paragraph 5121.08]

Thus, there are three terms to be understood and applied in practice in the determination of "market": replacement cost, net realizable value, and net realizable value less normal profit margin (sometimes called the "market floor").

Replacement or Reproduction Cost

The term "replacement cost" applies to purchased items, while "reproduction cost" applies to manufactured products. A retailer replaces his inventory. A manufacturer replaces his raw materials but reproduces his finished product.

Replacement cost is based on the assumption that goods will be bought in the open market. A market quotation should reflect the customary volume purchased at one time as well as the customary terms and manner in which purchased. It should include all costs necessary to bring the goods to their usual location, such as freight, duties, and other costs incidental to acquisition.

Reproduction cost means the costs of reproducing identical goods in the identical quantity and quality, irrespective of the advisability or desirability of duplicating them. It therefore involves factors such as stage of completion, current material and labor costs, and overhead allocation.

Net Realizable Value

Net realizable value is expected selling price less estimated costs to complete and sell. Estimated selling costs should include all directly identifiable costs, such as packing, shipping, and salesmen's commissions. Selling costs may be explicitly computed or the figure may be a fraction or percentage of selling price that is deemed to be a reasonable estimate in the light of past experience, budget, or forecast. Since net realizable value is at best a sum of estimates, use of a fraction or percentage of selling price is usually acceptable.

Normal Profit

Normal profit refers to gross profit or gross margin—sales less cost of goods sold. Theoretically, there can be some argument about what is a normal profit, but in practice that point can usually be established without too much difficulty by referring to performance over a recent period or to budget figures. There is probably less room for discretion and judgment in computing normal profit than in determining cost— and there is more room for tolerable error because the figure is needed only for the estimate of a "market floor."

Determining Market

Determining market requires comparing replacement or reproduction cost, net realizable value, and the "market floor." If net realizable value is lower, it is market; if replacement or reproduction cost is lower, it is market unless its use would result in a larger than normal profit margin; in that event, the "market floor" is market.

If net realizable value is the measure of market, it generally should not be further reduced by an allowance for an approximately normal profit margin. One accepted departure from that rule is the retail inventory method, which carries forward marked-down items at an inventory price that, it is expected, will yield what may be called the normal margin of gross profit for a particular line of goods or a particular department. Other instances may be encountered in which it is good business and good accounting to write down portions of an inventory to a point that may yield an approximately normal margin of gross profit, even though replacement cost is not below actual cost. On the other hand, writing down portions of an inventory below net realizable value with the result that profit is merely shifted from an earlier to a later period is usually unjustifiable.

Applying the test of market may require considering the course of prices after a balance sheet date to determine market at the balance sheet date. That does not mean, however, that losses that clearly belong in a subsequent period should be anticipated.

The following table illustrates the application of the rule of lower of cost or market:

	Illus. 1	Illus. 2	Illus. 3	Illus. 4
Cost	$1.00 *	$1.00	$1.00	$1.00
Replacement or reproduction cost	1.05	.98 *	.99	.94
Net realizable value	1.25	1.15	.95 *	1.20
"Market floor": Net realizable value less a normal profit	.99	.91	.75	.95 *

* Represents the value to be used for inventory purposes.

Net realizable value and net realizable value less a normal profit are determined as follows:

	Illus. 1	Illus. 2	Illus. 3	Illus. 4
Selling price	$1.30	$1.20	$1.00	$1.25
Less: Cost of completion and disposal	.05	.05	.05	.05
Net realizable value	1.25	1.15	.95	1.20
Normal profit (20% of selling price)	.26	.24	.20	.25
Net realizable value less a normal profit	$ .99	$ .91	$ .75	$ .95

Applying the Lower of Cost or Market

Cost or market, whichever is lower, may be applied to inventory in several ways, as indicated in Statement 7 of Section 5121:

> Depending on the character and composition of the inventory, the rule of cost or market, whichever is lower may properly be applied either directly to each item or to the total of the inventory (or, in some cases, to the total of the components of each major category). The method should be that which most clearly reflects periodic income. [Paragraph 5121.10]

We believe that the best practice in the application of cost or market generally continues to be to recognize, if practicable, the logical groups or classifications of items into which the inventories of a particular business naturally fall. That is because many, or perhaps most, product lines have to include some items deliberately sold at a loss as a necessary adjunct to obtaining sales of the profitable items.

IRS regulations provide that the lower of cost or market value be applied to each article in the inventory for tax purposes, but that requirement is not insisted on in practice if it is obviously not practicable. However, classifying inventory items into logical groups can be difficult in companies that make a large variety of products that do not fall into clear-cut categories. The discussion following Statement 7 of Section 5121 notes that "unless an effective method of classifying categories is practicable, the rule should be applied to each item in the inventory" (paragraph 13). The problems are much the same as those faced by companies trying to determine their "lines of business" to record sales and income by product lines, and a reasonable solution in most cases might be to use the same general classes for both purposes.

Purchase Commitments

Losses on unhedged·firm purchase commitments should be estimated and recorded as if the goods were in inventory:

> Accrued net losses on firm purchase commitments for goods for inventory, measured in the same way as are inventory losses, should, if material, be recognized in the accounts and the amounts thereof separately disclosed in the income statement. [Statement 10, Paragraph 5121.16]

Losses from purchase commitments cannot be measured unless inventories and commitments are compared with firm and probable sales orders. That comparison under the conditions addressed by Section 5121 more often than not leads to cancellation of purchase commitments and recording of an actual loss that is smaller than if the transaction were completed.

Hedging transactions are common in certain industries; many companies that are required to enter into firm purchase commitments for materials with fluctuating prices "hedge" their purchases. Manufacturers buy and sell futures on commodity exchanges to protect their purchase and sales orders against losses from fluctuations in market prices of raw materials. Futures are generally sold to hedge purchases and commitments to purchase raw materials; futures are generally bought to hedge the price of raw materials not yet purchased but required for goods sold at firm prices for future delivery. Although futures are usually contracts to purchase or sell stated quantities at specified prices and dates of delivery, they are customarily closed out prior to maturity to avoid physical delivery, and gains or losses resulting from price fluctuations are settled through the commodity exchange at the time a contract is closed.

If futures contracts are for the same commodities, though not necessarily the identical grades, as those carried in inventories and are entered into as part of a plan designed to decrease the risk of inventory loss, the hedging cost should be accounted for as part of the cost of materials. Realized gains and losses should be included in cost of goods sold. Unrealized profits or losses on futures contracts are usually not recognized specifically in the accounts but should be considered in estimating the cost and realizable value of inventory and in evaluating purchase commitments.

If futures contracts are entered into for a purpose other than to hedge inventory risks, they should be accounted for separately from inventories, and realized profits and losses from them should be reflected in other income or other expense. Unrealized profits should not be recognized in the accounts; unrealized losses should be recognized in the same way as those on purchase commitments.

DISCLOSURE OF INVENTORIES

Statement 8 of Section 5121 is as follows:

> The basis of stating inventories must be consistently applied and should be disclosed in the financial statements; whenever a significant change is made therein, there should be disclosure of the nature of the change and, if material, the effect on income in accordance with section 1051, *Accounting Changes*. [As amended, effective for fiscal periods beginning after July 31, 1971, by APB Opinion No. 20.] [Paragraph 5121.14]

Different methods of valuing inventories can have widely different effects on the determination of periodic income, and even within a method adopted there is often a large area of judgment and discretion. Management should select the inventory method deemed suitable to the enterprise over the long run and should then follow the method consistently from year to year.

However, that admonition cannot be applied rigidly and absolutely. Business operations and the inventories required to service them change and methods improve. Changes can be expected almost every year in the details of determining inventory values: for example, a change in the treatment of certain overhead items, a change in the information or rationale on which an estimate is based, or an unusual circumstance or condition to be taken into account. While the statement quoted above calls specific attention to the consistency standard and required disclosures, of course only material changes need to be disclosed.

The SEC is encouraging disclosure of the amount of income that is reinvested in inventory solely as a result of increases in prices between the beginning and end of a year—an amount often, and debatably, called "inventory profit."

• TYPICAL TRANSACTION SYSTEMS AND INTERNAL CONTROL

TYPICAL TRANSACTIONS

There are two major kinds of production systems and two major kinds of production objectives:

Systems:
The job order system, in which goods are made in the quantities and to the specifications called for by a job order—which can be for a standard item or for items having various degrees of customization.
The process system, in which goods are produced repetitively according to a schedule.
Objectives:
The objective of production for customer order, in which the production system is geared to the customer's specifications and a required delivery date, sometimes at the sacrifice of economy and efficiency.
The objective of production for stock, in which a stock of finished goods inventory permits buffering production from customers' demands so that it can be planned most economically and effectively.

Either kind of system can serve either objective, although the job order system most commonly goes with the customer order objective. The different systems and objectives give rise to somewhat different control features, but the similarities outnumber the differences. A process system may sometimes be controlled by job orders, and a job shop may have departments that are process operations, or jobs that run for such a long time or can be grouped with other similar ones so as to be scheduled the way a process system would be. Most systems designed to produce for stock have to provide for some customer order production; many customer orders are so large that production has to be geared to the building of a finished goods stock.

All production systems have in common the following five steps:

Identifying needs
Planning
Assembling facilities, people, and materials
Production
Moving and storage

There is literally an infinite variety of combinations and sequences of those steps, and the technological diversity of modern manufacturing causes them to appear in many forms. The following discussion of typical transaction systems and controls can give only the most generalized suggestion of the types of conditions that may be encountered.

Identifying Needs

Producing for Stock

When the production objective is to produce for finished goods stock, the identification of new production needs may be generated as an integral part of the system. The need may be signalled either by a periodic scrutiny of the stock levels ("period planning" ordering) or by noting when stock on hand reaches a predetermined minimum ("stock status" ordering).

The system can be informal, relying on the stockkeeper to look in the storage bins from time to time and decide what he needs. Or it can be formal and still physical and manual: the stockkeeper's review can be made according to a formal schedule and properly documented, or the predetermined amount of minimum stock can be identified so that it cannot be drawn down without signalling the need for replenishment.

Stock replenishment systems can be mechanized and systematized to a lesser or greater degree—some to an extraordinary degree—of sophistication. Manually posted inventory records can be used instead of physical inspection to identify needs. The control records can be mechanized or computerized; computerized inventory records offer the opportunity for highly sophisticated forecasting and modelling computations.

The necessity of identifying production needs gives rise to the primary reason for controls. The function of controls in safeguarding assets and providing accountability is generally recognized. It is not so generally recognized that there is a greater need for controls to operate the system effectively, and that the need is even more basic—as evidenced by the fact that it is still no very great surprise to discover poor inventory controls. Three types of controls are required for an effective stock replenishment production order system, and they are also the controls that provide accountability: controls over the basic data, controls over origination of orders, and supervisory controls.

Controls Over the Basic Data. Inventories need to be safeguarded by physical security and restricted access to make sure they will be there when wanted (that includes safeguarding them, using systematic storage or locator cards, from simply being mislaid). The duties of keeping the records should be segregated from the duties of physically handling the stores: it is usually more efficient to do so because the skills required for the two tasks are different, but it also enables the two activities to double-check one another. The amounts on hand must be verified periodically by physical count and reconciliation to the records. Controls are needed over the accuracy of the paperwork, such as double-checking or validity checking, proper authorization of receipts and issues, control totals over postings, control accounts periodically reconciled to detail accounts, and document control such as prenumbering. It will be noted that those controls are all among the basic control operations identified in Chapter 3.

Controls Over Origination of Orders. The minimum control over ordering is review and approval of production requisitions by a responsible and knowledgeable person who then authorizes initiating a production transaction. Once initiated, control over loss or misdirection of the requisition is desirable, either by a prenumbering system or a holding file of unfilled requisitions.

In informal systems, control over the inventory level and the amount of production requisitioned is left in the hands of the initiator of the requisition. Preferably, both of those highly significant factors should be controlled by means of well-developed techniques for calculating required inventory levels (through estimates of lead time and safety stock) and optimum production quantities [through, for example, the Economic Order Quantity (EOQ) calculation]. An auditor should be aware that those techniques exist and should have a general understanding of their basic principles because they are controls that help prevent a build-up of excess quantities in inventories.

At the least, inventory levels and order quantities should be set from time to time on some rational basis. In recent years computers have provided the means for "dynamic" inventory management—reforecasting demand and recomputing safety stock levels and EOQ's each time a reorder is signalled or sometimes on a monthly or quarterly basis.

Supervisory Controls. Usually an inventory control system that is loosely organized relies on direct supervision for most of its control. Highly organized systems are also dependent on supervisory control because the process of establishing them involves following strict rules, which may become unrealistic as circumstances change. Supervisory controls must be designed to assure continued functioning of the system and to detect conditions needing attention. Reports of "stock-out" conditions call for supervisory attention to why the reorder system did not function in time. Reports on "overstock" conditions call for supervisory attention to what caused the overstock and what changes in the reorder rules are required to correct it. EOQ cost factors and assumptions should be reviewed periodically to make sure they are current and realistic. Reports of physical count adjustments should receive supervisory attention and inquiry into the underlying causes of adjustments.

It will be noted that each of those supervisory controls serves the primary objective of keeping the operation of the system under control; it also contributes very importantly to supervising the asset safeguarding and accountability functions.

Producing for Customer's Order

The typical revenue transaction system, which starts with a customer's order, is described in Chapter 9. If a customer's order calls for production activity, it should be reviewed and approved—authorized —by production officials prior to its acceptance to make sure that potential production problems can be adequately handled.

There are industries with a degree of seasonality, in which some sales must be forecasted and goods manufactured in advance of receipt of orders. In those instances, the control problem is to strike the optimum balance between the possible cost of additional reorder and set-up and the possible cost of being left with excess inventory.

Planning

Whatever the source of the identified need, the result is a production requisition. After review and approval, the requisition becomes an authorization to produce. However, it cannot be an adequate execution instruction until it is converted into detailed plans.

Specifications

The first step is preparation of detailed drawings and specifications. In a process system, or production of standard items or items for stock, the complete plans and specifications should be on file. In a job shop the plans may have to be created anew, or they may be assembled in whole or in part from previous experience. If new plans are required, the design, engineering, and drafting staffs may have to be scheduled and controlled in much the same fashion as the actual process of production is controlled (described below). The specifications should determine exactly what material is required, how much is required, and where it is required.

Time and Cost Estimates

The next step is to estimate time and, preferably but not always, cost. For standard job orders and processes the estimates may be on file with the specifications. For many customer orders the time and cost estimates may have been prepared as a basis for the contract bid.

Time estimates have to be made to schedule production. They may be made only informally—some plants leave it to the foreman to order materials and schedule production when the production order arrives on his desk. However, preferred practice calls for detailed estimating, and estimating and planning are essential if complex projects are to be completed on schedule.

If cost estimates are not required as a basis for contract bidding, they may not be prepared even though time estimates are used for scheduling, on the theory that the cost of preparing them is not justified by their usefulness. In the authors' collective experience, profitability is so closely correlated with good cost estimating, and unprofitability with the reverse, as to suggest that cost estimates are almost always worthwhile, especially if production for a customer's order extends over a period of time. Cost estimates permit informed scrutiny of actual costs and the exercise of managerial control, and they are valuable for estimates of cost to complete for inventory valuation purposes.

Scheduling

The next step is to schedule production. Production scheduling may be done by the planners as implied by this presentation, it may be done by a separate group of production schedulers, or it may be done by the production foreman. Production scheduling may be formal and controlled, it may be very informal, or it may be anywhere in between.

The result of planning and scheduling is a production order—the detailed execution instructions. The production order must list the operations and the desired results. It may or may not include material requisitions, move tickets, travellers, instructions to cost accounting, expected move dates, or specific machines to be used.

Assembling Facilities, People, and Material

For some large orders, especially those involving on-site construction, this assembling step may follow the planning step as it does in this presentation. Most of the time, however, the people and the facilities are on hand and often so is the material in the raw material stores. All that is necessary in the individual production transaction is to bring the three together in one spot through planning.

Facilities

Chapter 12, "The Property Segment," describes the typical systems of acquisition and use of productive facilities. In the production process itself, any of several machines may be able to do a given job. Someone has to assign the work to be done in such a way as to balance the added direct cost of using a less efficient machine with the possible cost of leaving some machines idle. Tools and dies often require special attention: ordering the right ones so as to have them on hand on time; allowing for wear and breakage; guarding against over-use, under-use, or misuse.

People

Making sure that the right people are on hand is a highly skilled and specialized function of management: estimating the numbers of people required and their skills, deciding on pay scales, recruiting, training, and then handling contract negotiations and all of the other problems of personnel administration. The production function is to assign the right level of skill to the operation and it can be a complex scheduling of many specialized skills—toolmakers, set-up men, quality control inspectors, operators, and material handlers—to complete the work without disruption.

Material

Material is often provided by a raw material stock room. Enough raw material may be carried on hand to provide lead time for purchasing replenishment, or production planners may notify the purchasing department of material requirements. Raw material on hand is drawn for production as needed and is replenished by purchases. The raw material stores and initiation of the buying system are controlled in the same way as finished goods stock and initiation of the production system described above (Chapter 10, "The Buying Segment," describes the purchasing function).

If the required material is not carried in stores, a requisition for its purchase can go directly from production planning to purchasing. For a complex product or a large order, that can be an extremely complicated paperwork operation: a lengthy "bill of materials" is "exploded" into a procurement schedule, which may combine purchasing for raw material stores, subcontracting, blanket purchase orders, group purchasing, and the whole range of procurement possibilities.

Operational Controls

Planning and assembling the requirements for production are not part of the accounting system (except for raw material and tool inventories and, of course, the payroll of those involved in the process). Many auditors have gone through their careers without knowing how complex the functions are or how many people they involve, but those functions are of important direct concern to an auditor. Poor specifications can cause rework, unsalable stock, or returned merchandise. Poor estimates can give rise to excess cost in inventory, especially overruns on contracts; good estimates provide the basis for good estimates of cost to complete orders or contracts. Poor scheduling can likewise cause overruns and excess cost.

An auditor can evaluate accounting controls more effectively if he understands their close relationship to operational controls. He can evaluate the possibility of improved controls if he understands what it is reasonable to expect in various production circumstances.

Production

The production process generates many accounting entries. The more sophisticated the cost accounting system, the more accounting entries it requires. Sometimes accounting information can be integrated with operational production control data.

This section describes the steps in the execution of a typical production process and the accounting data that may be originated along the way. A later section describes the recording of the data and the uses that may be made of them.

Material must be assembled. Often a copy of the production order is the authorization to draw the material from the stock room, or sometimes material can be drawn simply on the signature of the requisitioning foreman. In either event, a document must be created to account for the movement of material, both for production control purposes and for accounting. The documents should preferably be numbered for detailed control, or at least batched under control totals.

Under some systems, separate copies of the production order authorize both the withdrawal from stores and the accounting entry for the designated amount of material, and there is no direct tie-in between the physical act of material issuance and the accounting entry for it.

In those cases there must be separate forms for nonstandard material issues.

If material is ordered directly for production, the production order, sometimes confirmed by an accompanying purchase order, notifies those concerned of the expected date of delivery. A receiving report notifies production and accounting when the delivery is actually received.

Machines must be set up in preparation for the production process. Set-up time may or may not be accounted for separately, depending on the informational needs of management which have been incorporated in the cost accounting system. Tools and dies are sometimes charged as direct costs, particularly in job order production systems in which the tools are likely to have been created especially for the particular order and sometimes specifically paid for by the customer. Most often, though, tools and dies are accounted for as capital items because they can be reused on different pieces of work. Usually documents are prepared to record what happens: a time report or job ticket for the set-up time and an issue slip or production order for the tool requirements.

Operations are performed and the time spent is recorded. Most often the basic record is the operator's time report or job ticket, on which are noted his identifying number, the operation or job identifying number, time spent, and sometimes quantity produced. Frequently the basic record is machine time, accounted for in addition to or instead of operator's time.

The quantity of production may be recorded in a variety of ways. The quantity called for by the production order, or the quantity determined by the operating time of the machine, may be recorded without actual counting. There may be a count—either manual or automatic—by weight, volume, or pieces processed by the machine, without distinction between good and unacceptable production. Or, good pieces only may be counted after inspection.

Reporting production is a real problem in a great many operations. Both managers of production control and cost accountants want good production counts, but in many cases the large volume of units, the inaccuracy of measuring devices, and the problems of distinguishing between good and bad units render it difficult, uneconomic, or impossible to report production accurately.

Inspection of results takes place at several stages and levels. Operators inspect for signs of problems as they complete their work. Supervisors may inspect output on a test basis. There may be specialists in quality control, or it may be necessary to employ the special skills and equipment of a laboratory to carry out tests for the quality of production. Formal, often elaborate, highly specialized techniques for quality control sampling are sometimes written into production contracts.

Production rejected as a result of inspection is reported for managerial cost accounting purposes. Sometimes the time spent reworking faulty items to meet specifications is also reported separately. Controlling production to minimize the amount of scrap and rework is an important element of production control management; adequate identification of it and accounting for it is an important element both of production cost and managerial accounting information.

Moving and Storage

Moving

Movement of production from one department to the next must be reported for operational purposes, but it is not often recorded for accounting purposes. Sometimes production must be moved out of a plant for processing that the company is not equipped to do. Those moves have to be documented and accountability maintained for purposes of managerial control. It is highly desirable that there be simultaneous accounting control, but often accounting control is established only at physical inventory time by accumulating and recording the managerial paperwork. In any event, good management calls for periodic reconciliation with outside processors of the quantities for which they are responsible.

Finished Goods Storage

After production is completed and has passed final inspection, it goes either to finished goods inventory or to a finished goods storage area to await shipment to a customer. The notice to production management may be a copy of the production order, signed off as completed, or it may be an inspection report or the receiving report of the finished goods storekeeper. The accounting document signifying an addition to finished goods may be any one of those documents, and it may be either the same as the one used for managerial purposes or another. The accounting document for withdrawal from finished goods is usually a copy of, or a document closely related to, the sales and shipping orders.

RECORDING AND ACCOUNTABILITY

A simple system that accumulates production costs and quantities produced and sold can provide an inventory figure adequate for financial statements at year end if it is consistently applied and if there are no major changes in operations. It can even be made to serve under problem conditions if measures are taken to identify or estimate costs that should not be inventoried. But without a cost system it is impossible to determine income during the course of a year or until some time well after the end of the year when the physical inventory is taken, summarized, and priced. The simple system provides no information for production or marketing management, and there is no way, short of time-consuming special studies, to explain unexpected changes in any of the relationships among elements of cost. Therefore, prevalent practice is to employ a cost accounting system for managerial information and for better product costing and more accurate and timely financial statements.

Raw Materials

Purchases are usually recorded in the accounts from vendors' invoices (discussed in Chapter 10, "The Buying Segment"). The quantities received may be recorded in the detailed inventory records from the invoices, from receiving reports, or perhaps from the storekeeper's independent physical counts. In the latter case, reconciling receipts recorded from that source to receipts recorded from invoices or receiving reports is a desirable control feature.

Raw material issues may be recorded from a report of production orders scheduled to start, which should be controlled by a comparison with production orders reported as actually started. Or they may be recorded from raw material storeroom issue slips, the numerical sequence of which should be accounted for. Occasionally, especially if raw material inventory is carried on computers, raw material usage may be measured by periodically—usually monthly—pricing the ending raw material inventory and adjusting the account balance through a charge to production.

Raw material accountability is exercised primarily by making sure that the inventory quantity records agree with amounts actually on hand. All items should be counted periodically and reconciled to the storekeeper's record. The reconciliations should be carefully made and differences investigated and explained as far as possible (see below for more detailed discussion of physical inventory taking).

The counts can be made all at one time or, if records are adequate, a few at a time spread over a planned cycle. Many companies count active items every time they reach reorder point, other items on an annual cycle, and a few small-value or slow-moving ones at less frequent intervals. An annual cycle for all, or very nearly all, items is still the most common practice. However, an increasing number of companies have established such comprehensive controls as to make annual counts unnecessary. They employ either a cycle or an annual statistical sample of counts, which verifies that perpetual records remain accurate enough to obviate more extensive counts.

Reviewing for slow-moving, obsolete, or damaged raw materials is the responsibility of production management; seeing that the reviews are made is the responsibility of the accountability function. An officer responsible for accountability should review and approve all adjustments and entries to the inventory accounts that are out of the ordinary. Periodically, provisions for safeguarding the investment in materials should be reviewed, both for physical safeguards and decisions on the amount and kind of insurance coverage.

Production and Work in Process

Material Costs

The entry for raw material issues is also the charge to production expense (or work-in-process inventory) for material costs—supplemented by charges through the voucher register for materials purchased directly. Depending on the structure of the cost system, material costs may be charged to a job order or to a material usage account in a process system. In either case, the standard cost of raw material used may be charged first to an intermediate account, which in turn is relieved at standard cost of standard quantities for production started to produce a "material usage variance."

Scrap is inevitable in most production processes. Efforts are made to minimize it in the first place, but once scrap has been created, physical control of it and recording and accountability are important to maximize cost recovery and thereby minimize production costs. Cost accounting is improved if scrap is identified with the operations or products creating it, but that is often impossible. In any event, scrap should be gathered, safeguarded, weighed and recorded, and disposed of with as much thoughtful effort as any other asset. Sometimes scrap is sold and sometimes it is recycled through the company's production process. In either case, the value recovered should be credited as a reduction of production cost.

Production Payrolls

The total cost of production payroll is accounted for through the payroll disbursements system (Chapter 10, "The Buying Segment"). Sometimes the distribution of payroll expense to detailed cost accounts also comes from the payroll disbursements entry, but more often the detail comes from job tickets or production reports. When job tickets are used the aggregate actual labor cost should be reconciled with a control total from payroll records. Production labor cost may be charged to job orders or departmental expense accounts. The system may provide detailed accounts for idle time, waiting time, set-up time, cleanup time, rework time, and so on. A standard cost system computes production labor at standard rates and amounts and, by comparison with actual costs, produces price, usage, and efficiency variances.

Production Overhead

Many different kinds of cost enter into overhead, and they are gathered in descriptive accounts as charges originate in the accounts payable and payroll journals and through journal entries.

The basis for charging overhead to job orders, departments, or work-in-process inventory is usually some measure of activity, most commonly direct labor hours or dollars. Many companies also employ a "material overhead" rate, which adds an overhead factor to materials charged to production. There are likely to be different overhead rates for different departments based on accounting or engineering studies.

In a standard cost system, overhead may be charged through several intermediate accounts to produce price, efficiency, and volume variances for managerial information. Those variances help to identify whether any overabsorbed or underabsorbed overhead should be "inventoried." Overabsorbed or underabsorbed overhead may be credited or charged in detail to job orders or departments, or it may be allocated to work-in-process and finished goods inventory on some overall basis. An appropriate fraction of overabsorbed overhead should always be allocated to inventories to prevent stating them in excess of actual cost; the allocable portion of underabsorbed overhead should be allocated to inventories unless it arises from elements of cost that should be written off as incurred.

Entries to record overhead absorption may be originated as a separate accounting task, but most often they are integrated with the entries for the data—payroll or material usage—on which the absorption rate is based.

Relieving Work-in-Process Inventory

Work in process is relieved and finished goods charged on the basis of completed production orders, inspection reports, or finished goods receiving tickets. The documents must be properly authorized and approved, and most systems have rules for documenting evidence of inspection according to quality control standards. Accurate counts are necessary for the transfer to finished goods inventory.

Partial completion of a job order may require that the cost of units transferred to finished goods be estimated and later adjusted to actual when the job order is closed out.

Sometimes production is shipped directly to a customer and the work-in-process account is relieved on the basis of billing, using standard cost or estimated actual cost. If contracts are accounted for as sales on the completed-contract method, costs are accumulated in a work-in-process account, with progress billings in a separate account, until the contract is completed and authorized for closing out to cost of goods sold. Under the percentage-of-completion method, contract cost is charged directly to cost of goods sold and revenue is recorded as described in Chapter 9. Contract costs are accumulated over time just as they are under the completed-contract method, except that closing out a contract does not give rise to an accounting entry.

Accountability for Work in Process

Physical inventory count of work in process is often difficult because it involves identifying a great many items in many different stages of completion. Goods may be scattered or they may be in hoppers, vats, or pipelines where access, observation, or measurement is difficult, or they may be in the hands of outside processors. Whatever the problems, there is no escaping management's responsibility to exercise accountability for the work-in-process inventory. Production management requires that someone know where each item is located and what its state of completion is, and the more difficult that production control is, the more essential it is to have a means of assuring that excess or "lost" costs do not build up in the work-in-process account. A physical inventory, properly summarized and priced, is by far the best practice, and most companies have found that, if adequately organized and timed, its cost and disruptive effect on the production process is not significant. A later section of this chapter outlines the considerations in planning and executing a physical inventory.

If production is to a customer's order and adequate records are available, an acceptable alternative is preparation of detailed estimates of cost to complete open production orders. Estimates of cost to complete often entail observation and physical counts of items on hand.

In those few instances where work in process is impossible to count because of the nature of the process, arrangements can be made to count the end result of each production order in process as it is finished and "work back" its results to validate the account balance as of the specified inventory date.

Finished Goods

Charges to finished goods are based on the same documents that relieve work in process plus, through accounts payable, charges for goods purchased from outsiders. Controls over the completeness of charges to finished goods are provided by numbered receiving reports or by reconciliation of charges to production reports.

Finished goods are relieved on the basis of filled sales orders or the storekeeper's issue slips; the latter should be reconciled to the sales orders. Occasionally, perpetual inventories (verified periodically by physical counts) are priced and the difference between that amount and the account balance is charged to cost of goods sold.

Accountability for finished goods is the same as that for raw materials: counts to correct the detailed records; reconciliation of detailed records to the control account balance; and review for discrepancies, slow-moving items, and other problems.

For enterprises that do not manufacture, the transaction system omits the work in process and production steps described above, but is otherwise much the same.

Material Belonging to Customers

Many companies receive material purchased by their customers, process it in various ways, and hold it pending customers' instructions. That material should be subject to the same control and accountability procedures as the company's own inventory.

PHYSICAL INVENTORIES

While physical inventories are often considered an audit requirement, good internal control requires the taking of a physical inventory at least annually and sometimes more frequently, depending on the type of business. The term "physical inventory" includes not only physical counting but also translating the counts into dollars, summarizing the dollars, and comparing the results with the accounts. A complete count of the inventory of a company, plant, or department may be made at one time while operations are suspended (a wall-to-wall inventory) or, if perpetual inventory records are maintained and other conditions are satisfactory, periodic counts of selected items may be made at various times during a year (a cycle count inventory), generally covering all items in the inventory at least once each year. Sometimes both types of inventory taking are used. Since the two methods involve somewhat different techniques, they are discussed separately in this chapter.

Inventories Taken at One Time

A complete inventory at one time is a large undertaking. It requires the cooperation of production, accounting, and storekeeping personnel since it usually involves shutting down a plant and physically rearranging inventory to facilitate counting. It is essential that someone with authority assume overall responsibility for taking the inventory. Often an "inventory committee" is organized, consisting of management representatives of production departments, controller's office and general accounting department, shipping and receiving departments, internal audit department, and the independent auditors. It is usually desirable to have someone from top production management responsible for rearranging the stock and making available employees who are familiar with it.

Inventories may be taken during the vacation period for factory employees, when production is stopped for some other reason, at a time when inventories are at a low level, at year end, or at a convenient month end prior to the balance sheet date.

Frequently production personnel count the inventories as they are rearranged, particularly if rearranging is equivalent to counting them. Sometimes the counts are made by clerical or accounting personnel, storekeepers, or internal auditors.

However the initial counting is organized, the counts should be verified. Some companies have a complete recheck by independent teams. Others assign foremen or internal auditors to make random counts as a test-check.

Inventory Program

An almost invariable requirement for a good physical inventory is advance preparation of a written program. To be most effective, the program should include instructions pertaining to:

1. Good physical arrangement as a means of simplifying the count;
2. Proper identification and description of stock, including stage of completion when appropriate;
3. Segregation or proper notation of slow-moving, obsolete, or damaged goods;

4. Identification and listing of inventory belonging to others;
5. Numerical control of inventory tags or sheets;
6. Practices to be followed in the verification of individual counts;
7. Practices to be followed in obtaining a proper cutoff of receipts and shipments, interdepartmental movement, and the related paper work; and
8. Practices to be followed in verifying goods in the hands of others.

In addition to those instructions for controlling and recording the inventory, the program should include instructions to the accounting department for summarizing quantities; pricing; extending (multiplying quantity times price) and summarizing the priced inventory; and checking of summarizing and pricing, including extensions and footings. Special attention may be required for consignments in or out, goods in transit, and goods in public warehouses or branches.

Requirements for the forms used in inventory taking vary, but experience with previous inventories should be applied to the design of forms that facilitate inventory taking. While it is possible to control physical counts otherwise, by far the best practice calls for the forms on which initial counts are recorded to be numerically controlled.

The inventory plan should provide for supervision adequate to assure that procedures for arranging and counting stock, pricing, and preparation of summaries of the counts are properly followed and that results are satisfactory.

The mechanics of counting vary. Seldom, if ever, can all individual items in an inventory be seen and counted; they are frequently in the packages or cartons in which they were purchased or are to be shipped, or they may be located in bins or stockpiles in large numbers that cannot be physically weighed or counted. The only rule that can be laid down is that a reasonable number of items should be counted; some packages should be opened and some items inspected, particularly if there are any unusual circumstances.

Differences between physical and recorded inventories should be investigated, and the possibility of leakage or pilferage should be considered. The records may be right and the count wrong so that no adjustments should be made without further investigation.

Inventories Taken Periodically Throughout the Year

The total "wall-to-wall" inventory may be replaced by periodic physical counts throughout the year if good perpetual records are maintained, controls over movement and paper work cutoffs are good, and all other circumstances are favorable. Generally, periodic counts should cover all items at least once in a year, but it is also good practice to count active items more often and inactive items less often. Procedures used in making periodic counts differ from those for inventories taken at one time. Rather than having production personnel rearrange and count all the stock in a plant, counts are usually made by relatively small groups of employees who soon become expert at counting inventories and possibly spend a large part of their time doing so. When periodic counts are made and found to be reliable, the perpetual records may serve as the equivalent of a complete physical inventory and are priced, extended, and summarized for comparison with general ledger accounts at or near the year end.

A problem frequently encountered in practice is obtaining a good cutoff by arranging for perpetual records to be posted promptly and accurately; otherwise the counts will result in apparent differences which are actually delays in recording. Employees making periodic counts usually should not know beforehand the amount shown in the perpetual records because they may tend to report that amount as their count. If a particular item to be counted is stored at more than one location, however, the locations should be reported to the employees making the count to minimize the possibility of errors in counting.

INVENTORIES IN PUBLIC WAREHOUSES

In addition to adequate insurance coverage on goods in custody of a public warehouse, controls should generally include preliminary investigation and continuing evaluation of the performance of the custodian. Statement on Auditing Procedure No. 37 (SAS No. 1, paragraphs 901.30 and .31), issued in 1966, suggests the following control procedures:

> Consideration of the business reputation and financial standing of the custodian.
>
> Inspection of the physical facilities.
>
> Inquiries as to the custodian's control procedures and whether he holds goods for his own account.
>
> Inquiries as to type and adequacy of insurance carried.
>
> Inquiries as to government or other licensing and bonding requirements and the nature, extent, and results of any inspection by government or other agencies.
>
> Review of the custodian's financial statements and related reports of independent auditors.

Review and update of the information developed from the investigation described above.

Physical counts (or test counts) of the goods, if practicable and reasonable (counts may not be practicable in the case of fungible goods).

Reconciliation of quantities shown on statements received from the custodian with the owner's records.

OTHER INVENTORIES NOT ON PREMISES

Other inventories not on the premises normally include inventories on consignment, in hands of processors or suppliers, and in branches. Those classifications of inventory should be carried in separate accounts supported by perpetual records. Additional control procedures may include monthly inventory reports, confirmation, and periodic physical tests. Controls over receipts and shipments should be similar to those discussed earlier in this chapter, even though shipments may be on memorandum only. To avoid possible duplication, special attention should be given to goods in transit.

INVENTORIES BELONGING TO OTHERS

All inventory belonging to others should be clearly identified, physically segregated, and counted as part of the physical inventory procedure. If the amount is significant and the activity frequent, a perpetual record should be maintained and all entries documented. Records of accountability for the property of others should be carefully maintained, particularly if the items are similar to, or there is commingling with, inventory owned.

DEFECTIVE WORK, SCRAP, AND WASTE

Good production control requires a system of inspection so that defective work may be detected promptly to prevent further accumulation of costs in completing a substandard or defective product. If defective items can be utilized in some other manner or sold as seconds, they should be segregated and quantity control should be maintained pending use or disposition. Similar control should be exercised over scrap and waste materials.

ITEMS CHARGED OFF, BUT PHYSICALLY ON HAND

Frequently, certain types of supplies, such as small tools, are charged to expense as purchased. Those items should be under physical control; unissued items should be subject to the same requisitioning and quantity control procedures as other inventories. Items of doubtful value written off, but on hand, should be segregated and under physical control until disposed of. A periodic physical inventory is as necessary an accountability procedure for those items as for any other inventory, but it is frequently neglected because the assets do not appear in the accounts.

RETURNABLE CONTAINERS

Returnable containers in which a company's products are shipped may be treated either as current assets subject to inventory adjustment or as fixed assets depreciated over their estimated useful life. Containers on hand should be checked physically in the same way as other inventories, including inspection of containers to determine their potential usefulness. Some companies include in the accounts containers shipped to customers with those on hand, setting up memorandum accounts indicating their location. The quantity of containers represented by those memorandum accounts should be added to those on hand and counted in determining the total quantity for inventory purposes. In some instances the seller may permit its customers to return containers on a freight collect basis or may have to expend a substantial amount for cleaning and reconditioning returned containers before they can be reused. If the estimated expense for freight, cleaning, and reconditioning of containers in the hands of customers is material, the containers may be valued on a reduced basis or a provision may be made for the amount of the estimated expenses.

• AUDITING PROCEDURES

OBJECTIVES

The objectives of procedures for auditing inventories are to provide evidential matter that is sufficient and competent to give an auditor reasonable assurance that:

Inventories physically exist, in good condition, unencumbered by pledge or lien.

The accounts reflect all property held for sale in the ordinary course of business and do not include the property of others or items billed to customers.

Cost of inventory items is measured in accordance with generally accepted accounting principles consistently applied.

Estimates of realizable value are carefully and consistently made.

Controlling auditing procedures for inventories and the production system is often difficult, both in the practical sense of managing the work while it is in progress and in the theoretical sense of maintaining the logical structure through which auditing procedures support the above objectives. That is because inventories are ordinarily such an important element in the determination of net income and financial position and because the number, variety, and complexity of factors bearing on their existence, cost, and realizable value are so great. Furthermore, precision in the valuation of inventories—as much as or more than in any other area—is not possible and thus judgments must be subjective.

THE AUDIT CYCLE

Even more than in other segments, functional tests of the production segment tend to contribute to confidence in the balance sheet accounts because physical controls, measurement of costs, and operational controls over preserving the realizable value of inventories all contribute directly to an auditor's objectives. An auditor can make tests of the existence, cost, and realizable value of inventories himself or he can rely on those made by the client. Thus there is a direct trade-off between the effectiveness of client procedures and controls and the amount of corroborative evidence to be gathered by an auditor.

Transaction Reviews

The number of types of transactions in the production segment depends on the complexity of the production process. A one-product, one-operation plant may have only three types of transactions: the raw material purchase/storage/issue transaction; the production material, labor, and overhead input/units of output transaction; the finished goods receiving/storage/shipping transaction.

On the other hand, a production process may consist of many different departments operating in different ways and producing different kinds of products, or even operating differently on the same kinds of products. Although systemization may reduce the number of types of transactions by providing the same kind of control procedures at an early point in the system, the characteristics of the production process frequently generate differences in reporting and control procedures.

Furthermore, an auditor may wish to trace transaction documents originating in various production departments to confirm his understanding of the system even though the types of transactions are not technically distinguished by differences in control procedures.

The following are examples—not a comprehensive list—of types of transactions that might be found in a production segment:

> Raw material purchases: usually reviewed in connection with the purchasing–accounts payable segment.
>
> Raw material issues: issues of standard quantities may be different from issues of nonstandard quantities.
>
> Labor reporting and payroll distribution.
>
> Overhead absorption.
>
> Piecework or incentive pay computations.
>
> Bill of materials ordering.
>
> Material received directly into production.
>
> Processing of customers' material.
>
> Production reporting and costing.
>
> Finished goods transfer reporting and costing.
>
> Job order close-out.
>
> Finished goods transfers to cost of goods sold: may or may not be integrated with revenue–accounts receivable recording.

Fully developed systems may be in use as accountability and valuation procedures. Counting, pricing, and summarizing of physical inventory is a complete system, subject to its own control operations (described in a preceding section), which an auditor reviews and functionally tests in connection with validating the existence of the inventory. There may be similar extensive systems for estimating cost to complete contracts or orders, verifying net realizable value, or identifying obsolete or slow-moving goods.

Each of those systems should be identified and reviewed as a basis for planning validation tests. If a system is activated only annually, as is often the case, the review is made of the *plans* for the validation process, and the tests made of the system itself serve all purposes.

As more fully discussed in Chapter 5, a considerable effort to identify significant types of transactions before testing commences contributes to an efficient and effective audit, but it is not essential. The transaction review itself and other steps of the audit provide means for identifying mistakes in the initial understanding.

Functional Tests

As discussed at length in Chapter 5, a control is important to an auditor only if reliance on it permits him to limit the amount of corroborative evidence he needs to gather through other tests. If the presence or absence of controls will not influence the remainder of his auditing procedures, an auditor has no need to make functional tests of controls, no matter how important the controls may be to the transaction system. That principle is particularly applicable to inventories because the unavoidable minimum of validation testing for existence, cost, and realizable value is extensive. Thus, often the reliability of underlying evidence of the cost accounting system and records of quantities has little impact on substantive tests. In those instances an auditor must consider carefully whether functional testing of the controls over underlying evidence adds enough to the basis for his opinion to justify the effort: for example, if physical inventory is taken at year end, functional tests of controls over movement of inventory might be unnecessary unless records of movement enter into determination of prices.

For that reason, and others mentioned earlier, the following discussion emphasizes the relationship of functional tests to the auditor's objectives. Since the range and variety of conditions encountered in practice are so great, two systems are used for illustration: the most rudimentary cost system and a highly organized standard cost system.

Rudimentary Cost System

For adequate inventory pricing, the minimum data required to be produced by an accounting system are properly classified cumulative totals of purchases, payrolls and other expenses, and units sold. Combining that information with units in opening and closing inventories, invoice prices of recent material purchases, and current labor rates produces an adequate allocation between cost of goods sold and cost of inventories (there are exceptions but the premise will do for illustrative purposes). In addition to observing the physical counting of the inventory and testing the summarization of quantities, an auditor needs functional tests as a basis for reliance on the accounting data used in pricing computations.

Functional tests of purchases, payrolls, and expenses were described in Chapter 10, "The Buying Segment." If those tests produce no reason to question the functioning or continuity of controls, an auditor has reasonable assurance that the underlying evidence of the accounting system can be relied on for inventory pricing as well as other purposes.

The accumulation of units sold is likely to be an integral part of the accounting system for the revenue segment and subject to the kinds of controls described in Chapter 9. Functional tests of those controls can simply be expanded to cover the accumulation of units as well as dollars of sales. Sometimes the accumulation of units is a separate process; then the system has to be reviewed, controls identified and functionally tested, and the results analytically reviewed by investigating fluctuations in the ratio of units sold to dollars of sales.

Thus, as long as controls over the purchasing and revenue segments are reliable, a rudimentary cost system calls for little or no functional testing beyond that described in earlier chapters—but in all likelihood both the client's validation of the inventory balance and the auditor's validation tests will have to be made at the end of the fiscal year rather than at an interim date.

Standard Cost System

A well-developed standard cost system requires much more data than the rudimentary system described above. For an auditor's purposes, a well-developed system (óf any sort, not necessarily a standard cost system) permits validation tests at any time during the year, although for reasons described in Chapter 4, both auditor and client usually prefer to make them during the last quarter of a fiscal year. The system must provide the details of:

> Transfers between raw materials and work in process and between work in process and finished goods.
> Distribution of material, labor, and overhead expenses to cost centers or job orders.
> Variance accounts identifying differences between actual and standard.

If the client has been applying the system effectively, the system's output would include analyses and explanations of variances.

Analyses of variances produced by a standard cost system are a form of exception reporting and thereby constitute a disciplinary control. The comparison of actual cost to standard costs through the analysis of variances should render the other control operations redundant for an auditor's purposes (there are exceptions to that conclusion; for example, variances that are not accounted for in detail do not serve to control the relationship between standard and actual costs). If the system produces variance analyses, an auditor's functional tests can be limited to testing their accuracy.

In deciding how much functional testing of the controls over that complex data system is required, an auditor should resist the temptation to test extensively. The system is large and complex and obviously important to the control of the most critical and difficult audit activity. Certainly functional testing of the cost accounting and unit control systems provides additional understanding of the client's operations and additional confidence in the functioning of the system. However, before conducting extensive tests, an auditor should measure each test against his objectives—reasonable assurance as to existence, cost, and realizable value of the inventories—and evaluate whether the additional understanding and confidence add substantively to the body of evidence he needs for that assurance. In many cases, the bulk of the assurance comes from observing the physical inventory and its pricing and summarization and from functional testing of the variance analyses. In other cases, the sole purpose of functional tests of movement controls is assurance of control between interim physical inventory taking and year end, in which event tests could most appropriately be made in that period.

Accordingly, a principal criterion in determining the scope of functional tests is the extent to which an auditor's assurance depends on the cost and quantity accounting systems. That dependence is greater when the client's annual accountability procedures (physical inventory, summarization, and pricing) are carried out at an interim date. The more effective the inventory accounting system, the longer the period of time an auditor may tolerate between validation procedures and fiscal year end.

Validation Procedures: Observation of Physical Inventories

For many years—since the *McKesson & Robbins* case precipitated the issue in 1939—the observation of physical inventories has been a required auditing procedure and therefore the principal focus of inventory validation testing. For a long time after 1939, auditors were expected to make voluminous and extensive test counts, sometimes virtually taking the physical inventory side-by-side with client personnel. In recent years the emphasis has shifted to observation and functional testing of the client's accountability procedures for physical verification of inventories.

The official position of the profession is now stated in paragraph 331.09 of SAS No. 1:

> . . . it is ordinarily necessary for the independent auditor to be present at the time of count and, by suitable observation, tests, and inquiries, satisfy himself respecting the effectiveness of the methods of inventory-taking and the measure of reliance which may be placed upon the client's representations about the quantities and physical condition of the inventories.

Validation tests of inventories may serve two purposes. Although they are primarily designed to provide corroborative evidence of the existence, cost, and realizable value of the inventories, they frequently also serve as functional tests of the client's accountability procedures. Separate tests may serve the two purposes, but often one test serves both.

Observing the physical inventory is the principal example of a procedure that serves both purposes. Whether the inventory is a "wall-to-wall" count of everything on hand at a given date, a statistical sample, or a system of cycle counts, an auditor's objectives are to be sure that the client's procedures are sound and to gather his own evidence of the existence and condition of the inventory. His approach, of course, must be tailored to the client's particular circumstances.

Plans for Wall-to-Wall Inventory Observation

The client has the primary responsibility for the conduct of the inventory and for making appropriate plans for its implementation. Because of the auditor's required participation, the planning should be a joint effort. Usually, an auditor's accumulated experience with physical inventory observation enables him to make a positive contribution to improving a client's plans; often a client who understands an auditor's objectives can suggest better ways to attain them.

Client and auditor should agree on the timing of the inventory, taking into consideration the factors described in earlier chapters: the inventory should be counted at year end if it is subject to extraordinary volatility of movement or quantities, or if there are weaknesses in the controls over accounting for movement. If controls are not weak, the count can be taken at any time other than the year end or on a staggered basis throughout the year; if it is taken at one time, usually both client and auditor have good reasons to prefer a month end in the last quarter of the fiscal year. The auditor should review and comment on the written instructions or a memorandum of inventory plans. If statistical sampling methods are to be used, an auditor should satisfy himself that the sampling plan has statistical validity acceptable to him as reasonable in the circumstances. Often the client executive responsible for the inventory holds one or more instructional meetings with those who are to supervise the actual inventory taking. It is usually helpful for the auditor to be present because he has to make his own plans for observing the inventory.

An auditor's manpower requirements are naturally greater if a complete physical inventory is taken at one time than if cycle counts or staggered inventories are taken. Audit manpower requirements must be determined in relation to the timing of inventories at various locations, numbers of counting teams fielded by the client, and difficulty of the observations to be made. If a client's internal auditing staff or outside inventory specialists participate in taking the physical inventory, an independent auditor may be able to reduce his manpower requirements to some extent. An auditor's plans encompass quality as well as quantity of staff: more experienced personnel or those familiar with an engagement are assigned to areas where problems have been encountered in the past or where difficulties of identification, observation, or control can be anticipated.

The importance of the planning process should be recognized; often the planning is almost as important as the actual observation. There is nothing more harrowing to client and auditor than the appearance of an unforeseen problem in the midst of inventory taking; every auditor can recall the late nights and weekends spent in the most uncomfortable circumstances before a problem inventory could be recounted or otherwise "cleared."

Observation of Wall-to-Wall Inventory Taking

An auditor must keep in mind his objectives in observing an inventory taking: to gain his own firsthand knowledge that the inventory exists and to observe that the count and description of the inventory are accurate and that both are properly recorded. An auditor is neither a stock-taker nor an expert appraiser of inventory quality, quantities, or condition; nonetheless, he cannot neglect the intelligent application of common sense. Well-arranged stock is more likely to be accurately counted than poorly arranged stock. Signs of age and neglect are often obvious, for example, dust on cartons or rust and corrosion of containers, and they naturally raise questions about the stock's usefulness or salability. An auditor should certainly know enough about his client's business before observing the inventory to be able to recognize at least in broad terms the product under observation and the measures appropriate to determination of its quality and condition. Thus, an auditor should spend some time in thoughtful examination of the inventory being counted. However, he must be careful that he, his client, and everyone else concerned recognizes that he is not acting as an expert appraiser.

An auditor should spend the bulk of his time observing the client's procedures in operation and the controls over them. He can note the diligence of the counting teams: the care with which they count, weigh, and measure; their ability to identify and describe the stock; the methods used to make sure that nothing is omitted or duplicated. He should observe the presence of supervisory personnel, execution of planned double-checking procedures, performance of cutoff procedures, control over inventory count documents, methods by which individual areas or departments are controlled and "cleared," and adherence to official instructions.

An auditor should make some test counts, both to confirm the accuracy of the client's counting and to record his own corroborative evidence of the existence of inventories for later tracing into the summarization. In the absence of specific reasons to do otherwise, an auditor records a small number of test counts in relation to the number of items in the inventory. However, he should recognize that such specific reasons are not uncommon. For example:

> The inventory may have some special characteristic, such as high value or volatility, that causes an auditor to consider it worthwhile to make his own counts or records;
>
> The client may lack enough responsible employees to do the necessary double-checking and may ask the auditor to fill that role; or
>
> As an additional safeguard or for its "psychological" effect, the client may specifically request the auditor to expand his counting activity.

Client inventory counts are commonly recorded at least in duplicate, with one copy left at the scene of the count and another gathered for summarization. Formerly, the auditor sometimes received a third copy which he retained for use in controlling the summarization process. That practice should seldom be necessary: if an auditor has such compelling reason to doubt a client's ability to perform and control the summarization process as to consider controlling it himself, he would serve his own and his client's purposes better by spending the time helping the client improve plans and procedures to the point where both could rely on them. Preferred practice is for the client to control the summarization and the auditor to make notations of tag or count sheet numbers or other control data on a test basis for later tracing to summarized records to provide corroborative evidence that the process was adequately controlled.

As part of his review of plans and his observation of the inventory taking, an auditor should note and evaluate the procedures followed in separately identifying and counting those items that are moving from place to place and goods on hand that belong to others: consignments, bailments, goods on approval, property of customers returned for repair or held awaiting delivery instructions, and so on. All items of that nature should be counted and recorded separately both because they are as subject to accountability procedures as the inventory itself and to preclude mistaken or purposeful substitution for inventory items.

As noted in an earlier section, adequately identifying work in process is likely to present particular difficulties. Concluding that a physical count of work in process is impossible for that reason is unacceptable, however, because the reason for the difficulties may be that the inventory is out of control. Production or operations personnel must be able to identify items in process and their condition or stage of completion in order to maintain control of the production process, and so they should be able to do so for physical count purposes as well. If they cannot, the possibility of inadequate production control is reason enough for both client and auditor to have serious difficulty in reaching a conclusion as to the work-in-process inventory balance without a wall-to-wall physical count at the balance sheet date.

That stricture, however, does not preclude any number of practical compromises to deal with the problems of work-in-process identification and valuation. Assumptions can be made that clearly, on the basis of experience and common sense, cannot be materially in error: goods in a given department can be assumed to have passed through an average state of completion; the variety of goods in a given department can be assumed to be of an average size, formula, or character; tote boxes, bales, or coils can be assumed to be of an average weight, and so forth.

Typical Audit Program

Following is a representative audit program for the observation of a physical inventory:

1. Physical arrangement. Make a general brief inspection of the premises. Note whether the arrangement of stock indicates that a good count is possible or probable. If the arrangement is extremely poor, recommend that the stock be rearranged.
2. Identification and description. Inspect some items of the stock, determine the source of the description, see that proper differentiation is made for the various stages of work in process, and check findings with production personnel. Conflicting answers to questions may cause doubt as to whether the client's employees taking the inventory are actually familiar with it.
3. Segregation or notation of slow-moving, obsolete, or damaged goods. Note provision for identification and segregation of those items; be alert for items not identified.
4. Control of tags or sheets. Determine that each inventory count team is charged with a sequence of prenumbered tags and that each team is required to turn in those unused or spoiled. Note whether employees account for all tags at the completion of the inventory. Ob-

serve whether items have been properly tagged or marked to avoid duplications or omissions.

5. Practices in verifying individual counts. Reperform some of the counts, noting whether quantities and descriptions are being carefully entered on the tags or inventory sheets. Record a number of counts, including some items of substantial value. In the event that differences between the limited test counts and the counts by client's employees indicate laxness, consider calling for recounts of the entire section in which the unsatisfactory condition exists. If inventory sheets are used instead of tags, select some items from the sheets to count on the floor and trace some items on the floor to the inventory sheets.

6. Practices in obtaining proper cutoff. At the time of inventory taking, visit the receiving and shipping departments, record the last receiving and shipping document numbers, and see that each department has been informed that no receipts after and no shipments before the cutoff should be included in inventory. Receiving and shipping departments should earmark materials that should not be included in the inventory. Make a subsequent check of the records of those departments after the inventory and compare the last receiving and shipping numbers with accounting department records. Manufacturing operations are sometimes suspended for the physical inventory; if they are not, special care must be taken to control the movement of inventory.

Statistical Sample

If other controls are effective enough to justify a client's restricting its accountability procedures to a statistical sample to confirm that the records represent goods physically on hand, an auditor should apply procedures similar to those for a wall-to-wall physical inventory, except that he must emphasize even more his observation and evaluation of the client's conduct of the sampling plan and concern himself over his ability to locate the stock sample. As a part of the planning process, he must understand and evaluate the statistical assumptions and then participate in the evaluation of the results and related judgments about the inventory as a whole.

Some auditors advocate taking an additional sample, statistically determined and evaluated, to validate the client's sample.

Cycle Counts

A cycle count system usually functions more or less continuously throughout the year according to a systematic plan or schedule, and its performance is documented by records and work sheets of counts and entries in the perpetual records. With effective disciplinary controls and documentation of their operation, an auditor has no practical or theoretical reason not to carry out his observation and test procedures at any time he chooses, including, if necessary, before or after the period under audit. Sometimes cycle counting is restricted to certain times of the month or year, in which case, of course, an auditor must plan his visit to coincide with the client's schedule.

All procedures applicable to wall-to-wall physical inventory observation can be readily adapted to cycle count observation. An auditor can review the cycle counting schedules, plans, and instructions; he can observe the physical arrangement and condition of the stock, the diligence and proficiency of the inventory counting teams in counting and identifying stock, and provisions for identifying and segregating slow-moving, obsolete, or damaged goods, controlling records of test counts, and preventing omissions or duplications. Because the entire stock is not being inventoried at one time, he must take steps to assure his proper identification of the items inventoried. He can make a few test counts either with or independently of the counting teams and can observe and, if he wishes, participate in the reconciliation of counts to perpetual records and the investigation of differences.

An auditor also needs evidence that the cycle counting procedures he has observed were functioning before and can be expected to function after his observation and that they are applied to substantially all inventory items. A formal schedule of counting and specific assignments (covering both personnel to do the job and responsibility for supervising it) is most persuasive, and some companies do have that degree of systemization and discipline.

Many companies, however, operate under a loose policy of "counting all items at least once a year" and assign the counting to the stock-keepers to do as time allows. In those instances, an auditor can review work sheets, entries in the perpetual records, and other evidence of the regularity of test counting and evaluate the results. The frequency of counting; absence of substantial differences over a period of time; absence of difficulties in cutoff of receipts, shipments, and transfers; quality of investigation of differences that occur; and quality of storeroom housekeeping and stock identification are all persuasive.

The review should be adequate to disclose the prevalence of poor performance, sloppiness, or irresponsibility which might raise doubts about the reliability of the cycle counting system. Those conditions are not at all unusual and should not be ignored if they exist. The authors have observed in a number of organizations a curious tendency toward what amounts to "negative supervisory control." Counting may be assigned to the newest, least experienced, and least responsible employees or it may be scheduled at night or on weekends when supervision and discipline are weakest.

Those conditions can constitute a weakness in accountability controls, and an auditor's response should follow the pattern described in Chapter 5. The preferred solution is a discussion with the client, leading to correction of the conditions. Alternatively, an auditor may expand the number of his own test counts to a sample sufficiently large to permit valid conclusions. If the sample contains no significant incidence of error, auditor and client may conclude that the cycle counting procedures function effectively even though they are not as well controlled as they might be; if there is a significant incidence of error, both auditor and client may be forced to conclude that either cycle counting procedures must be improved or a wall-to-wall physical inventory must be taken near the end of the fiscal year.

Difficult Inventories

Certain types of material—for example, logs in a river, piles of coal and of scrap metal, vats of chemicals—by their nature may be difficult to count, and an auditor may have to use ingenuity to validate quantities on hand. Measurement of a pile of metal may be unsatisfactory for a number of reasons: the pile may have sunk into the ground to an unknown depth, the metals may be of varying weights precluding the use of an average, or the pile may be of uneven density. Quality of chemicals and similar materials may be impossible to determine without specialized knowledge.

Clients sometimes use photographic surveys, engineering studies, chemical analyses, and similar specialized techniques to take physical inventory, and an auditor can observe the care and sense of accountability with which they are conducted. In some circumstances, an auditor may be guided by the client's system of handling receipts and disbursements from the piles. For example, the client may use a pile rotation system, in which metal is taken from a specified pile, and metal received is placed on other piles, until a pile is exhausted, at which time errors in the accounts are disclosed. If the pile rotation system functions satisfactorily, an auditor may be willing to rely to some extent on the accounting records.

In any event, both auditor and client should keep in mind that it is the client's responsibility to validate the inventory; the auditor's responsibility is to observe that validation.

Alternative Procedures If Observation of Physical Inventories Is Not Practicable or Reasonable

An auditor should consider carefully a decision that observation of inventories is impracticable or impossible. Experience has proven that observing inventories, while inconvenient perhaps, or expensive or difficult, is seldom impracticable. However, if a client does not or cannot take a physical inventory or if an auditor cannot be present at the inventory taking, he may (or in certain circumstances may not) be able to form an opinion as to the reasonableness of inventory quantities by the application of alternative procedures. Those alternative procedures fall into two basic categories:

Establishing other physical evidence which may be tantamount to observation of physical inventories; or

Establishing the validity of inventories through further examination of accounting evidence.

Procedures in the first category can be applied, for example, if an auditor is engaged to examine financial statements after the physical inventory has been taken. Subsequent physical tests may be a satisfactory substitute for observation of the inventory taking. An auditor may also examine written instructions for the inventory taking, review the original tags or sheets, and make suitable tests of the compilation.

Government requirements may prohibit shutdown and interruption of production for inventory purposes. If work-in-process inventory cannot be taken in the customary way for that or any other reason, an auditor may have to exercise ingenuity in finding a reasonable substitute. Quantity records maintained for labor bonus purposes may be priced and extended and the total compared with the control account; records of finished production may be examined after the inventory date to determine quantities produced. Those procedures combined with overall observation of the work-in-process inventory and understanding of the production control system may provide a satisfactory basis for an opinion.

In any event, an auditor must examine or observe some physical evidence of the validity of the inventory and make appropriate functional tests of controls over intervening transactions. If on the basis of those procedures and through his examination of the accounts and the system of internal control he is satisfied that inventories are fairly stated, he may express an unqualified opinion. On the other hand, there may be no practicable substitute for observation of inventory taking, and an auditor may have to express a qualified opinion or no opinion, depending on the materiality of the amount of inventory, and on whether the failure to observe was unavoidable or was due to management's decision to limit the scope of the audit.

Sometimes procedures for validating inventories must be based on examination of accounting evidence. For example, an auditor making an initial examination of a client generally has not observed the physical inventory at the previous year end, and the opening inventory is usually a principal factor in the determination of cost of goods sold for the current year. If reputable independent public accountants expressed an unqualified opinion on the prior-year statements, an auditor may accept that opinion and perhaps merely review the physical inventory sheets and summaries. If no examination was made for the preceding year, an auditor may have no alternative but to expand substantially his tests of accounting evidence to attempt to establish the validity of the inventories.

Those expanded tests may include a detailed examination of physical inventory sheets and summaries, including review and testing of cutoff data; examination of perpetual inventory records and production records; and review of individual product and overall gross profit percentages. In connection with the latter procedure, cost compilations of selected inventory items should be tested and significant changes in unit costs should be directly correlated to factors such as improvements in technology, mass buying economies and freight rate "breaks," changes in labor costs, changes in overhead rates, and so on. Changes in gross profit percentages should be further related to changes in unit sales prices and changes in the profitability of the sales mix, if applicable. If an auditor is unable to form an opinion as to the opening inventory, he may wish to qualify his opinion or give no opinion with respect to the results of operations for the year under examination.

Initial audit engagements involving filings with the Securities and Exchange Commission present further problems because audited income statements for three years are required. While recognizing the difficulties inherent in reporting on earlier years, the Commission clearly requires for an unqualified opinion that certifying accountants establish the validity of prior-year inventories through appropriate alternative auditing procedures. SEC Accounting Series Release No. 90 states:

> . . . Lost and inadequate records may give rise to questions as to the reliability of the results shown in the financial statements and may make it impracticable to apply alternative audit procedures. Alternative procedures must be adequate to support an unqualified opinion as to the fairness of presentation of the income statements by years.

If, as a result of the examination and the conclusions reached, the accountant is not in a position to express an affirmative opinion as to the fairness of the presentation of earnings year by year, the registration statement is defective. . . . If the accountant is not satisfied with the results of his examination he should not issue an affirmative opinion. . . .

In addition, Statement on Auditing Procedure No. 43 (SAS No. 1, paragraph 331.13), issued in September, 1970, makes an opinion as to the reasonableness of the current inventory a prerequisite to one on prior inventories.

Validation Procedures: Pricing and Summarization

Some time generally elapses between taking the inventory and pricing and summarizing. Usually the client takes time to investigate inventory differences, and an auditor may wish to participate; satisfactory explanations of differences between the accounts and the physical inventory may be the most important part of his examination. The auditor's test count and tag control work sheets provide his "control" that the counting he observed is reflected in the subsequent priced summary.

In deciding the extent to which he needs to test quantities and pricing to inventory summaries, an auditor is guided by whether the client has already made careful and competent checks; the best assurance results from test-checks that confirm the accuracy of the client's procedures. In examining inventories compiled by computer, an auditor can generally assume that their mechanical accuracy is greater than if compiled by hand. However, even though machine errors are rare, they do occur, and operators of machines or systems analysts may have made errors not detected by the system.

An auditor should plan his work so as to gather evidence that accuracy of summarization is reasonably assured: concentrating on larger items, testing some footings, scanning other footings and extensions for reasonableness, and watching for accumulation errors that could have a significant effect on the total amount of the inventory. He should determine that items included in and excluded from inventories are properly treated.

Summarization of Quantities

In testing summarization of physical inventory quantities, an auditor generally performs each of the following procedures to some degree, depending on his confidence in the client's procedures:

1. Tests of the inventory tags, for reasonable assurance that only tags

used for the physical counts are included in the physical inventory summaries.

2. Checks of the inventory summaries against the auditor's record of counts, and test-checks against the client's count sheets or tags; checks of conversions and summarizations of units.

3. Test-checks of quantities to perpetual records, if they exist, and review of differences. This is particularly important when inventories are taken prior to year end and perpetual records will be the basis for year-end inventory valuation.

4. Comparisons of quantities with those in previous inventories on a test basis to identify slow-moving items or abnormally large or small balances.

5. Reviews of usage records for further indications of slow-moving items. If the client does not maintain perpetual records, an auditor may examine purchase orders or production orders to determine how recently certain items of inventory were acquired.

6. Tests of the observance of cutoff procedures and the inclusion of in-transit items.

7. Reviews of listing of damaged or obsolete items.

8. Reviews and confirmation of customers' materials on hand and of client's materials in the hands of others.

Pricing and Summarization

Steps similar to the following should be employed in testing inventory pricing and summarization:

1. Tests for reasonable assurance that costs to be applied to inventories are reasonably computed in accordance with an acceptable method. In examining an inventory of purchased items, the auditor's tests should include reference to current invoices or purchase contracts. He will have reviewed and tested the client's cost system in connection with his functional tests and thereby reached a conclusion as to the adequacy of work-in-process and finished-goods costs computed by the system. Those costs should be traced on a test basis into the inventory pricing.

2. Tests of the application of prices to inventory quantities and the resulting extensions, footings, and summarizations.

3. Reviews and tests of the application of policies for identifying obsolete or slow-moving items. Many companies have formulas or rules of thumb that translate overall judgments into serviceable detailed applications, such as: all items over a year's supply, all items that have not moved within six months, or all items bearing certain identifying numbers as to date or class of product. An auditor must review whether the rules are realistic and sufficiently comprehensive as well as whether they are fully and accurately applied. In addition to reviewing and testing the client's rules, an auditor must apply his

understanding of the client's business to each segment of the inventory, to evaluate whether there are market conditions that might create problems of realizability in the normal course of operations. He may augment that understanding through discussions about salability with sales and marketing executives.

4. Review of the pricing of obsolete, slow-moving, scrap, and damaged stock to determine that it is not in excess of net realizable value. Past experience is usually the best guide to realizable value of items that have to be "jobbed off" or otherwise disposed of at salvage prices.

5. Review and tests of the determination of market prices. Tests may be made to determine whether market is lower than cost, as described in the following paragraphs.

Inventory prices (at cost) may be compared with net realizable value (estimated selling prices less costs of completion and disposal) of individual or major groups of products. Estimated selling prices may be tested against recent sales invoices—or preferably against latest customer orders—and evaluated for possible trends in prices. Estimated costs of completion and disposal may be tested for reasonableness by overall computation. Some auditors include a carrying cost for an average estimated period until sale as part of the cost of disposal.

Inventories priced at market should not be stated at more than net realizable value or less than "market floor" (selling price less cost of completion and further reduced by an allowance for an approximately normal profit margin). Consequently, an auditor need not determine the value of inventory at reproduction or replacement cost if there is acceptable evidence that, for individual or groups of products, the range between net realizable value and market floor is not great.

Replacement costs may be test-checked by reference to cost records, current invoices, or purchase contracts. Reproduction costs may be test-checked in a similar manner, supplemented by conferences with production and accounting employees.

Since net realizable value, market floor, replacement cost, and reproduction cost are all very general terms, and since the objective is an aggregate inventory figure that is fairly stated in relation to the financial statements as a whole, judgment and common sense in the application of broad statistical approximations have to serve in place of precision.

Retail Inventories

If the retail method of inventory accounting is used, the physical inventory is priced at retail and the totals are compared with the recorded inventory. Unusual shortages may require investigation to determine whether the retail method is functioning improperly or excessive physical losses are being incurred. An auditor should also review and make selected tests of the retail method computations outlined in the accounting principles section of this chapter.

Independent Experts

In special circumstances a qualified specialist or independent expert may be needed to establish quantity or value: for example, the value of an inventory of precious stones.

Inventories in Public Warehouses and Other Inventories Not on Premises

Stock held by others, such as in public warehouses, on consignment, or in hands of processors, should be substantiated by direct confirmation in writing from the custodians. An auditor should also consider the necessity of making supplemental inquiries if those inventories represent a significant portion of current or total assets or if a confirmation reply is not satisfactory. A confirmation reply might not be considered satisfactory if the holder is not believed responsible in relation to the amount of inventory in his custody, or if the holder, as public warehouses customarily do, confirms only that he has possession of certain packages bearing a description of the contents but without representation as to the contents. In addition, while negotiable warehouse receipts are usually trustworthy, withdrawals are not always noted on those receipts, and it is often advisable to request direct confirmation of withdrawals by letter.

The Committee on Auditing Procedure, in Statement No. 37 (SAS No. 1, paragraph 331.15), recommended that supplemental inquiries include the following, to the extent an auditor considers necessary in the circumstances:

1. Discussion with the client as to the client's control procedures for investigating custodians and tests of related evidential matter.
2. Review of the client's control procedures for performance of the custodian and tests of related evidential matter.
3. Observation of physical counts of the goods, if practicable and reasonable.
4. If warehouse receipts have been pledged as collateral, confirmation (on a test basis, if appropriate) from lenders as to pertinent details of the pledged receipts.

Special Considerations as to Work in Process

Relating work in process to accounting records can be difficult and entail troublesome pricing problems, even if a complete inventory is taken at one time. That difficulty is most pronounced if work in process, by its physical nature, is not easy to identify, such as if it does not take on the aspects of the finished product until shortly prior to completion, or simply if the cost system is poor. No set formula can be prescribed in those instances, and an auditor must relate the physical evidence to the records as best he can, relying to a greater extent on comprehensive tests of controls and accounting records.

Work-in-process inventories may be taken physically at some time other than when raw materials and finished stock are inventoried. In those circumstances an auditor should determine carefully, through tests of internal accounting controls and the accounting system, that proper credits have been made to work in process both for production transferred to finished stock and for shipments directly from work in process to customers, since unrecorded transfers at time of inventory may result in a misstatement of the inventory. Unless controls over relief of work in process are good, an auditor may insist that the entire inventory be taken at one time or undertake comprehensive tests of the records. He may be well advised to refer not only to the conventional accounting records but also to records such as those of production control or other departments that record the physical movement of inventories.

In reviewing uncompleted long-term contracts, an auditor should employ the procedures described in that connection in Chapter 9. Even when contracts in process are accounted for as inventory rather than on a percentage-of-completion basis, estimates of cost to complete are required to determine net realizable value and whether it is in excess of accumulated costs.

Inventory of Others

Goods belonging to customers or others should be counted and if significant in amount they should be confirmed with their owners. An auditor should be alert to the possibility of such goods and make certain that they are properly identified and segregated.

Purchase Commitments

As discussed in the accounting principles section of this chapter, unrealized losses on purchase commitments should be estimated and recorded. Purchase commitments are of two kinds: commitments with suppliers for materials to be used in the ordinary course of business, and futures contracts for the purchase or sale of commodities under which delivery usually is not made and which may represent either a hedge or a speculation. An auditor should review the record of purchase commitments, emphasizing long outstanding commitments; if the client does not maintain a record, the auditor should examine open contracts and purchase orders for materials. Purchase commitments should be related to inventories and to sales orders. For example, if purchase commitments have been made at prices in excess of current market prices, but nevertheless a normal margin of profit seems assured from the prospective sale of the finished article, no loss should be recorded. On the other hand, if purchase commitments are substantial and the inventory amount is excessive, or market or sale prices are declining, recording a loss on purchase commitments should be considered.

Inventory Certificate

It is standard practice for auditors to obtain written representations from clients as to inventory status and the accountability procedures employed. The inventory certificate confirms statements made by the client as to the method of taking inventory, ownership of the inventory, and basis of its valuation. It helps avoid misunderstandings over those matters between auditor and client. In addition, it reminds the client that the primary responsibility for inventories rests with him rather than with the auditor. Requesting an inventory certificate is a customary procedure, which in no way reflects on the integrity of the client.

In initial engagements it is desirable to obtain a similar certificate covering inventories at the beginning of the period.

The status of purchase commitments may be covered in the inventory certificate or the liability certificate discussed in Chapter 10.

The certificate should be designed to fit the individual circumstances. Since it is a client representation, it is typed on client stationery. It may take the general form shown on the next page, with appropriate variations, and should be signed by the chief financial officer and the officer in charge of inventories.

Analytical Reviews

Auditing inventories challenges an auditor's perception and analytical ability more than almost any other audit activity. The better an auditor understands a client's business, its operating problems, and the market and other economic conditions under which it operates, the better his ability to determine that the inventory is fairly stated in accordance with generally accepted accounting principles. That understanding can be brought to bear on specific inventory judgments in the design of analytical reviews.

MANAGEMENT REPRESENTATION—INVENTORIES

[Client's letterhead]

[Name and address of auditors]

Gentlemen:

In connection with your examination of the financial statements of [name of company] as of [balance sheet date], and for the [current period] then ended, I hereby state that the inventory as of [balance sheet date], of which the following is a summary,

.... $............

....

....

                         $............

was taken under my direction, and that to the best of my knowledge and belief:

1. The quantities are correct and were determined by actual count, weight, or measurement as at [physical inventory date]. [If a physical inventory was taken by statistical sampling methods or cycle counts, substitute a brief statement describing the method, its adequacy, and, in the case of cycle counts, the frequency and coverage of physical tests.];

2. The entire inventory is the unencumbered property of the company, has not been pledged as collateral, and includes no items billed by the company up to and including the balance sheet date nor any items held on consignment;

3. Each item or specified group of items of the inventory is priced at cost or market, whichever is lower, and not in excess of net realizable value;

4. The basis of pricing and method of computation are the same as were used at the end of the previous fiscal period. The general basis on which cost is determined is as follows [first-in first-out; average; last-in first-out, etc.];

5. No obsolete, slow-moving, damaged, or unusable materials or merchandise are included in the inventory at prices in excess of net realizable value;

6. The amount stated above is appropriate for presenting inventories in accordance with generally accepted accounting principles in the balance sheet at [balance sheet date].

Very truly yours,

_____

[Name of company]

_____   _____

[Date signed]   [Name of chief financial officer
signing and title]

Both internal and external data are abundantly available for designing and testing statistical, ratio, and other kinds of analyses.

An auditor should make every effort to use analytical reviews unique to the client under examination, but only on the basis of the most careful and penetrating understanding. The following paragraphs describe only those analytical reviews that are likely to apply to most inventories.

If standard cost systems or budgetary systems produce variance reports, the system has, in effect, performed a large part of the analytical review for an auditor by identifying the variances. He can then complete the review with a thoughtful perusal of the variance reports and analyses of reasons for variances.

Balances of purchases, sales, usage reports, and production costs should be compared from month to month. Fluctuations should be investigated and explained.

Significant ratios should be computed and compared from month to month and with the prior year. The ratios of cost of goods sold to inventory and to sales (or profit margin) are universally considered informative (they must be used with caution in a period of changing prices: results under FIFO will differ, perhaps significantly, from those under LIFO). In a great many industries, the computation of the ratio of total units to total value—i.e., average unit cost—is valid and informative, but if the "mix" of unit costs is likely to vary substantially, explaining fluctuations in average unit costs can be a greater effort than it is worth. If they are valid, average unit costs can be computed for sales, purchases, and inventory account balances.

Purchasing activity, including outstanding purchase commitments, should be reviewed for unusual conditions. An auditor may find commitments in excess of current requirements or current net realizable value, which require recording a probable loss. Outstanding commitments for unusual items or unusual quantities may alert an auditor to new products or contracts requiring his attention.

If available, sales forecasts and marketing plans can provide important information about salability and net realizable value of inventories. For example, the authors have experienced conditions in which marketing plans for a "new line" effectively rendered obsolete an inventory that otherwise appeared perfectly salable at normal profit margins. However, sales forecasts and marketing plans are often not highly organized or reduced to writing, and thus an auditor must take care not to waste his own or his client's time searching for material that is nonexistent or inconclusive. If his understanding of the client is adequate, he will know what he can expect and of whom he should inquire.

Activity Between Inventory and Year End

Analytical reviews must be particularly intensive and penetrating between an interim inventory date and the year end. Often it is more logical to make the required functional tests during that period. Although infrequent, it is not unusual for conditions to change sufficiently during that period to require additional validation tests at year end, sometimes extending to the point of retaking the physical inventory.

● STATEMENT PRESENTATION

INTRODUCTION

To the extent that they are current, inventories are carried in current assets, usually following accounts receivable. As discussed in the section on accounting principles, "current" refers to a period of one year or the normal inventory turnover period, whichever is longer. Therefore, inventories long in process (for example, leaf tobacco or bulk whiskey being aged) are included among current assets. Further, trade practice occasionally permits classification of certain products that may not actually be held for sale as inventories among current assets (for example, motion pictures or television films leased to others).

Noncurrent inventories are relatively uncommon but are encountered occasionally. An example is inventory of spare parts and replacements carried to service machines sold or leased; when related to machines on lease the inventory is carried as part of the property, plant, and equipment account. It is usual practice to estimate a year's sales of parts and classify that amount as a current asset and the balance (at lower of cost or market) as a noncurrent asset.

DISCLOSURE OF COMPONENTS

Usual practice is to disclose the amounts of raw materials, supplies, work in process, and finished stock unless the amounts are insignificant. For financial statements filed with the Securities and Exchange Commission, Regulation S-X requires disclosure, if practicable, of the amounts of the inventory components.

If progress payments under long-term contracts have been deducted from inventories, the amount deducted should be disclosed, thus indicating the gross amount of inventory on hand.

Under SEC Accounting Series Release No. 164, material amounts of work in process under long-term contracts must be separately disclosed, together with pertinent information as to any costs included in inventory not applicable to firm sales orders, any costs associated with claims or other unresolved negotiations, and any costs in inventory in excess of those recognized by the unit-of-delivery method.

DISCLOSURE OF BASIS OF VALUATION

The basis of inventory valuation (usually "cost" or "lower of cost or market") should be described briefly in the balance sheet; further disclosure of unusual aspects is desirable. The method of determining cost (for example, average cost, first-in first-out, last-in first-out, etc.) should also be indicated. When any unusual elements are included in the cost, the amounts should be disclosed and described. Examples are general and administrative expense, where its inclusion may be permitted in certain circumstances, or deferred manufacturing or production costs [see SEC Regulation S-X, Rule 5-02(6)].

Some companies that follow the LIFO method of valuation would like to indicate the difference between LIFO and FIFO parenthetically or in a note to the balance sheet. In the authors' opinion, that disclosure would be helpful because it would enable a reader to recompute the gross profit effect on a FIFO basis. However, IRS regulations, which require LIFO accounting in published financial statements as a prerequisite to its use for tax purposes, limit the kinds of disclosure that the Service deems appropriate, and so the proper objective of full disclosure must be tempered in the light of those restrictions.

ALLOWANCES

If inventories are reduced to a generally accepted basis by allowances, deduction of the allowances is usually not disclosed, but it may be, depending not so much on the significance of the allowances as on their nature. For example, disclosure of an allowance under the base stock method would be appropriate, but a substantial allowance for reduction of a relatively large contract in process to estimated net realizable value would usually not be disclosed in the balance sheet (see below for possible income statement disclosures).

This practice is distinctly different from that followed for receivables, where allowances are usually disclosed.

DISCLOSURE OF LIENS AND ENCUMBRANCES

Borrowings accompanied by pledges or other encumbrances of inventory should be stated as liabilities and the amount of inventory pledged should be disclosed. Examples are bank loans and advances by factors, finance companies, or customers. Retention of protective title by lenders should be disclosed. Ordinarily, borrowings should not be shown as a deduction from inventories; however, partial payments received on inventories under contracts with the government and others should be deducted from inventories.

DISCLOSURE OF ADJUSTMENTS IN THE STATEMENT OF INCOME

The reduction of inventory carrying value and purchase commitments from cost to market values results in a charge to income. Generally a charge of that nature is typical of the customary business activities of an entity, and consequently its effect should be reflected in the determination of income before extraordinary items. However, if the charge is abnormal, it may be desirable to set it forth separately within the cost of goods sold section of the income statement or to disclose it in a note to the financial statements. Chapter 18 describes the requirement for disclosure of year-end adjustments which affect the comparability of fourth-quarter earnings with those of earlier quarters; inventory adjustments may be includable in that note even if not abnormal or material in other respects.

LACK OF CONSISTENCY OR COMPARABILITY

Consistency in the application of inventory methods is of great importance, particularly to the determination of income. APB Opinion No. 20 (*AICPA Prof. Stds.*, vol. 3, Sections 1051 to 1051B) states that a change from the LIFO method of inventory pricing to another method should be reported by restating the financial statements of prior periods. Other changes in inventory methods (except a change to LIFO) should be reported by reflecting the cumulative effect of retroactive application of the new accounting method to the beginning of the year in the income statement of the period of change. In the latter instance, certain pro forma data computed by applying the newly adopted accounting principle retroactively also should be shown on the face of the income statement for the immediately preceding period or for all prior periods presented. In any event, disclosure should be made in a note to the financial statements of a material change in principle or in the application of a principle during an accounting period. Disclosure should include a brief description of the change and the accounting for it, the reason for the change, and the effect on net income. That effect is usually indicated by stating that net income (or income before extraordinary items, if applicable) and per-share amounts have been increased or decreased by a stated amount.

12

The Property Segment

PROPERTY, PLANT, AND EQUIPMENT;
DEPRECIATION AND DEPLETION;
DEFERRED CHARGES AND INTANGIBLE ASSETS;
RELATED ACCOUNTS

INTRODUCTION

The longest of the major segments is the one in which property or other assets are acquired and used directly or indirectly to produce revenue (or avoid additional expenditures) over a considerable period of time. Every business has to have "property, plant, and equipment" or "fixed assets" (the two terms are interchangeable but the latter is declining in usage)—tangible property expected to be used for several years. Many businesses also incur expenditures that do not result in tangible property but nevertheless are expected to produce revenue or reduce costs in future years. The expenditures may be for specific transferable property rights, such as patents, trademarks, or franchises, which are commonly known generically as "intangible assets." Or the expenditure may not result in a transferable right, and the asset is then usually described as a "deferred charge." The excess of the purchase price paid (cost) for a business over its tangible and identifiable intangible assets (including deferred charges) is called "goodwill" and is treated as an unidentifiable intangible asset. Expenditures recorded as long-term assets of any of those types are said to be "capitalized" and they are generally referred to as "capital assets."

The accounting objective is to allocate the cost of an asset on a systematic basis among the periods benefited by having the asset. Most assets tend to lose value over time: some are used up, wear out, or grow obsolete; the transferable legal right to others expires. Property, plant, and equipment are not used up in the same way as materials and supplies, and depreciation is usually not visible—or if it is, assigning a dollar value to it is difficult. Some assets actually appreciate in value. Therefore, accounting generally does not attempt to reflect the actual economic pattern of expiration of value. Instead it simply aims to allocate the *net* cost of an asset (acquisition cost less estimated recoverable salvage) over the periods of use in a systematic and rational manner. The major exception is cost of natural resources in which the depletion is usually physically observable or determinable and cost allocation can be related to physical events. Land is not physically used up, nor does it normally decline in usefulness over time, and so it is not subject to depreciation or depletion.

The subject of this chapter is accounting for the acquisition and use of property (including intangibles and deferred charges) acquired to be used in enterprise activities over a period of time. The subject matter does not include: property acquired for resale, whether in the ordinary course of business or otherwise (Chapter 11); property held for investment (Chapter 14); or, by accounting convention, property having a short useful life, which is usually defined as less than a year.

Several difficult problems and long-standing issues related to the property segment remain unresolved. Many believe that traditional accounting for depreciation and depletion does not adequately reflect significant economic events, such as price level changes or appreciation of property values. There is recurrent confusion about depreciation as an exercise in cost allocation and depreciation as a source of funds. The propriety of deferring various kinds of costs and the period over which they should be amortized is under continuing scrutiny. Accounting for the cost of exploration and drilling in the oil and gas and other extractive industries is an unresolved issue at present. Each of those issues is far too complex to be discussed thoroughly in this book, which must confine itself to accounting and auditing practiced today.

• ACCOUNTING PRINCIPLES

Accounting principles for the property segment revolve around the four kinds of economic events to be recorded and accounted for:

Acquisition, including construction, creation, or discovery.
Use or expiration of value through consumption or passage of time. (Amortization, depreciation, and depletion.)
Events requiring or permitting adjustment of recorded amounts.
Disposition.

ACCOUNTING FOR ACQUISITION

Cost or Fair Value at Acquisition

The general rule, which prevails in the preponderance of transactions, is that assets acquired are recorded at acquisition cost—the amount of cash disbursed, the fair value of other assets given up, or the present value of liabilities incurred. If the asset acquired has no cost—for example, donated property or property acquired by issuing stock—its acquisition should be recorded at fair value. The cost of an asset received in exchange for another asset can be measured by the fair value of the asset received if the latter is more clearly determinable; similarly, the fair value of stock issued can be used to measure the fair value of an asset acquired in exchange if the former is more clearly determinable. Whether the amount recorded is at cost or at fair value, it is usually described as cost. [The foregoing is the gist of paragraph 67 of APB Opinion No. 16 (paragraph 1091.67 of *AICPA Prof. Stds.*, vol. 3).]

Although there are difficulties in determining the fair value of most kinds of property and it is often impossible to do so with precision, the fair value rule usually results in a reasonable and practicable valuation for accounting purposes. In general, using fair value is superior to recording an asset acquired at the carrying amount of the asset exchanged for it. The major exceptions to that general principle are specified in APB Opinion No. 29, *Accounting for Nonmonetary Transactions*, paragraphs 20 to 23 (*AICPA Prof. Stds.*, vol. 3, paragraphs 1041.20 to 1041.23): (a) if fair value is not determinable within reasonable limits and (b) if the asset received is essentially a substitute for the asset exchanged—for example, a swap of inventory to facilitate sales to customers other than the parties to the exchange or a swap of similar productive assets. Paragraphs 25 and 26 of the Opinion tell how to measure the fair value of a nonmonetary asset.

The propriety of adjusting property accounts to give effect to the impact of inflation has been the subject of much discussion over the years. It is not currently acceptable to deviate from cost or fair value at the date of acquisition as the basis for accounting for long-term assets, except in the very few specific circumstances described in the subsequent section headed "Events Requiring or Permitting Adjustment of Recorded Amounts."

What Is Cost?

Cost of long-term assets includes all expenditures necessary to make the property usable by the acquiring enterprise. Cost of acquisition or construction includes not only the contract or invoice price but also such costs as those of preliminary engineering studies and surveys, legal fees to establish title, installation costs, freight, and labor and materials used in construction or installation. Technically, cash discounts should reduce cost. However, if not material to the cost of the property or to related items in the income statement, cash discounts are sometimes ignored in accounting for long-term assets and are recorded as income.

Financing Cost

Funds Used During Construction. In the area of regulated public utilities, the addition to cost of plant under construction of a computed amount termed "allowance for funds used during construction" or "interest charged construction," which includes both interest on borrowed funds and a reasonable rate for other funds when so used, is a well-established accounting as well as regulatory rate-making policy. The "allowance" (or "interest") is intended to compensate the utility for funds invested in its construction program, on which it would otherwise not earn any return during the construction period, and the credit portion of the entry is presently shown as "other income" in the income statement. This practice is predicated upon recovery of the capitalized amounts through increased future rates, which include the resulting higher depreciation expense.

Some non-utility companies, for example, real estate and motels, have adopted the policy of capitalizing interest during the construction period; retail land sales companies capitalize interest on land inventory. More widespread use of this accounting method has been forbidden (except for utilities) by the SEC in ASR No. 163, one of the few instances in which it has dictated an accounting method. The FASB is studying this subject and, until further pronouncement, companies other than utilities and those employing the practice prior to the SEC's prohibition may not capitalize interest on construction.

Interest on Funds To Finance Purchase. The interest rate is usually explicitly stated and easily recognizable if funds are borrowed and then used to acquire assets in completely separate transactions. In contrast, if the seller offers extended payment terms, in effect lending all or part of the purchase price, the part of total contracted payments that represents interest may or may not be recognized easily. In some purchase contracts, the interest rate may be unstated or different from a realistic rate of interest.

The general principle is that interest on funds borrowed to purchase an asset is not part of the cost of the asset acquired. The cost of the asset should approximate the present value of the payments required. Interest should be recorded as an expense as it accrues. Amounts included in the face value of a note payable or installment contract payable in excess of the present value of the obligation at date of acquisition are interest, not part of the cost, and should be recorded as a discount on the debt.

Even if interest is not explicitly stated, an interest factor is always present in long-term borrowing and is often a part of the purchase negotiations. The present value of the obligation to pay should be computed using the interest rate that entered into the negotiations if it is known and is not unreasonably high or low; otherwise, the cost should be recorded at the regular purchase price of the asset, if determinable, or the current interest rate for similar borrowing should be used to compute the present value of the payments. The effect of interest on the price in purchase and sale transactions is the subject of APB Opinion No. 21, *Interest on Receivables and Payables (AICPA*

Prof.Stds., vol. 3, Sections 4111 and 4111A); accounting from the side of the seller is discussed in Chapter 9 of this book.

Overhead and Indirect Costs

It is permissible to capitalize overhead as a part of the cost of items constructed for an entity's own use, but determining the proper amount to be capitalized requires judgment. The overhead rate should not be higher than the normal overhead for the company's regular product, nor should it increase the cost of a project above the purchase cost from outsiders. Usual and preferable practice is to include in cost of a project only the overhead (some of which may be administrative) of departments directly involved in the construction and incremental overhead costs. Selling, general, and administrative expense is not generally capitalized.

Investment Credits and Capital Allowances

Many countries provide investment incentives to encourage spending for productive assets. The characteristics vary from country to country: in some countries the incentives are outright grants; in others they are deductions or credits that reduce income taxes otherwise payable. The investment incentive in the United States is the investment tax credit, which reduces taxes otherwise payable.

Two methods of accounting for the U. S. investment credit are permitted: "flow-through," which treats the credit as an immediate reduction of income tax expense, and "deferral," which defers and spreads the credit over the life of the property in proportion to depreciation. Although the latter is tantamount to a reduction of cost, the credit is separately recorded. These methods are more fully described in Chapter 13, "The Income Tax Segment."

The nature of investment incentives arising in foreign countries should be determined and the effect should be accounted for in a manner consistent with their substance. Outright grants are either recorded as additional paid-in capital or as a reduction of the cost of the asset.

Cost of Assets Acquired Together

If a purchase price or other cost applies to more than one asset, the cost must be allocated among the individual assets acquired to permit proper classification and accounting for depreciation or amortization. That kind of purchase is often called a "lump-sum purchase," a "basket purchase," or a "package acquisition," and the total purchase cost is allocated among the individual assets in the group on the basis of fair value. When the aggregate of the fair values differs from cost, the cost is allocated in proportion to the respective fair values, as shown in the following example:

| | Fair Value | | Allocated Cost | |
			Case I	Case II
Asset X	$24,000	(60%)	$18,000	$30,000
Asset Y	14,000	(35%)	10,500	17,500
Asset Z	2,000	(5%)	1,500	2,500
Total	$40,000	(100%)	$30,000	$50,000

However, the above principle is modified when the acquisition is, in effect, the purchase of a business or segment of a business and thus a business combination in which the element of goodwill may be found. Business combinations are the subject of APB Opinion No. 16 and are discussed in Chapter 17.

Cost of Property, Plant, and Equipment

The elements of cost of acquiring or adding to the major types of property, plant, and equipment are briefly noted in the following paragraphs.

Land and Land Rights

Land accounts should show the purchase cost of land owned in fee and of rights, interests, and privileges held in land owned by others. They should include all costs directly attributable to the acquisition of the property and to conditioning it for use.

Land costs should include:

Commissions paid to real estate and other agents.

Costs of examining, insuring, and registering title, including attorneys' fees and other expenditures for establishing clear title.

Costs of removing, relocating, or reconstructing property of others to acquire possession.

Expenditures for draining and filling, installing buried bulkheads, and clearing and grading.

Costs of improvements such as streets, sidewalks, and sewers, whether constructed directly by the owner or by public authorities who levy special assessments to defray costs. (These are sometimes recorded separately as land improvements and may be subject to depreciation.)

If assessments for betterments are paid in installments, the entire amount of the assessment should be recorded and the unpaid balance shown as a liability. Interest, if any, on deferred payments should be treated as an expense as incurred. Assessments for transitory services, such as lighting, sprinkling, street cleaning, snow removal, and protection of trees, should also be treated as expenses.

It is sometimes difficult to distinguish between components of building cost and components of land cost: the cost of excavation for a foundation, for example, or the cost of landscaping and grading. The distinction, which may vary from one building to another, should be whether the value of the component is more likely to expire at the end of the life of the building than to diminish over a different period, if at all.

Recovery of Cost. During the course of clearing land to make it useful for the purpose acquired, timber, loam, gravel, or other salable material may be recovered. Since the clearing costs are costs of the land, amounts realized from the sale of the materials should be used to reduce the cost of the land.

Allocation of Cost of Demolished Buildings. If land and buildings are purchased with the intent to demolish the buildings, the cost of the land after demolition includes the total original cost of land and buildings, plus cost of demolition of the buildings, less salvage. If, however, the decision to demolish is made after the purchase, a loss rather than an additional cost of land may be involved. Part of the total cost of the land and buildings would have been allocated to the buildings put into use at the time of acquisition and partially depreciated afterward. The loss to be recognized would be the sum of the entire cost of removal of the buildings, less salvage, and the original cost allocated to the buildings at time of purchase, less accumulated depreciation to the date of demolition.

Land Held for Development or Sale. If unimproved property is held for development or sale, taxes and other carrying costs may or may not be added to the cost of the property, depending on the circumstances. Expenditures such as taxes and interest on funds borrowed to purchase the property are generally treated as additional cost of the property until the property is ready to be marketed or placed into service. Other items of cost of the property include the costs of grading and paving streets and installing water and sewer lines. Related administrative and preliminary selling expenses—such as advertising, publicity, printing, and the preparation of maps—should be treated as expenses as incurred.

If the property is to be sold by lots, the total cost of the property should be allocated to the salable lots on some basis such as anticipated selling prices (relative value), so that gain or loss on each lot sold may be measured. If development of the property is delayed as part of a well-defined plan, and not because development would be unprofitable, reasonable amounts of carrying charges may be included as cost of the property. The AICPA Industry Accounting Guide entitled *Accounting for Retail Land Sales* indicates that "the carrying amount of capitalized costs should not exceed net realizable value." This Guide should be referred to for additional accounting considerations related to retail land sales. Land held for resale becomes equivalent to stock in trade or inventory.

Buildings

The cost of buildings should include not only the cost of the structure itself but also the costs of all permanent equipment and fixtures necessary for the intended use of the structure, such as boilers, furnaces, air conditioners, elevators, permanent floor covering, wiring, and lighting fixtures. Sometimes all are included in a single account; sometimes each major component is recorded in a separate asset account so that each can be depreciated over its own useful life.

Machinery and Equipment

Expenditures for the purchase or manufacture of machinery and equipment should be capitalized as its cost, together with all costs of installation. The latter includes transportation expenses borne by the purchaser, labor charges, cost of materials and supplies consumed, and other expenditures incurred in unloading and readying the equipment for operation. Since the installation may include a period of test operation, the cost of a machine properly includes costs incurred during an experimental period; any returns received from sale of production during the test period are reductions in cost. For example, proceeds from the sale of energy generated by an electric utility during a period when a new generator is being tested should be credited to the asset account.

Costs of large tools, such as lathes, looms, and motors, are usually capitalized as machinery and equipment. Costs of small tools which have a relatively small individual value, such as jigs, dies, hammers, saws, and shovels, should either be carried in a separate account under that classification or be excluded from long-term assets; in either case they should be accounted for as described under "Small Tools" below.

Purchases Involving Royalty Agreements. Machines are sometimes purchased under agreements that provide for royalties to be paid on units of production. Those royalty payments generally are not costs of acquisition and should be included in operating expenses. On the other hand, if royalties may be applied against the purchase price and the intent is to purchase the machines, they should be treated as payments of the amount due. At acquisition, the cost (purchase price) of the machines must be estimated by considering factors such as the price of similar machines and the contracted or expected total royalty payments that may be applied to the purchase price; the effect of a reasonable rate of interest should also be considered.

Transportation Equipment. Costs of airplanes, automobiles, motor trucks, trailers, and similar equipment with a useful life of more than one year should be capitalized. The initial cost of accessories such as tires and batteries is ordinarily capitalized, and later replacements treated as expenses. To facilitate allocation of depreciation to appropriate expense accounts, many companies classify transportation equipment according to function, such as production, sales, or administration.

Furniture, Fixtures, and Office Equipment. Almost every business has numerous assets, such as desks and desk equipment, chairs, tables, partitions, shelves, bookcases, carpets or other floor covering, and safes, which are often lumped together as furniture, fixtures, and office equipment. That classification also often includes some machinery such as computers, copying machines, and internal communications systems. Of course, more detailed classification can be used, including classification by function, to facilitate allocation of related depreciation expenses.

Leasehold Improvements

Various expenditures are usually necessary to put leased property into a condition satisfactory to a lessee. Leasehold improvements can range all the way from relatively minor costs of painting and partitioning leased office space to the cost of a department store, hotel, theater, or office building erected on leased land. Leasehold improvements should be distinguished from furniture, fixtures, and office equipment because their usefulness to the lessee ends with the termination of the related lease.

Small Tools

Many hand tools and other portable tools may last for years, or they may break or be worn out, lost, or stolen almost as soon as they are put to use. Therefore, accounting for them as property, plant, and equipment to be capitalized and depreciated is often considered too difficult or impracticable. Some companies take physical inventories of tools periodically and adjust the accounts accordingly. Others treat small tools as supplies inventory and record their costs as expenses when they are put into use, considering as assets only new tools that have not been placed in service. Others charge all tool costs to expense as incurred. Still others capitalize all tool costs and depreciate them over a short period, such as two or three years. All methods are sanctioned by long-standing practice; the first method of periodic physical inventories is most likely to reflect actual cost of tools consumed.

Returnable Containers

Returnable containers include reels, drums, barrels, kegs, boxes, cartons, bottles, siphons, and other types of containers that are necessary in many businesses to ship products. Customers are expected to return them, and to provide an incentive for their return, a deposit is usually required, which is often more than the cost of the container. If goods in a returnable container are sold for cash, the buyer's deposit is generally returned when the container is returned. If goods in a returnable container are sold on account, the customer's account is usually credited when the container is returned. If the container is not returned, the seller retains the deposit.

Sizable containers of substantial construction, such as shipping containers and reels for heavy wire or cable, usually have expected service lives of longer than a year and are capitalized as depreciable assets. They are frequently carried in two accounts, one for containers on hand and another for containers held by customers.

Smaller, more fragile, and less valuable containers, such as carboys, barrels, and bottles, are usually accounted for as supply inventories, which are described in Chapter 11, even though they may have service lives of more than a year.

Minor Items

A good accounting practice is to establish a policy setting a minimum price of units of property that are to be capitalized. Otherwise, the accounts may become cluttered with innumerable items of small value. The cost of accounting for many minor items over their service lives may easily exceed the original purchase price. The size of the minimum amount usually varies with the size of the business and properties in use.

Costs Prescribed for Public Utility Companies

The uniform systems of accounts prescribed for public utilities regulated by the Federal Power Commission, Federal Communications

Commission, and state regulatory commissions require "original cost" accounting for property, plant, and equipment. That is, if plant assets composing an existing operating unit or system are acquired by purchase, merger, or otherwise, the original cost (cost to the person first devoting it to public service) must be recorded as cost of plant, and related accumulated depreciation and amortization are recorded in appropriate allowance accounts. Amounts paid by utilities in arm's-length transactions in excess of the net recorded original cost of plant are recorded in "plant acquisition adjustment accounts" and disposed of as directed by the regulatory commissions. For example, the Federal Power Commission requires such debit amounts related to depreciable plant to be amortized over a period not longer than the estimated remaining life of the properties to which they relate. The classification of this amortization in the income statement is usually determined by the applicable regulatory commission.

Repairs Versus Replacements or Improvements

Repairs and maintenance of property, plant, and equipment are operating expenses and should not affect the recorded cost of those assets. In contrast, replacement of those assets should preferably be accounted for by removing from the accounts the cost and accumulated depreciation of the replaced item and recording the cost of the new item.

The line between repair and replacement is seldom clear-cut. Some expenditures modernize buildings or equipment but do not really affect future operations. Other expenditures replace a part of an asset and at the same time increase the rate of output, lower operating cost, or extend the useful life of the whole asset. Still other expenditures are for substantial overhauling and reconditioning of assets, which may not result in expanded capacity of a facility but may materially extend its useful life and assure its continued productivity. Accountants have sometimes given different names—such as repairs, improvements and betterments, and rehabilitations—to different types of expenditures to distinguish among the various possible accounting treatments, but misunderstandings may still result. The practical solution lies largely in expediency and consistency.

The distinction between cost of assets and cost of repairs and maintenance may be based on certain physical characteristics. For example, the uniform system of accounts for air carriers classifies certain spare parts as "rotables"—assets having a depreciable life—and others as "consumables." Another approach based on materiality and bookkeeping expediency is to adopt a policy that an expenditure of less than a specified amount—for example, $200—should be recorded as an expense while an expenditure in excess of that amount should be capitalized in an appropriate account. Either policy should be explicitly adopted, reduced to writing, and consistently followed.

Preferably, large expenditures that are expected to affect the productivity, efficiency, or useful life of a plant asset should be capitalized and depreciated, and the cost and accumulated depreciation of replaced assets or parts should be removed from the accounts. Maintaining additional detail in property records to achieve that result may be necessary and is usually worthwhile.

However, identifying the recorded cost of replaced assets or parts is often impossible for many kinds of plant assets. If so, the expenditure may in effect be "capitalized" by charging it to the accumulated allowance for depreciation. This practice implies two assumptions that are unlikely to be true: that the cost of the original asset and of the replacement are comparable, and that the original asset was nearly fully depreciated. Its use therefore is not recommended when there is any alternative, although it is preferable to capitalizing the replacement without any recognition of the retirement.

Property Acquired as a Contribution or Donation

Contributed or donated property should be appraised to determine its fair value at time of receipt and recorded in the accounts at the appraised amount.

Property Obtained Under Long-Term Lease Arrangements

Obtaining the use of property under a long-term lease has become an increasingly popular alternative to acquisition. Leases may vary in length from those on land or buildings for twenty-five to ninety-nine years or more to those on computers or automobiles for three to five years or less. Provisions may vary from those in which the lessee assumes all expenses and most obligations of ownership except, for example, payment of mortgage indebtedness on the property, to those in which the lessor pays maintenance, taxes, and the like and may even furnish computer software, gasoline, or other elements essential to operating the leased asset.

Most leases are accounted for by recording rent expense as it accrues each period and recognizing prepaid or accrued rent, if necessary, as described in Chapter 10, but some leases are accounted for as substantially equivalent to installment purchases of the leased property. The cost of the property and the related liability are recorded at the present value of future payments under the lease. Rental payments during the term of the lease are accounted for as part interest and part payment of the liability; the cost of the asset (the capitalized value of the lease) is depreciated over the estimated useful life of the property.

The circumstances in which a lease is accounted for as in substance an installment purchase of the property are described in paragraphs 5351.09 through .12 of *AICPA Prof. Stds.,* vol. 3 (originally issued as APB Opinion No. 5, *Reporting of Leases in Financial Statements of Lessee,* in 1964). Paragraph 5351.09 is paraphrased in the preceding paragraph. Paragraphs 5351.10, .11, and .12 are difficult to paraphrase accurately and are quoted in their entirety:

.10 The property and the related obligation should be included as an asset and a liability in the balance sheet if the terms of the lease result in the creation of a material equity in the property. It is unlikely that such an equity can be created under a lease which either party may cancel unilaterally for reasons other than the occurrence of some remote contingency. The presence, in a noncancelable lease or in a lease cancelable only upon the occurrence of some remote contingency, of either of the two following conditions will usually establish that a lease should be considered to be in substance a purchase:

a. The initial term is materially less than the useful life of the property, and the lessee has the option to renew the lease for the remaining useful life of the property at substantially less than the fair rental value; or

b. The lessee has the right, during or at the expiration of the lease, to acquire the property at a price which at the inception of the lease appears to be substantially less than the probable fair value of the property at the time or times of permitted acquisition by the lessee.

In these cases, the fact that the rental payments usually run well ahead of any reasonable measure of the expiration of the service value of the property, coupled with the options which permit either a bargain purchase by the lessee or the renewal of the lease during the anticipated useful life at bargain rentals, constitutes convincing evidence that an equity in the property is being built up as rental payments are made and that the transaction is essentially equivalent to a purchase.

.11 The determination that lease payments result in the creation of an equity in the property obviously requires a careful evaluation of the facts and probabilities surrounding a given case. Unless it is clear that no material equity in the property will result from the lease, the existence, in connection with a noncancelable lease or a lease cancelable only upon the occurrence of some remote contingency, of one or more circumstances such as those shown below tend to indicate that the lease arrangement is in substance a purchase and should be accounted for as such.

a. The property was acquired by the lessor to meet the special needs of the lessee and will probably be usable only for that purpose and only by the lessee.

    b. The term of the lease corresponds substantially to the estimated useful life of the property, and the lessee is obligated to pay costs such as taxes, insurance, and maintenance, which are usually considered incidental to ownership.

    c. The lessee has guaranteed the obligations of the lessor with respect to the property leased.

    d. The lessee has treated the lease as a purchase for tax purposes.

.12 In cases in which the lessee and the lessor are related, leases should often be treated as purchases even though they do not meet the criteria set forth in paragraphs .10 and .11, i.e., even though no direct equity is being built up by the lessee. In these cases, a lease should be recorded as a purchase if a primary purpose of ownership of the property by the lessor is to lease it to the lessee and (1) the lease payments are pledged to secure the debts of the lessor or (2) the lessee is able, directly or indirectly, to control or influence significantly the actions of the lessor with respect to the lease. The following illustrate situations in which these conditions are frequently present:

    a. The lessor is an unconsolidated subsidiary of the lessee, or the lessee and the lessor are subsidiaries of the same parent and either is unconsolidated.

    b. The lessee and the lessor have common officers, directors, or shareholders to a significant degree.

    c. The lessor has been created, directly or indirectly, by the lessee and is substantially dependent on the lessee for its operations.

    d. The lessee (or its parent) has the right, through options or otherwise, to acquire control of the lessor.

Paragraph 5351.10 is the key provision. Paragraph 5351.11 is interpreted to apply only if the application of paragraph 5351.10 is unclear, and paragraph 5351.12 applies only if lessee and lessor are related.

In practice, the tests set forth in paragraph 5351.10 have been interpreted narrowly rather than broadly. No "material equity" is deemed to be created as long as the price of purchase options or the anticipated present value of renewal options is not less than cost of the property less depreciation expected to be accumulated up to the date of the options. Many long-term leases are carefully written to meet that test.

APB Opinion No. 5 has by no means settled the issue of recording leases as equivalent to installment purchases of property. Critics of the Opinion argue that several kinds of provisions in leases besides those that result in a material equity in the property by the lessee give leases the substance of purchases. They would conform accounting by lessees more closely to accounting by lessors by applying to lessee accounting criteria such as those in APB Opinions No. 7 and 27 (*AICPA Prof. Stds.*, vol. 3, Sections 4051 and 4052, respectively), which are discussed in Chapter 9. Leases would then be capitalized if, for example, the property is leased for substantially all of its useful life or if the lessee in substance pays the normal selling price of the property through the rentals under the lease. Both lessees and lessors have vigorously resisted extending Opinion No. 5 to require increased capitalization of leases, arguing that lessors' accounting does not necessarily govern lessees' accounting and that leases are executory contracts, the rights and obligations under which should not be recorded as assets and liabilities without considering whether rights and obligations arising from other executory contracts should also be recorded as assets and liabilities.

The Accounting Principles Board was unable to settle the issues involved and therefore referred the matter without prejudice to the Financial Accounting Standards Board. Until the FASB promulgates accounting policy in this area, APB Opinion No. 5 is the authoritative pronouncement on accounting for leases by lessees. The paragraphs on disclosure (16, 17, and 18) in that Opinion were superseded in 1973 by APB Opinion No. 31, *Disclosure of Lease Commitments by Lessees* (*AICPA Prof. Stds.*, vol. 3, Section 5352). Accounting Series Release No. 147, issued by the Securities and Exchange Commission, is also pertinent for items of required disclosure (see Chapter 16).

Property Costs in Extractive Industries

An extractive industry is one that "produces" by taking a material from an exhaustible deposit. The material may be sold in the form in which it is found or may be processed into another product. Extracting the material depletes the deposit, and "depletion" expense accounts for the cost of the part of the deposit extracted.

A deposit of natural resources is a major asset of an extractive concern, and depletion is often a major element in the cost of goods sold. Since a deposit must be found and developed before production can begin, certain pre-production activities and costs are much more significant in extractive than in manufacturing concerns:

Prospecting is exploration of a general nature intended to identify promising areas and properties for more particular exploration. Costs include salaries, equipment, and supplies for prospecting crews; rights of access to land to make geological and geophysical tests; and options to acquire rights to promising property.

Acquiring rights to explore and recover natural resources involves purchasing or leasing land and mineral rights or mineral rights alone. Costs include purchase price or bonus on signing a lease, various legal and title fees, brokers' commissions, and sometimes advance royalties.

Retaining leased rights to minerals usually requires specified performance or additional payments often called "delay rentals." Other "carrying costs" between acquisition of rights and beginning of production include taxes, legal fees, and minimum royalties.

Exploring to determine whether a promising area has deposits of commercial value involves some of the same methods as prospecting and therefore also involves some of the same kinds of costs. Ascertaining the content and size of a deposit requires obtaining physical access to it, often at several points, and involves the costs of activities such as drilling wells or cores, tunnelling, and removing overburden.

Developing a deposit for commercial production requires installing means of producing, handling, and storing or shipping the product or material in the deposit. It involves additional physical access to the deposit—more wells, tunnels and shafts, or overburden removal—as well as cleaning or processing equipment, roads, and perhaps supporting facilities such as repair shops and housing and food services for workers.

The various activities tend to overlap and intertwine, and some are more important than others, depending on the nature of the deposit and the extractive activities. For example, prospecting is often difficult to distinguish from exploring, and development usually continues after production starts. Discovery activities such as prospecting and exploring are relatively unimportant for resources in abundant supply, such as coal or sand and gravel, but are crucial for oil and gas and many metals. Development required before production begins is sometimes minimal if the deposit is easily accessible, as is most sand and gravel and some coal and metals, but is usually extensive for oil, gas, and mining, which require shafts and tunnels.

Accounting for pre-production costs by companies in the extractive industries is characterized by numerous exceptions and differences caused by variations in circumstances, traditional industry practices, and the like. Nevertheless, some broad observations are possible. Costs that are generally accounted for as expenses as incurred include prospecting costs other than some that are clearly related to property rights acquired, carrying costs and delay rentals, costs of unsuccessful exploration, and costs of unsuccessful development such as dry wells. Costs that are generally capitalized as costs of a deposit include some prospecting costs directly identifiable with acquired rights (especially if paid to an outside contractor), costs of acquiring mineral rights, costs of successful exploration, and costs of successful development. Some costs that are capitalized as incurred are later amortized before production begins or are written off as the related property rights are abandoned or the effort is otherwise deemed unsuccessful. Sales of products or materials produced during exploratory or developmental stages before commercial production begins are deducted from the capitalized cost.

Some major exceptions to those general practices are noted in the following subsections of this chapter and in Chapter 13. Accounting Research Study No. 11 (Robert E. Field, *Financial Reporting in the Extractive Industries*), Chapters 2 and 7, describes in more detail existing accounting practices in various extractive industries and discusses the impact of federal income taxes. The study also contains references to detailed descriptions of practices in specific industries.

Mines

The nature of mining operations is such that, once commercial production is achieved, production costs and development costs are often incurred together and may not be practically separable. As extraction proceeds, open pits become larger or shafts become deeper because working faces recede. More track, cars, and other equipment are needed to produce the same quantities of ore as at the beginning of production. Therefore, after production begins, development costs of mines are usually accounted for as expenses when incurred unless they significantly increase output or decrease cost of production. Mining companies that normally have insignificant prospecting and exploration costs often record them as expenses at the time of incurrence.

Stone, Sand, and Gravel

Companies producing stone, sand, and gravel rarely capitalize prospecting and exploration costs. In the first place, those costs are usually not significant. In the second place, they are often classified as marketing expenses: discovering suitable deposits near construction sites is essential to successful bidding on materials contracts because the relatively low value and heavy weight of the materials make transportation cost a vital factor.

Oil and Gas Rights

Leasing is by far the most prevalent means of acquiring rights to explore for, develop, or produce oil and gas, and oil and gas companies commonly use leases as the bases of cost capitalization. An undeveloped lease is recorded in the accounts at the sum of the bonus usually paid to the lessor on signing, the legal and other costs of obtaining the lease, and the cost of geological and geophysical work performed on the leased property. That total cost is amortized over the life of the lease unless production is achieved or the lease is relinquished earlier. At that time, the unamortized cost becomes part of the base for computing depletion for the productive wells or is written off if the lease is abandoned.

Costs of drilling and equipping successful wells are usually capitalized; those of unsuccessful wells are not. Most companies do not distinguish dry exploratory wells on unproved property from dry development wells on producing property even though at least some dry holes for development are necessary to define the characteristics of a deposit. A few companies do not capitalize so-called intangible drilling costs—such as labor and other costs having no salvage value—on successful wells; increasingly prevalent practice is to capitalize intangible drilling costs. Several companies capitalize all costs of discovering and developing oil and gas reserves, including the costs of dry holes. That method is called "full costing" and has been the subject of considerable controversy.

Full Costing Versus Successful Efforts

The vital difference between the "successful efforts" method, which is generally described in the preceding paragraphs, and the "full costing" method turns on the way pre-production costs are related to gas and oil reserves. The successful efforts method defines that relation narrowly and directly: only costs that directly result in the discovery and development of oil or gas reserves are costs of those reserves; since the largest part of pre-production expenditures does not result in reserves, those expenditures are deducted from revenue as incurred or as soon as they are known to be unproductive. Proponents of the method cite the high risk of failure involved in committing funds to the search for oil and gas and argue that losses should be recognized if costs are unproductive. They use leases and wells as the bases for accumulating costs, capitalizing costs of successful leases and wells, and writing off costs of unsuccessful ones.

In contrast, the full costing method defines the relation between pre-production costs and oil and gas reserves broadly and indirectly: all of those costs are necessary to find and develop the reserves that are discovered. Proponents of the method argue that a high risk of prospecting and exploratory failure is inherent in the search for oil and gas; unproductive efforts and dry wells are therefore an essential part of the discovery and development process, and their costs are essential costs of discovered reserves. They maintain that showing those costs as losses misrepresents the economics of the oil and gas industry.

Since the two methods produce entirely different accounting results, the Accounting Principles Board attempted to determine appropriate accounting in an effort to narrow the diversity of accounting practices in the extractive industries. The most important of the Board's tentative decisions was that an oil or gas field was the appropriate "cost center" for accumulating and amortizing costs. The field is significantly broader than the lease or well; for example, costs of dry development wells in proven fields are capitalized under that concept. However, the field is so much narrower than the company-wide or nationwide basis used in full costing that adopting the field as the "cost center" effectively rules out that method.

The Board's conclusion met substantial resistance; other efforts to reconcile these differences by the Board were also resisted. In the meantime and despite the Board's urging for a delay to allow it to try to settle the matter, the Federal Power Commission proposed and adopted an order applying the full costing method in its uniform system of accounts for Classes A, B, C, and D natural gas companies. The Accounting Principles Board ceased operations without issuing an Opinion on the subject, so the matter passed to the Financial Accounting Standards Board. The APB's Committee on Extractive Industries issued a booklet, *Accounting and Reporting Practices in the Oil and Gas Industry* (New York: AICPA, undated but issued in June 1973), describing the issues and the Board's attempts to resolve them.

Specialized Acquisition Arrangements

The oil and gas industry, and sometimes other extractive industries, are characterized by numerous specialized arrangements often dictated by desires to spread risks, obtain financing, or minimize income taxes. Those arrangements are often described in specialized terms such as working interest, overriding royalty, farm-out, carried interest, and ABC transaction.

Since those arrangements often involve acquisitions of interests in undeveloped or producing mineral properties, the acquisition cost to be recorded is frequently a question. Issues involved include whether only cash cost should be recorded or whether expected production costs required by the agreement should also be included, and whether costs of leases carry over as costs of retained interests if a portion of the rights under a lease is assigned. Readers should be aware of the existence of those arrangements, but in general they are too numerous, specialized, and complicated to describe in this brief section.

Costs of Timber and Timberlands

Cutting of timber depletes timberlands just as the extraction of mineral deposits depletes a mine or production of oil and gas depletes a reservoir or field. However, timberlands differ from mineral deposits and oil pools in that timber can be replaced, even though it takes time, and the trees grow both physically and in value during the replacement process.

The cost of timberlands includes the usual costs of acquiring property—purchase price, brokers' commissions, legal and title fees, and the like. It also includes development costs, such as access roads, and costs of removing diseased trees and thinning growth, less sales of timber cut during those activities. Once timber has been cut, costs of clearing and reseeding cut-over lands to insure second growth should be capitalized as cost of timberlands or standing timber and depleted when the new timber is cut.

The question of whether accounting should recognize accretion in value of timberlands from natural growth has been given considerable attention by accountants and others. If accretion were recorded, the carrying amount of timberlands would be increased each period, and the increase in value would be recognized as a specialized type of revenue. Depletion cost would be based on cost plus accretion rather than cost alone, as at present. Although there may be merit to recognizing accretion in the accounts, it is seldom, if ever, done in practice. (But see the section on depletion of standing timber, later in this chapter, for a description of the practice of taking accretion into account in computing depletion.)

Cost of Intangible Assets and Deferred Charges

Recording the acquisition of intangible assets is covered by paragraphs 5141.24 to .26 of *AICPA Prof. Stds.*, vol. 3 (originally issued as APB Opinion No. 17, *Intangible Assets*, in 1970):

Acquisition of Intangible Assets

.24 The Board concludes that a company should record as assets the costs of intangible assets acquired from other enterprises or individuals. Costs of developing, maintaining, or restoring intangible assets which are not specifically identifiable, have indeterminate lives, or are inherent in a continuing business and related to an enterprise as a whole—such as goodwill—should be deducted from income when incurred.

.25 *Cost of intangible assets.* Intangible assets acquired singly should be recorded at cost at date of acquisition. Cost is measured by the amount of cash disbursed, the fair value of other assets distributed, the present value of amounts to be paid for liabilities incurred, or the fair value of consideration received for stock issued as described in section 1091.67.

.26 Intangible assets acquired as part of a group of assets or as part of an acquired company should also be recorded at cost at date of acquisition. Cost is measured differently for specifically identifiable intangible assets and those lacking specific identification. The cost of identifiable intangible assets is an assigned part of the total cost of the group of assets or enterprise acquired, normally based on the fair values of the individual assets. The cost of unidentifiable intangible assets is measured by the difference between the cost of the group of assets or enterprise acquired and the sum of the assigned costs of individual tangible and identifiable intangible assets acquired less liabilities assumed. Cost should be assigned to all specifically identifiable intangible assets; cost of identifiable assets should not be included in goodwill. Principles and procedures of determining cost of assets acquired, including intangible assets, are discussed in detail in section 1091.66–.89.

Cost is generally determined as described at the beginning of this chapter.

Deferred charges are always recorded at cost at the time of the expenditure that gives rise to them. They are, by definition, costs carried forward to be matched with future revenue at an appropriate time, usually by amortization over time.

The elements of costs of acquiring or adding to the major types of intangible assets and deferred charges are briefly noted in the following paragraphs.

Patents

In the U. S., patents are granted for seventeen years. The costs of purchased patents are properly capitalized as assets, as are legal costs incurred in connection with internally developed patents. Legal costs of patents may include expenditures in connection with patent applications, litigation, or the licensing of patents. Other costs of internally developed patents are usually included in expense as they are incurred, particularly by businesses with research departments continually experimenting with new developments.

Legal and other expenses of patent application or interference suits may be deferred until a settlement has been made. If a patent applicant is successful in an interference proceeding in the Patent Office, the expenses of the proceeding should be considered as patent application cost. Expenditures for unsuccessfully defending or prosecuting patent infringement suits should be recognized as expenses when incurred or as soon as the outcome becomes apparent. If the defense or prosecution is successful, costs may be capitalized to the extent of the evident increase in the value of the patent. Costs of defending a suit that have been currently expensed over a relatively long period usually should not be retroactively adjusted because of a successful outcome.

Copyrights

Cost of copyrights may include expenditures for government fees and attorneys' fees and expenses. Many of the considerations that apply to patents apply also to copyrights. The term of a copyright is twenty-eight years in the U. S. and in certain circumstances it may be extended for another twenty-eight years.

Trademarks, Brands, and Trade Names

Trademarks, brands, and trade names should be recorded at cost, which includes attorneys' fees, registration fees, and other expenditures definitely identifiable with their acquisition. The determination of what portion of advertising cost may be considered a cost of developing trademarks and trade names, and consequently a capital expenditure, is generally so difficult that those items should be treated as current expenses. Some companies have capitalized advertising expenditures only to find on cessation or reduction of their advertising that the drawing power of a trademark or trade name has to be constantly nourished. They had in fact been capitalizing maintenance. It may be acceptable to capitalize unusual advertising and marketing costs that are clearly identifiable with the introduction of a new product or brand, but the period of amortization should be short, usually not longer than a year or a selling season.

Under federal statute, trademarks and trade names may be registered for a period of twenty years and then renewed indefinitely for additional like periods. They may also be registered under the laws of most states, some of which have no time limit on the effectiveness of the registration. However, there is a significant distinction between patents and copyrights on the one hand and trademarks and trade names on the other. The right to a patent or copyright arises from registration under a statute; the right to a trademark or trade name is a common-law right based on use. It is customary, therefore, to consider trademarks and trade names as being of value only so long as they are used. Usually they are carried at cost less accumulated amortization, but sometimes they are carried at nominal amounts.

Royalty and License Contracts and Franchises

Royalty and license contracts granted under patents and copyrights are not usually recognized formally in the accounts of the person to whom the rights are granted. Fees of attorneys for drafting the contracts may be capitalized, but in practice minor amounts are charged to expense. If an assignment of royalty and license agreements is obtained for a consideration, the cost of obtaining the assignment may be capitalized.

Franchises that are purchased should be recorded at cost, including legal fees and similar costs. Since losses are expected in the initial stages of many franchised operations and the success of the venture may remain in doubt for some time, careful analysis of all relevant factors is needed to determine whether the cost of a franchise should be recorded as an asset or an expense.

Covenants Not To Compete

Contracts for the purchase of a business sometimes contain provisions or covenants binding the seller not to engage in a competing business for a specified period. If the contract indicates that a definite portion of the purchase price has been paid for that type of agreement, the purchaser should normally record that amount as an intangible asset, appropriately described, and amortize its cost over the term specified in the contract. If a contract of purchase contains a no-competition clause but does not indicate a specific amount of consideration for it, the purchaser should allocate a reasonable part of the purchase price as payment for the covenant not to compete, which should then be recorded at cost as a separate asset to be amortized over the specified term.

Research and Development Costs

The practice of deferring research and development expenses became quite common in the 1950's and 1960's, especially among companies that were new, rapidly growing, technologically based, and investing heavily in research and development. Often the costs in an entire research and development budget were deferred and amortized over some arbitrary period, such as five years. Gradually, standards of sound practice tightened, requiring that deferred research and development costs be subjected to the same sort of tests for net realizable value as other assets—that is, deferred costs should not exceed net realizable value or recoverable cost of the asset. In October 1974 the FASB issued Statement No. 2, *Accounting for Research and Development Costs* (*AICPA Prof. Stds.*, vol. 3, Section 4211), which directs that all research and development costs be charged to expense as incurred, with one exception.

Some utility regulatory commissions permit or require deferral and amortization of significant nonrecurring research and development expenditures; where significant in the rate-making process, they presumably will continue to do so, with adequate disclosure, in accordance with Addendum to APB Opinion No. 2 (see Chapter 13) and as permitted by FASB Statement No. 2.

Statement No. 2 defines research and development as follows:

> Research is planned search or critical investigation aimed at discovery of new knowledge with the hope that such knowledge will be useful in developing a new product or service or a new process or technique or in bringing about a significant improvement to an existing product or process.

> Development is the translation of research findings or other knowledge into a plan or design for a new product or process or for a significant improvement to an existing product or process whether intended for sale or use. It includes the conceptual formulation, design, and testing of product alternatives; construction of prototypes; and operation of pilot plants. It does not include routine or periodic alterations to existing products, production lines, manufacturing processes, and other on-going operations, even though those alterations may represent improvements, and it does not include market research or market testing activities.

Deferred Start-Up Costs

Another practice that has become increasingly questionable after having been prevalent in former years is the deferral of various kinds of start-up and set-up costs. The theory was that the cost of starting up an operation or "setting up" to produce a product was as much an unexpired cost to be allocated to the period of use as the cost of the machinery and other property associated with the operation or product. The absence of objective criteria for its application has served to discredit it. Some companies went so far as to defer all losses on the grounds that they were in substance start-up costs or to defer cost overruns on contracts on the grounds that they were an investment in learning how to perform subsequent contracts more profitably.

Now those types of extreme practices are generally not acceptable and a deferral is to be considered clearly not in accordance with generally accepted accounting principles in the absence of a positive basis for believing that the costs are recoverable from future revenue. Examples of acceptable deferrals are costs incurred by an established company entering an established market, such as pre-opening costs of a new store incurred by an established chain of retail stores, and pre-operating costs incurred by a scheduled airline in readying ground-support and flight crews for a new type of aircraft. Pre-opening or pre-operating costs that may be deferred comprise those identified and documented as directly related to the specific event. FASB Statement No. 7, *Accounting and Reporting by Development Stage Enterprises (AICPA Prof. Stds.*, vol 3, Section 2062), articulated and confirmed the above outlined principles.

Deferred Moving and Relocation Costs

The cost of moving a company's operations from one location to another may significantly affect the income of the year in which the move is made. Since the move presumably benefits the company for several years, some companies defer the cost and amortize it over some short period, such as three years.

Goodwill

Only purchased goodwill is recognized in the accounts and is recorded at cost. Goodwill is most commonly recorded in business combinations accounted for by the purchase method. The APB has specified how goodwill is to be measured and in doing so has given it a definition as well:

> First, all identifiable assets acquired, either individually or by type, and liabilities assumed in a business combination, whether or not shown in the financial statements of the acquired company, should be assigned a portion of the cost of the acquired company, normally equal to their fair values at date of acquisition.
>
> Second, the excess of the cost of the acquired company over the sum of the amounts assigned to identifiable assets acquired less liabilities assumed should be recorded as goodwill. [APB Opinion No. 16 *(AICPA Prof. Stds.*, vol. 3, paragraph 1091.87)]

Goodwill is thus in essence another name for unidentifiable intangible assets. Intangibles that can be identified and assigned a fair value or cost do not belong in goodwill.

The paragraph also deals with the opposite situation, an excess of identifiable assets acquired less liabilities assumed over the cost of the acquired company:

> . . . the values otherwise assignable to noncurrent assets acquired (except long-term investments in marketable securities) should be reduced by a proportionate part of the excess to determine the assigned values. A deferred credit for an excess of assigned value of identifiable assets over cost of an acquired company (sometimes called "negative goodwill") should not be recorded unless those assets are reduced to zero value. [Paragraph 1091.87]

Section 5141 of *AICPA Prof. Stds.*, vol. 3 (APB Opinion No. 17, quoted earlier under the caption "Cost of Intangible Assets and Deferred Charges") specifically prohibits recording goodwill by capitalizing "costs of developing, maintaining, or restoring intangible assets which are not specifically identifiable, have indeterminate lives, or are inherent in a continuing business and related to an enterprise as a whole . . . ."

Cash Surrender Value of Life Insurance

Cash surrender value of life insurance should be stated at amounts determined by computation from tables in insurance policies. The computation usually involves discounting at the prescribed policy loan interest rate the cash surrender value shown for the end of the current policy year back to the statement date. The total cash surrender value should include accrued dividends from mutual insurance companies and additional cash surrender value acquired by applying dividends left on deposit with the insurer.

In most forms of life insurance other than term or group insurance, a substantial portion of each annual premium payment after a specified period is immediately reflected in increased cash surrender value. That portion of the premium not added to cash surrender value may be included in insurance expense or prepaid insurance and amortized over a suitable period. Care should be taken that amounts shown as prepaid insurance do not duplicate amounts included as cash surrender value.

Contingent Assets

Contingent assets ("gain contingencies" in FASB Statement No. 5) are potential assets whose realization and value are uncertain and the resolution of the uncertainty depends on future events. Many business concerns have claims in dispute that are considered collectible at least in part, such as those for tax refunds, upward price redeterminations, patent infringements, reimbursements under condemnation proceedings, and unfulfilled contracts. Probably the most frequently encountered contingent asset is a tax loss carryforward, which is contingent because realization depends on the uncertain future generation of sufficient taxable income.

Contingent assets may also arise if contingent liabilities become actual liabilities. For example, a guarantor who is required to pay because of a default by a primary obligor obtains a right of action against the primary obligor, although it may be of doubtful value.

Contingent assets are not recorded in balance sheets because "to do so might be to recognize revenue prior to its realization" [FASB Statement No. 5 (*AICPA Prof. Stds.*, vol. 3, paragraph 4311.17(a))]. However, they must be considered because if significant they should be disclosed in financial statements, usually in a note.

ACCOUNTING FOR USE: DEPRECIATION, MAINTENANCE, DEPLETION, AMORTIZATION

Depreciation

The Committee on Terminology of the AICPA defined depreciation for accounting purposes as follows:

> *Depreciation accounting* is a system of accounting which aims to distribute the cost or other basic value of tangible capital assets, less salvage (if any), over the estimated useful life of the unit (which may be a group of assets) in a systematic and rational manner. It is a process of allocation, not of valuation. *Depreciation for the year* is the portion of the total charge under such a system that is allocated to the year. Although the allocation may properly take into account occurrences during the year, it is not intended to be a measurement of the effect of all such occurrences. [Accounting Terminology Bulletin No. 1, paragraph 56]

The important points of the conventional definition of depreciation are:

Depreciation accounting is allocation of cost, not valuation.

The cost to be allocated is net cost: acquisition cost less anticipated recovery on disposition (salvage value or residual value).

The period of allocation is the estimated useful life to the enterprise.

The method of allocation must be "systematic and rational."

Thus, the accounting principles for depreciation rest on one fact (acquisition cost), two estimates (salvage value and useful life), and a judgment (selection of a systematic and rational method). Acquisition cost has been discussed above; the other subjects and their accounting implications are discussed in the following paragraphs.

Salvage Value

Most assets involve some recovery at the end of their service lives: scrap value at the very least, the secondhand market, or some reusable parts. Some cost may also be associated with dismantling, removing, or selling assets. The amount of recovery and related cost is virtually impossible to predict accurately, but a best effort to estimate it is unavoidable. The effort is necessary, first, to permit adequate evaluation of the wisdom of the acquisition, and second, for proper accountability.

In view of the inherent difficulties in estimating salvage value, most managements resort to general guides which are often formally adopted as accounting policies. For example, one possible policy is to ignore salvage value for the sake of conservatism in depreciation accounting; alternatively, salvage value may be assumed to average 10% or 15% or may be based on average experience over past years. The whole subject of depreciation accounting is so based on judgment and estimates and so likely to be altered by future events that general guides, rationally and responsibly used, usually serve adequately. They should, of course, be re-examined from time to time to make sure they continue to reflect a reasonable approximation of the likely course of events.

Estimates of salvage value should be based on conditions current at the time of acquisition: current price levels, current resale markets, etc. There is a tendency, especially in real estate, to assume constantly rising values; however, relying on such expectations for accounting purposes is presently not acceptable.

Useful Life

The useful life of depreciable assets is based on their usefulness to the company and thus is distinguished from inherent life or physical life. An asset may have a long inherent life, but expected obsolescence or other factors may limit its economic usefulness to the company. For example, a computer may be useful to an insurance company for about five to eight years, after which a larger, faster computer will foreseeably be needed and available. However, it may give satisfactory service in other industries for many more years. The useful life to the insurance company is five to eight years regardless of the experience of others.

Estimating Useful Life. Useful life, like salvage value, more often than not is impossible to predict with accuracy or certainty, and general guides are commonly used. They are heavily influenced by the service lives allowed by the Internal Revenue Service in computing income for tax purposes, the well-known "guideline lives."

Management has a responsibility for making estimates of useful lives that reflect as nearly as possible the economic circumstances of the particular enterprise. Neither accountants nor management should ignore conditions that make particular estimates possible or, more important, required because guideline lives are unrealistic. *For example:*

> If the life of an operation is clearly limited, the useful lives of the depreciable assets employed in it are similarly limited: a mine, oil well, or timberland may be worked out before the machinery employed would ordinarily be fully depreciated; a remote construction project

may be completed and require abandonment of much of the equipment; a new model that will make present equipment obsolete (a computer, an aircraft, even an office building) may be scheduled for delivery at a predictable date in the future.

Management's responsibility for accountability requires that actuarial estimates of useful lives be made if a company has assets that have been used over a period long enough to permit those estimates. The techniques are well developed and not difficult to apply, even without specialized expertise. For example, *Depreciation—Accounting, Taxes, and Business Decisions* by J. D. Coughlan and W. K. Strand (New York: The Ronald Press Company, 1969), Chapter 11, describes the techniques in terms intelligible to every accountant. Companies that lease or use a number of similar items—computers, vehicles, machines —can estimate useful lives actuarially. Estimates usually need not be made annually except when conditions are changing rapidly; every three to five years is usually often enough.

Companies subject to economic developments that can be expected to affect useful lives of their depreciable assets have a responsibility to evaluate those effects and to reflect them in depreciation policies. For instance, computer leasing companies were criticized a few years ago for failing to predict the effect of technological obsolescence on useful lives of computers. Regulations that are scheduled to take effect at a future date, such as environmental protection controls, may have similar effects on some depreciable assets.

Widely Varying Useful Lives. Actual useful life is known to vary widely for some kinds of items. Tools, dies, and molds may break the first time they are used or may last for many years. Machines on month-to-month lease may be returned in three months or stay in a lessee's factory for thirty years. Transportation equipment and some other kinds of depreciable assets are more subject to accidental destruction than other kinds of assets. There are two ways to account for that phenomenon: the "inventory method" and the "composite method."

The inventory method is commonly used to account for tools and spare parts. They are accounted for in the same way as an inventory of materials (Chapter 11), even though they may be classified as fixed assets. Tools issued or purchased during a year may be charged to expense, which is then adjusted periodically on the basis of a physical inventory of tools on hand.

The composite method, described in more detail on page 470, may be used for any group of assets, whether their useful lives are expected to vary or not. It consists of estimating the average useful life of the group, computing depreciation on that basis, and charging the acquisition cost of items taken out of service to the accumulated allowance for depreciation. The feature of the method that makes it useful for assets with varying useful lives is that as long as the estimated average life is reasonably accurate, items that remain in service for longer than their estimated useful life will offset those retired earlier.

Some companies capitalize the costs of tools and similar short-lived assets, depreciate them over some relatively short life such as three years, and write off the asset balance when fully depreciated. That is usually an acceptable practice for accounting purposes, considering the sums involved and the general imprecision of depreciation accounting. However, that method of accounting provides no cost or managerial information about tool usage, and it is therefore less desirable.

Leasehold Improvements. The useful life to the lessee of improvements to leased property can obviously never be longer than the life of the lease, unless the improvement can be removed and used elsewhere. Often it may be shorter: specialized equipment, such as air conditioning machinery, may have a useful life that is shorter than the term of the lease. The general rule therefore is that leasehold improvements are depreciated over the life of the lease (as more fully described below) or the life of the improvement, whichever is shorter.

The life of the lease is its original term without regard to options to renew, unless and until those options are actually exercised or it is obvious they will be exercised. Substantial expenditures made toward the close of a lease period may indicate that renewal is likely. When a lessee elects to exercise a renewal option, any unamortized portion of improvements should be distributed over the period between the date the option is exercised and the extended expiration date of the lease or over the remaining useful life of the improvements, whichever is shorter.

If a lease requires the restoration of the premises to their original condition, reasonable wear and tear excepted, the estimated expenses of restoration should be accrued ratably over the lease term.

Methods of Allocation

Two kinds of considerations arise in spreading the net cost of an asset over its useful life. One involves the method of allocating costs among accounting periods; the other involves how items are grouped to compute depreciation. There are five generally accepted methods of allocation: straight line, declining balance, sum of the years' digits, units of production or hours of service, and the seldom used annuity and sinking-fund methods. There are many variations of two basic methods of grouping items: the unit method and the composite method.

With some exceptions, each of the allocation methods may be applied to units or to composite groups.

Straight-Line Depreciation. Straight-line depreciation allocates an equal amount of the net cost of an asset to each accounting period in its useful life: for example, 10% of net cost a year for an asset with a ten-year useful life. The rate of straight-line depreciation is expressed either as a number of years—ten-year life—or an annual rate—10%. Straight-line depreciation is the simplest and most common method. Many companies that have tried other methods and changed back to straight-line depreciation appear to have concluded that the estimates and judgments needed for depreciation accounting are so broad and imprecise that nothing useful is gained from adopting more complicated methods.

Declining-Balance Depreciation. It is often argued that the value received from use of a productive asset is greater in the early years and less toward the end of its useful life, that cost of repairs and maintenance is higher in later years, and that risk of obsolescence increases rapidly after the first year or two of use. For all those reasons, many authorities believe that a depreciation method that allocates more cost to early years than to later years is more realistic than the straight-line method. The so-called declining-balance method is the most popular means of achieving that result.

Annual depreciation is computed by applying a constant rate to the declining undepreciated balance of cost—acquisition cost less accumulated depreciation. A rate of slightly more than double the straight-line rate is required to spread the same cost over the same period. Since the formula for computing the exact rate is complicated and double the straight-line rate is the maximum rate permitted for federal income tax purposes, that is the rate ordinarily employed in practice. Hence, the method is usually called "double declining balance."

The double declining-balance method results in an undepreciated "tail" of cost toward the end of the useful life, which can be roughly related to salvage value. Therefore, users of the declining-balance method often make no allowance for salvage value in the computation of depreciation.

Sum-of-the-Years'-Digits Depreciation. Depreciation computed by the sum-of-the-years'-digits method is similar to that produced by the declining-balance method in that it results in a greater proportion of depreciation during the earlier years than in the later years of useful life. The method differs from the declining-balance method in that it accumulates 100% of the amount being depreciated by the end of the estimated life. Therefore, the cost should be reduced by an estimated amount for salvage value before computing depreciation.

The sum-of-the-years'-digits method is applied as follows: depreciation is computed as a fraction of the net asset cost in which the numerator for each year is the remaining estimated life of the asset in that year and the denominator is an amount obtained by adding the years of estimated life numbered successively from one through the last year of expected life—hence, sum of the years' digits.

For example, if an asset has an estimated useful life of ten years, the sum of the years from 1 to 10 is 55, determined either by adding $1 + 2 + 3 + 4 + \ldots + 10$ or by the formula

$$n \frac{(n + 1)}{2}$$

in which n equals the estimated useful life. The respective annual depreciation rates are 10/55 for the first year, 9/55 for the second year, and so on to the tenth year when the rate is 1/55. Using the half-year averaging convention discussed later in this chapter, the respective annual depreciation rates are 5.0/55 for the year of acquisition, 9.5/55 for the following year, 8.5/55, and so on to the tenth year after year of acquisition when the rate is 0.5/55.

Comparison of Results of the Above Methods

The schedule below compares annual and cumulative depreciation for a single asset under straight-line, declining-balance, and sum-of-the-years'-digits methods, assuming an asset cost of $100, a 10-year useful life, and salvage value of $10 at the end of the useful life. For simplicity, a full year's depreciation is recorded for the first year.

Year	Straight-Line Method (Rate = 10%) Annual	Accumulated	Declining-Balance Method (Rate = 20%) Annual	Accumulated	Sum-of-the-Years'-Digits Method Annual	Accumulated
1	$9.00	$ 9.00	$20.00	$20.00	$16.36	$16.36
2	9.00	18.00	16.00	36.00	14.73	31.09
3	9.00	27.00	12.80	48.80	13.09	44.18
4	9.00	36.00	10.24	59.04	11.45	55.63
5	9.00	45.00	8.19	67.23	9.82	65.45
6	9.00	54.00	6.55	73.78	8.18	73.63
7	9.00	63.00	5.24	79.02	6.55	80.18
8	9.00	72.00	4.20	83.22	4.91	85.09
9	9.00	81.00	3.36	86.58	3.27	88.36
10	9.00	90.00	2.68	89.26	1.64	90.00

Other Allocation Methods

The three methods already discussed are by far the most prevalent methods of computing depreciation. Other methods that are considered acceptable for accounting purposes but that are less widely used include those based on output or activity and those involving interest and present values.

Units-of-Production or Hours-of-Service Depreciation. Because of a direct relationship between usage and physical wear, the useful lives of some kinds of assets can be estimated within reasonable limits in units of output or hours of service life. Technological or economic obsolescence is not anticipated within normal service life. Depreciation for a period is then computed as the ratio that the number of units produced or hours worked during the period bears to the estimated total number of units or hours in the estimated life. Output or activity methods are used in operations such as blast furnaces, coke plants, and the extractive industries. Some transportation equipment, such as heavy trucks, may be depreciated this way. Generally, not many classes of plant and equipment have useful lives that can be reasonably estimated in terms of units of production or hours of service: accordingly, the difficulties involved in computing depreciation usually preclude the use of those methods.

Annuity and Sinking-Fund Depreciation. Except for a few instances permitted by regulation, depreciation methods that use interest or present values are not acceptable. These methods are occasionally found in practice outside of the United States. The annuity method computes depreciation on the assumption that the net cost of an asset represents the present value of a stream of constant benefits from its use over its estimated useful life. The allowance for accumulated depreciation increases each period by an amount computed by deducting interest on the undepreciated cost of the asset from the level depreciation expense. The sinking-fund method is similar except that the depreciation expense is computed as the level amount that would need to be contributed to a sinking fund over the useful life of an asset to accumulate a replacement fund equal to cost less estimated scrap value; interest is computed on the hypothetical balance in the fund and is added to the depreciation expense to obtain the amount of increase in the accumulated allowance for depreciation. The sinking-fund method gives a different depreciation expense and interest amount than the annuity method, but the increase each year in the accumulated allowance for depreciation is the same under both methods. The annuity and sinking-fund methods result in increasing net depreciation expense because of the interest factor, a result that is just the opposite of that produced by the declining-balance and sum-of-the-years'-digits methods.

Depreciation of Additions and Retirements During a Year

In modern accounting systems, depreciation is often computed and recorded month by month, usually starting with the month after an asset is placed in service. Practices are also still encountered that were prevalent in earlier days when the labor of computing depreciation manually was a significant factor: one-half the annual amount of depreciation may be taken in the year of acquisition and one-half in the year of retirement, or depreciation charges may begin with the first of the year following the year of acquisition.

Grouping Assets To Compute Depreciation

Depreciation can be computed for each individual item of property or for groups of assets. The result is, of course, affected by the way assets are grouped, but depreciation by its very nature is so much a matter of estimate and judgment that the differing effects of grouping and averaging are accepted as long as a method is consistently employed.

Unit Method. The most specific and detailed depreciation computations result from the unit method, in which each item or unit is accounted for separately. The salvage value and useful life of the unit are estimated, and a depreciation rate is determined, usually using the overall method of allocation adopted by the enterprise for the class of asset. When the unit is retired, the asset and related accumulated depreciation are closed out; the undepreciated cost is compared with any salvage or recovery value, and a gain or loss is recorded on the transaction.

"Units" may be variously defined under the unit method. An entire building may be considered a unit, or each of its components may be treated as a separate unit. Each machine on an assembly line or the entire line may be a unit. The larger the unit, the more nearly the unit method of grouping approaches its major alternative, the composite method.

Composite Method. The composite or group account method is predicated on the theory that a group of similar or related items has a reasonably determinable average useful life: the actual useful life of some items will fall short of the general average but will be offset by useful lives of other items extending beyond the average. The composite method works best if the assets are segregated into appropriate classified or functional groups determined by circumstances. That segregation facilitates the initial determination of average useful life and provides a basis for subsequent periodic evaluation of the reasonableness of the life selected. The composite rate should be redetermined whenever substantial changes occur in the "mix" of the composite group—that is, in the proportionate dollar amount of long- or short-lived items—or whenever the ratio of accumulated depreciation to cost shows a persistent rising or falling trend, thus signalling a possible change in average useful life.

In a normal retirement under the composite method, the cost of property retired is removed from the asset account and charged to the accumulated allowance for depreciation, and costs of removal, less salvage value, are also charged to the accumulated depreciation account. As a result, the remaining undepreciated costs of assets retired before the average life are spread over periods beyond the average.

If assets in a composite group are retired because of casualty or "extraordinary obsolescence," a resulting loss should be reflected in income. The allowance for depreciation should be charged only with an amount equal to estimated depreciation, including normal obsolescence, accrued to the time of retirement, and the undepreciated balance of the cost, less salvage, should be recorded as a current loss.

Other Methods of Grouping. As the defined size of "units" expands and the generic or functional groupings of composite accounts are defined more narrowly, the unit and composite methods overlap. Many variations and combinations in the application of the methods of grouping have been designed in an effort to facilitate computation or to enhance accountability and managerial information.

One common variant is the "lapse schedule," in which the total of each year's additions to major plant classifications is set up on a separate work sheet or subaccount and depreciated as a group. If lapse schedules are used as a variant of the unit method, they facilitate the computation of gain or loss on retirement. If they are employed as a variant of the composite method, they facilitate periodic ratio analysis to verify that estimated useful lives continue to be realistic.

Consistency in Application

Once a sound depreciation policy has been decided on, it should be applied consistently until conditions change to such a degree that its application no longer produces reasonable results. Unless depreciation accounting is consistently applied, comparisons of income statements for the affected periods may be useless, misleading, or both.

Maintaining a consistent policy does not necessarily imply or require that rates of depreciation must be inflexible. Circumstances may arise that make it desirable to accelerate or decelerate depreciation charges. For example, if production is abnormally heavy, wear and tear may be greater than was expected when the rates were established because of less opportunity to repair and maintain equipment; if cessation of demand is foreseen or new models threaten the ability of old equipment to compete, an effort should be made to absorb undepreciated cost during the remaining useful life of the assets. Conversely, actual experience as time passes may indicate that the original estimates of useful lives were too conservative, and useful lives may be considerably longer than originally anticipated. In those conditions, studies should be made to determine whether useful lives have actually shortened or lengthened and to what extent changes in lives should be reflected in revised rates for existing facilities and for future acquisitions of similar facilities.

APB Opinion No. 20, *Accounting Changes (AICPA Prof. Stds.,* vol. 3, Sections 1051 to 1051B), revised and clarified accounting for changes in depreciation, among other accounting changes. A change in estimated remaining life or estimated salvage value is a "change in accounting estimate" which should be accounted for prospectively, not retroactively, by adopting the newly computed depreciation rate to spread the undepreciated balance over the remaining useful life. On the other hand, a change in depreciation method is a "change in accounting principle." The retroactive effect of the change should be computed and shown as a separate item between the captions "extraordinary items" and "net income" in the income statement for the year of change; the effect of adopting the new method on income of the period of change should be disclosed. Paragraph 22 and an Appendix to the Opinion contain examples.

Different Methods for Different Purposes

A company may properly decide to use different methods of allocation or grouping for different categories of assets. Using different depreciation methods for tax and financial statement purposes is widespread practice because the opportunity to defer tax payments through use of so-called "accelerated" methods of depreciation is a compelling reason for adopting those methods for tax purposes. Accounting for the tax effect of book-tax differences in depreciation accounting is described in Chapter 13.

Depreciation Allowances

It is now expected that depreciation will be accumulated in separate "allowance" accounts (formerly known as "reserve" accounts) and not, as in the past, credited directly to reduce the asset account. Usually there are separate allowance accounts for each classification of asset, and sometimes for each unit.

Maintenance

The level of maintenance and repairs affects the useful life of plant assets where obsolescence is a minor factor. At one extreme is the policy proclaimed many years ago by private railroads in arguing against depreciation accounting: a high level of maintenance keeps properties in a state of constant renewal which precludes the need for depreciation charges. At the other extreme is the policy often adopted when a decision is made to phase out a class of equipment: the property is "run into the ground" by minimizing maintenance outlays. Neither extreme is economical in most cases, but the possible range within normal limits is so wide that maintenance policy should be specifically taken into account in estimating both useful life and salvage value.

Some maintenance consists of large, infrequent overhauls: meticulous periodic overhauls of aircraft, rewiring a building, overhauling a boiler, renewing air conditioning, and the like. Some maintenance expenditures can be deferred for a few years as a matter of deliberate management decision: repainting, reroofing, repointing masonry, and the like.

Some accountants believe that both kinds of maintenance costs are an expense of current operations and should be accrued on the basis of periodic estimates of the amount and timing of work to be done. Others do not believe that deferred maintenance need be accounted for, because the level of maintenance affects useful life and salvage value, and therefore is reflected in depreciation charges. FASB Statement No. 5 (*AICPA Prof. Stds.,* vol. 3, Section 4311) did not address the subject, and must be interpreted for indirect guidance. If an asset is impaired by deferring maintenance, there is a loss contingency that should be accrued, either by depreciation or by provision for deferred maintenance. On the other hand, there is no liability in the true sense of that word. The issue is unclear, and should be carefully considered by accountants and auditors faced with conditions of deferred maintenance; in the meantime, accrual of deferred maintenance is not required.

Depletion

Depletion is the expired cost of an investment in natural resources, accounted for by amortizing the cost through charges to expense over the period during which the resources are extracted. Depletion is both similar to and different from depreciation. Both allocate the cost of long-term assets to the periods in which they are used or consumed. Depletion is almost always based on units of production, while depreciation only rarely is. Depreciation is amortization of the cost of man-made production facilities; depletion is amortization of the cost of natural resources. Enterprises exploiting depletable assets generally employ both depreciable and depletable assets. If plant and equipment remain idle, depreciation not only continues, but may be accelerated. In contrast, cessation of operations does not ordinarily affect the units of natural resources since they remain to be extracted in the future. Similarly, obsolescence rarely affects natural resources.

Methods of Computing Depletion

Since depletion is in essence the cost of natural resources extracted, depletion accounting must be primarily related to output or extraction. Spreading the cost over time usually is not acceptable. Two methods of depletion are commonly discussed: the production method and the percentage method.

Production Method. The most widely used method of computing depletion for accounting purposes (as distinguished from tax purposes) allocates cost on the basis of resources produced during a period relative to those remaining. It is comparable to the units-of-production method of depreciation and is usually called the production method of depletion. The depletion rate may be determined in relation to proven mineral reserves (that is, those actually assured) or in relation to not only proven reserves but also probable and possible reserves.

Under the former procedure, the unit rate applied to extractions during a year is determined by dividing the unamortized cost of the asset at the beginning of the year by the units of proven reserves at the end of the year plus the units extracted during the year. If, as extraction proceeds, development continues to be successful, that method will result in higher depletion charges in the earlier years of extraction than in later years.

If probable or possible minerals are included in the depletion computations under the latter procedure, the depletion rate may remain unchanged for a number of years or until conditions indicate the necessity for a change. If estimates of probable or possible minerals prove to have been optimistic, depletion charges will have been inadequate; if estimates prove to have been conservative, depletion charges will have been overgenerous. Because of those uncertainties, depletion rates should not be based on probable or possible minerals unless competent geological or other evidence has indicated a high degree of probability that the reserves are there.

Depletion may be computed on the unit of metal, such as a pound of copper or an ounce of gold, or on the mining unit, such as a ton of ore. The unit of sale is usually not a ton of ore but rather a pound or an ounce of metal contained therein, and the percentage of metal contained in ores in different sections of a mine may vary widely. Therefore, depletion rates applied to units of metal appear to produce more equitable results. Since value is inherent only in the metal (or other salable product), the prices at which mining properties are bought and sold depend not on tons of ore but rather on quantities of metal. If depletion is determined on the basis of tons of ore, the charge will be the same for a ton of high-grade ore as for a ton of low-grade ore, and consequently income may be distorted.

Percentage Method. Under the percentage depletion provisions of the Internal Revenue Code and Regulations, depletion is computed on the basis of a fixed percentage of gross income from the property (5% to 23%, depending on the nature of the product extracted), limited in most cases to 50% of net income from the specific property involved computed before any depletion allowance. Percentage depletion is a tax method and is not generally acceptable for accounting purposes. The difference between such "statutory" depletion and cost depletion for accounting purposes is of the type characterized in APB Opinion No. 11 (*AICPA Prof Stds.*, vol. 3, Sections 4091 and 4091A) as a permanent difference, for which tax allocation is not appropriate. (See Chapter 13.) It is being phased out of the tax law covering oil and gas interests but remains in effect for other minerals.

Development Costs

Until commercial operations begin, development costs are ordinarily not subject to depletion but are included in a property account or recorded in a separate account. Some development costs may be amortized over lives of leases or other basis before production starts, but not as depletion. Deferred development costs are then usually amortized simultaneously with mineral costs.

A mine is usually considered to have passed from a development to a producing stage when the major portion of mineral production is obtained from workings other than those opened for the purpose of development or when the principal activity of the mine becomes the production of developed minerals rather than the development of additional minerals for mining.

The Internal Revenue Code provides that a taxpayer may elect either to deduct expenditures for the development of a mine or other natural deposits (other than an oil or gas well), whether incurred before or after the production stage is reached, in the year they are incurred or to defer the expenditures and deduct them ratably as the ore or mineral is sold. If development expenditures are deferred in the accounts and deducted currently for tax purposes, the resulting tax benefit should be deferred and amortized over the same period as the deferred development costs.

Accounting for Depletion

The accepted theoretical method of accounting for depletion is to base the charge on extraction and include it in production costs; thus, as in the case of depreciation, an appropriate amount of depletion is included in inventory costs. However, depletion based on units extracted is sometimes charged directly to income rather than to cost of production and consequently is not included in inventory amounts. That procedure results in charging income with depletion on quantities that may differ from quantities sold. Depletion is also frequently charged to income on the basis of units sold rather than units extracted, and the portion of property costs applicable to inventories remains in plant assets. Those two alternatives may be used only if the differences from the accepted method are immaterial.

Probable Reserves: Mining Properties

Available information about ore reserves varies from mine to mine. Many large mines are developed extensively before extractive operations begin. Development gives a much greater assurance about quantity and quality of the deposit than exploratory drilling and may be necessary to assure commercial content sufficient to justify extensive investments in mining and milling equipment, smelters, power plants, railroad lines, and other necessary facilities. In smaller properties, however, often no more than a few years' supply is developed in advance of extraction, particularly if the mining company sells unprocessed ore or a concentrate rather than a refined product and thus does not need to justify so large an investment. Since production exposes (that is, develops) additional ore much more economically than development without production, extensive development may not be economically justified.

Without extensive development, the true nature of a deposit often can only be a guess. Thus, the terms "proven," "probable," and "possible" are often used to give a broad indication of the total potential reserves of mining property. Changes in costs of recovery and refining, in selling prices of ores or refined products, and in the technology of recovering metals from ores all affect the quantity of commercial reserves in a property. Despite numerous difficulties in estimating reserves, the attempt should be made; estimated depletion costs are better than no depletion costs.

Probable Reserves: Oil and Gas Deposits

Usable estimates of probable reserves of oil or gas can be prepared by geologists, usually separately for each lease or property unit. Depletion should begin to be recorded when production is obtained, computed at rates per unit of production applied to unamortized development, exploration, and perhaps prospecting costs.

Costs of drilling and lifting equipment may be depreciated on a units-of-production basis or over its estimated useful life.

Probable Reserves: Standing Timber

Cutting of timber depletes timberlands just as the extraction of mineral deposits depletes a mine. A proportion of the cost of the timber should be written off each year based on the quantity of timber cut during the year relative to the quantity standing at the time of its purchase. Allowance for the value, if any, of land should be made in determining the amount of the charge for depletion.

Although accountants and others have talked about accounting recognition of accretion in value of timberlands resulting from natural growth, it is seldom recorded in practice; thus, timber depletion is based on cost. However, it is not uncommon to take accretion into account in computing depletion charges, by estimating the "total yield" of a tract and spreading cost over the total estimated yield, which includes timber to be grown over the cutting period as well as that standing at time of acquisition.

Sums spent to clear and reseed cut-over lands to insure continued yield should be capitalized and depleted.

Amortization

Amortization is the term conventionally applied to the allocation of the cost of intangible assets and deferred charges to the periods during which they are useful. It is the same, both in concept and in methodology, as depreciation and depletion; technically speaking, "depreciation" and "depletion" are distinct types of the general category "amortization."

Sometimes amortization of intangible assets and deferred charges is accumulated in separate allowance accounts; more often it is credited directly against the cost of the asset.

Methods of Amortization

So-called "accelerated" methods of amortization are rare, although conceptually they are as acceptable as in depreciation accounting. Usually, intangible assets and deferred charges are amortized by the straight-line method or the units-of-production method.

Useful Lives

Depending on their nature, most deferred charges are amortized over rather short periods, such as three to five years.

The cost of internally developed patents may be distributed pro rata over their seventeen-year term or over the period between the date of application and the date of expiration, unless it appears that the patent will have a shorter period of commercial value; then the cost should be distributed over the period of expected benefit. The cost of purchased patents should be amortized over remaining legal life; those having no commercial value should be written off immediately.

Since trademarks, brands, and trade names can usually be renewed indefinitely as long as they are used, they have no fixed term. However, they are generally considered as being of value only if they are used. Their cost should be amortized over a reasonable period, the basis for which is a matter of judgment.

Copyrights usually diminish in value irregularly, and amortization often should be based on periodic revaluations of individual copyrights rather than on their statutory twenty-eight-year life.

Royalty and license contracts capitalized should be amortized over

the life of the agreement or over the expected period of utility, whichever is shorter.

Franchises should be amortized over the period of their duration
and charged off when they have demonstrably become worthless.

The Accounting Principles Board concluded in Opinion No. 17
(*AICPA Prof. Stds.*, vol. 3, paragraphs 5141.27 to .29) that all intangible assets have finite lives and their costs should be amortized.
If the useful life appears indeterminate, as the useful life of goodwill
often does, the maximum period of amortization should be forty years,
unless the intangible assets were acquired prior to November 1, 1970,
in which case amortization is not required until diminution of value
occurs. Irrespective of the amortization policy, if a material decline in
value appears to have occurred, write-down of the unamortized cost
is proper.

In accordance with FASB Statement No. 2 (*AICPA Prof. Stds.*, vol. 3,
Section 4211), "the costs of intangibles that are purchased from others
for use in research and development activities and that have alternative
future uses . . . shall be capitalized and amortized as intangible assets
in accordance with *APB Opinion No. 17*" (paragraph 4211.11).

EVENTS REQUIRING OR PERMITTING ADJUSTMENT
OF RECORDED AMOUNTS

The questions of whether and when it is appropriate to restate the
amounts at which property or other long-term assets are carried in the
accounts have been a recurring problem over the years. The values
of assets clearly do change, even disregarding the effect of changing
price levels, but when and how much they change is often impossible
to determine objectively. Accountants have not found a satisfactory
means to deal consistently with the entire problem of changing values.
Only three circumstances are presently recognized as appropriate bases
for restatement of property values: a purchase, an apparently permanent
decline in value, and a reorganization. Appraisals are sometimes recorded in the accounts even though doing so is not in accordance with
generally accepted accounting principles except in very limited circumstances.

Purchase

When property is purchased from an unrelated party, whether for
cash or in exchange for other property, the transaction is presumed to

give an objective measure of current value stemming from reconciliation of the conflicting interests of buyer and seller. A clearly defined exchange transaction has taken place which establishes a new "cost." Almost the whole of the chapter to this point has been concerned with recording and amortizing costs recognized in exchange transactions.

Decline in Value

A change in general business conditions or in the economics of the area in which property is located may make it impossible to recover the remaining cost of property either through revenue generated from its use or through its outright sale. Under the general accounting principle of anticipating losses, those conditions should be recognized when they occur. Usually, the conditions giving rise to the possibility are so prevalent as to be all too obvious: idle plant or excess capacity; a depressed or deteriorating neighborhood, region, or industry; continuing losses. However, only when it becomes clearly obvious that the remaining net book value of property cannot be recovered through sale or use should the loss be recognized by a charge to income. Depending on whether the property is expected to continue in use or be sold, its carrying amount should be written down to, but not below, estimated recoverable value or net realizable value. (Chapter 11, "The Production Segment," discusses the determination of net realizable value, which applies with little adaptation to plant and intangible assets as well.)

Reorganization or Quasi-Reorganization

In certain circumstances, the values of an entity's assets, liabilities, and equity accounts may be adjusted. The adjustment may be pursuant to a legal reorganization or a formal voluntary quasi-reorganization. Accounting Research Bulletin No. 43, Chapter 7A (*AICPA Prof. Stds.*, vol. 3, Section 5581) describes what constitutes a quasi-reorganization. In such a case, the assets may be adjusted upward as well as downward to estimated recoverable value or net realizable value, but neither more nor less.

Appraisals

Accountants generally reject appraisals as an accounting basis for properties because of the subjectivity involved in performing appraisals and because recording an increase in value of an asset usually is not permitted until realized. On the other hand, users of financial data find appraisals useful for many purposes, and financial statements reflecting appraisals will undoubtedly continue to be prepared. Accountants may properly assist in their preparation and use as long as the fact that appraised values are reflected, as well as the fact that the financial statements are not in accordance with generally accepted accounting principles, is clearly and properly disclosed. If appraised values are reflected in a balance sheet, depreciation should be computed on those values [APB Opinion No. 6, paragraph 17 (*AICPA Prof. Stds.*, vol. 3, paragraph 4072.01)].

ACCOUNTING FOR DISPOSITION OF ASSETS

Sale or Abandonment

If detailed records of property, plant, and equipment are maintained and depreciation is computed by the unit method, the accepted accounting treatment of retirements is well defined. At the time a unit of property is retired from service, the cost should be removed from the appropriate asset account, the related accumulated depreciation should be removed from the allowance for depreciation account, and the profit or loss, adjusted for salvage value and cost of removal and disposition, should be recorded as an income or expense item.

If a company computes depreciation by the composite method, the accepted accounting treatment of plant units retired in the normal course of business is to remove the cost of the unit from the appropriate property account and to charge that cost and the cost of removal, less salvage value, to the allowance for depreciation; no profit or loss is recognized. However, profits or losses should be recorded for abnormal or unusual retirements because composite rates do not provide for them. Examples of that type of retirement include disposal of items of a certain class because of obsolescence not considered in determining the composite rate, or the retirement of facilities used to produce a discontinued major product line.

Fully Depreciated Items

In the past, it was common to "write off" fully depreciated assets by removing the cost from the asset account and accumulated depreciation from the depreciation allowance account, leaving no amounts in the balance sheet. Preferable accounting is to carry in the accounts the cost of the asset and related accumulated depreciation for properties still in use and to write off assets only on physical disposition.

Involuntary Conversions

Property may be destroyed or stolen or may be expropriated or taken by right of eminent domain. The Internal Revenue Code refers to such events as "involuntary conversions," and the phrase has entered the vocabulary of accountancy. Since insurance coverage is commonly based on current values and governmental units normally reimburse property owners on the basis of current appraisals, proceeds from an involuntary conversion often exceed the cost of the property less related depreciation allowances. If the proceeds of an involuntary conversion are reinvested to replace the asset lost, no gain is recognized for tax purposes and the new asset is carried forward at the same "basis" (cost less accumulated depreciation) as the asset replaced, plus any additional funds used.

APB Opinion No. 29 (*AICPA Prof. Stds.*, vol. 3, paragraph 1041.04) specifically excluded involuntary conversions from that Opinion and its requirements so that, for financial reporting purposes, a gain may either be recognized or not. We prefer the latter treatment, consistent with the IRS provisions. If a gain is recognized, the "tax effect" (Chapter 13) should also be recognized—the deferred tax recorded on the gain should be amortized to the extent that depreciation deductions for tax purposes on the lower tax basis are less than reported depreciation on the new property.

● TYPICAL TRANSACTION SYSTEMS AND INTERNAL CONTROL

TYPICAL TRANSACTIONS

The property transaction segment consists of the following steps.

Authorization and Allocation of Funds

The acquisition of property usually requires a major use of funds and accordingly is supervised and controlled at a high level in an organization. Often the capital budget for property acquisitions is approved by the board of directors.

Some companies use well-developed techniques of capital budgeting to evaluate the economic feasibility of proposed acquisitions, both large and small. Other companies are less formal and more subjective and judgmental in their analysis. The extent of economic justification depends on the management style and preferences of those ultimately responsible for authorizing acquisitions of property; usually those preferences are formally expressed in company policy.

Acquisition

Routine or recurring purchases are usually handled by the purchasing department or a closely related department in the same manner and subject to the same controls as described in Chapter 10 for purchasing in general. Larger or more technically specialized acquisitions may be handled by specialists in engineering and contract negotiation.

Installation

Putting property in place and getting it ready for use may be as simple as delivering and plugging it in or as extensive as complete construction of a plant. Installation may be the responsibility of the seller and therefore part of the acquisition step.

Use and Maintenance

Proper use of property and maintaining it in efficient working condition is a critical and often complex and extensive managerial function which has a significant bearing on the financial and operational well-being of an enterprise.

Disposition

Disposition of property that has served its purpose is often neglected but effective realization of residual and salvage values can have an important effect on the profitability of an enterprise.

INTERNAL ACCOUNTING CONTROL

The recognition of need for property and economic justification of its acquisition are major management accountability functions. Internal accounting control starts with the authorization step and thus the following discussion of controls in the property segment begins at that point.

Authorization

A company's policy governing property acquisitions and procedures for implementing them should be well defined. Often the procedures provide for several levels of authority; the larger the expenditure the higher the level at which it will be authorized. Usually the procedures call for some kind of written request and specify the degree of economic justification that must accompany the request. Approvals of requests may be issued on an ad hoc basis as the requests are received, but it is preferable to compile them in a capital budget for formal review and approval. Sometimes a capital budget enumerates specific acquisitions, but most often it has to be prepared far in advance and thus necessarily consists of estimates or aggregates of probable acquisitions.

When a capital budget is approved, it becomes the authorization for the purchasing or other department to execute acquisition transactions. Thereafter the actual transactions are authorized by the persons responsible for the various segments of the capital budget.

Authorized acquisitions should be documented and the documents should be subject to numerical control. One common system is to assign a "construction work order" number or "appropriation" number to each authorization, even when no construction is involved. Often, control totals of "commitments" and "construction work in progress" are supported by holding files of open work orders, which can be reconciled periodically to the control total.

Acquisition and Installation

Acquisitions that are processed through the normal purchasing procedures are subject to the practices and controls described in Chapter 10 in connection with the buying segment. If an acquisition is complex or specialized enough to be the responsibility of a separate department, it should, for the same reason, be subject to special control efforts. Control over large-scale procurement has become a highly developed art over the last several decades, and "procurement" or "contract management" has become a profession in its own right. This discussion can only touch in the most general way on the kinds of controls that may be found in practice.

A contract, including all specifications, should be reviewed for completeness. The more complete the initial specifications, the less risk of costly unforeseen variations. The range of tolerable deviation from the specified standards should be spelled out and the time of delivery and quality of performance should be specified. Since higher quality or closer tolerances are almost always more costly, contracts are best reviewed by a team comprising different skills and points of view: purchasing specialists, engineers, production men, lawyers, and cost accountants. If a going concern is acquired or construction costs are to be audited, an auditor can often be a productive member of the team.

During construction, acquisition, or installation, a "clerk of the works" or "contracting officer" should supervise step-by-step compliance by the contractor with the terms of the contract. Sometimes the supervision can be supplied by an outside specialist, such as an architect; on other projects, the full-time attention of a whole staff of the purchaser's executives and employees is required.

There should be formal procedures for testing and accepting an acquisition, and compliance with them should be adequately documented and reviewed before the acquisition is legally accepted and final payment made.

Costs of acquisition should be accumulated in work order ledgers —purchases, payments to contractors, and "in-house" labor and overhead. Sometimes contractors provide detailed cost ledgers as part of the service under the contract. Accumulated costs should be balanced to the control account periodically and compared with the authorized expenditure.

Property, Plant, and Equipment Records

Property, plant, and equipment controlling accounts should be supported by detailed records showing the classification of plant assets. The most satisfactory control results from subsidiary accounts that are supported in turn by individual records maintained on cards or sheets containing pertinent information for each item of property, plant, and equipment in each classification. Those records should be kept for all items in use, including fully depreciated assets and assets leased from others. In addition to the dollar amount, the record for each plant item should include information such as date purchased or constructed, voucher or work order numbers, adequate description of the asset, unit number assigned, and location in the plant. Often those records also show maintenance and repair history. The detailed records should be balanced with the general ledger controlling accounts at least once a year.

Maintenance of detailed property records is generally recognized as preferred practice, except for small value items, and well worth its cost in terms of improved control over use and possible misuse of property. However, it is still common to find property accounts without supporting detail or with support only in the form of lapse schedules by year of acquisition (used to compute depreciation of all assets acquired in the same year as a unit).

Records of Use, Maintenance, and Repair

Good management involves maintaining careful records of use and maintenance history of equipment. The amount of use affects the amount of maintenance needed, and the maintenance history indicates what kind of repairs may be expected and whether maintenance costs are building up as the equipment is used. For accounting purposes, use and maintenance records are often ignored because accounting, for the most part, allocates costs on a "systematic and rational" basis that may not be directly related to use.

There are some notable exceptions to the generalization that records of use are seldom under accounting control: the use of commercial aircraft is required by regulation to be meticulously accounted for to make sure that periodic overhauls are undertaken after prescribed amounts of use, and cost accounting for overhauls is usually based on the records of use; rentals for many kinds of leased property are based partly on the amount of use (mileage for automobiles, units produced for machines, hours of service for computers, dollars of sales for retail stores, and so forth), and usage records are carefully controlled.

With those exceptions, accounting records and control functions related to use of equipment are usually very simple. They generally comprise: a standard policy, which may not even be written, for rates and methods of depreciation, depletion, and amortization; forms or schedules for computing entries and often a standard journal entry form for recording them; and procedures for periodically balancing details with control accounts, checking computations, and adjusting recorded amounts.

Every company should have a policy for periodic review of estimated lives, estimated salvage values, and depreciation methods selected; the policy should include requirements for documenting reviews made and conclusions reached. Most often, however, clients tend to rely on general industry or commercial practice, and reviews are not made unless an auditor carries them out in the course of his validation tests. It is better practice for an auditor to request that the client make them for the auditor's review.

Disposition of Property, Plant, and Equipment

Controls over the disposition of property no longer needed are important to any business, not only to preserve the accuracy of the records but also to make sure that assets are safeguarded, are not improperly disposed of, and are disposed of under the best possible terms. Too often, controls over disposition do not receive the attention they deserve. One reason is that disposals are infrequent occurrences, and property is either held throughout its useful life or is disposed of in relatively large batches such as an entire plant, assembly line, or building. Another is the belief—not valid in the case of many small items —that property is hard to remove and dispose of improperly. A related feeling is that accumulating depreciation takes care of accounting for the expiration of value of the asset whether it remains on hand or not. Accountability is obviously ill served by all those beliefs: controls can exist even though used infrequently; many costly items of equipment such as typewriters and tools are desirable, easily moved, and readily marketable; and charging off an asset is no substitute for safeguarding it.

The best control over dispositions is a work order system to document and account for retirements, plus the disciplinary controls of restricted access to the property and division of duties between those responsible for assets, those authorized to move, remove, or otherwise work on them, and those authorized to approve construction or removal work orders. Those controls can be embodied in a policy that no item of property may be released by the person responsible for it without a properly authorized work order. Retirement work orders should be reviewed by a plant engineer or someone similarly responsible and knowledgeable. The reviewer should evaluate the reason given for the disposition, the estimated cost of removal, and the estimated recovery for scrap or salvage.

A frequently encountered intermediate stage of control between little or none at all and a well-systematized and disciplined system of control consists of a written policy calling for documentation of removals and dispositions. The policy statement can be considered effective only if it is controlled by detailed records of assets on hand checked by periodic inventories of at least the movable and salable items.

Intangible Assets and Deferred Charges

Records and controls over accounting for intangible assets and deferred charges are similar to those for tangible property. Generally, both the accounts and the transactions entering into them are simpler than property accounts, and thus the records and controls can be more straightforward. A policy should specify the kinds of expenditures that are deferrable and amortization methods and rates; entries should be properly authorized and approved. Provision should be made for periodic review of balances, realizable values, and continuing validity of the deferral policy.

• AUDITING PROCEDURES

OBJECTIVES

The objectives of auditing property and related accounts are roughly parallel to those for other asset accounts: reasonable assurance that the existence, ownership, and authenticity of physical assets are as stated; that cost and its expiration through use are determined in accordance with generally accepted accounting principles; and that net realizable value or recoverability of cost has been taken into account. The existence of property is usually much easier to verify than inventories or receivables because of the permanent or semipermanent nature of most property; accordingly, that objective is not emphasized in auditing procedures for property. Questions of net realizable value are serious when they arise, but they arise only rarely. Therefore, the bulk of audit activity focuses on accounting for the cost of acquisitions and the expiration of cost through use of property.

Restating those objectives in terms related specifically to the property segment (including intangible assets and deferred charges), an auditor wishes to obtain sufficient competent evidence, both underlying and corroborative, that:

The cost or other basis of recording property is in accordance with generally accepted accounting principles.

Additions are authentic.

Accounting for the use and disposition of property is consistent from period to period and in accordance with generally accepted accounting principles.

Net book value is expected to be recoverable in the normal course of operations.

The property represented by the accounts exists, is owned by the enterprise, and is unencumbered except as indicated.

The last objective does not receive much attention in most discussions of auditing. It is generally agreed that an auditor does not need detailed evidence of the existence of all items of property. However, that does not mean he can ignore all evidential matter supporting the existence of property. Since buildings and equipment are likely to remain in place for a long time after acquisition, auditors tend to lean heavily and almost exclusively on evidence of physical acquisition. Continued existence is observed, though often not specifically or explicitly, as an auditor moves about the property in the course of his observations of physical inventory and other tasks. The possibility of encumbrances is considered both explicitly and implicitly in the course of reviews of minutes, loan agreements, and other possible sources of information about encumbrances.

THE AUDIT CYCLE

Transaction reviews and functional tests must be made to obtain evidential matter that gives reasonable assurance that the system works as planned and can be depended on to continue to do so and that the underlying evidence of the accounts may therefore be relied on. Since property recorded a number of years earlier, and its related depreciation, may be significant in both the current balance sheet and the income statement, an auditor may have to extend his review of underlying evidence back into the past if he has not made previous examinations. Some corroborative evidence must be gathered by substantive tests, although often less than is required for current assets.

All testing must be viewed as an integrated process and not as separate steps.

Transaction Reviews

The number of types of property transactions depends principally on the variety of a client's acquisition activity. In its simplest form, the acquisition transaction system may be fully reviewed in connection with the general purchasing system described in Chapter 10. Or several completely separate property acquisition activities may each give rise to a separate type of transaction. Major acquisition transactions, such as mergers, cannot be systematized and must be treated individually.

The complete property segment can be viewed as one type of transaction with the "cradle" the authorization of the acquisition and the "grave" the fully depreciated asset or retirement. Usually, however, it is more convenient to treat accounting for acquisitions, accounting for use, and accounting for disposition as separate types of transactions because assets are in each of the different stages of the segment at the time of a specific examination.

Functional Tests

In many companies, additions to property accounts are so few that they can be easily validated by vouching each one, and therefore functional testing is unnecessary. When additions are numerous and significant, good conditions of control over property accounts permit a minimum of corroborative evidence, and the functional tests thus assume considerable significance.

Unless a client's system of accounting for property is extraordinarily complex and varied, testing relatively few control functions should give an auditor confidence in the underlying data. The control function of authorization and approval of acquisitions is of particular interest to an auditor, whether it is carried out through a formal capital budgeting system or item-by-item approval of each invoice or work order. Controls over formal acceptance of an acquisition before it is paid for and recorded are of significance in assuring its authenticity. An auditor should test controls that assure compliance with accounting policies for determining costs and distinguishing between property additions and repairs, such as double-checking, reviewing, and approving invoices and work orders. He should also test controls over the regularity and accuracy of depreciation computations and entries.

A work order system is virtually indispensable if additions and retirements are many and varied. Generally, work order systems are an inherent part of a systematized capital budgeting and authorization process. Therefore, if a work order system exists and an auditor's tests of it are satisfactory, the expected result should be maximum confidence in the underlying evidence.

Following is an example of an audit program for functional testing of a work order system of controlling plant additions:

1. Select a representative number of completed and uncompleted work orders and determine that they have been properly authorized; examine vouchers and other evidential data in support of selected charges for evidence of review and approval; test the appropriateness of accounting classifications; and examine completion reports and related engineering data;

2. Test the mathematical accuracy of charges accumulated on work orders, the accounting for completed work orders transferred from construction work in progress to plant in service accounts, and the reconciliation of work order balances to the balance of the construction work in progress account at the end of an accounting period;

3. Make a test comparison of expenditures authorized or estimated with the actual costs charged to completed work orders as finally determined; review evidence of client's explanations of substantial variances; and, if variances cannot be explained satisfactorily, investigate further the accuracy of the accounting for expenditures; and

4. Compare date of completion of work order with date of approval for transfer to plant in service accounts, date of accounting transfer, and date of commencement of depreciation accounting.

If a client has no work order control system and additions to and retirements from property accounts are few in number, validating entries in the property accounts may be relatively easy, and therefore no functional tests would be required. If, however, a client has no work order system and additions and retirements are numerous, an auditor should seek the best among the alternatives described in Chapter 5: he first considers whether there are alternative controls that can be relied on; a detailed capital budget with comparison of actual to budgeted expenditures is an example. If not, he may have to expand his validation testing; perhaps a statistical or judgmental sample of entries in the property accounts may afford sufficient confidence in the accounting system to preclude further detailed validation testing.

If they exist, an auditor reviews and tests controls over re-evaluation of useful lives, salvage values, net realizable values, and recovery costs. Unfortunately, those re-evaluations are not made in a great many companies except at the request of the auditor.

Control over disposition of assets should be by means of a work order system, which can be tested as described above. If there is no work order system, retirements should be validated. Provisions for physical security over property assets should be observed and evaluated.

VALIDATION PROCEDURES

Examination of Opening Balances and Prior Years' Transactions

If financial statements are being examined for the first time, an auditor must decide to what extent it is necessary to examine plant accounts before the beginning of the year or years under examination. Since the amount of plant acquired in prior years and the related depreciation are likely to be significant in the current balance sheet and income statement, an auditor must have a basis for believing that both are fairly stated in accordance with generally accepted accounting principles.

If financial statements for earlier years have been examined and reported on by independent public accountants, reviewing the other accountants' working papers and the client's records should be sufficient to provide an auditor with an understanding of the accounting principles, policies, and methods employed.

In some cases—for example, if no audit was made in earlier years or the auditor is unknown—a new auditor's work should be a combination of transaction review, analytical review, and validation. He should review available plant records in enough depth to understand the accounting procedures and principles used and the consistency with which they have been applied since the inception of the existing plant. He may prepare or obtain analyses summarizing the annual changes in plant and depreciation accounts. He may examine evidential matter to support major additions and reductions. In particular, he should investigate unusual items in an effort to learn of revaluations or other major adjustments. He should pay particular attention to additions to property accounts acquired by issuing common stock of the company or by exchanging other property. In an initial examination, an auditor must make numerous other historical analyses—such as of long-term debt, capital stock, additional paid-in capital, retained earnings, and minutes of directors' meetings—and he should be alert for matters in those analyses that affect the property accounts.

Ownership

In an initial examination, an auditor should seek evidence that the principal plants are in fact the property of the client. If a client's historical record keeping is adequate, deeds, purchase contracts, and other evidence of ownership will be on file and retrievable. Sometimes, however, those documents get mislaid over the years as successive generations of management come and go and files are moved, rearranged, or culled. Even though few auditors are competent to judge questions of legal title, a brief visit to the registry of deeds may provide simple evidence that the property is registered in the name of the client and that there are no encumbrances against it. If no other evidence can be found, an auditor can ask his client to seek assurances from counsel concerning legal title to properties.

If an auditor's functional tests give him reason to be satisfied with control over acquisitions and additions to plant and equipment, his validation tests of the property accounts may be limited to scanning the capital budget and the property accounts and reviewing documentation for some major additions not scrutinized in the functional tests. If he is not satisfied about the reliability of controls, supporting data for additions should be examined for evidence of physical existence, approval and authorization, formal acceptance, propriety of accounting classification, and so on. Substantially all additions may have to be examined or a small number may constitute so large a fraction of the total that others can be assumed to be insignificant; alternatively, additions may be so voluminous that a statistical sample should be designed as a basis for inferring conclusions about the total.

Many clients must prepare, for SEC filings or tax purposes, schedules that summarize changes in asset and allowance accounts. Even if they are not required, summary schedules serve as convenient work sheets for organizing validation tests. For each major classification of property, both tangible and intangible, and the related allowance for depreciation, depletion, or amortization, the beginning balance is reconciled to the ending balance by identifying the total of each major type of addition, deduction, and transfer. Using a schedule of that type, an auditor can reconcile retirements to charges to the allowance accounts, and additions to the allowance accounts to depreciation, depletion, or amortization expense.

An auditor seldom finds it necessary to make a specific physical inspection of a plant, but if a client takes a physical inventory of plant assets, an auditor should take the opportunity to observe it. If he has reason to entertain serious doubts about the existence of assets reflected in the property accounts, an auditor should request that the client verify the physical existence and condition of the assets. The procedures for a physical inventory of plant assets are nearly identical to those described in Chapter 11 for inventories of materials.

The liability certificate described in Chapter 10 provides written confirmation from a client of the absence of undisclosed encumbrances on property.

Depreciation Accounts

Validation tests of depreciation accounts should start with a review of the client's methods and policies. It is preferable that policies be systematically documented, but if they are not they can be inferred from the computations and work sheets of the prior and current years. Depreciation rates and useful lives may be compared with those in general use by similar enterprises. Computations of depreciation expense should be tested, often by making approximations on an overall basis.

Useful Lives

An auditor should consider the reasonableness of useful lives. Many auditors tend to accept without question the useful lives of types of plant assets that are in common use throughout business—a ten-year life for furniture and fixtures, for example. Those depreciation rates are only rarely unrealistic, but unrealistic rates are encountered often enough that an auditor should never fail to examine critically the applicability of generally accepted rates to each client under examination. He ought first to consider whether known factors should limit or extend the lives of categories of plant assets. He should observe the pattern of gains and losses on disposition; a consistent record of one or the other could suggest that lives are too long or too short. For assets depreciated on the composite method, he should scrutinize the ratio of allowance accounts to asset accounts. Ratios are, of course, affected by the pattern of additions, but after an auditor allows for unusually high or low additions in certain years, a significant upward or downward trend in the ratio of an allowance account to a related asset account should indicate whether useful lives are too short or too long. Where either analysis suggests a possible problem, an analysis of actual useful life being experienced is called for.

Realizable Value

The realizable value of property should also be considered, not on an item-by-item basis, but overall by plant or product line. If a plant or product line is unprofitable, an auditor should consider evidence of the prospects for recovery of the operation or, if recovery does not seem likely, for salvaging the remaining net book value of the property through sale. If the prospects for both are poor, the plant may need to be written down to estimated realizable value.

The conditions that cause an auditor to consider that action are usually so extreme as to make the question of realizable value almost self-evident—for example, protracted periods of operating losses. Determining the right answer can be extremely difficult, however. There is bound to be a period when no conclusion can be reached about whether a depressed industry will recover. An auditor should not be hasty in insisting on a write-down of plant during a period of uncertainty, but if time passes and the client cannot discover evidence indicating a likely prospect for recovery, both good accounting practice and prudent business management call for anticipation of a probable loss.

Disposition of Assets

Entries to remove assets from the accounts should be vouched by examining evidence of approval, checking the acquisition cost to underlying records, checking computations of accumulated depreciation and resulting gain or loss, and evaluating the reasonableness of cost of removal and recovery from scrap or salvage. If a properly controlled work order system is in existence or if a large number of assets is disposed of at once, as in the case of a sale or abandonment of a plant, the entries can usually be validated by vouching a sample of the individual transactions.

Mines

In examining the amounts at which mining properties are carried, an auditor should be aware that costs incurred are not necessarily indicative of the economic value of property. Indeed, the value of property can vary significantly as a result of changes in market prices, improvements in extraction or reduction methods, discovery or development of additional ores in the property, and the like. An auditor should review the carrying value of mining properties in light of the existing ore reserves (as estimated by qualified engineers or geologists), present and prospective operating costs, and other pertinent factors to determine whether the carrying value exceeds future returns that can reasonably be expected from the properties. While an auditor need not examine engineering or geological records, he should be aware that such information is available in a well-managed mining company.

Depletion

An auditor should determine that the method of computing depletion is reasonable. If a mining enterprise consistently computes depletion on the basis of the best information available, its procedures may be considered reasonable. There can be no serious objection to changes in depletion rates resulting from bona fide revisions in estimates of recoverable mineral; those revisions may be made annually or less frequently.

An auditor should, if possible, receive a written statement from a geologist, mining engineer, or other responsible and informed person stating the depletion basis and indicating that the current depletion rate is reasonable. Mining experts are usually reluctant to commit themselves to an estimate of ore. Consequently, if the depletion allowance is based on not only developed ore but also estimates of probable and possible ore, an auditor may have difficulty securing a responsible written opinion concerning the depletion rate. A request for an opinion is reasonable—it is part of management's accountability function to see that estimates are made—and if it is not complied with, an auditor is on notice that the depletion rate may be inadequate or excessive.

In well-managed timber operations, the quantity of standing timber is verified (cruised) by qualified persons and, with that as a starting point, the depletion to be charged is computed. Adequate records show quantities of timber as well as dollar amounts, since an attempt to determine depletion based only on monetary values is hazardous. An auditor can examine records of the cruisers' reports and relate them to known conditions and prior experience in the area. Logging records can be related to sales, usage, and inventory reports.

Appraisals

As described in an earlier section, appraisals are not generally accepted as a basis for carrying values of property, but there are exceptions: a reorganization, quasi-reorganization, and allocation of a basket purchase price are examples. If appraisals are used to determine values, an auditor should secure a copy of the appraiser's report, inquire about the basis on which the appraisal was made, read the report to understand the basis on which it was made, and examine resulting adjustments to the accounts to determine whether they properly reflect the appraised amounts.

When an appraiser—or any other non-accounting specialist—is relied on for accounting values or estimates, an auditor should inquire into and evaluate the qualifications of the specialist, his relationship to the client, if any, and the assumptions and methods followed in developing, evaluating, and reporting the findings.

An entire plant may be acquired in exchange for stock of the acquiring company. In the absence of an appraisal, the problem of valuation is difficult unless there is a readily determinable fair value for the stock. Rather than delegate the valuation task to independent appraisers or company engineers, the board of directors may undertake to value the property and fix the value of the assets acquired. Since the directors may not be expert, an auditor should review their conclusions and available information and consider whether he should take exception in his report to the values established.

If, as a result of an appraisal, property, plant, and equipment accounts are revised downward, an auditor should investigate the basis for the revisions and review the entries recording the adjustments as comprehensively as if the adjustment had been upward.

ANALYTICAL REVIEWS

An auditor should tour each plant he visits, the main plants probably once a year and outlying or smaller plants from time to time over a period of years. One among several reasons for making a tour is to

observe the existence and condition of the plant as part of his validation of the property accounts.

The minutes of directors' meetings and executive committee meetings also provide evidence of matters affecting the property accounts.

The auditor should routinely inquire of those he encounters in the
course of his other tasks about past or prospective changes in operations
that might affect the plant accounts.

Balances of asset, depreciation and depletion allowance, and expense
accounts should be compared with the prior year and possibly month-
to-month to identify fluctuations and unusual entries calling for inquiry
and explanation.

Among the most important of an auditor's procedures are his review
of his knowledge of the client's operations and economic environment
and his correlation of developments in those areas to activity in the
plant accounts. He should make sure that he understands the business
reasons for additions and retirements and whether trends in operations
or in the environment are likely to affect the values at which property
is carried in the accounts.

SUBSTANTIVE TESTS OF INTANGIBLE ASSETS AND DEFERRED CHARGES

Tests and reviews of intangible assets and deferred charges are parallel to those for tangible property accounts. An auditor should review
schedules of activity, vouch additions, review amortization policies, and
test amortization computations. He should find documented support
for continuing to carry assets as intangible assets and deferred charges.
That support can never be conclusive because no one can predict precisely the realizable value of patents, goodwill, or pre-operating costs,
but conclusions should be supported by responsible factual data. Often
the existence of intangible assets can be confirmed by direct correspondence with attorneys or grantors of royalties, licenses, and franchises.
The existence of trademarks, trade names, and brand names may be
independently observable.

CASH SURRENDER VALUE OF LIFE INSURANCE

Cash surrender value of life insurance should be confirmed by direct
correspondence with insurance companies. A copy of the form developed for that purpose appears on the following page. The form

STANDARD CONFIRMATION INQUIRY
FOR LIFE INSURANCE POLICIES
Developed by
AMERICAN INSTITUTE OF CERTIFIED PUBLIC ACCOUNTANTS
LIFE OFFICE MANAGEMENT ASSOCIATION
MILLION DOLLAR ROUND TABLE

_____19____

Dear Sirs:

Please furnish the information requested below in items 1 through 9 (and also in items 10 through 12 if any of those items are checked) for the policies identified on lines A, B and C. This information is requested as of the date indicated. IF THE ANSWER TO ANY ITEM IS "NONE," PLEASE SO STATE. The enclosed envelope is provided for the return of one copy of this form to the accountant named below.

(Ins. Co.)_____

_____
(Name of owner as shown on policy contracts)

Information requested as of_____

(Accountant)_____

Request authorized by_____

		Col. A	Col. B
A.	Policy number		
B.	Insured		
C.	Beneficiaries as shown on policies (if verification requested in item 11) Col. A— Col. B—		
1.	Face amount of basic policy	$	$
2.	Values shown as of (insert date if other than date requested)		
3.	Premiums, including prepaid premiums, are paid to (insert date)		
4.	Policy surrender value (excluding dividends, additions and indebtedness adjustments)	$	$
5.	Surrender value of all dividend credits, including accumulations and additions	$	$
6.	Termination dividend currently available on surrender	$	$
7.	Other surrender values available to policyowner	a. Prepaid premium value	$	$
		b. Premium deposit funds	$	$
		c. Other	$	$
8.	Outstanding policy loans, excluding accrued interest	$	$
9.	If any loans exist, complete either "a" or "b" a. Interest accrued on policy loans	$	$
	b. 1.) Loan interest is paid to (enter date)		
	2.) Interest rate is (enter rate)		

The accountant will indicate by a check (✔) which if any of items 10-12 are to be answered

			Col. A	Col. B
☐	**10.**	Is there an assignee of record? (enter Yes or No)		
☐	**11.**	Is beneficiary of record as shown in item C above? (enter Yes or No*)	*	*
☐	**12.**	Is the name of policyowner (subject to any assignment) as shown at the top of the form? (enter Yes or No) _____. If No, enter name of policyowner of record. _____		

*If answer to 11 is No, please give name of beneficiary or date of last beneficiary change._____

Date_____ By_____ Title_____
For the insurance company addressed

provides space for confirming cash surrender value, names of insured and beneficiaries, existence of assignments or loans, and reservations of rights—all important matters in indicating whether the client has a right to record cash surrender value as an asset.

CONTINGENT ASSETS

An auditor may encounter contingent assets in ways so varied that specific auditing procedures cannot be prescribed. If contingent assets are encountered, an auditor should establish their existence and probable amount to the best of his ability by inquiry and examination of supporting written evidence. By definition, contingent assets may be uncertain as to both existence and amount, and thus an auditor will not need or be able to secure the kind of specific evidence he seeks for recorded assets.

• STATEMENT PRESENTATION

PROPERTY, PLANT, AND EQUIPMENT

The financial statements or a note should disclose the balances of major classes of depreciable assets, by nature or function, at the balance sheet date [APB Opinion No. 12 (*AICPA Prof. Stds.*, vol. 3, paragraphs 2043.01 and .02)]. No single description of property, plant, and equipment on the balance sheet has been accepted to the exclusion of others. "Property, plant, and equipment," "fixed assets," "land, buildings, machinery, and equipment," "general property," "properties," "plant, equipment, and real estate," and numerous other captions are found in published financial statements.

Nondepreciable property, such as land, should preferably be segregated from depreciable property, such as buildings and machinery. Real estate not used in the business should be stated separately. Material amounts of excess land, buildings, and equipment being offered for sale should be stated separately from property in use and at amounts not in excess of estimated net realizable value. Significant construction work in progress may be stated separately or, if included with completed projects, may be indicated parenthetically. If a company is in the business of buying and selling real estate, properties held for sale constitute inventory and should not be included in property, plant, and equipment.

Property purchased subject to a mortgage or other lien—that is, the mortgage is not assumed by the purchaser and so it is not a lien on any asset other than the mortgaged property itself—is sometimes recorded only at the purchaser's net investment. This method of recording "non-recourse" loans as a reduction of the asset amount is considered improper by some accountants, but the APB considered the question and failed to act on it.

Gross costs of facilities purchased under an installment plan should be shown as assets with an indication of a material lien. Unpaid installments should be shown as liabilities. It is not good practice to state only a company's equity in installment purchases, even though title to the property remains vested in the vendor until completion of the purchase contract.

Property Stated on Cost Basis

A long accepted principle of balance sheet presentation is that property, plant, and equipment is carried at cost less allowance for depreciation. Most companies append the words "at cost" to the principal plant caption to avoid the possibility of misunderstanding.

Property Stated on Other Than Cost Basis

If property, plant, and equipment accounts are restated pursuant to orders of regulatory bodies, plans of reorganization, or corporate readjustments, the nature and amount of the restatement should be clearly indicated.

Restatements of plant accounts may be made in connection with a quasi-reorganization. The fact of a quasi-reorganization should be disclosed by dating the new retained earnings account for a period of time, usually ten years (*AICPA Prof. Stds.*, vol. 3, Section 5582).

Appraised values may have been recorded in the accounts before the time when that practice became unacceptable. If so, the amounts of cost and appraisal increases should be separately disclosed.

Idle Plant, Reserve, and Stand-By Equipment

Plant assets in a balance sheet may include not only property in use but also unused property held with reasonable expectation of being used in the business. Segregating or indicating the existence of temporarily idle plant, reserve, or stand-by equipment is not customary. However, property abandoned but not physically retired and facilities still owned but no longer adapted for use in the business, if material in amount, should be removed from plant accounts and recorded separately at estimated net realizable value, appropriately described.

If a material portion of plant and equipment is idle with little likelihood of resuming operations, it should be stated separately with an appropriate caption.   Idle plant facilities involve a continuing expense, and creditors, stockholders, and others should be apprised of the fact that property, plant, and equipment exceeds apparent reasonable needs.

Fully Depreciated Items

Since an allowance for depreciation is at best an estimate, facilities may be operating after full depreciation has been recorded in the accounts.   One of the following treatments of fully depreciated plant may be adopted:

1. The amount of fully depreciated items may be included in the gross amount of property, plant, and equipment, and the related allowance for depreciation may be included in the accumulated allowance for depreciation.
2. The amount of fully depreciated items may be written off against the related allowance for depreciation, so that no amount appears in the balance sheet.

If the facilities are being used, the first method is preferable.   If the amounts involved are significant, it is appropriate to disclose them either parenthetically or in a note.

DEPRECIATION AND DEPLETION

Balance Sheet

Allowances for depreciation and depletion may be deducted from the costs of related assets or the total allowances may be deducted from total depreciable assets.   The balance sheet or a note should disclose accumulated depreciation at the balance sheet date, either by major classes of assets or in total [APB Opinion No. 12 (*AICPA Prof. Stds.*, vol. 3, paragraphs 2043.01 and .02)].   Depletion should be similarly disclosed.

Income Statement

The income statement, the statement of changes in financial position, or a note should disclose the amount of depreciation expense for the period covered by the income statement and include a general description of the depreciation methods applied to major classes of assets [APB Opinion No. 12 *(AICPA Prof. Stds.,* vol. 3, paragraphs 2043.01 and .02)]. Sometimes, depreciation is listed as a major element of cost in an income statement; sometimes the amount is shown parenthetically following cost of goods sold and general and administrative expense. An example of disclosure is:

> Note [referenced to depreciation expense]: In general, the company's policy is to depreciate its property, plant, and equipment over their estimated useful lives, using either the straight-line or sum-of-the-years'-digits method.

Many companies also disclose the method used in computing depreciation for tax purposes if it differs from the method used for accounting purposes.

The disclosure requirements of the Securities and Exchange Commission are somewhat different. Rule 3-16(m) of Regulation S-X asks for disclosure of not only the amount of depreciation expense and the methods used but also, "if practicable, the rates used in computing the annual amounts." Among other requirements of the same rule are disclosure of a company's accounting policy for maintenance, repairs, renewals, and betterments and its policy for "the adjustment of accumulated depreciation . . . at the time the properties are retired or otherwise disposed of, including the disposition of any gain or loss on sale of such properties."

Lease commitments should be disclosed in the notes to the financial statements in conformity with APB Opinion No. 31 *(AICPA Prof. Stds.,* vol. 3, Section 5352) and Accounting Series Release No. 147 (see "Leases" in the statement presentation section at the end of Chapter 16).

INTANGIBLE ASSETS

Intangible assets with specified terms of existence and those of indeterminate terms of existence should be shown separately on the balance sheet. They are assumed to be carried at cost unless otherwise stated. In financial statements filed with the Securities and Exchange Commission, the basis, whether cost or otherwise, should be specifically stated.

Financial statements should disclose the method and period of amortization of intangible assets. Rule 3-16(m) of Regulation S-X requires for financial statements filed with the SEC, disclosure of the accounting policy for amortization of intangibles, including methods and, if practicable, rates used in computing annual amounts.

Rights of way and franchises are important elements of intangibles of public utilities and are closely related to plant assets; therefore, intangible assets are generally included with plant assets in statements of public utilities. The excess of amounts paid by a parent company over the underlying book amounts of investments in subsidiaries may be shown in consolidated statements of public utilities as a separate item in one amount because of the impracticability of allocating it between tangible and intangible assets.

Occasionally, the unamortized cost of an intangible asset is reduced significantly in a fiscal year. The reason for such reduction should be disclosed.

CASH SURRENDER VALUE OF LIFE INSURANCE

Cash surrender value of life insurance is customarily classified as a noncurrent asset. Its usual purpose, to provide funds at the time of the insured's death, is distinctly noncurrent. The statement presentation of loans on insurance policies on the lives of officers is discussed in Chapter 16.

13

The Income Tax Segment

INTRODUCTION

Income tax has long been one of the most significant items in financial statements: frequently it constitutes a company's or an individual's largest single annual expenditure. Most often the expense is significant in the income statement, the current liability is significant in the balance sheet, and increasingly in recent years the credits and debits for deferred taxes are significant in their own right.

The Nature of Income Tax

The question of whether income tax is an expense to be recognized in arriving at net income, or a division of net income similar to dividends, has been settled in the U. S. (but not in some other countries) in favor of treating it as an expense. Questions about the nature of deferred tax accounts have been resolved by APB Opinion No. 11, issued in 1967: deferred tax credits are not liabilities or a type of equity or long-term financing, nor are deferred tax debits assets in the conventional sense. Rather, deferred tax debit and credit balances are treated as deferred charges and deferred credits, respectively.

It is helpful in understanding the accounting principles governing recognition of income tax to consider another fundamental question about the nature of income tax. The question is whether income tax is a cost of doing business for a period, levied by the government according to the rules and regulations in existence at the time of the levy, or whether the tax—or a relief from it—is the consequence of individual actions and transactions and should be accounted for in association with the accounting for those actions and transactions. If the former view prevailed, there would be no such thing as deferred tax accounting—whatever the tax return for the period showed as the liability would be the expense for the period. Instead, accountants have chosen the latter approach, which is reflected in the principle of "comprehensive interperiod tax allocation," largely because the tax consequences of individual transactions and options have become so important in the making of business decisions.

Accountants and Income Taxation

Professional accountants and auditors have long been prominent in the administration of income taxes, both in government and in the role of advisors to taxpayers. The general public probably identifies certified public accountants with income taxes more widely and frequently than with auditing and the attest function. That is because so much of income taxation is based on accounting theory and practice. However, income taxation is also a body of statutory and administrative law, and the provinces of the accounting and legal professions overlap in virtually the entire field of taxation. In actual practice, the field has become so complex that, more often than not, lawyers and accountants welcome the consultation and assistance of each other.

Auditors are expected to have the education, training, and experience to understand the types of taxes to which a business is subject; the statutory methods for determining amounts of tax payable; the alternatives available for minimizing taxes; the proper principles and methods of accounting for them; and, of course, the applicable auditing procedures. Many auditors seek the assistance and advice of tax specialists, but that practice does not relieve the auditor in charge of an engagement from reaching his own understanding of his client's tax affairs.

Many books have been devoted to the complexities of tax legislation. It is not practicable or necessary to try to repeat or even summarize here all the possible tax problems an auditor might encounter. It *is* practicable to indicate how the results of tax rules and related management planning should be accounted for and controlled, and how an auditor can apply his knowledge of taxation to assure himself that his clients' tax affairs are fairly reflected in the financial statements.

• ACCOUNTING PRINCIPLES

Income tax differs from other costs and expenses because it is based on the revenue received and costs and expenses incurred by an enterprise. It is, at least in part, a dependent variable. Significant transactions affecting the incidence of tax are to some degree under the control of management, allowing the ability to control the timing and amount of tax payments.

Problems in accounting for income taxes, in common with other costs and expenses, fall into two categories: how much to record and when to record. Those two problems complicate presentation of the balance sheet liability or deferred debit and credit accounts and the expense in the income statement. The actual liability is difficult to determine because of the complexities of the taxing statutes and regulations. The accounting is more complicated because of the number and variety of differences between generally accepted accounting principles and the treatment permitted or required by tax laws and related rulings and regulations.

Accounting for income taxes is presently governed by APB Opinions No. 11, 23, 24, 25, and Addendum to Opinion No. 2 (*AICPA Prof. Stds.,* vol. 3, Sections 4091, 4091A, 4095, 4096, 4062, and 6011). Every change in the Internal Revenue Code or other tax statutes must be evaluated to determine its treatment under those principles. For international companies, income taxes levied in foreign countries, under the laws and regulations of those countries, must likewise be evaluated

to determine their treatment under the accounting principles set by
the APB.

BACKGROUND

Tax Accounting Methods

Under the Internal Revenue Code, "taxable income shall be computed in accordance with the method of accounting regularly employed
by the taxpayer in keeping his books," unless the Internal Revenue
Service does not agree that the method used clearly reflects income.
In that event, it is empowered to recompute income using any method
that it believes clearly reflects income. That has been a general principle of income taxation since the enactment of the Sixteenth Amendment. If it were followed consistently, there would be few, if any,
related financial accounting problems. However, for very practical
reasons, there are so many exceptions to the general rule that it is often
easy to forget that it exists. The two main categories of exceptions are
those that result from public policy considerations and those that
result from the exigencies of administration of the tax statutes.

The Internal Revenue Code has often been used as an instrument
of public policy because of its universal and pervasive effect on the
economy of the country. For example, when investment in capital
goods needed encouragement, accelerated depreciation and the investment tax credit were incorporated in the Code; when exports needed
encouragement, Western Hemisphere Trade Corporation and Domestic
International Sales Corporations (DISC's) were created; when capital
outflows were to be discouraged, the Interest Equalization Tax appeared; when it appeared to be in the public interest to encourage
investment in extractive industries, percentage depletion was developed.
The list is virtually endless. Incentives and disincentives of that type
are based on fiscal, political, social, and economic considerations, not
on good accounting.

In addition, the problems of administering a complex and all-encompassing body of law and regulations have resulted in a vast number
of rules, precedents, and procedures. Some are arbitrary, but many
are practical solutions to the need for clearly understood methods of
dealing consistently with particular situations. Thus, the procedure
for changing an accounting method is different for IRS purposes than
under generally accepted accounting principles. Such judgmental
items as depreciation and amortization may be reduced to rules (ADR
depreciation, for example), which may or may not be consistent with

the requirements of generally accepted accounting principles. Or such methods as the installment sales method of reporting gains on sales for long-term receivables or the completed-contract method of reporting profits on long-term contracts may become accepted for tax purposes, with the consequence that equitable and consistent treatment of taxpayers requires their continuance long after their use has been restricted under generally accepted accounting principles.

Thus, despite repeated efforts at conformity, differences between income determined under generally accepted accounting principles and income reported for taxing purposes have become more prevalent, and how to account for them has become more complex.

Necessity of Estimates

Income tax recorded in the accounts is always an estimate—or more properly the sum of a large number of estimates—for two reasons. The first is that the computation of the current year's liability often takes a long time: three months, six months, even the maximum delay permitted by most taxing authorities, eight and one-half months, because large amounts of specialized data must be gathered and analyzed for use in computing taxes. In the meantime, for purposes of timely preparation of financial statements, estimates and judgments of amounts that will ultimately be reflected in the returns must be made. Secondly, revenue agents' examinations often extend over several years and informal and formal discussions of the resulting findings over several more years. It is not unusual to have several taxable years "open" for review at one time. Meanwhile, judgments have to be made at least annually of the adequacy of the tax liability in the balance sheet. Companies with a well-developed sense of accountability make those judgments with great care and attention to detail, and with the help of their auditors and sometimes tax counsel as well.

Inevitably, estimates have to be adjusted either in the light of new information or because the actual liability as finally determined is larger or smaller than the earlier estimate. In the past, there was considerable difference of opinion and even confusion about how adjustments of earlier estimates should be accounted for; this is no longer so.

Generally, adjustments are now charged or credited to expense at the time new information makes revised estimates possible, consistent with the treatment called for by APB Opinions No. 9 and 20 (*AICPA Prof. Stds.*, vol. 3, Sections 2010 and 1051 to 1051B) for changes in estimates. Sometimes a change in estimate affects items entering into the computation of deferred income tax (see below), in which case that account should be adjusted also. Occasionally, an adjustment of the estimated income tax liability is so significant as to call for separate disclosure either in the income statement or a note. In no circumstances should an adjustment of income tax liability be treated as an extraordinary item (except for the tax benefit effect of net operating loss carryforwards described below).

In rare cases, an issue involving the determination of income tax liability can be so novel or so complicated that its outcome cannot be predicted without a judicial resolution. When uncertainties are that great, the liability—for the unpredictable issue only—is ordinarily considered contingent and calls for disclosure in the financial statements and perhaps qualification in the auditor's report. In that event, at the time the uncertainty is resolved the resulting adjustment of the liability should be accounted for retroactively as an adjustment relating to prior periods.

HOW MUCH INCOME TAX TO RECORD

Since the tax is based on income, it cannot be calculated until pretax income is determined; the income tax accrual is usually the last entry in the accounts before the books are "closed." (Whenever post-closing adjusting entries are made, the "tax effect" of each entry must be recorded as well.)

Preferable practice requires examination of the tax accounts at an interim date, just as accounts receivable, inventories, and most other accounts are reviewed and validated before the year end. Specialists should analyze all of the pending issues, estimate the ultimate impact on tax liability, compare the total of those estimates with previously recorded amounts, and recommend any necessary adjustment. At the same time, possible tax-saving transactions or other actions or decisions should be considered. The tax effect of "permanent differences" (see next section) should be estimated for the current year, as well as any additions to or reductions from foreign income taxes to be recorded for foreign subsidiaries.

The year-end accrual determination can then be a simple matter of applying the statutory tax rates to pretax income and adding or subtracting the effect of permanent differences. The elements of deferred tax included in the accrual must be identified and segregated in both the income statement and the balance sheet.

The determining factors in how much income tax to record are, obviously, the amount and types of income to be taxed and the tax rates applicable to the various types. As noted above, differences may exist between income determined under generally accepted accounting principles and for tax purposes. Some of these "book-tax" differences are created when the *timing* of tax recognition differs from the *timing* of book recognition, and the differences are expected to be offset by corresponding differences in later periods. Those "timing differences" and the complicated problems of allocating the related tax effects are covered under the subsequent caption "When To Record Income Tax."

Permanent Differences

Other differences are *absolute* differences between taxable income and book income; these are called "permanent differences." Most permanent differences arise from differences in definition between taxable income and pretax accounting income (or, to say the same thing in another way, statutory provisions for specialized treatment of certain elements of income and expense). The following are examples:

> Some types of revenue may be exempt from taxation, such as life insurance proceeds and interest on municipal bonds.
>
> Some expenses may not be deductible for tax purposes, for instance, fines and penalties, premiums on life insurance, and amortization of goodwill.
>
> Some adjustments to revenue or expenses that are not recognized for accounting purposes may be specifically written into the Code, such as the deduction allowed to corporations for dividends received.
>
> Some taxable items may not appear in conventional income statements; for example, dividends paid from a subsidiary corporation to a parent corporation do not appear separately in consolidated financial statements, but may in some instances be a taxable item in the tax returns of the parent corporation.

Some permanent differences are precisely defined, while others involve highly judgmental estimates and allocations. Among the examples given above, there is likely to be little question about the treatment of such items as life insurance proceeds, interest on municipal bonds, amortization of goodwill, or the treatment of dividends received from subsidiaries. On the other hand, allocating revenue and expenses among corporate entities in an international group involves a high degree of judgment. The same may be true of computing percentage depletion.

Tax Rate Differences

Exceptions to the general statutory tax rate may also affect how much income tax expense to record. Examples are:

Some items are taxed at preferential capital gains tax rates rather than as ordinary income.

The investment tax credit (discussed further below) is a reduction in taxes to be accounted for either in the year the credit is allowable or ratably over the life of the investment.

Special incentives such as those provided for DISC's may result in permanent tax savings, for all practical purposes.

Income earned and reinvested in a foreign country may be taxed at a different rate from the general statutory rate in the U. S.

The presence of items of "tax preference" may require the payment of taxes even in the absence of taxable income.

Investment Incentives

The U. S. investment tax credit is an incentive to invest in productive assets and results in a reduction of tax liability, 10% (or 11% if elected) of cost of qualified property placed in service. The APB, in Opinions No. 2 and 4, has expressed a preference for deferring the investment credit and amortizing it to income by reducing tax expense ratably over the life of the property to which the credit relates—the "deferral" method. However, government policy and other considerations have been overriding, and as a result it is acceptable to reduce income tax expense by the full amount of the investment credit when it arises—the "flow-through" method. (The Revenue Act of 1971 prohibited any governmental body—such as the SEC—from specifying the acceptable accounting.) Most companies follow the flow-through method, although a few use the deferral method.

Under either method, some of the credit may not be an allowable reduction of tax liability in the year it arises because of statutory limitations. For control purposes, any unused investment credit should be entered in a memorandum account. Disclosure should be made of the accounting method used, the amount of the credit which reduces the provision for income taxes, and amounts (book and tax) of any unused credit carryforwards—see illustration later.

The investment tax credit is subject to "recapture" if property is disposed of before a specified length of time. An investment credit "recapture" becomes part of the current year's tax provision.

When there are timing differences between book income and tax income, accounting for the investment credit can involve questions of when to record the credit as well as how much. Those questions are discussed in the subsequent section of this chapter headed "Investment Credits."

Other countries may provide similar investment incentives from time to time. In some foreign investment incentive plans, the grant or credit may reduce the depreciable basis of property; as a result, subsequent taxable income will be increased in the amount of depreciation deductions not available by reason of the investment incentive. In that situation, a portion of the incentive is effectively taxed. This procedure was followed briefly in the U. S. when the original investment credit was enacted in 1962. In accounting for that type of incentive, the tax expected to be payable must be accounted for as a deferred credit even if the "flow-through" method is employed for U. S. investment credits. Another type of foreign incentive grant may result in either a deferred credit amortized to income over the life of the grant— for example, 10 years (with somewhat different income statement results than if the basis of the assets had been reduced directly)—or a contribution to the company's capital. In the latter cases, the full cost of the assets would be depreciable and the tax accounting would follow from the terms of the incentive. Each set of facts must be analyzed for compliance with the applicable accounting requirements.

Tax Benefits of Loss Carrybacks and Carryforwards

If the computation of taxable income produces a loss, the loss may be carried back to certain prior accounting periods or forward to certain subsequent accounting periods to reduce income taxes payable in those periods. When a tax loss is carried back to earlier years, the realization of the resulting tax refund is reasonably assured; the claim for refund is recorded as a receivable with a corresponding credit to the provision for income tax for the period. Since the realization of tax benefits from a tax loss carryforward is dependent on the future production of taxable income, it usually cannot be considered reasonably assured. Therefore, credits for carryforward tax benefits are usually not recorded until realized, but should be disclosed in a note to the financial statements. Conditions under which realization of a tax benefit from a carryforward could be considered reasonably assured are described in paragraph 47 of APB Opinion No. 11 (paragraph 4091.46 of *AICPA Prof. Stds.*, vol. 3), as follows:

> Realization of the tax benefit of a loss carry*forward* would appear to be assured beyond any reasonable doubt when both of the following conditions exist: (a) the loss results from an identifiable, isolated and nonrecurring cause and the company either has been continuously profitable over a long period or has suffered occasional losses which were more than offset by taxable income in subsequent years, and (b) future taxable income is virtually certain to be large enough to offset the loss carry*forward* and will occur soon enough to provide realization during the carry*forward* period.

Although rare, these conditions do occasionally exist. Auditors must satisfy themselves that there is a factual basis for the assumptions made and that realization is assured beyond any reasonable doubt.

When tax benefits resulting from a tax loss carryforward are realized in periods subsequent to the loss period, they should be accounted for as extraordinary item credits so as not to distort the customary relationship between pretax accounting income and tax expense (paragraph 4091.60 of *AICPA Prof. Stds.*, vol. 3).

Accounting for loss carrybacks and carryforwards can become complicated when there are timing differences between book and tax income. Those complications are discussed in the subsequent section of this chapter headed "Operating Losses."

WHEN TO RECORD INCOME TAX

The liability for income taxes payable or estimated to be payable should, of course, be recorded as soon as it comes into existence. A taxpayer is subject to income tax for any year or part of a year in which business is done; thus, the liability should be recorded in those periods even though the exact amount may not be determinable until later and may have to be re-estimated and readjusted a number of times.

Interperiod Tax Allocation

When timing differences exist, Opinion No. 11 requires comprehensive interperiod income tax allocation in financial statements (except as indicated under "Public Utilities" below). The aim of the allocation is to match the provision for income taxes in the financial statements for a period with the items of income and expense reported therein. Paragraph 8 of the Opinion (paragraph 4091.07 of *AICPA Prof. Stds.*, vol. 3) summarizes the problems involved, as follows:

> The principal problems in accounting for income taxes arise from the fact that some transactions affect the determination of net income for financial accounting purposes in one reporting period and the computation of taxable income and income taxes payable in a different reporting period. The amount of income taxes determined to be payable for a period does not, therefore, necessarily represent the appropriate income tax expense applicable to transactions recognized for financial accounting purposes in that period. A major problem is, therefore, the measurement of the tax effects of such transactions and the extent to which the tax effects should be included in income tax expense in the same periods in which the transactions affect pretax accounting income.

Definition of Timing Differences

The mechanism through which allocation is accomplished is the analysis of timing differences (defined below) and the assignment of the related tax effects of those timing differences to the various periods when the incidence of tax is expected to occur. As a result, entries for all tax effects are made in the current period to record amounts that may affect tax expense in the future. The Board, in opting for comprehensive allocation, specifically rejected the partial allocation concept, under which allocation would be required only for nonrecurring timing differences.

Opinion No. 11 encompasses all material timing differences, whether recurring or not. Timing differences are defined in paragraph 13 (paragraph 4091.12), as follows:

> Differences between the periods in which transactions affect taxable income and the periods in which they enter into the determination of pretax accounting income. Timing differences originate in one period and reverse or "turn around" in one or more subsequent periods. Some timing differences reduce income taxes that would otherwise be payable currently; others increase income taxes that would otherwise be payable currently.

Four major categories of timing differences exist. Appendix A to Opinion No. 11 (taken from Accounting Research Study No. 9, pages 8 to 10) presents examples of various types included in each of the categories, which are:

1. Revenue or credits taxed before being recognized in income for accounting purposes.
2. Revenue or credits taxed after being recognized in income for accounting purposes.
3. Expenses or debits deducted for tax purposes before being accrued for accounting purposes.
4. Expenses or debits deducted for tax purposes after being accrued for accounting purposes.

Methods of Allocating Income Taxes

Once the APB had determined that comprehensive allocation was appropriate, it was then faced with choosing from among three methods of application. The three methods, each of which has both attractive and negative features, are the "deferred method," the "liability method," and the "net of tax method." Accounting Research Study

No. 9 analyzes each extensively; Opinion No. 11 summarizes those analyses. Readers desiring greater theoretical background information about the "liability" or "net of tax" methods are referred to those publications. Because the APB adopted the deferred method, this chapter will focus on it. Except for the brief descriptions in the following paragraph, the other methods will be brought into the discussion only when it is essential to do so for clearer understanding.

The "liability method" considers tax allocation to be a process of estimating additional taxes to be paid in the future (or reductions of taxes otherwise payable); computations are therefore made on the basis of tax rates expected to be in effect when the timing differences reverse. The "net of tax method" reduces assets and liabilities by the amounts of current or estimated future tax effects on the theory that the tax effects are a major factor in their valuation.

The deferred method was adopted because it is oriented toward the current income statement and current tax rates. The Opinion requires calculating the "tax effect . . . measured by the differential between income taxes computed with and without inclusion of the transaction creating the difference between taxable income and pretax accounting income" (paragraph 4091.35). The method described is called the "with-and-without" method. Under it, tax cost or benefit is measured at the tax rate effective when the timing difference originates. There is no adjustment of deferred tax accounts for subsequent rate changes or other subsequent tax law changes.

Intraperiod Tax Allocation

The principle of tax allocation also applies within an accounting period to items that are treated separately from the ordinary elements of income and expense in financial statements. The tax effect should be matched with the item—that is, the tax effect of an extraordinary item, a prior-period adjustment, or a cumulative accounting change should be reflected against that item. Tax allocation within a period is measured by the difference between taxes computed before and after the item affected.

Interim financial statements—usually fiscal quarter-years—also present problems. These generally involve determining the appropriate rates and how to deal with seasonal losses. At the end of each interim period, the company should make its best estimate of the effective tax rate expected to be applicable for the full fiscal year. The effective tax rate should reflect anticipated percentage depletion, capital gains rates, and other available tax planning alternatives. No effect should be included for the tax related to significant unusual or extraordinary items that will be separately reported or reported net of their related tax effect in reports for the interim period or for the fiscal year.

The tax effects of losses that arise in the early portion of a fiscal year (in the event carryback of such losses is not possible) should be recognized only when realization is assured beyond any reasonable doubt (see previous discussion of this subject). An established seasonal pattern of loss in early interim periods should constitute evidence that realization is assured beyond reasonable doubt, unless other evidence indicates the established seasonal pattern will not prevail. The tax effects of losses incurred in early interim periods may be recognized in a later interim period of a fiscal year if their realization, although initially uncertain, later becomes assured beyond reasonable doubt. When the tax effects of losses that arise in the early portions of a fiscal year are not recognized in that interim period, no tax provision should be made for income that arises in later interim periods until the tax effects of the previous interim losses are utilized (such recoveries are not treated as extraordinary items). Changes resulting from new tax legislation should be reflected after the effective dates prescribed in the statutes.

Timing differences of the usual type previously discussed do not ordinarily affect quarter-to-quarter results unless a company's tax year differs from its accounting year. Normally, they are treated the same as if the interim period were a fiscal year.

Discounting Deferred Taxes

Deferred tax debit and credit accounts represent the cumulative tax effects of transactions recognized in different periods for tax and financial reporting purposes. Deferred taxes are not contractual obligations to pay money or to receive money from the Internal Revenue Service on fixed or determinable dates. They are not receivables and payables in the usual sense. Thus, despite its applicability to some extent elsewhere in accounting practice, discounting to present value is not applied to deferred tax debits and credits. APB Opinion No. 10 (*AICPA Prof. Stds.*, vol. 3, Section 4092) concluded that discounting is inappropriate, and footnote 3 of Opinion No. 21 reaffirmed that conclusion. Discounting deferred taxes would be essentially a variation of the liability method of tax allocation and would be inconsistent with the deferred method.

Grouping of Timing Differences

An "originating" timing difference creates or increases a difference between book income and tax income and therefore also, of necessity, a difference between the book and tax valuation ("basis") of a particular asset or liability. A "reversing" timing difference decreases a previously created book–tax difference. Paragraph 4091.36 requires either that each individual transaction resulting in a timing difference be designated as an originating difference or a reversing difference (the "individual transaction" method), or, alternatively, that all individual originating timing differences resulting from similar transactions and all reversing timing differences resulting from similar transactions be grouped and treated as single originating or reversing differences (the "gross change" method). Originating and reversing differences resulting from similar transactions are not grouped under this method. In some circumstances, the net change in cumulative originating *and* reversing timing differences during the period for a group of similar transactions may be treated as a single timing difference (the "net change" method).

Grouping of "similar timing differences" permits logical groupings by type of transaction (e.g., depreciation, installment sales, prepayments, deferrals) or type of item (e.g., buildings, equipment, leaseholds, development costs, advertising). Dissimilar transactions may not be grouped under any of the methods of determining originating and reversing timing differences. Different methods and groupings may be used for various transactions or groupings of transactions, but, once adopted, they must be followed consistently for the specific type of similar differences. Under the net change method, tax applicable to reversing differences is calculated on the basis of their effects on the current year's tax payable at *current* tax rates. Differences between this tax effect and the tax effects established in the prior years in which the differences originated are essentially ignored and therefore accumulate in the deferred tax debit or credit accounts. Under the individual transaction and the gross change methods, the deferred tax related to a difference is automatically charged or credited to current book income in the amount and at the tax rate established in the *prior year* when the difference originated. The financial statement results under the net change method thus differ from those under the other two methods, and the difference can be material even in the absence of statutory rate changes. It should be noted that the net change method is not in accordance with the theory underlying the deferred method of tax allocation, but it is sanctioned by Opinion No. 11.

The individual transaction method involves maintaining substantial records and detailed analyses of deferred tax accounts. Fewer records are required under the gross change and net change methods. The net change method is the simplest, from an administrative viewpoint. It may also have the effect of minimizing unusual fluctuations in income in years immediately after statutory tax rate changes have been enacted, especially where there are large gross changes but small net changes in cumulative book–tax differences (e.g., insurance companies which defer policy acquisition costs over a one- to two-year period).

Treatment of Operating Losses and Investment Credits

The theoretical simplicity of the deferred method of tax allocation (despite some computational complexities) is disturbed by two issues: the accounting to be followed when operating losses arise and when investment credits are generated.

Operating Losses

It is possible for profits to be reported in the financial statements and losses in the tax returns and vice versa. Practice has been confusing and the authoritative literature does not satisfactorily resolve the problems of determining amounts of taxes to be recorded in financial statements when either situation exists due to the effect of timing differences.

When taxable income is negative—a loss—the present Internal Revenue Code allows the loss to be carried back against income of the three prior years, resulting in refunds of taxes paid on that income. Any loss not carried back may be carried forward to offset up to five years' future income. If there are no timing differences between tax and book income, the accounting loss is offset by a credit provision in the income statement in the amount of the tax refund receivable. (See example 1 below.)

If pretax book income shows a profit when there is a tax loss due to timing differences—a not uncommon situation—and the tax loss carryback produces a refund receivable, both a provision for tax expense based on book income and the receivable are recorded. The resulting credits are made to the deferred tax credit account and are equal to the tax effect of the timing differences that created the book–tax difference. (See example 2.)

If no carryback refund is available or if tax losses exceed the carrybacks, a tax loss carryforward position arises. If book income is positive, the book provision for taxes should be based on that income at current rates (after allowing for permanent differences), thereby providing a deferred tax credit for some or all current timing differences. If and when the tax loss carryforward is used to reduce tax payable in future years, the remaining portion of the timing differences that gave rise to the tax loss should be "tax effected" by debiting the current liability and crediting deferred tax. (See example 3.)

Most of the authoritative literature has focused on the conditions just described: what is to be done when *tax* carrybacks and carryforwards arise. However, more complicated problems arise when *book* carrybacks and carryforwards are created that differ, due to timing differences, from the tax amounts.

If, instead of book profits and tax losses, there are losses for both book and tax purposes, but the amounts differ, a book carryback may be recorded, subject to the availability of prior years' book income and related book tax provisions and to the test of realizability. When the book carryback is less than the actual tax refund receivable, there is little doubt about realizability. (See example 4.) Even when the potential book carryback is greater than the tax refund receivable, either because the book loss is greater than the tax loss or because book tax provisions in the carryback period exceeded actual taxes paid, the credit may still be considered "realizable" to the extent that there are existing deferred tax credits that will reverse during the carryforward period. (See example 5.) To the extent that there are no such receivables or credits, a book carryback cannot be recognized because realization is not assured. (See example 6.)

Upon subsequent realization, the credit for reduction in taxes payable as a result of loss carryforward should be accounted for as an extraordinary item. In computing the amount of the extraordinary item, the tax benefit actually realized in the form of a reduction in current-year taxes otherwise payable should be adjusted downward to reinstate any unreversed deferred tax credits previously eliminated in computing a book carryback credit. See example 7.

The following examples illustrate the above principles (50% tax rate assumed for simplicity):

1. Book and tax losses the same; carryback refund available:

	Book	Tax
Current-year loss before taxes	($1,000)	($1,000)
Carryback tax refund receivable	500	500
Net loss	($ 500)	($ 500)

Accounting entry:

Tax refund receivable	$500	
Income tax expense (credit)		$500

2. Book income, tax loss (due to $2,400 timing difference); carryback refund available:

	Book	Tax
Current-year income (loss) before taxes	$1,400	($1,000)
Provision for income tax payable (refundable)	700	(500)
Net income (loss)	$ 700	($ 500)

Accounting entry:

Tax refund receivable	$500	
Income tax expense	700	
Deferred income tax		$1,200

3. Same as 2 above, but no carryback available:

Accounting entry:

Income tax expense	$700	
Deferred income tax		$700

Accounting entry if carryforward reduces tax payable in a future year:

Income tax currently payable	$500	
Deferred income tax		$500

4. Book loss less than tax loss (due to $700 timing difference); carryback refund available:

	Book	Tax
Current-year loss before taxes	($300)	($1,000)
Provision for income tax refundable	150	500
Net loss	($150)	($ 500)

Accounting entry:

Tax refund receivable	$500	
Income tax expense (credit)		$150
Deferred income tax		350

5. Book loss greater than tax loss (due to $600 timing difference); carryback refund available limited to $350; deferred tax credits on the books of $450 or more which will reverse in next five years:

	Book	Tax
Current-year loss before taxes	($1,600)	($1,000)
Provision for income tax refundable	800	350
Net loss	($ 800)	($ 650)

Accounting entry:

Tax refund receivable	$350	
Deferred income tax	450	
Income tax expense (credit)		$800

Memorandum: Unused tax loss carryforward = $300.

6. Same as 5 above, but reversing deferred credits limited to $200:

	Book	Tax
Current-year loss before taxes	($1,600)	($1,000)
Provision for income tax refundable	550	350
Net loss	($1,050)	($ 650)

Accounting entry:

Tax refund receivable	$350	
Deferred income tax	200	
Income tax expense (credit)		$550

Memorandum: Unused book loss carryforward = $900; unused tax loss carryforward = $300; deferred credits to be reinstated = $200.

7. In the year subsequent to example 5, book and tax income are large enough to absorb the tax loss carryforward:

	Book	*Tax*
Current-year income before taxes	$1,000	$1,000
Unused tax loss carryforward		300
		700
Provision for taxes	500	350
Net income	$ 500	$ 350

Accounting entries:

Income tax expense	$500	
Liability for tax currently payable		$500
Liability for tax currently payable	150	
Deferred income tax		150

Investment Credits

Accounting for the investment credit has previously been discussed under "Investment Incentives." Under the flow-through method, the financial statement provision for income tax expense is reduced by the full amount of investment credits applied against the tax otherwise payable. Under the deferral method, investment credits are deferred and amortized over the lives of the assets generating them, and the provision for tax expense each year is reduced by such amortization. The unamortized balance is reflected as a separate deferred credit in the balance sheet. (See "Public Utilities" for exceptions.)

The Internal Revenue Code limits the amount of investment credit that may be used to offset tax otherwise payable for a year to 50 per cent of the tax, except for public utilities, for which higher percentages are allowed under the Tax Reduction Act of 1975. Carrybacks and carryforwards of unused credits are allowed for a certain number of years. When pretax book income and tax income differ because of timing differences, the amounts of investment credit to be recognized for tax and book purposes may also differ. The amount of credit for tax purposes is limited by the amount of taxable income; for financial statement purposes, however, the controlling income limitation is the smaller of book income or taxable income. APB Opinion No. 11 did not cover this type of situation. It is the authors' opinion that investment credits should be calculated on a "with-and-without" basis, regardless of whether the deferral or the flow-through method is used. In effect, investment credits become another timing difference. Donald J. Bevis and Raymond E. Perry, in a monograph interpreting Opinion No. 11, *Accounting for Income Taxes (AICPA Prof. Stds.,* vol. 3, Section U 4091), state the issue clearly:

If tax allocation results in net deferred credits the differential calculations will recognize as income for financial accounting purposes, through a reduction in the deferred tax provisions, that portion of available investment credits that would have been allowable had taxes payable been based on pretax accounting [book] income. In effect investment credit carryforwards [for tax purposes] are being recognized as offsets against net deferred tax credits in a manner similar to that followed for operating loss carryforwards. [Paragraph U 4091.110]

A simple example illustrates the points. Assume the following:

1. Pretax accounting income equals taxable income before timing differences: $1,000.
2. No carryforwards of investment credits or operating losses from prior years exist.
3. Tax rate is 50%; surtax exemption is ignored.
4. Investment credit generated is $500, and life of the asset is 10 years.
5. Timing difference reducing pretax accounting income: $500.
6. Maximum credit allowable is 50% of tax before credit.

	Book Purposes		
	Deferral Method	Flow-Through Method	Tax Purposes
Income before taxes and timing difference	$1,000	$1,000	$1,000
Timing difference			500
Income before taxes	1,000	1,000	500
Provision for income tax, before allowance for investment credit:			
Currently payable	250	250	250
Deferred	250	250	
Subtotal	500	500	250
Investment credit:			
Against tax currently payable	(50)	(125)	(125)
Against deferred tax		(125)	
Net tax provision	450	250	125
Net income	$ 550	$ 750	$ 375

Accounting entries:

To record tax currently payable:
Income tax expense $250
   Liability for income tax $250

To record deferred tax:
Income tax expense   250
   Deferred income tax   250

Deferral method—to record investment credit:
Liability for income tax   125
   Income tax expense   50
   Deferred investment credit   75

Memorandum: Unused investment credit carryforward = $375.

Flow-through method—to record investment
   credit:

Liability for income tax	$125	
Deferred income tax	125	
Income tax expense currently payable		$125
Deferred income tax expense		125

Memorandum: Unused investment credit carryforward = $250 for book purposes,
   $375 for tax purposes.

As the example shows, if the amount of credit reflected in book income is greater than the amount offset against tax otherwise payable due to the effect of timing differences, that excess, up to 50% of the smaller of the income statement provision or the deferred credit in the balance sheet, will reduce the balance sheet credit account for deferred taxes. The excess investment credits thus recorded need not be actually used for tax purposes; by reducing the deferred tax, the investment credit booked is effectively used to reduce its future reversal.

Disclosure of amounts of carryforwards of unused credits and the years of expiration is required, but only of credits available for tax purposes. It is the authors' opinion that the relevant figure is the amount available to be reflected in future book income. Complete disclosure would encompass both amounts.

Deferred Tax Debits

A deferred tax debit may be recorded when there are originating timing differences resulting from revenue being recognized earlier, or expenses later, for tax purposes than for book purposes. This deferred debit is frequently related to a significantly larger credit—a liability, an allowance, or a deferred income account; or it may be related to a cost capitalized for tax purposes but expensed on the books. The debit will ordinarily be "realized" by matching it against the related credit in the future, when the timing differences reverse. However, the "net realizable value" test usually applied to assets in general is essential. When a company suffers losses for some years and the likelihood of continuing losses is high or liquidation is probable, deferred tax debits should not be recorded at the time differences originate, because they may not be "realizable" through tax savings when the timing differences reverse. Deferred debits related to investment credits should not be recorded unless the carryforwards are offset by deferred tax credits, and then they should be recorded as reductions of the deferred credits.

Tax Allocation in Special Areas

In 1972, the APB issued two Opinions, Nos. 23 and 24 (Sections 4095 and 4096 of *AICPA Prof. Stds.*, vol. 3), which extended tax allocation procedures to certain areas not covered by Opinion No. 11. These areas are:

1. Investments in common stock accounted for by the equity method (other than subsidiaries and corporate joint ventures).
2. Undistributed earnings of subsidiaries.
3. Investments in corporate joint ventures.

The Board concluded that all three are likely to give rise to timing differences because they represent earnings included in book income which have not been subject to various kinds of income tax that would have become payable on actual distribution from one company to another. However, the Board distinguished the latter two from the first (investments in "controlled companies") on the basis of the degree of control exercisable by the investor company.

Undistributed Earnings of Subsidiaries and Investments in Corporate Joint Ventures

Since the investor (parent) company can exercise a great deal of control over subsidiaries and joint ventures and therefore can determine their financial and operating plans, it is possible to establish a policy of permanently reinvesting earnings in a subsidiary or joint venture. In those circumstances (described in paragraph 4095.12), the transfer of earnings may be so clearly deferred indefinitely as to give rise to a permanent difference, and taxes that might be payable on distribution of the earnings to the parent company need not be provided for. The question of "how much to record" therefore depends on the company's intent. Unless there is sufficient evidence that the earnings are or will be permanently invested in the subsidiary's or joint venture's assets or that there is a permissible means of effecting a tax-free liquidation of the subsidiary or joint venture, tax should be provided as if all earnings had been distributed to the parent company.

Investments Accounted For by the Equity Method

On the other hand, since an investor cannot exercise that degree of influence over controlled but less than 50 per cent owned companies, the APB concluded that tax payable on ultimate realization of the investor's equity in earnings should be recorded at the time the earnings are recorded (see also Chapter 14). The tax may be computed as if the earnings were either received through dividends or realized through sale of the investment, whichever the evidence indicates is more appropriate.

Should changes in ownership percentages occur whereby a controlled company becomes a subsidiary or a subsidiary becomes a controlled company, the taxes provided on undistributed earnings should be adjusted accordingly through the tax provision in the year of change.

Tax Allocation Among Consolidated Companies

The general principles of tax allocation apply also to the various entities of a consolidated group of companies that file a consolidated return. Two basic methods are in use:

The source of income method, and
The separate return method.

Under the former, the tax is allocated among the various subsidiary companies and to the parent in proportion to the amount of pretax income (or loss) included in the consolidated total. Under the latter, each constituent calculates the tax that it would owe if it filed a separate return. All credits, special deductions, and other peculiar features of its own tax position are taken into account. The ratio of the separately determined amounts to the total calculated under this method is applied to the actual consolidated tax to determine the allocation.

Many parent companies, preferring not to rely on mechanical formulas, have established arrangements with their subsidiaries specifying allocations based on internally defined criteria; for example, some do not allocate credits to subsidiaries that suffer losses. Since liability for the consolidated tax is joint and several, the arrangements need not follow any precise pattern. Depending on the particular circumstances, a variety of alternatives is available and acceptable, as long as adequate disclosure is made in all unconsolidated or subsidiary company statements.

Public Utilities

Addendum to APB Opinion No. 2 (*AICPA Prof. Stds.*, vol. 3, Section 6011) permits public utilities to apply generally accepted accounting principles differently from non-regulated companies because of the rate-making process, which attempts to provide a specified rate of return to the affected utilities. Such differences usually relate to the time at which the regulatory commissions permit various items to enter into the determination of net income in accordance with the principle of matching costs and revenue. Accordingly, deferred income taxes and investment credits are recorded by public utilities only to the extent such deferred amounts are allowed as currently recoverable costs for rate-making. Examples of timing differences for which deferred income taxes need not be provided if they are not an allowable cost include: (1) overhead costs associated with construction which are capitalized for accounting purposes and expensed for tax purposes; (2) interest portion of the allowance for funds used during construction (interest charged construction) capitalized for accounting purposes; and (3) excess of tax depreciation attributable to the use of accelerated methods and shorter lives for tax purposes. However, in certain circumstances, since 1970 the Internal Revenue Code and Regulations have permitted accelerated depreciation, ADR lives, and investment credits on post-1969 plant additions only if a public utility elects (and a regulatory commission allows) deferred treatment of such timing differences and investment credits for accounting and rate-making purposes. As a result, some utilities follow a combination of deferred and flow-through accounting methods.

The Federal Power Commission revised its Uniform System of Accounts (effective in 1975) pertaining to the deferral of income taxes to substantially conform its prescribed accounting for interperiod income tax allocation with tax accounting for non-regulated industry (unless the regulatory commission having primary rate jurisdiction requires less than full deferral).

Other Areas

Two other areas were covered in Opinion No. 23 (*AICPA Prof. Stds.,* vol. 3, Section 4095): "bad debt reserves" of savings and loan associations, and "policyholders' surplus" of stock life insurance companies. The APB determined that tax allocation was not desirable in those areas because the originating timing differences "may not reverse until indefinite future periods or may never reverse" (paragraph 4095.05). If the differences do reverse, tax provisions should be made in those years, with appropriate disclosure in the financial statements or notes.

Loss Carryforward Benefits Following Acquisition, Reorganization, Etc.

Infrequently, but often enough to warrant discussion, reductions of taxes are obtained as a result of carryforwards of losses incurred:

1. By a subsidiary prior to its acquisition by another company in a business combination,
2. Prior to a quasi-reorganization, and

3. Representing prior-period adjustments which, in a previous year, had been charged directly to retained earnings.

If a company that has book and tax loss carryforwards is acquired in a purchase, any tax benefits obtained after the date of acquisition as the result of realization of the prior carryforwards should be accounted for as an adjustment of the purchase price (*AICPA Prof. Stds.*, vol. 3, paragraph 4091.48). APB Opinion No. 16, paragraph 88 (paragraph 1091.88), further provides that the adjustment to the purchase price for such tax benefits should be made to the goodwill account if created by the purchase (see Chapter 17).

Different considerations apply to acquisitions that are accounted for as poolings of interests, and the APB Opinions are not explicit on the subject. In these cases, there is no "date of acquisition" as such, and prior years' operations are combined. The SEC does not currently permit restatement of prepooling financial statements to give "pro forma" retroactive effect to such tax benefits. Therefore, unrecognized premerger (book) tax benefits of (book) loss carryforwards of parties to a pooling are still considered as (book) loss carryforwards to postmerger years, even though, on a pro forma combined basis, tax benefits could possibly have been recognized for such book losses in a premerger year or years. The extraordinary item treatment outlined in paragraph 4091.44 is appropriate and has become general practice.

Tax reductions obtained subsequent to the date of a quasi-reorganization as the result of carrying forward losses incurred prior to that date (or from deductions applicable to the excess of the tax basis over the new book basis of assets set at the date of the quasi-reorganization) should be excluded from the determination of net book income and should be credited to capital in excess of par value of common stock (paragraph 4091.49).

At times, a prior-period adjustment that has been charged directly to retained earnings (without tax effect) results in a tax benefit at a later date. That benefit is essentially an adjustment of the charge to retained earnings and should be accounted for as a prior-period adjustment rather than entering into the determination of current net income.

• TYPICAL TRANSACTION SYSTEM AND INTERNAL CONTROL

TYPICAL TRANSACTION

The typical income tax transaction system is simple, although adequate control of the important item of tax expense may become highly sophisticated and complex. The transaction system consists simply of disbursing the required amount of tax payment at the required time. A reminder list, often called a "tax calendar," helps to control the timing of payments. The amount is usually computed by a tax specialist and then authorized by a financial officer.

Balance sheet accounts recording tax liabilities and deferred debits and credits should be reconciled to an underlying detail schedule or subledger from time to time. The current liability account should be supported by a computation of estimated liability. The computation of liability for the current-year tax should preferably start with book pretax income and proceed through estimated permanent and timing differences to an estimate of taxable income and the tax payable thereon. The estimated tax payable is then reduced by any previous installment payments.

Usually, provision for possible additional liability which might result from revenue agents' examinations is included in the current liability account, although it may not become payable for some lengthy period of time. The amount of the provision should be supported by a detailed estimate of possible tax questions, or "exposures"—it should not be simply an accumulation of previous years' overaccruals and underaccruals.

Deferred debit and credit accounts should be supported by schedules that account for the various timing differences (either individually or by type, depending on whether the "individual transaction" method or the "gross change" method is employed) and the years in which they are expected to reverse.

Tax Compliance

The actual preparation of tax returns and monitoring of compliance with statutes may be a full-time task for a staff of specialists in a large company, or it may be delegated to an outside professional, such as a certified public accountant, lawyer, or tax specialist. The gathering of the necessary information, preparation and planning of returns, and payment of tax should be systematized, subject to specialized supervisory review, and controlled by a financial officer of the company. The officer responsible for monitoring tax compliance should also review the details supporting the balance sheet accounts described above.

Tax Planning

Adequate control of the significant item of tax expense requires extensive advance planning. The planning is facilitated and in part controlled by reminder lists of compliance requirements (due dates, elections to be made, information required, and the like), of alternatives and opportunities, and of open issues.

It is particularly important that companies maintain reminder lists of past decisions having future tax implications. That kind of list is sometimes called a "tax balance sheet" or a "tax surplus reconciliation." The authors were made aware of the importance of this type of reminder list when a client, in abandoning one of its lines of business, very nearly overlooked the tax benefit of a multimillion-dollar goodwill deduction because the goodwill had been written off for book purposes generations before.

Tax specialists—including auditors—maintain reminder lists of tax-saving opportunities, which they review periodically to make sure that a company has properly availed itself of all of the deductions, exemptions, elections, and the like permitted by the law.

• AUDITING PROCEDURES

OBJECTIVES

The objective in auditing the income tax accounts is to obtain reasonable assurance that the liability (or refund receivable) is fairly stated in the light of all the issues and unresolved questions, that the current-period expense and deferred debits and credits are fairly stated, and that all necessary related disclosures are made in the financial statements. The basic audit tasks are the same as for any other accrued liability: checking the basis and computation of the year-end liability and of the charge to expense for the period. For income taxes, however, the amounts involved are more likely to be significant, and the issues affecting them to be many, complex, and often debatable. As the section on accounting principles demonstrated, the analysis and evaluation of deferred tax debits and credits can be complicated and confusing.

THE AUDIT CYCLE

For taxes, compliance evaluation takes on a special meaning and importance. Control over meticulous and timely compliance with taxation requirements is necessary to minimize liability for taxes and to account for them accurately, especially when a company is subject to a multiplicity of taxing jurisdictions: federal, state, local, and foreign. However, transactions in the tax accounts are not numerous, and each one may be significant, so functional tests are likely to be omitted in favor of, or combined with, substantive tests.

For that reason, transaction reviews and functional tests are not separately described in this chapter. As emphasized in Chapter 5, there is no need to make functional tests when an auditor plans to validate the accounts rather than rely on controls. With the emphasis on substantive validation tests, however, it is easy for an auditor to overlook his professional responsibility to his client to make an evaluation of the system of internal control over taxes. That evaluation is usually a quick and easy task; once the need for it is recognized, an auditor can draw on his knowledge of taxation and his experience with other clients to conclude whether the client under examination has adequate controls for its needs.

Validation Tests and Analytical Reviews

The clear distinction between validation tests and analytical reviews, which can be drawn in discussing the audit of other segments, is not present in the tax segment. Much of the validation testing consists of analytically reviewing conclusions reached by the client, and much of the analytical review is carried out by means of checklists and similar validation-type procedures. The two types of substantive tests are therefore not covered separately in this chapter.

Account Analysis

As the starting point in his examination of the tax accounts and to provide an orderly framework for it, an auditor usually requests his client to prepare an analysis of the tax accounts through an interim date, which is subsequently brought up to year end. The analysis should show, for each kind of tax (including each type of deferred debit and credit) and for each year still "open," the beginning balance, accruals, payments, transfers or adjustments, and ending balance. The auditor then can review the analysis, and usually vouch the transactions entering into it, to see that prior-year overpayments and underpayments are properly identified, deferred debits and credits are properly identified and computed, and amounts currently payable are identified and paid on time. He should verify the validity of the tax and accounting principles employed and the mechanics of their application.

Updating the Auditor's Understanding

To make sure he has the fullest possible understanding of his client's tax affairs, an auditor should review the tax returns and related correspondence for all "open" years (in a recurring engagement he would review the most recent year and update his understanding of earlier years). Often the review can be combined with the auditor's participation in the preparation of the prior year's tax return or his technical review of the client's preparation. If a revenue agent's examination is in process, an auditor should inquire for reports or memoranda and review and evaluate any issues set forth.

An auditor is expected to have sufficient knowledge of the major taxing statutes to be able to evaluate the accrued liabilities for the various taxes to which a company is subject. Accordingly, for each examination, he must review changes in the law since the preceding examination and consider their application to the client. Here again, many auditors use reminder lists or checklists designed to insure consideration of all the factors commonly affecting the computation of tax liability. Sometimes an additional reminder list is employed for the purpose of making sure that the client has not overlooked tax-saving opportunities; sometimes the two lists are combined.

For many companies, an auditor's review of changes in the tax law in the light of his understanding of the client may result in a conclusion that there are no major judgments that need to be evaluated. However, in many companies—perhaps most major ones—transactions are varied and complex and there are inevitably many issues and uncertainties affecting possible assessments or refunds of prior years' taxes as well as the amount and timing of the current year's taxable income. An auditor should not decide those issues for himself. It is management's responsibility to evaluate them and reach a decision, and it is the auditor's responsibility to evaluate that decision.

Evaluating the Liability

The best way to evaluate such a complex and uncertain question as income tax liability is for the client's tax specialist to prepare an analysis of the issues in support of a recommended conclusion as to the amount of the probable liability for prior years' assessments and the amount by which the current-year liability will be affected by permanent book–tax differences. That analysis should then be discussed with the auditor and his tax specialist. Once the issues are sufficiently aired, explored, and understood, the specialists should jointly agree on and recommend to management the amount of accrued tax liability that most reasonably represents the probable outcome of all the issues and uncertainties. After review and approval by management, the accrued liability should be adjusted by a charge or credit to current-year expense.

It is common, but much less desirable, for the client to act as advocate for the most favorable tax treatment, thus forcing the auditor to judge the most likely outcome. Auditors' long-standing involvement in taxation qualifies them to exercise that judgment when necessary.

In either case, an auditor must reach his own conclusions about each of the issues affecting the liability. The function of the tax specialist may end with the estimate of the liability, but the auditor's function extends further, in two directions. On the one hand, he must evaluate the adequacy of the evidence supporting the decisions made —whether any data or matters affecting taxes have been overlooked and whether the evidence at hand is adequate for the purpose: for example, whether the evidence of management's intentions supports a decision to provide or not to provide for taxes on the undistributed earnings of subsidiaries. On the other hand, he must evaluate the adequacy of disclosures to be made in the financial statements (see statement presentation below) and the propriety of accounting principles employed in accounting for deferred debits and credits.

The section on accounting principles noted that it is common to base a year-end tax accrual and the resulting expense on an estimate which must be made before the actual liability for the year is computed and before deferred tax debits and credits are identified and computed. An auditor's interim review of prior-year experience and existing conditions should put him in a position to validate a computation of that year-end estimate. Sometimes, if issues are critical or resolution of them is moving fast, a second conference with the client's tax specialist may be called for. For the most part, the auditor should have very nearly reached his opinion on the adequacy of the tax liability and related expense by the time the year-end computation is available for his review.

Accruals for state and local taxes are reviewed in much the same way as federal income tax accruals, although they are less significant and therefore subject to a much less intensive and detailed analytical review. For companies operating in many states, the fact that any one individual state or local tax may be insignificant often obscures the significance of the aggregate state and local taxation. An auditor should make sure that, as well as evaluating individual accruals, he evaluates the client's ability to control and accurately account for all of the taxes to which the enterprise may be subject.

The broadening scope of taxation in the United States at all levels and the increasing complexities involved make it difficult for an auditor to maintain currency in the necessary expertise to fulfill the above requirements. This has led to considerable specialization within accounting firms, and the specialists needed to evaluate the particular client problems that arise should be consulted by the auditor regularly. Many firms require that, as a minimum, the annual tax accruals be approved by a tax specialist within the firm. Working papers covering current and prior-year tax accruals should be extensively prepared and reviewed regularly for changes in tax laws, regulations, and rulings.

• STATEMENT PRESENTATION

DISCLOSURE

Standards for disclosure of the details of income tax expense and the balance sheet deferred debit and credit accounts have been rising in recent years, as users of financial statements increasingly recognize the importance and complexity of those elements in financial statements. Since 1962, disclosure has been required of the amount of investment credit and the method of accounting for it. The Revenue Act of 1971 extended this requirement. Since 1967, APB Opinion No. 11 (*AICPA Prof. Stds.,* vol. 3, paragraphs 4091.59 to .63) has required disclosure of the tax effects of timing differences and of operating losses, extraordinary item classification of tax benefits resulting from operating loss carryforwards, and reporting of any unused operating loss carryforwards or other deductions or credits. Paragraph 4091.62 also contains the following sentences:

> [Disclosure should be made of] reasons for significant variations in the customary relationships between income tax expense and pretax accounting income, if they are not otherwise apparent from the financial statements or from the nature of the entity's business. The Board recommends that the nature of significant differences between pretax accounting income and taxable income be disclosed.

In those sentences the APB took a step toward comprehensive disclosure of the components of income tax expense. Not many companies acted on the recommendation. In 1973, the SEC published requirements for comprehensive disclosure in financial statements under its jurisdiction. The SEC's reasons were set forth in Accounting Series Release No. 149, which also quoted the first of the above sentences from APB Opinion No. 11 and observed that the new SEC requirements "may be necessary in order to reflect the spirit of Opinion No. 11." The disclosures, incorporated in an amended Rule 3-16(o) of Regulation S-X, are summarized as follows:

> Separate disclosure of U. S. federal, foreign, and other (state and local) income taxes.

For each of the above, separate disclosure of taxes currently payable, the tax effect of timing differences, the tax effect of operating losses, and the treatment of investment tax credits.

For timing differences, the estimated effect of each significant type.

A reconciliation between the total income tax expense reported in the financial statements and the amount obtained by applying the U. S. federal income tax rate to the reported income before tax.

Any excess of cash outlay for income taxes over income tax expense expected in the next three years.

The rule permits nondisclosure of immaterial variations and specifies various percentages for the measurement of materiality. It should be carefully consulted.

The SEC's rule provides useful information not generally available in the past. However, the inconsistencies and confusion noted previously in this chapter between "book" tax losses and "tax" tax losses are not clarified by the disclosure requirements of either Opinion No. 11 or ASR No. 149. In the authors' opinion, consistent adherence to the deferred method requires disclosure of these items on the "book" basis —that is, related to amounts reflected in the income statement—in accordance with the "with-and-without" basis of computing deferred taxes. Therefore, amounts of operating losses and investment credit carrybacks and carryforwards should be computed on a "book" basis, not a "tax" basis. Disclosure of significant differences between those bases would be informative; as noted above, ASR No. 149 requires it when "tax" expense is expected to exceed "book" expense.

The following, then, is the current status of required or desirable presentation of income tax accounts in financial statements.

Liability for Taxes

The estimated liability for income taxes is usually stated separately, entitled "Accrued income taxes," "Estimated federal, state, and foreign income taxes payable," or a similar caption. Under APB Opinion No. 10 (*AICPA Prof. Stds.*, vol. 3, Section 2032), the offset of government securities against taxes payable, formerly considered acceptable practice in a number of instances, is no longer acceptable except "when it is clear that a purchase of securities (acceptable for the payment of taxes) is in substance an advance payment of taxes that will be payable in the relatively near future, so that in the special circumstances the purchase is tantamount to the prepayment of taxes" (paragraph 2032.03).

Some part of the estimated liability may be technically noncurrent, but it is not usually segregated from the current liability.

Deferred Debits and Credits

Deferred income tax credits or debits should be included among current liabilities or assets to the extent that they relate to assets or liabilities classified as current, such as receivables, inventories stated on the percentage-of-completion basis, or product warranty liabilities. The deferred amount should not be classified as current when it is created by a noncurrent asset or liability (such as depreciation timing differences or an unfunded long-term pension liability).

The extensive disclosures described earlier apply mostly to the provision for taxes in the income statement, but the note is usually referred to in the balance sheet captions as well.

Income Tax Expense

Most companies show one figure in the income statement, referenced to a note setting out the detailed disclosures described above. The caption is usually something like "Provision for taxes on income."

In some companies, the complexities of deferred tax accounting are not great, and the required disclosure can be handled on the face of the income statement, somewhat as follows:

```
Provision for taxes on income:
  Currently payable:
    U. S. (less $xx investment credit)           $xxx
    Foreign                                        xxx
  Deferred (principally as a result of accelerated
    depreciation for tax purposes)                 xxx    $xxx
```

The tax effect of extraordinary items is sometimes set out as a separate caption deducted from the extraordinary items, and sometimes as part of the caption:

```
(Description of extraordinary item), less
  $xxx related tax effect                         $xxx
```

The tax benefit of a loss carryforward is an extraordinary item in the year in which the benefit reduces taxes otherwise accrued as payable.

Note Disclosure

The disclosures required by Rule 3-16(o) of Regulation S-X, summarized earlier, are required of registrants in all financial statements that reflect significant amounts of investment credits, permanent book–tax differences, timing differences, or the effects of loss carrybacks or carryforwards. In the authors' opinion, they are highly desirable for companies that are not registered with the SEC.

14

The Investment Segment

MARKETABLE SECURITIES, INVESTMENTS, UNCONSOLIDATED AFFILIATES, INVESTMENT INCOME, GAINS AND LOSSES, AND RELATED ACCOUNTS

TERMINOLOGY

Investment assets are held for various reasons and their description in financial statements differs accordingly.

Marketable securities or *short-term investments* are the terms often used to connote income-producing use of excess cash funds by an industrial or commercial enterprise. The terms usually imply a temporary condition and refer primarily to the purpose of the investment rather than to the nature of the securities held. The term "marketable securities" also refers to securities that are salable in ordinary circumstances with reasonable promptness—that is, those for which an organized and active market exists. Most short-term investments are in marketable securities for obvious reasons, but some long-term investments, including those held for purposes of control, are also in securities that are readily marketable at a quoted market price. Many marketable securities held in the ordinary course of business by brokers and dealers in securities are in substance inventories.

Investments is a term often used by companies that hold securities as a part of their principal business activity, including banks, insurance companies, mutual funds, pension trusts, and endowed institutions. Their investments usually consist entirely or preponderantly of securities that are readily marketable, but both the business purpose and the usual holding period of individual securities is longer term. Many industrial and commercial companies also maintain significant investment portfolios that are managed primarily for a long-term yield of interest or dividends and market price appreciation.

Long-term investments, investments in affiliates, or sometimes simply *investments* often appear as noncurrent assets in financial statements of commercial and industrial companies and generally represent holdings of securities for purposes of control, affiliation, or financing of enterprises related to the operations of the investing company.

Sinking funds, building funds, and other funds accumulated for specific purposes may consist of investments in securities.

Since the terminology is not precise and the types of investments tend to overlap, readers of financial statements must often look at classifications, descriptions in captions, and descriptive notes to discern the nature and purposes of a company's investments in securities. In this chapter, the terms "securities" and "investments" refer both to the entire subject matter of the chapter and to the particular kinds described above; the context makes clear which use is intended.

In 1973, the AICPA published two Industry Audit Guides, *Audits of Investment Companies* and *Audits of Brokers and Dealers in Securities.* Those Guides are a more comprehensive treatment of much of the material covered in this chapter.

• ACCOUNTING PRINCIPLES

ACCOUNTING FOR ACQUISITION OF SECURITIES

Cost

For the most part, securities acquired are purchased and are recorded at cost. Cost includes costs of purchase, such as commissions, transfer taxes, finder's fees, and other fees. Gifts of securities are significant in nonprofit institutions and are recorded at fair value at the date of the gift. Fair value is determined by reference to published quotations of market price on the date the gift is received or, if the security is not publicly traded, by appraisal as of that date. The recorded value of a gift is then commonly referred to as cost.

Accrued Interest and Dividends at Acquisition

Part of the price paid for an interest-bearing security usually constitutes payment for interest accrued to the date of purchase. Accrued interest included in a purchase price should be excluded from the cost of the securities acquired and accounted for separately as accrued revenue or income receivable.

Sometimes the price paid for stock includes a dividend that is "on," that is, it has been declared, but the stockholders of record to receive the dividend have not yet been fixed, a fact that can be determined from published market quotations. Technically, the portion of purchase price reflecting the dividend that is "on," and not yet "ex," should be treated as a receivable and the dividend, when received, credited against it.

Exchanges or Substitutions of Securities

The accounting for the acquisition of securities in exchange for other investment securities issued by the same or a different corporation depends on the circumstances. The general principle is that a security so acquired should be recorded at the fair value of the security surrendered. The fair value of the asset received may be used to measure this cost if it is more clearly evident than the fair value of the security given up. That accounting normally results in a new carrying value and in the recognition of a gain or loss on the asset surrendered [APB Opinion No. 29 (*AICPA Prof. Stds.*, vol. 3, paragraph 1041.18)].

There are, however, several exceptions to that general principle which affect accounting for securities acquired. Some are described in Section 1041. The security acquired should be recorded at the carrying amount—usually cost—of the security surrendered if neither fair value is determinable within reasonable limits (paragraphs 1041.20, .25, and .26) or if the exchange of securities is not "essentially the culmination of an earning process" (paragraph 1041.21). As defined in paragraphs 1041.21 and 1041.03, an exchange of investments accounted for by the equity method is an exchange of productive assets, which is not "the culmination of an earning process." Thus, an exchange of securities accounted for by the equity method does not result in a new carrying amount, while an exchange of securities accounted for by any other method does. Securities acquired are also recorded at the carrying amount of securities given up if the transaction is in substance the rescission of a prior business combination (implied in paragraph 1041.23.) Cost of one asset should not, of course, be substituted for cost of another if evidence of impairment of value exists, in which case the amount should be written down to recoverable cost, and a loss should be recognized.

Securities are sometimes acquired through conversion of other securities of the same issuer or as a result of a consolidation, merger, or other reorganization of the issuing corporation. Those securities acquired are also recorded at the cost of the securities surrendered, adjusted for any cash paid or received in the transaction or for a permanent decline in value.

Securities Received as Dividends

Occasionally, securities of one corporation are received as dividends on securities of another. Dividend income equal to the fair value of the securities received should be recognized, and that amount becomes the "cost" of the securities at the time of their receipt.

Stock Dividends Received

The effect of receiving a dividend on common stock in shares of the same common stock is merely to increase the number of units of ownership held without changing the investor's proportionate stockholding in the issuing company. There is no effective divestment of property or rights by the issuing corporation. No dividend income should be recognized, and the cost of the original stockholding should be apportioned between the new shares received and the old shares held. (In some cases income may result from stock dividends under the concept of apportionment contained in some state trust laws, which should be consulted in each instance.)

A dividend on common stock is sometimes received in the form of preferred stock of the issuing corporation. If no other preferred stock is outstanding, the effect is the same as a stock dividend of common stock on common stock, the same accounting applies, and cost is apportioned between the stock received and the original stock held. (The same reasoning applies to dividends in the form of warrants or rights to purchase common or preferred stock.) If shares of the preferred stock used in the dividend were previously outstanding, the preferable treatment is to recognize dividend income on the grounds that the dividend gives the investor an interest different from that represented by former holdings.

Securities Acquired Together

If more than one security is received in a transaction, the cost basis, however determined, should be apportioned to each security acquired in the ratio that its fair market value bears to the aggregate fair market value of all securities received.

Sometimes complex "packages" of securities are acquired: combinations of different kinds of stock or of stock, debt, and warrants. Allocating cost among the different securities is a difficult, specialized task, which is usually best performed by an investment banker if market quotations are not available. Allocating cost is particularly difficult for venture-capital types of investments in small companies, but good practice and the specific requirements of the Investment Company Act of 1940 for assignment of value to each security listed in reports to stockholders both require that it be done.

ACCOUNTING FOR HOLDING AND DISPOSAL OF SECURITIES

Securities Carried at Cost

In the financial statements of commercial and industrial companies and of some financial institutions, primarily banks, marketable securities and investments are carried at cost without adjustment except for amortization of bond premium or discount. (Investment companies carry investments at market value, sometimes without amortization, as described in a subsequent section.)

Amortization of Discount or Premium

If a debt security is acquired at a premium or discount, preferred practice is to amortize the difference between cost and face value of the security over its remaining life to maturity. The interest method of amortization is preferable.

The reason for amortizing premium or discount is to recognize the effective interest rate on a security. If instead a discount represents an allowance for the probability that the security will not be redeemed in full at maturity, amortization is inappropriate and amounts received as interest should be evaluated to determine whether they represent effectively partial recovery of cost rather than entirely current income.

Recognizing Investment Income

Interest income should be accrued as time passes unless its receipt is doubtful. Dividends should be recorded on the "ex dividend" date; they should never be accrued based on the passage of time even if experience indicates beyond a reasonable doubt that they will be received. Most companies record dividends as they are received and accrue dividends receivable only at the end of an accounting period. Dividends in kind should be recorded at fair market value. As already noted, stock dividends should generally not be recorded as income.

Sometimes an investor makes additional loans to or investments in an "investee," part of which is used to pay interest on outstanding loans. An investor should not recognize such interest as income if it appears that the investee is in financial difficulty and ultimate full repayment or recovery is not assured.

Disclosing Fair Value

The fair value of securities carried at cost should be determined from time to time for management purposes and should be disclosed in financial statements. Fair values should be watched for evidence of a decline in value that is other than temporary, which should be recognized by recording a loss. Securities that are carried as current assets should always be written down to market if a significant decline has taken place. Those carried as noncurrent assets need be written down only if the decline is not considered temporary (see SAS Interpretation published in January 1975). Opinion is divided on whether securities that have been written down can be restored to cost when market quotations recover. We prefer not to write them back up again.

Lending institutions, such as banks, finance companies, and insurance companies, make large numbers of loans which, individually, do not have readily determinable market values. It is customary to set up a "provision for loan losses" which is estimated and accounted for in much the same way as the "allowance for doubtful accounts" described in Chapter 9.

Gain or Loss on Disposal

Gain or loss is recorded when securities are sold or, in certain cases, when they are exchanged for other securities. The gain or loss is computed by deducting the carrying amount (cost or amortized cost) and costs of disposal from the proceeds, reduced by accrued interest or declared dividends, if any. If only part of an investment in a security is sold, cost is usually apportioned on the basis of average cost, first-in first-out, or identification of the cost of specific certificates. Occasionally, the last-in first-out method is used by stockbrokers. The average cost method has the merit of recognizing the fungible character of different lots of the same security and is generally considered preferable to the other two methods. The identified cost method permits considerable choice in the amount of gain or loss to be recognized if different lots of a security have been purchased at different prices. (See also the *Investment Company* Audit Guide, pages 39 and 40.)

The average cost method cannot be used for federal income tax purposes under current regulations. Thus, if the average cost method is used for financial statement reporting of sales of partial holdings, a difference arises between the book basis and tax basis of both the securities sold and the remaining holdings. Deferred tax accounting is necessary, and memorandum records of tax cost must be maintained coincident with the accounting records.

Accounting for Investments by Banks

Banks account for investment securities in the conventional manner: investments are carried at cost, income (mostly interest) is recognized as it is earned, and gains and losses are computed on each sale. A considerable body of opinion holds that most sales and purchases of investment securities by banks constitute adjustments of the portfolio for the purpose of adjusting income yield; therefore, gains and losses should be amortized over the average life of the portfolio so as to show an average yield in interest income. That issue was thoroughly discussed by the accounting profession during the course of preparing an AICPA Industry Audit Guide, *Audits of Banks,* and the proposed principle was not adopted.

Securities Carried at Market Value

For many years, some kinds of entities—principally mutual funds, insurance companies, and stockbrokers—have carried some or all of their investments at market value. The *Investment Company* Audit Guide (page 16) calls for all investment companies to report at value. The reason for this, which is implied rather than clearly stated in the Guide, is that investment is a major business operation, and the "performance" of that operation in preserving and enhancing value is an important fact. Therefore, complete reporting of the results of operations requires accounting for changes in market value. Insurance companies carry certain of their investments at market value because failure to recognize substantial accumulated "unrealized" appreciation or depreciation would misstate the actual values available to protect policyholders and creditors. The application of market value accounting by insurance companies is generally governed and restricted by statute or regulation: usually common and preferred stocks may be carried at market value, but bonds are carried at cost with amortization of premiums and discounts. Some endowed institutions carry investments at market value as part of the "total return" concept, which is described later in the chapter.

Some accountants believe that market values should be used for all investments other than those held for control or use in production. The subject was studied by the Accounting Principles Board: although most of those who participated in the discussions or commented on the various proposals agreed that investments should generally be stated at market values, serious differences of opinion arose regarding accounting for gains and losses from changes in market values, and the issue was not settled. Presumably, the Financial Accounting Standards Board will eventually consider the matter.

Determining Market Value

Using market value for investments rests mechanically on the availability of a means for obtaining market price quotations for publicly traded securities and appraisals of value for other securities. Usual practice is for an institution that needs market values regularly to arrange with a brokerage firm to supply quotations as needed. Closing prices are used for securities listed on a recognized stock exchange. An average of bid and asked prices, preferably from more than one broker–dealer, is usually used for over-the-counter securities, although some concerns use bid prices. Some securities, such as municipal bonds, have specialized markets, and quotations must be obtained from specialists. Quoted market values are not reduced for brokerage commissions and other normal costs of disposition. (See also the *Investment Company* Audit Guide, pages 33 to 35.)

Determining Fair Value

Securities that are not actively traded often present valuation problems. Examples are "venture-capital investments"; investments in "restricted" securities (issued under a covenant prohibiting public sale for a specified period of time) and unregistered securities (not registered with the Securities and Exchange Commission and, therefore, not freely tradeable); blocks of securities for which the market is "thin" (i.e., the number of shares normally available for trade is small in relation to the block to be valued, so that sale of the block can be expected to affect market prices); and blocks that represent effective control of the investee company. The Investment Company Act of 1940 requires directors of registered investment companies to value securities for which market quotations are not available "at fair value in good faith," and the *Investment Company* Audit Guide (pages 35 to 37) and SEC Accounting Series Release No. 118 give some guidance in doing so. The Release and the Guide describe fair value as the "amount which the owner might reasonably expect to receive from them upon their current sale" and cite examples of methods for ascertaining it based on multiples of earnings, a discount from the market price of a similar security that is freely traded, yield to maturity on debt securities, or some combination of those and other methods.

Periodic evaluation of untraded or restricted securities held is a serious responsibility for management purposes as well as financial reporting purposes for all companies where the value of investments is significant, and it deserves careful attention. In the past, it was often done informally or subjectively by the chief investment officer, but the subject has received much attention and discussion in recent years. As a result, more formal and objective procedures have evolved. Preferred procedure is for a brief factual analysis of the security and its prospects to be prepared by the member of management most knowledgeable about it; after review by other members of management, the analysis is presented to the directors together with a recommendation for valuation. While investment companies value all their investments at "market or fair value," there are many instances (venture-capital investments and real estate holdings are the most common) where cost may be the most appropriate measure of value in the absence of other evidence. (See the *Investment Company* Audit Guide, page 16.)

Investment Income and Gains and Losses

Accounting for dividends and interest on securities carried at market or fair value is much the same as for securities carried at cost. Interest and dividends, realized gains and losses on sales, and unrealized appreciation on securities still held are accounted for separately because they are often disclosed separately in financial statements and have different tax treatments and different availability for use or distribution. Gain or loss on sales is computed on the basis of cost, because realized appreciation is significant for legal and tax purposes; further, the distinction between realized and unrealized appreciation retains significance in accounting. Unrealized appreciation is usually excluded from net income and recorded directly in retained earnings or an equivalent equity account after provision for deferred income tax, if any, payable on the gain when realized.

Distributions by Investment Companies

A long-standing principle is that many investment companies act as a "conduit" between the companies in which they invest and their own stockholders for the purpose of "passing through" the net income and realized gains. As such, they can be relieved of federal income tax if they qualify and elect to be taxed as "regulated investment companies" and comply with the pertinent detailed regulations. The important requirement is that substantially all income (primarily interest and dividends) and realized gains be distributed to stockholders. Since the stockholders are taxed as though they themselves received the income and gains, the two sources must be kept separate, and distributions by an investment company must be identified as to source.

For accounting purposes, the distributing fund charges distributions of income against accumulated income and distributions of gains against accumulated gains. Recipients most often take both income and gains into income. Technically, both income and gains should be used to reduce the cost of the investment if they represent distributions of amounts included in the value of the shares at time of purchase, but that distinction is seldom practical and is usually ignored. The portion of costs of repurchases of capital shares equivalent to the amount on a per-share basis of distributable net investment income on the date of the transaction is charged to undistributed income. (See the *Investment Company* Audit Guide, pages 17 to 19.)

Some funds offer stockholders the option of receiving additional fund shares rather than cash in distributions of income and gains. The accounting for the fund is essentially the same as if the cash had been distributed and stock sold to the stockholder in the same amount. Opinion is divided on the proper accounting by recipients. For tax purposes, the fair market value of the distribution is income—or capital gain—and the stock received has the same tax basis as if purchased. The trust laws of some states require similar treatment. We believe that is also the preferable treatment for financial statement purposes, because it reflects the economic fact that income on the investment earned by the fund has been passed on to the investor. Others prefer stock dividend accounting; that is, no income is recognized and the cost of old shares is allocated among the old shares plus those received in the distribution. If that treatment is followed, the tax liability incurred because of the requirement that the distribution be taxed as income should be treated as an additional component of cost of the shares.

Some funds automatically reinvest realized capital gains and pay a related capital gains tax on behalf of stockholders: the so-called "deemed paid" distributions. The fund records the tax paid on behalf of stockholders as a reduction of the realized capital gains, the balance of which is credited to additional paid-in capital (and to capital stock if additional shares are issued). For tax purposes, a recipient is required to treat the entire amount of his share of the gain as capital gains income, to take his share of the tax paid as a credit against his tax liability, and to increase the tax basis of his stock by the net amount of the gain less tax. We believe that method is the preferable treatment for accounting purposes as well. Thus, a recipient records two entries on receipt of notice of a "deemed paid" distribution: (1) to increase the "cost" of the investment and record income for the deemed paid distribution and (2) to reduce federal income tax liability and "cost" of the investment for the tax deemed paid on his behalf.

Stock dividend accounting must also be considered acceptable: no income and no change in asset cost is recognized except to debit or credit any difference between the actual tax attributable to the distribution and the "deemed paid" tax credit. If stock dividend accounting is employed, separate records must be kept for the different tax basis.

Many mutual funds account for "income equalization": the small fraction of the price of each sale and repurchase of their own shares that represents undistributed ordinary income. That practice is explained and illustrated on pages 17 and 18 of the *Investment Company Audit Guide*.

Distributions by Endowed Institutions

Historically, endowed institutions have been presumed to be governed by "trust principles" of law and accounting in which the distinction between corpus and income must be rigidly and meticulously observed. Under those principles, realized gains are added to endowment principal, unrealized appreciation is seldom, if ever, accounted for, and interest and dividends are distributed to participating funds and used for the purposes of the institution. In recent years a body of opinion has developed that "corporate principles," both legal and accounting, should govern endowment funds. The principal implication of that view for accounting is that gains are considered income.

In the past, many institutions adopted a practice of "distributing" income at a stable annual rate which differed from the fluctuating actual interest and dividend income. The procedure involved crediting investment income received to an "income equalization account" and charging the account for amounts actually distributed. However, that type of "income equalization" accounting is no longer acceptable under the provisions of the AICPA Industry Audit Guide, *Audits of Colleges and Universities*, which requires that all investment income be distributed to participating funds.

In recent years, the "total return" concept of managing endowment funds appeared and gained some acceptance. This concept recognizes that many companies in whose stock endowment funds are invested have a financial policy of "plowing back" earnings rather than distributing them and that reinvestment of earnings enhances the value of the stock. Therefore, the concept calls for managing an endowment portfolio for "total return"—appreciation as well as interest or dividends. If a fund is managed for total return, some part of price appreciation on the stock in the fund may be recognized as income.

The legal status of the total return concept is currently in a state of change. It is clear that in some states strict trust principles apply and that no gains, realized or unrealized, may be used for current purposes. However, totally unrestricted discretionary funds which have been assigned to "function as endowments" may be used in any way an institution chooses. Other states have passed specific statutes to permit the current use of realized gains and in some cases of both realized and unrealized appreciation. Anyone concerned with accounting for and auditing of an endowed institution must keep informed on developments in the area.

The *College and University* Audit Guide calls for accounting for all gains distributed for use in current operations as transfers from endowment fund principal to current funds. Therefore, that method must be currently considered preferred accounting.

Securities Carried at Equity

Under the equity method, an investment is recorded at cost at acquisition and is then adjusted each period for the investor's proportionate interest in earnings, losses, and other changes in stockholders' equity of the investee corporation.

APB Opinion No. 18 (*AICPA Prof. Stds.,* vol. 3, Section 5131) prescribes the equity method for use in consolidated financial statements and in parent company financial statements "prepared for issuance to stockholders as the financial statements of the primary reporting entity" to account for investments in common stock of:

Unconsolidated subsidiaries, domestic and foreign,

Corporate joint ventures (defined in paragraph 5131.03), and

Other investments of 50 per cent or less of the voting stock in which the investor has the ability to exercise significant influence over operating and financial policies of the investee corporation.

The equity method does not apply if an investment is temporary, if common stockholders have lost control of an investee corporation because of bankruptcy or reorganization proceedings or similar reasons, or if foreign investments are subject to severe exchange restrictions, controls, or other uncertainties. Nor is the equity method a substitute for consolidation of subsidiaries that otherwise should be consolidated.

Opinion No. 18 is explicit on what the Board means by "the ability to exercise significant influence" over the policies of an investee corporation in which an investor holds 50 per cent or less of the voting stock:

Ability to exercise that [significant] influence may be indicated in several ways, such as representation on the board of directors, participation in policy making processes, material intercompany transactions, interchange of managerial personnel, or technological dependency. Another important consideration is the extent of ownership by an investor in relation to the concentration of other shareholdings, but substantial or majority ownership of the voting stock of an investee by another investor does not necessarily preclude the ability to exercise significant influence by the investor. The Board recognizes that determining the ability of an investor to exercise such influence is not always clear and applying judgment is necessary to assess the status of each investment. In order to achieve a reasonable degree of uniformity in application, the Board concludes that an investment (direct or indirect) of 20% or more of the voting stock of an investee should lead to a presumption that in the absence of evidence to the contrary an investor has the ability to exercise significant influence over an investee. Conversely, an investment of less than 20% of the voting stock of an investee should lead to a presumption that an investor does not have the ability to exercise significant influence unless such ability can be demonstrated. [Paragraph 5131.17]

The equity method of accounting usually does not apply to notes, bonds, and similar debt instruments. The Opinion is silent about its application to investments in preferred stocks.

The mechanics of the equity method can be handled in either of two ways. The simpler way is to adjust the investment periodically by the amount of the investor's share of the earnings or losses for the period, recording income or loss from the investment. Dividends received are credited to the investment account. However, since it is necessary to account for distributed earnings separately from equity in undistributed earnings for various reasons (SEC and federal income tax reporting, for example), it is common to include dividends received in an income account and to adjust the investment account only for the net change in underlying equity.

The equity method involves the same adjustments to underlying equity as are made in consolidating subsidiaries. A difference between cost and underlying equity at time of acquisition should be allocated to individual tangible and intangible assets and goodwill, and goodwill should be amortized according to the provisions of APB Opinion No. 17 (*AICPA Prof. Stds.*, vol. 3, Section 5141). Intercompany profits should be eliminated, entirely or to the extent of the investor's interest, depending on the circumstances. Income taxes that would become payable on receipt of undistributed earnings or on sale of the investment, whichever is more likely, should be recorded (*AICPA Prof. Stds.*, vol. 3, paragraph 4096.08). An impairment or decline in value of the investment that is other than temporary should be recognized in addition to the investor's equity in underlying income or losses.

Sometimes, recording an investor's equity in a series of losses reduces an investment carried at equity to zero. If the investor has no further financial responsibility beyond the initial investment, there is no need to record further losses. However, if the investor has a commitment to make further advances or investments, it may be necessary to record equity in continuing underlying losses.

It is often difficult to obtain reliable data on the underlying equity in an investment for accounting periods concurrent with those of the investor. Usually, the equity adjustment is determined from data for a period that ended from one to six months earlier. While it is desirable to have the lag as short as possible, there is no harm in a lag if the reporting periods are consistent from year to year and there is adequate means of communication about unusual gains or losses occurring in the lag period.

• TYPICAL TRANSACTION SYSTEMS AND INTERNAL CONTROL

TYPICAL TRANSACTIONS

The steps in the investment segment are more likely to be the same from one company to another than in any of the other segments. They can be expected to be rather formal and well organized, whether the purpose is short-term investment of temporary excess cash, long-term investment, or investment for purposes of affiliation or control. The segment begins with the selection and authorization of an investment; subsequent steps are: acquisition, safeguarding and accountability, accounting for income, appraisal, and disposition.

Selection and Authorization

If the investment function is not major—if it concerns only the temporary investment of excess cash, for example—it should be specifically delegated to an executive officer, often the treasurer, by vote of the board of directors.

If the function is major, as in insurance companies, investment companies, banks, endowed institutions, and pension trusts, it should be exercised by top officers or the board of directors. Often an investment committee of officers or directors employs an investment advisor; frequently it delegates to him the authority to make specific decisions about acquisitions and dispositions of investments. In the final analysis, however, the responsibility for investment decisions must rest with management.

The controls over investment selection, according to the classification described in Chapter 3, are authorization and pre-audit: authorization by the board may be for specific investments or it may be general authorization to an officer or advisor to make investment decisions; review and explicit approval of decisions made constitute a pre-audit control.

Acquisition

Investments in marketable securities are most often, but not always, acquired through banks and brokers who deal in formal markets. Control is exercised by some form of approved acquisition list, which may include maximum prices or minimum yields. Orders placed, receipt of the customary confirmation slip, and subsequent receipt of and payment for the security are noted on the list. In most companies, which have relatively few investment transactions, the acquisition list is maintained manually. For large investment activities, in which acquisition of a desired quantity of a single investment may require a number of transactions over considerable time, the control system over acquisitions may be formal and complex, including computerization.

Acquisitions of investments in other than marketable securities are almost always unique events. That is true even if a fairly large number of investments is acquired at one time, such as acquisitions of real estate for an endowment fund or investment portfolio. The selection of investments and the negotiation of acquisition terms are likely to be delegated to the same investment specialist. Control over his activities consists of pre-audit review and approval.

Safeguarding and Accountability

Physical safeguarding of securities is vital because many marketable securities are negotiable, and, even when it is not readily negotiable, a document evidencing legal ownership has a great value. Therefore, the control operations of restricted access and segregation of duties should receive careful attention. Securities should be kept in a vault, safe deposit box, or, at a minimum, fireproof safe. The custodian and other personnel who have access to the place of safekeeping should be independent of the functions of authorizing investment transactions, keeping investment records, handling cash, and maintaining the general ledger—preferably each of those employees should be independent of all the others.

If securities are kept in a safe deposit box, the number of people with authorized access to the box should be limited to the minimum consistent with orderly procedure. Two persons should be required to be present whenever the box is opened as a disciplinary control against error or misuse. A safe deposit box is preferable to an office safe because a bank's provisions for physical security and procedures for restricting and controlling access to the vault are naturally more extensive, systematized, and disciplined than most other organizations are able to maintain.

If securities are numerous it is usual to engage a bank as agent to maintain custody. Banks have facilities and procedures for safeguarding negotiable instruments and employ skilled specialists, all of which are expensive and inconvenient for a company to maintain. A custodian is responsible for maintaining both physical and recording accountability for securities held. However, accountability should not be left entirely to the custodian; the owner of securities should maintain a record as a check on the custodian's records. The custodian receives or delivers securities, detaches interest coupons or warrants, and performs other operations only on written instructions from the owner; those written instructions become the documentation for the custodian's function in the transaction system.

Accounting for Income

Accounting for income from publicly held marketable securities is a simple matter: interest is accrued periodically and dividends are recorded as received (or when they become "ex dividend"). At the end of an accounting period, the accounts are reviewed, the accrual computations double-checked, and dividends receivable recorded.

Published records of interest, dividends, and other distributions should be checked from time to time to make sure that all income is received when it should be. Often that task is left to the auditor and is performed as an expansion of his tests of investment income; it is usually less expensive and better systemization of control to have the double-checking control performed by an employee other than the one responsible for the initial accounting for income.

If an investment is accounted for on the equity method, copies of financial statements of the investee must be obtained for use as the basis for recording income or losses.

Appraisal

Appraisal of investments from time to time is necessary for managerial control and decision making; it is also required to determine market or fair value for financial statement purposes. If investments are few in number, relatively short term, and not a significant part of a company's operations, appraisals may be carried out informally by the officer responsible for investments. However informal they may be, appraisals should be conscientiously and explicitly performed. If investments are significant, appraisals should be formally executed and documented. The frequency of appraisals depends on the amount of activity in the investment segment and the frequency of issuance of financial statements: six-month intervals are generally considered the maximum; at the other extreme, some active investment portfolios are under virtually continuous appraisal.

Investments should be priced at market quotations (usually the list is classified by industry if voluminous) and the history of price and yield should be reviewed by one or more responsible officers. The Investment Company Act of 1940 requires that boards of directors determine the values of investment securities for which market values are not readily available.

The statutory requirement of the Investment Company Act notwithstanding, it was thought for many decades that securities could not be appraised or values determined in the absence of market quotations. The increasing number of investments without market prices, such as venture-capital investments and restricted securities, focused a great deal of attention on the subject of valuation in recent years. It became clear that management has a responsibility to itself, its investors, and the public to make an explicit appraisal of the value of each of its investments, and that good managements followed that practice.

Preferred practice is for the officer most knowledgeable about an investment to prepare a brief, factual description of the underlying conditions affecting its value: trend of sales, profits, and financial position; developments within the company or industry, and so forth. (See pages 33 to 39 of the *Investment Company* Audit Guide for a more extensive discussion of factors to be considered.) That analysis becomes the basis for a recommended valuation which is reviewed by others within the company and submitted to the directors for approval. A properly prepared analysis affords a reasonable basis for an experienced judgment, especially if it can be related to a series of earlier analyses.

Disposition

Disposition of investments usually follows the same procedures and is subject to the same controls as acquisition.

Records of Investments

The most basic record is the documentation of decisions to acquire or dispose of investments: the acquisition list or a copy of the vote of the investment committee or board of directors. If investment decisions are delegated to an individual officer, however, the acquisition list is often informal or even nonexistent. Brokers' advices and custodian receipts are always retained as part of the basic records. Approval of a transaction as authorization for payment is often evidenced by initialing the broker's advice.

Whether a portfolio is large or small, an investment ledger is desirable. The ledger should contain an account for each investment. The caption should describe the investment completely: full title of the issue; number of shares or face value; certificate numbers; interest or dividend rate; maturities or other features such as call, conversion, or collateral; cost; and required amortization of premium or discount. If the tax basis is different from the book basis, it may be convenient to record each in a separate section of the same investment ledger account. The detail of the investment ledger should be reconciled periodically with the general ledger control account. Larger portfolios usually have all this information computerized.

Some investments, such as mortgages, should be supported by a permanent file of documents controlled by a checklist of the contents: for example, note receivable (bond), mortgage, record of registering the mortgage, insurance policies, tax bills, and so on.

Exercise of the accountability function calls for periodic inspection of securities or other documentation of investments by persons other than those responsible for authorizing and executing transactions and maintaining custody of securities.

AUDITING PROCEDURES

OBJECTIVES

As in auditing other asset accounts, the objectives of auditing investments are reasonable assurance that they exist; are owned by the client, free of undisclosed restrictions or encumbrances; are carried at cost (or value where appropriate) determined in accordance with generally accepted accounting principles; and have a recognized market or other fair value. The principal differences in auditing investments are that the determination of market or fair value is critical and must be reflected in some way in the financial statements, and that they are evidenced by legal documents which may be negotiable or contain restrictions.

An auditor's objectives, therefore, are to obtain reasonable assurance that the investments are:

Owned by the client at the balance sheet date;

Not pledged or otherwise restricted;

Evidenced by appropriate documents on hand or held by other responsible parties for the account of the client;

Carried at cost or other basis in accordance with generally accepted accounting principles;

Recognized to have a market or other fair value determined as objectively as circumstances permit; and

Not stated in excess of fair value.

THE AUDIT CYCLE

The nature of the investment segment calls for emphasis on validation, resulting in an audit cycle that is usually much simpler than those for the major segments discussed in earlier chapters. Since the system must be understood and evaluated, the transaction review is essential. To the extent that an auditor intends to rely on controls, functional tests are necessary; however, investment activity is often validated in detail, thus precluding the need for functional tests. Investments held by mutual funds and other types of registered investment companies must be examined or confirmed 100 per cent under the Investment Company Act of 1940. Validation tests may be carried out at an interim date, but often they are concentrated on the year end if securities are marketable, both because of the volatility of the assets and because year-end validation is not burdensome.

Transaction Reviews

Most companies have only one type of transaction for each step in the handling of marketable securities and one type for each step in the handling of long-term investments. Large investment portfolios may include several types of transactions if transactions originate and are processed in separate departments: for example, bonds, government securities, real estate, and common stock.

Functional Tests

Certain investment segment control functions are of great concern to an auditor who wishes to limit his substantive tests or carry them out at other than year end. However, often the limited number of transactions, sensitivity of the asset, or client's request makes complete detailed verification of investment transactions desirable. In that case, an auditor does not rely on control functions and thus has no need to test them. Or, looked at another way, the control function is verified 100 per cent by the detailed examination.

As a matter of principle, preferred practice is for the client to make the 100 per cent detailed check and the auditor to make a functional test of the double-checking control feature. In that case, the controls in which an auditor is interested and the tests he makes are as follows:

Authorization and approval of acquisitions and dispositions.
> Trace a sample of investment transactions to minutes of meetings of directors or executive committee for authorization or approval.

Safeguarding of securities.
> Trace a sample of transactions to copies of instructions to custodian and custodian confirmations.
> Test custodian's controls over access to securities (or obtain assurance that access is limited and properly controlled).

Control over receipt of income.
> Verify income receivable for a number of investments by computation of interest and reference to published services for dividends; examine evidence of client's verification procedures.

Control over compliance with IRS requirements for eligibility as a regulated investment company (where applicable). (Those requirements are rather extensive, and strict compliance is of the utmost importance to an investment company that intends to maintain its tax-free status.)
> Examine client's checklist or control log for evidence of compliance; test-check computations; review for completeness.

VALIDATION PROCEDURES

If a company has a small portfolio and few transactions, it is customary for an auditor to count or confirm investments and substantiate all transactions in an investment ledger—purchases, sales, changes in units, and income. In other companies with large and active portfolios, however, a detailed examination can be extremely time-consuming and possibly unnecessary. Generally the size and importance of the portfolio warrant sound systems of accounting and internal control. Consequently, if internal accounting control and internal check are satisfactory, and functional tests substantiate the effectiveness of the system of control, an auditor may be justified in limiting his examination of security transactions to functional tests corroborated by a representative test-check of counts and confirmation of securities.

Marketable securities are more "volatile" than nonmarketable securities because they are usually negotiable, their values fluctuate, and they are subject to buying and selling activity. Therefore, the following discussion centers around marketable securities, but the same procedures apply also to nonmarketable securities.

Existence and Ownership of Securities

Auditing procedures designed to validate existence and ownership of securities include physical inspection of investments in stocks, bonds, notes, mortgages, and other debt instruments, or written confirmation from reputable depositaries holding securities for safekeeping or other purposes. If persons in a company's organization other than those who have responsibility for investments periodically inspect them, and an auditor has satisfied himself about the adequacy of the procedures by observation or on the basis of his own tests, another inspection may not be necessary. Generally, however, an independent count of securities on hand or under direct control of the client is advisable.

Count of Small Portfolios

Most industrial and commercial companies do not own numerous securities, and physical inspection is not difficult. An auditor usually obtains a list of securities supporting the general ledger balance at the date of the count and makes arrangements for the custodian to accompany him to the place where the securities are kept. The auditor examines the securities by checking them against the list. During the process, he normally observes evidence of internal accounting control and internal check: for example, an accurate security list, proper endorsement or evidence of ownership on the securities, proper division of duties between custodian and recordkeeper, adequate physical safeguards (such as use of a bank's safe deposit vault), and requirements for dual access to the securities. If those are in order, an auditor usually has no compelling reason to make the count at the balance sheet date or at the same time that other negotiable assets, such as cash, are counted.

In companies with few securities, control procedures may be, for that reason, informal or nonexistent. The treasurer or other principal officers may have authority to act for the company in buying or selling securities and also may have custody of or sole access to them. In those circumstances, an auditor may wish to make his count at the balance sheet date, or, if it is done at another date, to seal the vault or box during the intervening period. Banks generally seal a safe deposit box on an auditor's request and subsequently confirm to him that no access to the box was granted during the specified period. Furthermore, it may be desirable to make the count of securities simultaneously with the count of cash and other negotiable assets. A count is considered "simultaneous" if the securities are sealed or otherwise controlled until all the negotiable assets are examined.

Count of Large Portfolios

If a portfolio of marketable securities is relatively large and active, as in banks, insurance companies, investment companies, and stock brokerages, the count of securities may be a major undertaking requiring extensive planning, precision in execution, and a large staff of auditors. Although sometimes the count is made on the balance sheet date, usually the size and importance of the portfolio justify sophisticated internal accounting controls and internal check and, accordingly, the count may be made at another time. If an auditor deems it necessary in the circumstances, he may establish and maintain control of securities (or their movement) for the period between his count and the balance sheet date.

A list of marketable securities owned or held as collateral or for safekeeping at the date of the count should be prepared from the security records, preferably by the client. (Computer runs are frequently used for this purpose, and sometimes sophisticated computer audit programs are employed.) Securities counted should be checked against the list, which should adequately describe the securities, including aggregate principal amount of bonds and notes; number of shares of stock; denomination of bonds or par value, if any, of stocks; maturity dates of bonds; and interest and preferred stock dividend rates. If available, information as to location of the securities should be included on the list.

The auditor should maintain control over securities from the start of his count until it has been completed and checked to the list of securities and all exceptions have been investigated to the extent possible at the time. Responsible officials or employees of the client should be present during the count to reduce the possibility of later questions about the handling of securities.

In counts of large portfolios, an auditor must exercise care not only in determining the most expeditious plan of count, but also in setting up his controls with the least inconvenience to the client. Especially if a count is made without prior notice to the client, an auditor needs to ascertain the location of all marketable securities, establish controls at various points necessary to record movements of securities, and plan the sequence of the count.

A properly controlled plan may consist of stationing an auditor ("control" auditor) at each location to observe and record movements of securities. Other auditors perform the actual count. Bags, boxes, safes, or whole rooms may be sealed to be counted at a later time. The purpose of seals is not to make physical entry impossible but to indicate to the auditor whether the sealed item was disturbed.

If movement of securities is necessary before the count is completed, the control auditor should observe the withdrawal or deposit, determine the reason for withdrawal, and record the transactions in the working papers. If securities that have already been counted must be removed to be mailed to correspondents, brokers, transfer agents, or others, they should be recorded and controlled until they are turned over to the postal authorities. Relatively inactive securities may be counted and placed under seal in advance of the main count or placed under seal and counted after more active items have been examined.

The usual counting procedure is for the control auditor to release batches of securities to the counting auditors, keeping a record of batches released. The counting auditors count each issue of securities and call off the count to an auditor holding the security list. If the count and the list do not agree, the issue is recounted, sometimes by a different counter, until the listed amount is verified or it is determined that a difference exists.

In the process of counting the securities, an auditor should also examine them. He is not qualified to assume responsibility for the genuineness or authenticity of certificates or instruments representing securities investments. Certificates are commonly encountered in a wide variety of shapes, colors, types of engraving or printing, and quality of paper, and clever forgers have frequently succeeded in deceiving personnel of financial institutions experienced in handling securities. Nevertheless, an auditor should be alert to the possibility of spurious certificates. If any certificates appear to be unusual and if the auditor is unable to satisfy himself as to their authenticity by examination of purchase documents, income records, or the like, he should confirm them with the issuer or transfer agent.

Insurance companies and similar institutional investors frequently have in their portfolios registered instruments in large denominations that may have been reduced below face amount by partial payments. An auditor should request confirmation of the amount of those instruments outstanding if it appears that they do not have to be presented to the issuer or his agent for endorsement or reissue at the time a partial payment is received.

An auditor should note that certificates of stock and registered bonds are in the name of the client or an accredited nominee or, if they are not, that certificates are appropriately endorsed or accompanied by powers of attorney. Bonds with interest coupons should be examined on a test basis to determine that coupons not yet due have not been detached. If coupons presently coming due are not attached to the bonds, an auditor should inquire as to their location and either inspect them or confirm them with the holders. He should determine why coupons past due that are attached have not been presented for payment. Interest in default should be noted in the working papers for consideration in connection with the examination of accruals of income and carrying amounts of investments.

Differences between the count and the list of securities should be explored and the reasons identified and understood. Certain types of differences are normal and expected; for example, securities held by others, securities in transit, and entries to the investment ledger that do not coincide with receipt of securities ("cutoff" items). The holders of securities in other locations should be identified and requests for confirmation sent. In-transit and cutoff items should be related to recent transactions. Outgoing in-transit items should be confirmed with recipients. Securities received by the client through the mail for a few days subsequent to the date of examination should be examined to substantiate items in transit. Once an auditor is satisfied that all items on the security list have been counted or their location elsewhere confirmed and all differences have been reconciled, he may "release" control over securities.

Simultaneous Examination

An auditor should not overlook the possibility of substitutions, especially if disciplinary controls are weak. If examinations are being made of one or more trust accounts handled by the same trustee or in the same office, securities for all accounts should be counted at the same time. Similarly, if different auditors are employed to examine several accounts, they should make their counts simultaneously, if possible. Otherwise, material shortages may be concealed by temporary transfers from accounts whose securities are not being counted.

If a client is reluctant to permit an auditor to count securities of other accounts or is unwilling or unable to arrange for a simultaneous count by all auditors concerned, an auditor may identify securities owned by the client by accounting for certificate numbers of stocks and bonds. However, that procedure is difficult and time-consuming for a large portfolio with numerous purchases and sales.

Marketable securities owned or held as collateral or for safekeeping should be counted simultaneously with cash funds, undeposited receipts, notes receivable, and other negotiable assets if there is a possibility of substitution of one item for another.

Confirmation of Securities Not on Hand

Items on the list of marketable securities owned at the count date but not counted should be confirmed with the holders. When a client's entire portfolio is held by a custodian, confirmation procedures usually take the place of the security count, as discussed below.

Items not on hand ordinarily include securities held by banks as collateral for loans or for safekeeping, securities with transfer agents, and, if the client is a stockbroker, items with other brokers on loans or awaiting delivery. An auditor should determine the location of those securities at the examination date, the appropriate responsible person acting as custodian, and the reasons they are held by him. (If the securities are held by persons or organizations unknown to the auditor, he may consider it necessary to physically inspect rather than confirm.) Confirmation requests prepared by the client should be compared with the security records and mailed, in envelopes with the auditor's return address, on the date of the count or as soon thereafter as feasible. If a reply does not confirm information furnished by the client, the auditor should investigate and obtain a full and satisfactory explanation of reported differences. If no reply is received to initial requests for confirmation, second requests should be mailed and the items in question should be followed up until confirmations are received or the securities are otherwise accounted for satisfactorily.

In examining the accounts of financial organizations, an auditor should also confirm contracts for the purchase or sale of securities on a "when, as, and if issued" basis.

If the client's entire portfolio of securities is held in custody by a well-known, reliable financial institution independent of the client, the custodian should be requested to furnish directly to the auditor a list of securities held for the client at the examination date. The auditor should compare the list with the client's security records and account for differences noted. It is sometimes desirable to validate the custodian's confirmation by counting the securities. The most common reasons are when the portfolio is large in relation to the custodian's assets or when assurance as to the adequacy of the custodian's procedures is considered desirable. A letter from the custodian's auditor evaluating internal controls can satisfy the latter purpose. Joint counts with other auditors having a similar interest are possible.

If securities are in the custody of an affiliate or are under the control of a person or group of persons who take an active part in the management of the client, an auditor is not justified in relying solely on written confirmation from the custodian; he should employ auditing procedures outlined above for counting marketable securities under the control of the client.

Comparison of Count With Records

The list of securities owned or held as collateral or for safekeeping at the date of the count, if prepared by the client, should be compared in detail with the accounting records, both as to quantities and dollar amounts. After checking the computation of dollar amounts, an auditor should compare the total with the general ledger control account.

Investments in Subsidiaries, Affiliates, and Joint Ventures

Stocks, bonds, notes, long-term advances, and mortgages of subsidiaries, affiliates, and joint ventures should be substantiated by examining evidence of ownership or by direct correspondence with custodians. Since those investments are usually held over a long period, it is customary for an auditor to record certificate or bond numbers and other pertinent facts about them in the permanent working papers. Reference to that record when evidences of ownership are being examined may reveal transactions otherwise unknown to an auditor.

Notes and Mortgages

An auditor should examine mortgage notes (also known as "bonds") and the mortgages supporting them. He should determine whether the client is designated as payee and mortgagee or the note and mortgage have been assigned to him and the assignment recorded. Laws concerning mortgages differ in various jurisdictions and, while an auditor is not expected to pass on the legal sufficiency of a mortgage, he should be familiar with procedures, forms, and recording requirements customary in the jurisdiction in which he practices.

An auditor should inquire whether taxes or other assessments are in arrears and whether the mortgagee's interest in the property is protected by insurance. (Annual routine tax searches made by specialized service companies are a recommended control procedure.) If an apparently reliable recent appraisal of the mortgaged property is available, the amount should be compared with the unpaid balance of the loan.

An auditor may find it desirable to inquire about the financial responsibility of the maker and endorsers of notes secured by mortgages.

The mortgagee should keep informed as to the general condition of all properties on which he holds mortgages and as to circumstances affecting their values. That information may be requested by an auditor if payments against principal, interest, or taxes on mortgaged properties are in arrears or if the amounts of loans are out of proportion to the amounts of recent appraisals. If a loss on a mortgage seems to be in prospect, an auditor should inquire whether the mortgagee is taking proper steps to protect his interests—as well as, of course, seeing that the client makes adequate provision for the loss in the accounts.

Significant amounts due on notes and mortgages at the examination date should be confirmed by direct correspondence with debtors or mortgagors. Partial payments reducing the original amount may be endorsed on the note; however, since that procedure is not always followed, an auditor should rely on direct confirmation of the balance due. If the number of mortgages is large and internal accounting control and internal check are good, confirmation procedures may be on a test basis, and the auditor may examine correspondence and records of original purchases and collections of principal and income relating to some of the notes and mortgages not subjected to confirmation procedures. Although an auditor cannot accept responsibility for discovering forgeries, a review of those documents may disclose obvious irregularities.

Examination of Security Transactions

The accounting record of units and related dollar amounts of securities owned at the beginning of the period under audit should be compared with that shown in the working papers of the previous examination. Subsequent entries affecting units and dollar amounts should be substantiated by reference to original documents, such as brokers' advices of purchases or sales, bank advices, notices or published services concerning conversion privileges, stock dividends, rights issued, exchanges, capital adjustments and calls, and the like, or by computation of realized gains and losses and amortization of bond discounts and premiums. An auditor should determine that security transactions have been approved by the board of directors or designated trustees or officials. He should satisfy himself by reference to published services for dividends and rights and by computation of interest on bonds that all income from securities, receivable or accrued, has been recorded. As noted elsewhere, that examination is often made in detail; however, if the client's system of internal control is good, a test-check is preferable.

Substantiation of Cost

The cost of investments, marketable and otherwise, may be substantiated by reference to cash disbursements records and documents such as purchase authorizations, invoices, and brokers' advices.

Substantiation of Market Quotations

Whether marketable securities are carried on a balance sheet at market quotations or at cost with the amount at market quotations stated parenthetically or in a note, an auditor should satisfy himself that such amounts are fairly stated. Market quotations usually represent last sale prices on the balance sheet date or, in the absence of sales, either the last bid price or the average of the last bid and offered prices. Other bases, such as sales within a range of dates close to the balance sheet date, may be used in special circumstances. An auditor should satisfy himself as to the propriety of the basis selected by the company and should check the accuracy of the client's calculations. Prices used should be checked to published sources; if a published market price of a publicly traded security—for example, a municipal bond—is not available, an auditor may obtain direct confirmation of the quotation from brokers or other competent persons. In checking market quotations, it is preferable to refer to a publication or broker other than the one used by the client, to guard against the possibility of typographical errors in the listings. Footings and extensions should be checked.

Substantiation of Fair Value

Statement on Auditing Standards No. 1, paragraph 332.05(c), states that "If market quotations of security prices are based on a reasonably broad and active market, they ordinarily constitute sufficient competent evidential matter as to the current market value of unrestricted securities." If a security is traded only occasionally and in small quantities or particularly if the company's investment is significant in relation to the total issue or the total amount publicly held, the market may be considered "thin" and the sale of a substantial block of stock could have a material effect on the market price. The *Investment Company* Audit Guide and SEC Accounting Series Release No. 118 specify that market quotations are not to be relied on in that event and the securities should be valued in good faith by the board of directors.

A similar problem may arise in examining "restricted" securities or so-called "investment letter stock"—shares that have not been registered with the Securities and Exchange Commission for public sale and were purchased under a letter of intent that they were bought for investment and not for resale to the general public. Usually, letter stock is acquired at a price below the market quotation for registered stock of the same class and, although it may be sold in a private transaction, it may not be offered to the public without first being registered with the SEC. Valuation of letter stock is difficult for management to make, because the quoted market for unrestricted securities of the same class does not represent fair value for restricted stock except in unusual situations; a board of directors making the valuation often seeks the advice and assistance of competent independent experts in valuing that kind of securities.

An auditor should be alert to the terms and conditions under which security investments are acquired. If securities are purchased through brokers in apparently routine open market transactions, there is little likelihood of restrictions on their resale. If they are acquired privately or in large blocks, an auditor should inquire into the circumstances of the transaction. The securities may be letter stock or there may be repurchase options or other types of restrictions that might affect their marketability and valuation.

Substantiation of Valuations Made "In Good Faith"

In addition to the "thin market" and restricted or "letter" stock conditions, in which market quotations are available but are not a reliable measure of fair value, investment company portfolios sometimes contain securities for which there are no market quotations and that are stated at fair value as determined by management (technically by the board of directors, but in practice by management for directors' review and approval). The securities may be preferred stocks or debt instruments, sometimes convertible. The portfolios of some investment companies may consist entirely or principally of unquoted issues. Venture-capital investment companies and small business investment companies may invest heavily in new, small companies. Frequently those investments are made on the basis of long-term prospects which cannot be reflected in financial statements.

Valuations determined "in good faith" (the phrase used in the Investment Company Act and repeated in most subsequent discussions of the subject) necessarily reflect subjective and unverifiable judgments. The words of ASR No. 118 and of the *Investment Company* Audit Guide (which uses such phrases as: ". . . all appropriate factors . . . have been considered . . . ," ". . . no single standard can be laid down . . . ," and "this guide does not purport to delineate all factors which may be considered"; pages 35 and 36) emphasize the difficulty of being precise, even in describing the process. Auditors are thus faced with considerable uncertainties in both underlying and corroborative evidence. Nevertheless, an auditor can expect, and should insist on, the production of reasonable evidence supporting valuations.

In a properly managed investment company, extensive studies are conducted before an investment is made. Those studies include analysis and evaluation of the plans and prospects of the company, usually including income statement and balance sheet projections of how and when the investment may be expected to start to show a return. Sometimes a report of a professional investment analyst or appraiser is obtained. After an investment is acquired, there are periodic reviews, reports to the management committee or board of directors, and, frequently, audited financial statements.

That material usually provides the basis for objective evaluation of the investment by the board of directors. It can likewise serve as evidence on which an auditor can base a similar judgment. An auditor, however, is not an appraiser, and security valuations based on subjective judgment usually cannot be substantiated by auditing procedures. His objective is to be certain that the procedures followed in determining "fair value" are reasonable. Therefore, for securities carried at fair value as determined by the board of directors, an auditor "should review all information considered by the board or by analysts reporting to it, read relevant minutes of directors' meetings, and ascertain the procedures followed by the directors" (ASR No. 118).

Having satisfied himself that procedures followed are reasonable, an auditor usually qualifies his opinion as "subject to the possible effect on the financial statements of the valuation of securities by the board of directors . . ." in instances where the possible range of valuations is significant. Where the possible range of values could not be significant in the financial statements, an unqualified opinion would be appropriate. If the procedures followed (including documentation) are inadequate, an auditor must either qualify his opinion as "except for" or give a disclaimer or adverse opinion (*Investment Company* Audit Guide, pages 47 and 48). See also Chapter 19 on the auditor's report.

Valuation of Related Amounts

Bonds, loans, and advances are sometimes collateralized by negotiable securities, real estate, chattels, or other property, or payment may be guaranteed by a responsible person or corporation. An auditor should satisfy himself as to the existence of the collateral; if its value is an important factor in determining collectibility, he should determine that title to it is in transferable form and obtain evidence—which may on occasion go as far as physical inspection of the underlying property—that the value of the collateral or guarantee is reasonable in relation to the amount of the investment.

An auditor should consider the income tax status of the company and determine whether a portfolio stated at fair value in the financial statements should be reduced by the amount of federal and state taxes applicable to unrealized appreciation.

If marketable securities are required to be stated in a balance sheet at amounts determined by regulatory authorities (insurance companies, for example), an auditor should acquaint himself with the applicable regulations. The prices used by the company should be verified by reference to prescribed sources, and footings and extensions should be checked. An auditor should also satisfy himself that the difference between the cost of the securities and the prescribed amounts has been accounted for as required by the regulations.

Substantiation of Amounts Based on Underlying Net Assets

If the equity method is applied to an investment in common stock, or if summarized underlying net asset and income data are supplied as supplemental information, or if consideration is being given to recognizing possible impairment of an investment, financial statements of the investee company, examined and reported on by independent auditors, usually provide sufficient evidence of the investor's equity in net assets. Those financial statements also constitute evidence that may be used with respect to investments in notes, bonds, loans, and advances.

In some circumstances, an auditor may apply auditing procedures to an investee company to obtain evidence to support a client's investment. If the procedures are substantive, evidence thus obtained may be sufficient for his purpose.

Other Evidential Matter

Statement on Auditing Standards No. 1, paragraph 332.05(b)(i) states that "Unaudited financial statements, reports issued on examination by regulatory bodies and taxing authorities, and similar data provide information and evidence but are not by themselves sufficient as evidential matter."

Appraisals or evaluations of factors such as mineral rights, growing timber, or patents and similar intangible assets, if reflected in the cost of an investment, may also provide evidential matter.

ANALYTICAL REVIEWS

An auditor's review of the data supporting directors' valuations is as much an analytical review as a validation test.

An auditor should review analytically the account for each investment in the portfolio, observing the trend of values and comparing the income of the current period with the comparable prior period. While many investments, especially marketable securities, may fluctuate over a wide range in the course of a year, an investigation of fluctuations can often uncover errors or other events requiring recognition in the accounts. For example, a capital change may not have been picked up from the news services: a failure to record a two-for-one stock split might be discovered by an investigation of a sudden drop in the quoted market price of the security.

Other analytical reviews include reading minutes of the investment committee and finance committee of the board of directors as well as the minutes of meetings of the full board. An auditor should also obtain and read carefully any special agreements connected with investments.

The activity in control accounts should be reviewed analytically, especially between an interim date chosen for validation tests and the end of the fiscal year, for the purpose of identifying and investigating fluctuations and unusual charges or credits.

• STATEMENT PRESENTATION

BASIS OF CARRYING INVESTMENTS

The basis on which investments in securities are carried on a balance sheet—cost, market or fair value, the lower of cost or market, cost plus equity in accumulated undistributed earnings, equity in net assets, management appraisal, or other basis—should be clearly stated.

Marketable Securities

Commercial and industrial companies generally carry marketable securities at cost, indicating the amount at market quotations parenthetically in the balance sheet caption. If an allowance for an indicated decline in value is considered necessary, it should be shown separately.

Rule 5-02(2) of Regulation S-X sets forth the SEC's requirements for financial statements filed with it, as follows:

> Include only securities having a ready market . . . . State . . . the basis of determining the amount shown in the balance sheet and state the alternate of the aggregate cost or the aggregate amount on the basis of market quotations at the balance sheet date.

If the original cost of debt securities has been adjusted to reflect amortization of premium or discount since acquisition, a question may arise as to the appropriateness of "cost" as a description of basis. There is a similar question if arrearages of interest or preferred dividends that existed at the time of purchase were subsequently applied to reduce cost. In the opinion of the authors, it is permissible to describe the amounts resulting from those proper adjustments as "cost."

Institutions that receive gifts of marketable securities and record them at fair value at date of receipt generally describe the recorded amounts as "cost" in financial statements. Most nonprofit institutions present investments at cost, with market disclosed parenthetically, but some institutions present them at market, with cost shown parenthetically. The latter presentation permits, to some extent, a review of the performance of investment management because the increase or decrease in realized and unrealized appreciation of investments is disclosed in the accompanying statement of changes in fund balances.

Since publication of that Audit Guide, investment companies should present their investments at market or fair value, with cost indicated parenthetically or otherwise. Balance sheets of investment companies should be accompanied by a detailed list of investments showing, as a minimum, name and class of security, number of shares of stock or principal amount of bonds, and individual amounts at market quotations to support the aggregate amount of securities in the balance sheet. The list of investments of companies subject to the Investment Company Act of 1940 is required to contain specific and detailed information, as set forth in Section 30 of the Act, the regulations relating thereto, and Regulation S-X.

Stockbrokers follow the general practice in published balance sheets of carrying securities in investment and trading accounts at amounts based on market quotations without disclosure of cost. Other dealers in securities, for whom securities constitute so-called "stock in trade," frequently carry securities on hand at cost or market, whichever is lower. (They compute "cost or market" security by security for that purpose, whereas for most other disclosures aggregate cost is compared with aggregate market.) If securities carried on that basis are stated at cost, the amount at market quotations should be indicated parenthetically or otherwise.

Amounts of securities stated at management's appraisals of fair value should be identified in the detailed list of investments, or the total amount of those securities, if significant, should be disclosed and described as "at fair value as determined by management" or "as determined by the directors." If the aggregate of those amounts is material, the circumstances may require explanation or qualification of the auditor's opinion or a disclaimer or adverse opinion, as discussed in Chapter 19.

Marketable securities pledged or held in escrow should be disclosed on a balance sheet. Requirements for disclosure in filings with the SEC are set forth in Rule 3-16(c) of Regulation S-X: "Assets mortgaged, pledged, or otherwise subject to lien, and the approximate amounts thereof, shall be designated and the obligations collateralized briefly identified."

A provision for taxes on realization of unrealized net appreciation should be shown on the liability side of a balance sheet if securities are carried at amounts based on market quotations. If the amount at market is shown parenthetically or in a note to the financial statements, disclosure of the amount of those taxes should also be considered. If no taxes are expected (for example, because the company expects to maintain its qualification as a "regulated investment company"), that fact and the reason for it should be briefly stated.

The method used by investment companies for computing realized profits or losses should be disclosed. Rule 6-05 of Regulation S-X requires that, if a method other than average cost is used (see section on "Gain or Loss on Disposal" earlier in the chapter), the financial statements should disclose, if practicable, the profit or loss computed on the basis of average cost.

Long-Term Investments in Common Stock

Long-term investments in common stock generally are carried at cost or, if the equity method is applicable, at cost plus equity in accumulated undistributed earnings. If quoted market prices are available, the aggregate value at market quotations should also be disclosed, unless the investment is in a subsidiary, and there is no present intention of disposing of it. If there is more than one investment in common stock, disclosures wholly or partly on a combined basis may be appropriate.

Additional disclosures are generally necessary if an investment in common stock is accounted for by the equity method. The financial statements or notes thereto should include the name of each investee, percentage of common stock ownership, and the difference, if any, between the carrying amount of the investment and the underlying equity in net assets and related accounting for the difference. If investments in unconsolidated subsidiaries, in the aggregate, are material to an investor, summarized financial position and results of operations of such subsidiaries should also be furnished. Summarized financial data may also be necessary for a meaningful understanding of investments in corporate joint ventures or other investments of 50 per cent or less.

Rule 5-02(39)(b) of Regulation S-X requires that financial statements filed with the SEC disclose the amount of undistributed earnings of unconsolidated subsidiaries included in the parent's retained earnings. If unconsolidated subsidiaries are significant, adequate disclosure may require that their financial statements be included in filings with those of the parent company.

If an investor's present share of reported earnings or losses could be materially affected by a potential conversion of outstanding convertible securities, exercise of outstanding options and warrants, or other contingent issuances, that fact should be disclosed.

Preferred Stock, Notes, Mortgages, and Bonds

Investments in preferred stock are usually stated at cost; investments in notes, mortgages, and bonds are usually stated at face amount, adjusted for unamortized discount or premium. If a decline in market value of mortgaged property requires a reduction of the related mortgage, the asset should be shown on a balance sheet either gross less the reduction or net, preferably with the amount of the reduction indicated in the caption.

BALANCE SHEET CLASSIFICATION

Marketable Securities

Marketable securities may be included with current assets in balance sheets of commercial and industrial companies, even though there is no present intention of disposing of them within one year from the balance sheet date, if they represent part of the client's working capital. However, if such securities are held for long-term investment or special purposes such as sinking fund requirements or proposed plant additions and, therefore, are not part of the company's working capital, they should be separately shown among noncurrent assets with an appropriate descriptive caption.

Balance sheets of investment companies, banks, and insurance companies do not customarily classify assets as current or noncurrent.

Investments in Subsidiaries, Affiliates, and Joint Ventures

If investments in subsidiaries, affiliates, and joint ventures, whether or not marketable, are made for purposes of control, affiliation, or similar business advantage, they should be classified on the balance sheet among noncurrent assets.

15

The Cash Segment

INTRODUCTION

Cash can be viewed either broadly or narrowly. In the broadest sense, cash flow is the entire business history of a firm from initial cash investment inflow to final cash outflow in liquidation. For the purposes of this book, however, a narrow definition is more useful: the cash segment consists of the cash inflows and outflows that result from a given plan of operations, controlling and accounting for cash receipts and disbursements, and managing the resulting balances. The cash segment is thus the part of the overall cycle falling between the major transaction segments discussed in previous and following chapters; how-ever narrow it may be, it is as important to those segments as oil is to the moving parts of a machine.

The volume of transactions in the cash account is greater than in any other, and most of the activities of a business eventually begin or end there. Questions of valuation or judgment rarely arise in the de-termination of the amounts of cash, and the cash balance can be stated somewhat more precisely than most other accounts. Since it is the medium of exchange and highly mobile, cash is more susceptible to manipulation than other assets. Consequently, the safeguarding of cash through internal check procedures has received considerable at-tention through the years; indeed in the past it was the focus of a large fraction of an auditor's effort.

An auditor's responsibility for the cash item on a balance sheet does not differ from his responsibility for other balance sheet items; he should exercise his judgment to select and apply auditing procedures that will enable him to form an opinion about the fair presentation of cash in relation to the financial statements taken as a whole. In the past, many auditors spent an undue amount of time applying detailed auditing procedures to cash—for example, checking bank reconciliations at one or more dates, making one or more independent reconciliations, and examining cash receipts and disbursements and supporting vouch-ers for one or more months. Those procedures have their place, and in a few instances must be used to provide adequate audit evidence. But over the years they have increasingly taken on the character of "extended auditing procedures" rather than routine ones. The pur-pose of this chapter is to describe the various procedures for examining cash and to illustrate how and when they are employed pursuant to the audit logic set forth in earlier chapters.

• ACCOUNTING PRINCIPLES

CASH ON HAND AND ON DEPOSIT

Unless they are informed otherwise, readers of financial statements should be able to presume that the cash amount stated in a balance sheet is on hand or in banks and is immediately available for any pur-pose. It is not acceptable practice to treat funds received after the close of a period as cash and reduce accounts receivable correspondingly, al-though it has been defended on the ground that the receipts were for-warded by debtors before the close of the period and represented cash in transit. Similarly, outstanding checks should not include checks drawn prior to a balance sheet date but held for later delivery to creditors or checks drawn after but dated before the balance sheet date: such amounts should be restored to the cash balance and to liabilities. Those considerations are important if provisions of bond indentures, loan agreements, or preferred stock issues require that certain current ratios be maintained. A common practice in nonprofit organizations is to treat certain internal cash transfers as if they had been made at year end even though cash is transferred from one fund or account to another after year-end balances have been analyzed and reviewed. That practice need not be disclosed; it is nothing more than correctly accounting for the details of the total cash on hand.

Outstanding checks should not be listed indefinitely on bank reconciliations. A sound practice is to stop payment after a year has elapsed, return the amounts to cash, and record a liability for the unpaid amounts. The liability should be credited to income after expiration of the applicable statute of limitations unless state laws require other disposition. Dividend checks may require special treatment because the laws of some states distinguish between the liability for uncashed dividend checks and that for other uncashed checks.

Cash in Foreign Currencies

Foreign currency on hand and on deposit in foreign countries should be translated into dollars at the rate of exchange in effect on the balance sheet date. Translations are usually at official rates, if they exist. However, if transactions have been settled during the period principally at free rates of exchange or there are other indications that the free rate will be used for transactions in the future, that rate should be used. See "Translation of Foreign Balances" in Chapter 18.

Restricted Cash

Cash balances that are restricted as to availability or purpose should be separately accounted for. Details of the restriction should be maintained in the files to assure compliance. Common practice in earlier years was to commingle all cash funds during a year and to account for restricted amounts only at balance sheet dates. Now it is expected that terms of restrictions will be scrupulously followed. Those terms may or may not permit commingling: for example, compensating balances under loan agreements are not usually segregated, but amounts required to be set aside for "debt service" and "maintenance" under bond indentures usually are.

• TYPICAL TRANSACTION SYSTEMS AND INTERNAL CONTROL

Cash receipts form a part of the revenue segment and cash disbursements of the buying segment; each was discussed in that context in Chapters 9 and 10. The discussion in this chapter is parallel for the sake of encompassing the whole of the subject of accounting for, controlling, and auditing cash.

Because cash is the most negotiable and portable of all assets, it properly receives the most attention from those responsible for designing the disciplinary control operations of restricted access and segregation of duties. Those control operations are collectively termed "internal check." Because of their importance, we depart from the pattern of previous chapters and discuss the subjects of internal accounting control and internal check separately—although, as always, the conditions of control and supervisory control are likewise important.

INTERNAL ACCOUNTING CONTROL

Cash Receipts

Cash received by mail is usually in the form of checks; cash received over the counter, through collectors, or through salespeople may be in the form of either currency or checks. The initial step in the accounting control of cash receipts is to list them: collections by mail should be listed showing names and amounts (the customer's bill stub is commonly used for that purpose); receipts over the counter may be listed on cash register tapes or counter sales slips prepared in the presence of customers; receipts from collectors or salespeople not accompanied by listings should be listed on receipt. If more than one list or batch is prepared in a day, they should be identified for accountability; for example, by numerical sequencing of batches. Lists of receipts should be totalled, usually at least daily, and the totals should be compared with the corresponding totals of cash and checks received, cash book totals, deposit slip totals, and totals of credits to receivables or sales control accounts.

Since cash received should be deposited promptly in a bank account, items that are not suitable for immediate deposit, such as postdated checks or checks containing errors in amounts, should be separately listed and the two lists later reconciled with the deposit.

Counter sales slips, cashiers' receipts, and collectors' receipts should be prenumbered, and the numerical sequence should be accounted for.

Receipts should be recorded promptly and those at branch offices should be reported immediately to the main office. If receipts flow from a number of sources, such as collection departments, cash registers, vending machines, and ticket sellers, procedures should be adopted to insure the inclusion of receipts from all locations daily. For example, a control form or checklist should be prepared to flag missing entries.

Bank Accounts

All bank accounts should be formally authorized by someone clearly in a position to do so: often a vote of the board of directors is required. Discontinuance of accounts likewise should be formally approved. Authorization should include names of those who may sign checks. Lists of authorized check signers should be reviewed periodically by someone knowledgeable, to determine that employees' duties have not changed in ways that make their signing of checks improper or inconsistent with good internal control.

Disbursements by Check

A detailed listing of disbursements by check, showing payees and amounts, should be prepared and totalled daily or at other regular intervals. The list may be in the form of entries in a cash book, a written tabulation of requests for checks to be issued, a computer print-out, or an adding machine tape, perhaps supported by copies of checks issued. Totals on the list should be compared with credits to the cash control account in the general ledger and with debits to accounts payable or other control accounts. Transfers of funds between banks should be controlled to assure that both sides of transfers are recorded in the same accounting period.

Checks should be prenumbered and all numbers should be accounted for. When checks are signed, the signer should have written evidence in the form of approved vouchers that the payments liquidate liabilities and that the data on each check have been compared with related vouchers. The check signer should cancel the vouchers by appropriate means to prevent their reuse to support duplicate payments.

Disbursements of Currency

Disbursements made in currency are normally for advances, freight bills, and other petty expenditures or for wage and salary payments. Accounting control over currency disbursements is best maintained by keeping the fund (or funds) from which disbursements are made on an imprest system.

In an imprest system, the fund is maintained at a fixed amount as determined by the requirements of the particular circumstances. Disbursements from the fund are supported by vouchers signed by the recipients; depending on circumstances (or amount), advance approval may be required. The sum of unexpended cash in the fund and the vouchers for disbursements should always equal the fixed amount of the imprest fund. At regular intervals, or when the fund's cash nears exhaustion, the vouchers, with supporting documents attached, are presented for reimbursement from general cash. When the fund is reimbursed, the vouchers should be cancelled in some manner to prevent their reuse to support duplicate reimbursements. Imprest funds should be checked periodically and reconciled with general ledger control accounts.

Payments of payrolls in currency should be made from a specially designated imprest fund, usually provided by a withdrawal from general cash of the exact net amount of each payroll as previously computed. The net amount should be denominated and the bills and coins inserted in envelopes provided by the payroll office showing payee and amount of wages payable. After the envelopes have been prepared, the information on them should be compared with an approved payroll list. Signed receipts should be obtained from employees when they receive their envelopes. Unclaimed envelopes should be listed, and at regular intervals the currency in them should be deposited in a general bank account and a liability for unclaimed wages recorded.

Reconciliation of Bank Accounts

Periodic reconciliations of accounting records of cash in banks with amounts shown in bank statements are important elements of internal accounting control over bank deposits and disbursements by check. For internal accounting control purposes, reconciliation should include not only reconciliation of the balance as shown by the bank statement with that shown by the accounts at the same date, but also reconciliation of detailed items listed on the bank statement with detailed items recorded in the accounts during the period covered by the bank statement. The latter step assures recognition of all items recorded in the accounts, including offsetting items within receipts or disbursements, and of all items recorded on the bank statement. The preferred reconciliation procedure, the "Proof of Cash," which is increasingly recognized as primarily an internal accountability procedure, is described in detail under auditing procedures later in this chapter.

Readers will recognize in the foregoing paragraphs the control operations enumerated in Chapter 3: documentation (the initial listing of receipts and disbursements), authorization, numerical sequencing, pre-audit, control totals, comparisons, and reminder lists.

INTERNAL CHECK

Cash Receipts

Good internal check over cash receipts requires that persons who record amounts in cash receipts books or prepare bank deposits should be independent of those who post the related credits to accounts receivable records and general ledger accounts. Similarly, persons independent of other cash functions should perform the functions of preparing the initial detail listings of cash receipts and of obtaining authenticated duplicate deposit slips from banks and comparing them in total with cash book entries, listings of cash receipts, receivable control account totals, and credits on bank statements.

Checks should be endorsed as soon as they are received with an endorsement stamp including the notation "For Deposit Only." Each day's cash receipts should be deposited intact and without delay; authorized exclusions, as separately listed, should be reconciled with original listings and delivered to a responsible independent employee for review and disposition.

Deposit or collection items charged back by a bank as uncollectible should be delivered to an employee other than those who make deposits or record accounts receivable credits. Items charged back by a bank should be investigated by someone who has no responsibility for either cash operations or entries in cash books.

Banks should be instructed not to cash checks or money orders drawn to the order of the company or to accept them for deposit in payroll or other special accounts. Cash receipts of branch offices should be deposited in a bank account subject to withdrawal only by the home office.

Use of a "lock box" system—a service offered by many banks to reduce cash transit time, thus increasing the funds available to a company at a given time—also improves internal check for cash receipts. Company personnel do not have access to cash receipts because customers send their remittances to a post office box under control of the bank. The bank records deposits and furnishes the company with remittance advices and statement stubs or other correspondence from customers that serve to identify the receipts. Thus the required separation of functions and custodial control of cash are obtained.

Disbursements by Check

Unissued checks should be kept in a safe place with access restricted to those authorized to prepare checks. Checks should be prenumbered and the numbers accounted for as the blank checks are released for use. Checks should be protected against alteration by use of special paper and a protective writing device.

Persons authorized to sign checks, manually or in facsimile, should not have duties that include preparing or approving vouchers, preparing checks, recording and accounting for sequence of check numbers, or custody of unused checks. That separation of duties helps to assure that checks are issued only to pay approved liabilities and that all checks issued are recorded in cash disbursements records.

If a mechanical check signer is used, the die should be in sole custody of the person authorized to use it. That person should also be responsible to see that only authorized checks are signed.

Checks should be drawn specifically to the order of the creditors being paid or to custodians of imprest funds being reimbursed. They should never be drawn payable to "cash" or to "bearer." Drawing checks specifically limits their negotiability and provides an acknowledgment of receipt through payees' endorsements. Banks were formerly expected to make sure that checks were properly endorsed. Machine processing makes it no longer possible to examine every check, but if a check is made out to a specific payee, a bank that honors it with an improper endorsement, rather than the maker, is liable.

Signed checks should be kept in custody of the signer until mailed or delivered personally by the signer or someone under his control who is independent of all functions pertaining to cash receipts or payments, preparation of vouchers, preparation or distribution of payrolls, custody of cash funds, or general ledger posting. The check signer should cancel supporting vouchers by appropriate means to prevent their reuse to support duplicate payments.

Signing or countersigning checks in advance should be prohibited. The dangers of signing checks in advance are obvious, but are often ignored. Countersignatures are effective as an internal control procedure only if each signer makes an independent examination of checks and supporting documents. Although a countersignature affixed with proper understanding and discharge of assigned responsibility affords good internal check, signature by a single employee after careful examination of supporting vouchers offers greater protection than superficial countersignatures, which create an illusion of security and possible reliance by one person on functions not performed by another.

Disbursements of Currency

The primary responsibility for each petty cash fund should be placed in a single person whose duties should not embrace other funds, cash receipts, approval of disbursement vouchers, reimbursement of the fund, or authorizing, recording, or posting distributions of disbursements from the fund. No other negotiable assets should be in the custody of persons responsible for cash funds. Accommodation checks cashed by a petty cash custodian should be drawn to the order of the petty cashier and not to the company.

An internal auditor or other independent employee should count petty cash funds at unannounced intervals. The composition of the funds at those times should be reported to a responsible supervisor for review. Although a fund itself and expenditures from it may be petty, over a period of time misappropriations may become significant unless adequate safeguards are maintained.

Unclaimed wages, both cash and checks, should be held by an employee whose duties are divorced from payroll preparation and who handles neither cash receipts nor petty cash. If wages remain unclaimed after a specified period, the reason should be determined and the funds restored to general cash.

Reconciliation of Bank Accounts

Effective internal check requires that an employee who reconciles bank balances with account balances have no regularly assigned functions relating to cash receipts, cash disbursements, or vouchers; that he obtain bank statements directly from the bank; and that he make specific comparisons as part of the bank reconciliation procedure, such as comparing paid checks and other debits and credits listed on the bank statement with entries in the accounts, examining checks for signatures and endorsements, reconciling bank transfers, and other procedures described later under auditing procedures.

OPERATIONAL CONTROLS

Operational controls over cash contribute to the strength of accounting controls; therefore an understanding of operational controls, if they are present, gives an auditor additional assurance of the adequacy of the system for control of cash. The objective of operational control of cash is to obtain maximum use of cash by investing it, minimizing borrowing, or concentrating cash in deposits that "earn" the most in goodwill, banking relations, and bankers' services.

The principal tool of cash management is cash forecasting and budgeting: the effort to plan, in as much detail and as far ahead as possible, receipts to be expected and disbursements required. The objective is to schedule as precisely as possible the amount and timing of borrowings and cash available for temporary investments.

Variations from budget are under active and intense scrutiny by a cash manager; since his work is usually independent of the handling of and accounting for cash, operational control of cash constitutes a strong form of disciplinary control. Furthermore, cash management requires accurate daily figures of balances, transfers, and commitments, and that operational necessity for prompt and accurate reporting exerts pressure that enhances the effectiveness of accounting controls.

Good cash management requires bringing receipts under managerial control, in a central bank or otherwise, as quickly as possible. Bringing receipts under control depends on fast and accurate processing, including making bank deposits at least daily, lock box systems, and one-way depository banks. Management of cash disbursements calls for close control of invoices in process to make sure that payments are made precisely when due, neither earlier nor later. All of those steps are also desirable from the point of view of accounting control.

● AUDITING PROCEDURES

OBJECTIVES

The objectives of auditing cash are comparable to the objectives of auditing other asset accounts, that is, reasonable assurance that the asset exists, is the unencumbered and unrestricted property of the client, and is fairly stated (not necessarily precisely) in accordance with generally accepted accounting principles. As discussed more fully in Chapter 2, an auditor's examination cannot be relied on to disclose defalcations and other similar irregularities, although their discovery may result.

THE AUDIT CYCLE

As part of his initial understanding of the client, an auditor should determine the locations and approximate amounts of all cash funds, bank accounts, and other negotiable assets. He should also inquire whether cash or securities in the possession of the company's custodian include property of other organizations, such as an employees' association, or company property not recorded in the accounts, such as unclaimed wages, employees' savings, and the like.

The item "Cash" may comprise a substantial number of bank accounts used for general corporate purposes, and the records may be located at the general office, branches, or subsidiaries. Petty cash funds are frequently composed of balances in banks as well as cash on hand. Imprest funds, such as those for payrolls, freight bills, dividends, and the like, are also usually deposited in separate bank accounts. In short, the total of "Cash" may represent a large number of bank accounts, of which relatively few may constitute a large percentage of the total.

Transaction Reviews

Transaction reviews of the most common and voluminous cash transactions are carried out as part of auditing the revenue and buying segments described in previous chapters. As part of his preliminary understanding, an auditor should inquire about cash accounts and the activity flowing through them to identify all significant types of transactions not covered in the revenue and buying segments. He is likely to find several insignificant types of transactions: petty cash funds, other imprest funds, agency accounts for various incidental purposes, and so on. It is unusual, though a distinct possibility, for a transaction review of cash accounts to bring to light a previously unrecognized significant type of transaction; an example might be funds held for a significant community activity as a part of maintaining employee and community relations, or other large agency accounts.

The question of whether to review insignificant types of transactions is discussed in Chapter 5. It is not necessary to do so as a basis for an opinion on the financial statements, but it may be required by tradition or client expectations. An auditor should have an explicit agreement with the client about whether he is expected to review imprest accounts, agency accounts, and similar insignificant types of transactions and, if so, to what extent.

If those types of transactions are to be reviewed, the transaction reviews should be carried out as described in Chapter 5. The transactions should be reviewed from "cradle to grave" and the review and resulting understanding should be documented, preferably by means of flow charts. Since they usually originate and terminate completely within a cash account and not as part of a revenue or buying transaction, the "cradle" is likely to be the moment that a client becomes accountable for funds and the "grave" the moment of discharge of that accountability.

Functional Tests

The critical control functions should be tested in the manner and to the extent described in Chapter 5. The receipt and disbursement of funds must be authorized, transactions must be documented, and those in process must be properly recorded and their accountability maintained by periodic reconciliations to control totals. Functional tests should focus on controls over initial accountability, on periodic reconciliation to control totals, on controls over authorization and recording of disbursements, and particularly on evidence of supervisory controls which assure continuity of the basic controls.

Accountability controls consist of bank reconciliations, confirmations, and cash counts, which are also the principal tools for an auditor's validation tests. Those procedures are described in detail below under "Validation Procedures": the stronger the client's accountability controls, the more an auditor's reconciliations and cash counts take on the character of functional tests of the client's controls rather than independent validation tests.

Validation Procedures

Three procedures are available to validate cash balances, and a fourth is available to validate cash activity if an auditor does not have maximum confidence in the systems of control over cash activity:

Bank reconciliation,

Confirmation of balances with banks,

Cash count, and

Examination of a sufficient sample of cash transactions and reperformance of a sufficient sample of control functions to validate records of cash activity.

Those procedures are described in the paragraphs that follow. The extent to which they may be needed varies a great deal, depending primarily on the strength of the conditions of control and of the disciplinary controls; the range of variation is so great that it is not possible to offer definitive guidelines. The range is illustrated at the end of this section by contrasting an audit program for cash validation under conditions of effective control with one that might be required under conditions of weakness in internal control.

Bank Reconciliations

The reconciliation of cash balances in the accounts to those reported by a bank is a routine and generally accepted accountability procedure. An auditor has three alternative approaches to bank reconciliations and uses his judgment to choose among them. He may make an independent reconciliation himself if he believes it advisable to obtain completely independent evidence of the authenticity of a cash balance. He may simply review a client's reconciliations if he has sufficient confidence in the controls for preserving restricted access and segregation of duties. Or, he may review and test a client's reconciliations if his confidence in the controls falls between those limits.

1. *Independent Reconciliation.* The following procedures should be followed by a client in regular periodic reconciliations of bank accounts. The same steps are employed by an auditor to combine functional testing of cash transactions with an independent reconciliation, or reperformance of a client's reconciliation, which is a validation procedure. If the combination is not desired, only the steps related to reconciliation of balances at the end of a period are necessary.

a. Obtain the closing bank statement and paid checks for the period under examination directly from the bank and keep them under control until the reconciliation is completed. In selecting the period, an auditor may decide that a week (or some shorter or longer period) provides sufficient coverage.

b. Prepare a "Proof of Cash" working paper as illustrated below. This form of reconciliation has been developed for summarizing and controlling the examination of cash records for any selected time period, regardless of length, and can be used either as part of an auditor's independent reconciliation or in reviewing or testing a reconciliation prepared by a client.

XYZ CORPORATION

PROOF OF CASH
Month of December, 19—

	Balance Beginning of Period	Receipts	Dis- bursements	Balance End of Period
Per bank statement	$31,268	$42,687	$46,560	$27,395
Deposits in transit:				
Beginning	1,000	(1,000)		
End		2,000		2,000
Outstanding checks:				
Beginning	(3,917)		(3,917)	
End			4,560	(4,560)
Unrecorded charges and credits: Collection from customer on note, credited by bank during period, entered on books after end of period		(2,078)		(2,078)
Per books	$28,351	$41,609	$47,203	22,757
Audit adjusting entry # 1: Collection of customer's note				2,078
Per books as adjusted				$24,835

Note: Parentheses indicate subtractions.

An advantage of the form shown is that it provides a reconciliation of balances at the beginning and end of the period and with little additional effort effects a reconciliation of transactions during the period as recorded in the accounts with those reflected in the bank statement. An auditor is thus able to "prove" the propriety of the recorded transactions in the accounts to an independent source (the bank statement); hence the designation of the form as "proof of cash." Any other audit tests applied to the receipts, disbursements, or balances can be described on the form.

c. If the totals are not already shown in the bank statement, determine total receipts per bank statement by footing deposits and determine total disbursements by subtracting the closing balance from the sum of the opening balance and deposits. (Checks returned with the statement need not be added to determine total bank disbursements unless the proof of cash does not reconcile.) Enter those totals on the "Proof of Cash" form.

d. Obtain client's reconciliation as at the close of the preceding period and compare balances shown on that reconciliation with the corresponding amounts shown by the accounts and the bank statement; substantiate outstanding checks at the close of the preceding period by examining paid checks returned by the bank in the current period, investigating any still outstanding; and substantiate deposits in transit and other reconciling items at the close of the preceding period by reference to the current bank statement, bank notifications of charges and credits, and other supporting documents.

e. Compare daily totals of recorded cash receipts shown in the cash book with daily deposits appearing in the bank statement. If there are time lags between the receipt, recording, and depositing of collections, investigate any that appear unreasonable in the light of the company's usual practices. (Delay in depositing receipts constitutes inefficient cash management and exposes cash items on hand to risk of loss or misuse, such as "lapping" collections of accounts receivable —a method of continuously concealing a defalcation by crediting later collections to accounts whose collections were not previously recorded.) Enter unmatched cash receipts items or deposit items on the "Proof of Cash" form.

f. Compare paid checks returned with the bank statement with the disbursements record for check number, date, payee, and amount. The comparison determines not only which checks have not cleared the bank during the period but also that dates, payees, and amounts of disbursements as shown by the paid checks agree with those recorded in the disbursements record. That comparison should be made with a book of original entry (which may be a disbursements book, computer run, check register, check stub book, or file of duplicate checks) rather than a summary record. If a summary record must be used, an auditor should assure himself that existing control procedures make the summary record reliable. List checks outstanding at the end of the period, foot the list, and enter the total on the "Proof of Cash" form.

g. Examine transfers of funds within an organization, whether between branches, divisions, or affiliates. The examination should be made from paid checks, bank advices, or bank statements to the cash records and vice versa. An auditor should determine (1) that each transaction represented as a transfer is an authorized transfer in fact, (2) that debits and credits representing transfers of cash are recorded in the same period, and (3) that the funds are actually deposited in the receiving bank in the appropriate period. Transfers merit particular attention because "kiting"—depositing in a bank account a check drawn on another bank that is not recorded in the books as either a cash receipt or disbursement (and later reversing the procedure)—is a time-honored way either to cover a shortage due to defalcation or to simply overstate the balance of a bank account at a particular date.

h. Account for all checks issued in the sequence between the first and last checks drawn on the bank account during the period being examined.

i. Determine that the reconciliation foots and cross-foots (when the proof of cash reconciles, a mathematical proof has been obtained, making it unnecessary to foot the cash receipts and disbursements columns of the cash book) and that other items appearing in it are proper, bearing in mind particularly that a subsequent entry in the accounts that apparently offsets an item in a reconciliation is not necessarily proof of its correctness. It may merely transfer an error to some other account. Each adjusting entry, if material in amount, should be examined to determine its propriety. The propriety of reconciling items is not established merely by the fact that arithmetic reconciliation is effected by their inclusion.

j. If the end of the test period is also the balance sheet date, and a principal purpose of the reconciliation is validation of the cash balance appearing in the balance sheet, deposits in transit and outstanding checks revealed by the reconciliation should be substantiated by later comparison with a subsequent bank statement and accompanying paid checks. This is often done by means of a specially requested "cutoff" bank statement covering a period of a week or two. If that step is taken, the auditor should receive those documents directly from the bank. Checks outstanding at the date of the reconciliation that still are not returned with the subsequent bank statement, if material in amount, should be substantiated by reference to properly approved vouchers or other available documents. If the end of the test period does not coincide with the balance sheet date, it should not be necessary to follow up reconciling items because the client's procedures in that area are tested in step (d) above.

k. Items on the bank statement not accounted for in the foregoing reconciliation procedures—such as debits or credits followed by offsetting entries of identical amounts, which appear to be, or are claimed by the client to be, bank errors and corrections not so coded—should be scrutinized to determine their exact nature. If information in the client's office is inadequate, the auditor should request clarification from the bank as to their nature. For example, if internal control procedures are inadequate, an entire deposit might be withdrawn from the bank by an unrecorded (unnumbered) check that is subsequently destroyed when returned by the bank. The bank statement would then show an uncoded debit and credit for the same amount which might be claimed to represent a bank error and its correction.

l. Paid checks should be examined on a test basis for propriety of payee, signature, and endorsements. In examining paid checks, an auditor should pursue any seeming irregularities. He should investigate checks drawn to cash, to petty cash, to bearer, or to officers and employees other than for payroll or for reimbursement of imprest funds. Questionable items should be traced to supporting documents; a paid check in itself is not evidence of the propriety of the payment. Checks bearing second endorsements may also deserve further attention. If the second endorsement is that of an employee involved in disbursement, payroll, or authorization functions, it may indicate a fictitious payment of an invoice or payroll. Items of that type should be reviewed with a company officer. The auditor should determine that signatures on checks are apparently of those authorized to sign checks, and should review endorsements to see that they are in the name of the payee. Endorsements that appear unusual (a number of checks endorsed over to the same party, endorsements other than in the name of the payee) should be brought to the attention of the client.

m. Compare balances in the accounts with entries and balances in general ledger cash controlling accounts.

Banks often make available to their customers a variety of services, ranging from check sorting to complete reconciliations. Those services allow a client's reconciler and an auditor to spend less time on routine clerical tasks. Alternatively, there is no objection to having client employees whose duties do not involve cash disbursements sort the checks under an auditor's supervision.

Block proof bank account reconciliation. If the volume of payments by check is considerable (such as in payroll or dividend accounts), some companies use a block proof reconciliation method instead of the regular method described above. The essence of the block method is that checks are not accounted for individually but in total for a group or "block," representing either the checks issued during one or more days or a fixed number of checks in numerical sequence. Those block totals are recorded as checks outstanding. Then as checks paid are returned by the bank, they are sorted and totalled by blocks and the totals are deducted from the related outstanding amounts. At a reconciliation date, the block remainder amounts are available, but not a listing of individual checks supporting them.

Testing the accuracy of the amounts outstanding (generally on a limited basis) is the most practical method of examining the record of voluminous check payments. The auditor should obtain a bank statement and paid checks directly from the bank for a period deemed reasonable for clearance of most of the checks in the blocks to be tested. After the auditor identifies paid items by blocks, he may request an employee of the client who is independent of cash disbursement functions to prepare a list by check number and amount of unpaid items of selected blocks. That list, the total of which should agree with the block remainder amount, may be tested by review of the block files of paid checks. A few of the blocks recorded as closed may be tested to determine that all checks of the series are in the paid file.

Somewhat akin to the block proof method is the practice of issuing drafts to pay obligations and disbursing cash from the bank account only once a day for the total of drafts accumulated daily at the bank. That scheme reduces the number of bank checks to a minimum and simplifies the reconciliation process. Drafts payable that have been issued but not presented to the bank for payment are generally considered as outstanding checks and deducted from the amount of cash on deposit. In reviewing internal accounting control and internal check, an auditor may confine his examination of paid drafts to selected days, satisfying himself that each day's drafts were paid by the indicated bank check and were fully supported by appropriate evidence.

Reconciling "one-way" and imprest bank accounts. Generally, an auditor should not find it necessary to reconcile a "one-way" type of bank account if the account balance is kept to a nominal figure. In a "one-way" account, receipts are deposited by a branch, plant, or selling office and only the central office may withdraw funds by transfer into a general bank account. Evaluating and testing the procedures that insure the adequacy and continuity of control over deposits and transfers of deposits into general bank accounts should normally serve an auditor's purpose.

Similarly, an auditor should not ordinarily find it necessary to reconcile imprest bank accounts used for payment of payrolls, dividends, customer refunds, branch office expenses, and the like. Those accounts are usually limited to a nominal balance, and deposits are in amounts equal to the totals of checks drawn on the accounts. The increasing use of more sophisticated equipment enables many banks to return cancelled checks in numerical sequence with a list of the numbers of uncleared checks and in some instances (when the bank is furnished a computerized check register) to perform the reconciliations of imprest accounts (or regular accounts). Accordingly, an auditor generally need only review procedures and determine whether adequate safeguards appear to be in effect. As a part of his review, he may test evidence such as payrolls, dividend lists, refund documents, and vouchers supporting selected disbursements and compare serial number, date, and endorsement of paid checks with entries in supporting documents.

2. *Review of Client's Reconciliation.* The steps in reviewing a client's bank reconciliation include:

  a. Compare amounts on the reconciliation with original bank statements, cash books, and general ledger;
  b. Prove mathematical accuracy of the reconciliation; and
  c. Obtain bank statements directly from the bank for a subsequent period long enough to permit clearance of most reconciling items; compare paid checks dated before the end of the period with checks listed as outstanding; trace transfers of funds to account debits and credits, which should be recorded in the same accounting period; substantiate other reconciling items by reference to supporting documents; and consider further investigation of unusual outstanding checks not cleared.

3. *Test of Client's Reconciliation.* In addition to the review steps outlined above, an auditor may test the steps taken by the client in the original reconciliation. Generally, the tests are selected from the steps described under "Independent Reconciliation" and would normally involve reperformance of some or all of the operations.

Confirmation of Bank Balances

As a general rule, an auditor should confirm balances at year end by direct correspondence even though all year-end reconciliations may not be reviewed or tested. Since the confirmation form also seeks information about indebtedness to the bank, it is generally requested regardless of how small a balance may be and sometimes even if a bank account has been closed during the year. Except in unusual circumstances, obtaining confirmation of bank balances for functional tests of cash at an interim date should not be necessary.

Requests to banks for confirmation should be made using the Standard Bank Confirmation Inquiry form, which appears on the following page. That form is mailed to each bank in original and duplicate; the duplicate should be signed by the bank and returned to the auditor. Because of increased mechanization of bank accounting, the confirmation procedure can be expedited if the bank receives the confirmation form before the confirmation date and the exact name and number of the accounts to be confirmed are prelisted in item 1 of the form.

STANDARD BANK CONFIRMATION INQUIRY
Approved 1966 by
AMERICAN INSTITUTE OF CERTIFIED PUBLIC ACCOUNTANTS
and
BANK ADMINISTRATION INSTITUTE (FORMERLY NABAC)

_____19_____

Dear Sirs:

Your completion of the following report will be sincerely appreciated. IF THE ANSWER TO ANY ITEM IS "NONE," PLEASE SO STATE. Kindly mail it in the enclosed stamped, addressed envelope *direct* to the accountant named below.

Report from   Yours truly, _____

                                       (ACCOUNT NAME PER BANK RECORDS)

(Bank) _____   By _____
                                               Authorized Signature

_____

                              Bank customer should check here if confirmation of bank balances only (item 1) is desired.

_____

                                                  ☐

        Coopers & Lybrand   NOTE—If the space provided is inadequate, please enter totals hereon and attach a statement giving full details as called for by the columnar headings below.
Accountant   1251 Avenue of the Americas
        New York, New York 10020

Dear Sirs:

1. At the close of business on_____19____our records showed the following balance(s) to the **credit** of the above named customer. In the event that we could readily ascertain whether there were any balances to the credit of the customer not designated in this request, the appropriate information is given below.

AMOUNT	ACCOUNT NAME	ACCOUNT NUMBER	Subject to Withdrawal by Check?	Interest Bearing? Give Rate
$				

2. The customer was directly liable to us in respect of loans, acceptances, etc., at the close of business on that date in the total amount of $_____, as follows:

AMOUNT	DATE OF LOAN OR DISCOUNT	DUE DATE	INTEREST Rate	INTEREST Paid to	DESCRIPTION OF LIABILITY, COLLATERAL, SECURITY INTERESTS, LIENS, ENDORSERS, ETC.
$					

3. The customer was contingently liable as endorser of notes discounted and/or as guarantor at the close of business on that date in the total amount of $_____, as below:

AMOUNT	NAME OF MAKER	DATE OF NOTE	DUE DATE	REMARKS
$				

4. Other direct or contingent liabilities, open letters of credit, and relative collateral, were

5. Security agreements under the Uniform Commercial Code or any other agreements providing for restrictions, not noted above, were as follows (if officially recorded, indicate date and office in which filed):

_____

                         Yours truly, (Bank)_____

Date_____19____   By _____
                                                 Authorized Signature

The standard form has no space designated for reporting securities or other items held by the bank in safekeeping, as agent or trustee, or for collection for account of the client, nor does it request a statement of the bank account and cancelled checks. Accordingly, an auditor should request the client to address a supplementary letter to the bank covering those items or any others on which information is desired. The following example illustrates the format of the letter:

[Name and address of bank]

Dear Sirs:

Will you kindly furnish directly to our auditors, [name and address of auditors], the following information relevant to their examination of our accounts as of the close of business December 31, 19—:

1. The information requested in the enclosed Standard Bank Confirmation Inquiry form;
2. Statement of all securities or other items you hold for our account as of December 31, 19—, for collection or safekeeping or as agent or trustee; and
3. Statement of our account and the related paid checks for the period from January 1 to January —, 19—, inclusive.

Very truly yours,

[Name of client]
[Signature and title of officer]

Confirmation of Other Balances

It is common practice to request confirmation of cash on hand from other custodians of funds, often combining the request for confirmation of the fund balance with a request for notification of unrecorded expenses, if any.

Count of Cash and Negotiable Assets on Hand

Cash funds on hand, normally constituting one or more petty cash funds, are seldom significant in relation to the overall cash balance. Therefore, an auditor should generally not need to perform independent validation tests of the year-end balance of cash on hand. He may, nevertheless, wish to make functional tests of controls over the day-to-day operation of petty cash funds to obtain reasonable assurance that the activity in the funds is accurately and reliably recorded. Inadequate procedures and controls could result in improperly classified expenses in the income statement.

Some circumstances require physical counting of currency and cash items on hand. If cash funds on hand and undeposited receipts are significant in relation to the overall cash balance, and if controls are weak, there may be no alternative to a year-end cash count. Or the task may be too big for a client's staff to handle so that the auditor is requested to count the cash and negotiable assets as an adjunct to his regular examination. When an auditor finds that a cash count is required, he should coordinate that examination with the examination or confirmation of other negotiable assets such as marketable securities, notes receivable, and collateral held as security on loans to others. If simultaneous physical examination of negotiable assets on hand is not practicable, the auditor should establish control over all of them to avoid the possibility of a shortage in one group being covered up by the use of other assets already examined. Less active negotiable assets—such as reserve cash, notes receivable, or securities—may be counted in advance and placed under seal until completion of all counts. Occasionally it is necessary to permit movement of assets under seal; the auditor should control and record all changes. To preserve the integrity of the procedure, some auditors prefer to arrange, if possible, to count cash funds and other negotiable assets at a time not disclosed in advance to the custodians. The timing of preliminary audit work before the close of the fiscal year may be flexible and controlled by an auditor, thus affording opportunity, within limits, for a surprise count. In our opinion, the element of surprise is seldom pertinent to the objectives of an opinion audit.

An auditor should not assume responsibility for custody of cash or negotiable assets but should insist on continuous attendance by a representative of the client while those assets are being examined. After the count has been completed, the representative of the client should be given an opportunity to check it. Although auditors often obtain a receipt or acknowledgment from the custodian when funds are returned, it is usually not necessary. However, if for some reason a client's representative has not been present during the count, obtaining a receipt from him after he has verified the count is desirable. If the count discloses an overage or shortage in the fund, the auditor should ask for a recheck and acknowledgment by the client's representative of the accuracy of the count.

Counting cash does not normally require counting the contents of coin packages or all packages of currency notes. Vouchers in the fund may be reviewed for validity, reasonableness, and approval. Checks or vouchers not of recent date should be investigated.

The counting of undeposited receipts can be avoided by controlling those funds until deposited, obtaining an authenticated duplicate deposit slip, and later determining, either from a subsequent bank statement or by inquiry of the bank, whether any item deposited was subsequently charged back as missing or uncollectible.

Totals of funds and negotiable assets counted or confirmed should be reconciled with general ledger controlling accounts as of the date of the examination.

Examination of Cash Records

At times an auditor's functional tests may lead him to a conclusion that controls are not effective enough to rely on nor weak enough to be considered totally unreliable. That is probably more likely to occur in the area of cash controls than in other transaction systems, both because of the nature of cash and because the execution and recording of cash transactions is less likely to be an integral and inextricable part of a larger, often physical operation. It is also more likely to occur in small and medium-size companies in which one or a few people must handle all of the execution, recording, and accountability functions.

If the functional tests are inconclusive, an auditor can easily validate the cash balance at year end, and he can usually examine enough of the records of cash transactions to obtain evidence on which to base an opinion on whether the unexamined underlying records are reliable. In the absence of satisfactory functional tests, any such extended "vouching" is a validation test. That test may be made in conjunction with similar tests of revenue, expenses, and accounts payable, may be part of a "proof of cash" bank reconciliation, or may be performed as a separate procedure. In such circumstances, the auditor is seeking a basis for believing that the results are typical of those produced throughout the period under examination. The test results can be confirmed in the course of other validation tests. The sample may be judgmental (the reasons why judgmental samples are acceptable are discussed in Chapter 5) or may be designed statistically to provide a basis for inference.

Tests must be designed to fit the variety of accounting and control systems used. The following are typical tests:

> Compare the initial detail lists of cash receipts with duplicate bank deposit slips, cash receipts book, and accounts receivable posting. Some of the details as well as the control totals should be compared on a test basis to confirm that each batch is processed intact and promptly.

> Observe the actual cash receipts process (mail opening or counter receipts), the listing process, and the process of controlling receipts until they are deposited in a bank.

Compare paid checks with vouchers and supporting detail for agreement of payee and payment terms, proper attention to cash discounts, and evidence of adequacy of review and approval procedures.

Compare entries in voucher register and cash disbursements book.

Observe the actual check-writing process, the control procedures over checks before and after writing, and the procedures for controlling completed checks until they are mailed.

Trace handling and disposition of bank debit memos and credit memos for items such as checks charged back, service charges, and collections credited.

Validation Procedures: Effective Controls

If an auditor has reason to believe that he can place maximum reliance on cash controls—his preliminary understanding is confirmed by the results of functional tests of the revenue and buying segments, for example—cash validation procedures might be limited to the following:

Review and test records of client's bank reconciliations and cash counts at an interim date. Since that procedure is largely a functional test of the client's accountability procedures, the review may encompass all of the accounts or, if they are many, be limited to a representative sample. Usually, only some of the reconciliations and cash counts are actually tested.

Confirm year-end balances and compare with client's reconciliations.

Scan reconciliations for evidence of proper preparation and supervisory approval.

Request client to prepare a schedule of bank transfers before and after year end; test schedule to records.

Those validation procedures should be supplemented by the usual analytical reviews described below.

Validation Procedures: Weaknesses in Controls

If control weaknesses are found, the following procedures might be called for:

Prepare independent "proof of cash" reconciliation of bank accounts at an interim date.

Examine a sample of revenue, expense, and other transactions drawn from periods other than those selected for reconciliation.

Count significant cash funds at year end (auditor and client may agree on a count of insignificant cash funds in cases of extreme weakness, but it is not required for the auditor's opinion).

Obtain confirmation of bank accounts at year end.

Prepare independent reconciliation of bank accounts at year end.

Obtain cutoff bank statement two weeks after year end; trace year-end reconciling items to cutoff statement.

Analytical Reviews

Since cash accounts are not usually interrelated with many other accounts (they act as buffers and conduits for other activity), the analytical reviews are not as likely to produce important corroborative evidence as in other segments. The principal purpose of analytical reviews of cash accounts is to detect unusual transactions that might otherwise be overlooked.

Cash balances at the end of a period should be compared with one another and with cash budgets, if they exist, and significant unexpected fluctuations should be explained. If cash budget variance reports are prepared, they can be reviewed.

Entries in cash accounts should be scanned, especially for the period between interim validation tests and year end; unusual entries or unusual departures from standard entries should be investigated and explained. In particular, journal entries affecting cash accounts should be reviewed.

If an auditor has reason to suspect a practice of window-dressing the cash balance and related accounts, the totals of outstanding checks and other reconciling items in the bank reconciliations can be compared from period to period and significant fluctuations investigated for evidence of possible early cutoff or delayed closing of the cash books.

● STATEMENT PRESENTATION

DESCRIPTION OF CASH

In classifying cash, distinguishing among currency on hand, undeposited checks, cash in banks, and deposits at various locations is not necessary unless the balance sheet is prepared for a special purpose requiring those distinctions. The description of cash in banks as "demand deposits in banks" has merit in that it removes all question of restrictions. The reader of a balance sheet has a right to assume, however, that the item "Cash" is realizable in the amount stated and is completely and immediately available for operation of the business and payment of debts. The majority of published reports use the simple description "Cash."

Some companies regularly invest idle cash in readily marketable temporary investments, such as certificates of deposit, time deposits, or short-term cash-type securities (U. S. Treasury bills, etc.). It is considered acceptable practice to combine those kinds of temporary cash investments with cash in a single caption in the balance sheet, provided that the combining of items is disclosed and the investments are not of a nature (because of maturity or size) that makes it unrealistic to consider them as in effect readily available cash. We believe that amounts of temporary investments, if significant in relation to total cash, should also be disclosed, either parenthetically or in a note. In financial statements filed with the Securities and Exchange Commission, separate presentation is usually required.

SEGREGATION OF RESTRICTED CASH

Cash on hand sometimes includes balances with trustees, such as those for sinking funds, or other amounts that are not immediately available, such as those restricted to uses other than current operations, designated for acquisition or construction of noncurrent assets, or segregated for the liquidation of long-term debt. Restrictions are considered effective if the company clearly intends to observe them even though the funds are not actually set aside in special bank accounts. The facts pertaining to those balances should be adequately disclosed on the balance sheet, and the amounts should be properly classified as current or noncurrent.

Understandings with banks in connection with lines of credit often suggest that a company maintain a compensating cash balance at the bank, possibly amounting to 10% to 20% of the credit allowed. Formerly the existence of compensating balances was not disclosed in financial statements unless there was a binding agreement. A recent requirement of the Securities and Exchange Commission to disclose compensating balances was delayed for almost two years because of difficulties in defining and measuring the item. (For example, should compensating balances be reported in the full amount called for by the bank, or reduced by the normal "float" of outstanding checks?) In 1975, experience with the requirement is too limited to permit conclusions about the most practicable and effective ways of dealing with those problems. Showing the required disclosure in a note makes it possible to emphasize the measurement difficulties by stating an approximate amount. Compensating balances of cash should be segregated on the balance sheet only if they are legally restricted by the terms of the arrangement, and should be classified as current or noncurrent depending on whether the related debt is short term or long term.

Certain cash may be segregated in a bank account for which the client clearly acts merely as trustee, and the balance is not available for its own expenditures. An account of that sort may arise from employee savings plans. There is no objection to offsetting that cash against a related liability, provided all of the following conditions exist:

1. The trust status is indicated clearly on the records of the depositary;
2. Client's counsel is of the opinion that the account may be used only by the beneficiaries, whose claims may not be satisfied by any other assets; and
3. The records and internal control of the trust assets are sufficient to insure that the trust relationship is respected and that beneficiaries' interests are clearly recorded.

BANK OVERDRAFTS

Some accountants believe that an overdraft in a bank account should be included among liabilities and not be offset against balances in other bank accounts. We believe that an overdraft in one bank account may properly be offset by a balance in another bank account if the balance available to offset the overdraft is not restricted and is not part of a minimum balance requirement of a loan or other agreement. Any portion of an overdraft that is not offset by a free balance in another bank account should be included as a liability. Similarly, if an overdraft is in fact the bank's way of temporarily loaning funds to the client, it should be shown among the liabilities.

16

The Financing Segment

DEBT, EQUITY, RETAINED EARNINGS, AND RELATED ACCOUNTS

INTRODUCTION

The last of the major transaction segments to be considered comprises all the transactions involved in obtaining the financial resources necessary for an enterprise to function. That can range all the way from a single transaction—the initial capital to establish a nonprofit organization, which thereafter simply disburses all that it receives—through a whole range of increasingly complex combinations of financing activities to aggressive, large-scale, continuous selling of financing instruments that has been characteristic, in different ways, of public utilities, conglomerates, and mutual funds.

The traditional distinction between debt and equity is clear in most businesses. Equity stems from owners' invested funds plus earnings retained and reinvested; debt is the result of borrowing funds for specific periods, whether short or long term, although the individual loans are frequently renewed again and again for an indefinite period. Conventional accounting is built on that distinction, which continues to be significant and useful.

However, the distinction between debt and equity has become blurred and considerably less useful in certain businesses, especially large-scale public companies. In those companies, it is more realistic to view the various debt and equity financing instruments as an array of alternatives which financial managers should continuously marshal and remarshal to enhance the company's earnings record as well as its financial strength. Common stock becomes as much a financing instrument as bank loans, and convertible debt may have as many equity characteristics as preferred stock. In fact, financial managers adjust the legal characteristics of an instrument, whether formally designated as debt or equity, to achieve a desired (or required) balance of protection of principal and income with sharing of the risks and rewards of ownership. Instruments are designed to reconcile an enterprise's need for financial resources at minimum cost with investors' preferences for safety and reward. The result is a virtually continuous spectrum of financing instruments, ranging from straight borrowing through borrowing with equity features, borrowing with variable income features, stock with preferences as to income and principal, to common stock and even to promises of future stock.

Corporate finance is an exceedingly complex and sophisticated subject which deserves the extensive literature that has been devoted to it. It is not our intention in this chapter to attempt a summary description of so enormous a subject. Our description of financing instruments and their purposes is limited to that necessary to explain present accounting principles used to record them. Since they are much the same for many different types of financing instruments, the chapter does not go into detail to distinguish, for example, between trade acceptances and drafts drawn under letters of credit, between time and sight drafts, or between bonds and debentures.

For convenience, the following discussion of accounting principles is divided into sections dealing with short-term financing, long-term debt financing, equity securities financing, retained earnings, and, finally, promises and future commitments.

• ACCOUNTING PRINCIPLES

Accounting principles are required to answer three questions about transactions and events in the financing segment:

How should a transaction be classified?
When and in what amount should it be recorded?
When and how should the cost of financing be recorded?

Classification determines where in a balance sheet a transaction should be reflected or whether it should be reflected at all (for example, many leases are not recorded, but the details are disclosed in notes). The discussion of classification duplicates some of the material in the last section of this chapter, on statement presentation. It is necessary because adequate accounting principles for financing instruments are, more than in any other area, influenced by financial statement presentation and disclosure requirements.

Carrying amount involves questions of identifying and measuring values that may differ from those formally stated in transaction documents. Recording the cost of financing involves difficult questions of timing and even more difficult questions of what constitutes a cost, how to measure it, and how to report it. Accountants have yet to discover how to deal with the full range of those questions in a complete, consistent, and satisfactory manner.

SHORT-TERM FINANCING

Classification

Traditionally, short-term financing consists of borrowing to meet temporary or short-term needs. It is usually evidenced by notes, which are payable on demand or within a period of a year. Whatever the nature of the debt instrument, short-term debt is classified as a current liability because repayment is expected within the normal operating cycle using resources included in current assets. In recent years, short-term financing has been used increasingly for long-term purposes, either because long-term financing was not available on reasonable terms, or to provide a vehicle to accommodate severely fluctuating interest rates.

Notes payable to banks and financing institutions are classified separately from those payable to suppliers and others, which in turn are classified separately from notes payable to officers and affiliates. Separate classification stems from a general belief that different types of short-term financing are significant indicators of the financial policies of an organization.

Short-term loans under revolving credit agreements are technically short-term financing and current liabilities, but they may properly be classified as noncurrent or long term if the borrower has an unconditional right to renew for a total period of more than a year.

Loans on life insurance policies should be classified as current or noncurrent depending on the asset classification of the corresponding cash surrender value.

Trade acceptances and drafts drawn under letters of credit are usually more like accounts payable than short-term financing. They are used to purchase goods, and the financing feature is for the convenience of the seller. They should be separately stated if material; otherwise they are usually classified as accounts payable.

The portion of long-term debt due within a year is almost always classified as a current liability. The amount should be disclosed in the current liabilities section in those rare instances in which it is not so classified. One exception to that convention is if funds to pay a debt due within a year have been segregated and classified as noncurrent assets.

Offsetting Assets and Liabilities

The question of whether assets and liabilities may be offset or "netted" is recurrent because often an asset is held for the purpose of settling a liability or a debt is incurred to finance an asset—such as inventory, receivables, or equipment. As a general rule, assets and liabilities should not be offset because neither is exclusively related to the other: assets can be used for other purposes and debts are a lien on all assets as well as those specifically pledged. However, there are exceptions, and when assets and liabilities are clearly and exclusively related to each other, offset is acceptable. Examples are loans against cash surrender value of life insurance, accounts receivable sold with recourse, advances on long-term contracts, and certain types of leases.

Carrying Amount

There are few problems in determining the carrying amount of short-term financing. The amount of the liability is usually clearly stated in the instrument and both date of initiation and due date are explicit. If short-term financing is obtained by means of a "discounted" note, the liability recorded should be the face amount of the note less the discount, and interest at the effective rate should be accrued over the period of the note.

Cost

Similarly, there are few problems in determining the cost of short-term financing. The interest rate is usually clearly stated and there are few of the complicating rights and restrictions often associated with long-term financing. The practice of "compensating balances" described in Chapter 15 may obscure the true cost (or, alternatively, the true amount) of short-term financing, and that problem is currently being dealt with through disclosure.

LONG-TERM DEBT FINANCING

Conventionally, financing obtained for more than a year is used to finance longer-term needs, such as acquisition of plant or equipment. It is not uncommon, however, for long-term financing to be obtained for working capital needs or for working capital to be among the assets received in an acquisition for which long-term financing is obtained. The amount and kind of long-term financing appearing in a company's balance sheet is of interest to investors, lenders, bond rating agencies, and everyone who influences the supply of further financial resources. It is therefore important to financial management. Over the years, a great deal of ingenuity has gone into designing long-term financing that looks like something else. Much of that effort has recently been concentrated in the complicated field of leasing.

Classification

Each issue of long-term debt securities is likely to be for a relatively large amount and have sufficient characteristics differing from other issues to require separate accounting. Depending on the purpose of the financing and the conditions of the financial market at the time it is needed, long-term financing may take the form of term loans, bonds, debentures, installment loans, leases, or loans from stockholders. Any debt instrument may contain provisions for partial or complete repayment in installments over the period of the loan; bonds and debentures may require accumulation of sinking funds to repay the borrowing. Debt may be convertible into common stock or may include detachable or nondetachable warrants to purchase common stock of the borrowing corporation.

It is customary to account for each issue of long-term financing separately and to disclose the important characteristics of each in financial statements or notes. If individual issues of long-term debt securities are not significant, it is acceptable to group several issues together and make general disclosures about maturities, average interest rates, and the like.

If a company purchases its own long-term debt instruments, the liability should ordinarily be reduced as if it had been paid, and a gain or loss on retirement or other disposition of purchased debt should be included in current income—as an extraordinary item except when the purchases are made to satisfy sinking fund requirements. (The Federal Power Commission requires that any such gains and losses be amortized over the remaining life of the security issue unless the amortization principle is specifically disallowed for rate-making purposes.) Showing a company's own debt instruments acquired as an asset is acceptable in rare instances; for example, if the debt is acquired by and included in a sinking fund.

Carrying Amount and Cost

Problems arise in determining the carrying amount of long-term debt because the effective rate of interest for the use of money and the values of other rights received or given up in long-term financing transactions may be different from those stated in financing agreements. Since a formal borrowing agreement always specifies a due date and an amount to be repaid, which should generally be reflected in the accounts, variations in the carrying amount required to recognize a different economic substance must usually be reflected in other accounts, such as debt discount or premium.

Debt Discount and Premium

Debt discount or premium arises if the interest rate specified in a debt instrument differs from the effective rate of interest in the borrowing transaction. For example, the going rate of interest may change between the time an instrument is prepared and the time the funds are actually borrowed, or the parties may agree to specify an interest rate and to loan and borrow a sum different from the face amount of the instrument to give a different effective rate. Thus, although a difference between the face amount of a debt instrument and the borrowed funds may reflect a value placed on other rights received or given up in the borrowing transaction (as discussed below in relation to convertible debt and warrants), it is usually attributed to a difference in interest rates and accounted for as an increase or a decrease in interest expense. The difference is recorded as debt premium or debt discount and amortized as an adjustment of interest expense over the period to maturity of the debt, generally in proportion to the recognition of interest expense. If interest expense is capitalized during a period of construction (see Chapter 12), amortized discount or premium should also be capitalized during the same period.

The "interest method" of amortizing premium or discount is now the generally accepted method. It results in a periodic interest cost, including amortization of premium or discount, that represents a level effective rate on the debt outstanding (face amount plus or minus the unamortized premium or discount) at the beginning of each period. Various commonly encountered conditions require modifications in applying the general principle. For example, if debt matures in series or is payable in installments, amortization should be computed to obtain results approximating those of the interest method. The "bonds outstanding" method, which was widely used in the past, is a straight-line method and is no longer acceptable unless its results do not differ materially from those of the interest method [APB Opinion No. 21 (*AICPA Prof. Stds.,* vol. 3, paragraph 4111.14)].

Discount or premium on convertible debt is amortized in the same way as that on straight debt until conversion takes place. Then proportionate amounts of unamortized discount or premium are transferred to additional paid-in capital together with proportionate amounts of the debt.

If debt is retired before maturity, the balance of unamortized discount or premium should be written off to income at the time of retirement. The same accounting applies if debt is retired and refunded. APB Opinion No. 26, *Early Extinguishment of Debt (AICPA Prof. Stds.,* vol. 3, Section 5362) superseded prior authoritative pronouncements that expressed a preference for amortizing remaining unamortized discount over the remaining original life of the issue retired, but also permitted writing it off directly against income or amortizing it over the life of the new issue in certain circumstances.

If long-term debt is issued to finance the acquisition of property rather than to borrow funds, debt discount or premium may result. If so, it is not automatically determined by the transaction but must be "imputed," by imputing the effective interest rate on the debt. Determining imputed interest on payables is described in Chapter 12, "The Property Segment" (and on receivables in Chapter 9, "The Revenue Segment"). Once determined, an imputed interest adjustment recognized on a transaction is accounted for as debt discount or premium.

Some Problem Areas

Convertible Debt

Convertible securities are recurrently popular forms of financing because they offer advantages to both issuer and investor. An investor receives both specified preferences that serve to protect his investment and an opportunity, through the conversion feature, to share in growth in equity values. Since the feature of "down-side" protection and "up-side" opportunity is valuable to an investor, an issuer can obtain funds at less cost than through either straight debt or straight equity financing. To the extent that those mutual advantages are real, the cost savings to an issuer should be recognized.

Accountants had no satisfactory means for recognizing and accounting for the real costs of convertible debt before APB Opinions No. 14 and 15 (*AICPA Prof. Stds.*, vol. 3, Sections 5516 and 2011 to 2011D) were adopted in 1969. Conventional accounting previously offered opportunities to exaggerate the apparent cost savings of that type of financing because there was no generally accepted way to recognize the cost of the equity feature of a convertible debt instrument. *For example:*

> A corporation could issue a 3% convertible debenture at a time when interest rates were 6% or higher, accompanied by a right to convert $25 face amount of debentures into a share of common stock with a market value of $50. A high fraction of the debenture's value to an investor is obviously the right to obtain the $50 share of stock, rather than to receive the 3% interest. And there is clearly some cost to the company in giving up that $50 of potential equity investment in exchange for $25 in debt. Nevertheless, before 1969, the only cost the issuer had to reflect under conventional accounting principles was the 3% interest cost of the debt.

A great debate about how best to correct that obvious deficiency preceded the issuance of APB Opinions No. 14 and 15. A considerable body of opinion supported recognizing in the accounts a value for the conversion feature in a manner similar to that adopted for warrants in Opinion No. 14 (see the next two paragraphs). The Accounting Principles Board decided that the debt and equity features were so inseparable that it was neither theoretically nor practically feasible to separate them for accounting purposes. Instead, the Board adopted in Opinion No. 15 the concept of "common stock equivalents" for computing earnings per share (Chapter 18). That concept provided a means for recognizing the economic effect on per-share earnings of convertible debt having a substantial part of its value attributable to equity features.

Warrants

The Board concluded that debt issued with detachable common stock purchase warrants was different from convertible debt on both theoretical and practical grounds. Since the warrants were separable from the debt (and usually separately traded in open markets), values were separately determinable.

APB Opinion No. 14, therefore calls for determining the value of detachable stock purchase warrants and accounting for them as debt discount (or occasionally as a reduction of debt premium) and additional paid-in capital. The amount attributed to debt discount is amortized as an adjustment of interest cost, as described above. Since an issue of debt with detachable stock purchase warrants is a sophisticated financing transaction, it is seldom, if ever, undertaken without the advice and assistance of investment bankers who can also advise about the value to be assigned to the warrants.

Leases

Leases are a form of long-term financing, and the question of whether they should be capitalized as long-term debt has plagued the accounting profession for years. Some leases are now capitalized, but almost no one is satisfied with the current situation. As yet no satisfactory tests of which leases to capitalize have been devised, and the subject continues to be a troublesome and controversial one. The current state of accounting for property financed by long-term lease is discussed in Chapter 12, "The Property Segment."

If the circumstances call for capitalization of a lease, the present value of future rental payments is recorded as a long-term liability. Usually an interest rate appears somewhere in the calculations, proposals, and negotiations surrounding the creation of the lease, and that rate is appropriate for computing the present value of rental payments. Thereafter each rental payment is divided proportionately between reducing the liability and interest expense.

Commitments

Various commitments are customarily given and received in negotiating long-term financing. Typical commitments include: agreements to maintain a minimum level of working capital or net assets; to maintain adequate insurance; to maintain property adequately, sometimes through specified additions to maintenance funds; to pledge or mortgage certain property or to restrict the use of proceeds from its sale; to restrict leasing, borrowing, mergers, and the issuance or repurchase of other types of securities; to accumulate funds for repayment through a sinking fund; and to render reports and financial statements on specified dates. Such commitments are intended to protect the interests of security holders, and failure to comply is classed as an event of default which gives the security holders the right to demand immediate repayment and perhaps other rights as well.

Although those commitments do not directly involve accounting or accounting principles, they are important to accountants and auditors. First, they may require disclosure in financial statements. Second, failure to comply with them may have a serious effect on financial position if it causes acceleration of the maturity of the debt. Third, they may be important factors in encouraging or inhibiting changes in financial structure, financial statement presentation, or accounting principles.

EQUITY SECURITIES FINANCING

The owners' equity of a business is the excess of total assets over total liabilities (net assets) and is represented by the property or cash paid in as investment of the owners, together with increments or decrements arising from operations during the course of the business.

The discussion that follows is in terms of a corporate form of organization, the form that now predominates. Generally, similar principles apply to accounts and financial statements of partnerships and proprietorships even though they lack the legal separation of a business entity from its owners which distinguishes a corporation. Matters peculiar to those and other forms of organization are discussed briefly at the end of this section on accounting principles.

Terminology

The equity section of the balance sheet of a corporation reflects the interest of the stockholders of the corporation in its assets. Formerly considered as the "Capital" section, in published reports of corporations it is now generally entitled "Stockholders' Equity" or "Shareholders' Equity."

Accountants now prefer the terms "stockholders' equity," "capital," or "net assets" over the term "net worth," which was widely used at one time. Net worth has the disadvantage of suggesting present realizable value. Since the assets shown in most balance sheets prepared in accordance with generally accepted accounting principles are a mixture of known values (cash), estimates of current values (receivables), and unexpired and unamortized historical costs (inventories, fixed assets, and intangible assets), the owners' equity or excess of assets over liabilities as reflected by the accounts would only coincidentally approximate the present worth of a business.

Other terms for the various components of stockholders' equity have also been evolving. Many years ago, the Committee on Terminology of the AICPA recommended eliminating "capital surplus" and "earned surplus," both traditional terms using the generally misleading word "surplus." "Earned surplus" has now almost completely disappeared from financial statements, supplanted by "retained earnings," "undistributed earnings," or a similar term. "Capital surplus" has remained longer, perhaps because finding terms to replace it has proved more difficult. However, terms such as "paid-in surplus," which retains the disadvantage of "surplus," "additional paid-in capital," or merely "additional capital" have become more prevalent.

Classification and Carrying Amount

Stockholders' equity should be broken down into details that describe the nature and sources of the elements constituting the equity. The distinction of greatest importance relates to the origin of the equity, that is: (a) capital derived from contributions of stockholders—ordinarily further divided according to circumstances into "capital stock" and "additional paid-in capital," the latter category representing principally capital contributions in excess of the amounts assigned to capital stock—and (b) capital derived from or accumulated by the retention of earnings, most frequently called "retained earnings." Stock dividends or other actions that result in "capitalizing" retained earnings cause a transfer from the second category to the first. This chapter discusses the classifications of equity in terms of the three broad areas: capital stock and additional paid-in capital (in this section) and retained earnings (in the next).

Cost

It was once thought that the cost of financing through equity securities was the related dividend payments. It has been clear for some years that that is only part of the cost—and for many companies an inconsequential or nonexistent part.

"Dilution" is a commonly used measure in financial circles. It may be defined in the broad sense as any financing transaction that diminishes the remaining potential financial resources available to a business. No attempt is made to measure or account for dilution in that sense. However, the accounting profession has developed a means for measuring and accounting for dilution in the narrower sense of a financing transaction that actually or potentially dilutes a common stockholder's interest in a corporation. The computation of earnings per share, discussed at length in Chapter 18, is now widely used as a gauge of the cost of equity financing. It is a useful, but not a definitive, gauge. For example, the implication that an equity issue that does not dilute earnings per share is entirely cost-free must clearly be viewed with reservations.

One of accounting's uncompleted tasks is to devise an adequate means of reporting the economic cost of equity financing. Until it does, the use of earnings per share will continue to result in undue and often misleading emphasis on that single figure.

Capital Stock

Capital stock represents the part of the equity contributed by stockholders that a corporation is expected to maintain intact (other than as reduced by losses or by appropriate legal action) for the protection of creditors. The amount may be expressed as capital stock with par value or capital stock without par value, and the latter as having or not having stated or assigned value. It often does not represent the full amount contributed by stockholders.

Authorized stock is the maximum number of shares that a corporation may issue under the terms of its charter, and that number usually may not be increased or decreased without approval of the stockholders and appropriate charter amendment.

Issued stock, as the name implies, is that portion of the authorized stock that has actually been issued by the corporation. Issued stock may be reacquired by a corporation either through gift or by purchase from stockholders. Reacquired shares, unless retired, remain issued stock and are referred to as "treasury stock." From an accounting standpoint, outstanding stock generally is considered to be stock issued and in the hands of stockholders and does not include shares reacquired by the issuing corporation; however, from a legal standpoint, treasury stock may be considered outstanding until all necessary legal steps for its formal retirement have been accomplished.

Capital stock of a corporation is divided into shares, or proportionate ownership interests. Each owner of shares enjoys proportionately the same rights and privileges as other owners of the same class of stock. Stockholders usually receive certificates evidencing the number of shares owned.

Corporations often divide their capital stock into various classes. The most prevalent classes are common stock and preferred stock, which may in turn be divided into additional classes enjoying different rights. Occasionally, still other classes are authorized, such as debenture stock and founders' stock (see "Other Classes of Stock" later in this section).

The rights, privileges, and responsibilities of stockholders are governed by the laws of the state under which the corporation is organized and by the charter and by-laws of the corporation.

Par Value Stock

The par value of capital stock is a dollar amount assigned to each share. The par value has no inherent relation to the actual worth of the stock, nor does it necessarily fix the price at which a share will be issued. Par value is an arbitrary figure stemming largely from a legal technicality which today has little practical accounting significance. Many states do not permit capital stock to be issued originally at a price below par value. In states that do permit issue at less than par value, stock so issued may be classified legally as not fully paid, and the original stockholders may be liable to creditors for the difference between the price paid and the par value. That difference is known as "discount on capital stock." It is an undesirable feature and one that is easily avoided, and thus it is now uncommon.

Par value stock issued is recorded in a corporation's accounts at par value, and amounts received in excess of par are recorded as additional paid-in capital. Occasionally, the par value is ignored in accounting, and the capital stock account reflects the full amount contributed.

No Par Stock

Most states permit the issuance of stock without par value. Each certificate of no par stock merely states the number of shares that it represents. Some states require that the total number of shares authorized also be shown on the certificate.

No par stock issued may be recorded in the accounts of the issuing corporation at a stated or assigned value, which may be equal to or less than the subscription price of the stock. Sometimes a portion of the price paid is credited to additional paid-in capital and may be legally available for dividends. Payment of dividends from that source is discussed later in this chapter.

Another accepted method of accounting for issues of no par stock is to include in the capital stock account the entire net proceeds, notwithstanding the fact that stock may have been issued at different times and at different prices. Sometimes the above procedure is confined to the original issue and subsequent issues are recorded at the same stated amount per share, with the difference credited or charged to additional paid-in capital.

Expenses of Stock Issues

Underwriting discounts, professional fees, and related expenses are properly considered a reduction of the proceeds before determining the amount to be recorded as capital stock and additional paid-in capital. Those expenses include commissions to selling agents; fees of attorneys, engineers, or accountants; printing costs; SEC filing fees; and other expenses clearly and directly attributable to receiving the proceeds of the shares issued. If the net proceeds are below par or stated value, the difference should be charged first to available additional paid-in capital on issues no longer outstanding and then, if necessary, to retained earnings. Regulated utilities are required to record those expenses in a separate balance sheet account, which may be carried until the stock is retired or written off either directly to retained earnings or through systematic charges to income.

Common Stock

Common stock represents the residual ownership in a corporation. Common stockholders are not entitled to a distribution of earnings or assets until all prior claims of creditors and preferred stockholders are satisfied. If there is no preferred or other special class of stock, common stock and capital stock of a corporation are synonymous.

Common stockholders, by virtue of their ownership of a corporation, have certain basic rights: usually, to vote and thus to participate in the selection of management, to share in the profits of the business by receiving dividends declared by the directors, and to share in the distribution of assets in accordance with the terms of the charter when the corporation is dissolved. Depending on the laws of the state of incorporation or on the charter, common stockholders sometimes have a fourth right, called the "pre-emptive" right, which prevents dilution of the stockholders' equity without their consent: that is, they may have first call to purchase additional common stock issued by the corporation in proportion to their holdings at the time of a new issue.

Preferred Stock

Classes of stock that are granted certain preferences or privileges over those of the common stock or residual interest are known as preferred stocks. They may be accorded preference in dividends, in liquidation, in voting, or in other matters.

1. Dividend Preference. Holders of preferred stock generally are entitled to receive a specified dividend (expressed either in dollars per share or as a percentage of the par value of the stock) before dividends may be distributed to common stockholders. The payment of a preferred dividend is not automatic; it depends on declaration by the directors.

A dividend preference may be either cumulative or noncumulative. A cumulative dividend preference means that if a dividend is not paid in a given year, that dividend (and all other unpaid cumulative preferred dividends) must be declared and paid before the directors may properly declare a dividend payable to other stockholders. In contrast, if the directors fail to declare a noncumulative preferred dividend in a particular year, preferred stockholders lose their right to that dividend and are entitled only to their prescribed dividends in future years.

Unpaid cumulative preferred dividends should be accounted for in memorandum accounts, and the amount should be disclosed in financial statements.

A variation found in some preferred stocks might be termed "cumulative when earned." If the preferred dividend is earned in a year and the directors fail to declare it, no dividend may be paid until the directors pay the preferred dividend previously earned; however, if the preferred dividend is not earned in a year, the unpaid preferred dividend for that year does not affect future distributions.

A dividend preference may also be classified as participating or nonparticipating, and participation by the preferred stock may be either partial or full. A fully participating preferred stock receives its preference dividend for a year; then, after the common stock receives a prescribed amount (usually an equivalent amount per share), all further dividend distributions for the year are shared equally, share for share, by the common and preferred stock. A partially or limited participating preferred stock follows the same pattern as fully participating preferred stock except that its participation with common stock after a specified dividend has been paid to common stockholders is limited to a specified maximum amount per share. Once that limit is reached in a year, all additional dividends paid during the remainder of the year are paid to common stock only. Various classes of common stock are sometimes issued to achieve similar results.

A nonparticipating preferred stock is entitled to its preference dividend only, not sharing with the common stock in additional dividends paid. Unless the charter specifies otherwise, preferred stock is usually nonparticipating.

2. Assets on Liquidation. If a corporation is liquidated, proceeds from disposing of assets must be used first to settle creditors' claims. After claims of all creditors have been settled, preferred stockholders generally receive a specified amount per share before assets are distributed to common stockholders. The preference amount specified is often slightly larger in voluntary than in involuntary liquidation (bankruptcy). Preferred stockholders are also usually entitled to receive accrued or unpaid dividends before assets are distributed to common stockholders.

Preferred stock may also be participating with respect to distributions of assets when a corporation is liquidated. For instance, the preferred stock may initially receive $100 a share on dissolution; then, after the common receives $100 a share, the preferred stock may participate equally with the common in the distribution of remaining assets. The amount to which each is entitled depends on the preferred stock agreement.

If the liquidation preference is other than the par or stated value of the preferred stock, financial statements should disclose the aggregate liquidation preference (both voluntary and involuntary) on the face of the balance sheet. [Rule 3-16(f) of Regulation S-X.]

3. Voting. Unless a charter provides otherwise, preferred shares normally have the same voting rights as common shares. However, corporate charters commonly eliminate or restrict the voting power of preferred stock. Occasionally preferred stock is entitled to vote only under certain conditions, such as if dividends are not declared for a specified period or working capital, net assets, or earnings fall below a specified minimum. Preferred stock is usually given the right to vote on matters such as issuance of additional preferred stock or other senior securities, major sale of corporate assets, or changes in by-laws affecting the rights of preferred stockholders.

4. Convertibility. A privilege frequently granted to preferred stockholders is the right, at the option of the holder, to convert preferred stock into common stock of the corporation at a specified price or ratio.

A conversion privilege is added to make the preferred stock more attractive to prospective purchasers. Conversion generally must be effected within a specified period, and the conversion ratio may change over time.

5. Redemption. Many preferred stocks are redeemable after a certain date at the option of the corporation, sometimes in whole and sometimes in part selected by lot. The holder of stock that is called usually has a right to receive not only unpaid dividends but also a premium on redemption, which may be specified as a stipulated redemption price or as the par value of the stock plus a premium, depending on whether the stock is a par value or no par value stock.

6. Premium and Call Expense on Redeemed or Converted Preferred Stock. In general, premium and call expense on preferred stock redeemed should be charged directly to retained earnings. In certain circumstances, however, premium and call expense, in whole or in part, may be charged to additional paid-in capital or allocated between the two. Those circumstances normally involve the availability of additional paid-in capital that arose from the issue of stock of the class redeemed: a pro rata part of that additional paid-in capital may be used to absorb premium and call expense.

Convertible preferred stock on which a call for redemption has been given may be converted into common stock before the redemption date. The stockholder often finds it advantageous to convert rather than to receive cash from redemption because of the favorable market price of the common stock. The corporation may, in fact, have called the stock anticipating that most preferred stockholders would convert for that reason. Upon conversion, the excess of par or stated value of the preferred stock over par or stated value of the common stock issued in exchange, less expenses of conversion, should be included in additional paid-in capital. If the par or stated value of the common stock exceeds that of the preferred stock, all or part of the difference may have to be charged to retained earnings.

Other Classes of Stock

Various other types of stock are sometimes found in this country. Common stock may be divided into Class A, Class B, and sometimes Class C common stock. Often one or more of those classes have all the rights usually associated with preferred stock and are common stock in name only. On the other hand, the classes may vary only with respect to their voting privileges or the amount of dividends per share. Often, a class of common stock with a restricted right to receive dividends is convertible over a period into the regular class of common stock.

Debenture stock may be preferred stock under another name. If debenture bonds have no maturity date, they resemble preferred stock.

Founders' stock, now rarely seen in the United States, is usually issued to founders, promoters, or organizers of a corporation. It frequently claims a larger proportion of declared dividends than the remainder of the common stock; for example, 5% of the common stock —the so-called founders' shares—may be entitled to 15% or 20% of a total dividend declared on the common stock. Voting rights may or may not be the same as those of other shares.

Treasury Stock

Treasury stock is a corporation's own issued stock that has been reacquired by purchase or donation but not retired. Generally, treasury stock should be considered not an asset of the issuing company but a reduction of stockholders' equity. An exception to that rule may arise for treasury stock that has been acquired for the specific purpose of resale to employees or others; then it may be shown at cost on the asset side of a balance sheet if appropriately described. Reacquired stock remains treasury stock until it is retired, resold, issued to employees, distributed as a dividend, or issued for property. Treasury stock cannot be voted or receive dividends.

1. Recording Treasury Stock. Treasury stock may be recorded either at cost or at par or stated value of the issue. In the latter case, the difference between cost and par or stated value is accounted for as if the stock were retired (see below). Sometimes the purpose for which the treasury stock was acquired indicates the preferable accounting treatment; sometimes it is governed by law or custom of the state of incorporation. Some state laws prohibit purchase if legal capital is impaired.

2. Dividends on Treasury Stock. Ordinarily, no cash dividends are paid on treasury stock. Dividends paid through a dividend paying agent may include dividends on treasury stock, but upon receipt they should be applied to reduce the amount of dividend distributed; they are not dividend income to the issuing corporation.

Some companies prefer to issue stock dividends on treasury stock so that the treasury shares may retain the same proportionate ownership. That practice is permitted by some states and not by others; it is not essential for accounting. If stock dividends are issued on treasury stock, the accounting treatment should be the same as that for shares held by the public, as described in the section on stock dividends; the cost basis of the total treasury shares should not change, although the number of shares does.

3. Retirement of Treasury Stock. As a general rule, the applicable par, stated, or assigned value is deducted from the appropriate capital stock account on the formal or constructive retirement of treasury stock. Treasury stock with no par or stated value, often issued originally at varying prices per share, is deducted from the related capital stock account either at the amount originally recorded for the shares reacquired or, more usually, at the average recorded amount of all shares of the class. As a practical matter, determining the amount originally recorded for the specific shares reacquired is not always feasible.

An excess of cost over the amount originally recorded should preferably be charged proportionately to additional paid-in capital and retained earnings. The amount that may be allocated to additional paid-in capital is limited by the provisions of APB Opinion No. 6 (*AICPA Prof. Stds.*, vol. 3, Section 5542) to the sum of (a) all additional paid-in capital recorded on previous retirements and net "gains" on sales of treasury stock of the same issue and (b) a pro rata part of additional paid-in capital from initial issue, voluntary transfers of retained earnings, capitalization of stock dividends, etc., on the same issue. For the allocation, remaining additional paid-in capital applicable to issues fully retired (formally or constructively) applies pro rata to shares of common stock.

However, the Accounting Principles Board also stated that, although the allocation treatment described above appears "to be more in accord with current developments in practice" (paragraph 5542.13), it is alternatively acceptable to charge the entire excess of cost over par or stated value of treasury stock to retained earnings (because a corporation can always transfer amounts of retained earnings to additional paid-in capital) or additional paid-in capital (because the Board did not supersede ARB No. 43, Chapter 1B). Accordingly, an excess of cost over the amount deducted from the appropriate capital stock account may be charged to additional paid-in capital or to retained earnings or allocated as described above between the two, except in filings with the SEC. The SEC requires that an excess be allocated between additional paid-in capital and retained earnings or accounted for in accordance with the applicable state law.

If the par, stated, or assigned value of the stock retired exceeds the purchase price, the excess should be credited to additional paid-in capital.

Although the foregoing may be stated as generally accepted accounting principles, it is advisable to consult legal counsel when stock is retired so that accounting entries and financial statements conform to counsel's interpretation of applicable state laws, including a determination of whether retirement results in a reduction of the number of authorized shares.

4. Transactions in Treasury Stock. Frequently, treasury stock is reissued rather than retired. If the reissue price of the stock exceeds its cost when reacquired, the "gain" should be included in additional paid-in capital. "Loss" on reissue of treasury stock may be charged to additional paid-in capital to the extent that previous net "gains" from sales or retirements of the same class are included therein; otherwise, "loss" on the reissue of treasury stock should be charged to retained earnings.

Treasury shares may be issued in a transaction accounted for by the pooling-of-interests method (as long as they are not "tainted" by the presumption that their acquisition is related to the combination—Chapter 17) and should be accounted for as if they were newly issued shares. The cost of reacquiring them should be accounted for as if the shares had been retired.

Capital stock is frequently issued for services or assets other than cash. Determination of values to be assigned to noncash consideration, as discussed below, applies equally to treasury shares issued in similar circumstances.

Recording Consideration Received for Stock

If capital stock is issued for cash, the consideration received and the amounts to be recorded in the accounts are known. If capital stock is issued for services or for assets other than cash, the amounts to be recorded may not be so readily determinable. In principle, the consideration should be the fair value of the services or assets received, but in practice the fair value of the stock issued is often much more clearly evident and may usually be used as a measure of the consideration.

If the stock issued is actively traded and the number of shares does not represent a significant portion of the total shares outstanding, the fair value of the stock is generally reasonably clear. Frequently, however, those conditions are not present. For example, a new corporation may issue shares of capital stock for services or for intangible assets at the same time it issues other shares of stock for cash. The question then arises as to whether the amount to be recorded for the services or intangible assets may be measured by reference to the cash consideration received for the other shares. Although it is impossible to answer that kind of question without knowing the surrounding facts and the materiality of the amounts involved, we believe that consideration received for shares issued for cash, while evidential, is not always a sufficient indicator of the fair value of other assets or services received as consideration for other shares. It may therefore be necessary to rely on the fair value of the assets or services as the proper amount to be recorded, and appraisals may be required. In certain circumstances, transferors' costs or even nominal amounts may have to be used as appropriate values. Methods for determining the fair value of property, plant, and equipment acquired for stock are discussed in Chapter 12.

Business combinations are often accomplished through issuing capital stock. The preceding discussion applies to combinations accounted for by the purchase method. However, if combinations are accounted for by the pooling-of-interests method, a new basis of accountability does not arise (Chapter 17). Stock issued in a combination accounted for by the pooling-of-interests method should be recorded in the amount of the capital stock and additional paid-in capital of the company acquired.

Stock Subscriptions

Stock is sometimes issued on the basis of an agreement to pay a lump sum or installments at some time in the future. Those agreements are called stock subscriptions. Sometimes stock is issued at the time of subscription; usually it is not, and in some states it is illegal to issue stock that is not fully paid.

Stock subscriptions are usually recorded as accounts receivable because it is necessary to record them for control purposes. For financial statement purposes, stock subscriptions receivable should be deducted from capital stock issued or capital stock subscribed and additional paid-in capital, as appropriate, because the financing transaction has no economic substance until funds are received which can be used in the business.

Financing Through Minority Interests

A form of financing transaction that has appeared in recent years consists of selling an equity interest in a subsidiary company. That type of transaction is discussed at length in Chapter 17. If it is viewed as a financing transaction, the propriety of recording a gain on the sale of the equity interest may be questioned. However, the generally accepted accounting treatment has been to record a gain or loss on the sale if the parent sells part of its investment in a subsidiary but no gain or loss if the subsidiary sells its own newly issued shares. The "cost" of the financing is the future loss from consolidated net income of the minority interest in the subsidiary's income. The parent's share of any excess of proceeds over book value becomes part of consolidated paid-in capital.

Additional Paid-In Capital

The descriptive term "additional paid-in capital" includes all types or amounts of "capital" in excess of capital stock other than retained earnings. Other terms that are frequently used are "capital surplus," "capital in excess of par or stated value," "paid-in capital," and "paid-in surplus." As noted, there has been a significant trend in recent years toward replacing the term "capital surplus" with other terms.

The following types of transactions are characteristic of those in which additional paid-in capital may arise:

Issues of par value capital stock for consideration in excess of par.

Issues of no par stock in which part of the proceeds is designated as the stated or assigned value of capital stock and the remainder is allocated to additional paid-in capital.

Reduction of the par or stated value of previously issued stock, which may occur in or apart from a quasi-reorganization.

Conversion of securities with higher par or stated values than those into which converted.

Capitalization of earnings to the extent of amounts in excess of par or stated value of stock issued in stock dividends.

Additional paid-in capital of another entity in a business combination accounted for by the pooling-of-interests method (Chapter 17).

Grant of options to purchase stock at amounts that are less than the fair value thereof.

Value assigned to warrants upon issuance of debt securities with detachable stock purchase warrants.

"Gain" on reissue or retirement of treasury stock.

Subsequent realization of the tax effect of loss carryforwards arising prior to a quasi-reorganization but not recognized as of that date.

Windfalls arising from capital transactions such as tax benefits from premature disposition by optionees of stock acquired under qualified stock option plans and proceeds from "short-swing" profits recoverable under Section 16(b) of the Securities Exchange Act of 1934.

Additional paid-in capital also arises from the reissue of stock donated by stockholders or the donation of property to the corporation by stockholders, forfeited stock subscriptions, and assessments levied against stockholders in amounts in excess of par or stated value, all as discussed below.

We believe it is useful to preserve the contributed capital of each class of stock. Until a particular class of stock has been fully redeemed or retired, additional paid-in capital arising from transactions in it should be deemed to be allocated to that class and should not absorb charges from other classes (for example, premium and expense of called issues). After a class of stock is fully redeemed or retired, remaining additional paid-in capital applicable to that class may generally be used to absorb charges from other classes that have exhausted their own additional paid-in capital. Additional paid-in capital applicable to preferred stock that is converted to common stock becomes additional paid-in capital applicable to common stock.

Donated Capital

If a corporation's own stock (issued, fully paid, and nonassessable) is reacquired by donation and is subsequently disposed of, the proceeds of the reissue become donated capital, a form of additional paid-in capital.

Until donated treasury stock is reissued or retired, it may be entered in the accounts at no value or at a nominal amount of $1 with an offsetting credit to donated capital. The latter account should be adjusted as the shares are subsequently disposed of.

Donated capital sometimes arises from a direct capital contribution in cash or property from a stockholder, perhaps a parent company. If a public utility receives assistance from customers or municipalities in the construction of its facilities, the amounts are not usually shown as additional paid-in capital but are presented separately under a descriptive caption such as "Contributions for extensions."

Forfeited Stock Subscriptions

If a subscriber to capital stock remits a portion of the subscription price and fails to pay the balance, the corporation must act in accordance with the laws of the state of incorporation. In some states, the subscriber forfeits his payment after a certain period has elapsed, and the corporation may resell the stock. If the stock is resold at an amount that, together with the amount forfeited, exceeds par or stated value, a form of additional paid-in capital arises.

Stock Assessments

Even if shares of stock are fully paid and nonassessable, corporations occasionally levy a pro rata assessment on all shares outstanding. A levy might occur when a corporation is facing bankruptcy or is undergoing a reorganization. Since the funds are contributed by stockholders and are not part of capital stock, additional paid-in capital should be increased by the full amount received.

Other Transactions Affecting Additional Paid-In Capital

Some items may be properly charged to additional paid-in capital in accordance with generally accepted accounting principles. A number of those items have been previously discussed in this chapter. Examples of others are discussed below.

Dividends. Ordinarily, dividends are charged to retained earnings. In unusual circumstances, if permitted by statute and authorized by the directors, certain dividends may be charged to additional paid-in capital. Technically, those distributions are not dividends but returns of capital. Their treatment is discussed in the section captioned "Source of Dividends."

Organization Expenses. Organization expenses of newly formed corporations are sometimes charged to additional paid-in capital arising from the issue of stock at a premium, provided the directors authorize the charge and the laws of the state of incorporation permit it. The more usual method of disposing of organization expenses is to amortize them to expense over a short period, such as three to five years.

At one time, expenses incurred to effect a combination accounted for by the pooling-of-interests method could be charged against additional paid-in capital. APB Opinion No. 16 (*AICPA Prof. Stds.,* vol. 3, Section 1091) now requires that those expenses be charged against income in the period in which they are incurred.

Quasi-Reorganizations. A quasi-reorganization may be defined as a procedure recognized in accounting by which the accounts of a corporation are restated to the same extent as if a new corporation were created and acquired the business of the existing corporation; a new basis of accountability for assets, liabilities, and equity is established.

In 1934, in recognition of Depression-induced conditions, the AICPA formally adopted the following rule relating to surplus other than that arising from profits retained in the business:

> Capital surplus, however created, should not be used to relieve the income account of the current or future years of charges which would otherwise fall to be made thereagainst. This rule might be subject to the exception that where, upon reorganization, a reorganized company would be relieved of charges which would require to be made against income if the existing cor-

poration were continued, it might be regarded as permissible to accomplish the same result without reorganization provided the facts were as fully revealed to and the action as formally approved by the shareholders as in reorganization. [Accounting Research Bulletin No. 43, Chapter 1A, paragraph 2 *(AICPA Prof. Stds.,* vol. 3, paragraph 5511.01)]

The accounting principles for a quasi-reorganization or corporate readjustment were amplified five years later and are now found in ARB No. 43, Chapter 7A *(AICPA Prof. Stds.,* vol. 3, Section 5581).

Although the board of directors of a corporation may authorize the transfer of a deficit in retained earnings to additional paid-in capital without approval of stockholders, formal consent of stockholders is required for a quasi-reorganization. The effective date of a readjustment should be as near as practicable to the date consent is given; usually the close of the fiscal year is selected.

The adjustment should be made in such a way that income of subsequent periods will be fairly stated and will be comparable to that of a new corporation commencing operations under business conditions existing at the time of the reorganization. Assets should be carried forward at fair and not unduly conservative amounts, determined with due regard for the accounting to be employed thereafter. Maximum probable losses or charges known to have arisen before the date of the reorganization should be estimated and recognized; subsequent adjustments of those estimates should be recorded in additional paid-in capital.

Once the amounts to be written off in a readjustment have been determined, they should be charged first to available retained earnings; the balance may then be charged to additional paid-in capital. Frequently, the additional paid-in capital needed to absorb those charges is created by reducing the par or stated value of capital stock, approved by the stockholders at the time they give consent to the quasi-reorganization.

Implicit in the "new start" idea of a quasi-reorganization is the intention that no deficit should exist in any capital account and no retained earnings may be carried forward. A new retained earnings account should be established with a zero balance. Quasi-reorganizations are not expected to be repeated at frequent intervals, if ever.

Material transactions occurring after but relating to the period before a quasi-reorganization should not be reflected in the new retained earnings account. Dividends received from subsidiaries declared from earnings before the adjustment represent equity adjustments, not income. Retained earnings of subsidiaries at the date of a quasi-reorganization should not be carried forward as consolidated retained earnings in a consolidated balance sheet, but rather should be shown separately in the stockholders' equity section.

Plant accounts may be written down to more realistic amounts in a quasi-reorganization, with the result that depreciation charges in subsequent income statements are less than depreciation deducted for income tax purposes; the "tax benefit" of the excess depreciation deductions is then received by the reorganized company during the remaining life of the related plant. Similarly, if a company has suffered losses in the years immediately preceding a quasi-reorganization, those losses may be used by the reorganized company through loss carryforward provisions to reduce future taxable income. The "tax benefit" is customarily measured by the difference between the tax that would be payable with and without the deduction items affected by the reorganization. (Chapter 13 presents a discussion of "tax-effect accounting.")

If realization of those tax benefits is assured beyond reasonable doubt, they should be recognized as deferred charges at the date of reorganization and the tax benefits realized in each year subsequently credited to that account. If subsequent taxable income is not assured beyond a reasonable doubt at the time of reorganization (the usual case), the amount of tax benefit to be realized cannot reasonably be determined. In that event, tax benefits should be recognized only as realized through actual tax liabilities that are less than tax expense computed on the basis of recorded "book" income. At that time, the tax benefit realized should be added to additional paid-in capital because it results from events of or prior to the reorganization.

RETAINED EARNINGS

Retained earnings has been defined by the Committee on Terminology as:

> The balance of net profits, income, gains and losses of a corporation from the date of incorporation (or from the latest date when a deficit was eliminated in a quasi-reorganization) after deducting distributions therefrom to shareholders and transfers therefrom to capital stock or capital surplus accounts. [Accounting Terminology Bulletin No. 1, paragraph 34]

Appropriated Retained Earnings

Portions of retained earnings (representing an undivided portion of a corporation's assets) may be set aside by management for general or specific purposes. Those segregations are commonly referred to as appropriations of retained earnings or, despite the decrease in use of "surplus" in other areas of accounting, "surplus reserves." Examples of appropriations of retained earnings include appropriations for sinking funds, retirement of preferred stocks, working capital, and general contingencies. Retained earnings appropriations have little significance and are seldom used today; their only purposes are to comply with requirements such as those often included in agreements for bonds, notes, and preferred stocks, and to give some indication to stockholders of the amount of possible future losses. The principles applicable to those reserves are summarized as follows:

> Appropriations of retained earnings are not liabilities. An amount required to recognize an existing or reasonably estimable liability or loss should be classified as a liability, and an expense or loss should be recorded through a charge to income.
>
> Costs or losses should not be charged to appropriated retained earnings, and no part of an appropriation should be transferred to income or in any way used to affect the determination of net income in any year.
>
> When an appropriation or any part of one is no longer required, it should be returned to retained earnings.
>
> Appropriations should be classified in the balance sheet as segregations of retained earnings in the stockholders' equity section.

Unappropriated Retained Earnings

If a portion of retained earnings has been appropriated, the balance of retained earnings may be referred to as "unappropriated." Increases in unappropriated retained earnings result from net income and restoration of appropriations; decreases result from net losses, appropriations of retained earnings, dividends declared, and, under certain conditions, "losses" on transactions in a company's own stock. The only other transactions likely to affect the account are prior-period adjustments, the effects of combining corporations by the pooling-of-interests method (described in Chapter 17), and the effects of reorganizations or recapitalizations.

In years gone by, accountants used the retained earnings account freely for nonrecurring entries, prior-period adjustments, and unusual items, so as to preserve net income as a measure of periodic results of normal operations. The alternative view is now the generally accepted one, namely, that all charges and credits (except for rare instances of prior-period adjustments) should be reflected in the income statement. APB Opinion No. 9 (*AICPA Prof. Stds.*, vol. 3, Section 2010) presents the criteria for prior-period adjustments and a discussion and comparison of the two approaches to net income versus surplus entries. (See also Chapter 18, "Financial Statements.")

Reconciliation With Tax Records

For most companies, "tax surplus," or undistributed earnings and profits for tax purposes, differs from retained earnings in the balance sheet. The company may have been in existence before March 1, 1913, business combinations may have had different tax accounting, goodwill or other assets may have been amortized or otherwise written off without being deducted for tax purposes, or any of a number of other book–tax differences may have occurred (see Chapter 13). A company should maintain a memorandum record of its "tax surplus" to maintain good control over income taxes. The record is variously called a "tax balance sheet," a "tax surplus analysis," or a "Schedule M reconciliation."

Dividends

A dividend has been defined as a pro rata distribution by a corporation to its stockholders. Strictly speaking, only a distribution of earnings is a "dividend," but in common usage the term is applied to any pro rata distribution. Dividends may be classified as to the medium of payment (cash, property, or stock) or the source (retained earnings or additional paid-in capital).

The board of directors of a corporation decides the amounts and timing of dividends, taking into consideration the financial position and earnings of the company, the general business outlook, and future plans of the company. Often legal counsel passes on the legality of proposed dividend actions.

Dividends are declared by a formal vote of the board of directors, indicating the amount (or percentage of par) to be paid on each share, payment date, and record date. The declarations should be recorded in the minutes of the directors' meetings. Only persons owning stock as of the record date are entitled to receive dividends declared.

If a dividend other than a stock dividend is declared and public notice is given to the stockholders, the dividend is generally a legal obligation and may not be rescinded without the consent of stockholders entitled to receive the dividend. Accordingly, retained earnings is charged with the appropriate amount and a liability is recorded at the time of declaration. Stock dividends generally may be rescinded without stockholders' consent at any time before the additional stock is issued.

Accounting for dividends on treasury stock is discussed in the section on treasury stock.

Medium of Payment

Dividends may be paid in cash, in warrants or stock of the distributing corporation, in scrip, or in other assets. Payment of dividends in cash is by far the most common and accounting for cash dividends presents few problems.

Stock dividends are paid in capital stock of the corporation making the distribution. A dividend on one class of stock is usually paid in the same class of stock but is sometimes paid in stock of another class.

Dividend scrip is ordinarily an issue of short-term interest-bearing notes payable to stockholders in cash at a future date. Scrip dividends are occasionally paid by corporations that are otherwise in a position to pay dividends but lack cash or other assets suitable for distribution.

Occasionally, dividends are declared payable in other assets, such as inventory of the company or marketable securities of other corporations. Usually the difficulty of apportioning property other than securities among many stockholders owning various proportions of the outstanding stock discourages the payment of dividends in that manner.

Stock Dividends and Stock Split-Ups

Although stock dividends and stock split-ups may appear to be similar, they receive different accounting treatments. Accounting Research Bulletin No. 43, Chapter 7B (*AICPA Prof. Stds.*, vol. 3, Section 5561), defines a stock dividend as:

> . . . an issuance by a corporation of its own common shares to its common shareholders without consideration and under conditions indicating that such action is prompted mainly by a desire to give the recipient shareholders some ostensibly separate evidence of a part of their respective interests in accumulated corporate earnings without distribution of cash or other property which the board of directors deems necessary or desirable to retain in the business. [Paragraph 5561.01]

The Bulletin defines a split-up as:

> . . . an issuance by a corporation of its own common shares to its common shareholders without consideration and under conditions indicating that such action is prompted mainly by a desire to increase the number of outstanding shares for the purpose of effecting a reduction in their unit market price and, thereby, of obtaining wider distribution and improved marketability of the shares. [Paragraph 5561.02]

A stock dividend purports to distribute earnings of a corporation in a form other than cash; actually neither earnings nor assets are distributed. The percentage distribution is usually small and the issuance of the additional shares required to pay the stock dividend results in little or no decrease in the per-share market price of the stock. The accounting prescribed in the Bulletin, which is not required for closely held corporations, is as follows:

> . . . The committee therefore believes that . . . the corporation should in the public interest account for the transaction by transferring from earned surplus to the category of permanent capitalization (represented by the capital stock and capital surplus accounts) an amount equal to the fair value of the additional shares issued. Unless this is done, the amount of earnings which the shareholder may believe to have been distributed to him will be left, except to the extent otherwise dictated by legal requirements, in earned surplus subject to possible further similar stock issuances or cash distributions. [Paragraph 5561.10]

In our opinion, the time at which to determine fair value of the stock dividend shares and to make the appropriate transfer from retained earnings is the date of declaration of the stock dividend rather than the ex-dividend date or the date of payment. To compute the "fair value of the additional shares issued," consideration may be given to the dilutive effect of the additional shares on market value. That can be accomplished by dividing the market value of a present share by 1 plus the stock dividend percentage to get the fair value of an additional share.

The SEC has, in recent years, strongly objected to payments of stock dividends if a corporation had insufficient retained earnings to capitalize the fair value of a proposed stock dividend.

The accounting for stock split-ups in the Bulletin is:

> . . . Where this [reduction in the unit price of shares] is clearly the intent, no transfer from earned surplus to capital surplus or capital stock account is called for, other than to the extent occasioned by legal requirements. It is believed, however, that few cases will arise where the aforementioned purpose can be accomplished through an issuance of shares which is less than, say, 20% or 25% of the previously outstanding shares. [Paragraph 5561.15]

Stock split-ups are often more conveniently effected in the form of a stock dividend, such as a 100% stock dividend (two-for-one split). If the use of the word "dividend" cannot be avoided in transactions that are in substance stock split-ups, the transaction should be described as a "stock split effected in the form of a dividend."

The maximum amount legally required to be transferred to capital stock in a stock split-up is the par or stated value of the additional shares issued. If additional paid-in capital is less than the par or stated value of the shares issued, a charge against retained earnings may be required in a stock split-up. If the par or stated value is by formal action reduced in proportion to the share split or if no par stock is carried at the aggregate contributed capital amount, no change in the dollar amount of stated capital is required.

Sometimes outstanding shares of capital stock are reduced in a "reverse split." If par or stated value is not proportionately altered, a reduction in the capital stock account is recorded as additional paid-in capital.

Dividends Payable in Cash or Stock at Option of Stockholder

After a stock dividend (as previously defined), the percentage of total stock held by each stockholder in the class of shares distributed remains the same as before the distribution. A dividend payable in stock or cash at the option of the stockholder may not be a true stock dividend because it may not result in a pro rata distribution of shares; the proportions change if cash is taken by some stockholders. However, a corporation that gives stockholders the choice of a cash dividend or a stock dividend usually sets the terms of the offer in a way that the choice of stock is more attractive to the recipient.

If significant amounts of cash are paid in an optional distribution, the per-share amount of retained earnings to be capitalized for the entire distribution should be not less than the optional cash dividend.

Dividends in Property Other Than Cash

Retained earnings should be charged with the fair value of property distributed to stockholders as dividends if "the fair value of the non-monetary asset distributed is objectively measurable and would be clearly realizable to the distributing entity in an outright sale at or near the time of the distribution" [APB Opinion No. 29, paragraph 23 (*AICPA Prof. Stds.*, vol. 3, paragraph 1041.23)]. By implication, that treatment calls for simultaneous recognition in income of a gain or loss measured by the difference between fair value and book value of the property. The only exceptions are a distribution in a spin-off or other form of reorganization or liquidation or a rescission of a prior business combination.

Source of Dividends

Common business sense dictates that dividends should be paid to stockholders only from accumulated earnings. However, some dividends are charged to additional paid-in capital without clearly indicating the source of the dividend and without violating state regulations. Apart from the legality of dividends from capital, directors may be violating their trust if they declare dividends from capital contributions without clearly informing stockholders that the dividends are not distributions of earned income. Some states have legislation that requires notification of stockholders if dividends are paid out of capital.

Availability of Capital of Subsidiaries for Distribution by Parent Company

Companies often acquire subsidiaries that have substantial amounts of additional paid-in capital and retained earnings. Retained earnings of a subsidiary accumulated prior to acquisition should be excluded from consolidated retained earnings under the purchase method, and dividends paid to the parent company from capital accumulated by the subsidiary before its acquisition should not be treated as income but rather as a reduction of the parent's investment in the subsidiary.

There may be limitations on the payment by subsidiaries to a parent company of dividends from earnings after acquisition. Provisions of bond indentures and stock agreements of subsidiary companies may restrict the payment of dividends to all stockholders, including the parent.

Whether dividends may be paid to stockholders of a parent company from subsidiaries' retained earnings that have not been formally transferred to the parent in the form of dividends is a debatable question. Some states appear to permit the practice and others do not. The absence of recent court cases indicates either that directors assume that unremitted earnings are unavailable for dividends or that parent company retained earnings are generally adequate to meet dividend needs of most corporations. Legal counsel should be sought by those to whom the question is pertinent.

Liquidating Dividends

Dividends paid with the express intent of reducing the capital of a corporation and with a view toward partial or complete dissolution are known as liquidating dividends or distributions of capital. Accounting for those dividends should follow the intent expressed in resolutions of the directors or stockholders.

Dividends Paid From Amounts Specifically Included in The Price of the Stock

If specific amounts equal to accrued dividends per share are included in the prices at which shares of capital stock are issued with an intention of returning those amounts to stockholders as part of the first dividends to be distributed to them, the specified amounts should be shown as a liability and not included in the proceeds of the issue of the stock. The situation usually occurs if a corporation issues preferred stock at a price plus accrued dividends, and the first dividend is paid for a period beginning before the date the stock is issued. Also, certain types of investment trusts are required by their certificate of incorporation to segregate a portion of receipts from the sale of capital stock equal to the per-share amount of undistributed realized or unrealized net income. That procedure is designed to maintain for the benefit of the existing stockholders the per-share amount of distributable income that might otherwise be reduced on the issuance of new shares.

There appears to be no reasonable or practical basis for objection to those practices, even though the amounts received equivalent to accrued dividends technically might be considered premiums.

Dividends of Regulated Investment Companies

Investment companies often declare two types of dividends—one representing a distribution of investment income, the other a distribution of gains from sales of investment securities. The practice stems from provisions of the Internal Revenue Code pertaining to regulated investment companies, whose income from those two sources is taxed differently to the recipient stockholders and is substantially tax-free to the company if properly distributed currently as dividends.

Dividends of Extractive Industry Corporations Paid out of Capital

The statutes of some states permit companies engaged in the metal, timber, oil, and other extractive industries to determine distributable income without deducting depletion. Consequently, in those states the entire capital invested in wasting assets may legally be paid out in dividends. If that dividend policy is followed, the financial statements should disclose the amount of capital distributed as dividends in the current year as well as the accumulation of distributions to date. Tax regulations require that due notice must be given to stockholders if depletion is omitted and dividends are paid from capital. However, some companies omit depletion allowances in financial statements and make no attempt in paying dividends to distinguish between distributions of earnings and distributions of capital; we do not approve either of those procedures. Regardless of what is legally permitted by state laws and court decisions, paid-in capital should not be impaired by repaying to stockholders any of their contributed capital as dividends, unless that fact is adequately disclosed.

Constructive Dividends

Constructive dividends are distributions to stockholders in the ratio of their stockholdings without formal declaration of a dividend by the board of directors. Constructive dividends are mainly related to income tax determinations. Salaries or bonuses are often paid to officers who constitute practically all of the stockholders of a closely held corporation; if those payments are not based on the value of services but bear some relation to stockholdings, the IRS may consider them as distributions of profits and not as business expenses. Whatever the tax treatment, business purpose governs the accounting, but the effect on tax provisions usually should be disclosed.

Revaluation Surplus

In the past, companies occasionally restated property, plant, and equipment to an amount higher than cost less accumulated depreciation. The higher amount was frequently based on an appraisal, and excesses of appraised value over undepreciated cost that arose from increases in prices rather than excessive allowances for depreciation or other errors were credited to a revaluation or appraisal surplus. Appraisal surplus was considered by some accountants to be a form of permanent capital stemming from adjustments for price levels and therefore not available for transfer to retained earnings at any time. Others considered it to be a form of "unrealized" retained earnings that should be "realized" as depreciation on appreciation was included in measuring income. The practice of restating fixed assets to a basis higher than cost was looked on with disfavor by many accountants, and in 1965 APB Opinion No. 6 (*AICPA Prof. Stds.*, vol. 3, Section 4072) stated that no write-ups of fixed assets to reflect appraisal, market, or current values should be made except as part of a reorganization or quasi-reorganization.

EQUITY ACCOUNTS IN MERGERS, CONSOLIDATIONS, AND ACQUISITIONS OF SUBSIDIARIES

If two or more unaffiliated corporations merge or consolidate, the action may be accounted for, depending on the circumstances, by the pooling-of-interests method or as a purchase of a subsidiary (or its assets) by the acquiring company. The distinction between those methods and the applicable accounting principles are more fully discussed in Chapter 17.

Under the pooling-of-interests method, the individual components of the stockholders' equity sections of the balance sheets of the constituent companies are combined by classifications. An excess of the total of the combining companies' stated capital stock amounts over the amounts required for the stated or par value of the stock of the combined entity is credited to combined additional paid-in capital; conversely, if the par or stated value of the stock of the combined entity exceeds the respective totals of the combining companies, an insufficiency is made up first from combined additional paid-in capital, to the extent available, and then from combined retained earnings.

Under the purchase method, consolidated financial statements prepared after a purchase of a subsidiary eliminate all equity accounts of the subsidiary at the date of acquisition against the parent's cost. Therefore, only undistributed earnings of the subsidiary after acquisition are included in consolidated retained earnings (Chapter 17).

If a subsidiary is merged with or liquidated into its parent company, it is permissible to include in retained earnings of the parent company the subsidiary's undistributed earnings since the date of acquisition by the parent. Similarly, if two companies owned by the same parent company are merged and the resulting subsidiary is subsequently merged with the parent, the undistributed retained earnings of both subsidiaries after the dates of original acquisition may be included in the parent company's retained earnings.

If a corporation wishes to change its state of incorporation and for that purpose forms a corporation with the same corporate powers and capitalization in another state to acquire the business of the first corporation, it is permissible for the new corporation to begin operations with the retained earnings of its predecessor.

COMMITMENTS TO FUTURE STOCK ISSUANCE

Promises to issue stock sometime in the future are as much financing instruments as debt and equity instruments because they can be used to obtain needed services (usually) or funds at little or no apparent current cost. Options and warrants are the common types of those commitments.

Stock Options

Stock options represent rights given by a corporation—usually to a bondholder, stockholder, underwriter, officer, or employee—permitting the holder to purchase shares of stock of the corporation at a specified price, generally during a certain period, and in accordance with conditions set forth in the option. Options that are attached to bonds or preferred stocks to increase their marketability are usually referred to as warrants and are discussed in the next section.

Options to purchase stock may be granted to officers and employees of a corporation for reasons such as to compensate them for work previously performed, to create wider ownership of stock by the corporation's employees, and to induce continued employment and greater effort in managing the company so that its success will be reflected in higher market values of the stock. An option agreement usually provides that, during a specified period and upon performance by the grantee of certain stipulated conditions, a grantee may at his own election exercise the option in accordance with its terms.

Certain option agreements contain restrictions that take effect after exercise of the options, such as a requirement to continue employment or to hold the stock for a specified future period. The owner of restricted stock is effectively precluded from disposing of it until the restrictions expire.

The amount to be recorded for stock issued upon exercise of a stock option is the option price of the stock plus consideration received for the option. Consideration received for stock options is commonly in the form of services—usually of employees but sometimes of outsiders, such as underwriters—and the accounting problem involves measuring the amount of compensation of the affected recipients.

Accounting for employees' compensation in stock option transactions is discussed in Chapter 10 under that heading. The general outline of that accounting is summarized here. Stock option plans that involve all or a large number of a corporation's employees are often part of a program to secure equity capital or to obtain widespread ownership of stock by employees rather than to compensate employees; those "stock purchase" plans involve no element of compensation cost if they meet certain conditions specified in APB Opinion No. 25 (*AICPA Prof. Stds.*, vol. 3, Sections 4062 and 4062A). Other stock option plans involve no element of compensation for accounting purposes if at the date of grant of the option both the number of shares an employee is entitled to receive and the option or purchase price are known and the employee must pay at least the quoted market price of the stock at the date of grant to acquire it.

Compensation cost arises in stock option plans not meeting those conditions, especially plans in which stock is awarded to an employee without cash payment by him and those in which either the number of shares or the option price may vary after the date of grant. Compensation cost is usually measured by the difference between the quoted market price of the optioned stock at the date of grant or date of issue, depending on the circumstances, and the option price of the stock.

At the time an option involving compensation is granted, the total amount of compensation should be recorded as a deferred charge and as additional paid-in capital. See Chapter 10 for a discussion of when and how the compensation should be recorded as an expense. The SEC requires that the deferred charge be carried as a deduction from stockholders' equity rather than as an asset. If an employee forfeits his option, the applicable remaining deferred charge should be reversed and additional paid-in capital reduced.

Stock Purchase Warrants

Stock options that are freely transferable are generally called warrants. Stock purchase warrants may be issued to underwriters and investment bankers but usually are sold as part of a package of securities: for example, debentures or preferred stock with warrants attached. Like other options, warrants may have a limited or unlimited life. The inclusion of warrants as part of a package of securities generally results in greater salability and permits a lower interest or dividend rate on the prime security. The purchaser of the package ordinarily has the choice of detaching and selling the warrants, exercising them, or allowing them to lapse.

Occasionally debt security issues may include warrants that are not detachable; the security must be surrendered to exercise the warrant. Under APB Opinion No. 14 (*AICPA Prof. Stds.*, vol. 3, Section 5516), issuance of debt securities with nondetachable warrants does not require separate accounting recognition of the warrants.

Issuing debt securities with detachable warrants requires separate recognition of the value of the warrants in accordance with Opinion No. 14. A portion of the proceeds of the issue should be allocated to the warrants based on the relative fair values of the debt security and the warrants at time of issuance. The Opinion states that the "time of issuance generally is the date when agreement as to terms has been reached and announced, even though the agreement is subject to certain further actions, such as directors' or stockholders' approval" (footnote to paragraph 5516.15). The section under "Long-Term Debt Financing" captioned "Warrants" presents comments on the determination of fair values and the resulting allocation.

The proceeds allocated to the warrants should be accounted for as additional paid-in capital and the resulting difference between actual proceeds and the amount allocated to the debt security should be classified as unamortized debt discount or, if applicable, reduction in unamortized debt premium. When warrants are exercised, an appropriate amount (par or stated value of the stock issued) is transferred to the capital stock account. If warrants expire unexercised, no accounting recognition is called for, because the capital contribution resulting from the value attributable to the warrants remains with the corporation.

Recently, a number of companies have distributed stock purchase warrants to their stockholders. A major stock exchange has established as a condition for listing the underlying shares in that kind of distribution a requirement that the issuing corporation charge retained earnings with the fair value of the warrants, in effect equating the accounting treatment with that of a stock dividend.

CAPITAL OF BUSINESSES OTHER THAN CORPORATIONS

Business organizations other than corporations range from individual proprietorships to organizations tantamount to corporations. The more common types are individual proprietorships, business partnerships, limited partnerships, partnerships with transferable shares, and Massachusetts voluntary trusts with transferable shares. The last type mentioned so closely resembles a corporation that it is taxed like one for federal tax purposes.

As in a corporation, the types of capital and rights of participants depend on the articles of co-partnership or association and the laws of the state in which the business is formed.

CAPITAL OF NONBUSINESS ENTITIES

Nonbusiness enterprises include organizations such as churches, fraternal orders, educational institutions, hospitals, clubs, and governmental units. They may adopt one of several forms of legal organization but usually have no stockholders. In general, they are not-for-profit organizations and are usually not subject to income taxes.

The capital of nonbusiness entities arises from appropriations in the case of units of government, donations in the case of charitable institutions, or accumulations of fees or assessments which may be likened to retained earnings. The trustees may be permitted to use earnings from the funds and the funds themselves at their discretion, but often donors or statutes place restrictions on both income and principal.

Accounting for capital in those entities may not follow generally accepted accounting principles in all respects. Legal restrictions placed on the discretion of the trustees may require accounting treatment differing from that found in business enterprises. For example, profits or losses on the sale of stocks or bonds may be considered as changes in capital rather than credits or charges to income.

Trust Accounting

In trusts, the underlying objective is to account for the separate interests of income beneficiaries and remaindermen and often for several differing interests in each of those categories. Therefore, it is necessary to distinguish income transactions from those affecting principal and to account separately for each element of principal and income in accordance with the wishes of the initiator of the trust.

Fund Accounting

Frequently, the operations of nonprofit organizations are sufficiently complex to require accounting for several funds as separate entities or funds; for example, general funds, endowment funds, restricted funds, and plant funds. In a balance sheet, assets equal to the amount of each fund are separately stated. Transfers between funds, when legally permissible and properly authorized, should be recorded so as to recognize the funds as separate but related entities.

Several AICPA Audit Guides deal with nonprofit and governmental organizations. They offer authoritative guidance in the specialized accounting and auditing problems of those entities.

• TYPICAL TRANSACTION SYSTEMS AND INTERNAL CONTROL

TYPICAL TRANSACTIONS

A financing transaction system is likely to be short and relatively simple. Often authorizing a transaction, executing it, and recording it each involve only one step. The preparation for authorization and execution may be lengthy and complex: the study of whether to enter into a long-term financing transaction may take months or years, and once it has been decided on, the time and energy expended by lawyers, accountants, investment bankers, and the company's staff in preparing to execute the transaction may be tremendous. Nevertheless, actual transaction steps are short and simple. For most companies, an entire year's financing activity consists of a few large transactions. Even for those few companies—for example, mutual funds—in which the segment sometimes comprises a volume of data processing and accounting activity as large as the revenue or buying activity in the majority of companies, the system is likely to be short and consist of relatively few steps.

Authorization and Issuance of Financing Instruments

Since the principal purpose of the financing system is issuing legal obligations—both debt and equity—of an enterprise in exchange for cash or other property, control over authorization for issuance is even more critical than in other segments. The board of directors should always authorize a financing transaction specifically and explicitly. In fact, many legal jurisdictions, investment bankers, and institutional investors require that they do so. The board may authorize a type of financing and a maximum amount in general terms and then delegate to a financial officer the authority to execute the details. But the significance of financing transactions to an enterprise requires that the board assume direct and explicit responsibility for all authorization.

In the majority of businesses, which process no more than half a dozen financing transactions in a year, control consists simply of follow-up by the authorizing board or chief financial officer. In the terms used in Chapter 3, control is exercised by a "pre-audit" of transactions. The importance of the need for financing and the commitments made to obtain it assure close attention by top management. In many cases the lender or investor can be relied on to "audit" the authorization and validity of the investment instrument; for example, by insisting on certified copies of the vote of the board of directors. Often, however, the stockholder or bondholder is not in a position to assess the validity of the certificate he receives.

In other companies, the individual transactions required to implement a financing may be more numerous and correspondingly more extensive, and formalized systems of accounting and control may be needed. A number of short-term notes may be issued and repaid during a year; the company may act as its own registrar of bonds and stock; it may pay its own interest and dividends; numerous warrants or stock options may have to be accounted for.

In those instances, blank forms of financing instruments are usually kept on hand: notes payable, bonds, option agreements, and stock certificates. Since it is fairly easy to forge the execution of many of those documents, which once executed become negotiable obligations of the company, it is crucial to maintain restricted access to blank forms. In addition, blank forms should be subject to numerical control, preferably by being prenumbered in printing.

If the volume of transactions is large enough, authorization of transactions and issuance of instruments can be systematized as clerical functions. For example, new stock certificates can be issued routinely on receipt of cash or a corresponding number of old certificates. Control totals over issuing and recording of instruments should be computed and pre-audit or supervisory review of the propriety of each transaction should be made.

In view of the relatively high value and ready negotiability of most financing instruments, the expensive control step of pre-audit of each transaction is often considered worthwhile. Whether or not pre-audit is performed, close supervisory control of the transaction activity and control operations is essential.

Some companies have developed elaborations of the basic transaction of issuing stock for cash or in exchange for other stock: dividend reinvestment plans, in which dividends may be accumulated for a stockholder's account and additional shares purchased from the funds; "certificateless" plans, in which the cumbersome handling of certificates is replaced by a simple bookkeeping record; plans for purchase of stock on an installment basis, and other variations to serve particular purposes. Each of them, however voluminous the related data, involves a relatively simple accounting system. An account must be maintained for each participating stockholder; additions and reductions must be properly authorized, recorded in a journal or other book of original entry, and posted to the accounts; the accounts must be periodically reconciled to the control account; and statements of the accounts must be sent to stockholders from time to time.

The authorization and issue of financing instruments should be documented, both by executing the instrument itself and by initiating a proper record of it, for example, a register listing each item issued or a stub record similar to a checkbook. If instruments are reacquired they should be cancelled and appropriately filed; the cancelled instrument serves as documentation of reacquisition. Detailed accounts should be reconciled periodically to controlling accounts. Reconciliations should include all unissued, issued, and cancelled financing instruments.

Compliance With Securities Regulations

The issuance of securities to the public is highly regulated by the securities exchanges and by both the federal and state governments. Whether a company has an occasional major issue or actively trades its securities continually, periodic reviews of compliance with applicable regulations should be made. Often they are carried out by the company's accounting staff or by an auditor; in any event, they should always be supervised by legal counsel.

Interest and Dividends

Payments of interest and dividends should be properly authorized. Interest payments are authorized by the terms of the financing instrument. Dividends must be formally declared by the board of directors. Usually, the total interest installment or total dividend is deposited in an imprest fund and disbursements are then subject to the same controls as other cash disbursements (Chapter 10).

If interest is paid by redeeming coupons detached from bonds, the coupons received should be cancelled and retained.

Interest and dividends unclaimed for a reasonable period should be accounted for according to local law, which may permit writing them off by reversing the original accounting or may require that they be turned over to the state or continue to be carried as a liability. In all events, unclaimed items should be identified and removed from the active accounts, and the related imprest accounts should be reconciled.

Treasury Stock and Bonds

Reacquired and unretired financing instruments should be subject to the same controls as other negotiable instruments: they should be under restricted access, counted from time to time, and reconciled to a control account. Movement into or out of the "treasury" should be controlled.

Transfer and Disbursing Agents

The detailed and highly sensitive task of accounting for and controlling ledgers of bondholders and stockholders, handling treasury stock, and paying interest and dividends is most often delegated to independent agents such as banks. The independent agents take over the control responsibility from a company, but the need for control and responsibility for it remain the same. If independent agents are used, the company should maintain control accounts, require periodic reports from the agents, and compare the reports with the accounts.

Warrants and Options

Controls over warrants and options should be similar to those over the financing instruments themselves: careful authorization, control over unexecuted documents, a general record of activity, a ledger of outstanding balances, and periodic reconciliation of the ledger to control accounts.

Leases

Control over rental payments required under leases is maintained by a reminder list, which may be in the form of a register of leases by payment due date. Control over the information required for financial disclosures may be incorporated in the lease register or it may be maintained separately in the department responsible for leases.

Commitments

Control over compliance with commitments made in connection with financing is most commonly exercised by maintaining a reminder list. The reminder list is often maintained by the office of the treasurer, the official most likely to be responsible for financing activity. It may also be found in the controller's or accounting department or the office of legal counsel.

Stockholders' Equity Accounts

Most entries to retained earnings and paid-in capital accounts occur as an integral part of some other major entry: stock issues, retirements or conversions, dividend payments, or annual closing of the accounts. Accordingly, they are controlled by the controls over the initiating element of the entry. An unusual event giving rise to any other kind of entry in these accounts calls for authorization by the board of directors.

● AUDITING PROCEDURES

OBJECTIVES

An auditor's objectives in examining the financing segment are to obtain reasonable assurance that:

All commitments, both those connected with recorded financing (assets pledged, covenants, etc.) and those related to prospective or "off-balance sheet" financing, are identified.

All commitments are properly authorized and classified.

All transactions are recorded in the correct period and amount.

The cost of financing is accounted for in accordance with generally accepted accounting principles.

In principle, the financing segment is as much subject to the complete audit cycle as the others. In practice, however, more often than not all the transactions passing through the financing segment in a year can be examined and validated fairly easily (some exceptions are discussed below). Consequently, an auditor has no theoretical or practical reason to rely on internal control, and thus functional tests are not needed. That does not mean, however, that an auditor can ignore the first term of the audit equation: underlying evidence. Rather, it means that his basis for relying on underlying evidence comes from the detailed examination of transactions rather than from reliance on internal control.

THE AUDIT CYCLE

Transaction Reviews

However small the number of transactions in the segment, an auditor has to understand the system and confirm his understanding by making transaction reviews of each significant type of transaction. If the number of transactions is small and an auditor plans to validate or "vouch" every transaction, he may easily lose sight of the function of the transaction review. That function—confirming an auditor's understanding—is as necessary to a transaction segment consisting of a single transaction as it is to a large-volume complex system. In fact, it may be more significant because systemization is likely to be less strong and consistent in a seldom used system.

A low-volume financing segment is usually too short for an auditor to benefit from flow charting. The function of the transaction review can be carried out in the course of vouching financing transactions by observing how they are authorized, initiated, executed, and recorded. That observation should be documented, as should the procedures for preventing or detecting unauthorized transactions and errors. In a short transaction segment internal control is limited and easily observed; on the other hand, important weaknesses may be so subtle as to escape detection. For example, authorization for short-term borrowing may be formally delegated by the board of directors to a financial executive in accordance with sound principles of control, but the delegation may be loosely worded and general enough to permit virtually unlimited activities, some of which could be unauthorized and unrecorded.

The following are common types of transactions that might be encountered in the financing segment: short-term bank loans, acceptances, time and sight drafts, factored receivables, loans on pledged receivables, loans on pledged inventories, "floor plan" loans, installment loans, leases, long-term debt, stock issues evidenced by certificates, stock issues without certificates, stock options and warrants, and transactions incident to stock purchase and treasury stock repurchase plans.

An auditor should be particularly alert to financing transactions that are handled differently from other, similar transactions; he should make sure he understands the business reasons for differences encountered.

Functional Tests

Delegating the detailed accounting for the financing segment to agents has become so common that many auditors have never encountered a financing system that needs to be functionally tested. However, if a company with a large number of stockholders or debtholders and an active financing activity keeps its own records, an auditor must perform functional tests of controls as a basis for an explicit decision about the amount and kind of corroborative evidence he needs.

If pre-audit is used, an auditor can examine a sufficient sample of completed transactions to form an opinion on the quality of pre-audit. If pre-audit is not employed, an auditor can reperform other forms of control, for example, validity checks or double-checking, to obtain evidence of their reliability. Accounting for the numerical sequence of unissued, issued, and cancelled documents and reconciliation of detail accounts to control accounts can be tested.

Auditors sometimes scan files of correspondence from stockholders for evidence of inaccuracies in record keeping. For the most part, reasonable assurance that additions and reductions are under adequate control and that the detail is reconciled to the total should be sufficient because an auditor gives his opinion on the aggregate numbers appearing in financial statements and not on the details of the accounts. However, if there are serious inaccuracies in the detail accounts or if they are not reconcilable to the control account, the company may face possible legal action or liability which needs to be evaluated. There have been instances of capital stock records so seriously out of control as to precipitate regulatory agency action to protect stockholders.

SUBSTANTIVE TESTS

The following discussion applies equally to all kinds of financing transactions unless clearly inapplicable in the context or specified in the discussion. A convenient vehicle for substantive testing of the various kinds of financing transactions is an account analysis working paper:

a list of the notes, debt issues, or equities outstanding at the beginning of a period, and the additions, reductions, and outstanding amounts at the end of the period. Depending on the importance of each item, the list can be in detail or in the aggregate for each type of financing instrument. Often the list can be carried forward from year to year if changes are infrequent. It may incorporate all pertinent information about the financing instruments or that information may be summarized separately. An auditor should compare the list with the accounts and reconcile the total to the general ledger. He can, if he wishes, use the list to record the evidence of his other tests.

Validation Procedures

Validation procedures are usually carried out at year end because it is easy to do so and because the financing segment may be volatile and thus subject to changes on short notice. Often transactions are validated up to an interim date and then brought forward to year end.

An auditor should trace authorization for financing to a vote of the board of directors. If the directors have delegated authority for the details of financing, individual transactions should be traced to the authorizing officer's signature.

Copies of financing instruments should be obtained and scrutinized carefully. An auditor must ascertain that the classification of the financing and its description in the financial statements are proper. The instruments should be examined for commitments, which often accompany financing arrangements, and evidence of rights given or received, which might require accounting recognition or disclosure. If financing is in the form of a lease, the terms must be evaluated to determine whether it should be accounted for as a lease or as debt financing.

An auditor should trace the recording of receipt and repayment of financing into the accounts and compare those transactions with the authorization and terms of the instrument for timing and amount. Paid notes should be examined for evidence of proper authorization, documentation, and cancellation; interest expense, accrued and prepaid interest, and dividends declared should be checked by computation.

Outstanding balances should be confirmed, usually at year end. Confirmation should be requested from holders of notes and issuers of lines of credit, trustees under bond and debenture indentures, and registrars and transfer agents for stock issues. Outstanding stock issues often must be recorded with the Secretary of State in the state of incorporation, and confirmation can be requested from that office.

Amounts on deposit with dividend and interest disbursing agents should be confirmed; confirmation requests should include information about special terms and commitments, including collateral.

If lease commitments are capitalized, computations of the carrying amounts of assets and debt should be tested, and the terms should be checked to the underlying lease contract.

If several types of financing are outstanding, an auditor should check transactions in each against restrictions and provisions of the others. Dividend payments may be restricted by bond and note indentures; dividends on common stock may be affected by the rights of preferred stockholders or their rights may change with changes in capital structure or retained earnings accounts; certain transactions may require the consent of holders of senior securities, and so on. Often the opinion of company counsel is received as part of the letter from counsel described in Chapter 10.

The reconciliation of detailed stock ledgers to the control account should be reviewed and tested. Accounting for unissued, issued, and cancelled certificates should be similarly tested.

An auditor should check computations of shares reserved for issuance on exercise of options and warrants or conversion of convertible securities and of the basis for valuing stock dividends and split-ups. In checking those computations, the auditor should pay close attention to the interrelated effects of one issue on another and on the total amount of each issue authorized and outstanding. The accuracy of accounting for warrants, options, and conversion privileges exercised can often be checked by an overall computation based on the terms of the related instruments.

By the nature of financing commitments, an auditor cannot obtain positive assurance that he is aware of all commitments. If a client forgets to inform him of an obligation or deliberately conceals one from him, he will discover it only by chance. That chance is considerably improved by the use of auditing procedures that produce thorough and thoughtful knowledge of the client.

For the most part, auditors rely on the liability certificate described in Chapter 10 to remind clients of matters that need to be disclosed and of their responsibility to do so.

Defaults

Validation tests of financing transactions may reveal that one or more commitment or covenant has not been complied with. The financing instrument usually specifies what constitutes an "event of default" and what can happen in such an event. While ultimate legal remedies may be severe, the intent of the provisions of the agreement is to give the lender or investor adequate protection by restricting the investee's freedom of action in certain circumstances. Therefore, more often than not, an event of default will be "waived." An auditor should obtain specific confirmation of a waiver extending to the end of the succeeding year from the lender or investor, and the facts should be disclosed in the financial statements.

In serious cases, where an event of default is not waived, the debt may become immediately due and payable; if so, it must be classified as a current liability even though immediate payment has not been requested. The auditor must then determine whether his client can be considered a "going concern," or whether questions about ability to cure the default or repay the financing are unanswerable and therefore require recognition in his opinion (see Chapter 19).

Dividends

An auditor should determine whether proper procedures have been followed in accounting for regular cash dividends, stock dividends and split-ups, dividends payable in scrip, and dividends payable in assets other than cash. Auditors should be familiar with the types of problems that may arise from the declaration, recording, and payment of dividends and recognize when advice of counsel is needed. One of an auditor's responsibilities is to form an opinion on whether the intentions of the board, as indicated in the resolutions authorizing dividends, are properly reflected in the financial statements. The following paragraphs present examples of conditions that may be encountered.

Restrictive covenants of debentures and other debt instruments frequently restrict the payment of cash dividends in some manner (e.g., to earnings subsequent to the date of the instrument). The auditor should ascertain that dividend declarations do not exceed the amount of earnings available for dividends.

Holders of noncumulative preferred stock ordinarily have no claim to dividends in a year when the amount of the dividends has not been earned, except possibly when dividends earned in a prior year have been improperly withheld. Dividends paid on common stock may have encroached on the rights of holders of noncumulative preferred stock. If an auditor discovers that situation, he should remind the client of the terms of the preferred stock issue and suggest that counsel be consulted about a possible liability to holders of noncumulative preferred stock.

If the price of stock sold includes accrued dividends, an auditor should satisfy himself that the accrued dividends were correctly computed and that the accounting treatment is proper.

If a dividend on common stock is payable in preferred shares, an auditor should determine, usually by inquiry of counsel, that the corporation has complied with requirements for the consent of holders of senior shares and with the various formalities for the issuance of new or additional preferred shares. He should also determine that the capitalization of retained earnings related to the issuance of the shares is in accordance with generally accepted accounting principles.

If a preferred stock dividend is paid in common stock, an auditor should satisfy himself, usually by inquiry of counsel, that statutory requirements and provisions of the preferred stock agreement have been complied with and that the proper amount of retained earnings has been capitalized. A dividend on preferred stock, especially cumulative or participating stock, paid in common stock requires that directors give due consideration to the relative interests of the different classes of stockholders in determining the amount of retained earnings to be capitalized.

In the event of a stock dividend or stock split-up, an auditor must ascertain that the capital stock authorization is not exceeded and that consideration has been given to shares reserved for stock options and conversions of other issues.

Stockholders' Equity Accounts

Since analyses of stockholders' equity accounts appear in the financial statements and are subject to detailed scrutiny by security analysts and others, an auditor should validate each type of entry either individually or in the aggregate. Some entries, such as appropriations of retained earnings, are simply traced to the authorizing minutes of the board of directors. Other entries summarize a large volume of individual transactions and can be validated by means of an overall computation based on the authorizing instrument or vote of the directors: cash dividends, stock dividends, stock splits, warrants exercised, and securities converted are examples. Still other entries—the most common example is the exercise of stock options that were granted in the past at various times and various prices—are an aggregation of unique transactions and are best validated by an evaluation of internal control over the transaction system and by reconciling beginning and ending balances with the activity for the year. Each type of entry should be evaluated for compliance with loan agreements or other restrictive commitments.

Treasury stock should be confirmed with the custodian or, if there is no custodian, the client's count of treasury stock should be observed.

The effect on earnings per share of convertible securities, options, and warrants must be computed or the client's computations checked and documented in the working papers.

An auditor should review the terms of outstanding stock subscriptions and make sufficient tests of activity and balances to afford reasonable assurance that they are being complied with. It is preferable to confirm outstanding stock subscriptions receivable even though under generally accepted accounting principles they do not represent an asset but rather a memorandum entry in the capital section of the balance sheet.

Partnership Capital

An auditor's examination of partnership financial statements should include reading the partnership agreement. Ordinarily those agreements not only show the basis on which profits and losses are shared but also contain provisions concerning fixed amounts of capital to be maintained by the various partners, loans by partners in certain circumstances, interest on partners' capital and loans, limitations on withdrawals, and similar matters. An auditor should analyze and substantiate changes in partnership capital between statement dates and report a failure to carry out provisions of the partnership agreement.

Some partnerships conduct business without written partnership agreements. In those circumstances, an auditor should inquire whether the partners understand the bases on which the accounts are kept, particularly with respect to distributions of profits and losses and interest on partners' capital. It is good practice to ask all partners to sign the financial statements on which the partners' accounts appear or, alternatively, to confirm the balances in their accounts.

If partners' withdrawals are made in currency, partners should approve their accounts as they appear in the ledger. An auditor should suggest to partners that withdrawals be by check only and that personal bills be paid through personal bank accounts.

Capital of Nonbusiness Organizations

An auditor's procedures for nonbusiness organizations should be similar to those previously discussed. The terms of donations or bequests are frequently of considerable importance and should be reviewed to determine that restrictions are being observed.

An auditor should review changes in capital between balance sheet dates and apply other tests necessary to reasonably assure himself that items whose disposition is specified in articles of organization or incorporation, stipulations in bequests, or resolutions by trustees, directors, or members as embodied in the organization's minutes have been disposed of in accordance with the specific provisions.

Analytical Reviews

Minutes of the board of directors' meetings should be read and mention of financing transactions and entries to stockholders' equity accounts should be traced to the accounts or to appropriate disclosures in the financial statements.

Debt Financing

An auditor's files should contain a copy of every financing instrument, and he should read them and analyze their accounting and disclosure implications. The language of leases, indentures, and loan agreements can be highly technical and extremely complicated. Unusual accounting results, even unintended ones, are not uncommon. Often an instrument is designed to achieve a desired accounting and tax result. A careful study of financing instruments is so critical and so difficult that frequently the auditor in charge of an engagement asks another qualified professional to duplicate the analysis and check his conclusions. It is probably the rule rather than the exception that clients seek their auditors' interpretation of the accounting and disclosure implications of prospective financing instruments before they are executed.

Once the accounting and disclosure implications are analyzed and understood, it is usually possible to set up a work sheet which can be carried forward from year to year for computing and documenting compliance with pertinent commitments.

If the interest rate of a financing instrument is not clearly the going market rate for that type of instrument, an auditor's working papers should document his evaluation of its reasonableness. If the rate of interest must be imputed, the documentation for the imputed rate may be carried forward from year to year.

If a financing instrument is issued for property other than cash, an auditor should review the terms of the transaction, basis for recording, and evidence of approval by the board of directors. Usually, a transaction of that kind is significant enough to warrant careful review by an auditor during the planning stage. In that event, there is ample opportunity to suggest the appropriate basis for recording the property received and the kind of evidence that should be retained to support it.

In connection with analytical reviews of other transaction segments, an auditor reviews the accounting activity for fluctuations in account balances and flow of funds which offer clues to unusual entries or conditions. He should be alert in the course of those reviews to evidence of financing transactions not reviewed elsewhere.

Capital Stock

In an initial examination, an auditor should review the corporation's charter or certificate of incorporation, by-laws, and all pertinent amendments; the extent of the review of prior years' minutes of meetings of the board of directors and stockholders and other documents and of capital stock accounts depends on circumstances and whether the financial statements were previously examined by independent certified public accountants.

If capital stock is publicly held, it is advisable to review the registration statement filed with the Securities and Exchange Commission and the agreement with the underwriters. Those documents may disclose the existence of requirements, such as those for maintenance of minimum working capital or retained earnings, as well as restrictions on further financing transactions.

Many accountants advocate correspondence with the Secretary of State of the state in which a client is incorporated to obtain direct confirmation of the number of shares and classes of capital stock authorized.

An auditor should include in his permanent file of working papers information as to the kinds of stock authorized, the number of shares of each class authorized, par or stated values, provisions concerning dividend rates, redemption values, priority rights to dividends and in liquidation, cumulative or noncumulative rights to dividends, participation or conversion privileges, and other pertinent data.

Additional Paid-In Capital and Retained Earnings

In an initial examination, an auditor should analyze the additional paid-in capital and retained earnings accounts from the corporation's inception to determine whether all entries were in accordance with generally accepted accounting principles then prevailing. If, however, previous examinations have been made by independent certified public accountants, he may limit his procedures to a review of analyses made by the previous auditors. Entries in those accounts should also be reviewed for consistency of treatment from year to year. The analyses of additional paid-in capital accounts should segregate the balances by classes of stock outstanding. The auditor should retain those analyses in the permanent file of working papers so that changes in the current year may be readily reviewed for consistency with previous years.

• STATEMENT PRESENTATION

SHORT-TERM FINANCING

With a few exceptions, short-term financing is presented first in the current liabilities section of a balance sheet.

Notes Payable—Banks

For many years, no disclosure was called for beyond the caption. In 1973, the SEC started to require disclosure of the average interest rate on short-term debt, the maximum amount outstanding at any month end during a fiscal year, the total of the line of credit under which borrowings are made, and the details of any related compensating balances (see Chapter 15). It was once common to record the face amount of discounted notes payable and show the discount as a prepaid asset or deferred charge. Paragraph 16 of APB Opinion No. 21 (paragraph 4111.15 of *AICPA Prof. Stds.*, vol. 3) states a blanket requirement that discount or premium on all kinds of debt should be presented as a direct reduction from or addition to the face amount of the note.

Current Portion of Long-Term Debt

The long-term debt currently due should ordinarily be included in current liabilities and referenced to the note that describes the details of long-term debt (see below). It is acceptable to treat the portion currently due as noncurrent if the funds to pay it have been segregated and classified as noncurrent assets (for example, when bonds have been purchased for a sinking fund).

FASB Statement No. 6, *Classification of Short-Term Obligations Expected To Be Refinanced (AICPA Prof. Stds.*, vol. 3, Section 2033), defines terms and sets forth criteria for short-term financing that can properly be classified as long term. When the company intends to refinance on a long-term basis, there are two conditions for long-term classification. The first is when short-term financing is refinanced by issuing long-term or equity financing before the balance sheet is issued —obviously it is better to reflect the long-term nature of the financing by so classifying it. The second condition is most commonly exemplified by notes payable under a revolving credit agreement, which are technically short term and therefore current liabilities. When the loan agreement runs for more than a year from the date of the balance sheet, and the borrower has an unconditional right to renew the notes [under the conditions set forth in paragraph 11(b) of FASB Statement No. 6], it is acceptable to present the notes payable as long-term debt with appropriate disclosures describing the financing agreement.

Notes Payable—Other

If there are significant notes payable other than to banks, they should be presented separately following that caption. Disclosure of the nature of the note and of the creditor is usually called for.

Loans on life insurance policies should be classified as current or long term, depending on how the corresponding asset for cash surrender value is classified. Since a right of offset usually exists, it is acceptable, though less preferable, to deduct life insurance loans from the cash surrender value asset.

Loans collateralized by pledged accounts receivable or inventory should be classified as current liabilities and should not be offset against the assets. The amount of pledged assets should be disclosed, preferably in the caption of the affected assets or in a note.

Income Statement

Interest should be shown as a separate caption in an income statement if it is a significant amount; if it is not, it is usually included in the caption "Other expense." In statements to be filed with the SEC, amortization of debt discount or premium must be set out separately from interest expense. It is not customary to disclose the two amounts separately in other published financial statements.

Statement of Changes in Financial Position

Since short-term financing is an element of working capital, it is customary in a statement of changes in financial position to present only the net change in each item: for example, the net increase or decrease in notes payable would be presented as one item in the analysis of changes in working capital.

LONG-TERM DEBT

The details of long-term financing are important to those who study financial statements. Therefore, each significant issue, or sometimes a group of similar issues, is set forth separately on the face of the balance sheet or, perhaps more common when there are several kinds of long-term debt, in a note, which gives the details of a single caption in the balance sheet. If the details are presented in the balance sheet, it is usual to include the title of the issue, rate of interest, and due date.

Sometimes those items are all that need be disclosed about an issue of long-term debt. Usually, however, further disclosures are required. All significant features of each issue should be described, such as the call price, any premium on redemption, sinking fund provisions, subordination provisions, convertible features, or warrants. Any assets pledged as collateral should also be described—an exception is mortgage loans: if a loan is titled a "mortgage loan," the reader is expected to assume that all of the real property is pledged under the mortgage. If only a portion of the property is under the mortgage, that fact is usually disclosed.

Most long-term debt agreements contain commitments and restrictive covenants. It is not necessary to disclose all of those covenants, but the most restrictive one should be described: for example, if the agreement provides for minimum working capital and also a balance of retained earnings, only the one that would first restrict the company's financing activities need be disclosed. If the company is in default on any of its covenants and the lender has not waived the default, it should be fully described. Depending on the circumstances, the existence of an uncured default usually requires that the issue of long-term debt be classified as a current liability.

The SEC requires that the amount of debt falling due within each of the five years following the date of the most recent balance sheet be disclosed. Many companies are following that practice in their published financial statements whether subject to SEC jurisdiction or not.

Discount or premium is deducted from or added to the face amount of long-term debt; both amounts should be disclosed either on the face of the balance sheet or in a note. Debt issue costs are treated as deferred charges [APB Opinion No. 21 (*AICPA Prof. Stds.,* vol. 3, paragraph 4111.15)].

Reacquired debt is ordinarily shown as a reduction of the liability for the debt issue, unless it has been acquired for a sinking fund. Any gain or loss on the reacquisition is credited or charged to income.

Income Statement and Statement of Changes in Financial Position

Interest expense, if significant, should be shown separately in an income statement. It is not necessary to disclose separately the interest on each issue of debt, but interest on bonds, mortgages, and similar debt should be shown separately from other interest in SEC filings. Amortization of debt discount and expense should also be shown separately. A significant gain or loss on retirement of debt (other than for sinking fund requirements) is now required to be shown as an extraordinary item [FASB Statement No. 4 (*AICPA Prof. Stds.,* vol. 3, Section 2013)].

The effects of long-term financing activity are important, and so each major issue and retirement should be disclosed separately, not "netted"; borrowings are therefore shown as a source and repayments as a use of funds in statements of changes in financial position.

LEASES

Leases that are capitalized are accounted for as plant and as long-term debt and presented that way in financial statements. The information required by APB Opinions No. 5 and 31 (*AICPA Prof. Stds.,* vol. 3, Sections 5351 and 5352) for noncapitalized lease commitments should be presented in a note to the financial statements. That includes total rent expense charged to operations in each period for which an income statement is presented, with contingent rentals reported separately from minimum rentals; minimum rental commitments under noncancellable leases by major category of property for each of the succeeding five fiscal years, each of the next three five-year periods, and any remaining commitment; basis for calculating any variable or contingent rents; and any purchase options, guarantees, commitments, restrictions, or other important characteristics of the lease commitments. Opinion No. 31 recommends but does not require disclosure of the present value of minimum lease commitments and the average interest rate implicit in that computation.

The SEC's disclosure requirements set forth in Accounting Series Release No. 147 are more extensive and more stringent. Specific measures of materiality are set forth for the disclosures enumerated above (i.e., one per cent of revenue). If other measures of materiality are met (five per cent of total long-term debt and equity, three per cent effect on net income), then disclosure is required of present value of minimum lease commitments, average interest rate used, and the impact on net income of capitalizing all financing leases and recording straight-line depreciation and interest expense. The data collection and computation required for those disclosures can be extensive.

STOCKHOLDERS' EQUITY

The capital structure of an enterprise is important to owners, lenders, prospective investors, and often customers and creditors as well, and so financial statements present the capital accounts in considerable detail. The words of Accounting Terminology Bulletin No. 1, first published in 1949, are still valid as a succinct statement of the basic disclosure requirements. It is recommended that:

(1) The use of the term *surplus* (whether standing alone or in such combinations as *capital surplus, paid-in surplus, earned surplus, appraisal surplus,* etc.) be discontinued.

(2) The contributed portion of proprietary capital be shown as:
   (a) Capital contributed for, or assigned to, shares, to the extent of the par or stated value of each class of shares presently outstanding.
   (b) (i) Capital contributed for, or assigned to, shares in excess of such par or stated value (whether as a result of original issue of shares at amounts in excess of their then par or stated value, or of a reduction in par or stated value of shares after issuance, or of transactions by the corporation in its own shares); and
      (ii) Capital received other than for shares whether from shareholders or from others.

(3) The term *earned surplus* be replaced by terms which will indicate source, such as *retained income, retained earnings, accumulated earnings,* or *earnings retained for use in the business.* In the case of a deficit, the amount should be shown as a deduction from contributed capital with appropriate description.

(4) In connection with 2(b) and 3 there should, so far as practicable, be an indication of the extent to which the amounts have been appropriated or are restricted as to withdrawal. Retained income appropriated to some specific purpose nevertheless remains part of retained income, and any so-called "reserves" which are clearly appropriations or segregations of retained income, such as those for general contingencies, possible future inventory losses, sinking fund, etc., should be included as part of the stockholders' equity.

(5) Where there has been a quasi-reorganization, retained income should be "dated" for a reasonable time thereafter; and where the amount of retained income has been reduced as a result of a stock dividend or a transfer by resolution of the board of directors from unrestricted to restricted capital, the presentation should, until the fact loses significance, indicate that the amount shown as retained income is the remainder after such transfers.

(6) Any appreciation included in the stockholders' equity other than as a result of a quasi-reorganization should be designated by such terms as *excess of appraised or fair value of fixed assets over cost* or *appreciation of fixed assets.*

Corporations with long and complex financial histories may find it difficult to segregate stockholders' equity by sources and therefore may indicate it in one amount. If stockholders' equity is indicated in one amount, it is desirable to disclose in a note to the financial statements the reasons therefor and any known circumstances concerning its origin. Usually, however, it is possible to distinguish between undistributed profits (retained earnings) and capital arising from other sources.

Regulation S-X of the SEC sets forth in Rule 5-02 the requirements for statements of commercial and industrial companies filed with it:

> *Other stockholders' equity.* (a) Separate captions shall be shown for: (1) Paid-in additional capital, (2) other additional capital, and (3) retained earnings (i) appropriated and (ii) unappropriated.
>
> (b) If undistributed earnings of unconsolidated subsidiaries and 50 percent or less owned persons are included, state the amount in each category parenthetically or in a note referred to herein.
>
> (c) For a period of at least 10 years subsequent to the effective date of a quasi-reorganization, any description of retained earnings shall indicate the point in time from which the new retained earnings dates and for a period of at least 8 years shall indicate the total amount of the deficit eliminated.
>
> (d) A summary of each account under this caption setting forth the information prescribed in Rule 11–02 shall be given for each period for which an income statement is required to be filed.

Capital Stock

If there is more than one issue of stock, the classes should be stated in the order of the priority of their rights in liquidation, which is usually the same the order of priority in participation in earnings. Under this standard, preferred stock is usually stated first. The description of each issue of stock should include its legal title; whether it is par or no par value stock and the par value or stated or assigned value per share, if any; the number of shares authorized; the number and aggregate dollar amount of shares issued and outstanding; and, for preferred stock, the nature of the preference, the dividend rate, whether cumulative or noncumulative, and, in the circumstances discussed below, the redemption and liquidation amounts. The amount assigned to capital stock, regardless of class, may include amounts paid in excess of par or stated value. If shares of any class of stock are reserved for issue on conversion of other classes of stock or of bonds, the number of shares so reserved should be indicated in the description of the issue or in a note to the balance sheet.

No par value stock is stated on balance sheets in various ways. If no stated value per share has been assigned, the aggregate net proceeds from each class issued are usually indicated. State laws may require that a minimum value be ascribed to no par value shares. However, that is only a minimum value; if the corporation has designated a higher value, the higher amount should be shown in the balance sheet.

Many stock agreements contain restrictive and preference provisions. The balance sheet should describe adequately the various classes of stock so that owners of junior securities may ascertain the existence of prior liens in dividend distributions, redemptions, and liquidation. Frequently, those disclosures are provided in notes.

Redemption or Liquidating Prices Above Par or Stated Values

If redemption or liquidating prices of preference stocks are above their par or stated values, the facts should be clearly set forth so that holders of junior securities may ascertain the extent to which available capital will be reduced if senior issues are retired or the company is liquidated. It is good practice to indicate in dollars the aggregate excess of involuntary liquidation price of preference stock over par or stated value.

SEC Regulation S-X, Rule 3-16(f), requires that:

> . . . When the excess involved is material there shall be shown: (i) The difference between the aggregate preference on involuntary liquidation and the aggregate par or stated value; (ii) a statement that this difference, plus any arrears in dividends, exceeds the sum of the par or stated value of the junior capital shares and other stockholders' equity applicable to junior shares, if such is the case; and (iii) a statement as to the existence of any restrictions upon retained earnings growing out of the fact that upon involuntary liquidation the preference of the preferred shares exceeds its par or stated value.

As administrative policy, the Commission also requires, when the excess involved is significant, an opinion of counsel as to whether there are any restrictions on capital by reason of those differences and also as to any remedies available to stockholders before or after the payment of a dividend that reduces capital to an amount less than that by which the aggregate preference of the stock on involuntary liquidation exceeds its aggregate par or stated value.

Many companies show no par preferred stock on the balance sheet at the amount of preference in liquidation, rather than at a lower amount paid in or at a lower legal stated value. The difference should have been charged either to additional paid-in capital or to retained earnings, as permitted by the accounting principles described earlier in this chapter. One alleged advantage of stating no par preferred stock at the amount of preference in liquidation is that it simplifies the evaluation of common stock since all other capital, except amounts that may be applicable to unpaid cumulative dividends on preferred stock, is then identified with the common stock. Another advantage claimed is that it obviates the possibility of retained earnings being reduced by dividend declarations to an amount below that required to preserve the liquidation value of the preferred stock. If the client wishes to state no par preferred stock on the balance sheet at the amount of preference in liquidation and it is permitted by the statutes of the state in which the company is incorporated, the auditor can offer no objection providing the basis is adequately disclosed.

Some preferred issues require periodic redemption of amounts based on excess earnings determined in accordance with a prescribed formula or based on other terms of the charter. The amount of preferred stock that must be so redeemed within the next fiscal year should preferably be deducted from the capital section and shown among current liabilities.

Subscriptions to Capital Stock

If subscriptions to capital stock have been taken, and the stock is not to be issued until the subscription price has been fully paid, the obligation to issue the stock should be separately stated in the capital section of the balance sheet. The aggregate amount to be received for the stock and the number of shares to be issued should be indicated. The usual method is by means of a caption such as: "Capital stock subscribed, xxx shares, less $xxx subscriptions receivable."

If a subscriber has the right to cancel his subscription and to have refunded the amounts paid in, it is preferable to state the subscriptions at the amounts paid in, described as common (preferred) stock installments, and to disclose the number of shares subscribed, aggregate subscription price, and other pertinent provisions of the plan.

Discount on Capital Stock

Discount on capital stock is rare. Discount on other than preference stock generally should be deducted from the class of capital stock to which it relates; alternatively, it may be deducted from the total of capital stock and additional paid-in capital. If part of a class of stock is sold at a discount and the balance at a premium, discount and premium may be offset.

If the discount applies to preference shares, it is good practice to show it as a deduction from additional paid-in capital arising from other sales of the same issue (or from issues no longer outstanding) or as a reduction from retained earnings. There is no logical basis for writing off the discount by charges to income.

Unexchanged Stock in Recapitalization

Usually, after the date of a recapitalization, the new capital stock should be shown as though all the old shares had been exchanged, with an explanatory statement either in the body of the balance sheet or in a note indicating the number of old shares still outstanding, which for balance sheet purposes are assumed to have been exchanged, and the basis on which the exchange will be made upon receipt of old certificates. Disclosure should be made of any dissents entered by stockholders who disapprove the merger or consolidation plans and who have applied to the courts for an appraisal of stock values, as provided by state statutes. The capitalization should not reflect the exchange of shares held by dissenting stockholders.

Subordinated Indebtedness Treated as Capital

Corporations sometimes issue long-term debentures with provisions subordinating them to other corporate obligations, including general creditors. The debentures are frequently issued to stockholders who are willing to accept a subordinate position. In some instances, the interest on the debentures is payable only if earned and is noncumulative. If only common stock is outstanding, the debentures, on liquidation of the company, have substantially the standing of preferred stock.

It is sometimes argued that debentures of that type should be classified with capital rather than as liabilities. With one exception, the SEC has refused to accept that classification. The exception is capital notes issued by commercial banks, which may be grouped with capital stock under a heading such as "Capital notes and stockholders' equity."

The profession generally has agreed with the SEC's position, and subordinated debentures are rarely classified as capital. However, there may be instances where that classification is more realistic and informative; in the authors' opinion, there should be no objection to such a presentation as long as full disclosure is made.

Stock Warrants and Options

Terms of stock warrants and options granted should be adequately disclosed on the balance sheet, so that stockholders may know to what extent potential purchasers have options on stock that otherwise would be available for sale or issue. If option rights have been issued to officers and employees as compensation for services but have not been satisfied as yet by the issuance of shares, the amount of compensation should be shown in the capital section of the balance sheet as additional paid-in capital or in a manner similar to that for proceeds from subscriptions to capital stock. In the latter alternative, as the options are exercised, that amount will be relieved by transfer of appropriate amounts to a capital stock account and, possibly, to a paid-in capital account, adequately described.

Accounting Research Bulletin No. 43, Chapter 13B (*AICPA Prof. Stds.*, vol. 3, Section 4061), states the requirements for disclosure in financial statements with respect to stock option plans:

> In connection with financial statements, disclosure should be made as to the status of the option or plan at the end of the period of report, including the number of shares under option, the option price, and the number of shares as to which options were exercisable. As to options exercised during the period, disclosure should be made of the number of shares involved and the option price thereof. [Paragraph 4061.15]

The SEC requires much more extensive disclosures in connection with stock option plans.* [Rule 3-16(n) of Regulation S-X.]

Paragraph 6 of the New York Stock Exchange listing agreement requires the following disclosures:

> The Corporation will disclose in its annual report to shareholders, for the year covered by the report,
> (1) the number of shares of its stock issuable under outstanding options at the beginning of the year; separate totals of changes in the number of shares of its stock under option resulting from issuance, exercise, expiration or cancellation of options; and the number of shares issuable under outstanding options at the close of the year,
> (2) the number of unoptioned shares available at the beginning and at the close of the year for the granting of options under an option plan, and
> (3) any changes in the exercise price of outstanding options, through cancellation and reissuance or otherwise, except price changes resulting from the normal operation of antidilution provisions of the options.

Treasury Stock

The balance sheet should indicate the number of shares of stock held in the treasury and describe the issue. Treasury stock is commonly stated at cost and deducted from total capital; alternatively, it is stated at par value and deducted from the total outstanding amount of the

---

* See Louis H. Rappaport, *SEC Accounting Practice and Procedure,* 3rd Edition (New York: The Ronald Press Co., 1972).

related issue. If it has been acquired for the specific purpose of resale to employees or others, it may be shown separately on the asset side of the balance sheet, at cost, provided the reason for the treatment is disclosed in the balance sheet or in a note.

The laws of many states provide that treasury stock may be purchased only if the purchase does not impair legal capital; in some states an amount of capital equal to the cost of treasury stock is restricted for payment of dividends or other purposes. Such restriction should be disclosed in a note to the financial statements.

When treasury stock is legally retired and cancelled, the number of authorized shares is usually reduced accordingly. Retirement without cancellation does not reduce the authorization in some states, unless retained earnings have been reduced by the cost of treasury stock.

Legal considerations have substantial weight in determining the proper presentation of treasury stock in financial statements. An auditor should have some familiarity with the state laws concerning the accounting for and presentation of treasury stock and should consult with legal counsel when necessary.

Some corporations have sold substantial blocks of stock prior to the close of a fiscal year under an agreement to repurchase the stock at the same price shortly after the beginning of the new period. That procedure may be simply a form of window-dressing or the agreement may be so worded to protect the purchaser from loss on resale of the stock. In any event, commitments to repurchase a company's stock or to protect the purchaser from the effects of a falling market should be disclosed on the balance sheet or in a note.

Additional Paid-In Capital

The various forms of paid-in capital have been discussed previously in this chapter. It is desirable that each of them be separately stated in the balance sheet. If no one form of paid-in capital is particularly significant, it is permissible to combine them. However, so-called capital surplus arising from sources other than contributions or paid in, such as from appreciation or an appraisal, should be separately stated if material in amount.

Retained Earnings

Restrictions on retained earnings should be indicated in a note or parenthetically. Examples of restrictions that should be disclosed are those imposed by bond indentures, state laws, or charter provisions. Frequently, bond indentures include restrictions not only on the payment of dividends but also on use of assets for the purchase of capital stock. The amount of retained earnings free of those restrictions may be indicated, or the amount restricted may be stated. If provisions of those agreements are not presently operative, but are likely to result in a material restriction in the immediate future, a disclosure of the future applicability of the provisions is desirable.

Restrictions on the payment of dividends or stock purchases may be based on the availability of earnings accumulated subsequent to a specified date, on the corporation's ability to observe certain working capital requirements, or on other considerations. If agreements impose more than one type of limitation or if several issues containing different provisions are outstanding, disclosure may be made on the basis of the most restrictive covenant likely to be effective in the immediate future. If alternative provisions are nearly equally restrictive, reference should be made not only to the covenant currently operative but also to other types of restrictions imposed. A note similar to the following would be appropriate:

> The Company's loan indenture restricts the payments of dividends (other than stock dividends) and payments for reacquisition of capital stock to the lesser of:
> (1) the amount of earnings accumulated since December 31, 19—, which at December 31, 19— amounted to $3,000,000, or
> (2) an amount that will not reduce working capital to less than $10,000,000; at December 31, 19—, working capital, as defined in the indenture, amounted to $14,000,000.

Retained Earnings Appropriations

Terms of bond indentures, preferred stock agreements, or other contractual obligations often make mandatory the segregation from retained earnings of amounts otherwise available for dividends. Occasionally, amounts are voluntarily segregated from retained earnings by action of a corporation's board of directors. Whether the segregation is voluntary or involuntary, it results in an appropriated or allocated portion of retained earnings; as previously outlined in this chapter, the mere allocation of retained earnings does not alter its essential character. Any appropriation should be adequately described in the balance sheet, including a statement of the purpose of the appropriation.

It is permissible to characterize an appropriation as a reserve, but the term "reserve" does not indicate the purpose of the appropriation. Use of the term "reserve" in the description should alert readers of the balance sheet that the amount to which it applies is appropriated retained earnings, but the frequent misuse of the word makes it inadvisable to presume that its implications will be clear to readers of the statement.

There may be several "surplus reserves" and generally they immediately precede unappropriated retained earnings on the balance sheet.

Statement of Changes in Stockholders' Equity

Since 1967, APB Opinion No. 12 (*AICPA Prof. Stds.,* vol. 3, Section 2042) has required the following:

> When both financial position and results of operations are presented, disclosure of changes in the separate accounts comprising stockholders' equity (in addition to retained earnings) and of the changes in the number of shares of equity securities during at least the most recent annual fiscal period and any subsequent interim period presented is required to make the financial statements sufficiently informative. Disclosure of such changes may take the form of separate statements or may be made in the basic financial statements or notes thereto. [Paragraph 2042.02]

Some companies show the changes in retained earnings as a continuation of the income statement and the changes in capital stock and other paid-in capital in a note. An increasingly common practice is to present a schedule showing each of the capital accounts and numbers of shares for each class of capital stock in columnar form.

Dividends

It is customary to indicate the total dividend for each class of stock, the medium of payment if other than cash, and, if the dividends were paid in whole or in part out of capital other than retained earnings, to so indicate. Ordinarily, the amount or rate per share is indicated; Regulation S-X (Rule 11-02) of the SEC requires that per-share amounts be given and that the medium of payment be expressly stated.

Since there are many variations in the requirements of corporate agreements and state legislation, some companies may legally declare dividends out of sources other than retained earnings which, in the absence of accompanying explanatory comment, may be misinterpreted by uninformed stockholders as distributions of earnings. The circumstances and source of such dividends must therefore be adequately disclosed.

When a liquidating dividend has been declared and all the legal steps have been taken requisite to the reduction of the stock but the payments to stockholders have not been made, the balance sheet should show the outstanding stock at its reduced amount and the liquidating dividend as a current liability, adequately described.

Dividends declared but unpaid at the balance sheet date are deducted from retained earnings and included among current liabilities. Stock dividends declared but unissued at the balance sheet date are not shown among the liabilities; the amount to be capitalized may be shown as a separate classification in the capital section with an indication of the number of shares to be issued. If the shares are issued shortly after the balance sheet date and the statements are released some time thereafter, the balance sheet may give effect to the issuance of the shares, with appropriate explanation. It is permissible, however, not to reflect any change in the balance sheet as a result of the declaration other than to disclose in a note the nature of the declaration and the amount of retained earnings to be capitalized.

The balance sheet may reflect stock split-ups accomplished shortly after the balance sheet date, provided adequate explanations are given.

Dividends in Arrears

If unpaid dividends on preferred stock have accumulated, the amount unpaid, or the date since which unpaid dividends have accumulated, should be disclosed in the balance sheet. SEC Regulation S-X, Rule 3-16, requires that "arrears in cumulative dividends per share and in total for each class of shares shall be stated." That information may be indicated in a parenthetical note in the description of the preferred stock or in a note to the balance sheet.

CAPITAL OF BUSINESS PARTNERSHIPS

In a partnership, the balance sheet may show a summary of changes in each partner's capital since the date of the previous statement or a summary of changes in the combined capital; changes within the period in each partner's capital, including contributions, withdrawals, share of current profits or losses, interest credits or charges, and salary allowances, should be shown in detail in a supplementary statement.

CAPITAL OF NONBUSINESS ORGANIZATIONS

Capital of nonbusiness organizations is frequently stated on the balance sheet under headings sufficiently descriptive to indicate general restrictions on its use. Such capital may be stated as current funds, plant funds, or endowment funds, or in other classifications as indicated by restrictions on the accounts. Capital changes during the period should be disclosed, either on the balance sheet or in a separate summary. The balance at the beginning of the period, changes during the period, sources of additions, nature of distributions, and allocation of the balance at the date of the financial statements should all be shown.

Part III

REPORTS AND REPORTING

17

Business Combinations and Consolidated Financial Statements

INTRODUCTION

Many corporations conduct operations through subsidiaries because of legal or tax considerations or operating or financial advantages. A parent corporation may form subsidiary companies or they may result from business combinations. Business combinations are accounted for by either the purchase or the pooling-of-interests method, depending on relevant circumstances. Both methods may involve the transfer of stock between combining entities. If a company acquires control of another company through stock ownership, questions arise as to how to record the acquisition and how best to display the financial results of the combined enterprise.

Financial statements of a parent company alone are usually inadequate to disclose essential information if subsidiary companies conduct a substantial proportion of an affiliated group's operations or hold a significant part of the group's assets. On the other hand, statements of the parent company supported by separate statements of subsidiary companies may constitute so voluminous a mass of data and the interrelationships of the companies may be so complex that intelligent summarization is necessary for an understandable presentation of the financial picture. Consolidated or combined financial statements of a group of affiliated companies have been found to be the most useful and customary vehicles for the presentation of financial position and results of operations of such a group for most purposes. In some cases, separate statements serve useful purposes.

• BUSINESS COMBINATIONS

BACKGROUND

Business interests wishing to combine their operations may choose among many different means of effecting a combination, depending on legal, tax, accounting, and various other business considerations. The legal forms of business combinations vary widely according to the requirements of state laws; legal differences between mergers, consolidations, exchanges of stock, and purchases of stock or assets usually do not, although they may, affect the accounting treatment.

The Accounting Principles Board published in Opinion No. 16, *Business Combinations (AICPA Prof. Stds.,* vol. 3, Section 1091), compliance criteria and accounting requirements for business combinations. The Opinion specifies the circumstances in which each of two different mutually exclusive accounting methods, purchase and pooling of interests, is appropriate. Prior to the adoption of Opinion No. 16 (in 1970), the purchase method was always an optional choice. This section of the chapter is devoted to a discussion of the theoretical bases of the two methods, the various criteria for determining which method applies to a given combination, and the effects that each method has on the resultant accounting. Except to the extent that those effects differ, the accounting principles for preparation of consolidated financial statements described later in the chapter apply to all business combinations.

Under the purchase method, a new basis of accounting for assets and liabilities is determined, as described later in this chapter, recognizing current fair values. The pooling-of-interests method, on the other hand, recognizes a fusing of equity interests without the elements of purchase and sale and, as a result, establishes no new basis for the assets and liabilities of any constituent.

Opinion No. 16 was adopted by the APB only after considerable controversy within the profession concerning the desirability of permitting two methods of recording business combinations. Some felt that only the purchase method should be allowed, that all combinations were essentially acquisitions, and that new values should be established for acquired companies. Others recognized that abuses of the pooling-of-interests method had arisen and compromised on their elimination until more fundamental issues of accounting—such as current fair value concepts—could be settled. The controversy still lingers and the FASB has placed the item on its agenda for still further consideration.

POOLING-OF-INTERESTS METHOD

Pooling Concept

In a business combination accounted for by the pooling-of-interests method (often called a "pooling" for convenience), stockholder groups neither withdraw nor invest assets but in effect exchange voting common stocks in a ratio that determines their respective equity interests in the combined entity: they "pool" their respective interests. Paragraphs 28 to 30 of APB Opinion No. 16 (paragraphs 1091.28 to .30 of *AICPA Prof. Stds.*, vol. 3) describe the theoretical basis for the pooling method:

> . . . a business combination effected by issuing common stock is different from a purchase in that no corporate assets are disbursed to stockholders and the net assets of the issuing corporation are enlarged by the net assets of the corporation whose stockholders accept common stock of the combined corporation. There is no newly invested capital nor have owners withdrawn assets from the group since the stock of a corporation is not one of its assets. Accordingly, the net assets of the constituents remain intact but combined; the stockholder groups remain intact but combined. Aggregate income is not changed since the total resources are not changed. Consequently, the his-

torical costs and earnings of the separate corporations are appropriately combined. In a business combination [pooling] effected by exchanging stock, groups of stockholders combine their resources, talents, and risks to form a new entity to carry on in combination the previous businesses and to continue their earnings streams. The sharing of risks by the constituent stockholder groups is an important element in a business combination effected by exchanging stock. By pooling equity interests, each group continues to maintain risk elements of its former investment and they mutually exchange risks and benefits.

A pooling of interests transaction is regarded as in substance an arrangement among stockholder groups. The fractional interests in the common enterprise are reallocated—risks are rearranged among the stockholder groups outside the corporate entity. A fundamental concept of entity accounting is that a corporation is separate and distinct from its stockholders. Elected managements represent the stockholders in bargaining to effect a combination, but the groups of stockholders usually decide whether the proposed terms are acceptable by voting to approve or disapprove a combination. Stockholders sometimes disapprove a combination proposed by management, and tender offers sometimes succeed despite the opposition of management.

Each stockholder group in a pooling of interests gives up its interests in assets formerly held but receives an interest in a portion of the assets formerly held in addition to an interest in the assets of the other. The clearest example of this type of combination is one in which both groups surrender their stock and receive in exchange stock of a new corporation. The fact that one of the corporations usually issues its stock in exchange for that of the other does not alter the substance of the transaction.

Accounting for Assets and Stockholders' Equity

Since no new basis of accountability arises, the carrying amounts of the separate assets and liabilities of the constituent entities are brought forward into the combined entity. It is acceptable to make retroactive changes in *methods* of accounting for particular assets and liabilities of one or more constituents to make them uniform with the ongoing principles of the combined entity, provided the change would otherwise have been appropriate.

The combined retained earnings and accumulated deficits, if any, of the constituent corporations should be carried forward, except as otherwise required by law or appropriate corporate action. Adjustments of assets or stockholders' equity accounts that would otherwise be in conformity with generally accepted accounting principles are ordinarily equally appropriate if effected at the time of a pooling. However, it is inappropriate and misleading to eliminate a deficit of one constituent against its capital in excess of par while carrying forward the retained earnings of another constituent. Even though one or more of the combined companies continues in existence as a subsidiary, the new enterprise is nevertheless regarded as a continuation of all the constituent corporations; the rule applicable to purchased subsidiaries that retained earnings arising before acquisition are not part of consolidated retained earnings does not apply. However, if one of the constituent companies had acquired a subsidiary by purchase before the pooling of interests, the parent's share of the subsidiary's retained earnings before acquisition should not be included in retained earnings of the pooled corporations.

The capital stock or stated capital of the new parent may be either more or less than the total of the capital stock and stated capital of the constituent corporations. If more, the excess may be deducted first from the total of any other additional paid-in capital and then from the total retained earnings of the constituent corporations. If less, the difference should be added to paid-in capital. (The same accounting applies to a recapitalization other than a business combination.)

The statement of income of the combined corporations for the fiscal period in which a pooling occurs should ordinarily include the combined results of operations of the constituent interests for the entire period as if they had been combined at the beginning of the period. Financial statements for all prior periods presented should then be retroactively restated on a combined basis. Combinations occurring after the year end but before the issuance of the financial statements should not be reflected retroactively in the statements except in the unusual event that statements for the subsequent interim period including the pooling are published with or before release of the year-end statements. (That specific prohibition was written into Opinion No. 16 because of the occurrence of post-balance sheet poolings that gave rise to misleading implications.)

Criteria for Pooling-of-Interests Method

The concept of pooling of interests is clear and reasonably simple, but its application raises many questions. The great variety of conditions encountered in negotiating business combinations is further complicated by the economic and business consequences of the pooling versus purchase accounting decision, which leads businessmen to "structure" business combinations to achieve a desired result. Paragraphs 46 to 48 of Opinion No. 16 (paragraphs 1091.46 to .48 of *AICPA Prof. Stds.*, vol. 3) prescribe twelve specific criteria for a pooling, and paragraph 44 (paragraph 1091.44) states that a combination not meeting all the pooling criteria is to be accounted for by the purchase method—the methods are mutually exclusive. The Opinion supersedes all earlier pronouncements and criteria.

Earlier Criteria Dropped or Changed

The first sentence of paragraph 29 of the Opinion (paragraph 1091.29 of *AICPA Prof. Stds.*, vol. 3), quoted above, states that a pooling is in substance an arrangement among stockholder groups. No parameters for the sizes of the respective combining companies are specified (for example, that one company cannot be more than three times the size of the other as measured by assets, revenue, or income). The APB deliberated on that point and decided against specifying a size criterion, even though earlier pronouncements gave some consideration to relative size of constituents; practice had eroded that criterion because it had become apparent that relative size had no place in the formulation of an accounting principle.

Continuity of ownership and of management are other earlier criteria for pooling that are no longer required under the Opinion (however, the SEC has outlined certain holding period requirements for securities of publicly held companies, which are discussed below). Instead, the Opinion states that a combination agreement violates the pooling criteria if it requires a holder to either sell or retain shares issued in the transaction. All stockholders of the combined entity must have proportionately equal rights—including the right to sell or retain ownership; the risks and rewards of ownership attach to the shares rather than the owners: hence, the emphasis on the continuing existence of the proportionate share interests.

Under earlier pronouncements, contingent issuances of additional securities were commonplace in poolings. The amount to be issued was based on either future security prices of the acquiring company or future earnings of the acquired company. Since the objective of Opinion No. 16 is to preserve the proportionate interests of all combining stockholders in the future risks and rewards of ownership, contingent issues, which have the effect of altering such proportionate interests in the future, are prohibited, and the Opinion requires that all issues of securities must be fixed before the pooling-of-interests method applies.

Criteria Under Opinion No. 16

The criteria can be summarized into three categories: (1) independence and autonomy of the combining companies or the inherent ability of an entity to combine in a pooling; (2) the manner of effecting the plan, which involves the exchange of common stock as well as protection of corporate equity referred to above; and (3) the absence of planned post-combination transactions that have the effect of negating the exchange of common equity ownership interests. The criteria are discussed in the sequence outlined.

1. Independence and Autonomy of Combining Companies. The parties to a combination may not have significant investments (greater than 10%) in one another nor may they be owned or majority controlled by another corporation prior to entering into the plan of combination. A subsidiary company does not have the requisite independence; the combination of a subsidiary of one company with another company therefore does not meet the pooling criteria. That is considered to be more like the disposition of an asset for stock (from the point of view of the parent of the subsidiary) and the acquisition of an asset for stock (from the point of view of the issuing corporation). The Opinion includes an exception for a combining subsidiary that distributes stock of its parent to effect the combination because that is the same as if the parent effected the combination. An exception is also made for subsidiaries disposed of in compliance with a legal order to do so (usually as a result of antitrust litigation).

2. Manner of Effecting a Combination. The second group of criteria in Opinion No. 16 is concerned with preserving the combining equity interests before and during the time that voting common stock is exchanged between those interests to effect a business combination and with ensuring proportionate sharing of the risks of existing equity ownership.

None of the parties to a pooling of interests may make significant distributions to stockholders in contemplation of effecting the plan of combination (within a two-year period prior to initiation of a plan), if those distributions reduce the net assets and equity of the separate companies or the resultant combined entity. Prohibitions include sales or dispositions of significant portions of assets to third parties or spin-offs of assets or subsidiaries to stockholders; the corporate equities existing at the time of negotiations must be carried into the combined entity through an exchange of voting common stocks. Unless they are, a combination occurs with only a portion of the existing interests, which is not consistent with the concept of sharing of risks and rewards.

The same effect can occur if related business activities have been established in separate corporations owned by the same stockholders and not all are included in a proposed business combination. "Related" in that context has two meanings.

The more obvious meaning pertains to the components of an integrated business: for example, sales, manufacturing, etc. As a practical matter, an entity that is part of an integrated business cannot exist outside the framework of the entire business operation. The use of subsidiaries that function as independent profit centers in large corporations is common; smaller, closely held enterprises are motivated to use multiple corporations for tax or other reasons. A proposed business combination must include all entities in a business operation that are owned by the same stockholders or it must be accounted for as a purchase. The reason is that, unless all entities are included in a combination agreement, certain corporate assets are not brought into the combined entity.

The less obvious meaning of the word "related" refers to the status of the stockholder group. In many closely held company situations, families or individuals own numerous companies in the same or different industries. If entities that operate jointly in the same line of business are owned by "related" stockholders, exclusion of one from a business combination requires purchase accounting; if entities in different lines of business are owned by the same stockholders, exclusion of one does not preclude pooling. However, if entities in different lines of business owned by "related" stockholders are to be combined with another enterprise, the same accounting treatment must apply to all combinations—either they must be accounted for all as poolings or all as purchases. It is not acceptable to account for some entities as poolings and others as purchases.

The issuing corporation may exchange only its voting common stock for substantially all (90% or more) of the voting common stock of a combining company. Alternatively, the issuing corporation may exchange its voting common stock for all the net assets of another entity, with the understanding that the shares issued will ultimately be distributed in liquidation to the stockholders of the combining company. Not only must the exchange of shares be among the respective voting common stocks, but the ownership ratios of individual stockholders (within their own corporation) must not be altered by the exchange. Each individual holder must have the same percentage of ownership interest in the combined entity after the exchange as before. The combination agreement must place no restrictions or limitations on a stockholder's rights to collect dividends, vote shares owned, or (as noted above) dispose of those shares except to the extent that disposition may be precluded by law; for example, by the need for registration with the SEC. Because the underlying theory treats the formerly independent sets of stockholders alike, they must have identical rights, risks, and rewards.

Opinion No. 16 contains certain practical accommodations to recognize current business realities. One is the "substantially all" or 90%

test applied to the acquisition of stock of a combining company, which was adopted because of the difficulty of obtaining unanimous consent to a combination transaction. It gives dissenting stockholders the opportunity to seek available legal remedies and allows for inability to acquire an insignificant number of shares, while remaining consistent with the pooling concept as an exchange of stock.

Another accommodation permits obtaining indemnification provisions from the stockholders of combining companies whose stock is to be acquired. That is often effected (as part of the combination agreement) by placing a percentage of the shares to be issued in escrow. Technically, full and immediate sharing of risks and rewards among stockholder groups is required for pooling. However, escrow agreements for resolution of unknown contingencies or of warranties made by the stockholders of a combining company (other than as to future earnings) may be established to guard against error or misrepresentation of amounts of reported assets and liabilities and to provide a shortcut to legal remedies that exist regardless of the circumstances. Percentage and time limitations on the escrow and contingency provisions are outlined in the AICPA Accounting Interpretations published as a guide to the application of Opinion No. 16.

Flexibility is also allowed in the manner of obtaining the balance of shares once the 90% test has been met but a minority interest remains outstanding. Cash, debt securities, warrants, "tainted" treasury shares (discussed below), or a combination of some or all of those may be used to eliminate the minority interest. The per-share amounts of stock acquired for that purpose may differ from the ratio established for the exchange of shares initially consummated under the plan. There are only two restrictions concerning the elimination of a minority interest. First, no stockholder may dissent with a portion of his stockholdings and agree with another portion, thereby obtaining both stock and other consideration; he may obtain both stock and cash only to adjust fractional stockholdings. Second, elimination of the minority interest must not be part of the plan of combination. An unrelated elimination of a minority interest, however accomplished, must be accounted for under paragraph 43 of the Opinion (paragraph 1091.43 of *AICPA Prof. Stds.*, vol. 3), which prescribes that such acquisition is to be accounted for by the purchase method.

Many enterprises, especially smaller, closely held companies, have more than one class of common stock. Often, the second class of common stock has no vote although it receives identical dividends and is entitled to the same amount on liquidation of the company as the voting common. In other variations, companies have voting preferred, which may or may not be convertible into common stock, and which may have voting control, real or potential, of the company. Opinion No. 16 provides that callable or redeemable senior securities of a combining company may be called or redeemed as part of a pooling; the consideration may be cash, an identical security of the issuing company, or voting common stock of the issuing company. The call or redemption may be by either combining company. That type of transaction is not considered to be an impairment of the equity of the voting common stockholders because it can occur apart from a proposed pooling.

Moreover, the seemingly restrictive language of the Opinion can be interpreted more loosely to mean that senior securities may be eliminated from the capital structure of an acquiring company even if they are not callable or redeemable. A company with senior securities outstanding could undertake a recapitalization involving elimination of the senior securities pursuant to specific corporate action apart from a proposed business combination. Hence, it can be strongly argued that once the criteria are met with respect to the voting common equity, transactions in senior securities have no effect on the ability of a company to qualify for pooling accounting.

That argument can be extended to situations in which two classes of common stock or warrants or options are outstanding. If there are two classes of common stock, one class is usually (although not always) in control; a premium attaches to that class vis-à-vis the second class. Opinion No. 16 prescribes that the exchange of voting common shares must be among those classes of stock that control the respective parties to a combination. Accordingly, the exchange involving the second class of common may be at a different ratio.

Warrants and options of a combining company are claims on the existing equity and may be replaced by similar claims on the equity of the combined company. Although elimination of those claims, by either combining company, may result in changes to common stockholders' equity in apparent violation of the Opinion, a better interpretation is the one described above relating to debt that is neither callable nor redeemable—the elimination is an action that may be accomplished apart from a proposed business combination. The tests of impairment of the voting common stockholders' equity should run only to the voting common stock in control of a corporation. As long as amounts paid to eliminate claims are reasonable and related to the fair value of the respective securities, no violation of the pooling criteria has occurred. However, substance must always take precedence

over form; unrealistic amounts paid to existing stockholders to eliminate claims may be evidence of a part-stock, part-cash transaction, which
should result in using the purchase method.

Critical related provisions of the Opinion specify that for a combination to qualify for the pooling-of-interests method: (1) the exchange
ratio or formula for exchange of common voting stocks must be known
or able to be computed at initiation; (2) consummation of the plan
of combination must occur as a single transaction or plan within one
year of initiation; and (3) the combination must be fully resolved at
consummation, when the exchange of shares takes place. Contingent
issuances of shares (or other consideration) after consummation are not
permitted. On the other hand, a change in the terms of the plan constitutes a new initiation.

An exchange ratio that cannot be calculated depends on future
events and is therefore a prohibited contingency. If consummation is
expected to occur more than one year from initiation, the combination
can no longer be considered a single exchange of stocks between existing interests because remote factors influence the exchange.

There is an important distinction between contingencies related
to the financial position of a combining company at the date of consummation, which do not preclude use of pooling accounting, and
contingencies related to the occurrence of future events. Contingencies of the latter type are based on events after consummation and
may cause a large proportion of the shares issued to be contingent.
Those of the former type, in contrast, usually involve only a small fraction of the shares issued in a combination and are based on the need to
correct the exchange ratio to reflect more precise determination of
financial position at the date of consummation. For example, although
final determination of the status of a contested tax liability or warranty
provision may not occur until a date subsequent to consummation,
final resolution of the amount of the liability is indicative of the status
of the item at consummation and does not in any way affect or depend
on future reported income or future changes in security prices.

One kind of future event payout arrangement that does not
violate the pooling criteria is an agreement for reasonable compensation benefits to former stockholders of a combining company who become employees of the combined entity. Thus, if stockholders who
receive stock in a business combination are also employees of a combining company, reasonable adjustments to compensation levels paid
to similar employees by the issuing company are appropriate. So is
including those employee–stockholders in bonus or executive compen-

sation plans. On the other hand, stock options or bonus arrangements with nonemployee–stockholders based on future sales or profitability are contingent earnouts that preclude pooling. In all those situations, as in analyzing each section of the Opinion and relating a particular combination agreement thereto, care must be taken to determine that a subterfuge has not been created; the substance of every transaction must rule over its form.

Since it is possible to change an apparent exchange of stock into an effective cash acquisition by purchasing treasury stock in advance of the exchange, Opinion No. 16 restricts the reacquisition of stock by combining companies prior to a pooling. The Opinion permits treasury stock acquisition only for purposes other than business combinations. The test prescribed in the Opinion focuses on a "normal" or systematic pattern of purchases within the two-year period preceding initiation and between initiation and consummation. Accounting Series Release No. 146, issued by the SEC in 1974, sets strict guidelines for interpreting this rule.

Stock acquired during those periods in excess of that needed for reissuances is considered "tainted." The taint attaching to the stock may be removed if the shares are sold or reissued for valid consideration in a transaction other than a business combination to be accounted for as a pooling. If the "tainted" shares plus other restricted consideration exceed 10% of the number of shares to be issued in a business combination, pooling accounting is precluded. The 10% limit is part of the requirement, noted above, that no more than 10% of the voting common stock of a combining company may be obtained for other than voting common stock of the issuer; allowable treasury stock is diminished to the extent that other than voting common stock is issued for a combining company's voting common stock. There is only one 10% test, and it must be met in total, not separately for each kind of consideration used.

3. Absence of Negating Future Transactions. The third and final category of substantive compliance with the criteria in the Opinion relates to the absence, after consummation, of transactions that in effect negate the exchange of common equity ownership interests. For example, the issuing company may not tacitly or directly agree with stockholders of a combining company to convert shares into cash, either by repurchase from the stockholders or by guarantee of loans secured by the shares. Arrangements of that kind convert an exchange of shares among stockholder groups into the purchase of one company by another.

Under Opinion No. 16, the right to sell an asset is an inherent right of ownership and immediate sale of stock (to persons other than the corporations involved) after consummation of a pooling does not violate the pooling. The intent of those provisions is to allow for changes in circumstances of stockholders, who may number in the many thousands.

The Securities and Exchange Commission, however, in Accounting Series Releases No. 130 and 135, has reverted somewhat to its previous position that continuity of ownership, at least for a period until combined operations can be reported to the public, is necessary in poolings of public companies. The basis for the SEC's position is that an immediate sale of a substantial portion of stock received in a business combination is in substance the sale of stock by the issuing company followed by the purchase of the combining company. According to that logic, immediate disposition of shares received by stockholders in a business combination negates the sharing of risks and rewards of ownership by one group of stockholders, and pooling accounting is inappropriate. Nothing in Opinion No. 16 or the related Interpretations prohibits an issuing company from registering the shares issued with the SEC for public sale or listing the shares on an exchange, as long as the basic criterion concerning absence of arrangements negating the exchange of equity securities is met.

Applying the Criteria

Opinion No. 16 and the Accounting Interpretations supporting it prescribe that the pooling criteria are to be evaluated at two points in time—at initiation (which is rather rigorously defined, depending on the form of transaction) and at consummation. The more important date is consummation, that is, the date shares are exchanged. If the combination is to be accounted for by the pooling-of-interests method, certain types of transactions are prohibited between initiation and consummation and certain tests must be met at the exchange date. Use of the pooling method is precluded if:

Consummation occurs more than one year from initiation, even though a shorter time was anticipated at initiation, unless legal or regulatory authorities have intervened;

"Tainted" shares (unreserved treasury stock in excess of 10% of the shares to be issued in the combination) are on hand at consummation;

There are plans to dispose of significant assets after consummation of the combination; or

A substantial percentage of the shares issued is to be placed in escrow in the absence of specifically unresolved contingent liabilities or uncertainties.

Other examples could be noted, but the implications of those cited lead to one conclusion: a transaction planned as a pooling may be converted to purchase accounting and vice versa. Careful planning and monitoring of planned business combinations is necessary to obtain the desired result.

"Pooling Letter"

The New York Stock Exchange requires auditors for each company listed on the Exchange to attach to the listing application for the shares to be issued a "pooling letter" that gives explicit approval to the treatment of the business combination as a pooling. Although that procedure is not applicable to companies not listed on the NYSE, it points out the importance of a careful review of the criteria for a pooling before the transaction is consummated.

Accounting for Expenses of Poolings

Opinion No. 16 changed previous practice with respect to expenditures related to pooling transactions. Formerly, they were considered to be costs of issuing common stock rather than operating expenses. Paragraph 58 of Opinion No. 16 (paragraph 1091.58 of *AICPA Prof. Stds.*, vol. 3) provides specifically that those costs are to be charged to expenses in determining the combined net income of the period of combination.

Transition

Certain transitional provisions of Opinion No. 16 apply to situations that existed at October 31, 1970, and had to be resolved prior to October 31, 1975. Under those provisions, part-pooling, part-purchase accounting, which had grown up under prior pronouncements as an attempt to account for exchange offers that consisted partly of common stock and partly of other consideration, was retained until October 31, 1975, for companies meeting certain criteria. Part-pooling, part-purchase accounting is prohibited with the expiration of those provisions.

PURCHASE METHOD

Since the pooling-of-interests and purchase methods are mutually exclusive, a business combination that does not meet the specifically defined pooling criteria is automatically accounted for as a purchase. Regardless of the form of a purchase transaction, there are generally two sets of somewhat related problems in purchase accounting—determining the total cost of an acquired company and determining the portions of that cost to be allocated to assets acquired and liabilities assumed.

Determining Cost of an Acquired Company

Total cost of an acquired company is clear if the consideration exchanged is cash. Determining total cost is more difficult if other consideration is used, liabilities are incurred, or various equity or debt securities are issued. The general principles for recording an acquired company are the same as those for recording the acquisition of assets generally. They are summarized in Opinion No. 16 (*AICPA Prof. Stds.*, vol. 3, paragraph 1091.67) and Chapter 12 of this book. Briefly, an acquired company is recorded at cost. Cost in acquisitions for other than cash may for practical reasons " 'be determined either by the fair value of the consideration given or by the fair value of the property acquired, whichever is the more clearly evident' " (paragraph 1091.67). APB Opinion No. 29, *Accounting for Nonmonetary Transactions* (*AICPA Prof. Stds.*, vol. 3, Section 1041), provides additional discussion and information about applying the "fair value" principle, even though that Opinion is not directed toward business combinations.

If an acquisition is consummated by issuing stock of the acquiring corporation, the stock should be recorded at the fair value of the consideration received for it. That measurement is often difficult, however, when private companies are acquired. If the acquiring company is a public company whose shares trade freely and are widely quoted, it is far easier to establish value for the stock issued by the public company than for the assets of a closely held company. Accordingly, in that situation, total cost is usually determined by the market quotations of the stock issued. Value at market quotations may be adjusted to fair value by considering factors such as size of block of stock issued, volatility of the market, and other variables. If a closely held company acquires a public company, as sometimes occurs, determining cost can be extremely difficult, and the Opinion gives only limited guidance.

"Downstream Mergers"

Infrequently, but often enough to create accounting problems and confusion, a "downstream merger" or "upstream acquisition" occurs: that is, the corporation that issues securities (the ostensible acquirer) is actually the company being acquired because the company ostensibly being acquired is larger and its stockholders and management will control the resulting combined entity. The transaction is usually structured in that way either to retain tax benefits of net operating loss carry-forwards of the surviving corporate entity (or other tax reasons), which might be lost if the transaction were to follow the more conventional form, or to provide stockholders of a closely held company with an avenue to public ownership. Paragraph 70 of Opinion No. 16 (paragraph 1091.70 of *AICPA Prof. Stds.,* vol. 3) states the controlling accounting principle:

> . . . The Board concludes that presumptive evidence of the acquiring corporation in combinations effected by an exchange of stock is obtained by identifying the former common stockholder interests of a combining company which either retain or receive the larger portion of the voting rights in the combined corporation. That corporation should be treated as the acquirer unless other evidence clearly indicates that another corporation is the acquirer.

That is, substance prevails over form, and in a "downstream merger" it is the assets of the ostensible acquirer which must be revalued as the ones purchased.

Contingent Consideration

Problems may arise in accounting for contingent consideration in a business combination treated as a purchase. As already noted, a combination in which some elements of the transaction remain unresolved when shares are exchanged between the parties (except for escrow arrangements to provide for certain contingencies) must be accounted for as a purchase.

In the interest of making the best financial arrangements, companies have often delayed the measurement and payment of the total purchase price of an acquired company. The resulting contingency agreements can be reduced for accounting purposes to two types: those based on future earnings of the acquired company and those based on future security prices of the acquiring company.

In the former, significant uncertainty about the total purchase price exists at the date of acquisition. There is no assurance that the acquired company will attain or maintain specified levels of earnings (for purposes of "earning out" the additional consideration) during the contingency period. Accordingly, recording the additional consideration is inappropriate until it is determinable. That adjustment of cost of the acquired company is a change in estimate, which under APB Opinion No. 20 (*AICPA Prof. Stds.,* vol. 3, Sections 1051 to 1051B) is accounted for currently and prospectively rather than retroactively.

In the type of contingency agreement based on future security prices of the acquiring company, the distribution of additional cash or securities results in no change in total purchase cost from that recorded at consummation. The maximum anticipated consideration can be determined from the terms of the combination agreement; subsequent issuances do not change the acquisition price because they are based on the assumption that the value of the acquiring company's securities has not reached (or remained at) the level anticipated when the transaction was originally consummated. An example emphasizes the point:

A combination agreement stipulates the issue of 100,000 shares of common stock at a time when the value of a share is $10. It also provides that additional stock must be issued if the value of a share is not at least $20 in three years. Cost of the acquisition recorded at consummation is $2 million, not $1 million. If the market value of the stock is $16 at the end of three years, 25,000 additional shares will be issued to the sellers and recorded at $16 a share, or $400,000. At the same time, the recorded amount of the 100,000 shares already issued will be reduced from $20 to $16 a share; the total cost remains $2 million.

The distinction between a purchase and a pooling of interests is sharpest in the area of contingent consideration. Obviously, in the example described above, the selling stockholders of the acquired company are protected for three years from certain risks in holding common stock of the issuing company. There is no proportionate sharing of risks, a key requirement for use of the pooling-of-interests method.

We point out in the discussion of earnings per share (Chapter 18) that various types of contingent issues of stock must be recognized in computing both primary and fully diluted earnings per share. The EPS effects of contemplated purchases involving the potential issue of common stock or securities convertible into common stock should be carefully considered. Transactions may be structured so that the purchaser or seller may have the option of issuing or receiving additional consideration in shares or in cash. The conditions of an agreement and the provisions of APB Opinion No. 15, *Earnings Per Share (AICPA Prof. Stds.,* vol. 3, Sections 2011 to 2011D), dictate the appropriate computation.

Allocating Cost of an Acquired Company

After total cost has been determined, it must be allocated among the various assets acquired, liabilities assumed, and senior equity securities, if any, of the acquired company that remain outstanding. The general procedure is to assign a fair value to all specific tangible and identifiable intangible assets, a present value to liabilities assumed based on their respective terms, and an appropriate value to senior equity securities that remain outstanding. The excess of the fair values of assets acquired over liabilities assumed and senior equity securities is then deducted from the purchase price of the acquired company to determine an anomalous accounting item which is commonly called "goodwill."

General Principles

Paragraph 88 of Opinion No. 16 (paragraph 1091.88 of *AICPA Prof. Stds.*, vol. 3) details and formalizes valuation techniques for individual items. The paragraph applies to all business combinations accounted for by the purchase method, and the general principle of stating all assets acquired and liabilities assumed at fair value should be presumed to apply to all purchase transactions. Fair value is, of course, a difficult term to define or describe because its accurate application to each classification of assets and liabilities depends partly on the nature of the item. The principles stated in the paragraph are not new, but some of them have not been used frequently. The paragraph is quoted in its entirety:

> General guides for assigning amounts to the individual assets acquired and liabilities assumed, except goodwill, are:
> a. Marketable securities at current net realizable values.
> b. Receivables at present values of amounts to be received determined at appropriate current interest rates, less allowances for uncollectibility and collection costs, if necessary.
> c. Inventories:
>   (1) Finished goods and merchandise at estimated selling prices less the sum of (a) costs of disposal and (b) a reasonable profit allowance for the selling effort of the acquiring corporation.
>   (2) Work in process at estimated selling prices of finished goods less the sum of (a) costs to complete, (b) costs of disposal, and (c) a reasonable profit allowance for the completing and selling effort of the acquiring corporation based on profit for similar finished goods.
>   (3) Raw materials at current replacement costs.
> d. Plant and equipment: (1) to be used, at current replacement costs for similar capacity [12] unless the expected future use of the assets indicates a lower value to the acquirer, (2) to be sold or held for later sale rather than used, at current net realizable value, and (3) to be used temporarily, at current net realizable value recognizing future depreciation for the expected period of use.

---

[12] Replacement cost may be determined directly if a used asset market exists for the assets acquired. Otherwise, the replacement cost should be approximated from replacement cost new less estimated accumulated depreciation.

e. Intangible assets which can be identified and named, including contracts, patents, franchises, customer and supplier lists, and favorable leases, at appraised values.[13]

f. Other assets, including land, natural resources, and nonmarketable securities, at appraised values.

g. Accounts and notes payable, long-term debt, and other claims payable at present values of amounts to be paid determined at appropriate current interest rates.

h. Liabilities and accruals—for example, accruals for pension cost,[14] warranties, vacation pay, deferred compensation—at present values of amounts to be paid determined at appropriate current interest rates.

i. Other liabilities and commitments, including unfavorable leases, contracts, and commitments and plant closing expense incident to the acquisition, at present values of amounts to be paid determined at appropriate current interest rates.

An [acquiring] corporation should record periodically as a part of income the accrual of interest on assets and liabilities recorded at acquisition date at the discounted values of amounts to be received or paid. An acquiring corporation should not record as a separate asset the goodwill previously recorded by an acquired company and should not record deferred income taxes recorded by an acquired company before its acquisition. An acquiring corporation should reduce the acquired goodwill retroactively for the realized tax benefits of loss carry-forwards of an acquired company not previously recorded by the acquiring corporation.

[13] Fair values should be ascribed to specific assets; identifiable assets should not be included in goodwill.

[14] An accrual for pension cost should be the greater of (1) accrued pension cost computed in conformity with the accounting policies of the acquiring corporation for one or more of its pension plans or (2) the excess, if any, of the actuarially computed value of vested benefits over the amount of the pension fund.

APB Opinion No. 21 (*AICPA Prof. Stds.*, vol. 3, Sections 4111 and 4111A) provides guidance on discounting receivables and payables. Inventories may present special problems, especially if the acquired company has been using LIFO. Determining fair values of plant and equipment is a complex and specialized task, and the results are difficult for auditors to evaluate because evidence supporting the values is usually much more judgmental than that supporting values of receivables or inventories. Often for plant and equipment, and sometimes for inventories, professional appraisals may be necessary.

Valuation of liabilities is usually simpler than valuation of assets because amounts to be paid are fixed and recorded. The major problem is choice of an appropriate interest rate to decide whether a discount or premium should be considered, a matter discussed in APB Opinion No. 21. Senior equity securities remaining outstanding should be valued as if they had been issued at the time of the combination. Deferred credits and provisions for future expenses must be estimated following the principles described for those items in Chapters 9 and 10.

Auditors must carefully test the evidence used to support values assigned to assets and liabilities of an acquired company. Appraisal values of intangible assets especially should be closely scrutinized. Customer lists, favorable leases, franchises, and the like may have an intrinsic value to an ongoing enterprise that is extremely difficult to appraise adequately apart from that enterprise. Industry experience may have led to certain off-the-cuff valuation techniques, which do not necessarily suffice to support fair values for financial statement presentation.

Tax Consequences

The last sentence of paragraph 87 of Opinion No. 16 (paragraph 1091.87 of *AICPA Prof. Stds.*, vol. 3) contains a concept that was not unknown but was seldom applied to accounting for business combinations before the Opinion was issued: "The effect of taxes may be a factor in assigning amounts to identifiable assets and liabilities (paragraph 89)." Paragraph 89 (paragraph 1091.89) elaborates:

> The market or appraisal values of specific assets and liabilities . . . may differ from the income tax bases of those items. Estimated future tax effects of differences between the tax bases and amounts otherwise appropriate to assign to an asset or a liability are one of the variables in estimating fair value. Amounts assigned to identifiable assets and liabilities should, for example, recognize that the fair value of an asset to an acquirer is less than its market or appraisal value if all or a portion of the market or appraisal value is not deductible for income taxes. The impact of tax effects on amounts assigned to individual assets and liabilities depends on numerous factors, including imminence or delay of realization of the asset value and the possible timing of tax consequences. Since differences between amounts assigned and tax bases are not timing differences (section 4091.12), the acquiring corporation should not record deferred tax accounts at the date of acquisition.

Despite its seemingly permissive and inconsequential tone, the foregoing applies to virtually all business combinations accounted for by the purchase method, whether a transaction is taxable or tax-free under the Internal Revenue Code. If a transaction is taxable (for example, payment of cash for stock or assets), the valuation techniques prescribed in Opinion No. 16 and the tax laws and regulations result in assigning differing amounts to the various assets (including goodwill) for tax and accounting purposes, even though total cost is the same. The IRS prescribes a proportionate allocation of cost to all acquired assets, including goodwill; Opinion No. 16 requires that valuation procedures be applied to various assets and liabilities, with goodwill as the difference between the sum of those allocations and the purchase price. Applying paragraph 89 to tax-free purchases magnifies the problem.

If a purchase is a tax-free reorganization, the tax bases of the assets and liabilities of the acquired company carry into the consolidated enterprise, while new valuations are assigned for financial reporting purposes. The respective accounting valuations may be higher or lower than the tax bases. To reflect the liability for taxes in income properly, such valuations for accounting purposes should be adjusted by the tax effect of the difference in bases for accounting and tax purposes. Those adjustments necessarily affect the measure of goodwill.

The tax effect should be computed at the statutory rate at the date of acquisition, not at the corporation's effective tax rate, which may differ because of permanent differences such as the excess of percentage depletion over cost depletion. In addition, the tax rate adopted should not be the rate expected to be in effect in the future when the affected items will be amortized to income.

Paragraph 89 prescribes a net-of-tax procedure for valuing assets and liabilities which appears to be contrary to APB Opinion No. 11 (*AICPA Prof. Stds.*, vol. 3, Sections 4091 and 4091A), discussed in Chapter 13. The paragraph states in explanation that an acquisition does not give rise to "timing differences." Accordingly, no deferred taxes are recorded at consummation of an acquisition, and the tax effects that appear similar to those of timing differences in other circumstances are merely variables in determining the appropriate carrying values. The tax effect is therefore properly offset against or added to the assigned amounts of assets and liabilities to determine their fair values for purposes of allocating the cost of an acquired company. As the assets "expire" and are charged to expense, or as the liabilities are discharged, the tax effects of related taxable income or deductions are accounted for in those periods as "permanent differences."

Goodwill

Goodwill has traditionally represented excess earning power—earning power in excess of that attributable to individual recorded net assets. It was formerly computed as the excess of the purchase price of an acquired company over the book value of its net assets as recorded in the accounts immediately before acquisition. Goodwill acquired could therefore be described as internally generated excess earning ability that under generally accepted accounting principles was not (and still is not) recorded in the financial statements before being measured in the purchase and sale transaction represented by the acquisition.

AICPA pronouncements, including Chapter 5 of ARB No. 43 (1953) and ARB No. 51 (1959) in addition to Opinion No. 16, currently require recording specifically identifiable assets and liabilities at fair values at the time of acquisition. Opinion No. 16 prescribes that goodwill be computed by deducting those fair values from the purchase price of the acquired company; thus goodwill is a remainder. It represents the earning ability of unidentifiable (intangible) assets, whose presence is inferred from an excess of cost over the net value of identifiable assets and liabilities involved.

Goodwill, along with other intangible assets, has traditionally been a suspect asset. Many years ago, it was generally written off to stockholders' equity immediately or at least amortized rather rapidly.

More recently, ARB No. 24 (1944) discouraged immediate write-off of goodwill and similar intangibles, especially to additional paid-in capital, and Chapter 5 of ARB No. 43, paragraph 9, held that "Lumpsum write-offs of intangibles should not be made to earned surplus [retained earnings] immediately after acquisition, nor should intangibles be charged against capital surplus [additional paid-in capital]." APB Opinion No. 9 (1966; *AICPA Prof. Stds.*, vol. 3, Section 2010) prohibited direct write-offs of assets to retained earnings. Long before Opinion No. 16, the practice of writing off goodwill had diminished and then almost completely disappeared except for a few items of goodwill that had lost their value and were treated as extraordinary items. Moreover, since amortization of goodwill was optional unless a determinate life became apparent, substantial amounts of goodwill recorded in acquisitions were carried forward at cost.

Presently, Opinion No. 17, *Intangible Assets (AICPA Prof. Stds.*, vol. 3, Section 5141), issued as a companion to Opinion No. 16, requires that goodwill be amortized over not more than forty years from acquisition. Impaired value of acquired goodwill should still be recognized by write-down or write-off. The major change instituted by the Opinion was to require that amortization commence at acquisition for all goodwill acquired after October 31, 1970; goodwill acquired before that date need not be automatically amortized. The reasoning of the Opinion can be summarized easily: no asset lasts forever, the useful life of goodwill is usually indeterminate, and forty years is a reasonable maximum arbitrary period for amortizing costs of intangible assets whose useful lives cannot be otherwise estimated.

Negative Goodwill

The cost of an acquired company may, of course, be less than the fair value of its assets less liabilities—so-called "negative goodwill."

Before Opinion No. 16, an excess of net fair value or net book value of assets acquired over cost was usually amortized to income over a relatively short period or treated as an estimated allowance for expected losses of an acquired operation, to be offset against losses as they occurred. Before ARB No. 51 accepted that accounting (and particularly before it became general practice to use fair values instead of book values), the excess was often recorded as additional paid-in capital.

Paragraph 87 of Opinion No. 16 (paragraph 1091.87 of *AICPA Prof. Stds.,* vol. 3) now specifies the accounting for negative goodwill:

> . . . The sum of the market or appraisal values of identifiable assets acquired less liabilities assumed may sometimes exceed the cost of the acquired company. If so, the values otherwise assignable to noncurrent assets acquired (except long-term investments in marketable securities) should be reduced by a proportionate part of the excess to determine the assigned values. A deferred credit for an excess of assigned value of identifiable assets over cost of an acquired company (sometimes called "negative goodwill") should not be recorded unless those assets are reduced to zero value.

Since the Opinion effectively requires that the excess of fair value of assets acquired over cost be allocated to costs of noncurrent assets (other than investments in marketable securities), it is in effect amortized to income over the lives of those assets. To the extent that a portion of the excess is allocated to land on which production facilities have been constructed, it may be reflected in income only at some remote future time—if the property is sold—because the cost of the land is not amortized. If all noncurrent assets acquired are written down to zero, a remaining excess should be shown on the balance sheet between long-term debt and stockholders' equity and amortized to income as prescribed by Opinion No. 17.

The procedures described earlier under "Tax Consequences" also apply when the fair value of net assets acquired exceeds the cost of the acquired company. Practically, the adjustment of carrying values for tax effects must be made before the amount of the excess can be determined for offset against the costs of noncurrent assets as prescribed in paragraph 87.

Revaluing Accounts When Stock Changes Hands

The development of new financing approaches, as described in Chapter 16, has created new accounting problems. Among the new approaches is the practice of a company's selling to the public a portion of the common stock of a wholly owned subsidiary, usually at a price in excess of the book value of the stock. The question of whether the transaction should be treated as a type of financing, rather than a sale and recognition of a gain, was noted in Chapter 16. A closely related question is whether the transaction gives rise to goodwill in the accounts of the subsidiary.

Traditionally, a company was acquired and thereafter retained forever, sold as a unit to a third party, or liquidated. Goodwill was assumed to be an asset solely of the acquiring or parent company. Financial statements of the acquired company were on a separate company basis and remained the same (on its books) as before the acquisition. Revaluation of the assets acquired and determination of the parent's portion of goodwill arose only in consolidation and goodwill was recorded in a consolidating entry reflecting that the parent's investment in the acquired company exceeded the reported net book value of the company. When the subsidiary was sold, the goodwill disappeared from the consolidated balance sheet along with the net assets of the subsidiary, and gain or loss thereon was computed and recorded. The theoretical problems of minority interests in goodwill were ignored.

Those problems cannot be ignored if an interest in a subsidiary is sold in a public offering or for any other reason the subsidiary is required to present separate financial statements. It is impossible to ignore the fact that a transaction has taken place, establishing a new basis of accountability, whenever a business is sold or acquired in an arm's-length transaction, even though nothing has occurred within the entity itself to warrant a new basis of accountability. The occurrence of a sale and purchase, rather than internal changes or lack of them, must be the basis for recording changes in cost. The abrupt revaluation of assets, of course, affects comparability of the net income stream of the acquired entity, but it is preferable to ignoring the accounting result of changed ownership.

The principle of recording asset values and goodwill in the accounts of a company to reflect the purchase of its stock by another entity or group of stockholders has been called the "push-down" theory. At present, the question of how far it should be carried is unanswered. In 1973 the SEC proposed and then withdrew a rule that revaluation should be required whenever 50% or more of a company's stock changes hands in a single transaction. Until all of the ramifications of the push-down theory are fully explored, we would prefer to see its implementation limited to 100% (or nearly 100%—the pooling theory's 90% would be a good precedent) transactions.

Financial Statement Disclosure of a Purchase

A note to the financial statements for the period in which a purchase occurs should disclose that fact and also the pro forma revenue, income before extraordinary items, net income, and earnings per share as though the companies had been combined in the current and preceding periods. That disclosure may require recomputing such items as depreciation and amortization, interest expense, and income taxes on a pro forma basis [Opinion No. 16, paragraphs 95 and 96 (*AICPA Prof. Stds.,* vol. 3, paragraphs 1091.95 and .96)]. In addition, the SEC has asked for disclosure of the acquired company's contribution to earnings in the period of acquisition and the subsequent period.

• CONSOLIDATED FINANCIAL STATEMENTS

INTRODUCTION

Authoritative pronouncements covering consolidated financial statements include Accounting Research Bulletin No. 51, *Consolidated Financial Statements (AICPA Prof. Stds.,* vol. 3, Section 2051), issued in 1959, and Accounting Principles Board Opinion No. 18 (Section 5131), issued in 1971. Opinion No. 18 superseded certain paragraphs in Opinion No. 10, which was issued in 1966 and had provided some guidelines for the adoption of the equity method of accounting for unconsolidated subsidiaries. Certain problems relating to foreign subsidiaries are covered in ARB No. 43, Chapter 12 (Section 1081). The SEC has supplemented the AICPA's authoritative pronouncements with its own consolidation requirements for registrants in Regulation S-X. This section draws on all those sources.

The basic principles underlying the preparation of consolidated financial statements are the same whether a corporation forms subsidiaries, acquires them in business combinations accounted for as purchases, or unites with other enterprises in business combinations accounted for as poolings of interests.

Although consolidated statements seldom reflect legal realities, they reflect economic realities better than separate financial statements in this day of complex business enterprises. ARB No. 51 (*AICPA Prof. Stds.,* vol. 3, paragraph 2051.02) contains a "presumption that consolidated statements are more meaningful than separate statements and that they are usually necessary for a fair presentation when one of the companies in the group directly or indirectly has a controlling financial interest in the other companies." APB Opinion No. 18, though a pronouncement on the equity method, probably encourages consolidation of subsidiaries, since often subsidiaries required by the Opinion to be accounted for by the equity method can as easily be consolidated. For example, paragraph 14 of Opinion No. 18 (paragraph 5131.14 of *AICPA Prof. Stds.,* vol. 3) gives consolidation a significant boost:

The Board reaffirms the conclusion that investors should account for investments in common stock of unconsolidated domestic subsidiaries by the equity method in consolidated financial statements, and the Board now extends this conclusion to investments in common stock of all unconsolidated subsidiaries (foreign as well as domestic) in consolidated financial statements. The equity method is not, however, a valid substitute for consolidation and should not be used to justify exclusion of a subsidiary when consolidation is otherwise appropriate.

The pronouncements of the AICPA and Regulation S-X presume an order of desirability of presentation of the operations and financial position of a parent and its subsidiaries: consolidation of all subsidiaries is generally desirable; controlled companies not consolidated should be accounted for on the equity method; the cost method should be used only on the basis of strong justification.

CONSOLIDATION POLICY

The essential test for consolidation of a subsidiary is control. ARB No. 51 (*AICPA Prof. Stds.*, vol. 3, paragraph 2051.03) defines control as ". . . ownership by one company, directly or indirectly, of over fifty per cent of the outstanding voting shares of another company. . . ." The SEC, in Regulation S-X, Rule 1-02(g), extends the definition to ". . . the possession, direct or indirect, of the power to direct or cause the direction of the management and policies of a person, whether through the ownership of voting shares, by contract, or otherwise." The number of situations in which control is exercised with ownership of less than 50% of the shares, or in which control is absent with ownership of more than 50%, can be expected to be small.

Opinion No. 18 prescribes the equity method for investees that are less than 50% owned but over which the investor is presumed to exercise significant influence. The presumption of significant influence begins at a holding of 20% (Chapter 14). Under the equity method, an investor's interest in an investee's operating results is included in the investor's net income. It is presented on one line rather than in the various accounts of the investor.

It should be noted that the concepts of "control" and "ability to exercise significant influence" are quite different; in general, use of consolidation versus the equity method should follow accordingly. However, that distinction does not definitely answer the accounting question of whether to consolidate—some controlled investments are not consolidated but are instead accounted for by the equity method.

The decision of which subsidiaries to consolidate and which to account for by the equity method is often not at all clear-cut. Authoritative pronouncements leave room for differences of opinion and exercise of judgment. Some trends are quite clear, but significant disagreements remain, as the following examples show.

Foreign subsidiaries operating in countries having no exchange restrictions, which previously could be excluded from consolidation simply because they were foreign, should now be consolidated. Real estate and certain financing subsidiaries, which may have large amounts of debt and high debt/equity ratios, should be consolidated if their operations support the consolidated group's primary operations; those "whose principal business activity is leasing property or facilities to parent or other affiliated companies" [APB Opinion No. 18, paragraph 15 (*AICPA Prof. Stds.,* vol. 3, paragraph 5131.15)] must be consolidated.

Subsidiaries in lines of business different from the major activities of the consolidated group (such as a credit and financial operating subsidiary that provides services and generates revenue on a basis substantially different from the parent company and its integrated manufacturing operations) may be excluded from consolidation but should be accounted for by the equity method. Some accountants argue that a credit subsidiary is an integral part of its parent's business of manufacturing, wholesaling to dealers, and retailing to ultimate consumers and therefore that its operations should be fully consolidated with all others of the group; this is not general practice.

The SEC's Rule 4-02 of Regulation S-X states that "the registrant shall follow in the consolidated financial statements principles of inclusion or exclusion which will clearly exhibit the financial position and results of operations of the registrant and its subsidiaries . . . ," thus invoking the profession's generally accepted accounting principles, including ARB No. 51 and APB Opinion No. 18. However, the SEC still requires separate financial statements for subsidiaries engaged in certain financial activities, as specified in Rule 4-02(e).

If conditions make it appear impossible or improper either to consolidate a controlled corporation or to use the equity method to account for an investment of 20% or more of voting stock, those conditions must raise substantial doubt about recoverability of the investment as well as the degree of control. Those investments usually should be carried at cost and should be evaluated to determine whether the prospects for recoverability warrant retaining the cost or reducing it to a lesser amount or to zero.

CONSOLIDATION PROCEDURES AND PROBLEMS

The procedures for preparing consolidated financial statements, including the appropriate elimination of intercompany balances, transactions, and profits, are generally well known and understood. However, certain unusual transactions do arise from time to time that deserve some comment.

Piecemeal Acquisition

Sometimes acquisitions occur in steps; that is, ownership of a subsidiary is obtained over a period by acquisitions of shares at various dates in separate transactions. By definition, a subsidiary acquired that way must be accounted for by the purchase method. Determining equity in net assets and income allocable to the investor while the shares held constitute a minority interest presents some problems. Before APB Opinion No. 18, acceptable practice was to include earnings related to shares previously owned in income when control was obtained, either on a pro rata basis related to dates of acquisition of the shares or as if all the stock had been acquired in a single purchase at the time control was obtained.

That is no longer possible under Opinion No. 18, which changes the key date to the time an investor obtains an interest—usually 20% of the voting stock—that permits exercise of significant influence over the policies and decisions of the investee. An investor's share of investee income related to stock acquired before significant influence can be exercised may still be recorded either pro rata or as if all the stock were acquired at the time significant influence was obtained. Thereafter, however, each acquisition must be accounted for separately. That is necessary for several reasons: to eliminate profits on transactions between investor and investee; to amortize goodwill and other costs in excess of book value arising from the purchase of shares of the investee; and [under APB Opinion No. 24 (*AICPA Prof. Stds.*, vol. 3, Section 4096)] to record deferred taxes, as appropriate, on income of the investee. In other words, the so-called step-by-step method must be used in the period between "significant influence" and "control."

Theoretically, the "push-down" principle described above raises the question of when in the course of a piecemeal acquisition the assets and liabilities of the subsidiary should be revalued to reflect current fair values. In practice, revaluation is seldom attempted until control is obtained (and sometimes not then—see page 699); until then, the excess of cost of shares acquired over the equity of those shares in the book value of underlying net assets is amortized against the investor's recorded equity in income or loss of the investee. That practical short-cut seldom results in a material distortion of income. It is inconvenient and sometimes difficult to determine the necessary figures for each purchase of shares and then to disentangle the investor–investee accounting when control is achieved, but that accounting, or a reasonable approximation, is required.

Changes in Parent's Interest in Subsidiary

As already noted in this chapter, sale by a parent of a portion of a subsidiary company's stock to third parties and issue by a subsidiary of previously unissued shares to persons outside the consolidated group are increasingly common financing devices. Both types of financing result, one directly and the other indirectly, in a reduction in the parent's percentage of ownership. Although the substance of the two transactions appears similar on the surface, accounting for them in consolidated financial statements has diverged.

If a parent sells stock of a subsidiary, the net assets of the subsidiary remain unchanged. The parent merely relieves the investment account of the carrying amount of the shares sold and records a gain or loss on the sale. Thereafter, an increased share of investee income will be attributed to minority interests in future consolidated income statements. If the subsidiary issues additional stock, the parent disposes of nothing, but the net assets of the subsidiary increase, and the parent's share of them may increase or decrease, depending on the relationship among the per-share price of the stock issued, the existing per-share book value of the subsidiary, and the percentage of ownership reduction. Usually, the parent has a reduced percentage of ownership in a proportionately greater dollar net equity, resulting in an increase in the underlying equity and therefore the carrying value of the investment in the subsidiary.

That increase (or decrease) requires adjustment of the relative interests of the parent company and the minority stockholders when the subsidiary's assets are carried into the consolidation. Some have argued that the parent might record a gain or loss to reflect the change in carrying value of its investment in the subsidiary, but in practice the transaction is reflected as a direct charge or credit to stockholders' equity, usually additional paid-in capital. The SEC has insisted that credits resulting from a subsidiary's issue of its shares to outsiders must be excluded from income. Depending on the original purchase price, whether goodwill resulted at the time of acquisition, the parent's percentage of ownership reduction, and related factors, the mechanical computations for that kind of transaction can become quite complex. In our opinion, different accounting treatment for transactions that differ in form but not in substance appears anomalous. It is to be hoped that the profession will undertake to clarify that and related issues—such as the "push-down" theory—at an early date.

A similar and related problem, for which the computations can also be complex, involves the transfer of assets or common stock of partially owned subsidiaries among one another or between parent and subsidiary, resulting in an increase or decrease in the parent company's percentage of ownership. Those transactions cause not only computational difficulties in preparing consolidated financial statements but also the substantive problem of determining whether a partial acquisition of a minority interest has occurred, which is a purchase transaction, or merely a reallocation of existing ownership interests within a consolidated group [paragraph 43 of APB Opinion No. 16 (paragraph 1091.43 of *AICPA Prof. Stds.,* vol. 3) and Accounting Interpretations No. 26 and 39 thereto (Sections U 1091.099 and .151)].

Minority Interests

Two related problems concern minority interests in a subsidiary included in consolidated financial statements. One is the valuation of the minority interests; the second is the inclusion in the minority interests of senior equity securities of the subsidiary not owned by the parent company. Both problems may exist apart from a business combination, but both are often initially met as a result of a business combination.

One of the conditions for accounting for a business combination by the pooling-of-interests method is that an outstanding minority interest in a combining company's voting common stock cannot be greater than 10%. Since the net assets are brought into the combined entity's financial statements at their existing book value, the minority interest in the voting common stock is the proportionate share of the acquired company's net assets at previous book value. To the extent that senior equity securities of the subsidiary company remain outstanding after a pooling, they too are included in the minority interest at their previous carrying amounts.

After a business combination accounted for by the purchase method, however, accounting for a minority interest in common stock and senior equity securities that remain outstanding may differ substantially from both that required after a pooling and that generally used after a purchase before APB Opinion No. 16. The differences result from stating the assets and liabilities, including senior equity securities that remain outstanding, of an acquired company at fair value and from the recognition of goodwill.

If less than all of the common equity ownership of a company is acquired in a purchase, it is not clear at what point the valuation of the minority interests in consolidated financial statements must reflect changed accounting bases of the underlying assets and liabilities. Clearly, the "push-down" theory applies in computing minority interests but it is not clear whether it should be applied when 50% or more of the stock is acquired, or only when all but a small fraction—say, less than 20%—is acquired.

Before Opinion No. 16, minority interest often denoted a proportionate interest in the book value of an acquired subsidiary's net assets. Some companies attributed part or all of an excess of cost over net book value of an acquired company to individual assets, as prescribed in paragraph 10 of Chapter 5 of ARB No. 43, but apparently many did not. However, since the income of a subsidiary in consolidated statements now reflects the revalued assets and liabilities, the minority interest must also reflect the changed values.

New costs of assets acquired and present values of liabilities assumed are determined at least partly from the values assigned to senior equity securities included in the total purchase price. Those securities should, therefore, be included in a minority interest at the new carrying value. Amortization of premium or discount that is created when senior equity securities are fair valued has been discussed but seldom, if ever, practiced. The need for amortization depends on the terms of the issue, the period over which it may or must be called or redeemed, the nature of preferential dividend claims, and other factors.

Transactions Between Affiliates

Transactions between affiliated entities are among the most difficult to analyze and account for. Inter-entity receivables, payables, revenue, and expenses must be eliminated in preparing consolidated financial statements. Inter-entity profits should be eliminated unless the related items have passed outside the group. Elimination is required because it is improper to show profits not involving entities outside a related group. All of the principles for consolidated statements apply also to investments accounted for by the equity method except that inter-entity profits are eliminated only to the extent of an investor's percentage of ownership rather than in full as they are if the investee is consolidated. Combined financial statements may be required for fair presentation in some circumstances.

Inter-Entity Allocation of Income Taxes

The allocation of income taxes among separate components of a consolidated group of companies has received considerable scrutiny. The issue has become more significant as separate statements of partially owned subsidiary companies have achieved wider public distribution than previously because of public ownership of their securities. The mechanical complexities of the allocation process are exaggerated if tax and accounting bases of assets and liabilities differ substantially, as may often happen in a purchase.

Apportionment of the total tax reported in consolidated financial statements of a parent company and its subsidiaries, including the deferred tax effects of timing differences, is necessary to prepare separate financial statements of the individual companies. The objective of the method used should be equitable allocation of tax cost among components. The two most commonly used methods of distributing tax cost among members of a consolidated group are:

1. On the basis of the ratio that the portion of the consolidated taxable income attributable to each member of the group having taxable income bears to the total consolidated taxable income (with no credit to loss companies)—referred to as the "source of income" method.
2. On the basis of the percentage of total tax that the tax of each member computed on a separate return would bear to the total amount of the taxes for all members of the group so computed—referred to as the "separate return" method.

Both methods generally yield satisfactory results. The method of allocation used and the amount of tax that would be paid on a separate return basis should be disclosed in separate entity statements, and it is good practice to document the method by written agreements among the parties affected.

A number of problems may arise in the course of allocating taxes, such as losses of an individual member that can be carried back or forward, deferral of profits on intercompany sales, and differences in timing of taxable revenue or deductions. It is not feasible in this chapter to discuss the possible effects of those complications on the allocation computation: the logic of the "source of income" or "separate return" method is usually a reliable guide.

Noncash Contributions to Joint Ventures

We have previously noted the development of the practice of subsidiaries issuing their own stock or parent companies selling the stock of subsidiaries to third parties. A variation on that form of financing is the joint venture—a parent company joins with another corporation in forming an entity to succeed to the operations of a division or subsidiary of the parent. Depending on the result of negotiations between the parties, the other company usually contributes cash and the parent contributes assets having an agreed value—which value usually is not the amount at which the parent company carries the assets in its financial statements. The cash may or may not be contributed directly to the joint venture. Questions of the propriety of recording gains on those transactions must be analyzed closely, and the rights and obligations of the venturers must be considered in determining the appropriate accounting for the venturer contributing property.

Joint ventures may be in either corporate or partnership form. Either way, accounting for a joint venture by the equity method is appropriate, subject to slight modifications for partnership ventures. An accounting procedure that is a variation on both the equity method and consolidation has received much attention in certain industries, specifically real estate and natural resources. It is a consolidation technique known as proportionate or pro rata consolidation. Full consolidation is usually inappropriate if joint ownership of an entity leaves no single investor in control. Under proportionate consolidation, a venturer records his share of the assets and liabilities of the venture; the full asset and income totals are not included in the venturer's consolidated statements and therefore no minority interest relative to the investment need be shown. However, an appropriate provision for income taxes on undistributed corporate joint venture income may be necessary in an investor's income statement.

The SEC has, in the past, distinguished between corporate and partnership joint ventures and has sanctioned the use of proportionate consolidation accounting only for the latter.

Parent Guarantees of Subsidiary Debt

Creditors of subsidiaries or investees often insist on a guarantee by the parent company of a subsidiary's loans. Alternatively, creditors may lend directly to the parent, with the funds in turn advanced to the subsidiary or investee; collateral for the loan may be required in the form of a parent's stock certificates for the subsidiary's stock. Those matters and other related types of transactions require full disclosure in both the separate statements of the subsidiary or investee and the consolidated statements.

"Deconsolidation" or "Decombination"

Obviously, the coined terms "deconsolidation" and "decombination" refer to situations in which inclusion of a subsidiary in consolidated financial statements is no longer appropriate and accounting recognition must be given to its removal. The subsidiary may have been formed by the parent company or it may have been acquired by purchase or combined in a pooling of interests.

Deconsolidation refers to removing the amounts of individual items (such as cash, receivables, liabilities, and sales) of a subsidiary from the consolidated totals of similar items. It involves presenting the net investment of the parent company and the results of operations of the unconsolidated subsidiary as single-line items in the balance sheet and income statement, generally on the equity method; occasionally, the cost method may be required. At the point of deconsolidation, the carrying amount is the same for both equity and cost; cost, in that context, refers to acquisition cost of the investment plus accumulated earnings, less accumulated losses, amortization of goodwill, and dividends received to the date of deconsolidation.

Deconsolidation may result from loss of control by a parent (for example, as a result of bankruptcy), a decision to dispose of a subsidiary at a reasonably determinable time in the future, or other reasons. If a loss on disposition of a subsidiary is anticipated, the equity method may not be appropriate; writing down the investment in the subsidiary to net realizable value may also be necessary, in accordance with the provisions of APB Opinion No. 30 (*AICPA Prof. Stds.,* vol. 3, Section 2012).

Decombination has a more restricted connotation, though deconsolidation may be used to report the results of a decombination. Two related coined words—depooling and depurchase—are often used. A decombination is the undoing, within a short period after the date of consummation, of a business combination and all the terms under which it was originally consummated. All parties to the business combination revert to their pre-existing status.

If the transaction was originally accounted for by the pooling-of-interests method, the depooling returns to the issuing corporation the stock issued to effect the combination and returns to the stockholders who received that stock shares of stock (or assets) of the company disposed of. Financial statements of the issuing company are restated for all periods to exclude the operations of the depooled company. In a depurchase, an amount equivalent to the original consideration is returned to the purchaser, and the acquired assets are returned to the seller. It may be appropriate, depending on the facts of a particular situation, to estimate and record a loss in the latter circumstances.

The concept of a decombination breaks down if substantial time elapses between consummation and decombination, or consideration returned is not identical to that received due to subsequent dispositions, or, in a depooling, the combining company is not returned to the identical group of stockholders. With respect to a depurchase, there is an additional argument that gain or loss should be recognized regardless of the form of the transaction. Some also contend that depurchase is not a valid concept because the original exchange of consideration by the parties resulted in a new basis of accountability; to the extent that errors or misrepresentation colored the original exchange, depurchase is merely a substitute for legal remedies otherwise available.

18

Financial Statements

INTRODUCTION

This chapter deals with the most common form of financial statements, often called "all-purpose financial statements": statements prepared for general use by credit grantors, investors, and the interested public. Since the users often are not identified or identifiable at the time statements are prepared, and since users' needs are many and varied, all-purpose statements have been developed over the years to serve as many needs as possible. That objective inevitably calls for many compromises.

The particular needs of special groups can be met, and unique presentations can be provided when they are needed, by "special-purpose financial statements." The variety of form and content in those statements is limited only by the imagination and ingenuity of the accountants responsible for preparing them. Nevertheless, special-purpose statements are more readily understood when the conventions and disciplines of all-purpose statements are observed as a starting point and departures are carefully explained.

This chapter describes how all-purpose financial statements should be presented, not how they are used. Financial statement analysis is a separate subject in itself.

We do not offer examples of financial statement presentation in this chapter because that necessary service is so effectively provided by the AICPA annual publication, *Accounting Trends and Techniques*.

Financial statements of publicly held companies are included in annual reports to stockholders. Representations in those reports should be consistent with the information contained in the financial statements and an auditor should read the proofs to assure himself of this consistency.

AUTHORITATIVE STATEMENT

In 1970, the Accounting Principles Board approved Statement No. 4, *Basic Concepts and Accounting Principles Underlying Financial Statements of Business Enterprises*. That admirably comprehensive and exhaustive document, now incorporated in Sections 1021 to 1029 of *AICPA Prof. Stds.*, vol. 3, begins the discussion of financial statements with the following definition:

> Financial statements are the means by which the information accumulated and processed in financial accounting is periodically communicated to those who use it. They are designed to serve the needs of a variety of users, particularly owners and creditors. Through the financial accounting process, the myriad and complex effects of the economic activities of an enterprise are accumulated, analyzed, quantified, classified, recorded, summarized, and reported as information of two basic types: (1) financial position, which relates to a point in time, and (2) changes in financial position, which relate to a period of time. Notes to the statements, which may explain headings, captions or amounts in the statements or present information that cannot be expressed in money terms, and descriptions of accounting policies are an integral part of the statements. [Paragraph 1022.02]

The Statement then discusses such fundamentals as the environment of financial accounting; the objectives of financial accounting and financial statements; the basic features and basic elements of financial accounting; generally accepted accounting principles, divided into pervasive principles, broad operating principles, and detailed principles;

and the characteristics and limitations of financial accounting and financial statements. Many of those subjects are reduced to carefully worded statements codified and classified by letter and number. Everything contained in the Statement is fundamental and necessary to an understanding of accounting and auditing. It is assumed to be part of the body of knowledge possessed by a user of this book. It is used as the framework of this chapter, which summarizes very briefly the well-known and generally accepted features of financial statements, and emphasizes and discusses those which have presented unusual or difficult questions in practice.

General Characteristics and Limitations of Financial Statements

The Statement (paragraph 1022.27 of *AICPA Prof. Stds.*, vol. 3) sets forth "some of the more important present characteristics and limitations of financial accounting and financial statements." In condensed form, they are:

Financial statements are primarily historical.

Financial statements are general-purpose, that is, designed to serve the common needs of a variety of users.

Financial statements are fundamentally interrelated (a concept discussed in detail in Chapters 2–5).

Information is classified according to presumed needs of users.

Financial statements summarize large numbers of transactions.

Financial statements are expressed in terms of the monetary unit of the country in which they are issued; changes in purchasing power are not reflected.

Several different measurement bases are used in financial statements; current value or liquidating value may sometimes be used but is not a primary measurement base.

The accrual basis rather than the cash basis is preferred.

Estimates and informed judgments are often employed to assign dollar amounts in financial statements.

As far as possible, estimates and judgments are related to data derived from verifiable events.

Financial statements are prepared on a conservative basis: unfavorable events are recognized as they occur while favorable events are not recognized until realized.

The economic substance of transactions should usually prevail over legal form (see "Related Party Transactions" later in this chapter).

Many of the terms used in financial statements are common words to which accountants have given technical meanings.

Financial statement users are presumed to be generally familiar with business practices, the terminology of accounting, and the nature of the information reported.

Certain other basic characteristics of financial statements are covered elsewhere in the professional literature, and some of them in more detail earlier in this book:

Financial statements are those of a "going concern" unless otherwise stated. Therefore, amounts on balance sheets represent apportionment of income and expenses between periods, not necessarily liquidating values or replacement values. Reasons to doubt the going concern assumption cannot be ignored: accountants customarily prepare financial statements on the going concern assumption.

The principle of conservatism, enumerated above, extends to anticipating losses and not anticipating profits and to a healthy skepticism about valuations and estimates, but it does not extend to creating "hidden reserves" which defer profits to future periods.

Financial statements are the responsibility of management, not the auditor (a point explained in Chapter 1).

Financial statements are historical, not prophetic; accountants must guard against any implication to the contrary and leave it to users to decide the extent to which the historical record is an indicator of future performance; in that connection, disclosure of material nonrecurring items is necessary.

Matters not material to the understanding of the financial statements may be ignored; the judgment of materiality, one of the most difficult in accounting, is discussed at length in Chapter 2.

Those characteristics represent decades of pragmatic compromise among conflicting needs and objectives. Once they are recognized as just that, and as being subject to change in response to changing needs, much of the criticism leveled at the overall usefulness of financial statements from time to time falls into perspective. Financial statements are useful, but they are most useful to those who recognize their limitations; when the needs of a large number of users change, the form and content of financial statements must also change.

Conditions for Fair Presentation

Section 1027, which deals with broad operating principles, outlines the following conditions for fair presentation:

The qualitative standard of *fair presentation in conformity with generally accepted accounting principles* . . . is particularly important in evaluating financial presentations. This standard guides preparers of financial statements and is the subjective benchmark against which independent public accountants judge the propriety of the financial accounting information communicated. Financial statements "present fairly in conformity with generally accepted accounting principles" if a number of conditions are met: (1) gen-

erally accepted accounting principles applicable in the circumstances have
been applied in accumulating and processing the financial accounting information, (2) changes from period to period in generally accepted accounting
principles have been appropriately disclosed, (3) the information in the
underlying records is properly reflected and described in the financial statements in conformity with generally accepted accounting principles, and
(4) a proper balance has been achieved between the conflicting needs to
disclose important aspects . . . in accordance with conventional concepts
and to summarize the voluminous underlying data into a limited number of
financial statement captions and supporting notes. [Paragraph 1027.15]

Those four conditions constitute a large part of the subject matter
of this book. The first condition, the application of generally accepted
accounting principles, occupies the first section in each of Chapters 9
through 16 and all of Chapter 17. The second condition, consistency
and disclosure of inconsistencies, was discussed in Chapter 2 under the
second standard of reporting. The third condition, financial statement presentation of accounting information, is covered in the last
section of each of Chapters 9 through 16 and in the balance of this
chapter. The fourth condition, the balance between more complete
disclosure and more meaningful summarization, can never be conclusively defined or measured. That balance is, essentially, what accounting is all about—and maintaining it and adjusting it in response to
changing needs is the essence of an accountant's skill.

PRINCIPLES OF FINANCIAL STATEMENT PRESENTATION

Section 1027 contains twelve principles of financial statement presentation. They are reproduced here, together with our comments on
certain details and on the practical problems of implementing them.

Basic Financial Statements

R-1. *Basic financial statements.* A balance sheet, a statement of income, a
statement of changes in retained earnings, a statement of changes in financial
position, disclosure of changes in other categories of stockholders' equity,
descriptions of accounting policies, and related notes is the minimum presentation required to present fairly the financial position and results of
operations and changes in financial position of an enterprise in conformity
with generally accepted accounting principles.

Much other information is useful and is often presented, and the
discussion about whether various additional items—such as income by
line of business or order backlog—should be added to the required

minimum continues unabated. At present, the above items constitute the definitive list of required financial statements. The list applies to all reporting entities, with certain variations as to form—for example, for nonprofit institutions, the statements of changes in financial position and of changes in fund balances (the institutional equivalent of stockholders' equity) can often be combined in a "statement of changes in funds" or something similar. The balance sheet, income statement, and statement of changes in financial position are usually comparative, presenting at least two years and sometimes more in one statement.

The attempt to make basic financial statements "all-purpose statements" inevitably results in a compromise that is in some degree unsatisfactory to almost all users. Notwithstanding the problems of compromise, the usefulness of a basic, universally recognized, virtually standardized format appears to be generally accepted. That standard format serves as a recognizable departure point for other, nonstandardized information that may be required by or offered to special-purpose users.

In other times, variations and innovations in the format of the basic financial statements were fashionable and even officially encouraged. In recent years, it appears that the easier communication that results from standardization is more highly valued, and the number of unusual statements published is not large. Instead, the profession has encouraged the use of supplementary statements, and the data presented in supplementary sections of published reports have steadily expanded in volume and variety.

The next three statements of principles of presentation cover the balance sheet, the statement of income, and the statement of changes in financial position. The drafters of Section 1027 omitted a separate comment on the statement of changes in retained earnings and related disclosures of changes in other categories of stockholders' equity, although APB Opinion No. 12 (AICPA Prof. Stds., vol. 3, paragraph 2042.02) makes it explicit that those statements—or notes presenting the necessary data—are required for fair presentation of results of operations in accordance with generally accepted accounting principles because changes in the capital accounts are as much a part of the "operations" of a business as changes in any other accounts.

Traditional presentation was a separate statement for each "surplus" account, with changes in capital stock shown in either the balance sheet caption or a note. Alternatively, many companies present combined statements of income and retained earnings, in which retained earnings changes are shown as an extension of the income statement following net income.

In recent years, the practice has been growing of showing a "statement of stockholders' equity" with several columns for the number of shares and dollar amount of each class of stock and the dollar amount of each "surplus" account. Each change appears on a line in one or more of the columns with a descriptive caption. That form of statement has the advantage of bringing together in one schedule all of the capital changes, many of which affect two or more capital accounts simultaneously. It sometimes has the disadvantage of being complicated and hard to follow.

Complete Balance Sheet

R–2. *Complete balance sheet.* The balance sheet or statement of financial position should include and properly describe all assets, liabilities, and classes of owners' equity as defined by generally accepted accounting principles.

The major groupings in balance sheets are highly conventional and may be observed in the balance sheet of any commercial or industrial company. The fact that the organization is so conventional and so widely used constitutes a potential danger in those instances where it is not appropriate. Financial characteristics of some enterprises differ so markedly from the majority as to call for different balance sheet presentations, and for those enterprises the conventional groupings would be misleading. Nonprofit institutions, banks, real estate companies, utilities, and investment companies are the most common examples. In balance sheets of the first three types of companies, the subtotals of current assets and current liabilities are often omitted to emphasize the belief that conventionally defined working capital is not a significant financial statistic. In balance sheets of utilities, plant is often the first asset stated and in those of investment companies, investments are stated first—in both cases to emphasize that those are the most important assets. In nonprofit institutions, assets are marshaled opposite the sources or categories to which their use is restricted so as to emphasize the fiduciary nature of institutional financial management.

The sequence of items in balance sheets has evolved traditionally from an attempt to present them in order of liquidity. With the few exceptions noted, of which the foregoing are examples and not a definitive enumeration, balance sheets commonly start off with cash, followed by marketable securities if they represent temporary cash investment, accounts and notes receivable, inventories, and prepaid expenses. Those categories are totalled as current assets. After the subtotal of current assets, the most common order of presentation is property, plant, and equipment, less allowances for depreciation; investments in affiliates and other long-term investments; other assets; deferred charges; and, lastly, intangible assets, including goodwill.

Short-term debt commonly heads the list of liabilities, sometimes followed by the installments of long-term debt due within a year (although, for no apparent reason, the current portion of long-term debt appears just as often as the last item of current liabilities and sometimes elsewhere in the list). Those items are followed by accounts payable and accrued liabilities—sometimes combined and sometimes shown separately—dividends payable, accrued taxes, and unearned revenue. Those are totalled as current liabilities. Current liabilities are followed by long-term debt, deferred taxes on income and any other deferred income or long-term liabilities, minority interests, preferred stock, common stock, other paid-in capital, and retained earnings. The last four accounts are usually subtotalled as total equity or total stockholders' equity.

Significant items should be set out separately from the conventional categories: for example, income tax refunds receivable, if significant, are usually shown separately from other accounts receivable. Captions should be simple, commonly understood terms, preferably those that have been defined in the authoritative literature of the profession. Vague and ambiguous terms—such as "value"—should be avoided.

Working Capital

The excess of current assets over current liabilities, called "working capital," has always been of prime interest to users of financial statements, particularly grantors of credit (except in certain industries where it is deemed irrelevant). The working capital figure is useful because it identifies the relatively liquid portion of the total enterprise capital which provides a margin or buffer for meeting obligations within the ordinary operating cycle of the business. It has its limitations, however, because unusual assets or liabilities can distort working capital.

The most common form of balance sheet does not set forth the figure for working capital, but instead shows the totals of current assets and current liabilities clearly enough to permit easy computation. Another, less common form, called a "statement of financial condition," shows current assets first, followed by current liabilities, the total of which is subtracted to show working capital. In either case, the changes in working capital and its components are shown in the statement of changes in financial position (see below).

Balance Sheets Presented Without Other Statements

Balance sheets alone are required for various purposes, usually related to giving evidence of solvency and financial responsibility. Issuers that are not otherwise required to publish statements are often reluctant to disclose any more details of income or capital changes than are required, usually for reasons of confidentiality.

It is acceptable to issue balance sheets without other statements, and for auditors to report thereon, as long as all required disclosures relating to financial position are included in the balance sheet or notes. For example, it is necessary to disclose the principal components of property, plant, and equipment and any unfunded vested pension benefits, but not the amount of depreciation or pension expense for the period ended on the balance sheet date.

Complete Income Statement

R–3. *Complete income statement.* The income statement of a period should include and properly describe all revenue and expenses as defined by generally accepted accounting principles.

That statement is misleadingly innocuous. Financial statements, and particularly the income statement, are an important means by which users gauge a company and its management's stewardship of resources and potentiality for future success. Consequently, the disclosures in the income statement should be so fashioned, with a proper balance between significance and detail, as best to facilitate that evaluation. As the length and complexity of the following discussion demonstrate, the income statement has been a subject of recurrent extensive debate in the profession and of a number of formal pronouncements. Accounting Research Bulletin No. 32 was issued in 1947, supplemented by ARB No. 35 in 1948 and ARB No. 41 in 1951. Those pronouncements were updated and revised extensively by APB Opinion No. 9, *Reporting the Results of Operations,* issued in 1966 (*AICPA Prof. Stds.,* vol. 3, Section 2010), and that in turn by Opinion No. 30, issued in 1973 (Section 2012).

The reasons for so much discussion and restatement and refinement of previous decisions are two: first, the difficulty of deciding what kind of income statement is most useful to the largest number of readers and, second, the necessity to re-examine previous conclusions in the light of changing needs and in recognition of new conditions and circumstances.

For several decades, the discussion revolved around whether all items of income and loss should be included in the determination of net income and, if not, which items should be included in income versus which should be charged or credited directly to retained earnings: the so-called "all-inclusive" vs. "current operating performance" debate. The "all-inclusive" school appears to have won decisively, at least for the moment. With the very limited and carefully defined exceptions of prior-period adjustments, correction of accounting errors, and certain (very limited) changes in accounting principles that are effected by restating prior years' statements, it appears settled that all items of revenue and expense recognized in an accounting period should be reflected in the income statement of that period. However, the basic question is not settled, but merely shifted from debating whether certain unusual items should be reflected in income or retained earnings to debating how and where in the income statement they should be reflected. The current answers to that question are described below, following a description of the conventional income statement captions.

Income statements almost invariably begin with sales, usually shown as "net sales"—meaning net of returns, discounts, and allowances. Sometimes it is followed by other income and a total for revenue.

Formerly, the sales caption was almost always followed by cost of goods sold and the difference between the two was set forth as gross profit. Now it is increasingly common to omit the gross profit subcaption and to show cost of goods sold as the first of a group of costs and expenses: selling, general, and administrative expenses; research and development expenses; interest expense, if significant; and a miscellaneous category. (*Accounting Trends and Techniques,* the AICPA annual survey of reporting practices, suggests that the latter presentation—the "single-step form"—is favored over the "multiple-step form" by better than two to one: 415 surveyed companies compared with 185.) Depreciation expense and pension expense are required to be disclosed, and sometimes they are shown as items in the foregoing group. More often they are disclosed in a note, because there are both theoretical and practical problems in segregating them from the major categories of costs and expenses. (There are also theoretical problems in determining how much of the annual provisions for depreciation and pension cost are carried into inventory and therefore not charged to expense for the period; in practice the problem is usually ignored and the annual provisions are reported as the annual expenses.)

Sometimes the provision for income taxes is shown as one of the grouping of costs and expenses, but it is much more common to total the expenses and show a subcaption for "income before income taxes" followed by the provision for income taxes—that subcaption is required in filings with the SEC, with certain exceptions.

In the absence of the special categories of income, expense, and loss that have come into being in response to changing needs and conditions, net income follows the provision for income taxes in the income statement. For many years there was a concerted effort in the profession to highlight the net income figure by making sure that subcaptions, spacing, and potentially equivocal wording offered no possibility of confusion. With the proliferation of special categories of income statement items directly preceding the net income line, described in the following paragraphs, the trend toward emphasizing the single net income figure may have reversed.

The first step in the counter-trend was APB Opinion No. 9 (*AICPA Prof. Stds.*, vol. 3, Section 2010) which prescribed the all-inclusive income statement but created within the income statement a new category of "extraordinary items." Extraordinary items were to be shown separately as an element of net income for the period and were distinguished from "prior-period adjustments," which were excluded from net income. Experience with Opinion No. 9 proved that the definitions and criteria were not sufficiently precise to prevent ambiguity and even misuse—it was alleged that some companies were planning and timing transactions so as to use the extraordinary item category to relieve operating income of current or future charges that it might otherwise bear. As a result, APB Opinion No. 30 (*AICPA Prof. Stds.*, vol. 3, Section 2012) set up a new and narrower definition of extraordinary items and also provided for separate income statement captions for income or loss from operations of a discontinued segment of a business and gain or loss on disposition of such discontinued operations.

In the meantime, other kinds of special categories were appearing, some as types of operating income and expenses, and some as unique special categories. APB Opinion No. 11, *Accounting for Income Taxes* (*AICPA Prof. Stds.*, vol. 3, Sections 4091 and 4091A), called for the tax benefits of operating loss carryforwards to be reported as extraordinary items when realized. Opinion No. 18 (*AICPA Prof. Stds.*, vol. 3, Section 5131) called for an investor's equity in earnings of unconsolidated 20% to 50% owned companies and joint ventures (see Chapter 14), except for an investor's share of extraordinary items, which should be reported as an extraordinary item, to be shown as a separate caption in the income statement. Opinion No. 20 (*AICPA Prof. Stds.*, vol. 3, Sections 1051 to 1051B) called for the cumulative effect of a change in accounting principle to be shown in the income statement between the captions extraordinary items and net income, except in the very few cases in which a change in accounting method is applied retroactively. Thus, a company may have several captions just before the net income amount, each of which may be significant in relation to net income. They are presented net of related tax effects and are reflected in the accompanying earnings-per-share table. Each of those categories is described briefly in the following paragraphs.

Extraordinary Items and Prior-Period Adjustments— APB Opinion No. 9 (Section 2010)

The "all-inclusive" and "current operating performance" schools of thought are described in paragraphs 8 through 15 of Opinion No. 9. That Opinion reconciled the two viewpoints by concluding in favor of the all-inclusive statement (with the few exceptions noted), but requiring all-inclusive statements to segregate extraordinary items so as to present a record of current operating performance. Thus, if extraordinary items are present, the last three captions in an income statement would be as follows:

Income before extraordinary items		$xxx
Extraordinary items	$xxx	
Less: Applicable income tax	xxx	xxx
Net income		$xxx

The Opinion [now superseded in part and amplified in part by Opinion No. 30 (Section 2012), summarized in the following section] defined extraordinary items as:

> . . . events and transactions . . . . of a character significantly different from the typical or customary business activities of the entity . . . . which would not be expected to recur frequently and which would not be considered as recurring factors in any evaluation of the ordinary operating processes of the business. [Paragraph 21]

Explicitly excluded were adjustments of estimates and valuations, regardless of size, such as write-down of inventories, contracts in process, or receivables. As previous chapters have demonstrated, making those estimates and evaluations is a recurring responsibility of management, and so they are considered to be "of a character . . . typical of the customary business activities of the entity" (paragraph 22).

Also excluded from the income statement were prior-period adjustments, which should be charged or credited to retained earnings as of the beginning of the first period presented in a set of financial statements and, when statements of prior periods are presented, reflected in the periods in which they arose. Paragraph 23 of the Opinion states:

> Adjustments related to prior periods—and thus excluded in the determination of net income for the current period—are limited to those material adjustments which (a) can be specifically identified with . . . the business activities of particular prior periods, and (b) are not attributable to economic events occurring subsequent[ly] . . . , and (c) depend primarily on determinations by persons other than management *and* (d) were not susceptible of reasonable estimation prior to such determination. Such adjustments are rare in modern financial accounting. [Italics added for emphasis.]

The paragraph goes on to say that prior-period adjustments usually result from a contingency in a prior period, the accounting effect of which could not be determined during that and intervening periods, and that usually a contingency significant enough to be treated as a prior-period adjustment would have called for disclosure in the financial statements published during the periods of uncertainty and in most cases for a qualified auditor's opinion on the statements of those periods. The Opinion also makes it clear that recurring adjustments of estimates and valuations are not prior-period adjustments. However, errors in previously issued financial statements resulting from mathematical mistakes, mistakes in the application of accounting principles, or oversight or misuse of facts that existed at the time the statements were prepared should be corrected retroactively and the statements should be restated, with disclosure of the corrections.

Extraordinary Items—APB Opinion No. 30 (Section 2012)

In the years after the publication of Opinion No. 9, experience with the extraordinary item category, coupled with the economic events of the late 1960's and early 1970's, revealed problems in determining which transactions constitute extraordinary items, measuring their accounting effect, and adequately disclosing them. In 1972 and 1973, the Board re-examined the whole subject and reaffirmed the conclusions presented in Opinion No. 9 as to the "all-inclusive" income statement. It was felt that, without altering those conclusions, the problems noted would be resolved, or at least mitigated, by more precisely defining the extraordinary item category and by specifying the accounting for the disposal of a segment of a business, which is discussed below.

The definition of extraordinary items was very much narrowed. A transaction is presumed to be ordinary unless "the evidence clearly supports its classification as an extraordinary item" (paragraph 19). To qualify as extraordinary items, transactions (in addition to being material) must be *both* unusual in nature *and* infrequent in occurrence in light of "the environment in which the entity operates" (paragraph 20).

The latter phrase is intended to emphasize that no transaction can be definitively categorized as an extraordinary item solely on the basis of its inherent nature. A transaction is ordinary or extraordinary only in the light of its relation to the activities of the entity, and many transactions can be extraordinary for one company and ordinary for another. The main thrust of that provision was aimed at companies that seemed to have extraordinary items every year, thus raising questions about which caption on the income statement measured current operating performance.

In 1975, it is too early to evaluate the practical effect of the narrower definition. Several of the dissenters to the Opinion noted that both "unusual" and "infrequent" are subjective terms which are likely to be difficult to use. The same could be said of the phrase "the environment in which the entity operates." All three terms are clear in principle but likely to be cloudy in practice.

Having refined the definition of extraordinary items and thereby excluded many transactions that are either unusual or infrequent, but not both, paragraph 26 of the Opinion provides for "line item" disclosure of material transactions in those categories in the body of the income statement, but not net of taxes—that is, before the caption "income before income taxes and extraordinary items." That disclosure was always required implicitly under the third standard of reporting, but Opinion No. 30 made it explicit.

Discontinued Operations—APB Opinion No. 30 (Section 2012)

After the large merger movement of the late 1960's, there was a smaller but still widespread movement to discontinue or dispose of operations that were unsuccessful or for some other reason no longer contributed to corporate objectives. At first those transactions seemed to fit easily into the category of extraordinary items defined by Opinion No. 9, but there were serious problems in measuring the amount and timing of revenue, expense, and loss items entering into a given disposition, and different solutions led to different accounting treatments.

In response to those problems, Opinion No. 30 calls for the results of continuing operations to be reported separately from those of discontinued operations (for current and prior years), and the gain or loss on disposition separately from both. Income statements presenting discontinued operations would thus look as follows:

Income from continuing operations before income taxes	$xxx
Provision for income taxes	xxx
Income from continuing operations	xxx
Discontinued operations (Note ___):	
Income (loss) from discontinued operations (less applicable income taxes of $xxx)	$xxx
Loss on disposal of discontinued operations including provision of $xxx for operating losses during phase-out period (less applicable income taxes of $xxx)	xxx xxx
Net income	$xxx

Paragraph 13 of the Opinion defines the term "segment of a business" as it relates to qualifying for the foregoing separate accounting and distinguishes it from normal-course-of-business disposals of assets and phasing-out of product lines. Generally speaking, a segment of a business is a separately identifiable entity, physically, operationally, and financially—the Opinion points out (paragraph 13) that the existence of difficulties in separately identifying and accounting for the operations being discontinued ". . . strongly suggests that the transaction should not be classified as the disposal of a segment of the business."

Losses on disposal of a discontinued segment should be reflected when management commits itself to a formal plan of disposition, whether by sale or abandonment. At that date—known as the "measurement date"—three losses must be determined or estimated and recorded: (1) operating losses to the measurement date (including any write-downs that would normally be made in any event—such as markdowns of inventory to market); (2) estimated operating losses from operations of the segment from the measurement date to the disposal date (normally not beyond one year); and (3) estimated losses on disposal of the assets of the segment, including all costs, expenses, and write-downs directly associated with the decision to dispose (severance pay, additional employee pension and relocation expenses, lease terminations, crash liquidations, etc.). Item 1 and that portion of Item 2 occurring prior to year end would constitute the first caption in the previously illustrated income statement classification. The remainder of Item 2—the expected future operating losses during phase-out—would be included in the second classification, separately disclosed. Any net gains from disposal (less operating losses from measurement date) should be recorded *only when realized.*

The Opinion contains a number of other injunctions and definitions designed to reduce possible differences in accounting treatment and to discourage relieving present and future income of recurring charges. While the Opinion removes some of the area for subjective judgment and therefore differing conclusions, there can be serious problems in determining amounts to be shown in the discontinued operations category. Full disclosure of the judgments and allocations entering into the calculation of the amounts shown is required in filings with the SEC, and it is good practice in published financial statements in general.

In addition to the amounts that should be disclosed in the financial statements, the notes to the financial statements for the period encompassing the measurement date should disclose:

1. The identity of the segment of the business that has been or will be discontinued,
2. The expected disposal date, if known,
3. The expected manner of disposal,
4. A description of the remaining assets and liabilities of the segment at the balance sheet date (preferably segregated in the balance sheet), and
5. The income or loss from operations and any proceeds from disposal of the segment during the period from the measurement date to the date of the balance sheet.

For periods subsequent to the measurement date and including the period of disposal, notes to the financial statements should disclose the information listed in 1–4 above and also the information listed in 5 above compared with the prior estimates.

Tax Benefits From Loss Carryforwards— APB Opinion No. 11 (Section 4091)

Accounting for income taxes is discussed in Chapter 13. Among the points covered is the fact that losses may be carried back to earlier years or forward to later years for tax purposes. The tax benefits resulting from carryback of losses are assured at the time the loss is incurred, and so they are recognized in financial statements in the year of loss by showing the estimated refund (or reduction in deferred tax liability) in the income statement as a negative provision for income taxes. The tax benefits of loss carryforwards are not assured until taxable income is realized in future periods (except in certain circumstances), and so they usually are not recognized in the income statement until the period in which the carryforward is applied to reduce taxes— either taxes currently payable or provisions for deferred taxes.

Since those tax benefits do not relate to current operating performance, paragraph 45 of Opinion No. 11 calls for reporting them as extraordinary items. Thus, in a year in which a loss carried forward results in a tax benefit, the line in the income statement captioned

"Provision for income taxes" shows a provision for income taxes (including deferred taxes) that would have been required without benefit of the loss carryforward, and the amount of the loss carryforward benefit is shown separately as an extraordinary (credit) item.

Equity Accounting for Investments— APB Opinion No. 18 (Section 5131)

The equity method of accounting for investments in unconsolidated 20% to 50% owned corporations and joint ventures is described in Chapter 14. Paragraph 19 of Opinion No. 18 states that an investor's share of the earnings or losses of investees should be shown as a single amount in an income statement. However, if an investee has extraordinary items, and the amount thereof is material in relation to the investor's results of operations, the investor's share of the extraordinary items should be reported as an extraordinary item in the investor's income statement. Since an investor's equity in net income of investees is after the investees' provision for income taxes, use of the equity method results in a minor form of net-of-tax accounting within the body of the income statement. According to *Accounting Trends and Techniques,* a clear majority of companies (about 60%) show equity in earnings of investees as an item of "other income"; the second most common presentation (about 25%) is after income taxes but before net income.

Effect of Accounting Change— APB Opinion No. 20 (Section 1051)

Types of accounting changes were discussed in Chapter 2 in connection with the second standard of reporting—the consistency standard. Before Opinion No. 20 was published in 1971, the treatment of accounting changes varied, but the alternatives seldom, if ever, included the one required by Opinion No. 20: reflecting the cumulative effect of a change in accounting principle in the income statement. Paragraph 20 of that Opinion calls for presenting the cumulative effect, computed as defined in the Opinion, on a line in the income statement between the captions "Extraordinary items" and "Net income."

In dealing with accounting changes, Opinion No. 20 makes some careful distinctions and emphasizes the point that continual restatement of prior-period data dilutes public confidence in financial statements and may confuse users. It provides that restatements of prior-period financial statements should be limited to (1) corrections of errors and prior-period adjustments (as previously discussed); (2)

changes in the reporting entity (as when the principles of consolidation are changed and previously unconsolidated subsidiaries are consolidated for the first time, or when a pooling of interests takes place); and (3) certain limited types of accounting changes when the advantages of retroactive treatment outweigh the disadvantages, as follows:

A change from the LIFO method of inventory pricing to another method.

A change in the method of accounting for long-term construction-type contracts.

A change to or from the "full costing" method of accounting used in extractive industries.

All changes made (simultaneously) when a company *first* issues financial statements publicly for any one of the following purposes: (a) obtaining additional equity capital from investors, (b) effecting a business combination, or (c) registering securities.

All other changes in the application of accounting principles require that the cumulative effect on prior retained earnings from retroactive application of the new principle (now referred to as the "catch-up" adjustment) be reflected in the current income statement. However, whenever the catch-up adjustment is used, pro forma income statement data for all periods presented (including historical summaries—usually five years) must be provided as supplementary information showing the effect on income which would have occurred (including the effect on taxes, bonuses based on profits, etc.) had the change been in effect in prior periods. Pro forma per-share data are also required. In unusual cases, pro forma data may be omitted if they are not determinable.

Accounting changes are required to be made effective at the beginning of the year in which a change is made, and the note disclosures, fully describing the change and its rationale (changes must be made to "preferable" methods), must state the effect on the current year's income.

The Opinion also carefully distinguishes between a change in accounting principle and a change in estimate; the latter, if distortive, should be disclosed and accounted for currently or currently and prospectively, as appropriate in the circumstances. Sometimes an estimate change causes a concomitant principle change; when this occurs, the entire adjustment is considered a change in estimate.

Summary

If a company experienced transactions in all of the categories discussed in the preceding paragraphs, the result could be an income statement approximately as shown on the next page.

Sales	$xxx
Cost of goods sold	xxx
Selling, general, and administrative expenses	xxx
Research and development expenses	xxx
Interest expense	xxx
Equity in earnings of investees	xxx
	xxx
Income from continuing operations before income taxes, losses from discontinued operations, extraordinary items, and cumulative effect of accounting change	xxx
Provision for income taxes	xxx
Income from continuing operations before losses from discontinued operations, extraordinary items, and cumulative effect of accounting change	xxx

Discontinued operations:		
Income (loss) from operations of discontinued Division X (less applicable income taxes of $xxx)	$xxx	
Loss on disposal of Division X including provision of $xxx for operating losses during phase-out period (less applicable income taxes of $xxx)	xxx	xxx
Income before extraordinary items and cumulative effect of accounting change		xxx
Extraordinary items (less applicable income taxes of $xxx)		xxx
Cumulative effect of accounting change		xxx
Net income		$xxx

The earnings-per-share table would then be as follows:

Earnings (loss) per common share:	
From continuing operations before extraordinary items and cumulative effect of accounting change	$xxx
From discontinued operations	xxx
Income before extraordinary items and cumulative effect of accounting change	xxx
From extraordinary items	xxx
From cumulative effect of accounting change	xxx
Net income	$xxx

[Following the income statement would be a presentation, on a pro forma basis, of the effect of the accounting change on each of the preceding years presented (usually four), including per-share amounts. See APB Opinion No. 20, paragraphs 41–44 for illustrations.]

Complete Statement of Changes in Financial Position

R–4. *Complete statement of changes in financial position.* The statement of changes in financial position of a period should include and properly describe all important aspects of the company's financing and investing activities.

For many years the "statement of source and application of funds" has been recognized as an informative and frequently useful statement. In 1963, in Opinion No. 3, the Accounting Principles Board recommended but did not require its inclusion in published financial statements. The recommendation was reasonably successful, the practice spread, and in 1971 the Board issued Opinion No. 19, *Reporting Changes in Financial Position (AICPA Prof. Stds.,* vol. 3, Section 2021), which made the statement a required part of the basic financial statements of a profit-oriented entity purporting to present fairly financial position and results of operations (it is not required if only financial position is presented) in accordance with generally accepted accounting principles. At the same time, the Opinion broadened the concept of the statement and recommended that its title be "statement of changes in financial position."

The statement should disclose all important financing and investing activities as well as important sources and uses of cash or working capital. Examples of noncash financing activities required to be disclosed are acquisitions of property by issuing securities or in exchange for other property, and conversions of debt or preferred stock to common stock. The Opinion offers complete flexibility as to whether the statement should present changes in cash, cash and investments, or working capital, and it offers considerable flexibility as to format. The one requirement as to format is that the working capital or cash provided from (used in) operations be prominently disclosed, with that provided from or used by extraordinary items disclosed separately immediately thereafter.

The Opinion seems to express a preference for presenting funds provided from operations by first showing income or loss before extraordinary items and adding back items that were recognized in determining income or loss but did not provide or use funds (most often depreciation and provision for deferred taxes), approximately as follows:

Income before extraordinary items	$xxx
Add expenses not requiring outlay of working capital in the current period [e.g., depreciation]	xxx
Working capital provided from operations for the period exclusive of extraordinary items	xxx

That form of presentation is by far the most common. An acceptable alternative begins with total revenue that provided funds and deducts operating costs and expenses that required the use of funds. Since the preferred and most widely used treatment unavoidably implies that expenses (primarily depreciation) not requiring the current outlay of funds are a source of funds, some consider the alternative presentation more precise and less subject to misunderstanding. Nevertheless, the preferred treatment is so generally accepted that it must be the recommended one, and the problem of convincing financial statement users that depreciation is not a source of cash must be dealt with through other channels.

Changes in elements of working capital are treated differently from changes in most other accounts. The *net* change in each element of working capital should be presented, either in the body of the statement if it shows the flow of cash or as an accompanying tabulation if it shows the flow of working capital. For most other accounts, gross changes should be shown: for example, outlays to acquire property should be shown separately from proceeds on disposition of property; long-term debt borrowed should be shown separately from debt repaid; outlays for purchases of subsidiaries should be identified and shown by major categories of assets acquired and obligations assumed; conversions of securities should be shown; and issues of securities for assets other than cash should be presented both as a source and as a use of funds.

Accounting Period

R–5. *Accounting period.* The basic time period for which financial statements are presented is one year; "interim" financial statements are commonly presented for periods of less than a year.

A year has long been the basic period for financial statements: this is logical and natural since it embraces the four seasons without repetition. The professional literature generally refers explicitly or implicitly to annual statements. Company management and auditors have developed their accountability procedures, including the necessary estimates, valuations, and judgments, in relation to an annual cycle of reporting and auditing.

Over recent years, as the tempo of the financial community has increased and expectations for up-to-the-minute information have heightened, quarterly summaries of key financial statement data have become common. The emphasis on interim financial reporting was coupled with tighter legal and regulatory requirements for immediate disclosure of significant events and transactions. The SEC and stock exchanges now require the promulgation of quarterly data. In 1975, professional attention is focused on developing more accurate and meaningful reporting between annual financial statements.

As most of the chapters of this book have demonstrated, considerable skill is required in the preparation of meaningful and informative annual financial statements—particularly in allocating revenue and expenses to present, past, or future periods. Interim financial statements compound the problems many times over: more allocations have to be made, more estimates and judgments are involved, and the aggregate numbers are smaller so that they are more easily distorted. Nevertheless, the needs of the financial community must be met, and so those problems must be dealt with. As a result, the Accounting Principles Board issued Opinion No. 28 (*AICPA Prof. Stds.*, vol. 3, Section 2071) to provide guidance. The following paragraphs outline its provisions.

The thrust of the Opinion is to require the same attention in interim financial statements as in annual ones to the principle of matching costs and revenue and the pre-emptive principle of anticipating losses as soon as they can be identified. In a few instances, the standards of annual reporting may be modified in the light of practical difficulties of applying them to interim reports. For example, judgments, estimates, and valuations that are impracticable to make more often than once a year may be extrapolated to interim figures. Other than that, items should be deferred or accrued in interim statements only if doing so would be appropriate in annual statements, and write-downs, losses, and extraordinary items should be reflected in full in the interim period in which recognized, with appropriate disclosure. Materiality is generally judged in relation to the full-year figures; items material in interim statements but not expected to be material in annual statements (for example, extraordinary items or accounting changes) should be separately disclosed in the interim statements.

The difficulties of accounting for inventories in interim statements are recognized. The Opinion provides for anticipating estimated year-end results in interim accounting for inventories carried at LIFO and for overabsorbed and underabsorbed overhead or other variances, so that interim figures will not be distorted by the large fluctuations that are possible in those accounts. The Opinion also provides for recognizing the annual cycle in accounting for losses from declines in market values of inventories: declines need not be recognized if there is reason to expect them to be so temporary as to be eliminated within the year; if a decline is recognized in one interim period and the price recovers in another before the end of the fiscal year, it is acceptable to recognize the recovery as a gain.

The Opinion allows the use of estimated gross profit margins in determining interim figures for inventories and cost of goods sold. That provision was considered necessary in recognition of the reality that the cost accounting systems of some public companies do not provide adequate data for interim determination of inventories or for other reasons it is impracticable. As systems improve, this condition is expected to diminish.

Income taxes should be provided for on the basis of an estimated effective rate for the full year. The Opinion also contains guides to minimum disclosures of summarized interim data. In paragraph 31 (paragraph 2071.31 of *AICPA Prof. Stds.,* vol. 3) the Opinion calls for an innovative and interesting disclosure:

> When interim financial data and disclosures are not separately reported for the fourth quarter, securityholders often make inferences about that quarter by subtracting data based on the third quarter interim report from the annual results. In the absence of a separate fourth quarter report or disclosure of the results . . . for that quarter in the annual report, disposals of segments of a business and extraordinary, unusual, or infrequently occurring items recognized in the fourth quarter, as well as the aggregate effect of year-end adjustments which are material to the results of that quarter . . . should be disclosed in the annual report in a note to the annual financial statements.

The whole disclosure requirement is interesting and informative, but of particular note is the reference to "the aggregate effect of year-end adjustments." Year-end adjustments arise for many reasons other than weakness of a company's control and accountability systems, but if they are significant and recurrent, they may imply a less than adequate system. That implied disclosure provides a strong incentive to public companies to strengthen systems so as to eliminate year-end adjustments. Until interim determinations become more precise, it is desirable to disclose the effect of adjustments and other unusual items on the fourth quarter results so that users may be better able to evaluate trends discernible from comparison of quarterly figures.

The profession is currently studying the auditor's position vis-à-vis interim financial statements and a number of proposals have been advanced. The SEC and the public, and some auditors including the authors, feel the need for an auditor's involvement in some form. We have no doubt that the auditor's association with interim reports will be defined before long, but it is still too early to predict the form it will take.

Consolidated Financial Statements

> R–6. *Consolidated financial statements.* Consolidated financial statements are presumed to be more meaningful than the separate statements of the component legal entities. Consolidated statements are usually necessary for fair presentation in conformity with generally accepted accounting principles if one of the enterprises in a group directly or indirectly owns over 50% of the outstanding voting stock of the other enterprises.

Formerly, it was common to present separate financial statements of legal entities, with investments in affiliated companies carried at cost. That is the "legal entity" basis of preparing financial statements and for years it was the subject of considerable controversy. Since the 1960's, because of the proliferation of subsidiary companies and affiliated entities, the "economic entity" theory has become generally accepted. Chapter 17 discusses consolidated financial statements at length.

Equity Basis

R-7. *Equity basis.* Unconsolidated subsidiaries and investments in 50% or less of the voting stock of companies in which the investors have the ability to exercise significant influence over investees should be presented on the equity basis.

Accounting for investments on the equity basis was discussed in Chapter 14.

Translation of Foreign Balances

R-8. *Translation of foreign balances.* Financial information about the foreign operations of U. S. enterprises should be "translated" into U. S. dollars by the use of conventional translation procedures that involve foreign exchange rates.

It has always been necessary for purposes of consolidation to convert financial statements initially prepared in foreign currency to U. S. dollars. The first basic question is whether to make the conversion and consolidation; if that question is answered in the affirmative, a series of questions follows on how to do it and how to report it. The questions have been addressed from time to time, in Chapter 12 of ARB No. 43 (*AICPA Prof. Stds.,* vol. 3, Section 1081) in 1953, paragraph 18 of APB Opinion No. 6 (also Section 1081) in 1965, Statement No. 1 of the Financial Accounting Standards Board in 1973, and, in 1975, an exposure draft of a much more comprehensive statement of the FASB.

Earlier practice was to record income from foreign sources only to the extent that funds were received or unrestricted funds were clearly available for transfer to the U. S. It was considered conservative practice to look carefully at any other foreign earnings before including them in U. S. financial statements.

Current practice is to consolidate foreign subsidiaries and to record a parent company's equity in income of unconsolidated foreign affiliates and investees unless there is strong reason not to do so. Section 1081 requires disclosure of significant foreign items included in the U. S. statements: net assets, sales, and net income or loss, for example. Many companies show more than that minimum information about foreign operations. APB Opinion No. 23 (*AICPA Prof. Stds.,* vol. 3, paragraph 4095.14) requires disclosure of undistributed earnings of subsidiaries (to the parent)—both foreign and domestic—if U. S. income taxes to be incurred upon such distribution have not been provided for, as well as disclosure of why provision need not be made for U. S. taxes that would be payable upon transfer of those earnings to the parent company.

Foreign currency gains and losses realized as a result of completed transactions flow into income in the normal course of conventional accounting; unrealized gains and losses arise from "translation" of financial statements stated in foreign currencies to U. S. dollars. Unrealized losses should be recorded as charges to income. Paragraph 1081.11 stated a preference for crediting unrealized gains to a suspense account. That preference has not explicitly been superseded by later pronouncements, but it is probably common practice now to credit translation gains to income, and it would be required by the FASB's proposed statement.

The traditional translation method, which is set forth in Section 1081, has come to be called the "current–noncurrent" method. Current assets and liabilities are translated from foreign currency amounts to U. S. dollars at the "current" exchange rate in effect on the balance sheet date. Long-term assets and liabilities are translated at the exchange rate in effect when the assets or liabilities arose—the "historical" rate. Depreciation is calculated on the basis of assets translated at the historical rate—thus in effect deferring recognition of translation gains or losses on long-term assets until the assets "expire."

The current–noncurrent method recognizes the possibility of using historical rates for inventories if using current rates would result in recognizing translation gains before the assets "expire." The "lower of cost or market" rule, referred to in paragraphs 1081.15 and .16, would tend to require recognition of exchange losses but not of exchange gains, but only after taking into account the effect that exchange fluctuations may have had on the market value or replacement cost of the inventory items. Another exception to the current–noncurrent distinction is provided for long-term debt issued in connection with the acquisition of fixed or other noncurrent assets shortly before a presumably permanent change in an exchange rate: both assets and debt may be restated at the new rate.

Section 1081 calls for translating income statements at average exchange rates. If translation gains and losses are credited or charged to income, the size of a translation gain or loss in relation to other income statement items varies depending on whether beginning rates, ending rates, or average rates are used for translating the statement.

Until the issuance of APB Opinion No. 30 (*AICPA Prof. Stds.*, vol. 3, Section 2012), exchange gains and losses resulting from major revaluations or devaluations (as distinguished from year-to-year fluctuations) were treated as extraordinary items. Paragraph 23 of Opinion No. 30 specifically excludes them from the extraordinary item category.

During the 1960's an alternative translation principle called the "monetary–nonmonetary" method gradually gained recognition. It was given official sanction by paragraph 18 of APB Opinion No. 6 (*AICPA Prof. Stds.*, vol. 3, paragraph 1081.12). The principal differences from the current–noncurrent method are use of the current rate for the translation of long-term debt and long-term accounts receivable—accounts that are stated in "monetary" terms—and use of the historical rate for "nonmonetary" current assets such as inventories.

Statement No. 1 of the FASB notes the existence of the different methods of translation and concludes that additional disclosure in published financial statements should be made until the differences between the various methods are resolved. Paragraph 6 of the Statement (paragraph 1082.06 of *AICPA Prof. Stds.*, vol. 3) enumerates disclosures, as follows:

> A statement of translation policies including identification of: (1) the balance sheet accounts that are translated at the current rate and those translated at the historical rate, (2) the rates used to translate income statement accounts (e.g., historical rates for specified accounts and a weighted average rate for all other accounts), (3) the time of recognition of gain or loss on forward exchange contracts, and (4) the method of accounting for exchange adjustments (and if any portion of the exchange adjustment is deferred, the method of disposition of the deferred amount in future years).
>
> The aggregate amount of exchange adjustments originating in the period, the amount thereof included in the determination of income and the amount thereof deferred.
>
> The aggregate amount of exchange adjustments included in the determination of income for the period, regardless of when the adjustments originated.
>
> The aggregate amount of deferred exchange adjustments, regardless of when the adjustments originated, included in the balance sheet (e.g., such as in a deferral or in a "reserve" account) and how this amount is classified.
>
> The amount by which total long-term receivables and total long-term payables translated at historical rates would each increase or decrease at the balance sheet date if translated at current rates.
>
> The amount of gain or loss which has not been recognized on unperformed forward exchange contracts at the balance sheet date.

The Financial Accounting Standards Board has issued for comment an exposure draft of a lengthy statement on exchange translation. The statement contains a number of controversial points which should be resolved before it becomes effective, and it introduces new terms and concepts which are difficult to grasp without careful study. When those shortcomings are surmounted, the statement will deal comprehensively with a complex subject. If the statement becomes effective without major changes in its conclusions, it will require the following changes from current practice:

The monetary–nonmonetary method will be the only acceptable method.

Inventories will be stated at the lower of historical cost, translated at historical rates, or market, translated at the current rate.

Exchange gains and losses, including changes in the market value of unperformed forward exchange contracts, will be reflected in net income and not deferred.

The complexity of the income tax consequences of currency fluctuations will be recognized and accounted for, and the tax effect of gains and losses will be disclosed.

Classification and Segregation

R–9. *Classification and segregation.* Separate disclosure of the important components of the financial statements is presumed to make the information more useful. Examples in the income statement are sales or other source of revenue, cost of sales, depreciation, selling and administrative expenses, interest expense, and income taxes. Examples in the balance sheet are cash, receivables, inventories, plant and equipment, payables, and categories of owners' equity.

The discussion in Section 1027 following Statement R–9 contains Substatements A through E. They define gains and losses; call for separate disclosure of components of working capital, extraordinary items, and net income; and note that assets and liabilities should not be "netted" one against another unless a right of offset exists. Those subjects have been covered elsewhere in this and the foregoing chapters.

Other Disclosures

R–10. *Other disclosures.* In addition to informative classifications and segregation of data, financial statements should disclose all additional information that is necessary for fair presentation in conformity with generally accepted accounting principles. Descriptions of accounting policies and notes that are necessary for adequate disclosure are an integral part of the financial statements.

This Statement refers to the notes to financial statements, including the "summary of significant accounting policies" required by APB Opinion No. 22 (*AICPA Prof. Stds.,* vol. 3, Section 2045) and described later. Decades ago, the notes were called footnotes because they were just that: brief, occasional addenda of information that could not fit conveniently into the body of financial statements. As the variety and complexity of financial events and transactions have grown, paralleled by a growth in demand for more comprehensive information, notes have necessarily grown. It is generally recognized that financial statements cannot "present fairly in accordance with generally accepted accounting principles" without the necessary accompanying note disclosures; their extensiveness should not be criticized unless, of course, they are overdone. The notes should not contradict or correct the statements themselves (SEC ASR No. 4).

The discussion in Section 1027 following Statement R–10, and other professional literature before and since its publication, contains statements such as the following:

> Disclosure principles carry an implied responsibility to present information so that its significance is apparent to a reasonably informed reader.
>
> .   .   .
>
> A mass of detailed information, overly compressed information, and language that may be a barrier to communication are unsatisfactory.

The truth of those statements is evident and generally accepted. If notes appear to be carefully worded so as to be legally and technically informative, but not so as to be readily understood by the average user, the notes can approach substandard reporting if they are incomprehensible; however, technical accuracy is important.

Customary or routine disclosure is discussed throughout the foregoing chapters under specific topics; *disclosure of changes in accounting principles* was discussed in Chapter 2 in connection with the second standard of reporting.

Related Party Transactions

Disclosure of material transactions with related parties is now explicitly required in financial statements by SAS No. 6, *Related Party Transactions*. The Statement broadens the definition of related parties to include principal owners and management, their immediate families, and others who can significantly influence management policies. The required disclosure includes the nature of the relationships, effects of current-period changes in terms, open amounts, and terms and manner of settlement. No special accounting is required, but all such transactions should be scrutinized to see that the accounting reflects their substance, particularly if they involve exchanges of similar property or unusual terms.

SAS No. 6 states that the auditor is responsible for applying specific auditing procedures to (1) determine the existence of related parties, (2) identify material transactions with such parties, and (3) obtain satisfaction as to their purpose, nature, and extent and their effect on the financial statements. The procedures would include obtaining an understanding of the business purpose and examining evidential matter that should extend beyond inquiry of management. Procedures frequently followed include an evaluation of relevant controls as well as review of potential sources of information, such as proxy material, stockholder listings, and minutes of the board of directors and executive or operating committees.

Disclosure of Subsequent Events

Substatement 10C is as follows:

Disclosure of subsequent events. Disclosure of events that affect the enterprise directly and that occur between the date of, or end of the period covered by, the financial statements and the date of completion of the statements is necessary if knowledge of the events might affect the interpretation of the statements, even though the events do not affect the propriety of the statements themselves.

How to handle subsequent events has been a troublesome question for many years. SAP No. 47, issued in 1971 and now Section 560 of SAS No. 1, clarified the question and offered some guidelines. Experience thereunder and the financial community's need for knowledge of subsequent events are still unfolding, and so that pronouncement should not be taken as the last word on the subject.

SAS No. 1 defines two types of subsequent events; actually it covers three, plus the important difference between events of those three types occurring before the financial statements are issued and similar events occurring thereafter. The three types of events are those that should be recorded in the accounts and reflected in financial statements, those that should not be recorded but should be disclosed in financial statements, and those that should be neither recorded nor disclosed.

Events To Be Recorded. The first type of subsequent event is succinctly described in paragraph 560.03 of SAS No. 1 as follows:

. . . those events that provide additional evidence with respect to conditions that existed at the date of the balance sheet and affect the estimates inherent in the process of preparing financial statements. All information that becomes available prior to the issuance of the financial statements should be used by management in its evaluation of the conditions on which the estimates were based. The financial statements should be adjusted for any changes in estimates resulting from the use of such evidence.

Most auditors recognize their responsibility to seek out and use all available information right up to the conclusion of an examination to improve their judgment of management's valuations and estimates reflected in financial statements. Managements of some companies are not as well aware of their responsibilities. Even those who take ac-

countability seriously may feel that an inventory valuation or an estimate of future expenses, once made, is out of the way until the next
scheduled review. They may be quite sincerely surprised to find that
subsequent events should be taken into account and earlier judgments
altered if necessary.

SAS No. 1 illustrates the distinction between events that reveal or
clarify conditions existing at the balance sheet date and those that represent new conditions. The illustration used is a receivable uncollectible because of a customer's bankruptcy subsequent to the balance sheet
date, which is in the first category because the debtor's poor financial
condition existed at the balance sheet date, compared with a similar
receivable uncollectible because of a disaster occurring to the debtor
after the balance sheet date, which is a new condition. The SAS notes
that making the distinction requires "the exercise of judgment and
knowledge of the facts and circumstances" (paragraph 560.04).

The distinction is often a fine one and the judgment difficult to
make. For example, if market conditions deteriorate subsequent to
year end, is that a new condition, or does it reveal a condition inherent
in the inventory at year end which calls for adjusting it to net realizable
value? Similarly, if a subsequent event occurs that reveals reasons for
estimated expenses to be deemed inadequate, should they be adjusted?
The answer in both cases must be: it depends on the facts and circumstances. In any event, the alternative to adjustment is disclosure.

Rarely, but occasionally, an event of the type that should be reflected
in the accounts occurs after an initial release of condensed earnings
figures but before the release of the printed annual report. In that
situation, the event and its effect on the figures previously released
should be disclosed in another press release and in a note to the financial statements. The auditor's report on the financial statements should
retain the original date, prior to the initial release, usually supplemented by a later date referring to the note describing the subsequent
event (discussed more fully in Chapter 19).

After statements have been issued, all events should be considered
those of the subsequent period, even though they affect valuations reflected in the prior balance sheet (with the exception of those rare
uncertainties, described earlier in this chapter, that give rise to prior-
period adjustments). One serious, though very rare, exception is an
event that brings to light facts that existed prior to the issuance of the
statements and that would have been reflected in them if known. In
that instance, immediate public disclosure of the facts should be made
and the financial statements should be reissued as promptly as possible.
An auditor's responsibility in such an event and alternative courses of
action are described in the following chapter.

Events To Be Disclosed. The second type of subsequent event is a new condition that should be reflected in the financial statements of the year in which it occurs but that is significant enough to cause prior-year financial statements to be misleading if not disclosed. Those conditions include all events or transactions having significant financial impact. Examples given in SAS No. 1 include issues of debt or stock, acquisition of a business, and casualty losses.

Occasionally an event of that type may be so significant that the auditor's report should call attention to it in an explanatory middle paragraph. Sometimes adequate disclosure can be made only by means of pro forma data giving effect to the event as if it had occurred at the balance sheet date: a major acquisition, merger, and recapitalization are examples.

Events Not To Be Disclosed. Events that do not affect interpretation of financial statements should not be disclosed because describing them in notes can cause misleading or confusing inferences. Strikes, changes in customers or management, and new contracts and agreements are examples of events that ordinarily should not be disclosed in the financial statements although management may have a responsibility to make public disclosure apart from financial statements.

Since every event ultimately has financial impact, it is often extremely difficult to distinguish between events that should and those that should not be disclosed. Because users of financial statements have in recent years called for increased disclosure of financial information, management, legal counsel, and auditors have tended to decide more and more borderline cases in favor of disclosure.

Once financial statements have been issued, they should not be restated unless the event in question falls within the narrow definition of an error correction or a prior-period adjustment or is one of the few changes in accounting principle that are effected by restating prior years' statements. When an accounting principle is changed in a subsequent period, APB Opinion No. 20 (*AICPA Prof. Stds.,* vol. 3, Sections 1051 to 1051B) generally calls for pro forma disclosure of the retroactive effect of the change on income before extraordinary items and net income, but not for restatement.

Disclosure of Accounting Policies

Substatement 10D is as follows:

Disclosure of accounting policies. Description of the accounting policies adopted by the reporting entity is required as an integral part of the financial statements.

A description of accounting policies has been a feature of some annual reports for a number of years, although standards and methods varied. In recent years, the increasing needs of financial analysts and other users of financial statements have been evidenced in complaints about the diversity of accounting alternatives on the one hand and the rigidity of accounting principles on the other. While working to narrow the alternatives, the APB recognized that complete uniformity was impracticable and probably unattainable. It further recognized that accounting principles and the methods of applying them so significantly affect financial position and results of operations that the usefulness of financial statements depends to a large degree on users' understanding of the accounting principles and methods behind them. Therefore, in 1971 the APB issued Opinion No. 22, *Disclosure of Accounting Policies (AICPA Prof. Stds.,* vol. 3, Section 2045).

That Opinion requires a description of "all significant accounting policies" as an integral part of financial statements purporting to present fairly in accordance with generally accepted accounting principles. That means, according to paragraph 12 of the Opinion, to "identify and describe the accounting principles followed . . . , the methods of applying those principles . . . , and important judgments as to appropriateness of principles relating to recognition of revenue and allocation of asset costs to current and future periods . . . ." The Opinion goes on to specify the following particular disclosures: a selection from among existing acceptable alternatives; principles or methods peculiar to an industry; unusual or innovative applications; basis of consolidation; depreciation methods; amortization of intangibles; inventory pricing; translation of foreign currency; and recognition of revenue from franchising and leasing operations.

In 1975, experience with the Opinion is limited. An initial observation is that disclosures appear to be more general than apparently envisioned by analysts and the APB. Hopefully, additional experience will sharpen and improve disclosure practices. Nevertheless, the Opinion is a large step in the right direction—that of permitting diversity if adequately justified and disclosed.

Form of Financial Statement Presentation

R-11. *Form of financial statement presentation.* No particular form of financial statements is presumed better than all others for all purposes, and several forms are used.

As noted under Statement R-1 above, in recent years the advantages of standardization have seemed to outweigh the virtues of experimentation and innovation. Audit guides have been published which standardize the format of financial statements for many industries having unique traditions, conventions, or particular characteristics to be recognized. An issuer of financial statements or an auditor reporting on them risks a charge of failing to "present fairly in accordance with generally accepted accounting principles . . ." by departing from the standard form of financial statement presentation. Therefore, that move should be made only for sound and compelling reasons.

Earnings Per Share

> R–12. *Earnings per share.* Earnings per share information is most useful when furnished in conjunction with net income and its components and should be disclosed on the face of the income statement.

Earnings per share (EPS) of common stock is a statistic, not an accounting result. It has been presented in connection with financial statements for many years in annual reports and prospectuses for public offerings of stock. Since 1966, when APB Opinion No. 9 "strongly" recommended it, and 1969, when Opinion No. 15 made it mandatory, the figure and its computation have been embraced by the auditor's opinion.

Until fairly recently, EPS was a simple computation, and it usually appeared separately from the financial statements—in a summary of financial highlights, for example. Over the years, and particularly in the last two decades, the figure has taken on more and more importance in the minds of investors as a prime ingredient of the price–earnings multiple. As a result, issuers of financial statements and the accounting profession have paid increasing attention to the figure, and more and more complexities, alternatives, ambiguities, and other complications have entered into its computation.

A principal complication revolved around the effect on the earnings per share computation of financing instruments that were not common stock but derived some or all of their value from a right to obtain common stock on favorable terms. It was clear that ignoring that relationship meant failure to account for part or all of the cost of an element of the financing, but conventional accounting, until recently, contained no methodology for doing otherwise. The concept that a security other than common stock could enter into the earnings per share computation was recognized but seldom acted on in practice. In the meantime, the proliferation of financing instruments related to common stock and deriving some of their value from the value of the common stock made the single earnings per share figure often unrealistic and sometimes misleading.

For a few years before the publication of APB Opinion No. 9, the SEC was requiring in registration statements under its jurisdiction a supplementary computation of earnings per share to reflect dilution resulting from conversions of convertible securities and exercise of options and warrants to purchase common stock. In 1966, Opinion No. 9 recognized both the concept of "residual securities" which should be treated as common stock and the potential dilution from shares issuable upon a variety of contingencies. Experience with Opinion No. 9 demonstrated the need for refinement, modification, and revision of the concepts, so Opinion No. 15 was issued in 1968. Both are now incorporated in Sections 2011 to 2011D of *AICPA Prof. Stds.*, vol. 3. The Opinions brought a number of new concepts, terms, and definitions into being, to deal with a complicated subject; Section 2011 is very intricate and involved. It is accompanied by four appendices and more than one hundred "interpretations." The following paragraphs summarize its basic provisions.

Disclosure Requirements

All companies are required to report earnings *or loss* per common share on the face of the income statement, with a few exceptions where it is clearly inapplicable: mutual companies, registered investment companies, nonprofit institutions, government-owned companies, and wholly owned subsidiaries. Opinion No. 15 also does not apply to separate statements of parent companies accompanied by consolidated financial statements or to special-purpose statements. The Opinion requires presentation of per-share data only for income before extraordinary items and net income, but most companies also report per-share figures for all items entering into the difference between those two figures. In addition, APB Opinion No. 20, *Accounting Changes,* requires presentation of per-share amounts for the cumulative effect of a change in accounting principle, and Opinion No. 30, *Reporting the Results of Operations,* requires presentation of per-share data for income from continuing operations when operations of a segment of a business have been discontinued.

For companies with simple capital structures, the computation is based on net income (loss) adjusted for claims of senior securities, such as dividends on preferred stock, divided by the weighted average number of common shares outstanding during the period. A "simple capital structure" is defined as a capital structure that contains an insignificant number of securities having rights or potential rights to receive common stock on terms that would dilute earnings per share.

For purposes of the computation, significance is defined as "dilution"—reduction in EPS—of 3% or more.

A company with securities having outstanding claims or potential claims to receive common stock that would dilute EPS by 3% or more must present "primary earnings per share" and "fully diluted earnings per share": the so-called "dual presentation," together with a note describing the basis of calculation. Primary EPS is based on the outstanding common shares plus securities defined as "common stock equivalents" (similar items were formerly called "residual securities") that have a dilutive effect. ("Anti-dilutive" common stock equivalents—those that would result in issuance of common stock on terms that would increase EPS or reduce loss per share—are excluded from the computation.) Fully diluted EPS is based on a pro forma calculation giving effect to all contingent issuances of common stock that might potentially dilute EPS.

Common Stock Equivalents

Many securities are not technically common stock but contain provisions enabling a holder to become a common stockholder. If, through that right, a security derives a large part of its value from the value of the common stock rather than from its own intrinsic "investment" value, it is defined as a common stock equivalent. There are three basic types of common stock equivalents.

1. Convertible Securities. When a convertible security is issued, a computation is made to determine whether it is a common stock equivalent; that determination is not changed as a result of subsequent events. The general principle is that a convertible security (preferred stock or debt) is a common stock equivalent if its cash yield, expressed as a percentage of its market price or fair value, is significantly below the yield of a similar security without the conversion feature. That measurement is difficult to make in individual cases, so for the sake of simplicity, objectivity, and uniformity of application, Opinion No. 15 arbitrarily set up the bank prime rate of interest as the benchmark. A convertible security is a common stock equivalent if its yield based on market price is less than two-thirds of the bank prime interest rate at the time it is issued.

A computation of primary EPS that includes convertible securities as common stock equivalents should adjust earnings for the effect of conversion: interest on convertible debt, less related tax effect, should be added back to reported net income for purposes of the computation; dividends paid on convertible preferred should be eliminated from the computation. That is the so-called "if converted" method of computation.

2. Options and Warrants. Options and warrants are always common stock equivalents because they derive their value entirely, or almost entirely, from the right to obtain common stock. They have substantial value if the exercise price is much below the market price of the related common stock; they have little or no value if the exercise price is above market value of the related common stock. (Until they expire, warrants will usually have some market value if a potential rise in the price of the common stock exists; that value will fluctuate in relation to the common.) If options or warrants have substantial value, they are likely to be exercised and the equity of common stockholders diluted because the proceeds received on exercise are less than the value placed on the common stock by the marketplace. On the other hand, if they have little or no value, they are unlikely to be exercised, and even in the event that they are, the proceeds received may not "dilute" the equity of existing common stockholders.

To recognize the circumstances described above, the APB, in Opinion No. 15, adopted an ingenious method: the so-called "treasury stock" method of computing EPS. Under that method, the effect of assumed exercise of all outstanding options and warrants is imputed in the calculation of primary earnings per share in the following manner: the number of shares of common stock issuable upon exercise is added to common stock outstanding; the exercises are presumed to have taken place at the beginning of the period; the proceeds receivable from such exercises are then divided by the average market price of the stock during the period being reported on to derive the number of "treasury shares" that presumably could be purchased therefrom; and that number is then deducted from the total shares outstanding and issuable.

Obviously, if the average market price of the common stock during the period is not greater than the average exercise price of options and warrants, as many shares would be repurchasable under the treasury stock method as are issuable upon exercise of the options and warrants. Thus, options and warrants are dilutive only if more shares are issuable upon their exercise than could be repurchased: that is, if the average market price is in excess of the average exercise price. As a practical shortcut through that reasoning process, the Opinion states that those common stock equivalents need not be reflected in primary EPS until the market price of the common stock has been in excess of the exercise price for substantially all of three consecutive months prior to the end of the period being reported on. Once the computation of EPS has been made for a period, it should not be retroactively adjusted as a result of subsequent changes in market price of the common stock, although the effect of the same options or warrants on the EPS computation will vary from period to period depending on the relationship of exercise price to market price.

Opinion No. 15 recognizes that the proceeds received from exercise of options and warrants might be used in many different ways by different companies and that the treasury stock method is a highly arbitrary choice made for the sake of simplicity, objectivity, and comparability. Though arbitrary, this is a logical and practical solution to the problem of providing a completely new methodology for recognizing an important financial fact unrecognized in conventional accounting. It should prove useful until a better and possibly more general solution is found to the problem, described in Chapter 16, of adequately accounting for the cost of equity financing.

The treasury stock method should be used to incorporate options and warrants in the computation of primary earnings per share in all cases except where it is clearly inappropriate. The Opinion specifies two such situations. The first is obvious: if a warrant or option permits or requires the tendering of debt or other securities in exchange for its exercise or requires that the proceeds from exercise be used to retire debt or preferred stock, it is in substance a convertible security and the "if converted" method should be used to the extent conversion of such debt or securities is required. The treasury stock method should be used for any excess proceeds.

The second exception relates to options or warrants that represent a potentially large fraction of common stock outstanding and issuable. Since repurchase of a large fraction of a company's outstanding common stock at the market price is likely to be impossible, the treasury stock method is not an adequate measure of potential dilution in that situation. Opinion No. 15 arbitrarily limits the use of the treasury stock method computation to 20% of the number of shares of common stock outstanding (not including shares potentially outstanding after exercise of options and warrants) at the end of the period being reported on. If the proceeds from exercise of all outstanding options and warrants are more than enough to repurchase 20% of the outstanding common stock, the balance of funds potentially receivable should enter into the EPS computation on the assumption that they would be used first to reduce borrowings and then to invest in U. S. Government securities or commercial paper. That pro forma calculation should be combined with the 20% treasury stock calculation, whether or not either is anti-dilutive; the total should enter into the EPS calculation only if it is dilutive.

3. Contingent Shares. Sometimes shares of common stock are held in escrow or are issuable contingent on certain events, usually related to a level of earnings or market price of the stock. If the conditions are currently being met, shares contingently issuable should be treated as common stock equivalents in computing both primary and fully diluted earnings per share. If shares are issuable contingent on a higher level of earnings than is currently being achieved, they should be treated as "other potentially dilutive securities" and should be included in the computation of fully diluted earnings per share, discussed in the following section. If the number of shares issuable depends on market price of the stock, the price at the close of the period being reported on should be used to compute the number of shares to be included in the computations. In contrast to treasury stock method computations, which are not subsequently restated for changes in market price of the stock, EPS figures based on contingent issuances *should* be restated if the number of shares contingently issuable subsequently changes.

Fully Diluted Earnings Per Share

The purpose of the second computation in a dual presentation is to show maximum dilution, so *only* dilutive securities are included in it. Fully diluted EPS should be presented only (1) if any contingent issues *other than* common stock equivalents are outstanding during the period or (2) if any common stock was issued during the period as a result of conversions, exercise of options and warrants, and the like. Contingent issues that might be potentially dilutive consist of all convertible debt or preferred stock (whether or not common stock equivalents), options and warrants, and all agreements to issue shares upon contingencies such as a specified higher level of earnings or change in market price. The reason for the requirement that fully diluted EPS be presented for any period during which conversions of debt or securities or exercise of options or warrants occurred is to show the potential full-year effect on EPS, as if the issuance had occurred at the beginning of the period.

Since the purpose of the fully diluted EPS computation is to present maximum potential dilution, the price of common stock at the end of the period should be used in the treasury stock method calculation in connection with options and warrants if that price is higher than the average during the period.

Previously Reported EPS

Primary or fully diluted EPS should not be retroactively restated for subsequent *changes in the market price* of the stock that affect either the securities to be included in the computation or the amount of potential dilution. In contrast, if the *number of shares* contingently issuable *changes* either because of changes in the contingency or changes in the market price of the common stock, previously reported EPS should be retroactively restated. Other occasions for retroactive restatement of previously reported EPS figures are to give effect to prior-period adjustments, stock dividends, splits, and the like, poolings of interests, or reduction in number of shares contingently issuable as a result of expiration of an agreement.

Conclusion

Appendix A to Section 2011 gives computational guidelines; Appendix B, a summary discussion of differing points of view; Appendix C, illustrative disclosures, and Appendix D, definitions. Section U 2011 gives a 51-paragraph overview of APB Opinions No. 9 and 15, and 102 interpretations. The length of that supplement is an indication of the practical complexities of implementing the Opinions. The complexities are caused not so much by the Opinions themselves as by the wide variety of circumstances and cases with which they deal. The disclosures required in connection with a dual presentation are likewise complex and also reflect the complex nature of the subject matter. Paragraph U 2011.353 of *AICPA Prof. Stds.,* vol. 3 presents a summary of those disclosures.

When a company has outstanding many different types of securities, some of which may be common stock equivalents and dilutive convertibles, together with contingent issues and other complexities, the computations of primary and fully diluted EPS may be so complicated as to require an exposition in the notes to financial statements showing how the amounts were derived; sometimes this explanation is given in condensed form. In filings with the SEC, a special exhibit is required presenting the computation in all cases where the computation is not readily apparent from data given in the financial statements and notes.

19

The Auditor's Report

INTRODUCTION

An auditor's report is the formal result of all his efforts. There are many other results—the direct and indirect impact of audits on the control, accountability, and public reporting practices of companies, for example—and some people maintain that these are more significant, but the report is the specific identifiable focal point for an auditor and for all those who rely on his work. It is also referred to as a "short-form report" or an "opinion." The term "certificate" also still appears occasionally; auditors have discouraged its use because it implies a degree of precision and certainty which, as a practical matter, cannot be achieved.

Since so much meaning is concentrated in the few words of a report, its phraseology is highly stylized and has been stereotyped for many years. A standard form of report was first recommended by the AICPA in 1933, and its wording has been unchanged since 1948. Absolute standardization is desirable so that every auditor communicates exactly the same message to every reader. Any deviation from the expected wording inevitably raises questions in the minds of attentive readers, and standardization is intended to prevent inadvertent or unintentional raising of questions. One of the continuing efforts of the profession, currently the responsibility of the Auditing Standards Executive Committee, is finding better ways to set out separately and highlight any nonstandard words in the report so that intended raising of questions is unmistakable.

This chapter covers the standard report—often called an unqualified report or opinion—matters that require explicit attention in issuing a report, and the handling of variations from the standard report. The general term "qualification" or "qualified opinion" is used for any deviation from the standard report that is intended to convey an opinion that is other than a "clean" opinion, although, as described in this chapter, some accepted deviations are not technically qualifications.

STANDARD REPORTS

The basic form of standard report is as follows:

[Addressee]

We have examined the balance sheet of X Company as of December 31, 19—, and the related statements of income and retained earnings and changes in financial position for the year then ended. Our examination was made in accordance with generally accepted auditing standards, and accordingly included such tests of the accounting records and such other auditing procedures as we considered necessary in the circumstances.

In our opinion, the aforementioned financial statements present fairly the financial position of X Company at December 31, 19—, and the results of its operations and the changes in its financial position for the year then ended, in conformity with generally accepted accounting principles applied on a basis consistent with that of the preceding year.

[Name of Firm]

January xx, 19—.

The first paragraph is called the "scope paragraph" and the second the "opinion paragraph." Some auditors use a one-paragraph report in which the opinion is given first to emphasize its importance.

A standard report asserts that an auditor understands the standards of his profession and has made an examination that measures up to them; that the financial statements being reported on present what they purport to present fairly, in accordance with generally accepted accounting principles; and that those principles have been applied on a basis consistent with that of the preceding year. In short, a standard report signifies that the auditor found no problems or deficiencies, either in carrying out his work or in the financial statements under examination, of which he believes a reader of the financial statements should be aware.

Routine variations in the wording of the standard report are: the party or parties to whom it is addressed, the identification of the statements reported on, the period(s) covered (usually two years), and the dating. An auditor should not alter any other words of the standard report unless there are problems or unusual conditions to be highlighted—and then his alterations should follow the carefully drawn rules described in the following sections of this chapter—because any departure from the standard words is usually regarded as some sort of warning to the reader.

Addressing the Report

The report may be addressed to the client company itself, to its board of directors, or to its stockholders. Practically speaking, the address of a published report has little or no significance. However, we believe that an important point of principle is involved in addressing the report to the stockholders: that an auditor's ultimate responsibility is to the stockholders rather than to the company or its directors.

Sometimes an auditor is retained to examine the financial statements of a company that is not his client. In that case, the report should be addressed to the client and not to the company being examined or its directors or stockholders (but see the discussion in Chapter 2 of the necessity for making sure that all parties to that kind of examination understand the auditor's responsibility).

Identifying the Statements

The statements should be clearly identified, usually in the scope paragraph. The exact name of the company should be used and the statements examined should be enumerated: generally, balance sheet, statement of income and retained earnings, and statement of changes in financial position. If any other statements are covered by the report, they should also be enumerated; for example, some companies present a separate statement of changes in stockholders' equity accounts. Sometimes it is more convenient to refer to an accompanying list or index that enumerates the statements, in which case the first sentence of the scope paragraph would read:

> We have examined the financial statements of X Company listed in the accompanying index.

The enumeration of the statements need not be repeated in the opinion paragraph.

Period(s) Covered

The periods reported on should also be specified. In annual reports it is common to report on two years for comparative purposes. Statements prepared in connection with proposed issues of securities, particularly those regulated by the Securities and Exchange Commission, usually cover more than two years; for example, five years of comparative income statements or summaries of earnings. The simplest, and increasingly prevalent, phraseology is to enumerate the years covered in both paragraphs of the report: ". . . as of (at) December 31, 19X1 and 19X2 and for the years then ended." Where only one balance sheet is presented, accompanied by statements of income and retained earnings and changes in financial position for several years, the identification can be ". . . as of (at) December 31, 19X1 and for the x years then ended."

We believe it is desirable to emphasize in recurring annual reports that each year's financial statements are examined separately and that a current examination does not cover the preceding year. Therefore, we use a scope paragraph that covers only the current year's statements and add one of the following sentences at the end of that paragraph:

> We previously examined and reported upon the financial statements of the Company for the year ended December 31, 19X1.

> ───────

> We made a similar examination of the financial statements for the preceding year.

Then the opinion paragraph covers both years, with minor changes in wording, as follows:

In our opinion, the aforementioned financial statements present fairly the financial position of X Company at December 31, 19X1 and 19X2, and the results of its operations and the changes in its financial position for the years then ended, in conformity with generally accepted accounting principles applied on a consistent basis.

Dating the Report

Inevitably, an auditor's report is rendered on a date later than the end of the period being reported on because it takes time for the books to be closed, final auditing procedures to be completed, and financial statements to be prepared.

Importance of Dating

In the past, there was room for considerable difference of opinion about when reports should be dated, and there were seldom compelling practical reasons for fixing the date precisely. Currently, with auditors being held to increased standards of responsibility, and with increased demands for prompt, accurate information, the dating of the auditor's report has become more important. That is because the opinion speaks as of its date, and so it establishes—and ends—the period for which an auditor takes responsibility for reporting that the statements appropriately disclose events subsequent to the period being reported on. Obviously, he cannot be responsible for events occurring after his field work ends and his opinion has been given. (SEC filings, in which the report is dated when the audit is completed but the "expertising" of the filing carries responsibility up to the effective date of the registration statement, are a partial exception.)* The nature of an auditor's responsibility for subsequent events and the procedures he can undertake to execute it are discussed below following the discussion of selecting the date.

Selection of Date

The date of a report should be the date when audit field work is completed: that is, when all substantive auditing procedures carried out on the client's premises come to an end. Sometimes that date is largely a matter of judgment because there are always loose ends to be tidied up, last-minute inquiries to be made, closing discussions and conferences to be held, and so forth. In most cases, however, the date is quite clear: it is the date when the principal auditor agrees finally

* For SEC reporting requirements, see Louis H. Rappaport, *SEC Accounting Practice and Procedure*, 3d Ed. (New York: The Ronald Press Co., 1972).

with the responsible client executives on the form and content of the financial statements. That usually requires a formal or semiformal "clearance" conference, which establishes the date of the report. For public companies, that conference usually takes place on or just before the date of the release of summary earnings figures to the press, thus even more emphatically fixing the date.

Pressure for fast communication of financial data has been pushing the release date for summary figures of publicly held companies earlier and earlier. A date twenty to twenty-five days after the end of the fiscal year is common for many commercial and manufacturing companies; ten to fifteen days is the expected period for commercial banks. Usual practice, as described more fully in Chapter 4, is for auditor and client to agree on the financial statements—and usually on the wording and content of the press release—prior to any public statement. It then may take several weeks for the published annual report containing the financial statements to be prepared, printed, and mailed, but the auditor's report carries the date on which agreement was reached (unless new information is incorporated in the statements—see "Updating the Report" below).

Subsequent Events and Related Auditing Procedures

If an opinion must be given within two or three weeks of the end of the fiscal year, the amount of auditing that can take place in that interval is obviously limited. Much of an auditor's examination must be essentially complete by the time the fiscal year ends. This practice calls for careful planning by the auditor. With effective internal control, fast, accurate, and efficient closing procedures, and prompt communication of reliable financial information, an auditor can complete his examination and express his opinion almost as soon as financial statements can be pulled together.

However, many companies cannot or do not choose to achieve that ideal. Their accounting systems may require extensive validation work, or they may encounter problems in closing the books or making the necessary valuations, estimates, and judgments. It may take eight weeks, twelve weeks, or even more for an auditor to complete his examination and make his report. During that time he must keep current with client affairs so as to have a basis for an opinion that, as appropriate, subsequent events are properly reflected in the financial statements he is reporting on. The treatment of subsequent events in accordance with generally accepted accounting principles was described in the preceding chapter.

Keeping current is easy and virtually automatic if an auditor is involved in client affairs to the extent that inevitably results from the effective practice of auditing as described in the early chapters of this book. If he is not involved to that degree, no procedures short of a complete audit examination of the subsequent period can provide reasonable assurance that he has recognized all subsequent events not voluntarily disclosed to him. Whether an auditor is involved and informed or not—and in the whole range of possibilities between those extremes—certain specific procedures are necessary to provide some evidence that certain subsequent events are adequately recognized and dealt with. Those procedures are spelled out in paragraph 560.12 of Statement on Auditing Standards (SAS) No. 1. They may be summarized as follows:

Read all the available information bearing on the client's financial affairs: interim financial statements; minutes of meetings of stockholders, directors, and any appropriate committees; pertinent variance and other management reports, and the like. An auditor who understands his client knows which areas are sensitive or volatile and what information about them is likely to be available.

Make inquiries—the more specific the better—about financial events, unusual entries in the accounts, accounting principles, potential problems discovered during the examination, and the like. An auditor who has developed a close working relationship with his client can make those inquiries easily and expeditiously.

Obtain formal letters of representation from client officers and legal counsel, either describing subsequent events or disclaiming knowledge of any. Most auditors include the representation about subsequent events in the "liability certificates" (described in Chapter 10) requested as part of year-end auditing procedures.

Although not specifically covered in paragraph 560.12 of SAS No. 1, it is sometimes necessary to make analytical reviews or even validation tests of a recognized problem area. Usually, their purpose is to form an opinion on a client's measurement of the impact of a subsequent event; for example, validation tests of a client's estimate of the impact of a decision to discontinue a line of business made subsequent to year end. Sometimes those tests are required to assure an auditor that a possible subsequent event did not occur; an example is tests of the net realizable value of inventories due to changed market conditions subsequent to year end.

Many auditors attach enough importance to the representation letters referred to above to ask that they be dated the same day as the report. Obviously, it is then too late to act on any new information contained in them. Therefore, usual practice is for client executives, auditor, and legal counsel to cooperate in preparing representation letters in draft for review and discussion prior to the opinion date. The formal letter, dated the same day as the report, can then be routinely signed and delivered.

Updating the Report

Ordinarily, there is no need to update a report once it is issued. Even in SEC registrations under the Securities Act of 1933, the original issue date is usually retained even though a "keeping current review" is conducted very much along the lines of the auditing procedures for subsequent events described above.*

Occasionally, however, subsequent events that call for disclosure occur between the date of the report and the actual issuance of the financial statements. In that event, either the report must be updated or it must be made clear that the opinion does not cover the new disclosure. There are three ways to handle the reporting of that kind of subsequent event:

1. *"Double dating."* The auditor can cover the subsequent event in his opinion by updating it only with reference to the note describing the subsequent event. That is a cumbersome procedure, but it serves to call attention to the new information. Double dating is the most common way of handling the matter. The date of the report would then read as follows:

   January 25, 19—, except as to the
   information presented in Note Y for
   which the date is March 12, 19—.

   Usually, double dating serves to cover subsequent events that are recorded and reflected in the financial statements as well as those that are only disclosed in notes.

2. *Redating.* The entire report can be redated. Most auditors feel that the implied assumption of additional responsibility for the period between the original date and the subsequent event is to be avoided, and so this course is seldom followed except when the additional time period is very short.

3. *Unaudited disclosure.* The subsequent event can be excluded from the opinion and the necessary disclosure can be made in the last note to the financial statements, which can be clearly labelled as describing an event subsequent to the date of the auditor's opinion.

---

* For detailed discussion of keeping current reviews, see Rappaport, cited earlier.

Discovery of Information After a Report Is Issued

Sometimes an auditor gives his opinion and subsequently discovers or is told of the possibility ". . . that facts may have existed at that date [his report date] which might have affected his report had he then been aware of such facts" (SAS No. 1, paragraph 561.01). That situation is quite different from subsequent discovery of new conditions or situations not existing at the date of his report, for which an auditor has no responsibility. While the distinction is clear, in practice it is often difficult to tell, at least initially, whether new information refers to a new condition or a pre-existing one.

The new information is often fragmentary, hearsay, or otherwise suspect. If it comes from a source other than the client, the situation is obviously awkward at best and potentially explosive and dangerous at worst, and an auditor in this situation may find it desirable to seek the advice of legal counsel.

Subject to that advice, an auditor should ordinarily first see his client and discuss the information, requesting the client to make any necessary investigations. Usually clients comply at once, but occasionally a client may refuse to believe the information, to discuss it with the auditor, or to make any investigation.

If a client cooperates and the information is found to be reliable and to have existed at the date the auditor's report was rendered, and if the financial statements have been issued, it may be decided to issue revised financial statements and auditor's report. The revisions should be described in a note to the financial statements and the auditor's report should refer to it. If financial statements for a subsequent period are about to be issued, the revision can be incorporated in those statements, as long as disclosure of the revision is not thereby unduly delayed.

An auditor's report accompanying revised financial statements would read as follows:

> In our opinion, the aforementioned financial statements, revised as described in Note X, present fairly. . . .

The report should, of course, be redated. Some auditors believe it is important to highlight the fact of the revision more. That can be done by expanding the dating to refer to the revision in the same way as described above for a subsequent event.

If determining the effect on financial statements requires prolonged investigation, or if the information is so significant that no delay is tolerable, the client should notify all persons likely to be relying on the financial statements of the problem that is under investigation. Usually, that would include stockholders, banks, and, for publicly held companies, the SEC, stock exchanges, regulatory agencies, and perhaps the press.

If a client's management refuses to cooperate in an investigation, an auditor is left with the difficult judgment of whether his information is reliable enough for him to proceed independently. He should seldom try to make it without the advice of his own legal counsel, which should also guide his subsequent actions. If he decides to proceed, he should notify management and each member of the client's board of directors of the circumstances of his decision to withdraw his report and of his contemplated action. Unless the board takes action to do so, he should write to the SEC, stock exchanges, and any regulatory agencies to notify them of the situation and the withdrawal of his report and to request that steps be taken to accomplish the necessary public disclosure (usually his notification is made public at once). He should also notify in writing any others known to be relying, or possibly in a position requiring immediate or eventual reliance, on the financial statements and his report. The public disclosure following notification to the SEC is intended to take care of all unknown interested parties.

Paragraph 561.09 of SAS No. 1 states the guidelines for disclosure by an auditor to known interested parties. If possible, the disclosure should describe the information and its effect on the financial statements and the auditor's report. The description should be precise and factual and should avoid references to conduct, motives, and the like. Section (b) of paragraph 561.09 describes disclosure if precise and factual information is not available:

> If the client has not cooperated and as a result the auditor is unable to conduct a satisfactory investigation of the information, his disclosure need not detail the specific information but can merely indicate that information has come to his attention which his client has not cooperated in attempting to substantiate and that, if the information is true, the auditor believes that his report must no longer be relied upon or be associated with the financial statements. No such disclosure should be made unless the auditor believes that the financial statements are likely to be misleading and that his report should not be relied on.

Discovery of Information Between Report Dates

In the course of interim work on an annual audit engagement, or on a special assignment, an auditor may occasionally discover information indicating that, through error or omission, interim financial information reported to the public (such as that filed quarterly with the SEC on Form 10-Q) is significantly misleading. He may have a responsibility to notify the management of his client (including the board of directors), and management is responsible for making any necessary revisions publicly. Precisely what an auditor's responsibility may be when a client refuses to take such action is not presently clear; he should certainly consult his legal counsel on the matter. If he becomes publicly associated with the incorrect data, as he would be when his opinion on previously audited statements is included in a public document (registration statement or proxy statement), he should withdraw from that association, which may mean withdrawing his opinion or refusing the formal consent required in SEC filings. Furthermore, depending on the circumstances, he may even consider resigning from the engagement.

VARIATIONS ON THE STANDARD REPORT

The fourth standard of reporting, discussed in Chapter 2 as part of the body of generally accepted auditing standards, reads as follows:

> The report shall either contain an expression of opinion regarding the financial statements, taken as a whole, or an assertion to the effect that an opinion cannot be expressed. When an overall opinion cannot be expressed, the reasons therefor should be stated. In all cases where an auditor's name is associated with financial statements, the report should contain a clear-cut indication of the character of the auditor's examination, if any, and the degree of responsibility he is taking.

The standardized language of the conventional report affords precision. The professional literature, both at the time of publication of the fourth standard of reporting and since then, has attempted to provide similar precision in describing departures from the standard report. Authoritative pronouncements were set forth in Section 500 of SAS No. 1 and in SAS No. 2, *Reports on Audited Financial Statements*. There are two kinds of problems to overcome in obtaining adequate precision and clarity of communication.

First is the problem of trying to find a limited number of precisely defined qualifying or limiting phrases that will cover all possible situations. For professional auditors, who have studied and understand the meaning and usage of the common qualifying phrases that have been developed, the effort has been largely successful. However, new conditions keep appearing, and when they do a period of uncertainty ensues while auditors experiment and decide whether the new conditions can be covered by an existing type of qualification or a new phrase is required.

The second problem is communicating to the public the meaning of the qualifying phrases and the distinctions between them. The meaning of a highly stylized phrase can be understood and agreed on by practitioners, but it is useless unless it is equally recognized and understood by most readers. SAS No. 2 (paragraph 32) calls for explaining all variations from the standard opinion, other than a consistency exception, in a middle paragraph. Doing so clearly highlights the variations and provides an unmistakable place for full description. It probably sacrifices precision of phraseology, but it should improve both disclosure and communication.

Definition of Terms

SAS No. 2 classifies the variations from the standard report, sometimes referred to as a "clean" opinion, as qualified opinions, adverse opinions, disclaimers of opinion, and piecemeal opinions.

Qualified Opinions

Some accountants believe that any modifying phrase in the opinion paragraph qualifies the opinion in one way or another. Others make a distinction between those phrases that point to a diminution in the quality of the financial statements—and in that sense qualify the opinion—and those that merely explain some characteristic of the opinion, such as reference to the report of other auditors as part of the basis for the opinion. In practice, an auditor should try to avoid modifying phrases in the opinion paragraph other than the types of qualifications described below; explanations about the basis for the opinion are better made in the scope paragraph.

There are four basic reasons for qualifying an opinion: departures from generally accepted accounting principles, departures from consistent application of accounting principles, limitations on the scope of the examination, and uncertainties affecting the financial statements that cannot be resolved. The first three are referred to as "exceptions" (and usually begin with the words "except for") and the last as "subject to" qualifications. Examples of each are given in a later section of the chapter. A fifth reason for departing from the standard report is not a qualification: sometimes an auditor believes it is important to emphasize a point by commenting on it in his report. It is rarely done because it can be misconstrued as a qualification.

Adverse Opinion

An adverse opinion is a flat statement that financial statements *do not* present fairly what they purport to present. It is required when an auditor has sufficient evidence for a belief that the statements are misleading. Paragraph 513.02 of SAS No. 1 (and several other references in Section 500 of that Statement) specifically states that he cannot side-step an adverse opinion simply by disclaiming an opinion.

Adverse opinions are rare. It is obviously better for all concerned to correct the conditions before such an opinion is issued, and it is usually within the client's power to correct them. In practice, adverse opinions are usually restricted to statements prepared for special and limited purposes, whose users need a particular kind of statement that is at variance with generally accepted accounting principles and are able to understand what is involved thereby. Examples are financial statements showing appraised values of property and statements employing specified accounting principles required and agreed to by parties to a particular transaction, such as a business combination involving unusual terms or agreements among the parties.

Disclaimer of Opinion

If an auditor does not have enough evidence to form an opinion he must so state in his report and disclaim an opinion. A disclaimer can result either because the scope of an auditor's examination was seriously limited or because there are major and pervasive uncertainties that cannot be resolved. While SAS No. 2 indicates that usually a "subject to" opinion is appropriate when there are uncertainties, an auditor may decide to decline to express an opinion in some cases.

Paragraph 514.03 of SAS No. 1 and paragraph 45 of SAS No. 2 state that *all* substantive reasons for a disclaimer must be given. The intention is to make it clear that an auditor should not give only one reason for a disclaimer (such as an inability to make an audit) if he has more than one and that he especially should not blanket unfavorable reasons by citing only a relatively innocuous one. Particularly, it would be misleading for an auditor to issue a disclaimer if he had a basis for an adverse judgment; he must make the judgment and describe his reasons therefor.

The kinds of uncertainties that call for a disclaimer must be distinguished from the necessary estimates of future events, which are a normal management responsibility, and also from those specific uncertainties that can be isolated, defined, explained, and understood—and that therefore result in a qualified opinion. When the possible effect of one or more uncertainties on financial statements is so complex or pervasive as to be impossible to assess, a disclaimer may be appropriate.

Disclaimers resulting from uncertainties, while not common, are an accepted feature of financial reporting. They are considered acceptable because the evidence that would cure the defect simply does not exist and because the financial statements can be useful even though they are so seriously affected by an uncertainty that no opinion is possible. A disclaimer because of an uncertainty might be worded as follows:

> Because of the possible material effect on the aforementioned financial statements of [describe or refer to a description of the condition], the outcome of which is uncertain, we do not express any opinion on the company's financial statements.

Disclaimers because of scope limitations, on the other hand, are acceptable only in certain limited circumstances. If evidence exists that could have been examined by an auditor so as to form an opinion, it is considered unacceptable for either client or auditor to sidestep that opinion by limiting the scope of the examination, because choosing to do so is deliberately choosing to render the opinion worthless. On the other hand, when evidence is too difficult to obtain or is irrelevant to the purpose for which statements are required, a scope limitation disclaimer can be acceptable because it is not a matter of deliberate choice. The most frequently encountered examples arise in limited examinations and initial engagements; other accepted examples are statements prepared by an auditor without audit and when the auditor lacks independence because of a relationship to the client.

Limited Examinations. Sometimes a client needs an auditor's report for certain limited purposes, in the light of which all parties are willing to accept a disclaimer of opinion. Probably the most common example results from omitting observation of physical inventories because that procedure can be relatively expensive and a client (or potential user) may consider it irrelevant for his purposes. A middle paragraph should describe the limitation and the opinion paragraph should contain the disclaimer (SAS No. 2, paragraphs 45 to 47). *For example:*

> . . . and such other auditing procedures as we considered necessary in the circumstances, except as explained in the following paragraph.
>
> In accordance with the terms of our engagement, we did not observe physical inventory taking nor did we employ alternative procedures with respect to inventories at the beginning and end of the year.
>
> Because the inventory at those dates enters materially into the determination of financial position, results of operations, and changes in financial position, the scope of our work was not sufficient to enable us to express, and we do not express, an opinion on the aforementioned financial statements.

An auditor faced with a request for a limited examination should ask the client what his objectives are and should be especially careful to make sure that the reasons for and effects of a disclaimer of opinion are thoroughly understood. A client willing to accept a disclaimer based on omission of inventory observation may have unrealistic assumptions about the purpose of the audit; for example, he may believe that it assures him as to other aspects of the statements or as to the absence of defalcations and similar irregularities.

While an auditor must stand ready to serve his client in any way appropriate, we believe limited engagements likely to lead to a disclaimer should be approached with reluctance because of the high risk that the responsibilities will be misunderstood by inference. In most cases, a client's needs can be served by designing a special engagement in which responsibilities can be spelled out explicitly. See, for example, the discussion of reports on internal control in Chapter 20.

Initial Engagements. In an initial engagement for a new client, an auditor is likely to begin work well after the beginning of the year under examination. If the opening inventory has a material effect on income for the year (as is the case in most manufacturing and commercial enterprises), an auditor either has to try to gather evidence on which to base an opinion on the opening inventory or disclaim an opinion on the income statement and statement of changes in financial position. When he is able to form an opinion on the opening inventory—as is usually the case when he is succeeding another reputable auditor—there is no need to cover the point in his report. (See Chapter 11 for discussion of appropriate auditing procedures.)

Sometimes client and auditor may agree that it is not worth the time and cost to examine the opening inventory—or that it is not possible. In that event, the auditor's report, following the form shown in SAS No. 1, paragraph 542.05, would read as follows:

> We have examined the balance sheet of X Company as of December 31, 19X2, and the related statements of income and retained earnings and changes in financial position for the year then ended. Our examination was made in accordance with generally accepted auditing standards, and accordingly included such tests of the accounting records and such other auditing procedures as we considered necessary in the circumstances, except as stated in the following paragraph.
>
> Because we were not engaged as auditors until after December 31, 19X1, we were not present to observe the physical inventory taken at that date and we have not satisfied ourselves by means of other procedures concerning such inventory quantities. The amount of the inventory at December 31, 19X1, enters materially into the determination of the results of operations and changes in financial position for the year ended December 31, 19X2. Therefore, we do not express an opinion on the accompanying statements of income

and retained earnings and changes in financial position for the year ended December 31, 19X2.

In our opinion, the accompanying balance sheet presents fairly the financial position of X Company at December 31, 19X2, in conformity with generally accepted accounting principles applied on a basis consistent with that of the preceding year.

Unaudited Financial Statements. An independent auditor frequently prepares financial statements for clients as a professional service separate and apart from auditing—in a sense, the ultimate form of limited examination. Even if the auditor's name is not on the financial statements, if he prepared them he is inevitably associated with them, and he should do everything within his power to prevent any possibility of a misunderstanding. Each page of the statements and notes should be marked "unaudited" and a disclaimer should either be placed directly on the statements or be attached to them. Section 516 of SAS No. 1 discusses unaudited financial statements and includes, in paragraph 516.04, the following example of a disclaimer:

> The accompanying balance sheet of X Company as of December 31, 19—, and the related statements of income and retained earnings and changes in financial position for the year then ended were not audited by us and accordingly we do not express an opinion on them.

If an auditor knows of disclosures not made in the statements or departures from generally accepted accounting principles, either the deficiencies should be corrected or the auditor should describe them in the disclaimer. The following are examples of descriptive last sentences that may be included in disclaimers:

> The financial statements are intended to be restricted to internal use, and therefore they do not necessarily include all disclosures that might be required for a fair presentation in conformity with generally accepted accounting principles.

> The financial statements have been prepared on a modified cash basis and therefore are not in conformity with generally accepted accounting principles.

The second example above illustrates the fact that a description of deficiencies is likely to result in an adverse opinion accompanying a disclaimer of opinion. This is particularly important when the auditor knows the statements are misleading for any reason.

The fact that financial statements are unaudited and an auditor so states does not, of course, justify association with statements that an auditor knows are false or intended to mislead or contain departures from generally accepted accounting principles that are not disclosed. Also, the "internal use" explanation cannot be used blindly: it is obviously unprofessional to give internal use as a reason for omitting disclosures if an auditor has reason to believe the statements may be used otherwise.

If prior-year financial statements are unaudited but are included with audited current-year statements for comparative purposes, either the prior-year statements should be marked "unaudited" or the auditor's report should contain the following disclaimer on the prior-year statements:

> We did not examine the financial statements for the year 19— and accordingly do not express an opinion on them.

If the statements are clearly marked, the disclaimer is unnecessary because the opinion specifically identifies only the current-year statements. The same applies to reports, such as those commonly filed with the SEC, covering audited financial statements that are associated with statements of prior years or interim periods that are unaudited. Provided the unaudited figures are clearly so labelled, there is no need to include a disclaimer of opinion.

The foregoing discussion, which is a summary and condensation of Section 516 of SAS No. 1, describes the handling of unaudited financial statements under the fourth standard of reporting. However, the decision in the case of *1136 Tenants' Corporation v. Rothenberg* suggests that this treatment may not be sufficient. In that case, the court stated that an accountant who undertook to do mere "writeup" work, but not an audit, might be held liable to his client if in the course of such writeup work he discovered a material irregularity in the client's financial statements but failed to report it to the client. In other words, it may not be sufficient in these circumstances to issue a disclaimer, even one explicitly stating that not all relevant disclosures have been made.

Either way, the case is a warning to auditors to be doubly careful about implied responsibilities whenever they are associated with unaudited financial statements. Auditing standards should be observed where applicable—as in the exercise of "due professional care"—accountability procedures (which are defined in paragraphs 320.43 to .48 of SAS No. 1) should be carefully considered, and an auditor should make sure that he has fully evaluated the information presented to him and answered any questions raised as to adequacy of disclosure, conformity with generally accepted accounting principles, and consistency of application. Also, the case emphasizes the need for a carefully drafted engagement letter specifying the auditor's limited responsibility. The AICPA has published (1975) a *Guide for Engagements of CPAs to Prepare Unaudited Financial Statements,* which should be consulted.

When an Auditor Is Not Independent. Occasionally, an auditor prepares financial statements for an organization in which he is an officer, director, part owner, significant creditor, or otherwise related. Since he lacks independence—the requirement of the second general standard—he must disclaim an opinion. Independence is such an elusive and subjective quality that the profession has deemed it best to permit no exceptions to the rule of absolute disclaimer of opinion in the absence of independence. An auditor should not attempt to mitigate the lack of independence—by describing the reason for it, for example, or by describing auditing procedures that he carried out.

Section 517 of SAS No. 1 covers that condition and gives, in paragraph 517.03, the following example of a disclaimer of opinion:

> We are not independent with respect to XYZ Company, and the accompanying balance sheet as of December 31, 19—, and the related statements of income and retained earnings and changes in financial position for the year then ended were not audited by us; accordingly, we do not express an opinion on them.

Section 517 emphasizes again that a disclaimer in such instances does not permit an auditor to ignore departures from generally accepted accounting principles: if he knows of them, the auditor should either insist on revision of the statements, disclose his reservations in the disclaimer, or refuse to be associated with the financial statements.

Piecemeal Opinion

A piecemeal opinion is the complement of a qualified opinion: that is, a qualified opinion gives an opinion on the financial statements as a whole and makes exceptions for certain items, while a piecemeal opinion disclaims or is adverse on the financial statements as a whole and gives an opinion on certain items. Piecemeal opinions were formerly not uncommon, but they presented so many problems that paragraph 48 of SAS No. 2 prohibits them.

The SAS states as a reason that ". . . piecemeal opinions tend to overshadow or contradict a disclaimer of opinion or an adverse opinion. . . ." Besides that, piecemeal opinions took specific items out of the context of the financial statements as a whole, thus implying a greater degree of precision about those items under conditions that usually entailed a lesser degree of certainty. Also, the defect in the financial statements as a whole which caused the disclaimer or adverse opinion tended to destroy or call into question the interrelated, corroborative nature of accounts upon which the audit logic depends. When all of these deficiencies are balanced against the limited usefulness of piecemeal opinions, the profession is well off to abandon them.

Adverse Opinions Versus Disclaimers

There is a fundamental difference between exceptions, which affect the quality of the financial statements, and uncertainties, which affect the auditor's opinion. If exceptions become so great as to make the financial statements useless, an adverse opinion is called for. On the other hand, if uncertainties are so pervasive as to cause the opinion to be useless, a disclaimer of opinion may be called for. Those are fine distinctions, as illustrated by the following paragraphs.

The tabulation below helps keep in perspective the distinctions among "subject to," "except for," "disclaimer," and "adverse" opinions:

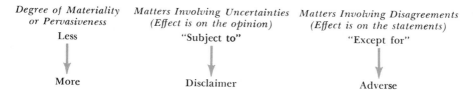

Degree of Materiality or Pervasiveness	Matters Involving Uncertainties (Effect is on the opinion)	Matters Involving Disagreements (Effect is on the statements)
Less	"Subject to"	"Except for"
↓	↓	↓
More	Disclaimer	Adverse

Unresolved uncertainties do not necessarily involve disagreement between client and auditor, but rather affect the degree of assurance of the opinion and call for a report "subject to" the uncertainty or occasionally for a disclaimer due to pervasiveness of the uncertainty. On the other hand, departures from generally accepted accounting principles are forms of disagreement about the quality of the financial statements which call for an "except for" qualification or, if necessary, an adverse opinion.

Qualified Opinions Versus Adverse Opinions or Disclaimers

Paragraph 513.02 of SAS No. 1 contains the following sentence (emphasis supplied):

> An adverse opinion is required in any report where the exceptions are *so material* that in the independent auditor's judgment a qualified opinion is not justified.

Materiality, a concept discussed at length in Chapter 2, would obviously exist before the question of a qualified opinion versus an adverse opinion or disclaimer could arise. What then does the phrase "so material" mean? The authoritative literature of the profession is as silent about that question as it is about the definition of materiality.

An auditor considering the question of whether problems are "so material" as to require an adverse opinion or disclaimer of opinion, rather than a qualification, should consider at least the following criteria:

> The usefulness of financial statements containing problems.
> The auditor's assessment of users' ability—and his own, for that matter —to understand the problems.
> The auditor's ability to measure the potential impact of the problems.
> The auditor's ability to describe his reservations about the financial statements with clarity.
> The extent of the auditor's disagreement with his client's handling of the matter.

Usefulness of the Financial Statements

An exception, unexamined item, or uncertainty impairs the usefulness of financial statements to some degree. If the impairment is only partial, a qualified opinion is acceptable; if it is so large or so pervasive as to make it difficult for a user to reach any meaningful conclusions from an analysis of the statements, a disclaimer or adverse opinion is required. A misstatement or an uncertainty about a single item—for example, deferred taxes in the balance sheet—might be quite large and still be covered in a qualified opinion because the problem affects only a few readily identifiable accounts. A material misstatement or uncertainty about inventories, however, would affect net assets, the current ratio, gross profit, income taxes, net income, and net assets and would likely be considered so pervasive as to require a disclaimer or adverse opinion.

Ability To Understand the Problem

If the problem is a common one, or for any other reason is readily understandable, an auditor is more likely to be able to give a qualified opinion than if a problem of the same magnitude is novel or unique. If a problem is readily understandable, an auditor may be able to conclude that readers can be expected to understand and properly evaluate the qualification: for example, the aggregate realizable value of investments by a venture-capital investment company is usually a material uncertainty but not an uncommon one; on the other hand, the recoverability of a major investment in a new, untried, high technology product may be considered unique to a company and therefore more difficult to understand. Furthermore, if a problem is common, the ability of an auditor and users of financial statements to assess the range of possible outcomes is greater. The foregoing example illustrates that point as well; another example is an income tax issue having a series of precedents in case law compared with a first-of-its-kind lawsuit involving product liability or environmental protection.

Ability To Measure the Potential Impact

If an auditor can calculate with reasonable assurance the outer limits of the possible impact on financial statements of an uncertainty or disagreement (the practical outer limits, that is; many suits, for example, claim amounts that are clearly unreasonable), he has some basis for a decision as to whether he can give a qualified opinion. If he cannot measure the potential maximum impact, he must assume that the item might be so pervasive or so material as to require an adverse opinion or a disclaimer.

The Auditor's Ability To Describe the Defects

If the problem can be pinpointed, quantified, and all of its ramifications described either in a note to the statements (preferably) or in the auditor's report, a qualified opinion is appropriate.

Extent of an Auditor's Disagreement With a Client's Decision

If a problem is within the client's ability to correct, either by further investigation or by improving the financial statement presentation, an auditor has to recognize a narrower range of tolerance than for items that are beyond the control of the client or are the subject of legitimate differences of opinion. Paragraph 21 of SAS No. 2 makes it clear that failure to estimate is unacceptable—only an impossibility of reasonable estimation is an acceptable basis for a "subject to" opinion. Also, if an uncertainty exists for a period of time and a client has not moved toward its resolution without clear business reasons for the inaction, an auditor must necessarily take a more pessimistic view of the outcome.

If a matter is a flat violation of generally accepted accounting principles, for example, or if an uncertainty is clearly resolvable with reasonable effort, an auditor's judgment of whether it is "so material" must be stricter than if there is room for judgment, difference of opinion, or error.

Sometimes the judgments involved in choosing between an "except for" and a "subject to" qualification can be difficult when the basis for the choice is itself a matter of judgment. For example, disputes over interpretation of income tax regulations that affect provision for income taxes are common. If the amount involved is material, an auditor is likely to find it difficult to decide whether he should express a "subject to" qualification because of an uncertainty that can only be resolved by a future court decision, or whether he must evaluate the tax case, reach a judgment on its merits, and state an "except for" opinion if his client does not agree.

Examples of Variations From Standard Report

As noted earlier, there are four basic reasons for a qualified opinion: departures from generally accepted accounting principles, departures from the consistency of their application, limitations on the scope of the examination, and uncertainties that cannot be resolved. Those conditions are covered in Sections 540 to 547 of SAS No. 1 and paragraphs 10 to 27 of SAS No. 2. SAS No. 2 cites three other reasons for departing from a standard report. Two are not qualifications, but explanations: when the opinion is based in part on the report of another auditor and when a matter needs emphasis. The third reason, departure from a promulgated accounting principle, is a variation of the departure from generally accepted accounting principles.

Some of those matters have been discussed at length in earlier chapters. The following paragraphs take up the discussion as it relates to the resulting wording in an auditor's report.

Departures From Generally Accepted Accounting Principles

The first standard of reporting is as follows:

> The report shall state whether the financial statements are presented in accordance with generally accepted accounting principles.

The standard opinion makes that positive assertion; thus, any departures from generally accepted accounting principles must be noted as "exceptions" to the assertion. Departures are rare in practice because most companies feel that an auditor's opinion qualified because of a departure from generally accepted accounting principles carries intolerable implications and so they use accounting principles that are generally accepted. Nevertheless, instances of departures sometimes occur; the most common ones are described in the following paragraphs.

Regulated Companies. Since 1962 [in Addendum to Opinion No. 2 entitled *Accounting Principles for Regulated Industries (AICPA Prof. Stds.,* vol. 3, Section 6011)], it has been recognized that, for public utilities and some other regulated industries, the rate-making process is a condition, not present in other industries, which justifies reporting on the basis of accounting principles that are at variance with generally accepted accounting principles for non-regulated companies (see Chapter 13). Sometimes regulations in those and other industries require variances that are not related to the rate-making process. When that occurs an auditor has no alternative but to render a qualified or an adverse opinion explaining his reason. The reason should be readily understood by users of financial statements.

Having explained the departure in a middle paragraph and referred to it in the opinion paragraph, it is acceptable for an auditor to report on conformity both with generally accepted accounting principles and with the prescribed accounting procedures. In that event, the opinion paragraph might read as follows:

> In our opinion, except for the effects resulting from the mandated use of the accounting principle described in the preceding paragraph which is at variance with generally accepted accounting principles, the aforementioned financial statements present fairly the financial position of X Company at December 31, 19—, and the results of its operations and the changes in its financial position for the year then ended, in conformity with generally accepted accounting principles and with the regulations of the ABC Agency applied on a basis consistent with that of the preceding year.

If, however, the effects on the financial statements of the departure from generally accepted accounting principles are so material that the auditor does not have a basis for a qualified opinion, he has to express an adverse opinion as to conformity with generally accepted accounting principles; he may still report on conformity with the prescribed procedures. An adverse opinion paragraph might be worded as follows:

> In our opinion, because of the materiality of the effects on the financial statements of the accounting principle described in the foregoing paragraph, the aforementioned financial statements do not present fairly the financial position of X Company at December 31, 19—, or the results of its operations or changes in its financial position for the year then ended in conformity with generally accepted accounting principles. However, the statements present fairly the assets, liabilities, revenue, and expenses of X Company at December 31, 19—, and for the year then ended, in conformity with the system of accounts prescribed by the ABC Agency applied on a basis consistent with that of the preceding year.

That kind of discrepancy between accounting principles and systems of accounts prescribed by regulatory agencies and generally accepted accounting principles was once common. Differences are gradually being ironed out as regulatory agencies adopt generally accepted accounting principles or as authoritative pronouncements of the profession give recognition to the particular needs of certain industries—as in the case of the rate-making process mentioned above. This type of exception is therefore becoming rare.

Inadequate Disclosure. Under the third standard of reporting:

> Informative disclosures in the financial statements are to be regarded as reasonably adequate unless otherwise stated in the report.

Thus, if an auditor believes that disclosures are inadequate, he is required to so state and to make the necessary disclosures in his report. Since clients always choose to make the necessary disclosures rather than to have them appear in the auditor's opinion, the authors cannot from their experience supply an example of this type of disclosure in an auditor's report.

One example of inadequate disclosure that was not uncommon in the past is the omission of a statement of changes in financial position. A number of companies did not agree with Opinion No. 19 of the Accounting Principles Board, which required that statement as one of the basic financial statements, and chose to accept the qualification rather than publish the statement. As the statement has proven generally useful in practice, this kind of qualification is also becoming rare.

Departures With Which an Auditor Agrees. Since 1964, members of the AICPA (by action of their governing Council) have been expected to report departures from accounting principles promulgated in the Opinions of the Accounting Principles Board and in the predecessor Accounting Research Bulletins as departures from generally accepted accounting principles. That expectation is now incorporated in Rule 203 of the AICPA Code of Professional Ethics and the related interpretations; it also now applies to the pronouncements of the FASB, successor to the APB. It is covered as a special case in paragraphs 18 and 19 of SAS No. 2.

Sometimes a departure from an accounting principle promulgated by an official body, or from some other generally accepted accounting principle, is required to present clearly and intelligibly a particular fact or condition. If auditor and client agree that a certain treatment is required to make the statements not misleading, it is permissible for the financial statements to reflect the departure, provided the departure and its effect are disclosed either in a note to the financial statements or in the auditor's report. The reason for believing that the departure from generally accepted accounting principles is justified should be stated. The auditor should then express an unqualified opinion.

One example to come to the attention of the authors is the report on a company's financial statements for the year ended December 31, 1973. A middle paragraph therein read as follows:

> In October, 1973, the Company extinguished a substantial amount of debt through a direct exchange of new equity securities. Application of Opinion No. 26 of the Accounting Principles Board to this exchange requires that the excess of the debt extinguished over the present value of the new securities should be recognized as a gain in the period in which the extinguishment occurred. While it is not practicable to determine the present value of the new equity securities issued, such value is at least $2,000,000 less than the face amount of the debt extinguished. It is the opinion of the Company's Management, an opinion with which we agree, that no realization of a gain occurred in this exchange (Note 1), and therefore, no recognition of the excess of the debt extinguished over the present value of the new securities has been made in these financial statements.

Note 1 read (in part) as follows:

> *Extinguishment of Debt:* In October, 1973, the Company issued 50,000 shares of 6% Prior Preferred Shares, par value $100, in exchange for the outstanding $5,000,000 of 6% senior subordinated notes. It also issued 18,040 shares of convertible $6 Serial Preference Shares, Series A, stated value $100 a share, in exchange for $1,300,000 and $504,000 of outstanding 6% convertible subordinated debentures and 5¾% convertible subordinated debentures, respectively. The Company expensed the unamortized balance (approximately $148,000) of the deferred financing costs associated with the issuance of each of the three classes of subordinated debt to the extent that such unamortized balances were allocable to the debt so extinguished.
>
> Opinion No. 26 of the Accounting Principles Board of the American Institute of CPA's states that the excess of the carrying amount of the extinguished debt over the present value of the new securities issued should be recognized as a gain in the statement of operations of the period in which the extinguishment occurred. While it is not practicable to determine the present value of the new equity securities issued, such value is at least $2,000,000 less than the face amount of the debt extinguished. However, the terms and provisions of these new equity securities are substantially similar to those of the debt securities extinguished, both on the basis of the Company's continuing operations and in the event of liquidation. It is the opinion of the management, therefore, that no gain as a result of this exchange has been realized or should be recognized in the financial statements.

In this case, the auditor did not, in his opinion paragraph, in any way qualify his opinion as a result of the described departure from a promulgated accounting principle. Such departure disclosures are required only when the particular circumstances clearly fall within the principle's intent.

Departures From Consistency

The second standard of reporting is:

> The report shall state whether such principles have been consistently observed in the current period in relation to the preceding period.

The consistency standard was discussed at length in Chapter 2. In contrast to departures from generally accepted accounting principles, which are rare in practice, consistency exceptions do occur fairly often. Companies from time to time change managements, operating philosophies, or judgments about which accounting principles are best for the company. Any significant change in accounting principle, or method of application of a principle, is a departure from the consistency standard and must be referred to in the auditor's report.

The words used for the consistency exception depend on the method of accounting for the change. The methods of accounting for a change in accounting principle are described in APB Opinion No. 20 (*AICPA Prof. Stds.*, vol. 3, Sections 1051 to 1051B) and in Chapters 2 and 18. In brief, a company making a change in accounting principle must disclose the nature of the change, the effect of the change on income, and why the newly adopted principle is preferable. In a few specified instances, the change should be made by retroactively restating financial statements of prior periods; in other instances, the change has only prospective effect. Except in those instances, a change is to be accounted for by recording the cumulative prior-period effect in net income of the year of change.

If an auditor is reporting only on the year during which a change of the latter type is made, the opinion paragraph should read approximately as follows:

> . . . in conformity with generally accepted accounting principles which, except for the change, with which we concur, in the [accounting principle] as described in Note X to the financial statements, have been applied on a basis consistent with that of the preceding year.

SAS No. 2, in paragraph 32, excludes consistency exceptions from the requirement that the matter be explained in a separate paragraph of the report.

If an auditor reports on two or more years, he should make reference to the change as long as the year of change is covered by his report. If the year of change is other than the earliest year being reported on, the wording should be as follows:

> . . . in conformity with generally accepted accounting principles consistently applied during the period except for the change, with which we concur, in the [accounting principle] as described in Note X to the financial statements.

If the year of change is the earliest year being reported on, there is no inconsistency during the periods presented, but an auditor should nevertheless make reference to the change with the following words:

> . . . in conformity with generally accepted accounting principles consistently applied during the period subsequent to the change, with which we concur, made as of January 1, 19—, in the [accounting principle] as described in Note X to the financial statements.

An auditor's concurrence in an accounting change is implicit unless his report states otherwise, but paragraph 546.01 of SAS No. 1 requires that concurrence be made explicit with the phrase "with which we concur."

It should be noted that, while Section 1051 of *AICPA Prof. Stds.*, vol. 3, prescribes that a note to the financial statements explain clearly why a newly adopted accounting principle is preferable, the authoritative literature of the profession does not require an auditor to satisfy himself as to that preferability. He is required only to see that disclosure of a reasonable justification of preferability is properly made. That requirement should seldom cause problems because an auditor is sure to have been involved in the consideration of a proposed change, at least in helping to draft the explanatory note and more likely in suggesting a change to a preferable method in the first place.

If a change in an accounting principle is reported by restating prior years' financial statements, the opinion must be worded accordingly. The following is an example of an opinion paragraph covering one year:

> . . . applied on a basis consistent with that of the preceding year after giving retroactive effect to the change, with which we concur, in the [accounting principle] as described in Note X to the financial statements.

An opinion covering two or more years would be as follows:

> . . . applied on a consistent basis after restatement for the change, with which we concur, in the [accounting principle] as described in Note X to the financial statements.

An alternative form that is used to report on restated financial statements covers the restatement in the scope paragraph, with the following words at the end of the standard scope paragraph:

> We have previously examined and reported on the financial statements of the company for the preceding year, which have been restated with our concurrence for the change in the [accounting principle] outlined in Note X to the financial statements.

The purpose of a consistency exception is to alert readers to the fact that a change has been made. If the auditor concurs in the change, the exception does not necessarily signal a problem that affects the quality of the financial statements other than the comparability of one period with another. Changes are rarely made that are not in accordance with generally accepted accounting principles, but paragraphs 546.04 through .11 of SAS No. 1 cover reporting by means of qualified and adverse opinions in that event. If an auditor does not concur in a change, he would need to report in the manner described in those paragraphs.

A correction of an error in application of an accounting principle should be reported as a change in accounting principle in which the reporting auditor concurs. A correction of an error of fact should be reported in the same manner as a subsequent event requiring publication of revised financial statements and auditor's report; that is, the correction of the error is reported in a note to the financial statements and referred to in the auditor's report (see "Updating the Report" and "Discovery of Information After a Report Is Issued" earlier in this chapter).

An acquisition or disposition of a business or a segment of a business is not an inconsistency, but it may require disclosure. A change in consolidation policy not resulting from an acquisition or disposition is an inconsistency. APB Opinion No. 20 requires that kind of change to be reflected by restatement of prior periods, and the auditor's report should cover it accordingly.

The basic concept of the pooling-of-interests method (Chapter 17) requires that financial statements of prior years be restated to reflect an acquisition accounted for as a pooling. If they are not restated, there is an inconsistency in the year of the pooling and thereafter. Since APB Opinion No. 16 calls for restatement, failure to do so results in a departure from generally accepted accounting principles as well as an inconsistency.

First Examinations. If an auditor is making an examination of a company for the first time, his examination should be extensive enough to permit an opinion on consistency with the prior year. Conditions that would prevent an auditor from forming that opinion would usually also prevent him from forming an opinion on the balance sheet at the beginning of the period. In that case, he would have to disclaim an opinion on the income statement and statement of changes in financial position. The most probable cause of that kind of problem is either inadequate financial records or limitations imposed by the client. The following is an example of the opinion that might result:

> . . . and such other auditing procedures as we considered necessary in the circumstances, except as indicated in the following paragraph.
>
> Because of major inadequacies in the company's accounting records for the previous year, it was not practicable to extend our auditing procedures to enable us to express an opinion on results of operations and changes in financial position for the year ended December 31, 19—, or on the consistency of application of accounting principles with the preceding year.
>
> In our opinion, the accompanying balance sheet presents fairly the financial position of X Company at December 31, 19—, in conformity with generally accepted accounting principles.

In a company's first year of operations, the consistency standard is obviously inapplicable. The standard report is used and the phrase "applied on a basis consistent with that of the preceding year" is omitted.

Limitations of Scope

An examination can be limited by client-imposed restrictions, by circumstances beyond the client's control that preclude an auditor from employing the auditing procedures he would otherwise consider necessary, or because part of the examination was made by other auditors.

Client-Imposed Restrictions. The most common client-imposed restrictions are limitations preventing observation of physical inventories, confirmation of accounts receivable, or examination of a significant subsidiary. Usually, if scope is limited by client-imposed restrictions, an auditor should disclaim an opinion because the client's election to limit the auditor's scope implies also an election to limit his responsibility. A middle paragraph is required and the disclaimer should take the form illustrated on page 756. In some circumstances, the limitation may not be so pervasive as to require a disclaimer, as discussed in earlier sections of this chapter, in which case an "except for" qualification may be appropriate, as follows:

[Scope paragraph]: Except as explained in the following paragraph, our examination . . . and such other auditing procedures as we considered necessary in the circumstances. . . .

[Separate paragraph]: We were not able to observe the taking of certain portions of the physical inventories as of December 31, 19xx (stated at $_____), and December 31, 19xl (stated at $_____), ... Due to the nature of the Company's records, we were unable to satisfy ourselves as to those inventory quantities by means of other auditing procedures.

[Opinion paragraph]: In our opinion, except for the effects of such adjustments, if any, as might have been determined to be necessary had we been able to observe all physical inventories . . . .

Occasionally a scope limitation may apply to a single isolated transaction or account, or to an area of lesser significance, so that a qualified opinion is acceptable. In that event, the qualification should be stated so that it clearly relates to the effect of the item excepted on the financial statements and not to the scope limitation. That is because relating the qualification to the scope limitation leaves unanswered the question of the possible effect of the item on the financial statements, which is the subject of interest to readers (SAS No. 2, paragraph 40). *For example:*

. . . and such other auditing procedures as we considered necessary in the circumstances, except as stated in the following paragraph.

In accordance with the terms of our engagement, we did not examine records supporting the company's investment in a foreign company, stated at $_____, or its equity in earnings of that company, $_____, which is included in net income as described in Note B to the financial statements.

In our opinion, except for the effect of possible adjustments, if any, to the carrying value or equity in earnings of the above-mentioned investment, the aforementioned financial statements present fairly . . . .

Conditions Precluding Necessary Auditing Procedures. Sometimes an auditor is not able to carry out procedures that he customarily considers necessary in the circumstances as a basis for a standard report. The most common instances are when conditions make it impracticable or impossible to confirm accounts receivable or observe inventories or when there is not enough information available to support an opinion on the carrying values of long-term investments.

In the past, an auditor was expected to state in the scope paragraph of his opinion that receivables had not been confirmed or inventory not observed even though he had satisfied himself as to those accounts by other means and was therefore able to render an unqualified opinion. In 1970, Statement on Auditing Procedure No. 43 (now Section 542 of SAS No. 1) recognized that there was no real significance to that disclosure and therefore no need to make it. Paragraph 542.02 states that no comment need be made, although if an auditor wishes to disclose the circumstances of his engagement and to describe the other procedures he may do so. A significant potential problem is involved in describing alternative procedures: in doing so, an auditor may intentionally or unintentionally shift to the reader the responsibility for deciding whether the procedures were adequate in the circumstances. It is better for the auditor to decide what is adequate and not to comment on it except as an explanation of a qualified opinion.

If an auditor cannot satisfy himself by means of alternative auditing procedures as to an account to which he is precluded from applying conventional procedures, he has to describe the problem and qualify his opinion or disclaim an opinion. The usual practice is to describe the problem in a middle paragraph and refer to it in the scope paragraph and the opinion paragraph. A scope limitation should always be described entirely within the auditor's report, in contrast to the treatment of qualifications related to information presented in the financial statements, which are usually described in a note to the statements and only referred to in the report. That is because a qualification based on a scope limitation arises from the auditor's activities, and limitations on them, rather than from the financial statements themselves. However, as noted earlier, the qualification itself should be stated in terms of its effect on the financial statements rather than in terms of the scope limitation. *For example:*

We have examined the balance sheet of X Company as of December 31, 19X2, and the related statements of income and retained earnings and changes in financial position for the year then ended. Our examination was made in accordance with generally accepted auditing standards, and accordingly included such tests of the accounting records and such other auditing procedures as we considered necessary in the circumstances, except as stated in the following paragraph.

Because we were not engaged as auditors until after December 31, 19X1, we were not present to observe the physical inventory taken at that date (stated at $_____) and we were unable to satisfy ourselves by means of other procedures concerning inventory quantities.

In our opinion, except for the effect on the financial statements of possible adjustments, if any, which we might have proposed had we been able to observe opening inventory . . . .

Part of Examination Made by Other Auditors. Chapter 2 described at length the alternative courses of action open to an auditor and how to decide among them when part of an examination is made by other auditors. In reporting on his action: if an auditor decides not to make reference to that circumstance, which means that he assumes responsibility for the work of the other auditors, his report is not affected; if he decides to make reference to the examination of the other auditors, the standard report is expanded as follows (SAS No. 1, paragraph 543.09):

. . . and such other auditing procedures as we considered necessary in the circumstances. We did not examine the financial statements of B Company, a consolidated subsidiary, which statements reflect total assets and revenues constituting 20 per cent and 22 per cent, respectively, of the related consolidated totals. These statements were examined by other auditors whose report thereon has been furnished to us, and our opinion expressed herein, insofar as it relates to the amounts included for B Company, is based solely upon the report of the other auditors.

In our opinion, based upon our examination and the report of other auditors, the accompanying [financial statements] present fairly . . . .

Since reliance on other auditors is a scope limitation that does not result in a qualified opinion, SAS No. 2 does not require that the explanation be set out in a separate paragraph.

The disclosure is lengthy and somewhat awkward and much expanded from reporting practice of some years ago when it was customary only to state that part of the examination had been made by other auditors. Employing more than one auditor inevitably results in divided responsibility and risk of misunderstanding or omission. However, the practice is sometimes followed to take advantage of specialized expertise or when the principal auditor is not located in areas served by other auditors, and in the light of the professional literature it is acceptable. See Chapter 2 for discussion of additional procedures required when other auditors are relied on.

Uncertainties

Management is expected to evaluate and reach a reasoned conclusion on all matters affecting financial position and results of operations, and an auditor is expected to review and form an opinion on those conclusions. However, some matters are simply not determinable, either by management or auditor, and others are determined by management on the basis of evidence too slight or subjective to be reviewed by an auditor. Both kinds of matters give rise to "subject to" opinions, or disclaimers when the uncertainties are pervasive.

If the outcome of a matter having an impact on financial statements depends on the decisions of others, it may be impossible, for management and auditor, to reach a valid conclusion about it. The most common events of that kind are lawsuits and tax disputes. The mere existence of an unresolved question does not relieve management or auditor from the responsibility of forming a judgment about the outcome if at all possible—for many disputed tax issues, for example, the outcome is reasonably determinable by an informed analysis. However, in some cases, the best possible efforts result in a judgment that no valid conclusion can be formed. In that event, the uncertainty should be described in a middle paragraph of the report, even though it is also described in a note to the financial statements, and the opinion paragraph should read approximately as follows:

> In our opinion, subject to the effect on the financial statements of any adjustments that may result from the final determination of the uncertainty referred to in the preceding paragraph, the aforementioned financial statements present fairly . . . .

Some important financial statement matters are determined by management based on estimates and judgments for which there is little or no objective evidence for an auditor to review. The most common examples are realizability or recovery of assets such as plant or deferred charges. Long-term investments can be an especially troublesome item because the determination of value is subjective, judgmental, and highly specialized. Chapter 14, "The Investment Segment," discusses the problem at length, pointing out that management has a responsibility for making its judgments as objective and rational as possible, and for documenting them, and that an auditor has a responsibility for understanding his client's business well enough to be able to form an opinion on those judgments. Nevertheless, there are occasions when an auditor feels he cannot take a position for or against a client's conclusion reflected in the financial statements, because it is outside his expertise.

If the uncertainty is the auditor's rather than management's, the opinion must be either qualified or disclaimed, as illustrated in the following examples:

> In our opinion, subject to the uncertainty described in the preceding paragraph, the aforementioned financial statements present fairly . . . .

Because of the possible material effect on the financial statements of the uncertainty described in the preceding paragraph, we do not express any opinion on the company's financial statements taken as a whole.

Going Concern. The concept that financial statements are prepared on the basis of a "going concern" is one of the basic tenets of financial accounting (paragraphs 1022.17 and 1025.04 of *AICPA Prof. Stds.*, vol. 3). That is the assumption that assets will "expire" and liabilities will be liquidated in the ordinary course of continuing business activity. Because the going concern assumption is so basic, the standard auditor's report does not make reference to it.

However, when a company becomes insolvent or operates for long periods with a net outflow of cash or is unable to meet currently maturing obligations, the going concern assumption must be questioned. That question immediately raises a number of questions about realizable value of assets, the order of payment of liabilities, and the proper classification and carrying amounts of both; the unexpired historical carrying amounts may become inappropriate (usually they are in excess of liquidation values). Reasonable assurance that the company will not have to suspend operations—a "going concern opinion"—must be explicitly considered, and if it cannot be reached, the auditor's report must be qualified to report that fact.

Two kinds of events create "going concern" problems. One is operational uncertainties—progressive deterioration in a firm's financial health, due to operational factors, changing markets, or aging and inefficient plant. That results in, among other things, declining earnings or losses, reduced cash balances, and increasing inability to meet current liabilities on a timely basis. This set of events can occur quite suddenly—within a year—or develop over a long period of time. In its early stages it is likely to appear temporary and not serious; identifying the point at which the going concern question must be recognized is one of the most challenging judgments an auditor is called upon to make. Failure to comply with bond indenture provisions—such as maintaining working capital limitations—often results in a technical default that, unless waived, can accelerate maturities and cause a "going concern" problem.

Another type of operational uncertainty results when a newly organized company has not yet achieved success and a solid financial position. In this case, the realizability of its assets (which are usually specialized plant and equipment, inventories, and sometimes deferred charges) can be questionable and the company's continuation not at all assured.

Another kind of event leading to questions about the ability to continue in business is external—an occurrence beyond the control of an enterprise, and potentially beyond its financial capabilities as well. Governmental actions, mandatory product recalls, or lawsuits of various kinds could all result in that kind of potential catastrophe.

In many situations, a "going concern" qualification is unnecessary because the problems are diagnosed early enough for corrective action or the enterprise is able to show that it can otherwise overcome its difficulties. When doubts about the ability of a company to continue as a going concern cannot be satisfactorily resolved, they sometimes, but not always, constitute a pervasive uncertainty. SAS No. 2, paragraphs 21 through 26, 35, 39, and 45 (and the various footnotes thereto) describe several circumstances in which a qualified opinion or disclaimer of opinion may be appropriate, but provide an auditor only broad suggestive guidance about analysis of the going concern problem and wording of any opinion he might wish to express in the circumstances. The authors believe that the same guidelines as are described in the section on "Qualified Opinions Versus Adverse Opinions or Disclaimers" can be applied. If, as frequently is the case, the problem causing the going concern question can be adequately measured and described, then a "subject to" qualified opinion is appropriate. Otherwise, the middle paragraph should describe the problem and the pervasiveness of its effect, and a disclaimer of opinion should follow.

The format and suggested wording of an auditor's qualified opinion or disclaimer of opinion on a company with a "going concern" problem are much the same as those outlined previously in this chapter for other nonstandard opinions. After the usual scope paragraph, an explanatory middle paragraph might read as follows:

> The aforementioned financial statements have been prepared on a going concern basis which contemplates continuity of operations and realization of assets and liquidation of liabilities in the ordinary course of business. Because of significant and continuing operating losses, and the imminent maturity of debt as described in Note B to the financial statements, the company's ability to continue as a going concern is dependent upon the attainment of profitable operations and arrangement of satisfactory financing.

Of course, other descriptive language could be added for different circumstances. After the explanatory middle paragraph, if a disclaimer is issued, the opinion paragraph would read as follows:

> Because of the materiality of the matters referred to in the preceding paragraph, we do not express an opinion on the aforementioned financial statements.

If a qualified opinion is issued, the paragraph would read as follows:

> In our opinion, subject to the effects of any adjustments to the financial statements resulting from the matters discussed in the preceding paragraph, the aforementioned financial statements present fairly . . . .

SUMMARY

As the discussion in this chapter amply demonstrates, the profession has worked long and hard to establish standardized phraseology having precise meaning to cover every possible kind of situation. Notwithstanding that effort, users of financial statements continue to misunderstand or fail to understand what an auditor's report says and does not say. As business affairs continue to expand, diversify, and grow more sophisticated, the problems of precise communication can be expected to multiply rather than diminish. The continuing work of the Auditing Standards Executive Committee, the cognizant authoritative body of the AICPA, is therefore of great and growing importance in refining further an auditor's only formal means of communication with the great body of users of financial statements.

20

Special Reports and Special Reporting Problems

INTRODUCTION

The variety of types of reports and letters that an auditor may be called on to prepare is literally infinite; the more his special kind of skill and experience is understood and used, the greater the diversity of out-of-the-ordinary reports and reporting situations he will encounter. While formerly the professional literature dealt almost exclusively with reporting on financial statements or other financial presentations, now the broadening scope of auditors' activities is reflected in Institute committee statements on tax and management advisory reporting problems and in the coverage in Statement on Auditing Standards (SAS)

No. 1 of letters to underwriters, reports on internal control, and other special reports.

Until a few years ago, most special reports were intended for management only or for a limited and explicitly identified group of outsiders. Recently, more and more special reports have been given increasing circulation to the public and to regulatory agencies. As greater importance is attached to the reports and as the number of parties relying on them increases, the weight of legal and financial responsibility imposed on auditors increases correspondingly. For example, letters to underwriters and letters on internal control originated years ago as almost casual favors to interested parties, generated as a by-product of an audit. Now those letters assume virtually the same importance, since they are auditors' attestations, as the report on financial statements.

The trend toward increasing reliance on special reports poses problems for an auditor. The problems are not so much in the basic work he has to do to be able to report as requested, but in his assessment of how users will view the reports so that he can appropriately communicate conclusions. To cite a currently controversial example:

> Auditors of hospitals or real estate developers are often asked to review and report on projections of the financial results of operating prospective facilities. An auditor's report is valuable to those who make or review decisions on whether to finance new facilities because it provides useful objective assurance that the projections are accurately and responsibly prepared and that the assumptions are properly identified. The report may be rendered informally—even orally—or as formally as a conventional report on financial statements. An auditor needs to know by whom and how his report is to be relied on. The amount of information he can give, the degree to which he can base his conclusions on judgments, and the precision of language all depend on the legal responsibility he undertakes. Since that has not been clearly defined, the form and content of a standard report on such work cannot be settled.

Special reports are defined in SAS No. 1 (paragraph 620.01) as ". . . reports for which the wording of the usual short-form report may be inappropriate . . . ." That is certainly an all-encompassing definition: we interpret it to cover every written communication in which an auditor makes a statement based on professional judgment— either judgment of the work required to support the statement or judgment of the conclusions reached. In this chapter we cover the types of reports most commonly encountered in practice. They are discussed generally in the order of presentation of Section 600 of SAS No. 1, as amended by later Statements on Auditing Standards and Auditing Interpretations.

Applicability of Auditing Standards

The standards of the profession (enumerated and discussed in Chapter 2) apply with equal rigor to *all* of an auditor's work—the only exception is the practical fact that some of them are not relevant in some special reporting situations. The theoretical and practical necessity for that discipline is obvious as soon as it is pointed out, although it is easy to overlook when an auditor's work, and resulting reports, take him into areas far removed from conventional financial statements. Paragraphs 620.02, .03, and .04 of SAS No. 1 make the point, although less emphatically than we believe it merits.

The general standards—adequate training and proficiency, independence of mental attitude (for which "objectivity" seems to us a preferable term), and due care in the performance of the work—all are clearly applicable in every professional effort.

Of the standards of field work, the first and third—planning and timing of field work and sufficiency and competence of evidential matter as a basis for any opinion—are also clearly universal in their applicability.

The second standard—a proper study and evaluation of internal control—is generally, though not universally, applicable. Whenever a professional report involves a system of business activity, the auditor must obtain an understanding of the system and its controls to make adequate professional judgments. However, some reports, such as those on the accounting or tax treatment of prospective transactions, do not involve a control system.

The standards of reporting are more specific and therefore cannot be as universally applied. The first standard—adherence to generally accepted accounting principles—obviously applies only to financial statements that purport to present financial position and results of operations, or items drawn therefrom; the preceding chapter deals with adherence to this standard under various conditions. The second standard—consistency—applies whenever a report relates to accounting principles in use. The third and fourth standards—adequacy of informative disclosures and the requirement for a clear-cut indication of the degree of responsibility taken by the writer—while stated in terms of financial statements, can just as well be viewed as generally applicable to every report written by an auditor—or any other professional, for that matter.

LONG-FORM REPORTS

Years ago, the so-called "long-form report" was at least as common as the short-form report, and perhaps even more so. It went out of general use some time ago. Many auditors advise their clients against long-form reports because the same information is ordinarily available from the client's records and reports. Nevertheless, long-form reports are still useful in some circumstances, particularly in medium-sized, closely held organizations.

In the traditional long-form report, the basic financial statements were supplemented by a variety of additional material in narrative and tabular form, for example, details of the subaccounts comprising financial statement captions, statistical data, explanatory comments, financial analyses, possibly some operational data, and occasionally a description of the auditor's procedures. Some long-form reports combined the account details, analytical comment, and audit scope explanation under each account heading, while others separated those subjects in different sections of the report.

Section 610 of SAS No. 1 deals with long-form reports and serves two purposes. First, it provides guidelines for clearly establishing the degree of responsibility an auditor takes for data other than the basic financial statements, including how he can make sure that he only expresses an opinion and does not make factual statements. Second, it requires an auditor to make sure that data presented in long-form reports are consistent with the basic financial statements and are not presented in such a way as to suggest that the long-form report contains data not contained in the basic financial statements that are necessary to fair presentation.

In our experience, some long-form reports are useful historical records of a company's financial activities. Since the useful material can always be prepared by a qualified member of the client's staff as well as by an auditor, long-form reports should be internal wherever possible. In many companies, however, especially smaller ones, the auditor may be the only one among those concerned with financial statements who has the skill and experience to identify and analyze the significant data for a historical report, and he provides a useful service to his client in doing so. He should make sure that the objective of the long-form report and his function in preparing it are clearly understood and that an unwarranted degree of significance is not attached to it.

Having helped his client think through whether a long-form report is useful, and, if so, what information it should contain, an auditor has to make clear his relationship to that report. In the words of the fourth standard of reporting, ". . . the report should contain a clear-cut indication of the character of the auditor's examination, if any, and the degree of responsibility he is taking." Preferred practice is the following:

The examination should be restricted to that required for a short-form report on the basic financial statements, without additional procedures relating to the long-form report.

The short-form report and the financial statements covered by it should be included in the long-form report, with both clearly distinguished from the supplementary data comprising the long-form report.

The short-form report should be supplemented by a statement of the auditor's relationship to the supplementary data. That may be done by adding a third paragraph to the standard report, as follows:

The financial statements referred to in the foregoing opinion are set forth on pages _____ to _____, inclusive, of this report. Our examination was made primarily for the purpose of rendering an opinion on these basic financial statements, taken as a whole. The other data included in this report on pages _____ to _____, inclusive, although not considered necessary for a fair presentation of financial position, results of operations, and changes in financial position, are presented primarily for supplemental analysis purposes. This additional information has been subjected to the audit procedures applied in the examination of the basic financial statements and, in our opinion, is fairly stated in all material respects in relation to the basic financial statements taken as a whole [or state that the information has not been subjected to the audit procedures applied in the examination of the basic financial statements, stating the source of information and the extent of examination].

Alternatively, this paragraph may be placed between the basic financial statements in the report and the supplementary data. If this is done, it should be separately signed and dated (using the same date as for the basic financial statements; also, the first portion should be modified to read along the following lines:

Our report on our examination appears on page _____ [referring to the page on which the short-form report appears]. This examination was made primarily for the purpose of rendering an opinion on the basic financial statements, taken as a whole, shown on pages _____ to _____ of this report [referring to those pages which include the basic financial statements]. The data included in this report on pages _____ to _____, inclusive, although not [etc.].

Consolidating Statements

Often statements are prepared showing in tabular form the accounts for each of the companies entering into consolidated financial statements, together with the necessary eliminations and reclassifications. Sometimes, but rarely, an auditor makes a complete examination of each of the companies; in that event, a standard opinion on each can be issued referring to the companies by name or collectively. It is much more common, however, for an auditor to be engaged to examine and report on the consolidated financial statements and to report also on the consolidating statements, without necessarily examining each subsidiary specifically. In that event, the auditor has to make clear in his report the limits of the responsibility he takes for the individual company amounts.

A report on consolidating statements could read as follows:

Qualified Report as to Omission of Auditing Procedures

We have examined the consolidated and individual balance sheets of Parent Company and its subsidiaries as of December 31, 19___, and the related statements of income and retained earnings and changes in financial position for the year then ended. Our examinations were made in accordance with generally accepted auditing standards, and accordingly included such tests of the accounting records and such other auditing procedures as we considered necessary in the circumstances, except that we were not present to observe inventory taking of the ABC Company at the close of the year nor did we satisfy ourselves concerning such inventories by alternative auditing procedures. Neither omitted procedure was considered necessary to form an opinion on the consolidated financial statements.

In our opinion, the accompanying statements, other than those of the ABC Company, present fairly the consolidated financial position of Parent Company and its subsidiaries and the individual financial positions of such companies at December 31, 19___, and the results of their respective operations and changes in financial position for the year then ended, in conformity with generally accepted accounting principles applied on a basis consistent with that of the preceding year. Because of the limitations in our examination of inventories of the ABC Company, we are not in a position to express an opinion on the fairness of the financial statements of that company, taken as a whole.

CASH BASIS OR MODIFIED ACCRUAL BASIS STATEMENTS

Cash basis or modified accrual basis statements ordinarily do not purport to present fairly financial position and results of operations in accordance with generally accepted accounting principles. The exchange of cash in completing a transaction does not necessarily coincide with the economic event giving rise to the transaction. APB Statement No. 4, *Basic Concepts and Accounting Principles Underlying Financial Statements of Business Enterprises,* indicates in paragraph 121 (paragraph 1025.08 of *AICPA Prof. Stds.,* vol. 3) that the accrual basis is necessary to properly measure financial position and results of operations. Nevertheless, some organizations—primarily not-for-profit entities—keep their accounts on a cash or modified accrual basis because they believe they do not need the informational refinements of complete accrual accounting and, therefore, do not find the extra effort worthwhile. In other organizations, usually entities formed for special purposes by specific groups, such as certain partnerships and joint ventures, the particular purposes of the interested parties are better served by cash or modified accrual basis accounting.

Cash basis and modified accrual basis statements should display prominently on their face a notation concerning the method of their presentation. In the absence of such information, readers may incorrectly assume that the statements have been prepared on the accrual basis, in accordance with generally accepted accounting principles. The nature of any omissions and, where practicable, the net effects of the omissions on the statements should be described in a note to the statements. Because cash basis and modified accrual basis statements are not in accordance with generally accepted accounting principles, conventional terminology, which would have the effect of describing nonexistent circumstances, should not be used. Accordingly, "balance sheet" is inappropriate; "statement of assets, liabilities, and capital" should be used. Similarly, the terms "income statement" and "statement of changes in financial position" should be replaced by other appropriate title.

An independent auditor may express an opinion on financial statements prepared on the cash or modified accrual basis. The scope paragraph of his report should indicate, using the descriptive language noted above, the statements examined, and the opinion paragraph should state that the financial statements present fairly the assets and liabilities, revenue and expenditures, and changes therein arising from cash (or modified accrual) transactions. No reference to generally accepted accounting principles should be made in these circumstances; such reference might lead readers to make incorrect inferences about what the statements purport to present. Since non-accrual basis statements may be prepared on a consistent basis from period to period, a statement as to consistency is appropriate.

In situations where an auditor believes that misleading inferences might be drawn from cash basis or modified accrual basis statements, he may wish to add a middle paragraph to his report stating specifically that the statements do not present financial position and results of operations in conformity with generally accepted accounting principles. SAS No. 1, paragraph 620.06, provides an example of such a paragraph.

Implicit in the above discussion is the assumption that there are significant differences between conventional financial statements and those prepared on the cash or modified accrual basis. If, however, the differences are insignificant, the basis of presentation and the terminology used may be conventional, and an auditor may issue a standard two-paragraph report. The note disclosing the method of preparation should state that differences between the basis employed and the accrual basis are insignificant.

If the differences are material but standard terminology is employed, cash basis or modified accrual basis statements lose their status as "special reports" under Section 620 of SAS No. 1 because they purport to present financial position and results of operations in accordance with generally accepted accounting principles. In those circumstances, the auditor must explain the departures from generally accepted accounting principles and appropriately qualify his opinion or give an adverse opinion. Paragraphs 15 to 17 of SAS No. 2 outline the factors to be considered in arriving at that reporting decision.

Although that course is a theoretically possible alternative, it is seldom acceptable in practice. Rather than issue statements accompanied by a qualified opinion or an adverse opinion, a client should be urged to prepare statements along the lines suggested above for cash basis or modified accrual basis statements, using sufficiently explanatory terminology.

Some cash basis statements are prepared for entities that have poor control over receipts. For example, clubs and charitable organizations commonly rely on members to collect or solicit funds and believe that internal control and internal check procedures are impossible or inconsistent with the trust implicit in membership. In those instances, the AICPA Industry Audit Guide for *Voluntary Health and Welfare Organizations* requires an auditor to consider qualifying or disclaiming an opinion.

INCOMPLETE FINANCIAL PRESENTATIONS

Reports on incomplete financial presentations are discussed in paragraphs 620.09 and .10 of SAS No. 1. The term may be defined broadly as presentations of data drawn from financial statements prepared in conformity with generally accepted accounting principles but shown separately from the statements. The type of data presented in this way is not ordinarily given prominence in financial statements; examples are profit-sharing calculations, contingent payments of various kinds, and adherence to bond indenture provisions.

An auditor's report on such data is often required for a variety of business purposes, usually to assure a particular party to an agreement that certain accounting requirements have been met. Each report must be tailored to its particular purpose and subject matter, but a few general principles are common:

> The report should indicate the extent of the examination of the data. In many cases, the scope paragraph of the short-form report is appropriate because the report is being issued as an adjunct to a recurring annual audit report. When it is not (usually because the examination is a special one or because procedures in addition to "normal" ones were called for), a brief description of the scope and limitations of the special-purpose examination should be set forth.
>
> The report should specify what data are being presented.
>
> The report should state the basis on which the data have been prepared and whether they are presented fairly on that basis. It should not refer to conformity with "generally accepted accounting principles" unless the scope of the examination is sufficient to make that assertion.
>
> The report should refer to the governing instrument, if there is one, with words such as ". . . in accordance with Section X of the ABC Agreement dated_____ . . . ." If the information has been prepared on some basis other than, or in addition to, generally accepted accounting principles and/or the governing instrument, it should be described.

When reporting on a single figure or a limited number of figures, an auditor must determine whether to extend his auditing procedures in order to report unreservedly on the data presented. Alternatively, he should explicitly state in his report that the data are "fairly presented" only in relation to the financial statements taken as a whole, adding in some cases that his examination was not specifically directed to obtaining or verifying the information being reported on. In addition, an auditor may wish to express "negative assurance" on the information, stating that nothing came to his attention that indicated that anything was amiss in the information presented.

REPORTS ON PRESCRIBED FORMS

Many federal, state, and local regulatory agencies and taxing authorities prescribe forms on which the entities under their jurisdictions must report. The particular requirements of each agency govern the format of the reports. By law or by administrative practice, an agency may also require attestation of the data by an auditor. Frequently, the format in which data are presented is not in conformity with generally accepted accounting principles or the wording of the auditor's report is not in conformity with the profession's standards of reporting.

Since an auditor cannot and should not subordinate either to the requirements of a form, he sometimes has problems in bridging apparent inconsistencies between the two.

If a form does not call for attestation, as in the case of most tax returns, auditors usually sign the printed statement, sometimes called the "jurat," although some auditors prefer to substitute their own statements. (Others report on tax returns as if they were special-purpose or cash basis financial statements, either routinely or in cases where there is reason to believe the returns may be given to banks or others in lieu of financial statements.)

If a form requires an auditor's attestation, and the prescribed format or auditor's report is not satisfactory, it is often possible to alter the form or make insertions in either or both the form and the auditor's report to make them mutually satisfactory to the auditor and the recipient authority. Some authorities may accept separately prepared financial statements and auditors' reports, filed as attachments, instead of those prescribed by the form.

As professional societies have gained recognition, it has become increasingly common for them to work with governmental agencies both to improve the content of reports and to conform the prescribed forms to professional standards.

REPORTS ON INTERNAL CONTROL

For decades, auditors have reported the results of their evaluations of internal control to clients. Many regard an audit as deficient if constructive suggestions for improvement do not arise from it. In the past, those reports were often informal, even oral, and when they were written, even rather formally, there was no standardization.

Reports on internal control have assumed much greater importance in recent years as more people—management, directors, regulatory agencies, customers whose interests are affected, and even the general public—have realized the potentially dangerous consequences of weaknesses in internal control (see the introductory pages of Chapter 3 for examples). Clear standards and limitations were therefore needed, and Section 640 of SAS No. 1 has been the result.

That section distinguishes between the general public on the one hand and on the other hand those who have a direct interest in internal control, the training and experience to understand it, and the means to take action to correct deficiencies in it as a result of a report: management, directors, regulatory agencies, and other auditors. A report on internal control is clearly less useful to the general public: it is subject to misinterpretation and misunderstanding; it places undue emphasis on that subject at the expense of other important areas of management; and the action to be taken is indirect at best.

After discussing at some length the question of whether reports on internal control are or can be useful to the general public and the possible problems and dangers in their publication, the SAS concludes (paragraph 640.10):

> Considering the conflicting views discussed above and the limited experience with such reports, the decision as to whether reports on an auditor's evaluation of internal accounting control would be useful for some portion or all of the general public in particular cases or classes of cases is the responsibility of management and/or any regulatory agencies having jurisdiction.

The length of the discussion in the SAS and the above quoted explicit refusal to take a stand on the subject indicate its transitional nature. It is recognized that there is some kind of information in which the public has a legitimate interest, but what that information is, and how best to communicate it, is not yet clear.

The SAS recommends a standard form of report on internal control so as to minimize the risk of misunderstanding if the report is to be distributed beyond the direct group of users. The recommended form, which is lengthy, is set forth in paragraph 640.12, and there is no need to reproduce it here. Its main points are as follows:

The purpose of the review of internal control should be made clear: usually its purpose is part of the audit logic leading to an opinion on financial statements.

The objective of internal control is reasonable, not absolute, assurance; cost must be balanced against benefits, a process that requires judgments by management.

Readers should be warned of the inherent limitations in the evaluation of any system of internal control; the recommended form gives examples.

Readers should be warned that a study may not necessarily disclose all weaknesses in a system.

Any material weaknesses observed should be enumerated.

The section further suggests how comments should be presented.

Paragraph 640.13 states that an auditor may exclude certain weaknesses from his report if he concludes that action by management is not practicable in the circumstances. It proposes modified wording of the report in that event, the intent of which is to show that only those material weaknesses that are capable of being corrected practicably (or for which no such conclusion has been reached) are listed:

> However, such study and evaluation disclosed the following conditions that we believe to be material weaknesses for which corrective action by management may be practicable in the circumstances.

The carefully hedged and qualified words in the recommended report may strike readers as negative indeed. Their purpose is to emphasize that extra effort is called for to prevent readers from assuming that a report on internal control is a certification of the absence of possible error. The words are aimed at doubt about possible inferences on the part of users, not about the auditor's ability to make the evaluation. Thus, SAS No. 1 does not require use of the recommended form outlined in paragraph 640.12 for reports to those who can be expected to understand their limitations, such as other auditors and members of management.

REPORTS TO REGULATORY AGENCIES

Regulatory agencies charged with enforcing and administering statutes, regulations, and funding programs have been turning more and more to independent auditors to examine and report on various matters in addition to the financial statements of entities subject to their jurisdiction, such as operating practices and compliance with the agencies' regulations, as well as internal control. The following are some examples:

> Reports to the SEC on Form N-1R by registered investment companies.
> Reports to the SBA on Form 468 by SBIC's.
> Reports to HUD under its various programs, such as cost certification reports (Form 2330).
> Reports to HEW by grant recipients under programs such as the National Defense Student Loan Program and the Educational Opportunity Grants Program.
> Reports to the Department of Labor under JOBS contracts.
> Reports to the Environmental Protection Agency on construction grants.

Agency requirements may be nonspecific, such as a "long-form report" or a "report on internal control." Increasingly, however, the requirements are detailed and specific and cover compliance with regulations as well as internal control. Frequently, agencies prescribe forms or questionnaires to be used; if the criteria set forth therein are sufficiently detailed and susceptible of objective application, an auditor may express a conclusion on the adequacy of procedures employed by the client in complying with an agency's requirements.

Section 641 of SAS No. 1 provides guidelines for reporting weaknesses in internal accounting control where agencies have established appropriate criteria. It also indicates that an auditor should include a statement describing the restricted nature of his report.

Because many agencies require a large amount and wide variety of information to be reviewed and reported on, an auditor must be concerned about the degree of responsibility he can assume for each item. Several degrees or gradations of attestation have been worked out in experience with the earliest forms. *For example:*

> Some numerical information can be precisely verified and an auditor may so state.
>
> Some numerical information cannot be precisely verified, but may be found to be "reasonably stated in relation to the financial statements taken as a whole."
>
> Compliance with some regulatory requirements can be verified; for example, the extent of insurance coverage.
>
> Some items cannot be verified without an unreasonable extension of effort, but an auditor may give negative assurance with words such as: "Our examination was not specifically directed to verification of the required information; however, in the course of our examination, nothing came to our attention . . . ."
>
> In other instances, no amount of auditing procedures could afford a basis for an opinion; for example, whether or not an entity had engaged in transactions with prohibited parties. An auditor must limit his expression to an even lesser degree of assurance by making an even more explicit and comprehensive disclaimer, with words such as:

The procedures which we applied were not of sufficient scope to enable us to express an opinion, and we do not express an opinion, as to the answers to the following items:

Items 1.13; 2.05; 2.24(b), (c); 2.25(a)(1), (b)(1), (c); and 2.32.

However, in connection with our examination, nothing came to our attention which causes us to believe that the accompanying answers to such items do not fairly set forth the information they purport to show.

OPINIONS ON ACCOUNTING PRINCIPLES

An auditor is often requested to give a formal opinion on an accepted or preferred method of accounting, either for a hypothetical situation or for a specific proposed or completed transaction. Perhaps the most notable examples are the reports required by the SEC when a company changes an accounting principle, and by the New York Stock Exchange in connection with the accounting for a business combination as a pooling of interests. Quite often those reports must be lengthy and highly detailed if they are to deal adequately with the complex subject matter.

It is important to record the facts on which the opinion is based because proposed situations and transactions have a way of changing subsequently, with possible implications for the opinion given. When an auditor is basing his opinion on precedent, regulation, or other authoritative source, full and accurate citations should be given. Any applicable alternatives should be outlined, the auditor's reasoning for selecting among them should be carefully presented, and his opinion should be set forth clearly and unequivocally.

Example of Pooling Letter

We have reviewed the Agreement and Plan of Reorganization between X Corporation, Y Corporation, and Shareholders of Y Corporation dated as of [date], along with information and representations submitted to us in memoranda by the companies. The Agreement is to be consummated through the issuance of up to _____ shares of X Corporation Common Stock on [date].

In our opinion, based upon the aforementioned information presented to us, this combination conforms in substance with the principles, guides, rules and criteria of APB Opinion No. 16, and we concur in the treatment of this combination as a pooling of interests.

OPINIONS ON TAX CONSEQUENCES, PROPOSED SYSTEMS, AND OTHER MATTERS

Independent accountants have long engaged in tax practice (see Chapter 13) and therefore they are frequently requested to issue formal opinions on the tax effects of prospective situations and transactions. An opinion may be required for purposes of a client's tax planning or to evaluate the effect of the proposal on financial statements. Opinions on tax matters should be prepared following the same principles noted above for opinions on accounting principles. However, the discussion of precedents and regulations and their effects on conclusions reached is likely to be more detailed and specific because of the importance of case law in tax matters.

An auditor is often asked to evaluate a proposed accounting system or computer program. Most auditors encourage their clients to seek a review of controls to be built into a system. As in the preparation of reports in general, auditors should be careful to avoid the possibility of misunderstanding. The subject matter and the auditor's assignment should be explicitly identified; the facts should be stated, the alternatives examined, the reasoning explained, and the conclusion clearly set forth.

As the two foregoing paragraphs illustrate, the variety of matters on which an auditor may be asked to report is limited only by the breadth of expertise he offers to clients. While an auditor may recognize that opinions issued by tax specialists, actuaries, or management consultants are different from audit opinions, users may not. Therefore, the same standards should apply to all substantive reports, whatever the subject matter. Since conditions and subjects cover such a wide range, standardization is not possible, and writers must rely on rigorous logic and clear expression to prevent misunderstanding.

REPORTS ON FORECASTS, PROJECTIONS, AND PRO FORMA STATEMENTS

A financial *forecast* is a statement presenting the most likely outcome of a given set of underlying assumptions, which have been evaluated for reasonableness in determining the expected results. A *projection* presents the mathematically computed financial effects of given assumptions. A *pro forma statement* presents the effects of specific hypothetical conditions or prospective transactions on historical financial statements. The distinctions among those terms are not generally recognized and the terms are often used interchangeably; however, the distinctions are important ones.

Auditors are particularly cautious concerning their association with reports on forecasts, projections, and pro forma statements. That caution may seem inconsistent with their readiness to issue opinions on proposed accounting methods, anticipated tax effects, or control aspects of prospective actions. The reason for the difference is that opinions on specific matters are not likely to be of any use, and therefore not distributed, to anyone other than direct users, who are presumed to be knowledgeable recipients. Forecasts, projections, and pro forma statements covered by an auditor's opinion, on the other hand, are likely to be distributed to persons who may not have significant expertise, with the implicit expectation that these third parties will rely on the auditor's association with the data.

The financial community's interest in forecasts, projections, and pro forma statements is growing, and consequently attitudes toward them are in the process of change. It is to be expected that if their use expands, methodology will improve and better ways will be found for auditors to report on them. The SEC and AICPA are currently working on resolving the thorny problems related to this subject. The following discussion is therefore likely to be outdated in the near future.

Pro Forma Statements

Pro forma statements giving effect to proposed transactions are sometimes used in prospectuses, proxy statements, and other public documents. No doubt they are employed more often in less widely circulated, special-purpose statements. A pro forma statement is often the only way to illustrate the effects of proposed transactions. Examples are an important business combination, whether accounted for as a purchase or a pooling of interests; a divestiture; incorporation of a partnership or a proprietorship; a recapitalization, refunding, or reorganization; and an accounting change—all may be impossible to describe intelligibly without the use of pro forma statements.

Guidelines for reporting on pro forma statements were published by the AICPA in 1923 and remain in effect today. An auditor may issue an opinion on pro forma financial statements if the proposed transactions are subject to definitive agreement among the parties, if the interval between the date of the statements and consummation of the transactions is relatively short, if the auditor has no reason to believe that subsequent events might interfere with consummation, and if the character of the transactions is clearly disclosed. Although the condition is not explicitly stated in the guidelines, most auditors, including the authors, will express an opinion on pro forma financial statements only if the underlying historical financial statements have been examined in accordance with generally accepted auditing standards.

Thus, under the proper conditions, it may be appropriate for an auditor to express an opinion on pro forma financial statements. However, there are situations when a report on pro forma adjustments only, accompanied by a clear disclaimer of opinion, may be useful; an auditor should be guided by circumstances.

The following is an example of an opinion on a pro forma balance sheet:

> We have examined the accompanying pro forma balance sheet of X Corporation as of December 31, 19___. This balance sheet is based upon the accompanying balance sheet of X Corporation as of the same date, which we have previously examined and reported upon under date of January ___, 19___, and the pro forma adjustments identified in the headnote.
>
> In our opinion, the pro forma balance sheet referred to above presents fairly, in accordance with generally accepted accounting principles, the financial position of X Corporation as it would have appeared at December 31,

19___, had the transactions set forth in the related pro forma adjustments identified in the headnote been consummated at that date.

With appropriate modifications in wording, this form of opinion could also cover a pro forma income statement.

When pro forma statements are intended to reflect the effects on historical financial statements of hypothetical conditions (such as a different form of organization or capitalization) rather than prospective transactions, an opinion might read as follows:

> We have examined the balance sheet of X Corporation as of December 31, 19___, and the related statements of income and retained earnings and changes in financial position for the identified periods then ended. Our examination was made in accordance with generally accepted auditing standards, and accordingly included such tests of the accounting records and such other auditing procedures as we considered necessary in the circumstances.
>
> In our opinion, the financial statements referred to above present fairly the financial position of X Corporation at December 31, 19___, and the results of its operations and changes in its financial position for the identified periods then ended, in conformity with generally accepted accounting principles applied on a consistent basis.
>
> We have also read the pro forma adjustments to the financial statements referred to above as of December 31, 19___, and for the identified periods then ended and, in our opinion, those adjustments have been properly made and applied.

Forecasts and Projections

Forecasts are so useful and so widely demanded by the financial community that pressure is building to require them for various purposes and to develop standards for their preparation and use. Since forecasts can be easily abused, concurrent pressure is building for auditors to be associated with them in some manner or other.

The profession has had a long-standing rule of not expressing opinions on forecasts. Rule 204 of the Code of Professional Ethics states:

> A member shall not permit his name to be used in conjunction with any forecast of future transactions in a manner which may lead to the belief that the member vouches for the achievability of the forecast.

However, in a subsequent interpretation (204-1), the Ethics Committee of the AICPA made it clear that a member may associate his name with a forecast as long as there is full disclosure of the source of information, the major assumptions made, the character of the work performed by the auditor, the degree of responsibility he takes, and a clear disclaimer of opinion about the achievability of the forecast.

At present, the Securities and Exchange Commission has departed from its previously long-standing prohibition, except in very limited circumstances, of forecasts in documents filed with it. Several statements by members of the Commission and the staff have made it clear that the SEC intends to permit, and perhaps even require, forecasts in the not too distant future. The SEC has also proposed standards for reporting forecasts on Form 8-K; guidelines covering auditors' reporting responsibilities have not yet been well articulated by any authority, but are under study by the AICPA.

In many public and private transactions not subject to SEC jurisdiction, projections are now accepted and even required. The most common examples are real estate syndications and certain kinds of feasibility studies in connection with proposed institutional financing. Both issuers and users of that kind of financial projection apparently believe it is useful to have an auditor's name associated with it, and therefore auditors have been under pressure to develop a suitable means for doing so.

Current practice is for an auditor to issue a report associating himself with a projection and including in the report a disclaimer of opinion as to achievability and sometimes as to the appropriateness of the underlying assumptions. Since reports are requested and fees paid for their preparation, they evidently communicate something meaningful to potential users, even though an opinion is disclaimed. It seems clear that the report's usefulness must be based on the presumption that an auditor would not have associated himself with the projection if he knew of any significant problems or errors in the assumptions. That presumption is reasonable: an auditor who associates himself with forecasts and projections should be knowledgeable enough about the subject matter to have some basis for believing that the assumptions are not unreasonable.

Following is an example of a report in which an auditor associates himself with a projection while disclaiming an opinion on the validity of the assumptions and the achievability of the projections:

Mr. Executive, President
Developers, Inc.
Address

Dear Mr. Executive:

At your request, we have prepared the following projections for a proposed limited partnership to be known as XYZ Investors:

1. Projected Sources and Uses of Funds.
2. Projected Income (Loss) and Cash Flow.

3. Projected Income (Loss), Cash Distributions, and Cash Generated per Unit of Investment.

4. Projected Gain per Unit of Investment.

These projections are based on information and assumptions as to future events supplied by you and on assumptions relating to local and federal income tax matters, all of which are set forth in the notes to the projections.

The projections are mathematically accurate and fairly reflect the aforementioned information and assumptions. The selection of assumptions requires the exercise of judgment and is subject to the uncertainty that changes in economic, legislative, or other circumstances may have on future events. Variations of such assumptions, especially in local and federal tax laws and regulations, could significantly affect the projections; to the extent that the assumed events do not materialize, the outcome may vary substantially from that projected. Accordingly, we express no opinion on the validity of the assumptions or the achievability of the projections.

Thus, an auditor in theory disclaims an opinion, but in practice implies some assurances by his willingness to associate himself with the projections. This difference between theory and practice makes many auditors uncomfortable, and it is likely that the profession will take steps to resolve it before long. Since users are pressing for additional assurance of the reasonableness of assumptions, it is likely that the resolution will move in that direction.

In the meantime, more and more auditors are giving "negative" assurance, using wording such as the following:

. . . However, no information has come to our attention that would indicate that the assumptions are unreasonable or inappropriate.

Our belief, which is not universally accepted, is that there is little difference in users' minds between negative assurance and positive assurance, so on occasion we issue reports such as the following:

Assumptions used for purposes of the projections represent estimates of future events and are subject to uncertainty as to possible changes in economic, legislative, and other circumstances. As a result, the identification and interpretation of data and their use in developing and selecting assumptions, from among reasonable alternatives, require the exercise of judgment. In our judgment, based on our study, the assumptions used for purposes of the projections are reasonable and appropriate and the projected outcome is therefore reasonable. To the extent that the assumed events do not materialize, the outcome may vary substantially from that projected, and accordingly we express no opinion on the achievability of the projections. In addition, this report should be evaluated in the light of any events and changes in circumstances occurring after the date of the report.

The ability to give that assurance requires industry expertise, often in combination with skills other than auditing. In any event, the above quoted disclaimer of opinion on achievability should be stated.

British Experience

Since 1969, practice in the United Kingdom has permitted, and in some cases even encouraged or required, auditors to give opinions on forecasts included in prospectuses and other published statements. The suggested "standard" report is as follows:

> To the Directors of X Limited:
>
> We have reviewed the accounting bases and calculations for the profit forecast [for which the Directors are solely responsible] of X Limited for the period [specified] set out on pages [enumerated] of this circular. The forecasts include results shown by unaudited interim accounts for the period [specified]. In our opinion, the forecasts, so far as the accounting bases and calculations are concerned, have been properly compiled on the footing of the assumptions made by the Board set out on page [identify] of this circular and are presented on a basis consistent with the accounting practices normally adopted by the company.

Officially, the auditor takes responsibility only for the "accounting bases and calculations." However, it appears to be generally understood that auditors would not give the quoted opinion unless they were also satisfied that the assumptions were not unreasonable.

Thus, in spite of substantial and very significant differences in professional attitudes and standards, legal responsibilities, and the business climate, British practice is not much different in fact from that in the United States. The British give opinions limited to the accounting bases and calculations of forecasts, while U. S. auditors disclaim an opinion or give negative assurance on forecasts. But issuers and users in both countries believe that it is the association of the auditor's name with the forecasts that is important rather than the words he uses. This attitude is clearly expressed in a paper published by D. R. Carmichael in the January 1973 *Journal of Accountancy* entitled, "Reporting on Forecasts—A U. K. Perspective":

> The accountants interviewed overwhelmingly agreed that the report is only an instrument of attestation. The critical factor is association of an accounting firm's name with a forecast and the exact wording of the report is of lesser significance. [Page 40]

LETTERS TO UNDERWRITERS

The requirements of the Securities and Exchange Commission covering responsibilities for disclosures to be made in prospectuses and registration statements under its jurisdiction are complicated and very strict.* For that reason, all parties to an SEC filing go to great lengths to make sure that they comply with the requirements.

Underwriters have had a long-standing practice of seeking specific assurance from lawyers and accountants that the SEC rules and regulations have been complied with. It has also long been a common practice for underwriters to seek "comfort" from an auditor on financial information in registration statements not covered by the auditor's opinion and on events subsequent to the opinion date.

As public expectations have grown and been reflected in legal and other attacks on those associated with disclosures, underwriters and their counsel have sought to obtain more and more "comfort" from auditors. It is formally expressed in a letter called a comfort letter (some lawyers still use the phrase common in earlier, more austere times: "cold comfort" letter). While the comfort letter may originally have been an informal or semi-formal helpful gesture on the part of an auditor, it now carries tremendous weight. Auditors must therefore be especially careful not to assume unwarranted responsibility, either express or implied. The legal responsibility attaching to comfort letters is so uncertain that at least one lawyer of the authors' acquaintance claims that an auditor should not enter a conference to decide on the contents of his letter without being accompanied by his legal counsel.

Avoiding Misunderstanding

Section 630 of SAS No. 1 is based on Statement on Auditing Procedure No. 48, which was published in 1971 to provide guidelines for minimizing misunderstandings in connection with comfort letters. The importance that had become attached to comfort letters by that time is reflected in the length and details of the 53 paragraphs in the section. It states what kinds of matters may properly be commented on by auditors in comfort letters and what the form of comment should be, suggests forms of letters and how to go about preparing them, and offers recommendations on how to reduce or avoid misunderstanding as to responsibility. The following paragraphs summarize and para-

---

* For details, see Louis H. Rappaport, *SEC Accounting Practice and Procedure*, 3d Ed. (New York: The Ronald Press Co., 1972).

phrase that section; the treatment in this book is not intended to provide adequate guidance to those concerned with comfort letters. That guidance is contained in the Rappaport book cited earlier.

Comfort letters are required not by the SEC but by underwriters acting under the responsibilities imposed on them by the SEC; they are not "filed" with the SEC. Often they are required as part of an underwriting agreement. If the scope of the letter is specified in the agreement, an auditor who subsequently finds he cannot comply may be in the position of appearing to be responsible for a client's failure to keep his part of the underwriting agreement. An auditor can avoid that embarrassing position if he makes it clear at the outset that the comfort letter could be a problem and that he is prepared to help to arrange for an adequate letter and to forestall possible misunderstandings by advising the underwriter on which procedures are possible and which are not.

Preferably, as soon as an underwriting is in prospect, the auditor, underwriter, and client should meet to discuss the possibilities for a comfort letter. In the past, before the importance of comfort letters was recognized, it was sometimes difficult to arrange such a conference, but now all parties usually recognize their respective objectives. The underwriter wants to have as much comfort as possible, the client wants to avoid unnecessary problems and delays in the underwriting, and the auditor wants to have his position clearly understood. Furthermore, an auditor who understands his client in the breadth and depth presumed throughout this book can usually benefit both underwriter and client by clarifying what is possible and what is not possible. In the authors' experience, that kind of early conference often results in timely recognition of desirable clarifying changes both in the registration statement itself and in the underwriting agreement.

The auditor should obtain a copy of the underwriting agreement as soon as it is in draft form. Once he understands and accepts the draft agreement, he should draft his letter in as exact and final form as possible. Drafting the letter makes clear to all parties what they may expect and affords opportunity for discussion and changes in advance of execution of the contemplated procedures. The underwriting agreement may be changed or the contemplated procedures may have to be modified. In either event, the purpose is to assure the smoothest possible execution of subsequent steps in the underwriting.

Preparing and reviewing a draft letter also gives an auditor the opportunity to emphasize that responsibility for the sufficiency of procedures carried out in the comfort review is the underwriter's, not the auditor's. The purpose of that is to preclude allegations in support of a claim against the auditor that the underwriter relied on the auditor for the sufficiency of the procedures if they subsequently appear to have been insufficient. An auditor must take great care to make clear to all parties that he can advise on review procedures but cannot assume responsibility for adequacy or sufficiency. That cautious position may seem extraordinarily defensive, but only to those unacquainted with the aggressive demands of some underwriters. The following wording is suggested in a footnote to paragraph 630.07 of SAS No. 1 to call attention to that division of responsibility:

> In the absence of any discussions with the underwriter, the accountants should outline in the draft letter those procedures specified in the underwriting agreement which they are willing to perform. In that event, this sentence [in paragraph 630.07] should be revised as follows: "In the absence of any discussions with [name of underwriter], we have set out in this draft letter those procedures referred to in the draft underwriting agreement (of which we have been furnished a copy) which we are willing to follow."

Dating

Underwriting agreements usually specify a "closing date" on which the agreement is to be consummated and a "cutoff date" shortly before the closing date—perhaps five business days earlier. A comfort letter is expected to speak as of the cutoff date and to be dated on or just before the closing date. The letter should make clear that the period between the cutoff date and the date of the letter is not covered by the procedures and disclosures set forth in the letter.

Addressee

The underwriting agreement often specifies to whom the letter should be addressed. Sometimes it is addressed to the lead underwriter, sometimes to the client, and sometimes to both. An auditor should not agree to address his letter to anyone else without first consulting his legal counsel.

Contents of the Letter

Comfort letters generally cover some or all of the following: the auditor's independence; compliance with the applicable statute and published rules and regulations; unaudited financial statements and schedules; changes in specified financial statement items during the period subsequent to the latest statements contained in the filing; tables, statistics, and other financial information; and an understanding about the restricted circulation of the letter. The auditor's letter usually "tracks" the underwriting agreement precisely. The following paragraphs illustrate a typical comfort letter.

Introductory Paragraph

A typical introductory paragraph is as follows:

We have examined the consolidated financial statements and schedules of X Company ("the Company") and subsidiaries as of December 31, 19X0, and for the three years then ended, and the related summary of earnings for the five years then ended included in the Registration Statement (No. _____) on Form _____ filed by the Company under the Securities Act of 1933 ("the Act"); our reports with respect thereto are also included in such Registration Statement. Such Registration Statement, as amended as of [date], is herein referred to as "the Registration Statement." In connection with the Registration Statement: . . . .

Independence

It is customary to make an assertion as to independence, approximately as follows:

We are independent certified public accountants with respect to X Company within the meaning of the Act and the applicable published rules and regulations thereunder, and the answer to Item _____ of the Registration Statement is correct insofar as it relates to us.

The item referred to is the statement that the experts who are named in the registration statement have no other relationship with the registrant.

When the auditor is reporting on a subsidiary or predecessor company rather than the company named in the registration statement (and particularly when the auditor is no longer associated and therefore does not need to be independent currently), the assertion would begin along the following lines:

As of [date of the accountants' report] and during the period covered by the financial statements on which we reported, we were independent . . . .

Compliance

It is also customary to require comfort on compliance with SEC requirements as to form, which may be done as follows:

In our opinion, the financial statements and schedules and the summary of earnings examined by us and included or incorporated by reference in the Registration Statement comply as to form in all material respects with the applicable accounting requirements of the Act and the published rules and regulations thereunder.

In the rare case of a material departure from the published requirements, either the paragraph would include the phrase "except as disclosed in the Registration Statement" or the departure would be disclosed in the letter. Normally, a departure would not be considered unless representatives of the SEC had agreed to it in advance; in that event, the agreement should be mentioned in the comfort letter.

Unaudited Statements and Subsequent Changes

Section 630.16 of SAS No. 1 gives a number of guidelines for commenting in comfort letters on unaudited financial statements and subsequent events. The guidelines and illustrative comments are as follows.

1. Negative Assurance. Comments on unaudited statements and subsequent changes should be limited to negative assurance because an auditor has not made an examination in accordance with generally accepted auditing standards. The following is an example of negative assurance:

Nothing came to our attention as a result of the foregoing procedures, however, that caused us to believe that:

a. (i) the unaudited financial statements, summary of earnings, and schedules described . . . above, included in the Registration Statement, do not comply as to form in all material respects with the applicable accounting requirements of the Act and the published rules and regulations thereunder; (ii) said financial statements are not fairly presented, or the information in said summary is not fairly summarized, in conformity with generally accepted accounting principles applied on a basis substantially consistent with that of the audited financial statements and summary of earnings; or (iii) said unaudited schedules, when considered in relation to the basic unaudited financial statements, do not present fairly in all material respects the information shown therein; or

b. (i) at May 31, 19X1, there was any change in the capital stock or long-term debt of the Company and subsidiaries consolidated or any decreases in consolidated net current assets or net assets as compared with amounts shown in the March 31, 19X1, balance sheet included in the Registration Statement or (ii) for the period from April 1, 19X1, to May 31, 19X1, there were any decreases, as compared with the corresponding period in the preceding year, in consolidated net sales or in the total or per-share amounts of income before extraordinary items or of net income, except in all instances for changes or decreases which the Registration Statement discloses have occurred or may occur.

(It should be noted that the reference to changes in specific financial statement items has replaced what was previously a general statement to the effect that there was "no material adverse change in financial position or operations.")

2. Enumerating Procedures. The procedures carried out by the auditor, which should have been agreed on in advance, as described above, should be set forth in the letter. The following is an example:

For purposes of this letter we have read the 19X1 minutes of the stockholders, the Board of Directors, and [include other appropriate committees, if any] of the Company and its subsidiaries as set forth in the minute books as of June 25, 19X1, officials of the Company having advised us that the minutes of all such meetings through that date were set forth therein, and have carried out other procedures to June 25, 19X1 (our work did not extend to the period from June 26, 19X1, to June 30, 19X1, inclusive), as follows:

a. With respect to the three-month periods ended March 31, 19X0 and 19X1, we have:
  (1) read the unaudited consolidated summary of earnings for these periods included in the Registration Statement;
  (2) read the unaudited consolidated balance sheet as of March 31, 19X1, and unaudited consolidated statements of income, retained earnings, and changes in financial position for the three months then ended and the related unaudited schedules included in the Registration Statement; and
  (3) made inquiries of certain officials of the Company who have responsibility for financial and accounting matters as to (i) whether the unaudited financial statements, summary of earnings, and schedules referred to under a(1) and (2) above comply as to form in all material respects with the applicable accounting requirements of the Act and the published rules and regulations thereunder; (ii) whether said financial statements are fairly presented, and the information in said summary is fairly summarized, in conformity with generally accepted accounting principles applied on a basis substantially consistent with that of the audited financial statements and summary of earnings included in the Registration Statement; and (iii) whether said unaudited schedules, when considered in relation to the basic unaudited financial statements, present fairly in all material respects the information shown therein.

b. With respect to the period from April 1, 19X1, to May 31, 19X1, we have:
  (1) read the unaudited consolidated financial statements of the Company and subsidiaries for April and May of both 19X0 and 19X1 furnished us by the Company, officials of the Company having advised us that no such financial statements as of any date or for any period subsequent to May 31, 19X1, were available; and
  (2) made inquiries of certain officials of the Company who have responsibility for financial and accounting matters as to whether the unaudited financial statements referred to under b(1) above are stated on a basis

substantially consistent with that of the audited financial statements included in the Registration Statement.

The foregoing procedures do not constitute an examination made in accordance with generally accepted auditing standards. Also, they would not necessarily reveal matters of significance with respect to the comments in the following paragraph. Accordingly, we make no representations as to the sufficiency of the foregoing procedures for your purposes.

3. Precise Terminology. Vague, broad, and uncertain terms such as "review" should not be used. Either terms should be defined in the letter or they should be precise enough to preclude misunderstanding: for example, "read" or "compare" instead of "review."

4. Specific Identification. Any financial statements, schedules, or other data to which the letter refers should be specifically and explicitly identified and the auditor's responsibility with respect to each item should be clearly stated. The following is an example:

We have not examined any financial statements of the Company as of any date or for any period subsequent to December 31, 19X0; although we have made an examination for the year ended December 31, 19X0, the purpose (and therefore the scope) of such examination was to enable us to express our opinion on the financial statements as of December 31, 19X0, and for the year then ended, but not on the financial statements for any interim period within such year. Therefore, we are unable to and do not express any opinion on the unaudited consolidated balance sheet as of March 31, 19X1; interim consolidated statements of income, retained earnings, and changes in financial position for the three months then ended; interim consolidated summary of earnings for the three-month periods ended March 31, 19X1 and 19X0; the related schedules included in the Registration Statement; or on the financial position, results of operations, or changes in financial position as of any date or for any period subsequent to December 31, 19X0.

5. Negative Assurance Related to an Audit. Negative assurance should not be given unless the auditor has made an examination in accordance with generally accepted auditing standards for a period including or immediately prior to that to which the negative assurance relates. That is because an auditor must have a fully formed body of evidence to which he can relate his comfort letter procedures before even negative assurance can be offered. The body of evidence must be his own—he may not give negative assurance with respect to data associated with financial statements that have been examined by other accountants.

6. Limited Effectiveness of Procedures. Negative assurance is ordinarily requested for various kinds of subsequent events. The auditor's procedures cannot be relied on to disclose all subsequent changes, and the letter should make that clear. An appropriate manner of doing so is shown in the conclusion of the illustrative paragraph under "Enumerating Procedures" above.

7. *Working Papers.* Obviously, working papers should be prepared to support the assertions made in comfort letters and to provide evidence of the procedures followed.

Other Considerations

A comfort letter should not repeat the standard opinion or give negative assurance on it because doing so clouds the relative responsibilities for subsequent events and could give rise to misunderstanding. The letter should not give negative assurance as to "adverse changes"— a phrase formerly in common use—because the term is too broad and imprecise. The letter should refer to changes (either increases or decreases) in specified items such as illustrated under "Negative Assurance" above.

It is essential that terms be defined as precisely as possible and that everything feasible be done to make sure that all parties understand the terms. The "change period" to be covered by the comfort letter and the financial statement items to be covered should be specified. What constitutes a change should be defined, including what period or date is to be compared to what earlier period or date.

In the rare case in which the SEC accepts financial statements covered by a qualified opinion, the comfort letter should refer to the qualification. The auditor has to consider the effect of the qualification on the items reported on by the comfort letter.

When other accountants have examined a portion of the accounts, the principal auditor (and sometimes the underwriters as well) usually gets from the other auditors comfort letters that duplicate as closely as possible the one he is to issue. The principal auditor then states in his comfort letter that he has read the letters of the other accountants and has not performed any procedures other than reading those letters in connection with the matters examined by the other accountants.

Tables, Statistics, and the Like

Many underwriters would like auditors to give comfort on every numerical figure appearing in a registration statement. However, many of those are beyond the competence of an auditor, acting as auditor, to comment on. It is proper for an auditor to comment on information expressed in dollars or derived from dollar amounts and

on other quantitative information obtained from accounting records that are subject to the internal controls of the company's accounting system or derived directly from those data by analysis or computation. Auditors should not comment on matters involving the exercise of management judgment, such as explanation of the reasons for changes in income, operating ratios, and the like.

As with all other comments, the procedures followed by an auditor in support of his comments on tables, statistics, and the like, should be clearly set out in the letter and agreed on in advance. They should also be accompanied by a disclaimer of responsibility for sufficiency of the procedures.

The expression "present fairly" should not be used in comments concerning tables, statistics, and the like. As discussed more fully elsewhere in this book, "present fairly" is meaningful only in relation to a specific frame of reference—for an auditor, that frame of reference is accordance with generally accepted accounting principles. Without that qualifying phrase, "present fairly" is too broad and imprecise and likely to give rise to misunderstandings.

Concluding Paragraph

To avoid the possibility of misunderstanding as to the purpose and intended use of the comfort letter, SAS No. 1 recommends, in paragraph 630.42, and it is customary to conclude with, a paragraph along the following lines:

> This letter is solely for the information of, and assistance to, the underwriters in conducting and documenting their investigation of the affairs of the Company in connection with the offering of the securities covered by the Registration Statement, and is not to be used, circulated, quoted, or otherwise referred to within or without the underwriting group for any other purpose, including but not limited to the registration, purchase, or sale of securities, nor is it to be filed with or referred to in whole or in part in the Registration Statement or any other document, except that reference may be made to it in the underwriting agreement or in any list of closing documents pertaining to the offering of the securities covered by the Registration Statement.

APPENDIXES

A

Statistical Sampling Procedures

An auditor's use of statistical sampling in performing audit tests may be appropriate in certain circumstances, as outlined in Chapter 5. The purpose of this Appendix is to provide additional guidance concerning the suitability and application of statistical sampling techniques. It is not intended as a full exposition of the theory and application of mathematical statistics in auditing, which is an extensive, highly technical subject. Several excellent texts are available for more detailed reference.*

DEFINITION OF RISK

It is necessary at the outset to distinguish sampling risk from audit risk.

Sampling Risk

By definition, sampling involves detecting or estimating a particular occurrence, quantity, or amount by examining fewer than all of the items in the population that is subject to the test. The tester thus incurs the risk that the facts developed from the sample are not truly representative of conditions in the whole population because the sample itself is not typical or representative. An auditor incurs two types of sampling risk. The first (which statisticians call "alpha risk") is the risk of deciding that a client's financial statement figure is misstated (or that his internal control system is inadequate) when the figure is in fact fairly stated (or the control system is in fact adequate).

---

* See, for example, Herbert Arkin, *Handbook of Sampling for Auditing and Accounting*, 2nd Ed. (New York: McGraw-Hill Book Co., Inc., 1974).

The second (called "beta risk" by statisticians) is the risk of deciding that a client's financial statement figure is fairly stated (or that his internal control system is adequate) when the figure is in fact a material misstatement of the actual value (or the control system is in fact inadequate as a basis for reliance).*

Audit Risk

In addition to sampling risk, audit risk includes possible inaccurate measurement or misinterpretation of the facts revealed by the test, as well as an incorrect assessment of the significance of the test in relation to the audit objective. Audit risk is no different in statistical sampling than in any other auditing procedure.

MEASURING SAMPLING RISK

Since all sampling involves some sampling risk, all audit tests require as objective an assessment of that risk as possible. If statistical sampling techniques are employed, the likelihood that a sample reflects particular qualities of the population can be measured statistically; likewise, the risk that the sample does not reflect the characteristics of the population can be measured. An auditor can specify in numerical terms the criteria he wants his test to meet. He can decide (1) how closely he wants to estimate the amount of an account balance or the rate of occurrence of a characteristic (precision), and (2) the probability that his estimate is in fact that close to the true balance or occurrence rate (the reliability). Measurements of reliability and precision are not possible in nonstatistical sampling applications. However, auditors who prefer not to use statistical methods believe that audit risk can be controlled adequately through other methods.

STATISTICAL SAMPLING APPROACHES

Sample Selection

There are several generally used methods of obtaining statistical samples, all of which have a basis in the mathematics of probability. All depend on the known, usually equal, opportunity of each item in a defined population being included in the sample selection. Such

---

* The term "actual value" and references to the actual state of the control system relate to values or circumstances that an auditor would know if he were to audit *all* of the account and transaction values or occurrences of control procedure performance in the population under examination.

samples are called probability or random samples. Unrestricted random selection, systematic selection, and stratified random selection are the most frequently used selection methods. (These are discussed more fully later in this Appendix.)

In selecting statistical samples, the auditor should remember that:

(a) The only method of sample selection suitable as a basis for mathematical evaluation is probability sampling, where each item in the population being tested has an equal or known chance of being chosen as a sample item.

(b) A probability sample can be selected in almost all audit situations. An auditor should not abandon potential statistical applications because of difficulty in deciding how to select a sample. He should, however, weigh the costs of sample selection along with other costs against the degree of audit assurance to be achieved from the sample results.

(c) Often, some of the items selected for inclusion in a sample are not available for examination. Alternative auditing procedures should be applied to missing items (or non-responses in the case of positive confirmations). If this is not possible, the missing items should be treated as exceptions.

As a practical guide, most statistical sampling results have little auditing significance unless they are based on sample sizes in excess of fifty items. On the other hand, if sample sizes determined by statistical calculations seem excessive, the auditor should re-examine the criteria he set and modify them or explore alternative methods.

Evaluation of Results

A random method of sample selection does not of itself constitute a complete statistical sampling application. In addition, techniques for establishing the sample size and for objectively appraising the sample results are required. Several approaches are available. The choice among them depends on the objective of the test and the nature of the data being tested. Some samples may be evaluated under more than one approach. An auditor should carefully select the approach or combination of approaches that will yield in the most efficient manner the kind of information he needs.

Sampling for Attributes

An *attribute* is a *quality characteristic* of a transaction or a control event. For example, a client's control procedures may call for the review of vouchers and for the reviewer to initial the voucher to indicate agreement of the amount of the invoice with the amount of the disbursement. The initial itself is an attribute of the voucher, and actual agreement of the invoice amount to the disbursement amount is also an attribute (in this case indicating that the review initial was properly made).

Attribute measurement is simple—either the attribute exists or it does not; the initial was written on the voucher or it was not; the invoice and disbursement amounts agree or do not. This measurement, when made on a sample of vouchers, is expressed as a proportion; e.g., 2% of vouchers in the sample were not initialed, or 6% of the vouchers did not agree with disbursement amounts.

One important feature of attribute measurement is that it does not generally produce statements about dollar values. Attribute measurement gives the auditor information about the frequency of control compliance errors and facilitates his decisions about internal control. However, some auditors use a sampling plan known as "dollar unit sampling" in which the population items are defined as each dollar in a total, and the sample theoretically is from a population of dollar units. In dollar unit sampling, a ratio of dollar errors can be converted into an expression of dollar amounts. This method of sampling, which is too complex for a full explanation in this Appendix, is one way to effectively combine the concepts of attributes sampling with the objective of dollar measurement.

Attributes sampling may be used in functional tests of some disciplinary controls (especially the discipline of supervision discussed in Chapters 3 and 5) and in functional tests of basic controls. In particular, attributes sampling may be applied to obtain evidence of compliance with control procedures that are supposed to be in effect.

Samples selected for attribute measurement purposes may be mathematically evaluated using different approaches, three of which are briefly explained below.

Attributes Estimation

An auditor may wish to estimate the rate of error occurrence as a part of his basis for deciding what degree of reliance to place on a system of internal control. The measurement statement takes the general form of an expression of a probability that the actual error rate in the population is between some calculated upper and lower limits. In order to be useful, both the probability measure and the upper and lower limits must be meaningful in the auditor's judgment.

Acceptance Sampling

An auditor may be most interested in measuring the probability that the actual error rate is simply less than an upper limit (i.e., a maximum acceptable upper precision limit). The auditor may need only to attain a desired probability (i.e., reliability) that the actual error rate is less than a rate that in his judgment is tolerable in a satisfactory system of internal control as a basis for determining the degree of reliance to be placed on the system.

Discovery Sampling

In some rare situations, an auditor may be interested in finding at least one example of a particular attribute that holds some special importance. For example, suppose an auditor wanted to find a voucher filed among the paid vouchers when in fact it had not been paid. He might design a plan to "discover" such an example by random selection of vouchers in the paid file, looking for absence of an attached check copy. The mathematics of attribute discovery evaluation enables him to express, for a given sample size and population size, a probability of finding at least one such voucher provided that the error occurs at a specified critical rate.

Special tables are available for making the calculations; for example, if out of a population of 5,000 paid vouchers a sample of 1,000 is selected at random, the auditor has a 97% probability of finding one example if 15 such errors exist (a critical rate of 0.3%). The discovery sampling objective usually calls for samples larger than those used for the estimation and acceptance evaluations, and discovery sampling is not ordinarily employed except when the error is of such special critical importance that one example must be found, even if at a high cost.

Sampling for Variables

The term *variables* sampling is commonly used when referring to a quantity characteristic, e.g., the measurement of dollar amounts. An auditor may wish to make an estimate of a dollar total or he may wish to make a decision about the fair statement of the client's representation of a dollar figure. In the latter case, the auditor usually is concerned about deciding that the client's financial statement figure is materially misstated when in fact it is fairly stated (the "alpha risk" decision error) or about deciding that the client's financial statement figure is a fair statement of the actual value when in fact it is a material misstatement (the "beta risk" decision error).

The important difference between sampling for variables and sampling for attributes is that variables sampling measures dollar amounts and contributes direct evidence to the decision about the client's figure, whereas attributes sampling measures error rates but not the magnitude or direction (i.e., overstatement or understatement) of the errors. Variables calculations may utilize the *mean-per-unit* measure, the *difference* measure, or the *ratio* measure. These are described more fully later in this Appendix.

Alternative Methods

When considering the use of any sample tests, an auditor should remain alert to opportunities to obtain better or less expensive information. The most obvious alternative to sampling machine-readable data is to use computers to process all of the machine-readable data. The feasibility of converting manual records to machine media should also be considered. (Only the information of audit interest need be converted.)

SAMPLING PLAN

When an auditor decides to use variables sampling techniques for validation testing or attributes sampling techniques for functional testing, he should carry out the following steps in designing, implementing, and evaluating his test.

1. Establish the Objective of the Test

Each test should have a specific, stated objective; statistical techniques are selected on the basis of that objective. For example, in testing the value of inventory there may be two objectives: (a) to determine the frequency (error rate) of incorrect unit costs, and (b) to determine the amount of error caused by using incorrect unit costs. Attribute measurement is applicable for the first objective and variables measurement (using the difference measure) may be applicable for the second. In fact, both types of sampling measurement can be based on the same sample. A possible finding is a high frequency of errors, say 50%, but a small net dollar effect due to offsetting errors. The high incidence of pricing errors may lead the auditor to test more items simply to satisfy himself that the offsetting is characteristic of the inventory.

The inventory pricing example, however, does not necessarily encompass *all* audit objectives regarding inventory. The limited tests described above enable the auditor to decide whether the inventory is priced and extended without material misstatement, but they do not include other objectives, such as deciding whether the inventory is properly stated at lower of cost or market. For the latter objective, the procedures would have to include consideration of lower of cost or market unit prices, not only the unit cost prices. The usefulness of any sampling test depends on a clear recognition of the relationship between the test objective and the corresponding audit objective.

2. Define the Population

In using statistical sampling techniques, test results can be projected only to the population from which the sample is selected. Thus, the population must be carefully defined to ensure that all items about which the auditor wishes to draw a conclusion have an equal or known chance of being selected in the sample.

For example, the client may have removed some cards from a file of perpetual inventory cards from which a sample of inventory items is drawn. If those cards are not made available for selection, any projection of sample results will (possibly misleadingly) relate only to that portion of the population included in the file. Similarly, if the sample items are selected from a listing of inventory part numbers, it is necessary to investigate and track down any missing items to avoid restricting the usefulness of the sample results.

An auditor may make a judgment to test more heavily from among the items of greater value or importance. This judgment can be implemented by stratifying the population. "Stratification," the process of separating the population into various segments, often increases the efficiency of sampling where there are considerable differences among the amounts being measured, as is often the case with accounting aggregates. Therefore, an auditor should look for opportunities to stratify. For example, he may determine that he can achieve his objectives efficiently by auditing all items in a stratum of high dollar value items and combining this 100% test with some sampling of strata containing lower dollar value items. He may choose to express his results by stratum, or (preferably) he may employ statistical computations to arrive at a conclusion about the entire population.

3. Define the Characteristic Being Measured

An auditor should carefully define the quality or quantity characteristic being measured and determine a means of measuring it. For example, in a test of controls, the characteristic might be evidence of failure to comply with the control, or it might be the absence of evidence of compliance (such as approval signatures or initials). In a test of inventory valuation, the characteristic might be the difference between the audited dollar value and the client's corresponding book value for each inventory item examined. In a test of the aging of accounts receivable, the characteristic might be the portion of the value of each account that falls into a specific age category.

In the above examples, and in all samples, acceptable conventions of measurement, such as estimating piece counts by scale weight, or accepting quantities marked on sealed packages, may be used. The measurement technique should be the same for all items selected for any given test.

The usefulness of any final sample result reflects the accuracy and soundness of the judgments made in defining the population and the characteristic to be measured in relation to audit objectives. In the past, statistical sampling was often misunderstood or misused because of auditors' failures to define those essential facts rigorously enough, rather than because of difficulty in applying the techniques.

4. Estimate the Sample Size

Sample size must be large enough to provide meaningful results, but not so large as to cause excessive work. In judgmental sampling the auditor can arbitrarily select a sample size, but the question of whether it is adequate to meet his objectives is not measurable and is therefore based on judgment. Statistical sampling techniques provide mathematically verifiable quantitative aids for estimating the sample size needed to achieve the desired precision and reliability. The adequacy of the sample size in meeting those specifications, however, can only be determined after all the sample items are examined and the results evaluated mathematically.

While statistical techniques define and quantify the areas of judgment, an auditor must nevertheless exercise judgment in deciding what he wants to achieve in applying sampling techniques. In addition to the size of the population, the factors influencing the estimate of sample size are:

(a) The desired reliability and confidence level,
(b) The desired sampling precision,
(c) The variability of the characteristic being measured (i.e., the population "standard deviation") or the estimated rate of occurrence of the characteristic in the population.

Once these factors have been determined as discussed below, the sample size may be estimated from tables in a recognized statistical text or by using formulas or appropriate computer timesharing programs. Different techniques and situations require different sample sizes; obviously, the sample must be sufficiently large to meet the audit objective.

Reliability and Precision in Variables Sampling

These concepts are quite complex because they are expressed in two forms: first, as *desired* reliability and *desired* precision, meaning that they are statements of the auditor's judgment, and second, as *achieved* reliability and *achieved* precision. In the first sense, they are predetermined criteria for evaluating sample results and are expressed *before* the auditor does any sample selection and auditing work; in the second sense, they are the results of calculations performed on audited data *after* sampling and auditing work has been performed.

Furthermore, reliability is measured by one minus the "beta risk" expressed as a percentage; that is, the reliability of a test would be 95% if there were a 5% risk of deciding that the client's financial statement figure is a fair statement of the actual value when in fact it is a material misstatement. There is another probability, which is commonly called "confidence" or "confidence level," and many auditors understand these terms to refer to the probability that is measured by one minus the "alpha risk" expressed as a percentage. Thus, "confidence level" is the probability of deciding that the client's financial statement figure is a fair statement of the actual value when that is in fact the case. For example, if the alpha risk is 15%, the confidence level is 85%.

In variables sampling, desired *precision* is functionally related, through mathematical relationships, to both reliability and confidence level and to the amount that an auditor considers material. The auditor's determination of an amount considered a material misstatement depends on his professional judgment and is in no way determined by mathematical calculations.

The relationships of these judgments to sample size are as follows (in each case, "all other factors constant," including the standard deviation discussed below):

(a) The higher the desired reliability, the larger the sample.

(b) The higher the desired confidence level, the larger the sample.

(c) The greater the amount considered material, the smaller the sample.

For a fixed sample size and a fixed confidence level, the greater the desired reliability, the greater (i.e., smaller number) the desired precision.

Most audit application designs require that the auditor establish the criteria for reliability, confidence level, and material amount, and then calculate the sample size using a table or a mathematical formula. Once sample size has been determined in this manner, the auditor must consider the cost of auditing the number indicated and decide whether proceeding on this basis is the most efficient way to accomplish the audit. Sometimes statistically determined samples appear to be quite large in an intuitive sense.

Reliability and Precision in Attributes Sampling

The basic reliability concept in attributes sampling is not as complex as it is in variables sampling, because evaluation tables that incorporate relevant probability measures are readily available. The precision concept in attributes sampling is also simpler; essentially it is the auditor's judgment of a maximum rate of error that can be allowed in a system of control that is considered reliable for audit purposes.

This last concept is often termed the "maximum acceptable upper precision limit." It requires the auditor to express his belief that some rate of error, say 5%, can exist and he can still call the system of control satisfactory. Of course, 5% is not a general guide; the rate of acceptable error may be very low, e.g., .1%, or much higher, e.g., 12% or more, depending on the importance of the attribute being tested. As a general rule, the more likely the error is to produce a financial misstatement, the lower the maximum acceptable upper precision limit.

The auditor must also be able to make a statement about desired reliability. Reliability in attributes sampling is the probability that the actual error rate in the population is less than an achieved (calculated) upper precision limit based on the results of auditing the sample. It is defensible to set desired reliability high, say 95% or 99%. Essentially this reduces the risk (one minus reliability) of deciding that a population error rate is low enough to be acceptable when it is actually too high for justifiable reliance. When reliability is 99%, the risk of this erroneous conclusion is 1%. Thus, the auditor can minimize the risk of a decision error about the population error rate at the cost of using larger sample sizes.

The foregoing explanation is based on the design of an acceptance sampling plan. Having specified desired reliability, maximum acceptable error rate, and expected error rate (discussed below), the auditor can consult a table for the required sample size. The relationship of sample size to the decision criteria is as follows (in each case, the expected error rate and the other criterion are "constant"):

(a) The higher the desired reliability, the larger the sample.
(b) The higher the maximum acceptable upper precision limit, the smaller the sample.

Standard Deviation and Estimated Rate of Occurrence

In addition to judgments about reliability, confidence level, material amount, and maximum acceptable upper precision limit, the auditor must also make an estimate of the variability in a population. Variability is a technical statistical measure that describes an important feature of a data population.

In variables measurement, the variability is most often expressed by the "standard deviation," which is a measure of the range and dispersion of dollar values among the individual items in the population. The greater the range of values, the greater the standard deviation. For example, inventory items in one clothing store might range in price from $5 to $250, and the average price of all items might be $150. Another clothing store may carry a more expensive line, having item prices from $10 to $1,000, but the mix of items may be such that the average price is also $150. The second store has greater variability and a greater dispersion of item prices below and (particularly) above the $150 average, and thus the standard deviation measurement will be greater than in the first store.

Sample size varies directly with the standard deviation measurement. Thus, with the same judgments as to reliability, confidence level, and material amount, the auditor would calculate a larger sample size for the inventory of the second store than for the first store.

In sampling for attributes, the variability measure is expressed in the auditor's judgment of the "estimated rate of occurrence" or "expected error rate." The greater the estimated rate of occurrence (up to 50%), the greater the standard deviation of an attributes population.

Sample size varies directly with the expected error rate. Thus, with the same judgments as to reliability and maximum acceptable upper precision limit, the greater the expected error rate, the larger the sample size.

As an example, consider two clients, both of which required a reviewer's initials on vouchers to show evidence of a check for agreement of invoice amounts to disbursements. Suppose that for both clients the situations were such that the auditor decided that desired reliability should be 95% and the maximum acceptable upper precision limit should be 8% for reliance on the control. If the auditor has reason to believe that errors occur at a 2% rate for client A and at a 4% rate for client B, then the sample for client B would be larger. A general rule is that the narrower the spread between the estimated rate of occurrence and the maximum acceptable upper precision limit, the greater the sample size. Sometimes this spread is called "required precision."

5. Determine an Unbiased Method of Sample Selection And a Means of Identifying the Selected Items

Once the sample size has been estimated, a method for selecting the sample items must be chosen. The sample should be representative because the objective is to infer the actual population value or rate of occurrence. Without a 100% examination, the auditor can never be absolutely sure that his sample reflects accurately the characteristics of the population. As a general rule, however, the larger the sample, the less risk there is of distorting or omitting a population characteristic.

A random sample—defined as one selected in such a way that each item in the population has an equal or known chance of selection—generally achieves the desired representativeness. There are several acceptable methods for selecting a random sample, three of which are briefly explained below.

Unrestricted Random Sampling

In this method, sampling units are drawn from the entire population and each item has an equal chance of being selected. The most common technique of random sampling is to choose numbers from a table of random numbers and associate these with items in the population. This can be done only after the auditor has established a relationship between the numbers and the items in the population; i.e., every item in the population must have a corresponding number in the table. Computer-based random number generators and tables can also be used to obtain associated random numbers.

Systematic Selection

Systematic selection—drawing every nth item (where n is equal to population size divided by sample size)—can be an alternative to unrestricted random sampling. It should be used only if the auditor can determine that there is no periodic, cyclic, or other biased arrangement of the characteristic being tested. Modification of the nth item selection method, such as using multiple random starting points, can reduce the possibility that the sample might be biased because of some unknown pattern existing in the population. The use of two or more random starts is recommended in order to avoid reproducing a biased population arrangement in the sample. For example, a choice of every 40th payroll check from a payroll that had the same order every time could produce n selections of the same person.

Stratified Random Sampling

This method involves dividing the population to be tested into separate segments and drawing samples (usually of different sizes) from each as if it were a separate population. The segments generally are determined as a matter of audit judgment. For example, an auditor may decide to audit all customers' account balances that individually exceed the amount of misstatement considered material. In an attributes sample, the auditor may choose to audit all disbursement approvals on a special-purpose bank account for foreign payments.

In both of these examples, the stratification is a judgmental dividing of a population into segments that have some special importance. The high-value customer accounts are considered important enough to require complete coverage, while other accounts may be sampled; the special-purpose bank account involves disbursements that are importantly different from other disbursements. Such stratifications are applications of common audit sense that can be accommodated by statistical methods.

6. Locate and Examine the Selected Items and Investigate Exceptions

After the auditor has located the selected items, he must audit each one. Any errors made in examining the sample will be projected to the final results and may be magnified into an erroneous conclusion about the population. Such errors are generally known as "nonsampling errors" and they can occur regardless of the sampling method used.

The auditor must determine the cause and the audit significance of each exception. Doing so is much easier if the objective, the characteristic being tested, and the means of measuring it have been rigorously defined. It may be impossible if they have not. On the other hand, an auditor must be careful not to let those definitions blind him to other, unexpected implications of an exception. If unanticipated characteristics should be found, they may be subject to adequate evaluation by means of the sampling technique in process, or a new sample and a different technique may be required.

7. Evaluate Sample Results, Making the Appropriate Audit Decision

The auditor must statistically evaluate the test results to determine whether he has achieved his desired precision and reliability requirements. He must determine how good his estimate of sample size, established in step 4 on the basis of an estimated standard deviation or expected rate of occurrence, was by calculating the "point estimate" (the sample result) and the statistical estimate of its achieved precision. The three most widely used techniques for evaluating variables sampling results are: *mean-per-unit estimation, difference estimation,* and *ratio estimation.* Mean-per-unit must be used when few or no differences are found in the sample. The method of calculating the point estimate for each of the techniques differs:

> For *mean-per-unit estimation,* the point estimate is the average audited value of the sample items multiplied by the number of items in the population.
>
> For *difference estimation,* the point estimate of the difference is equal to the average of the differences multiplied by the number of items in the population, and the point estimate of the actual total amount is the client's recorded amount plus the point estimate of the difference. (The average difference may be either positive or negative.)
>
> For *ratio estimation,* the point estimate is calculated by multiplying the client's total value by the ratio of the aggregate audited value of sample items to their aggregate book values.

The achieved precision of each of the above variables estimates is then calculated using formulas, tables, or computer programs, to obtain an interval measurement around the point estimate. Achieved precision is a function of reliability, confidence level, sample size, and the standard deviation of the sample items (which may be different from the estimated standard deviation used before in the calculation of sample size).

When attributes are being measured, the point estimate is the ratio of errors in the sample (the sample error rate). Some evaluation tables, however, do not contain this ratio but instead incorporate combinations of sample size and *number* of errors found. The sample error rate may be different from the estimated rate of occurrence used before to calculate sample size. Calculation of achieved precision and of the *computed upper precision limit* (in acceptance sampling plans) is made easy by consulting tables that give the upper and lower limits of an interval for the desired reliability.

When the auditor has obtained evidence from the audit of the sample and has made statistical calculations based thereon, he is ready to use his findings for a decision about the fair statement of a client's financial figure or about the reliability of an internal control system. An auditor is most concerned that he might incorrectly decide that a client's figure is fairly stated or that the control system is reliable (i.e., the "beta risk" decision error). This decision error may have serious consequences, because once having reached the positive conclusion, an auditor is not likely to continue work in order to confirm or reconfirm the decision. He can be somewhat less concerned about committing the "alpha risk" error because this negative decision generally leads to further work, e.g., extended auditing procedures if internal control is thought to be inadequate or different procedures designed to determine the amount of a financial statement adjustment. If the alpha risk error has in fact occurred, the auditor usually has other chances to detect it.

Audit decisions generally do not rest entirely on evidence contained in statistical calculations. At present, the art of statistical applications in auditing is not sufficiently developed to maintain that *all* evidence is captured and analyzed by statistical methods. Thus, any indicated decision based on statistical results must be accompanied by a warning: "This decision is appropriate provided that it is supported and not directly contradicted by evidence obtained by other methods."

A complete explanation of statistical evaluation methods and calculations is beyond the scope of this Appendix, but several reference books and manuals may be obtained from other sources. For purposes of illustration, however, two limited examples of evaluation and decision are given below.

Evaluation: Variables Sampling

Suppose that the auditor decided to use the mean-per-unit measurement method in connection with the audit of an inventory consisting of 10,000 different types of items which the client represented as $875,000, stated at cost. Suppose also that as matters of audit judgment and estimate he established the following:

Desired reliability	95%
Desired confidence	85%
Material amount	$50,000
Estimated standard deviation	$ 100

Based on these data and appropriate mathematical calculations, the sample size would be 2,757, calling for the audit of quantities, prices, and extensions of the random items selected on an unrestricted basis. Making the proper calculations, the required precision in this case is $23,500. (In fact, required precision will always be less than the amount considered material when desired reliability is greater than 50%.)

Assume now that the sample produced a point estimate of audited item values in the amount of $870,000, and that achieved precision was $23,500 (i.e., the standard deviation of items in the sample was $100.) The auditor can conclude that this evidence indicates that the client's recorded value is a fair statement of the actual value; that is, that the recorded amount is not different from the unknown actual value by a material amount ($50,000), with an associated probability of being wrong in this decision of (in this case) *less* than 5%, i.e., the achieved reliability is greater than 95%.

The general rule in this case (restricted by the presumption that the sample standard deviation is equal to the estimated standard deviation) is that when the client's recorded amount is within the interval defined as the point estimate plus and minus $23,500, the evidence indicates that the recorded amount is a fair presentation and no adjustment is necessary. If, however, the client's recorded amount is not within the interval (which would occur if the point estimate were less than $851,500 or greater than $898,500), the evidence would indicate that the sample may have come from a population of actual values having a total actual value of $825,000 (if the point estimate were less than $875,000), or of $925,000 (if the point estimate were greater than $875,000). If the auditor were to accept the client's recorded value when the point estimate was, for example, $840,000, the beta risk of decision error would be greater than 5% and the achieved reliability of the test would be less than 95%. However, evidence from other sources may be combined in the decision process to overcome this statistical calculation of risk.

Evaluation: Attributes Sampling

Suppose that the auditor decided to use the acceptance sampling design to test the effectiveness of an internal control procedure that called for a supervisor to initial vouchers as indication of agreement of the supporting documents with the amount of the cash disbursement. Assume that there were 5,000 paid vouchers in the period being tested. Suppose also that as matters of judgment and estimate he established the following:

Desired reliability	99%
Maximum acceptable upper precision limit	8%
Estimated rate of occurrence	3%

Based on these data, the sample size would be about 150 vouchers to be audited for the attribute of interest.

Assume now that the audit of these 150 vouchers resulted in detection of 5 missing initials (or initials placed when documents were not actually in agreement). Whenever the estimated rate of occurrence is actually realized in a properly determined sample (as in this example), the auditor can conclude with the desired reliability (99%) that the actual but unknown error rate in the population is less than the maximum acceptable upper precision limit (8%).

If the sample of 150 contained fewer than 5 errors, the achieved (calculated) upper precision limit would be less than 8%, and if more than 5 errors were found, the achieved (calculated) upper precision limit would be greater than 8% (in both cases, with 99% reliability). In the latter case (with 8 errors, for example), the calculated upper precision limit would be 12%, and the auditor could conclude the following: the probability is 99% that the worst likely error rate in the population is 12%, and because this is greater than the desired maximum acceptable upper precision limit of 8%, the inference is that errors in the system are too frequent to justify reliance. As a practical matter, the auditor need not audit all 150 vouchers if among the first vouchers selected (say, the first 50) he finds 6 or more errors; at that point he already knows that even if he finds no more errors, his maximum acceptable upper precision limit criterion will not be satisfied with 99% reliability.

DOCUMENTATION

Statistical sampling techniques should always be adequately documented in the working papers. Minimum documentation should include:

A statement of the objective of the test.

The reasons for the choice of reliability and precision.

The method of estimating sample size.

The method of selecting sample items.

A listing of the sample items and any differences or exceptions noted.

The evaluation of sample results.

The audit conclusion reached.

ILLUSTRATIVE EXAMPLE

To illustrate the procedures followed in a statistical sampling application, assume a particular audit situation.

The client is a distributor of automotive parts. Inventories with an aggregate value of $1,200,000 are material to the financial statements. In the past, the auditor had been able to match perpetual inventory record balances to observed counts, and to trace the counts forward, through pricing and summarization, to an extended value reconcilable to the general ledger control account.

This year, however, due to temporary operating problems, there is doubt about the accuracy of recent postings to the ledger cards. Correction of the condition is not foreseen for three months. Meanwhile, the auditor needs assurance concerning the recorded inventory value at December 31, the balance sheet date.

The auditor will subject the entries in the general ledger control account to auditing procedures including tests of gross profit factors and examination of product mix. Reconciliation of the perpetual ledger balances to physical quantities would require a review of all current postings, as well as a search for all unposted transactions. There is not enough time for this process. On the other hand, the auditor can count, price, and extend a sample of the 5,000 inventory articles relatively quickly.

Thus, the auditor decides to use statistical sampling techniques as a basis for making a decision about the actual value of the total inventory. He believes that a misstatement of the inventory in excess of $80,000 would be material to the financial statements taken as a whole. Because he can place little reliance on the client's records, he believes it necessary to require 99% reliability of the test. Furthermore, because it would be inefficient to have to extend procedures at a later date, he also believes it necessary to require 98% as a confidence level in the test. These judgments cause desired precision to be $40,000.

In other words, the auditor has decided in advance that he will accept the client's inventory book value as fairly stated with respect to quantities, pricing, and extensions, if it falls within his estimated value, plus and minus $40,000, based on findings from a sample of sufficient size to meet his reliability and confidence level requirements. If the book value does not fall within this measurement interval, the auditor will have to decide what additional work, if any, is required.

In order to design and implement an effective statistical sampling plan, the auditor must understand the client's system. He would consider the following:

(a) The inventory is maintained in the company's own warehouse. A separate area is maintained for the expensive items (approximately fifty items totalling $200,000). The inventory count was taken by the client using prenumbered tickets.

(b) The client will manually price the inventory tickets by reference to purchasing department records which include vendor name, latest price paid, quantity, and date of last price change. The auditor, as a result of his testing, is satisfied that these records are well kept and can be relied on.

(c) The auditor will be able to recount and price any tickets selected for testing.

Statistical sampling plans should include the steps outlined in this Appendix. All steps should be well documented. The auditor may employ work sheets similar to those shown on the following pages.

DESCRIPTION OF TEST

Test of inventory quantities, pricing, and extensions.

TEST OBJECTIVE

To estimate the actual value of inventory in order to ascertain that inventory is not materially misstated.

POPULATION

Definition of population: 5,000 prenumbered inventory tickets from physical inventory.

Procedures used to determine that population is intact (i.e., all items about which the auditor wishes to make a conclusion have a chance of being selected): Reviewed numerical sequence of inventory tickets.

Stratification (if more than one stratum): (1) 50 items maintained in separate area totalling approximately $200,000. (2) Remaining 4,950 items totalling approximately $1,000,000.

SAMPLE SELECTION

Unrestricted Random Selection

Random number table used: N/A

    Starting point in table:
        Page _____ Line _____ Column _____

    Termination point in table for presample:
        Page _____ Line _____ Column _____

    Termination point in table for main sample:
        Page _____ Line _____ Column _____

    Pattern (direction) followed in using table: _____

Other method: _Timesharing random number generator used._

Systematic Selection

Starting points: _____ Skip interval: _____

Method used to determine starting points: _____

Procedures used to determine that the population is not ordered: _____

Other method (describe): _____

SAMPLE SIZE DETERMINATION

Desired reliability: _99%–selected as we can place little reliance on the client's records._

Desired precision: _$40,000 (equal to one half of materiality)._

Method of estimating standard deviation: _Presample of 50 items from stratum 2._

Estimated standard deviation: _$50_

Method of estimating sample size: Formulas found in an appropriate

text.

Estimated sample size:

      Stratum 1 (all items)   50

      Stratum 2   712

                              762

EVALUATION OF SAMPLE RESULTS

Method of evaluation: Mean-per-unit estimation

Audited value of stratum 1 (actual value of 50 large items)	=	$210,000
Estimated value of stratum 2 (average audited value of 712 items times 4,950)	=	$980,600
Point Estimate		$1,190,600

Achieved precision: $35,700 (based on stratified sampling estimation calculations)

Confidence limits: We are 98% confident that the actual value of inventory is between $1,154,900 and $1,226,300.

(The probability is 98% that the actual population value is between $1,154,900 and $1,226,300, and therefore the risk is 1% or less that the $1,200,000 recorded amount is misstated by $80,000. The achieved reliability of the test is thus 99% or more.)

CONCLUSIONS

Client's inventory of $1,200,000 falls between the two limits and is fairly stated.

B

Major Methods of Accounting
for LIFO Inventories
and Related Matters

Accounting for LIFO inventories has become an extensive subject. The principles and the general description of methods are simple to state, but the detailed application of them involves many choices of classification and computation. Discussion here is restricted to a general description of methods. Details of application are illustrated in the tax regulations and specialized texts on the subject.

The basic theory underlying the LIFO method is that operations require a minimum quantity of inventory at all times and that the first inventory sold is that most recently purchased. The basic inventory is carried at the price at which it was originally acquired; the practical effect during a period of rising prices is to eliminate from inventory and include in current expense an amount approximately corresponding to what would otherwise be the increase in valuation of the inventory under most of the other accounting methods of determining cost.

Most common among the several different methods of applying LIFO are unit basis, dollar value, and retail LIFO.

UNIT BASIS LIFO

Under the unit method, purchased inventory is segregated into natural groups or pools of items on the basis of similarity in type of goods, and manufactured inventory is segregated on the basis of similarity in raw materials used, factory processes through which product passes, or style, shape, or use of finished product. The method is most useful for basic raw materials such as steel, copper, etc. Computations for each pool are made separately.

In the year of adoption of LIFO, the cost of the opening inventory is determined for each pool, computed on the basis previously in use (FIFO or average). All units contained in each pool are considered to have been acquired at the same time for the same price, and the unit price is obtained by dividing the inventory cost by the total number of units in the pool.

To the extent that the number of units on hand at the end of the year does not exceed the number on hand at the beginning of the year, the inventory cost is obtained by multiplying the number of units on hand at the end of the year by the average unit price at the beginning of the year. If the number of units in inventory at the end of the year is greater than at the beginning, the increment may be valued by one of the following methods:

> The actual cost of goods purchased or produced during the year in the order of acquisition or production,
>
> The actual cost of goods purchased or produced during the year in the reverse order of acquisition, or
>
> The average cost of goods purchased or produced during the year.

Those three methods are, respectively, a FIFO method, a LIFO method, and an average method within each year to determine the cost of a LIFO "layer."

Increments in units on hand from year to year form successive inventory "layers." If inventory is decreased, the most recently added inventory layer is the first layer eliminated to accord with the theory that the last goods acquired are the first goods sold. As long as the number of units in inventory is never reduced below the number on hand at the beginning of the year of LIFO adoption, the original unit cost prices remain frozen in inventory. Once inventory is liquidated and not replaced before the year end, however, the original cost is lost. Reacquisition is generally treated the same as any other increase in inventory—as a new layer. Contemplated reacquisition following an involuntary liquidation is discussed later.

DOLLAR VALUE LIFO

The use of a physical unit of measurement is simple, but it has theoretical and practical deficiencies. Its practical application is impossible in a company that manufactures or distributes a large variety of products that may change in character from year to year. Therefore, a computation based on dollars, rather than units, and the changing value of those dollars, is considered more accurate and theoretically sound. The use of the dollar value of units or of inventory components (material, labor, and overhead), rather than the physical units, as a yardstick to measure changes in inventory makes LIFO practicable regardless of the complexity of the inventory. Also, it makes possible a measure of pure price changes that can be obscured by production efficiencies under a unit method.

Under dollar value LIFO, the closing inventory of each pool is valued at opening inventory prices and the total dollar value of the pool is compared with the value of the comparable opening inventory to ascertain whether inventory has increased or decreased. An alternative to pricing the entire closing inventory at both closing prices and opening prices is to convert the closing inventory at closing prices to a closing inventory at opening prices by an index number developed from an inventory sample. A representative cross section of inventory is priced at both opening and closing prices, and an index number of change in price level is derived by dividing the valuation at closing prices by the valuation at opening prices. Applying that index number to the total closing inventory valued at closing prices approximates the value of the closing inventory at opening prices.

There are other ways of developing acceptable index numbers, based on documented overall changes in material prices or wage rates. Since one of the principal features of LIFO is the resulting tax saving, any method adopted must be acceptable for tax purposes. The regulations are extensive and illustrate the various possible alternatives.

If the closing inventory quantities valued at opening inventory prices are less than the opening inventory value, the closing inventory so determined is the LIFO inventory. If the closing inventory stated at opening inventory prices has increased, the increment is restored to current prices by multiplying by an index number computed from (a) prices of first purchases during the year; (b) prices of last purchases during the year, or (c) average prices during the year, depending on the method chosen to value the increment. The index number shows the upward or downward movement of (a), (b), or (c) as compared with prices at the beginning of the year. The increment, as adjusted by the index, is a new layer and is added to the opening LIFO inventory to determine the closing LIFO inventory. Computations for years after the year of election can be made with reference to the opening LIFO inventory of the year of election—the basic inventory—or through use of a cumulative index.

RETAIL LIFO

The retail LIFO method is a dollar value method adapted for use in conjunction with the retail method of determining cost. For income tax purposes, stores that do not qualify as department stores usually must compute an index of the change in price level from their own data on prices and quantities. In certain circumstances, retailers who qualify as department stores and specialty stores may use published indices in place of self-computed indices. An approved index number prepared by the Bureau of Labor Statistics is applied to departmental inventories stated at retail to determine the change in value of the inventory stated in terms of base-year retail prices, thus computing the increase or decrease during the year in departmental inventories stated at base-year retail prices. An increase is converted to retail prices at the end of the year by the current year's index. The retail price is reduced to cost by a method similar to the retail method discussed in Chapter 11, except that markdowns are deducted from purchases at retail to arrive at a net cumulative markon percentage that approximates cost rather than lower of cost or market—that is required to conform to a federal income tax requirement. The cost of the increase or layer is then added to the LIFO inventory at the beginning of the year to obtain the LIFO valuation at year end.

The method works by first determining every increment in inventory at base-year retail prices, then converting each increment to its current-year retail prices, and finally reducing it to cost by the net markon method. Accordingly, if year-end inventory at base-year prices shows a decrease, the LIFO inventory at the beginning of the year is reduced by eliminating the appropriate portion of prior years' increments (layers), in reverse chronological sequence, to obtain the LIFO cost at year end.

RELATED MATTERS

Inventory Pools Under LIFO

Every election of the LIFO method of inventory valuation necessitates consideration of the inventory pools to be used. Broad classifications permit the maintenance of substantially equivalent quantities of inventory on hand from year to year regardless of substitutions or changes in the mix of various components of the inventory. Narrow classifications may lead to substantial liquidations of portions of the basic inventory despite increments in other portions. The economic objective of eliminating from income the effect of price level changes related to inventories is better served by broad pools.

Provision for Replacement of Liquidated Inventories

One disadvantage of LIFO is that decreases in inventory may cause large increases in net income. The increase in income may be distorted if the liquidation is involuntary, i.e., due to circumstances beyond control, as it would be, for example, if caused by the inability to get goods because of a strike, embargo, or other factors, and management undertakes to reacquire the goods when they become available. In such a case it is good practice to record an allowance for the excess of current replacement costs of inventory that have been involuntarily liquidated over costs determined under LIFO whether or not allowable for tax purposes. The provision for replacement would be a charge to cost of goods sold with an offsetting credit reflected in the balance sheet. A company that is also on the LIFO basis for federal income tax purposes should be sure that the allowance is shown in its financial statements in a way that does not jeopardize its right to continue on the LIFO basis for tax purposes.

Considerations on Adopting LIFO

LIFO has been adopted by many enterprises in which prices of finished products change with or vary in direct proportion to the cost of the basic raw materials, for example, processors of nonferrous metals, oil producers, and cotton textile manufacturers.

Many other companies have adopted LIFO because of the tax advantages to be gained when tax rates are high and prices are rising. Probably a great many more companies would have adopted the method for tax purposes except for a requirement that LIFO also be used in a taxpayer's annual financial statements. In a period of rising prices, the use of LIFO results in reporting lower net income than under other methods, a consideration that sometimes outweighs tax savings.

The tax regulations governing LIFO also provide that inventories may not be written down to market for tax purposes if market is lower than cost on the LIFO basis. It is permissible to record in the accounts an allowance equal to an excess of LIFO inventories over market, but the allowance is not deductible for tax purposes. The effect of the requirement is to more or less permanently prohibit a deduction for an inventory write-down that would otherwise be allowable, and thus it removes some of the incentive to adopt LIFO.

The tax and financial reporting considerations involved in changing to the LIFO method are of utmost importance and should be studied carefully. LIFO should not be adopted for purely theoretical reasons or solely for the sake of an immediate tax saving.

Index

disclosure of, 732–34
Subsidiaries
  acquisition of, 633–34
  consolidated statements, 697–98
  consolidation of, 694–95
  obligations of, guarantees, 313–14
  parent guarantees of debt, 701
Substantive tests, 95, 107; *see also* Analytical
    reviews, Validation procedures
Successful efforts method, 454–55
Suggestion letter; *see* Management letter
Sum-of-the-years'-digits method of deprecia-
    tion, 467–68
Supervision, 180–81
Supervisory controls
  built-in, 74
  electronic data processing, 164
  superimposed, 74
Supplies, 368
Suspense debits and credits, 354

Tax balance sheet, 529
Tax calendar, 528
Tax consequences of business combination,
    688–89
Tax Reduction Act of 1975, 521
Tax surplus, 627
  reconciliation, 529
Taxation, income; *see also* Income tax, fed-
    eral
  accountants and, 505–6
Taxes, income; *see* Income tax
Taxes other than income taxes, 298
Test deck, 168
Tests; *see* Auditing procedures
Tests of compliance; *see* Compliance tests
Timber, standing, 477
Timberlands, 456
Time budget, 178
Timesharing computers, 174–75
Timing differences, on federal income tax
  definition, 514
  grouping, 516–17
Title, legal rule of, 369
Tools and parts, 368
Trace routine, 169
Trade acceptances, 289, 603
Trade names
  amortization, 478
  costs, includable, 458
Trademarks
  amortization, 478
  costs, includable, 458
Training, 17
Transaction reviews, 93, 109–19
  auditing, 90
  cash, 583
  financing, 643–44
  frequency, 118–19
  functional tests, 118
  inventories, 409–10

investments, 555
  making, 116–17
  number to review, 117–18
  property, plant, and equipment, 489
  for purchasing and accounts payable,
    325–27
  revenue, 242–44
  sampling, 146
  working papers, 183–84
Transactions, types of
  apparently identical, controlled differ-
    ently, 115
  that combine or divide, 115
  identified late in the audit, 116
  originating in different ways, 114
Transfer and disbursing agents, 641
Transitional rules for business combina-
    tions, 682
Travel expenses, 348
Treasury stock, 611, 617–19
  dividends, 617–18
  recording, 617
  retirement, 618–19
  statement presentation, 661–62
  tainted shares, 619, 681
  transaction systems and internal control,
    641
  transactions in, 619
Trial balance, 183
Trust accounting, 638
Tuition, 212, 262

Ultramares Corp. v. Touche, 49–50, 51
Unamortized debt discount and expense,
    354
Unaudited disclosure, 750
Unbilled receivables, 208, 272
Unclaimed dividends, 350
Uncollectible accounts, 216–17
Underlying evidence, 23, 108
Understanding, 4–11, 103
Underwriters, letters to, 799–807
  addressee, 801
  comfort letter, 799–800
  contents, 801–7
  dating, 801
Unearned revenue, 208, 211, 263–64, 273
Unexpired costs, 283
Uninsured claims and losses, 351
Unit method of grouping assets, 470
Units-of-production method of deprecia-
    tion, 469
Unrealized appreciation
  appraisal of plant; *see* Appraisals
  income tax on, 570
  investments in marketable securities, 545
Unrealized profits and losses
  foreign balances, 727–30
  intercompany, 213–14, 699
  in inventories, 372

CONTENTS
